A DESERT NAMED PEACE

History and Society of the Modern Middle East

A DESERT NAMED PEACE

The Violence of France's Empire
in the Algerian Sahara, 1844–1902

BENJAMIN CLAUDE BROWER

Columbia University Press

New York

COLUMBIA UNIVERSITY PRESS
Publishers Since 1893
New York   Chichester, West Sussex
Copyright © 2009 Benjamin Claude Brower
Paperback edition, 2011

Library of Congress Cataloging-in-Publication Data
Brower, Benjamin Claude.
A desert named peace : the violence of France's empire in the Algerian Sahara, 1844–1902 /
Benjamin Claude Brower.
p. cm. — (History and society of the modern Middle East)
Includes bibliographical references and index.
ISBN 978-0-231-15492-5 (cloth) — ISBN 978-0-231-15493-2 (pbk.) — ISBN 978-0-231-51937-3
(ebook)
1. Algeria—History—1830–1962. 2. Sahara—History—19th century.
3. Algeria—Colonization. 4. French—Algeria—History—19th century.
5. Algeria—Ethnic relations—History—19th century.
6. Violence—Algeria—History—19th century.
7. Slave trade—Algeria—History—19th century.
8. France—Colonies—Africa, North. 9. France—Territorial expansion.
10. Imperialism—History—19th century. I. Title. II. Series.

DT294.B76   2009
965'.03—dc22   2009007514

CONTENTS

Part 3: Slavery in the Algerian Sahara Following Abolition

139

Part 4: Imagining France's Saharan Empire

197

PREFACE

How to withstand mourning for our friends, our colleagues, without first having sought to understand the why of yesterday's funerals, those of the Algerian utopia? The white of a sullied dawn.
                              —Assia Djebar, *Algerian White* (1995)

Like all books, this one has a history. It begins in the late 1990s, when the war between Algeria's military-led government and the armed groups who claimed to fight in the name of an Islamist revolution degenerated into unintelligible violence. In a rare piece about the conflict to appear in the *New York Times*, correspondent Roger Cohen described this period as follows: "There is an air of gruesome ritual to the Algerian conflict. Each year, with the onset of Ramadan, the killing intensifies, and with the massacres come unresolved questions about responsibility and an international outcry." Cohen's article appeared in 1998, following the mass murder near the city of Relizane, a farming region, where some of the cruelest and most incomprehensible acts of violence occurred in an internal war that was then beginning its sixth year and had already claimed roughly one hundred thousand lives. In a series of attacks, assailants entered small villages at dusk, just as the muezzin announced the call to evening prayer, and slew the entire population of each hamlet. Terrified neighbors heard cries through the night. When they investigated at morning's light, they found whole families dead, their corpses horribly mutilated. Reflecting on this wave of killings, Cohen continued, "Terrorism has gained all the appearances of complete arbitrariness, losing any military or moral logic," concluding that this violence serves "only the causes of instability and murkiness."[1]

The Algerian violence began in early 1992, when the government suspended an election process that promised to bring to power the Islamic Salvation

Front (Front du salut islamique, or FIS), an alliance of Islamist political parties that enjoyed widespread popular support. Combat groups formed and began an armed struggle against the state, with attacks against police stations and military bases. Assassinations soon followed. Anyone associated with "douly" (a word for the state that came to have a pejorative connotation), including army conscripts, police officers, and civil servants, fell in the sights of various armed assailants, as did intellectuals, feminists, musicians, and entertainers, who were associated with "al-ghazu al-thaqafi," the West's cultural invasion. Meanwhile, the government had started an aggressive program of repression. Rumbling Soviet-made tanks seized strategic parts of the capital, while security forces occupied mosques in violent displays of the state's power designed to intimidate. Indiscriminate and widespread roundups ensued. Wearing a beard was grounds for arrest. People held in government detention were tortured and many disappeared.[2] At this stage the mass rallies and heated debates that had characterized political life since 1988 largely ceased, replaced by nameless corpses dropped along roadsides, which silently greeted Algerians each morning.

Early on this violence claimed the lives of the *innocent*—feminists, singers, teachers, lawyers, foreigners, and countless simple citizens—and by 1998 it targeted the *inconsequential*—the aged and the ill, children and their parents.[3] As the journalist and novelist Juan Goytisolo wrote following a visit to Algeria, the victims were "men, women and children who lived with nothing and died for nothing."[4] Their lives being worth so little, both sides reaped the political capital of their deaths, and a civil war became a war against civilians. Each massacre had the effect of effacing the original cause of the war—a quite ordinary struggle for power—and threw it into the realm of a metaconflict beyond question or critique, negotiation or resolution. They created what philosopher Jean-François Lyotard has called *differend*, and the only solutions seemed to be final ones: eradication of an enemy ever more difficult to specify.[5] Foreign reporters shunned the country and world leaders looked away from the fighting. With the violence becoming increasingly brutal, it seemed as if the gods themselves demanded blood.

Although this horrifying conflict called out for immediate answers, the intensity of the violence and the occult circumstances in which the killings occurred provided little opportunity to articulate a coherent set of questions. This information deficit was filled by sensationalism and rumor.[6] Foreigners living outside Algeria stressed the former. Frenchman Bernard-Henri Lévy, a philosopher serving the mass media, published multipage, voyeuristic spreads in *Le Monde* on the pain of others, bearing titles like "Le Jasmin et le sang" (Jasmine and Blood). And Canadian author Robert Young Pelton got his book *The World's Most Dangerous Places* mentioned on the *New York Times* best-seller list, telling puerile stories about Algeria, the "world's most dangerous place."[7] On the other hand, people in Algeria—those actually threatened by the violence—saw their lives consumed by rumor.[8] People throughout the country, like villagers along the Chélif River, circulated stories of terrorists possessed of superhuman powers while they watched state-security forces kill unknown men along rural roads in not very discreet assassinations.[9] At the same time, critics of the government began to ask: "Who is killing whom?" This was less a question than an accusation of state complicity in the massacres at Bentalha (22–23 September 1997) and Raïs (29 August 1997), where entire communities were slaughtered while state security forces stationed nearby did nothing to protect them.[10] Bitter rounds of accusations followed, amplifying the situation's confusion.

For me this gave new meaning to a historian's comment, made in a quite different context: "There are times when for once the formulation of problems is more urgent than their solution."[11] A conference held at Cornell University in 1996, where I had just arrived as a graduate student, set me on the path that ended with this book. This conference brought together artists and intellectuals who discussed the Algerian conflict in an emotional atmosphere marked by urgency, frustration, and despair.[12] The debates moved me, an American witnessing events playing out far away. I came to Cornell to work on questions of historical memory and trauma, and it was simple enough for me to seek understanding in Algeria's past. It was here, I thought, that the political and social fields in conflict originally formed. Surely in these decades long past there was a response to Algerian novelist Assia Djebar's "Why?," a question she posed in 1995, following the murders of three friends.

At the end of this project, I did not find the anticipated answers—simple ones—but I have been disabused of many certainties with which I began. I found no "taproot" of violence, one that can be pulled up and eliminated, nor did I find the "Labroussian paradigm" that might bestow violence in Algeria with structural truths. That much was to be expected. Another false certainty I developed during the course of my research—one that I relinquish painfully— was that the violence had neared its end. Contrary to so many hopeful expectations, peace has not come to Algeria. The violence grinds on, mutating into new forms rather than disappearing.

Algiers, mid-morning, 11 April 2007. Two explosives-packed vehicles explode at separate locations in the Algerian capital. Together the bombs claim some two dozen lives, shattering the decade-long peace the city had enjoyed since the government gained the upper hand on security. This spectacular act of violence rudely shocks residents of the capital, who had come to see terrorism as a far-off problem limited to Algeria's rural *wilāyas* (provinces). It shocks me also. I look out onto the street and see ambulances rushing the wrong way up the one-way street, their drivers urgently waving oncoming traffic out of the way. A telephone call confirms the worst: "Don't go outside."

I had just arrived in the Algerian capital days earlier by boat with my family to begin a three-month research trip involving newly inventoried documents in the national archives. The visit's length and the fact that our children accompanied my wife and me were the expression of our confidence that Algeria had rounded a corner. The sight of Algiers from the sea confirmed this belief. Gleaming white from its recent repainting, Algiers ("Alger la blanche") was a much different place than the city I had first visited in 2000. Then it appeared tired and foreboding, a place where nighttime fell far too early, draping the poorly lit city in darkness and bringing with it a long wait for morning light. Seven years later, Algiers is a different city, one living up to the modernity traced out in its colonial-era colonnades decorating the port, the sweeping lines of the *Monument of the Martyrs,* and the majestic profile of the El-Aurassi Hotel, both built after Algerian independence in 1962 and giving the city its proud skyline. International banks had returned to Algiers, a French hypermarket had opened its doors, and Asian auto dealers now filled their gleaming showrooms with Algerian buyers eager for the new models. Although something of a Luddite by nature, I did not pause to regret Algeria's transformation into a consumer society nor to bemoan the ills of materialism that come with it. Not being from Algeria, I had little to mourn, not even my own fantasies. In this explosion of the new—named Nokia, Daewoo, Carrefour, and China State Construction—I saw, first and foremost, security and stability.

Following the attacks of 11 September 2001, the world is told that everything has changed. Two bombs go off in Algiers on 11 April 2007 and *nothing* seems to have changed. More people have been lost forever to their families and their country's future—that is certain. But has a new era of violence dawned in Algeria or did a previous one never end? In any event, the pain of the 1990s is not over for those mourning the roughly two hundred thousand victims of the conflict. Families of means pay for a newspaper announcement in memory of lost loved ones, while the poor live their "persisting tragedy" in silence.[13] Inarguably the Algerian conflict has mutated, and there is new logic to violence today. But the feeling of anxiety and anger remains: "We are going to continue like this for how long?," one man exclaimed on the radio news the night of 11 April. Time will tell.

We live with a degree of violence today that has become ubiquitous, pushed into people's lives both as a result of events, conflicts accompanying the global redistribution of power following the Cold War, and because—yet again—violence and its rhetoric yields valuable political currency both for those holding power and those contesting it. After the April bombings, thousands pour out into the streets of Algeria to demonstrate their solidarity in the face of a renewed threat. The government welcomes this expression of the people's will but scrambles to head off the critical questions that will come in its wake, sending out bulletins announcing that the last terrorists have been "eliminated" (The Last Man Standing: Chérif Gousmi, d. 1994; Djamel Zitouni, d. 1996; Antar Zouabri, d. 2002; Nabil Sahrawi, d. 2004, Samir Moussaab, d. 2007, etc.). Police and soldiers continue to pay a heavy price in this struggle, and newspapers report their successes in articles that express less their author's confidence than the need to say something—anything to counter the *horror vacui*. But emptiness seems to be the rule, and people learn to live with it. The fear and anger that marked the first week following the bombing gives way to—or coexists alongside—a blasé feeling, testifying to the fact that human emotions are quickly exhausted, leaving behind an enduring residue of profound numbness.

The why of Algeria's funerals? This type of book cannot begin to provide all the answers. In any case, it is not placed before the reader as a moral obligation. The history of violence should be about trying to learn lessons, not give them.

Sidi Amar Sud, Chélif Valley, Algeria (April 2007)
Princeton, New Jersey (April 2008)

ACKNOWLEDGMENTS

This first book could not have been written without the support of many individuals, and it is a pleasure to acknowledge their help. This project began as a dissertation funded by a Mario Einaudi Pre-Dissertation Grant, a Sicca Grant, and an Einaudi Dissertation Fellowship—all from Cornell University's Institute for European Studies. The French-American Foundation's Bicentennial Fellowship enabled me to work in various archives. The Department of History at Cornell provided funding in the form of a Barret Fellowship, a Bowmar research fellowship, and a LaFeber-Silbey Grant. Cornell's Peace Studies Program and the Andrew W. Mellon Foundation supplied funding that enabled me to complete the dissertation. The Department of History at Texas A&M University and the Melbern G. Glasscock Center for Humanities Research at Texas A&M both came through with much-appreciated funding. The final revisions to this book were made during part of my stay at the School of Social Science at the Institute for Advanced Study, Princeton, New Jersey. My time in this extremely stimulating and supportive environment was made possible by funding from the National Endowment for the Humanities.

My project came together in discussions with friends, colleagues, and mentors in many locales. It would be impossible to express my thanks to all of those whose input helped shape this book. First, I owe a special debt of gratitude to dissertation committee members Steven L. Kaplan, Dominick LaCapra, and John H. Weiss. I would also like to thank Lucette Valensi, who supported me in my early dissertation research and then traveled to Ithaca, New York, to be present at my defense. The encouragement of these scholars was essential to the dissertation's completion, and they have remained unflagging intellectual supporters of my efforts as the dissertation became a book. Needless to say, I alone am responsible for the views expressed herein, as well as for any oversights and errors.

I would like to thank the colleagues and many close friends who have given generously of their time: Lahouari Addi, Leslie Adelson, Hamou Amirouche, Terry Anderson, Henriette Asséo, Anne Berger, Ross Brann, Cynthia Bouton, Terry Burke, Allan Christelow, Sherm Cochran, Julia Clancy-Smith, Dennis Cordell, Caroline Douki, Nelly Furman, María Antonia Garcés, Sandra Greene, Mohammed Harbi, Peter Holquist, Isabel Hull, Yasmina Khadra, Alexander Sydney Kanya-Forstner, Zaïm Khenchelaoui, Martin Klein, Philippe Minard, Isabelle Merle, David Powers, Robert Resch, Joan Scott, David Schalk, Michael Steinberg, Susan Tarrow, Enzo Traverso, Jean-Louis Triaud, Larry Yarak, and Oumelbanine Zhiri. This group of scholars provided advice and criticism that both inspired and pushed me to maintain a sense of rigor and commitment. I would also like to acknowledge the help of Sakina Drihem, Bouabdallah Khouidmi, and David Powers with Arabic-language documents. At Columbia University Press I wish to thank the anonymous readers of my manuscript for helpful suggestions. Acquiring editor Peter Dimock and editorial assistant Kabir Dandona were supportive from first to last. Freelance editor Henry Krawitz provided much-appreciated copyediting input. I owe a debt of gratitude to Tsering Wangyal Shawa of Princeton University Library for his help with the frontispiece map.

The staff at various repositories facilitated my research: Daniel Hick and his colleagues at the Centre des archives d'Outre-Mer (Aix-en-Provence); the Service historique de l'Armée de terre (Vincennes); the Centre des Archives nationales (Paris); the Bibliothèque nationale de France, Arsenal (Paris); the Département des cartes et plans at the Bibliothèque nationale de France, Richelieu (Paris); the Bibliothèque nationale d'Algérie, El-Hamma (Algiers); the Archives nationales d'Algérie (Algiers); and the U.S. National Archives in College Park, Maryland. My appreciation also goes to Guy Durand at the Archives de la Chambre de commerce de Marseille and to Boulamouar Dahia, librarian at the *zawiya* of El-Hamel. I would also like to thank the helpful teachers at the *zawiyas* of Aïn-Madi and Ouled-Djellal. Bob Parks extended a warm welcome at the Centre d'études maghrébines en Algérie, Oran.

Friends on three continents have supported me throughout the travails associated with this book. In Algiers I'd like to thank the Abrouk family for their graciousness and unfailing assistance. Bouabdallah Khouidmi has played an especially important role in helping me to develop my ideas in an ongoing conversation that spans nearly a decade. My thanks to the Khouidmi family and all my friends at Sidi Amar, and the Djemoui family of Djelfa, for their kind hospitality. In France I would like to thank the Talbi family, along with Alain and Annie-Claude Rouzier, Kamel Eddine Benhamouda, Daouda Gary, Mouloud Haddad, Madjid Chemirou, Dalila Rebhi, Bakhta Moukraenta, Ahmed Oulddali, Fatiha Sifou, and Fatima Cherak. The generosity of the Drihem family was a source of great inspiration. My work in the United States was facilitated by Aïcha Rahmouni, Federico Finchelstein, Tracie Matysik, Chris Bilodeau, Eleanor Kaufman, Jared Poley, Rick Keller, and Richard Schaefer. In Princeton my family and I could not have asked for a warmer friendship than that offered by Lakhdar and Melica Brahimi.

To my family goes my deepest appreciation. There are few people whose impact on my work has been more profound than that of my brother, Brady, my closest interlocutor. My sister-in-law Amy Jamison has seen this project through many stages, including some of the most difficult and trying moments. My parents have been a constant source of encouragement and support. For their immeasurable contribution I dedicate this work to them. Despite their young ages, my three daughters—Claudia, Hanan, and Sana—have enriched this work in their own inestimable ways. My final thanks go to my wife, Sakina Drihem. This book would have been a pale shadow of its present form without her persistent support, commentary, and insight.

NOTE ON TRANSLITERATION OF ARABIC

My transliteration of Arabic words strives for clarity, not elegance, and reflects the fact that many words and names come down to us with uncertain spellings and vocalizations. Technical terms in Arabic that are not found in an unabridged English-language dictionary have been transliterated according to the guidelines in the *International Journal of Middle East Studies* (IJMES). With commonly repeated words, like *zāwiya*, I have dropped diacritical marks in the interest of readability. I have used the French spelling of *Ouled* ("children of . . .") rather than the transliteration *Awlād*, to reflect local pronunciation and usage in French-language sources.

There are a handful of common English renderings of personal names of Algerians. I use them when they exist, such as "Abdelkader." I have given other well-known personal names both in their common rendition in the French-language sources and in transliterated form at first occurrence, following the IJMES system. I have cited other Algerian personal names as presented in the French sources.

Place names and names of topographical features correspond to the spellings of the *Michelin Map: Algeria and Tunisia* 743 (St.-Armand-Montrond, France: Imprimerie Clerc, 2007) and *Michelin Map: Africa North and West* 741 (St.-Armand-Montrond, France: Imprimerie Clerc, 2007). These are the names that appear in latin characters on Algerian road signs and maps. However, colonial-era place names, such as Géryville (today's El Bayadh), have been maintained in the interest of consistency with source material. Wherever they exist I have used common English spellings for cities, such as "Algiers" and "Timbuktu."

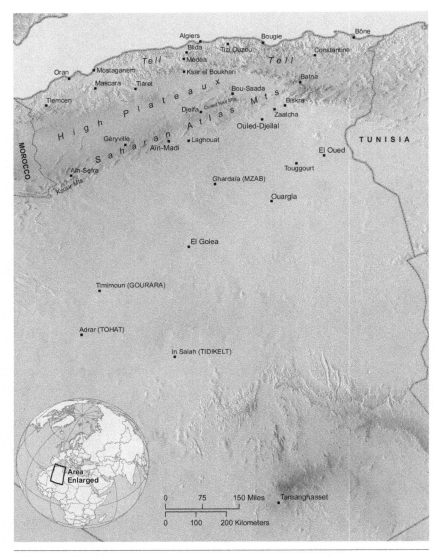

Map of Algeria [Tsering Wangyal Shawa and Benjamin Claude Brower]

A DESERT NAMED PEACE

INTRODUCTION

Understanding Violence in Colonial Algeria

. . . this land was a desert and a witness . . .
—William Faulkner, *Intruder in the Dust*

He was only a few days into his 1881 Algerian tour when Guy de Maupassant wrote, "As soon as one sets foot on this African soil, a singular desire invades you, to go further, to go south."[1] The thought came to Maupassant in Oran, a city he found banal, weary. More than two centuries of Spanish rule, only ending in 1792, had left Oran too familiar, its streets and people too European. Although it burned under a brilliant Mediterranean sun, Oran recalled Paris, reminding Maupassant of the intolerable life he had left behind. Disappointment gave way to ennui. It was not long before he fled. Driven by an irrepressible desire for the sun, for the "furious dazzlement of the light," Maupassant traveled to the Sahara. It was a long trek, made faster by the recently built railway, and Maupassant hoped to see the fantastic scenery painted by Eugène Fromentin and partake of the desert's exotic pleasures, both of which would be intensified by the fact that the Sahara was at this moment in full rebellion.

At Saïda, his first stop, Maupassant encountered "a little town after the French style," oddly placed in this land where the sun, "ferocious ravager," left nothing. The heat rising in the desert had "devoured the flesh of these valleys, leaving only stones and dust, where nothing can grow" (15). Saïda's French façade soon lifted, revealing a poor garrison town where ruined Alsatian peasants roamed the dirty streets by day, half-mad with grief and regret for the land they had left. At night packs of "starving and ferocious" feral dogs descended on the town and terrified all passersby. Maupassant spent a fitful night here; the unrelenting heat prevented him from falling sleep and the cries of the dogs unnerved him. "They bark at times in a continuous way, fearful to hear, enough to drive one crazy. Then other cries are heard, the shrill yelps of jackals, and above it all one hears the strong and singular voice of the hyena imitating the dog's cry in order to attract and devour him" (16). Farther south at Aïn-el-Hadjar were the silent ruins of the Compagnie franco-algérienne's factory, which once processed halfa, or esparto grass. Its workforce of landless Spanish peasants recently massacred, the factory was now home to jackals and vultures, which preyed on the weak and the wayward. Farther south, at Tafraoua, was a ramshackle fort, broken telegraph poles, and scattered bales of halfa, the desert crop that European investors had hoped would make them rich. Swept along by a sirocco, "the burning air of the desert," Maupassant stumbled over the bleached bones of would-be settlers and the rotting corpses of camels. At Oued-Fallette, deeper in the Sahara, he left the rail line, the locomotive inert on its tracks like "a fat black beast lying down on the dry sand," and set off on foot into the "deserted and gloomy land." Maupassant pressed on lethargically into the desert, "always toward the south" (21).

Setting out as the great Romantic in search of a strange and harsh land, Maupassant's oriental fantasy would meet with the reality of French colonialism in the Sahara. Like Gérard de Nerval's *Journey to the Orient* three decades earlier, Maupassant's voyage was undertaken in an effort to escape both himself and his society in a legendary "ailleurs." This elsewhere was the Sahara, which promised a change of scene and even deliverance. But in place of the inner discoveries Maupassant sought, he found a real country ravaged by war and economic disaster, where death and despair hung heavy. Here his romantic quest became a self-consciously ironic one, his writing a knowing parody of the tales of Byron or Chateaubriand's *René*, the wandering "mal du siècle" incarnate. Having seen the famed Sahara destroyed by the wars of colonialism, Maupassant's romantic voice became a critical one. The colonial effort to remake the Saharan steppes with farms and factories, he argued, was absurd. Such efforts yielded only heartache and ruin. French colonialism had brought modernity to Algeria—market economies, social stratification, bureaucracy—but it did not give the people who lived there "civilization." Algerians in particular, the descendents of the people who lived in the regency of Algiers prior to its demise in 1830, benefited little from Western education or European science, technology, and medicine. Instead, French rule had transformed them into impoverished rebels who now tore the country apart. They acted "neither out of hate nor religious fanaticism," as the military and settlers claimed, "but out of hunger." Maupassant continued: "With our system of colonization, consisting as it does in ruining the Arab, looting him without respite, hunting him without mercy and making him die of misery, we must expect to see many more insurrections" (23; translation modified).

Maupassant's outrage was compounded by the fact that such misrule forced the poet to make an ignoble retreat.

Maupassant's was not the typical understanding of France's path to Saharan empire. The predominant conception of the day shared only his desire for the sun. The expansion in the Sahara, many thought, was driven by an irresistible force, namely, fate. As Auguste Margueritte, a lieutenant colonel commanding the desert base at Laghouat, wrote eloquently in an 1860 report, "If we want to consider how we have thus far accomplished the conquest of Algeria and pushed successively our Domination just to the Algerian Sahara, we are obliged to observe that this great event was produced, so to speak, outside our will and plans."[2] As this narrative would have it, the French were magically drawn to these sublimely desolate lands of rocks and sand.

While Maupassant returned safely to write about his "journey to the sun," the same year another group, a survey mission for the trans-Saharan railway led by Colonel Paul Flatters, suffered a different fate. Some have claimed that Flatters, the son of a sculptor, liked to think of himself as an artist and was mentally confused by the desert's spectacular wonders when he marched into an ambush with more than a hundred French and Algerian troops. It is just as likely, however, that ambition blinded this officer, who misread the political signs and failed to maintain defensive ranks in his haste to make it across the Sahara, personally leading the way to French empire across the feared desert.[3] On 16 February 1881, at a site near the modern city of Tamanghasset, a group of Tuareg attacked and routed the mission. The initial assault was devastating, and those who survived (Flatters did not) started a long, ten-week trek back north to Ouargla, the nearest French base. Deep in the Sahara, without camels, weighted down with the mission's money (which they stubbornly refused to abandon), harassed by their enemies, and suffering from hunger and dehydration, a handful of survivors straggled back. The defeat stunned the French. They expected the Tuareg—whom they had come to know through ethnographic studies as a noble class of mounted warriors—to stand by their French allies. The shock of defeat was redoubled when word leaked out that the survivors had stayed alive by killing and eating the weakest members of their group. Even the last surviving Frenchman, a noncommissioned officer named Joseph Pobéguin, participated in the grisly meals. He first refused to join in the cannibalism but later agreed on condition that the victim's heart and liver be reserved for him.

By the time Maupassant and Flatters came to the Sahara, the French had devoted forty years of effort to establish control over the desert to the south of their Algerian colony. Lacking political support, know-how, and resources, planners thought to expand their influence over these lands incrementally, without major military engagements. It was to be a bloodless "conquest," and it came to be known as the "pénétration pacifique," a peaceful penetration. Whereas France's control over northern Algeria had been hard won after decades of costly and brutal war, the history of colonialism in the Sahara would be different. Sparsely populated, without lands suitable for farming or other resources that might attract the hordes of settlers and speculators who had so muddled things in the north, expansion into the Sahara would be an affair reserved for military, scientific, artistic, and commercial elites, that is, those best able to persuade local people of the benefits of French colonialism. It did not turn out that way. Colonial expansion into the Sahara brought few of the promised edifying results and was far from peaceful. Instead of a mutually beneficial encounter, French expansion into the deserts of North Africa was characterized by violence.

DEFINING COLONIAL VIOLENCE

Most often, studies of colonial violence concentrate on the coercive actions of European states and their agents.[4] There are empirical as well as ethico-political justifications for this emphasis. Certainly in terms of scale the violence perpetrated by Europeans—what historian Caroline Elkins has called the "dreadful balance sheet of atrocities"—is weighted heavily on Europe's side.[5] The facts in Algeria are worth stressing in this respect. Thanks to the work of demographic historian Kamel Kateb, we know that around 825,000 Algerian lives were ended because of the violence of the first forty-five years of the French occupation, and an equal number died in the famines and epidemics triggered, in large part, by the colonial-induced economic mutations suffered by Algerian society.[6] When the emigration of people who fled colonial rule is counted, Algeria lost a total of nearly half its precolonial population, from about four million people in 1830 to the roughly two million Algerians (indigènes) counted in 1872.[7] (On the other side of the ledger, during the same period the French army lost a total of 118,000 men in combat and due to illness.)[8] Thus, in terms of sheer numbers the actions of European agents dominate the history of colonial violence.

Amplifying the need to understand European violence is the tendency of historians working in former colonial states to marginalize their country's colonial past, writing national histories dominated by events occurring in Europe.[9] This is especially true in France. Although there is a dynamic field populated by several generations of historians working on French colonial history, whose works fill booksellers' shelves and the pages of French-language journals, the best-known and most powerful historians (e.g., Roger Chartier, Arlette Farge, Daniel Roche, Pierre Nora, Jacques Revel, and Alain Corbin) concentrate on French fields within Europe.[10] This is part of a larger problem of canon formation, allocation of state resources, the academic job market, and so forth, which has produced what Caroline Douki and Philippe Minard have called the "resserrement franco-français."[11] Moreover, influential scholars working in areas outside the hexagon tend to not deal with French colonialism. Of the prestigious chairs held by specialists of non-European societies at the Collège de France, only Henry Laurens, the chair of the Contemporary History of the Arab World, works on French colonialism. Unlike his predecessor, Jacques Berque, Laurens does little work on the French presence in the Maghreb, the most important colonial region for France. In this respect Algeria is a special case. France relinquished its colony in Algeria following a long and costly war, but it rarely mentioned this past in public discourses, a history that became "the gangrene and the oblivion" of French memory.[12] When colonial memory returned several decades ago, it showed the distortion of these years of repression. After Algeria's descent into civil war filled French news broadcasts and newspapers with stories of ghastly violence, the door opened to fully revanchist readings of the colonial era. As historian Mohammed Harbi has argued, "Unable to conceive relations of equality with postcolonial societies, nostalgists of colonialism renew the stereotypes in giving themselves over to the pleasures of retrospective predictions."[13] This reached new levels in 2005 when the French National Assembly and Senate—caught up in electoral politics and the struggles about security, citizenship, and identity—passed the 23 February 2005 law requiring that the national curriculum include lessons on the "positive role" of French colonialism.[14] As the late historian Claude Liauzu wrote, this law represented a "law against history."[15]

The aim of this book is not to right the course of history and memory. There is no need to write a "légende noire" of French colonialism to counter the "légende rose" informing the February law and other revisionist accounts.[16] Others have already amply documented the crimes of the French in Algeria in work that began more than fifty years ago during the Algerian revolution, when Algerian nationalists decried French "genocide," and it has continued to this day.[17]

This book has a different focus, namely, measuring and explaining the violence of Algeria's colonial past. It treats colonial violence not as a single whole but as a question with multiple parts. While the limits of sources ensure that this book starts from a French perspective, these documents come from a colonial archive that, contrary to stereotypes, is infinitely complex and speaks in a profusion of voices. This approach is also inspired by the novels of William Faulkner, like *The Sound and the Fury, Light in August,* and *Intruder in the Dust.* The bleak tapestry of Southern society Faulkner described in these texts reveals patterns of poverty and racial conflict, along with local political struggles and the larger economic and social forces that intersected, uprooted, and destroyed otherwise confined lives. Although the society described by Faulkner was strictly split down racial lines, he rejected a dualist perspective to recount the violence of segregation. Like *The Sound and the Fury,* my book tells one story in four parts, representing four facets of the same problem. The reader will recognize in what follows that I make no pretentions of formal innovation. But this structure presents a "single story, several times told."[18]

The four parts of this book cover the history of the Saharan lands that became a part of France's Algerian colony in the second half of the nineteenth century.[19] The first examines how the French took control of the Sahara through military campaigns involving immoderate forms of violence, including massacres, even as they first conceived of the Saharan conquest as a peaceful penetration. The second seeks new understandings of anticolonial resistance through the case study of an Algerian attack on a French village. This minor and forgotten episode is marked by the brutality of the assailants as well as the obscurely shaded purpose of their actions. The third deals with the violence of indigenous forms of slavery and the accommodation with colonialism that preserved it in an era of abolition. The fourth shows how cultural struggles in France, linked to a fascination with the extreme and the archaic, infiltrated colonial planning with particularly dangerous results.

Taken together, these parts examine the *multiple* logic of violence in colonial Algeria. My argument begins with the recognition that violence is not a singular phenomenon and assumes many forms. This is particularly true in colonial settings, where violence emerges from many contexts and responds to multiple forms of logic, each one a special case. The fact that French colonialism in Algeria never produced a universal regime of shared norms or banished nonsynchronous spaces illustrates this point. Moreover, it never succeeded in reducing the social complexity of the country to simple dichotomies. As Franz Fanon recognized, Algeria under French rule was a "compartmentalized world," with Algerians and French living vastly different and unequal lives. However, it was not the simple "Manichean" one that he saw near the end of the war of independence (1954–62), when revolutionary violence finally defined the social binary necessary for a nationalist victory.[20] Thus, there are limits to talking about violence during Algeria's colonial period within categories such as "proactive" and "reactive," as in previous studies of modern violence.[21] A multiplicity of actors and relations of force defined colonial society and shaped its violence. Telling this story requires crossing the disciplinary fields separating European, Middle Eastern, and African history. This is a project with hazards, but it is necessary to understand a place like Algeria, a Mediterranean borderland that does not fit neatly into current fields of research. Analyzing the violence of the colonial era also entails thinking differently about the rise of the French colonial state and its impact. It was not a seamless institution. Although the entire country felt the effects of colonialism—no region was untouched—its weight was distributed unevenly. Hardly the robust disciplinary grid they claimed to be, during the entire period covered by this book French institutions and colonial practices remained disjointed, marked by contradictions and incoherence.

These facts and their implication for the study of violence emerge with clarity along the frontiers of what the French empire made into the Algerian Sahara, far from the logistical centers of French power. Here colonial rule was invariably incomplete. Coercive power remained a mainstay of the new regime, seeking social contours of dominators and dominated. But a great deal of violence eluded the logic of colonial oppression and anticolonial resistance. As one might expect, this included the violence of smugglers and bandits, groups that adapted to French rule even as the French tried to deploy them to serve their own ends. But it also included the violence of local political entrepreneurs, like the people studied in the second part of this book, who sought to carve power and influence out of the social mutations triggered by French rule. When colonial administrators failed to achieve a monopoly of violence, they supplemented coercion by exploiting cleavages in Algero-Saharan societies, using them as arteries to distribute colonial power. This often ended in violence, albeit one that does not correspond to uprisings of the "wretched." In other cases colonial policies targeted institutions of social cohesion, seeking to break down indigenous social norms, but the violence unleashed by this anomie remained tied to endogenous, precolonial dynamics and idioms. Violence during the colonial period thus reflected the social makeup of the country itself, and it expressed a variety of political strategies, tensions, hopes, and anxieties. The individual case of colonial Algeria shows the truth of what philosopher Etienne Balibar has observed about violence and power more generally: "There are layers of violence which do not gravitate around the alternative of power versus counterpower, although they inevitably return in them—*infect* them, so to speak."[22]

A definition of colonial violence unfolds in several stages. At its most basic level it consists of processes, yielding forms, in other words, as phenomenon with effects. But it is not a single, unified thing, something with structural coherence that the historian might use to draw the grand panoramas of the past. Therefore, in order to define colonial violence in a study like this, it is useful to first identify actions and actors. In this book the *actors* are those who both perpetrated and suffered the effects of violence, that is, its victims. The logic of colonialism tried to reduce these actors to colonizer and colonized, the binary that represented the ultimate expression of colonial politics and society during the first fifty to sixty years of the French occupation. As I will demonstrate, establishing this divide was the work of the earliest forms of French violence, beginning in 1830. This binary held sway in many cases, and it channeled violence between the two parties with terrifying efficiency. In other instances, however, violence did not respond uniquely to this duality but showed many "fields of overlapping and intersecting forms of subjection," like power itself.[23] In this book I examine several salient occurrences. For example, the case of Saharan slavery shows that slave-owning and slave-trading notables were at the center of a diffuse and indistinct violence, and they did not immediately draw their logic from the colonized-colonizer dynamic—although with the threat of abolition looming, they were hardly outside of colonialism. The social tensions produced by slavery in an age of abolition provided a handy opening where colonial rule could invest itself in local society. Colonial administrators and Algero-Saharan notables engaged in a process of accommodation wherein they negotiated the power differential of the new order, while slaves and other socially subaltern peoples of color continued to suffer the violence of slavery. In other situations colonial actors pursued different projects, which display displacements of earlier or unrelated conflicts. A case in point is the French army officers and explorers who deployed the idioms of European Romanticism to frame their actions in the Sahara, importing the cultural struggles of the metropole into the desert.

The *action* of colonial violence—violence itself—is difficult to define. Violence has no essential nature and one cannot state exactly what it *is*. The word itself is derived from the French "violence." According to the *Grand Robert*, when French authors first used it in the thirteenth century they meant the "abuse of force." Modern definitions vary in both French and English but agree that violence is force that injures living beings and ideas, or damages property, and they all convey the original French sense of abuse. But the traits of violence are not constant over time, and its meanings and methods, its purposes and effects, have changed considerably over the course of history.[24] Norms have also shifted. What constitutes violence has not remained steady. Sexual violence in particular has been redefined substantially in the last two centuries.[25] So, too, have interpretations. Historian Fernand Braudel, for example, famously wrote that war in the early modern Mediterranean was only the slow pulse of larger historical forces, a sort of conversation linking rival powers, a view difficult to reconcile in the *longue durée* with the Mediterranean that Braudel knew after 1945, when so many wars, civil and "uncivil," spilt the region apart.[26]

My main focus on violence in this book is its relationship to power and the production of social inequalities. I am especially interested in instances where physical force constitutes political power. Many of my sources speak to the fundamental link between violence and power, what Etienne Balibar has called the dialectic of *Gewalt*, or the "violence-of-power."[27] At the same time, my inquiry into the historical conditions for violence in colonial Algeria seeks multiple forms. I agree with those who argue that violence cannot be reduced to its physicality, pain and death. Anthropologists Nancy Scheper-Hughes and Philippe Bourgois have argued that "violence also includes assaults on the personhood, dignity, sense of worth or value of the victim."[28] Forms of psychosocial coercion used to control another person's labor and sexuality can be added to this list. Thus, my field of analysis includes what Pierre Bourdieu has named symbolic violence, forms of domination that use signification as an "auxiliary" to physical force.[29] Finally, I find it helpful to be attentive to what anthropologist Paul Farmer has called structural violence, the less visible form of violence imbedded in history, institutionalized racism, and gender inequality that "withers bodies slowly."[30] Although they are an important part of colonial violence, symbolic and structural forms of violence are typically overshadowed by the sheer physical force wielded by European militaries and their anticolonial double, those who took up arms against them.

In terms of theory and method, therefore, my argument moves forward without presumptions, nor does this book take aim at particular paradigms, either to shift them or establish new ones. Instead, it draws from several different perspectives in order to better understand a particular historical problem. This book will not give the reader the source from which flows the darkness of colonial violence, a morally satisfying but historically dubious project. But it should get us closer to the set of questions and events, terms and structures, necessary to understand violence in Algeria's history.

FRENCH VIOLENCE IN ALGERIA UP TO THE SAHARAN CONQUEST: THE "FIRST" FRENCH-ALGERIAN WAR

The story of colonial violence in the Sahara begins where another one leaves off, the "first" French-Algerian war beginning in 1830 and roughly ending in 1848.[31] Fought against a broad range of armed Algerian opposition, France's victory resulted in control of the northern lands of Algeria, a place known as the Tell. In terms of violence, the actions of French actors dominate the conquest of the Tell and set the tone for the period of Saharan expansion that followed. While later chapters of this book seek different vantage points, it is useful to introduce this first part of the story primarily from the French perspective.

Numerous factors brought France to Algeria in 1830. One explanation draws on a political history that began decades earlier and thousands of kilometers away. The expedition of 1830 represented one of many aftershocks of the French Revolution that reverberated into the next century and beyond.[32] Having taken back the throne that the Revolution forced Louis XVI to vacate, the Bourbons struggled to reconstitute a monarchial authority devastated by regicide, war, and new rising classes and their political agendas. The Restoration's first king, Louis XVIII, embraced pragmatism and sought equilibrium, but his brother, Charles X, came to power in 1824 determined to roll back the Revolution. This project faced many difficulties. Practicing absolutist politics in the face of an opposition with fresh memory of the Revolution—when, as Anatole France wrote, the "voice of the people was the voice of God"—posed many challenges, to say the least.[33] Charles X hoped that by beating the drums of imperial conquest in Algeria he might make a claim on nationalism and use it to rally people to support the shaky edifices of his regime. In other words, although he would not reconcile himself to the Revolution, Charles X had learned some of its lessons. These included the domestic uses of foreign wars. As his minister of war acknowledged in the 1827 proposal to seize Algiers, "it goes without saying that it is useful sometimes to remind France that military glory survived the revolution and that a legitimate monarchy . . . also knows how to float its battle flags in far-off countries."³⁴ Thus in the postrevolutionary era, war would be as much about shaping public opinion, containing its "subversive words," as it would be about larger geostrategic concerns.³⁵ Cultivating sentiments of militarism and national chauvinism—legacies of the Revolution and Napoleonic era valuable for all forms of modern politics—helped the struggling regime create a climate useful to the modern state, what Roger Caillois has called "excess, violence, outrage."³⁶

Given the fact that Charles X's main enemies were in France, he did not think through the purpose of the expedition in Algeria itself. An ad hoc response of a dying monarchy, the French expedition to Algiers lacked clear strategic goals. It had a military plan to seize Algiers, one that dated back to 1808, when Napoleon first thought of landing there.³⁷ But few could say what the army might do when and if it defeated the Ottoman dey. Symptomatic of this opacity of mission was the fact that the Algiers expedition lacked an ideology. The confluence of many orders of political thought issued during the French Revolution determined the site of the expedition.³⁸ The most important originated in Bonaparte's 1798 expedition against the Mameluke regime in Egypt, which gave Mediterranean conquest "new elevation and grandeur," as the monumental first volume of the *Description de l'Egypte* announced in 1809.³⁹ This text, written by Joseph Fourier with the help of the archeologist Jacques-Joseph Champollion and corrected by Napoleon himself, announced a new idea of empire. Based on the emancipatory mission of the Revolution, conquest in the southeast Mediterranean involved, according to Henry Laurens, the "liberation of the people of the Orient from their local despots, the Mamelukes, and more generally . . . from Ottoman domination."⁴⁰ Unlike the ancien régime's mercantilist schemes of empire, Bonaparte promised cooperation in Egypt and put the ideas of "enlightened internationalism" on his standards.⁴¹ These assumed a basic harmony of interests among peoples united against ignorance, suffering, and despotism. The political values of 1789, as well as modern science and technology, would produce a spirit of fraternity in Egypt and lead to "a solid and glorious peace" throughout the Mediterranean.⁴² But Bonaparte's appeals to Arabo-Egyptian patriotism against the Mamelukes and Ottomans did not signal his commitment to ideas of self-determination, as the bloody suppression of the Cairo revolt of October 1798 showed. Egyptian aspirations would first have to pass through the crucible of "regeneration," wherein Egyptians would be reborn to a modern future. The rebirth was expected to be a long one, focused less on the sort of moral regeneration that mobilized revolutionaries in France—for example, when they planned their virtue-forming festivals—than on the development of the infrastructure of a modern state.⁴³ There were canals to be built, along with irrigation projects, ports, schools, and armies. Bonaparte presented himself as the midwife in this process, and for this he made claims on the offspring, a country producing resources needed by France, representing French interests in the eastern Mediterranean.[44]

Events forced the French army out of Egypt in 1801. Three decades later, when it again arrived on the southern shores of the Mediterranean, French generals tried to adapt Bonaparte's program to Algeria even as they fought against revolution in France. They lifted almost word for word the language of social revolution from Bonaparte's Egyptian campaign. This is amply manifest in the 1830 proclamation by the commander of the army, General de Bourmont, to "the inhabitants of Algiers and the people of the tribes," a document in Arabic prepared for him by translators. In it he announced: "Our presence among you is not to fight you; our goal is only to make war on your Pacha. . . . You are not ignorant of the excesses of his tyranny ["ghāyāt taḥkimihi wa qabh ṭab'ihi," translated in French as "les excès de sa tyrannie, la dépravation de sa mauvaise nature"], the depravation of his bad character. . . . The proof [of these] is that the most beautiful estates, lands, horses, arms, clothing, jewelry, etc., are all for him alone." The document concluded by stating that God had ordained the fall of the Ottomans "to deliver you from the worries and the misery that oppress you."[45]

The Convention of 5 July 1830 reaffirmed these principles. This text, by which France negotiated the surrender of Hussein Dey (al-Husayn ibn al-Husayn, d.1838) and thereby first made its claim to sovereignty in Algeria, announced in unambiguous terms a new rule based on just laws protecting property and promoting cultural respect (called "tolérance" in other texts).[46] "The exercise of the Mohammedan religion will remain free. The liberty of the inhabitants of all classes, their religion, their property, will experience no harm. Their women will be respected."[47] The idea behind this text was to distinguish the 1830 mission from the Crusades, or the later wars of the Hapsburgs and Romanovs against the Ottoman Empire, narrated in the idioms of religious struggle, namely, the cross versus the crescent. As minister of war, Marshal Soult later wrote, "Christendom, a name that has been evoked, dreamed in other times of religious conquests on the Barbary Coast. Today it is a matter of pacific conquests of civilization, useful to the vanquished as well the victors."[48] Guaranteeing protection for women, it was hoped, would further signal the differences: the French army did not come to Algiers to rape and pillage.

Yet they did not come to liberate either. Despite its language of emancipation, the army that landed in 1830 was aligned with the Restoration, not the Revolution. It was led by Général de Bourmont, who rallied to support the most vehement counterrevolutionaries after 1789, like the Prince de Condé, and later led royalist armies in western France. "Liberation" was anathema to him. As historian Gabriel Esquer wrote a century later, despite what Bourmont said to the Algerians, he recognized that the expedition was simply "a diversion . . . a way to avoid revolution."[49] It failed famously. Less than a month after Bourmont's victory, Paris bristled with the barricades that announced another revolution, and on 30 July 1830 the Bourbon Restoration came to an end. Charles X abdicated and revolutionaries offered the throne to the duc d'Orléans, Louis-Philippe. The new king vowed to give France a liberal constitutional monarchy in tune with the changing political and social needs of the country, a project he continued until he, too, fell victim to the revolution of 1848.

France's first four years in Algeria have generally been characterized as a period of disorder. Eugène Pellissier's memorable lines of 1854 best express this thinking: "The northern hordes that wrested from the Roman Empire its debris acted with more wisdom and reason" than the French in Algeria.[50] Seen from the French perspective, the occupation was indeed disorderly and expensive. But France's confusion represented opportunity for others. Thus, when vague news of the revolution of 1830 arrived in Algiers on the morning of 11 August in a letter from an Algerian merchant in Marseille, some Algerians were heartened.[51] These were notables who, although not welcoming French armies, thought desirable change might result from their presence. Louis-Philippe's expressed moderation and ascendant liberals' embrace of property as a fundamental right seemed to offer a different set of possibilities for the French projects in Algeria than had the Bourbons. Algerian merchants like Ahmed Bouderba (Ahmed Bu Darba) and former Ottoman officials like Hamdan Khodja (Hamdan ibn 'Uthman Hujah, ca. 1775–ca. 1839) anticipated new possibilities following the defeat of the Ottomans.[52] Although they differed in many respects, Khodja and Bouderba, like the reformers farther east studied by Albert Hourani, looked north across the Mediterranean to "the new Europe of industry, swift communications, and political institutions, not as a menace so much as offering a path to be followed."[53] In Algeria aspirations centered on the Egyptian example after 1798. The overthrow of the Mameluke government and the isolation of Egypt from the Ottoman Empire ushered in new opportunities for the country, especially for certain classes of Egyptians. These were represented by Muhammad Ali Pasha, governor of Egypt (Muhammad 'Ali Basha, 1769–1849), a forward-looking leader who some Algerian elites saw as expressing their own hopes.[54] Certain French commentators, like the scholar Adrien Berbrugger, agreed with the Algerians.[55] The fact that France supported the national aspirations of Poles, Greeks, and Belgians in Europe gave them further reason to be optimistic that their own goals might be moved forward by events.

Finding an Egyptian solution for Algeria largely depended on getting French troops out of the country, like Bonaparte's army had been forced out of Egypt. This was a distinct possibility. The British were not happy to see the French flag in Algeria, and many politicians in Paris would have supported Louis-Philippe had he walked away from battles that were not his own. At the beginning of a new era, influential political figures thought France had a continental, not a colonial, future. In his insightful yet overlooked 1973 dissertation historian

Marwan R. Buheiry pointed to the fact that French critics first called for their country to "decolonize" in the 1830s, using the term more than a century before the struggles following the Second World War made it common usage.[56] They looked back to the disasters of the revolutionary and Napoleonic eras, when France lost most of what remained of its first colonial empire, wealthy colonies like Saint Domingue, which exploded in revolution. They argued that the government needed to divert the resources being spent in Algeria to modernize their own country and ensure France's future in the coming industrial era. Moreover, Algeria grew the same types of crops as in France, and the climate did not look promising for the tropical plants that could make this place an Eldorado comparable to the old sugar colonies. And even if something valuable like cotton might thrive in the Maghreb, as some vainly hoped, neomercantilist schemes in Algeria threatened to prolong the economic archaism of the ancien régime with "feudalism of the modern era," as the colonial critic Amédée Desjobert put it in 1837.[57] Finally, the end of slavery loomed on the horizon, making colonies obsolete according to this view. The free trade promised by economic liberals offered a much better, more modern way to secure things like the sugarcane and fibers needed by French refineries and mills.

However, Louis-Philippe considered the political risks of evacuating Algeria more formidable than staying put. Turning his back on the army's most important victory since it was muzzled by the Congress of Vienna presented incalculable dangers. The landings aroused great enthusiasm in cities like Marseille, where commercial interests anticipated making their fortunes in Algeria. Others worried that Britain would step in if France left, fears that roused currents of nationalist fervor. The latter held that it was empire as much as industry that made Britain a threat to France. If France wished to remain a great power, it would have to compete with its cross-Channel rival globally, controlling territory and people.

In the end, the same domestic political problems faced by Charles X came to haunt Louis-Philippe, influencing his decision to stay in Algeria. Having come to power on the barricades, Louis-Philippe faced troubling questions about his legitimacy, and foreign conquests offered him a valuable tool to consolidate power. Algeria provided the luster of imperial conquest necessary for his family to hold on to the throne. In the short run, in 1834 his government decided upon what they called "occupation restreint" (restricted occupation).[58] This limited the French presence to Algeria's major Mediterranean ports—a strategic move that helped France control the western entrance to the Mediterranean. Moreover, the Orléanist monarchy could extract considerable symbolic value from its occupation of the "Barbary Coast" by expelling the corsairs, which Europeans and Americans considered "pirates" and "brigands." Rather than being viewed as the expression of a dangerously resurgent imperial France—something that might rally the great powers to take action against it—the conquest of Algeria could figure as part of larger European-led struggle against disorder in the world. As a note addressed to the Parliament in 1835 stated, "In conquering Algiers France delivered humanity from the infamy of piracy. This generous nation has lavished its blood and treasury to implant Civilization on the debris of the most monstrous despotism."[59] There were practical considerations as well in that the port cities were easily controlled. France faced more daunting prospects in the interior of Algeria. It was an immense country. Just the northern lands of the Tell, not counting most of the southern steppes and the Sahara, covered over two hundred thousand square kilometers, a massive area roughly half the size of metropolitan France itself.[60] Mountains dominated the geography and Algeria lacked navigable waterways and had few roads, making for slow, difficult, and dangerous communication with the interior. Sending military forces into these lands would require huge expenditures and entail considerable risks. Rather than move them inland, the restricted occupation allowed Louis-Philippe to pull his forces back to the relative safety of the coast.

A COLONIAL LOGIC TO EARLY FRENCH VIOLENCE

In one of his last books historian Mahfoud Kaddache emphasized that Algerians experienced the fall of Algiers not as the "prise d'Alger" (seizure) celebrated in the history lessons he learned growing up in colonial Algeria but as a "perte" (loss).[61] Indeed, lamentation was the typical reaction of Algerians to the fall of the city. Ahmed Efendi, a mufti residing in Algiers, wrote, "God protect Muslim countries from such a frightful spectacle."[62] Another witness recounted the "panicked terrors" of Algiers's population in a haunting poem that concluded "my heart is in mourning for Algiers!" Some blamed the weakness of the dey and the Ottoman regency of Algiers itself for the defeat.[63] Situated "at the margins of empire," as historian Suraiya Faroqhi puts it, this state dated back more than three hundred years, with janissaries, corsairs, and local rulers holding power as a vassal principality of the Ottoman Empire.[64] By the nineteenth century the regency of Algiers consisted of Algiers and the three provinces, or *beylicks*, of Titteri, Oran, and Constantine, roughly covering Algeria's modern-day borders with Tunisia and Morocco. After the Hussein Dey's defeat in Algiers, surviving Ottoman leaders like Ahmed Bey (Ahmad ibn Muhammad Sharif, 1784–1850) of Constantine welcomed refugees from the French conquests to his capital and prepared to face the invaders by reorganizing his army and government.[65] In the west the famous Algerian leader Abdelkader ('Abd al-Qadir ibn Muhyi al-Din al-Jaza'iri, 1808–1883) forged a coalition of Algerian forces that represented a powerful challenge to France.[66] Bearing the title Amīr al-Mu'minīn (Commander of the Believers), Abdelkader combined war and diplomacy to wrest the beginnings of a self-governing Algerian state from the French and his Algerian rivals, making him the iconic figure of Algerian nationalism.[67]

Although expressed in the idiom of lamentation, it was not an experience of humiliation, a blow suffered by the Dar al-Islam (abode of Islam), that made the fall of Algiers such a loss to Algerians. Algiers was not the first Muslim city in North Africa to succumb to Christian rule, and its fall does not begin a trite story of the "roots of Muslim rage."[68] Rather, the year 1830 represented a traumatic moment for Algerians because of the harsh forms of subjugation they experienced at the hands of the French. These occurred almost immediately. The signing of the Convention of 5 July 1830, which ended the war between the French state and the regency of Algiers, should have brought an end to armed operations and violence, but it was followed by a wave of looting. French soldiers and officers, eager to get their share of the city's riches, led it and local criminal elements joined them, profiting from the collapse of the Ottoman government's police force. They were effective. The treasury of the dey, the grand prize claimed by the French state, had been estimated to hold as much as 500 million francs, but only 48.7 million francs made it into the coffers of the French government.[69] In the days following the fall of Algiers, eyewitnesses reported looting by officers like General Loverdo, who was seen leaving the city with six mules loaded with stolen goods.[70] Others reported French troops plundering marble columns and fountains to take back to France.[71] According to some sources, soldiers even looted the Swedish consulate's residence as well as the homes of the foreign diplomatic corps in Algiers.[72]

This free-for-all put in doubt the claims of the convention. French violence no longer appeared to be about state-building, nor was the looting law-instating or law-preserving.[73] In the months that followed, the military sequestered homes, seized mosques, and destroyed whole neighborhoods, all with scant legal justification.[74] In 1830 alone military engineers destroyed 90 buildings in Algiers, and the following year they leveled another 335.[75] Owners were labeled "absent" or "unknown," and few received compensation. Religious institutions suffered a similar fate. The decree of 7 December 1830 claimed for the French state the *ḥubus*, or properties held in usufruct by mosques and Islamic pious foundations. Their confiscation put a good part of Algiers under the full or partial domain of the French government.[76] This outright assault on property in Algiers violated the convention and led many people to flee the French-controlled city. The trickle of refugees who departed in the early days of July turned into a veritable flood. From an estimated population of thirty to forty thousand in 1830, the number of Algerians living in Algiers fell by more than two-thirds, reduced to some twelve thousand people in 1834.[77] Reflecting on this period, historian Larbi Ichbouben noted somewhat ironically that the liberation promised in 1830 "was a matter of 'liberating' the city of its own [people]."[78]

The violence came with important implications for the forms of power of the colonial state. By the standards of the day, the conquest of Algiers enjoyed legitimacy. An 1827 diplomatic incident between the Ottoman dey and the French consul (the "coup d'éventail" [fan slap] made famous by colonial historiography) provided what was necessary for a justified war, and the landings and seizure of Algiers represented a legitimate rite of war. A rite of peace, the convention, duly followed. This brought to an end one system of laws and sovereignty and created a new one based on the respect of property and legal protections for Muslim institutions.[79] However, the army's looting and immediate violation of the convention signaled the fact that it considered itself exempt from the law, the very law its force had inaugurated. This amounted to a portentous announcement that the new regime did not plan to rule based upon affirmation and consent, law and legitimacy, institutions thought to be typical of the modern state. Instead, it prepared a specific set of institutions for colonial rule inspired by the most unsophisticated forms of power.

Apart from the forced expulsion of Algiers's Ottoman-Anatolian populations, whom the French obliged to leave shortly after they arrived, there is little evidence to show that soldiers beat, killed, or sexually assaulted people in Algiers in the first month of the occupation. However, with the brutal sack of Blida, sixty kilometers from Algiers, in November 1830 all this changed. Soldiers led by General Bertrand Clauzel, Louis-Philippe's choice to command the African army, killed randomly in the hours following their arrival in this town. Pell-mell executions of people assembled as prisoners followed, which included firing squads and sabering and bayoneting of those who survived. This improvised slaughter dragged on for more than six hours.[80] Several days later, when French troops billeted in Blida came under counterattack, the indiscriminate killing recommenced with a vengeance. French troops descended on one neighborhood and killed everyone. Eight hundred Blideans were slaughtered as recompense for the twenty-one French soldiers killed in action that day.[81] Apologists for the army downplayed the massacre.[82] (One even claimed that Blida's people killed each other.[83]) But a reporter writing in the army publication *Le Spectateur militaire* described the attack in blunt terms that expressed the author's reprobation. French soldiers initiated this slaughter, the reporter wrote, and Blida's entire population "were all treated like the enemy," contrary to the codes of military conduct.[84] When troops departed, they left the town deserted. The reporter concluded: "This unfortunate town can be considered no longer to exist."[85] Those who survived the murderous violence, "the debris of the population," returned to Algiers under the army's protection.[86] In the spectacle of their shocked looks and wounds they testified to the omnipotence of French power and its macabre benevolence.

The violence at Blida did not serve to defeat enemy forces or control territory, both typical goals of military violence. Few of the people killed had taken up arms against the French, and the leaders of the territories France sought to control had already ceded them by the time the second massacre occurred. But the violence did have a political purpose. It recorded a crude sort of message, inscribing its meaning on the bodies of victims, people who became "debris." These survivors served as a grim symbol, a memento mori announcing the new regime's massive and inscrutable power, which was almost godlike in intensity.

It is not clear whether or not the Algerians, the intended recipient of such violence, ever got the message. Ultimately, this violence was probably less about impressing people about to be colonized than a way for the French army to impress itself, a sort of autoerotic display. In any case, many within the French military contested this strategy. For example, when General Pierre Berthezène took command of the African army he put a stop to the tendency toward violence. Succeeding General Clauzel in February 1831, Berthezène considered new relations with Algerians not subject to the logic of force and domination. To his mind the way to proceed was simply to "respect the capitulation of Algiers [the Convention of 5 July 1830], give back to the pious foundations the property wrongly taken by the state, pay indemnities to the dispossessed proprietors, [and] render justice to the most humble."[87] Berthezène represented a different view of the colonial state, one that was more in tune with the trend toward softer forms of power occurring in Europe. Thus, he proposed a new twist on the military idea of "rigor" in Algeria: "the most rigorous justice," law exercised with integrity and rectitude, would be the watchwords of his administration.[88] However, Berthezène's policies provoked hostility with the minister of war repeatedly pressing his commander to take a harder line.

In less than a year Berthezène was out and his successor, the duc de Rovigo, had taken up the firm policy with zeal. Reacting to unconfirmed reports in April 1832 that the Ouffia, a pastoralist group camped near Algiers, had robbed Algerian travelers allied to France, Rovigo dispatched a battalion of the Foreign Legion and a squad of Algerian auxiliaries on an early-morning punitive raid. The raid turned into mass murder: the Ouffia were entirely "destroyed," as Rovigo later remarked with satisfaction.[89] Operating under old rules of military entrepreneurship resurrected for Algeria, wherein booty figured into the pay of troops, soldiers plundered the Ouffia camp and took their herds back to Algiers, where they sold the spoils and shared the profits.[90] To celebrate this "victory," Rovigo ordered merchants to keep their shops open late that night.[91] Although some rebuked Rovigo for this arbitrary slaughter, their criticism did not move the French general. "I know that this does not please everybody," he wrote. "They do not find it philanthropic. Maybe it would have been more liberal to let the army be decimated little by little and give time to these brigands to civilize themselves," thereby masking the brutality of his actions with irony and sarcasm.[92]

This process displays little Foucauldian sophistication. The main expression of colonial power in Algeria remained the "right to *take* life or *let* live."[93] The modes of power that Foucault has shown transformed Europe came very late to Algeria.[94] Despite the hubristic claims of Alexis de Tocqueville that by 1847 France had lifted what he called the "veil" hiding the secrets of Algerian society, the sort of knowledge necessary for more diffuse forms of modern power did not emerge until well into the French occupation.[95] It only arrived during the last decades of the nineteenth century in the form of reform projects to regulate Algerian piety, among other things. Even then, these were accompanied by fragmented and imperfect institutions and techniques. In this respect, the 1945 Sétif massacre, a state-led, eight-week pogrom that claimed the lives of between twenty and thirty thousand Algerians at the end of the Second World War, is emblematic of a power that saw itself more as a purveyor of death than a regulator of life.[96]

Nevertheless, Foucault's reasoning concerning the productivity of power holds true in these early years of colonial Algeria. The violence of power certainly destroyed, but it helped French colonialism produce itself with a specific *episteme*. Violence functioned in conjunction with the ethnographies, political announcements, laws, and visual images that marked exclusions, exceptions, and difference. It served a specific function. The violence done to Algerians reflected the meanings that had circulated in texts written by colonial planners, army officers, in-house orientalists, government officials based in Paris, and so on. But it also placed them on real bodies. Violence fixed the power relations of colonial society in unambiguous ways, making them plainly visible to the naked eye.

The "enframed" order of appearances in Algeria was thus saturated by the order of force. This provides a different version of "colonising" than the one Timothy Mitchell has written about concerning Egypt.[97] There was little in the first fifty years of French rule in Algeria that gave colonial power a coherent or orderly image. In most cases colonial projects failed in very visible ways. Insects and frost destroyed newly introduced tropical and industrial crops; workers showed up late at their jobs—or not at all; soldiers, consumed by alcohol and illness, deserted, disappeared, or simply changed sides by accepting Abdelkader's invitation to convert to Islam and join his cause.[98] Even the great works, like farms, meant to showcase the perfected institutions of France and produce the "world-as-exhibition," were unsuccessful. Carefully plotted out on administrators' desks in Paris and Algiers, rural settlements were abandoned by French families when they could not make ends meet. Large "capitalist" colonies like the Société genevoise turned out to be schemes to grab land and government subsidies.[99] In the Sahara, where water scarcity provided the opportunity to superimpose the colonial framework, the French managed to sink new wells in an effort to make the desert blossom, but they could not control what happened afterward. This included not only the unpredictable hydrological effects of new wells on fragile aquifers but also the very political text of these projects.

In one revealing case the French caretaker for a state-built well and rest station (caravanserai) fatally undermined the symbolic order of colonial power. An unscrupulous and brutal man, he prostituted his wife and daughter to all passersby. "The mother and the daughter give themselves to all, Europeans, or [indigenous] Mzabis and Jews, and this even in the presence of each other," wrote an infuriated local officer worried about the effect this would have on France's image.[100]

When the order of appearances failed, many of the military men who led the colonial project felt more comfortable relying on the order of physical force, which produced the results they sought. It simplified the country's considerable social complexity and the violence against law, property, and people engendered the social hierarchies of the new order. The logic of this violence reflected a simple schema: there were those who were subject to arbitrary force and those who wielded it. As expressed by one author in 1833, in French Algeria there was a "peuple vainqueur" and a "peuple vaincu."[101] Like all binaries, this one separating the victors from the vanquished was not absolute. During the course of the next 132 years that France remained in Algeria, it would be contested, crossed, and ignored to serve various ends. These included those of the colonial state. At the end of the century governor-generals like Jules Cambon (served 1891–97) and his successors found the colonial binary less helpful and sought reform.[102] But the violence of the first years of the occupation produced the lasting outlines of a colonial subject as a thing apart. The subject to be liberated announced prior to 5 July 1830 did not entirely vanish, but in its place there appeared a subject with more definite features — a *subjected* one.

THE "INDIGENOUS QUESTION"

Within the first five years of the French occupation, this subject became known as the "indigène."[103] The word, which translates into English as "native," arrived in the French language as an adjective from the Latin *indegena*, meaning "originally from the country."[104] In some usages it was innocuous, and it could even support anticolonial politics, like Voltaire's reference in *Essai sur les mœurs* (1769) to those in Arabia "who were truly indigenous" in contradistinction to outsiders. But by 1830 there was a telos taking form around the word that ensured its importance among colonial idioms. This came from earlier colonial experiences across the Atlantic. Commenting on Euro-American settlements in North America, Abbé Raynal first used the word in its substantive form in 1770. The noun "indigène" was used by Raynal to refer to Native Americans.[105] Rather than simply calling them by their group name, as he often did, or simply "Indiens," like other authors at the time, Raynal used "Indigènes" as a proper noun to characterize Native Americans as a group that was weak, decadent — even disappearing as a result of the influx of Euro-American settlers.[106] Such meanings evoked ideas about the course of history and social change that were part of a larger movement, the quest for new beginnings when "modern" became a value to kill and die for. After 1789 this animated the struggle against the outmoded, archaic, and all that was "ancien": refractory clergy, aristocrats, British cottagers, and the "idiocy of rural life."[107]

The term "indigène" also permitted colonial commentators to speak of Algeria's inhabitants in the aggregate, not as a people but as a *population*. Prior to the French landings they had been known by several terms. The flurry of letters between Istanbul and Paris leading up to the French landings called them "Algériens," as did official publications of the Ministry of War published in 1830.[108] The author of Bourmont's "Arabic Proclamation of 1830" addressed himself to "āṣdiqā'inā sūkān al-Jaza'ir wa sha'b al-maghāribat" (Our friends the inhabitants of Algiers and the people of the Maghreb).[109] After 1830 the term "Algerian" fell out of favor with French writers, as did "Maghrebi." Used in its specialized sense, "Algerian" could refer only to people living in the city of Algiers and not the outlying populations, who fell into French sights after 1830.[110] When used in their general sense, "Algerian" and "Maghrebi" implied social unity and might validate claims of people like Abdelkader and Ahmed Bey that they represented legitimate national interests. Instead of "Algériens," colonial leaders preferred to see people "without relations among themselves" and "without unity."[111]

There were times when colonial planners found it useful to see social complexity in Algeria, and they had the terms to express it. When they arrived in 1830, they recognized "Maures," "Juifs," "Turcs," and "Kolouglis" or "Colousis" (Kulughlān, descendents of mixed Turkish and local Algerian couples), "Noirs" and "Nègres" (African people of color, often slaves) as inhabitants of the cities. Within the interior colonial authors identified people they called "Bedouins" and "Arabes," "Berbères" and "Kabyles" (variously spelled as "Cabylès," "Qaba-ïles" or "Cabaïles").[112] Planners who embraced divide and conquer politics, a haphazard project some called the "Turkish system," relied on these terms.[113] However, as the history of Algerian opposition to the French revealed, these categories failed to assign a stable political personality to the various groups the French identified as allies and enemies (most often, but not exclusively, expressed in positive characteristics for Berberophone peoples and negative ones for Arabophones). Moreover, the need to express the macrosocial colonial order ensured that "indigène," as noun and adjective, retained a prominent place.

By 1833 "indigène" became part of the "indigenous question," an explosive phrase used to discuss the fate of Algerians under French rule. In the summer of 1833 the government convened a special commission to recommend policy in Algeria. It asked its members to consider three broad solutions to the "question des indigènes": (1) "mildness" (douceur), or "seek to use the indigènes, and later merge them into the European populations"; (2) "push-back" (refoulement), or "banish them from all the territory that we occupy"; and (3) "extermination" (extermination), or "a continual war that will destroy them."[114]

"Mildness" was the most ambiguous solution, signifying opinions that ranged from cooperative relations between Algerians and French to the forced "submission" (soumission) of Algerians.[115] Those who looked to Algerians as a source of labor emphasized the latter sense. As one writer later put it, "The resigned and vanquished is very close to becoming an associate."[116] "Push-back" was first mentioned in 1830 by the geographer Aristide Michel Perrot, who proposed, "the push-back into the African interior of the barbarous hordes of the coast."[117] The idea circulated within administrative circles for some time thereafter before the African Commission took it up again in 1833.[118] For his part General Clauzel publicly expressed his support for this option. Either the local people "will consent to live with the Europeans or they will move away [s'éloigneront]. . . . In either case the settlers from Europe will obtain their lands at a good price."[119] The last idea, "extermination," first came to public notice in 1832. Authors from Marseille, who spearheaded the campaign for aggressive and expansive colonization in Algeria, proposed this solution. They outlined the project of extermination in articles published in the *Sémaphore de Marseille* in early August 1832 and reprinted in the *Tribune* and the *Quotidien* of Paris at the end of the month.[120] According to commentators, these articles called for "colonization by the extermination of the former owners of the land."[121] In general, these authors did not explain how to achieve it. Some ambiguity existed in the verb "exterminer," resulting from one of its Latin connotations *ex-terminus*, meaning "out," or "beyond the frontier." But the Latin *exterminare* also simply meant "to destroy." This sense was borne out in the *Sémaphore* article and in French practices that used military-led mass murder to "exterminate" — kill, destroy, and disperse — Algerian communities.

THE PRACTICES OF TOTAL CONQUEST, 1839–47

Following the outbreak of a new round of war in 1839, one that continued until the last days of 1847, Paris abandoned the restricted occupation and French policy became the "absolute conquest of Algeria."[122] This meant occupying Algeria's interior, a project requiring a huge commitment in terms of resources, one the government was ready to make at this point.[123] This change in policy added momentum to plans for a settler colony. Settling the Algerian interior with Europeans solved both the practical issues of security — with settlers spreading out and securing the land — and provided the symbolic justification for the massive expenditures of the war, transforming the budget's negative bottom line into hallowed sacrifices made for a higher good.[124] The change from a restricted occupation to a full-blown settler colony fundamentally altered the terms of the indigenous question. French relations with Algerians were no longer limited to concerns about security and trade. A settler colony necessitated a far-reaching control of the land and its people.

This led to the return of debates about extermination and push-back. A settler colony, a "colonie de peuplement," again triggered thoughts of "dépeuplement." Thus, commanders wrote that the use of military force should be calculated not to defeat the enemy on the field of battle but systematically to exterminate or push back Algerians. They included people like Lieutenant Colonel Lucien-François de Montagnac, who articulated his own scenarios about how this might occur. Following a series of bloody encounters with the Ouled Attaya near Philippeville, Montagnac described "how to make war on Arabs" as follows: "Kill all the men down to the age of fifteen, take all the women and children, put them on boats and send them to Marquesas Islands, or somewhere else; in a word, annihilate all who will not grovel at our feet like dogs."[125] Some officers put this sort of thinking into practice during campaigns. These campaigns consisted of punitive raids the French called "razzias," utilizing an Arabic term to name practices that had originated in the wars in western France during the Revolution and the Napoleonic campaigns in Spain.[126] The declared purpose of such raids was to break the rural economy and consequently the capacity of people to resist. French troops burned crops, emptied silos, stole herds, and cut down fruit and olive trees, thereby ensuring economic ruin. But they also sought to destroy Algeria's social fabric. Even as the French repeatedly denied Algerians any sense of national community, they recognized that social cohesion represented the real threat to their rule. Disarticulating traditional social networks like the "'ashīra" (tribe) and targeting social bonds like "'asabiyya" (feelings of solidarity) became part of the process of conquest. Terror became the army's most important weapon in this struggle: kidnapping, summary executions, outright murder, torture, and sexual assaults produced *metrus atrox*, the sense of "terrible fear" that commanders thought would destroy existing social bonds and result in a docile population.

The practices of the razzia easily lent themselves to the logic of extermination, and in several cases French troops committed acts of mass murder. The best known example, the Dahra asphyxiations, illustrates these patterns of thought in action.[127] These occurred in June 1845, when a French column led by Colonel Aimable Jean Jacques Pélissier pursued a group, the Ouled Riah, in the rugged Dahra Mountains located in the western part of the country. The Ouled Riah took refuge in a deep cave, refusing the terms of surrender offered by Pélissier, who ordered his men to build a huge fire at the cave's entrance. The goal was not simply to smoke out the Ouled Riah, however; this "enfumade" had a more murderous intent. Soldiers stoked the fire through the night, and by morning the smoke had succeeded in asphyxiating nearly a thousand people, including men, women, and children. In a letter written just after this event, Governor-General Bugeaud identified the "great repercussions" of the asphyxiations. "It is a cruel extremity," he wrote, "but a horrifying example was necessary to strike terror among these turbulent and fanatical montagnards."[128] Their gruesome mass deaths stood as a testament to the radical dissymmetry of colonial power.

This act of mass murder expressed certain dimensions of the standard military thinking of the day, dominated by theorists like Baron de Jomini. Taking his lessons from the Napoleonic campaigns, Jomini taught a new generation of officers that the "fundamental principal of war" was the aggressive use of force physically to overwhelm enemies and psychologically to dominate them with the collateral effects of violence, shock, and fear.[129] Although Jomini personally abhorred irregular "little wars," fighting in Algeria proved amenable to his theories about shock and force. The lessons of the Vendée, Spain, Italy, and Haiti were not lost on the generation that came to Algeria.[130] (Much of the African army's leadership—including Clauzel, Rovigo, and Bugeaud—participated in these campaigns.) There was also the particular context of Algeria, an exoticized place that people like Marshal Soult, the minister of war, felt was an essentially violent place where the rules of military engagement were fundamentally different. In Europe Soult said the massacre of civilians was "hideous, abhorrent. In Africa, it is war itself."[131]

Extermination was in the air at the time. Members of Parliament publicly called for "a war of extermination." Later anthropologists in Paris discussed the possibility of a population die-out in Algeria, where the "Arab population tends to disappear," and people like Dr. Eugène Bodichon in Algiers hoped for the day there would be an Algeria without Algerians.[132] (Before the First World War some authors thought that climate change, cooling temperatures, snow, and ice would make Algeria a killing field for Algerians. "Mohamed Shivers!," one article announced.)[133] The idea that people faced with European colonization would become extinct even had a romantic cachet about it thanks to novels like James Fenimore Cooper's *Last of the Mohicans*, which enjoyed great success in French translation.[134] Its description of the sublime beauty of the American wilderness captivated several generations in France, where everyone had read "son Cooper," and those who came to Algeria often referred to the novel.[135] Cooper slated a poetically tragic fate for Native Americans. As he wrote in the 1831 introduction to *The Last of the Mohicans*, their disappearance represented "the seemingly inevitable fate of all these people, who disappear before the advances, or it might be termed the inroads of civilisation, as the verdure of their native forests falls before the nipping frost."[136] The significance of this thinking was not lost on French readers. When this introduction was made available to the French reading public in an 1846 edition, the translator removed whatever ambivalences remained in Cooper's words by translating "the *seemingly inevitable* fate of all these people" as simply "le sort *inévitable* de ces peuples."[137]

For Georges Sand *The Last of the Mohicans* represented Cooper's "conscious stricken cry; 'in order to be what we are, we had to kill a great people and devastate a mighty land.'"[138] But telling a story of extermination as a Greek epic produced a fetishistic site for readers confronted by the brutal realities of modern settler colonialism, effectively blotting out the trauma of colonial expansion and giving the whole project an aesthetic of the sublime and, with it, a new sort of politics.[139] And just as the American example influenced the Algerian case, events in Algeria traveled back to America. Following a trip to Algeria in 1846–47, Domingo Faustino Sarmiento, future Argentine president and prominent liberal intellectual (and an avid reader of Cooper), decided his country would "eliminate the 'Bedouins of America'"[140] (Argentine fascists in the twentieth century would take this up again.)[141]

While the actions of the French colonial state indisputably contributed to the extreme violence witnessed in the twentieth century—part of the "European genealogy" of Nazi violence brilliantly sketched by historian Enzo Traverso—there is no direct path leading from Algeria to Auschwitz, as some have suggested.[142] France never embraced a policy designed to exterminate Algerians, nor was there a systematic effort to push Algerians entirely out of the country and take their land. A settler colony needed land, to be sure, but early on colonial planners identified other means to obtain it, such as sequestration and confiscation or, more efficiently, by putting land on the market through the individuation of land tenure and new land codes.[143] Labor was the more important variable for success in Algeria, and colonial planners expected Algerians to provide the manpower needed by settlers and the state. Thus, in 1846 Dr. Auguste Warnier, a voice of harsh settler opinion, looked forward to the day when Algerian labor, driven by poverty, came on the market and Algerians would become the "docile instruments" of French settlers.[144] This made wholesale expulsion or extermination of Algerians undesirable. Political obstacles to such a project loomed as well. While the government rarely failed to defend the murderous actions of its army in the 1840s, Louis-Philippe sought a quick resolution to the Algerian war, full of glory and imperial grandeur, not wonton slaughter. As we shall see, the army's excesses were cause for considerable political embarrassment.

The Department of Indigenous Affairs (aka the Bureaux arabes) perhaps best represents the state's view of the indigenous question and its solutions. In 1841 Eugène Daumas took over direction of this freshly reorganized military bureaucracy, which had direct authority over French-named local Algerian leaders and handled relations with the remaining independent tribes. Although the pro-Algerian, or "arabophile," sentiments of this corps have been exaggerated, its mission was distinctly at odds with a policy seeking extermination or expulsion.[145] Daumas headed the office throughout the 1840s, the deadliest years of the military campaigns. Like virtually every other officer in Algeria, Daumas agreed that violence should be primary in relations with Algerians, but he believed that such violence should be about controlling people, not eliminating them.[146] The colonial triad (order, authority, and economy) represented the most important elements in Daumas's thinking about the indigenous question, none of which made extermination or expulsion desirable. Ultimately he believed that Algerians, resigned to their defeat, would be absorbed by French ways and customs. If Algerians "disappeared," he wrote in 1853, it would be "among us."[147]

Finally, there was General Thomas-Robert Bugeaud himself. He was not, as some biographers have claimed, the reluctant agent of colonial violence, a true advocate of the moderate "juste milieu" politics.[148] Bugeaud is correctly understood as one of the most dangerous men ever to have set foot in Algeria. He led the army as Algeria's governor-general from late 1840 until 1847. During this time he did as much as any individual to intensify the scope and range of the army's violence. Bugeaud's call to arms in 1840 — "We need a great invasion, an invasion like that of the Franks, like that of the Goths" — reflected a military philosophy that recognized few limits.[149] He personally led troops on murderous raids and encouraged junior officers to follow the harshest line of conduct toward Algerians, covering up their actions when necessary to avoid scandal.[150]

Nevertheless, Bugeaud recognized the importance of Algerians as a source of labor, as military and administrative auxiliaries, and even as settlers themselves.[151] This is most clearly expressed in a letter of 1846 addressed to General de La Rue, the king's commissioner, wherein Bugeaud bluntly discusses the question of push-back and extermination. "We cannot push back the Arabs like we said once. . . . The whole French army would not suffice to get the job done. We can no more exterminate them, and even if we could, our morals, our philanthropists will not permit it. We must in all necessity live with them."[152] The equivocation evident in Bugeaud's statement ("even if we could") reflects the lingering influence of his earlier defense of extreme violence and his scorn for his critics, whom he saw as weak-kneed "philanthropists." However, Bugeaud rejected a policy of extermination or expulsion less as a moral problem than as a practical and political impossibility. The solution to the indigenous question he outlined to de La Rue was an unequal absorption of Algerians into a colonial system dominated by France, a process he called "mélange," which implied "entwining the Arabs with us." This, Bugeaud argued, would "destroy the cohesive force of nationality," yielding atomized individuals of no political consequence. The real battle would be won, he thought, through the incorporation of Algerians into a market-based economy, with its norms of private property, individual land tenure, and surplus-oriented production for French markets: "The first thing to do along these lines is to make them property owners, and to give them, little by little, the taste of built property and [illegible] well-cared for crops. . . . This is assuredly one of the best methods to bring to an end the insurrection that our slow but permanent invasion produces."[153]

There was nothing progressive about this plan, which words like "association" and "assimilation" capture poorly. It reflected a wide range of thinking resulting in a great deal of violence — death, social and cultural destruction — that typified the experience of French colonialism in Algeria. How it played out in the south, in the desert lands of the Sahara, is the subject of the next chapter.

PART 1

The "Pénétration Pacifique"
of the Algerian Sahara, 1844–52

Solitudinem faciunt pacem appellant.
[They make a desert and call it peace.]
—*Tacitus*

Il a fait de notre pays un désert. [He made our land a desert.]
—*French translation of Kabyle poem, recorded in the 1850s*

[1]

THE PEACEFUL EXPANSION
OF TOTAL CONQUEST

France's expansion into the Algerian Sahara began with war. On 14 March 1844 a column of three thousand French soldiers arrived at Biskra, a strategic oasis located in the Ziban region at the desert's edge, southeast of the city of Constantine.[1] The son of Louis-Philippe, the duc d'Aumale, led the troops. The young, twenty-two-year-old general still glowed from his victory the previous year against Emir Abdelkader, the famous "prise de la smala" (16 May 1843), and he was confident that this expedition to the faraway Sahara would bring further glory and add imperial luster to the family name. The Orléans family, this fragile "dynasty without a past," sought lasting legitimacy, and military conquest in a far-off and exotic desert land was one way to increase public favor and blur the fact that it owed its political life to the Parisian barricades that had toppled the Bourbon Restoration in 1830.[2] Less important in this grand scheme of French politics—but significant to the struggle against Abdelkader—were Aumale's military goals. Although a remote oasis, Biskra afforded Aumale the chance to kill two birds with one stone. He would oust Muhammad Seghir (Muhammad al-Saghir ibn Ahmad), whom Abdelkader had named his French governor, or *khalifa* (*qalīfa*) for the Ziban and reinstall the Ben Ganah family, the region's traditional rulers, who had rallied in support of France.[3] With the Ziban placed under allied rule, Aumale hoped to return north through the Aurès Mountains and seek the main prize, Constantine's Ahmed Bey. The capture of this fugitive leader—who had inflicted the humiliating 1836 defeat on General Clauzel and who stubbornly continued to resist after the fall of Constantine in 1837—would be a major victory and sure to be warmly hailed in the capital.[4]

Fortune accompanied the young general. Although the itinerary posed many dangers (including a perilous traversal of the Aurès Mountains through the gorge of al-Kantara and dangerously stretched supply lines), the first stage of the operation went in Aumale's favor. When the inhabitants of Biskra saw the large force outside their doors, factions sympathetic to the Ben Ganahs won the day, and they sent delegations bearing dates to meet the French. When French forces entered the oasis, they did so without firing a shot. Buoyed by his success, Aumale negotiated the submission of Biskra and left behind a small detachment of "tirailleurs indigènes," supplemented by 275 of Muhammad Seghir's men, who had changed sides. Under the command of a Ben Ganah leader (supervised by two French officers), the garrison received orders to hold this far-off post. Aumale boasted that the conquest was "entirely peaceful."[5]

Governor-General Bugeaud, Aumale's superior and the architect of the Saharan expansion, was exuberant. His skillful maneuvering around recalcitrant officials in Paris had paid off. The southeastern region appeared well on its way to submission and the outpost at Biskra promised to extend French influence well into the Sahara and beyond. As Bugeaud reported to the minister of war, "The submission of the Ziban is an event much more important than one might think in France. It was detrimental for our overall domination to have left the flag of Abdelkader fly there for so long; this gave people a weak impression of our power, and it was a permanent danger for our security in the province of Constantine." Bugeaud promised other advantages as well: "Economically speaking, it is also very important; our tax resources will increase, and our commerce sees the doors of the desert open before it."[6]

All of this had been achieved with little bloodshed. In Bugeaud's view, the hostages taken from among Biskri families guaranteed that their kin would offer no opposition in the future. The painless occupation would be just as easy on the government's coffers. The rich palm gardens of the Ziban represented a sizable tax base, and the mission had already taken 150,000 francs in forced contributions and confiscations. Moreover, experimenting in indirect rule, Aumale decided to install a hybrid occupation force. Overseen by an Arabic-speaking French officer (who were known as "Africains"), locally recruited soldiers ensured order, while Ahmed ben Ganah remained the actual head of the region with his traditional title of Shaykh al-Arab. As Aumale boasted, "Things were organized in a manner that allow us to give the Cheikh el-Arab the authority necessary for him to rule with confidence, albeit in a manner that our commandant can exercise continual surveillance over his actions."[7] The Ben Ganahs could deal with complex local issues the French little understood, while the French officer ensured that he ruled according to French interests. Aumale did not need to point out that this occupation method would pay for itself and require a minimum of French manpower.

When the mission's reports and letters appeared in the official *Moniteur universel*, Bugeaud happily took this as a sign of the government's satisfaction. He had undertaken the operation with little communication from Paris, and his bold decision to lead the move southward with the king's son was vindicated in terms of the successful and easy victory. Attaching the Orléans name to these triumphs helped his political standing with the monarchy, a move that Bugeaud had carefully calculated. With the French flag planted peacefully at the entrance to the desert by Louis-Philippe's son, Bugeaud's claims that his leadership in Algeria had brought progress — indeed, that the costly war had rounded a corner in the Sahara — received a sympathetic hearing at the Tuileries Palace. With improved tactics and a newfound ability to project power to the interior of Algeria, Bugeaud gave substance to his claims that the hard-fought battles for Algeria's northern lands were a thing of the past. Outflanked to the south, the remaining Algerian rebels would recognize the futility of resistance and lay down their arms. A new era of peace lay ahead for the Algerian colony.

THE RESTRICTED OCCUPATION AND THE SAHARA

It was a turn of events that frustrated officials in the capital welcomed. The 1830s had not gone well. Vague as they were, Louis-Philippe's promises of 1834, when he decided to stay in Algeria in a limited occupation, remained unrealized a decade later. Criticism mounted that the government lacked clear vision. Already in 1840, when the restricted occupation was abandoned, one deputy disparaged the conquest's first decade by saying, "we had neither a plan nor a system."[8] The government could not articulate its goals in Algeria. The claims of some, that the territories might fit into revived mercantilist schemes, seemed unfounded, and many observers doubted that France needed to embark upon another "New France" settler colony, the memory of the North American debacle still not forgotten.

Notwithstanding the critics, there was a system and plan for Algeria. The ordinance of 22 July 1834 gave the colony an official name — the unwieldy Possessions françaises du Nord de l'Afrique — and a system of rule through royal ordinances. It organized administration under the auspices of the minister of war, who appointed Algeria's governor-general.[9] The governor-general of Algeria occupied a powerful position, overseeing authoritarian political institutions. He controlled combat forces and stood at the head of a military-dominated bureaucracy responsible for finances, justice, commerce, and the police. Although answering to the government in Paris, the governor-general influenced policymaking for Algeria, and he could rule by emergency decree.[10] The independence, power, and visibility of this office made it one of the most attractive commands in the French army.

The 1834 plan limited French control to coastal cities (such as Bône, Bougie, Algiers, and Oran), and after 1837 the inland eastern capital of Constantine was added. The focus was on Algeria's northern lands, known locally as the Tell, where a Mediterranean climate provided sufficient rainfall for settled agriculture.[11] This was first divided into various *beyliks* or *agaliks*, led by traditional elites and former Ottoman leaders who recognized French sovereignty, or by French-appointed Algerian notables who answered directly to the governor-general.[12] The Treaty of Tafna (30 May 1837) recognized Abdelkader's authority over the western Oran region and ceded him control of the territory south of Algiers. The Sahara did not figure in these plans. To the extent they thought about the dry southern lands known as the Sahara (al-Ṣaḥrā), which included both the desert and the southern steppes and high plains (High Plateaux), planners attached them to the Tell. In the Sahara a dry climate dictated a pastoral life and, where possible, irrigated cultivation of date palms, neither of which promised much to the French.

In many ways the restricted occupation continued traditional patterns of Mediterranean colonization exemplified by the seaport colony.[13] Such "gateways" linked the sea and the interior, serving as points of contact and exchange. Although colonial planners did not draw direct inspiration from this example (unlike the Roman one),[14] they hoped that the restricted occupation — the first experiment with a "pénétration pacifique" in Algeria — would allow France to maintain an unobtrusive and low-cost presence.[15] This would not upset the European powers (especially Great Britain, which anxiously watched post-Napoleonic France's first overseas conquest) or require a large and politically dangerous military commitment.

Historian Frederick Cooper's observation that "European policy is as much a response to African initiatives as African 'resistance' or 'adaptation' is a response to colonial interventions" is borne out by the fate of the restricted occupation.[16] The failure of the intermediaries through whom France sought to extend power to act subserviently doomed this project. For example, Hajj Ahmed, the bey of Constantine, refused the role offered him. Instead he used the interval to reform his administration and army in preparation for a showdown with the French. For his efforts the Ottoman Empire named Ahmed "Basha," and in 1836 he won a startling victory over the French.[17] Meanwhile, the emir Abdelkader forged an even more powerful challenge to the French.[18] Heading a coalition of rural and urban elites, Abdelkader combined armed engagements (he was at war with the French 1832–34, 1835–37, and 1839–47) with diplomacy to wrest territory and concessions from Paris and forge the birth of an independent Algerian state.[19]

By the end of the decade, Louis-Philippe's restricted occupation had ended. Ambitious military leaders chafed under the limitations placed upon them. Abdelkader sought to realize his own plans, which were increasingly

TABLE 1.1 Algeria: Governmental Expenses and Receipts,
1831–40 (francs)

	Ministry of War	Ministry of the Navy	Ministry of Finance	Total Expenditures	Receipts
1831	15,451,424	2,000,000	37,000	18,285,424	1,098,697
1832	20,312,447	2,000,000	46,000	23,155,447	1,758,008
1833	22,720,196	2,000,000	51,000	25,568,196	1,784,833
1834	23,620,471	2,500,000	51,000	26,968,196	2,038,341
1835	22,654,026	2,960,000	51,000	26,462,026	1,607,499
1836	25,299,161	3,000,000	58,000	29,154,161	1,436,240
1837	37,505,637	4,451,000	97,000	42,850,637	1,827,198
1838	38,428,381	3,000,000	100,000	42,325,381	2,054,596
1839	41,287,748	8,600,000	111,000	44,786,748	1,494,838
1840	58,105,909	2,600,000	162,000	61,664,909	1,494,838
Total	305,385,400	33,111,000	764,000	341,221,125	16,595,088

Source: *Le Moniteur universel*, 30 April 1840.

at odds with the French. Moreover, the project was costing enormous sums (see table 1.1).

The first decade of the occupation of Algeria had cost the government almost 350 million francs—a major sum. Despite this expense, the most precious commodity in Algeria, namely, security and order, remained elusive. Due to the political situation large stretches of the country were too dangerous for trade or travel. The French did not enjoy security far outside the areas they occupied, which at this time were limited to Constantine and the major Mediterranean ports of Oran, Algiers, Bône, and their immediate hinterland. The impossibility of the situation was underscored in 1839 when the fragile peace between Abdelkader and the French worked out in the Treaty of Tafna was definitively broken. Governor-General Vallée made his provocative "Portes de fer" march through territories he disputed with Abdelkader. The emir retaliated with bloody raids on unprotected European settlers in the Mitidja Valley, near Algiers. Abdelkader's admonition to Vallée prior to his offensive ("Warn your travelers, your isolated settlers") did little to offset the shock left in the wake of the killings.[20] The emir's forces spared few, leaving hundreds of decapitated bodies throughout the Mitidja's remote farms.

Bugeaud's Total Conquest, 1841–44

When the legislature met in January 1840, the deputies could scarcely contain themselves. Their rage over events in Algeria was compounded by lasting bitterness from the divisive 1839 elections and the dangerous international situation brewing in the eastern Mediterranean, the result of Muhammad Ali's confrontation with the Ottoman Empire in Syria. In stormy sessions deputies heaped scorn upon the restricted occupation and called for vengeance. They had the king on their side. Louis-Philippe, feeling more confident, prepared to make a major military commitment in Africa. For the first time the government mentioned its readiness to send as many as one hundred thousand troops to Algeria.[21]

The debates continued throughout the summer.[22] By year's end Marshal Soult, the minister of war, set aside his reservations (viz. the threat of a military coup coming from the army in Algeria) and named Bugeaud to serve as Algeria's governor-general on 29 December 1840. Bugeaud had already seen extensive service in Algeria and had coveted the powerful position at the head of the Algerian colony for some time. He had prepared the way for his nomination by using his seat in the Chamber of Deputies to attack French timidity and offered himself as an alternative leader.[23] Posing as an opponent of expansion in North Africa, Bugeaud claimed that if politicians chose to stay there, only an all-out effort could see the mission through. As he put it in an oft-quoted speech to the Chamber of Deputies: "There remains only absolute domination, and the subjugation of the country. . . . The possession of Algiers is a mistake; but as you choose to commit it . . . you must commit it grandly."[24]

Thomas-Robert Bugeaud (1784–1849) was descended from a Périgord family that had obtained titles of nobility in the early eighteenth century.[25] When his family experienced financial ruin during the Revolution, Bugeaud looked to a military career. In the turbulent decades that followed, he ascended to the highest halls of power (he was made Maréchal de France in 1843). He adjusted his politics to weather the Restoration, and under Louis-Philippe he became known as a conservative advocate of the "juste milieu," a centrist expression of opposition to liberals and legitimists that resonated among many of the aristocrats, pseudo-nobles, and elite bourgeois that made up the "regime of the notables."[26] Accordingly, Bugeaud liked to present himself as the incarnation of traditional virtue, which he located in rural culture. He was particularly fond of expressing himself in countrified tropes, many of which bordered on the absurd. "There is more real progress for the people in a head of cabbage or a turnip," he wrote after the revolution of 1848, "than in all the theories of the Proudhons, the Louis Blancs, the Considérants, and other great Doctors."[27] While some snickered at his bumpkin pretensions, they recognized that Bugeaud was a shrewd politician and one of the most ambitious men of his day. (Some may even have recalled that the turnip made possible the agricultural revolution!)[28] Marshal Soult, in particular, kept close tabs on the governor-general, and Bugeaud's ambition often strained their relationship.[29]

Bugeaud won the powerful command of the African army with promises to end the war in Algeria as quickly as possible. He accused his predecessors of failing to grasp the essence of "African warfare" and lacking the will to deploy the force necessary to subdue Algerians. He argued that the conventional rules of warfare meant little in Algeria. The lessons of the Vendée campaigns and Napoleon's "Spanish ulcer" showed that the only way to crush irregular resistance was to wage war against civilian populations.[30] Bugeaud had spent many years on the Iberian Peninsula and swore that he would not wince in the face of the cruelty needed to ensure victory.[31] Accordingly, when he arrived in Algiers he promptly ordered his troops to destroy crops, cut down orchards, steal herds, and empty food reserves. Soldiers understood they could beat, rape, and kill the old and defenseless as they wished. In order to spread feelings of insecurity, troops had specific orders to kidnap women and children. "You have frequently defeated the Arabs; you will defeat them again," Bugeaud told his troops upon arrival. "But it is not much to make them flee; they must be vanquished."[32]

The tone for such tactics had been set for some time. As was mentioned previously (see introduction), early debates on the Algerian occupation in the 1830s considered pushing back or exterminating Algerians.[33] Seething over the deaths in the Mitidja Valley, extremist politicians later called for "a war of extermination" against Abdelkader.[34] Other commentators provided a vocabulary to serve Bugeaud's needs. Wanting to stress the exotic nature of warfare in Algeria and the ability of French troops to adapt to "African" rules of combat, they had taken to calling French punitive raids "razzias."[35] This represented more than the importation of an Arabic word into French. It was a bold claim that the French army in Africa had somehow transformed itself to do battle here. Accordingly, Bugeaud boasted to Algerians, "I am as much an Arab as you are" and claimed that he adapted his tactics from traditional Maghrebi practices.[36] But, as he stressed to his enemies, his means exceeded their capabilities. "I can remain on campaign longer without returning for supplies. Your vast solitudes, your steepest mountains, your crags, your deepest ravines cannot frighten me. . . . Like a river of fire I will scourge this land in all directions."[37]

Bugeaud's razzias not only brought increased devastation but significantly transformed the character of military engagements in North Africa. Gone was the combination of surprise, shock, and less lethal economic and symbolic violence that had accompanied the direct attacks on property and persons in the *ghazw*.[38] A closer inspection reveals that Bugeaud did not limit his attacks to foodstuffs and supply routes, as he claimed. Instead he and his commanders counted on especially spectacular demonstrations of their capacity to inflict pain and suffering upon their enemies.

When political opposition to Bugeaud's war was heard—strong voices did not fail to materialize—he skillfully defended his actions by arguing that such tactics were, in fact, the most humanitarian. "These actions even have a humane aspect because, by the intimidation that they produce, they will bring the war to a more rapid conclusion."[39] He argued that the "Arabs" were naturally "bellicose," and that they understood and respected only force. Negotiations were futile. Peace would come only when Algerians were crushed militarily. While some rightly suspected that Bugeaud was trying to exaggerate the role of the army in Algeria—and thereby secure his own position in the military—pundits from Père Enfantin to Alexis de Tocqueville accepted the logic of this argument. And Bugeaud won over many with his contention that only after the war could the projects of the "philanthropists" take root in this hostile soil.[40] As he articulated his mission, "Our empire is founded upon force alone; we do not have, we cannot have, any other effect upon the Arabs; we can only continue in Africa by force."[41]

The First Round: Biskra and Laghouat, 1843–45

Three years later these efforts began to bear bitter fruit. Those who had fought with Abdelkader or had tried to chart a nonaligned course were devastated by the French razzias. The emir abandoned Tagdempt and Mascara in 1841. Following the capture in 1843 of his "smala" (*zmāla*: household; here referring to the emir's mobile administration), Abdelkader sought refuge in Morocco. Discouraged, the ranks of those ready to march under his banner thinned out.

Nevertheless, in 1843 the battle for the northern Tell was far from conclusively settled in France's favor. Abdelkader was on the run, but much of the country—like the mountainous Kabylia region around Tizi Ouzou and the mountains southeast of Constantine—escaped French control. Woe to the European who ventured into the Collo region, north of Constantine, without heavy escort.[42] Moreover, in the so-called "soumises" regions widespread insecurity remained. The disparaging comment made by Louis Veuillot in 1841 still rang true throughout Algeria: "Algiers is yours, and provided that night is far away, you can stroll out for a league or so in the region."[43] Violent and costly, Bugeaud's "pacification" had not brought peace.

The governor-general's response was to expand the war. He looked southward across the arid and mountainous lands, where rebels had found safe haven. Firm control of the Tell, he reasoned, was to be had when his troops controlled its southern approaches. This was not a hospitable region. The High Plateaux— or "Little Desert," as the French called it—a wide stretch of arid steppes punctuated by salt flats, separated the Tell and the mountains of the Saharan Atlas. Water was scarce and edible fodder for stock animals even more so. Furthermore, the sparsely populated region lacked villages that French troops could raid for food supplies (a standard means of military procurement in the field). Asserting French power over these lands would not be easy.

There was also the political challenge. Relations between Bugeaud and Parliament had deteriorated by 1843, and the government's support for the Algerian campaign had become increasingly ambivalent. While the monarchy liked sharing in the glory of Bugeaud's victories, many in the council were wary of his political ambitions.[44] It had taken the shock of the 1839 deaths in the Mitidja Valley to rally support in Paris for the full occupation of the comparably rich lands of the Tell. Convincing politicians of the necessity for sending columns of French troops into the desert would be difficult. Its sterile lands attracted few settlers. Skepticism in the capital mounted as people questioned the logic of Bugeaud's wars for peace.

Bugeaud skirted the problem by disguising his moves in a series of incremental half measures and faits accomplis. By the winter of 1843–44 he had stationed garrisons in a line of "temporary" outposts to form an arc along the northern edge of the High Plateaux, stretching from Sebdou in the west (near Tlemcen), across to Boghar in the center (near Ksar El Boukhari), to Batna in the east. Bugeaud hoped that these bases, less than 150 kilometers from the coast, might be seen as mere tactical advances and thus escape criticism. However, as he confided to Adolph Thiers in April 1843, "The theater of war is carried much farther."[45] These advanced bases served operations farther south. More important, they were where people living in the Saharan Atlas Mountains and in the desert purchased vital grains. The emir might be able to hide farther to the south, but with the grain markets in French hands Bugeaud calculated that he would have difficulties finding provisions. This would deliver a cheap victory. Explaining his move to a colleague, Bugeaud cited local lore: "He who is master of the Tell is master of the desert."[46]

In the spring of 1844 the governor-general prepared to make the move south across the High Plateaux. His report to the minister of war, drafted well after the operations were already underway, stated: "The inhabited part of the desert is necessarily ours politically . . . [and] we must reign everywhere where Abdelkader reigned."[47] The potential objections to the Saharan expansion were numerous. First was the question of its legality. Relations had not been established with most of the region's leaders, and many might have legitimate claims to independence. This issue had to be resolved. Bugeaud's justification was simple. Having once paid tribute to Ottoman authorities, desert leaders were therefore under the zone of influence won by the rights of the conquest of the Algerian regencies.[48] It was an expedient answer, but the minister of war, little concerned about the details of sovereignty, accepted Bugeaud's explanation. A more important question was how much it would cost and what was to be gained. Bugeaud peddled the plan with considerable rhetorical flourish: "The desert will cost us nothing to govern; commercial exchanges will suffice and pay us a few taxes. If we do not dominate there, Abdelkader will go and control it and the storm clouds will form here and rain upon us. They must be destroyed at their source."[49]

The tempest metaphor fit in well with colonial rhetoric used to describe Algerian social movements. This rhetoric helped Bugeaud conceal the fact that he had scant knowledge of the economic resources of the region. Claiming that the occupation would pay for itself was based upon pure hearsay. Furthermore, Bugeaud had only a vague idea of the military capabilities of the Algero-Saharan societies, and their political dispositions were poorly understood at best. Bugeaud had enough experience by this time to know that promises that came from the local notables—for example, that they could establish order effectively and cheaply—often turned out to be exaggerated. Destroying the "source" of the emir's "storm clouds" would depend not on the simple matter of planting the French flag in the desert but on the ability to project a sustained military presence into this region. While army commanders offered hubristic assessments of their ability to operate in the far south, basic logistical questions remained unresolved. As the commandant of Médéa would later admit, "We did not know that winter is the key season of the Sahara, like the summer is in the Tell."[50]

Bugeaud concealed this information from the government. Rather than moving ahead cautiously, he redoubled his moves south. In March 1844, as Aumale approached Biskra, an offer of alliance came from the Ben Salem family at Laghouat. Like Biskra, Laghouat was a "door to the desert." Strategically situated directly south of Algiers, it controlled access from the central portion of the High Plateaux to the commercial centers in the Mzab and beyond. Bugeaud invited a representative of the Ben Salems (Jahi ben Salem, brother of the family's leader, Ahmed) to Algiers and assured him of his support.

The history of the events leading up to the offer, which remained unknown to Bugeaud, reveals the motives and limitations of the alliance.[51] The Ben Salems were part of the old and powerful Ouled Zaanoun clan of Laghouat and the principal members of the Ouled Hallaf (Awlad Ahlaf) faction (Ṣaff) who had struggled with their rivals, the Ouled Serghin (Awlad Serkin), to control the strategic oasis since the early eighteenth century. Complexity marked oasis politics, which were driven by the interplay between local and regional powers. Because local elites rarely achieved stable hegemony, they called upon outside forces to shift the balance of power decisively in their favor. Ottoman beys used threats and favors to play the factions off against each other in order to advance their own influence in this far-off but strategic settlement. Thus, by the beginning of the French era in Algeria, the factions had a long history as a vehicle for the power of outsiders, whom local leaders tried to deploy to their own advantage. In 1828 Ahmed ben Salem (Ahmad ibn Salim, d. 1856) assumed leadership of the Ouled Hallaf through a shrewd combination of alliances, military force, and a strategic marriage with the daughter of the leader of the Ouled Serghin. At the head of the Ouled Hallaf and tied to the Ouled Serghin by marriage, Ahmed ben Salem emerged as Laghouat's primary leader. His tenure, however, was short-lived. In 1837 Abdelkader marched on Laghouat, rallied enemies of Ben Salem, and expelled him. In his place the emir named as his governor Hadj Larby (al-hajj al-'Arbi) of the Ouled Serghin. The tenure of this candidate did not last long, and soon the Ouled Serghin forced Larby to flee. Once again factional divisions ensured that power was not concentrated in any single pair of hands. Frustrated with the volatile Saharan situation, Abdelkader called upon a powerful military ally from a nearby town to destroy Laghouat, kill its leaders, and rule from a new seat at a distance from the oasis's volatility. Word of the pending attack reached Laghouat in time and the town united and expelled the emir's ally. In 1839 Ahmed ben Salem returned to Laghouat and established a shaky rule hostile to Abdelkader's local allies. As an expression of his opposition to the emir and in order to overcome the structural insecurity of his position, Ahmed ben Salem looked to a French alliance. In his offer to the governor-general he wrote, "All the Muslim Sultans that I have trusted have betrayed me; I may find stability in the justice of the French Sultan."[52]

Bugeaud jumped at the offer. In mid-April 1844 he ordered General Marey-Monge, the commandant of Médéa, to prepare an expedition to invest Ahmed ben Salem as the *khalifa*. He made the decision on his own authority. Days afterward Bugeaud informed Paris of his plans: "If this affair turns out favorably, as I have reason to hope, it will spread our authority far throughout the desert, from Touggourt to Laghouat and Aïn-Madi. It is only through domination that we will be able to open our commerce to relations with the interior of Africa. We also needed to take from Abdelkader the resources that he might have been able to find in this country, and to eliminate even the appearance that he had any power left here."[53]

The minister of war did not protest the fact that this notification came after Bugeaud started the operation. According to some historians, Minister of War Soult was happy to have Bugeaud off on military campaigns, where he posed less of a political threat.[54] Yet Soult might have questioned Bugeaud's optimism. A series of Algerian notables had already been handed control over zones in the south, and none of them had successfully ruled there.[55] The belief was far-fetched that an alliance with the Ben Salem, combined with the Ben Ganah at Biskra, would spread the net of French control over the entire High Plateaux and as far south as Touggourt. Ben Salem's position had negligible power, and he depended on Bugeaud's ability to back him up with military force.[56]

The governor-general concealed these problems from superiors and went forward with his plans. On 24 May 1844 the French flag was unfurled at the ksar of El-Haouïta, near Laghouat. In a public ceremony conducted in French and Arabic, Ahmed ben Salem received the seals of the French *khalifa* and was named head of the central Algerian Sahara.[57] Reporting on this success, General Marey-Monge triumphantly proclaimed that the region had been organized "without any losses in men, horses, or mules."[58] Like Biskra, victory was measured in terms of the bloodless triumph. "What strikes me as remarkable in this operation," Marey-Monge concluded in his report, "is, first of all, the fear inspired by our troops and then the confidence that our discipline and our word inspired. Finally, and most important, [I was impressed with] the general opinion that we are superior, and [their confidence in] the wisdom of our administration, and the advantages that lie in rallying to [support] us. This situation stems from the manner adopted recently of waging war, from the prosperity of our tribes, who have successively submitted to us, and from the manifest disorder that reigns among the remaining hostile populations."[59]

Marey-Monge, an early member of the Department of Indigenous Affairs and the founder of the "spahis" (mounted Algerian gendarmerie), was not above panegyrics.[60] He suggested that the "manner adopted recently of waging war" produced fear among desert peoples, which combined with an attraction for the reputed honesty and efficiency of French administration. This combination of fear and confidence—what Bugeaud called the "shadow of the bayonets"—was enough, in his opinion, to ensure that the Sahara's populations would receive their new masters warmly.[61]

Failure of the First Effort: Laghouat and Biskra

It would take more than intimidation and Panglossian talk to make the Algerian Sahara French. The fate of the first garrison at Biskra was the most immediate and dramatic example. During the night of 11–12 May 1844, two months after Aumale's main column had departed, the locally recruited force he left to defend Biskra mutinied.[62] Under cover of darkness they infiltrated the citadel where the garrison's two French officers and surgeon slept, and killed them.[63] Those "tirailleurs indigènes" who were not in on the coup (many were from Biskra and joined their kin) were also killed. (Only one Frenchman, a noncommissioned officer named Sergent-major Pelisse, escaped.) Mutineers looted the garrison's stocks of arms and ammunition before they cleaned out the fort's food supply and treasury (totaling 68,000 francs).[64] It was a week before a French detachment arrived from operations in the nearby Aurès Mountains and retook Biskra.

Similar trouble occurred at Laghouat—with less dramatic results. Reflecting differences in opinions among the commandants of the Divisions of Algiers and Constantine on how best to administer Algerians, Marey-Monge did not leave a French contingent behind to supervise the French khalifa. This did not leave French soldiers exposed in case of a revolt. On the other hand, Ben Salem lacked sufficient force to rule effectively in the face of a powerful opposition.

Fearing a coup, in April 1845 the vulnerable *khalifa* fled Laghouat.[65] In this case a bloodless conquest was followed by a bloodless defeat.

These failures demonstrated the challenges that lay before the French in the Sahara. In the case of Biskra, Bugeaud had to swallow the bitter pill that only a permanent French garrison of five hundred soldiers could ensure control of the region.[66] The cost was daunting, as was the commitment of troops. The Aurès Mountains and Kabylia had not yielded, and inhabitants promised to mount a stiff resistance. Moreover, Abdelkader had convinced Morocco to support his struggle, leading to the Franco-Moroccan War of 1844, which opened the possibility that subduing the emir might involve a much larger struggle across North Africa. The proliferation of war in the north cast in a totally new light a host of questions that had dogged the first round in the Sahara. Many revolved around costs, logistics, and the capacities of potential allies, while others raised more serious doubts. What were the strategic advantages? Was the desert as rich as was claimed? Would local populations passively accept French rule? Most important, would moving into the desert instead of bringing peace to the Tell open a Pandora's box of conflict in Algeria? Three years into the total conquest, Bugeaud pursued an ever more elusive victory.

OPPOSITION IN PARLIAMENT, 1844

Colonies (nos): s'attrister quand on en parle.
—Gustave Flaubert, *Dictionnaire des idées reçues*

Louis-Philippe hoped to build part of his dynasty's foundations by having his sons lead the way to French glory in North Africa. But in order to build the political capital of the Orléans family, colonial campaigns had to be victorious. Stalemates, standoffs, and defeat paid the bitterest political dividends. While the government could count on support for the Algerian colony from such powerful individuals as Alexis de Tocqueville and Adolph Thiers and groups like the Chamber of Commerce of Marseille, French society at large expressed a great deal of ambivalence toward Algeria throughout this period. This mood combined with the general political volatility of these long years of "Revolutionary France" to make Algeria a point of contention.[67] In particular, the government's opponents seized upon setbacks in the Sahara to point to the inconsistencies and contradictions involved in the whole Algerian project, if not in the regime itself. Moreover, as details of the campaigns filtered back to France—details that belied the image of glorious colonial conquest—many began to express a deeper sense of moral outrage. For some time critics of the Algerian project had envisioned the worst-case scenario. Even in the bellicose days of 1840 some opposed what they feared might be a Sisyphean struggle in Africa. As one deputy argued in May 1840, "The conquest of Algeria is disastrous madness, a ruinous fantasy, an enterprise without goals, without results."[68] Four years later the same apprehensions were raised, and the mounting costs of the war had increased the numbers of those ready to oppose the war in Algeria. Already Bugeaud's command came under intense scrutiny for its excesses in violence and cost, and the fear of military adventurism was on many minds. Moreover, at the same moment as Bugeaud was waging unrestricted war in Algeria, François Guizot, the minister of foreign affairs (1840–1848), had brilliantly shown how a "politique pacifique"—careful diplomacy in place of military force—could yield excellent results.[69] Under Guizot's tenure the threat of a continental war receded and the volatile situation in the eastern Mediterranean stabilized. This threw an especially unfavorable light on the intractable conflict in Algeria.

Even before word of the Biskra debacle reached Paris on 7 June 1844, the Saharan expansion had provoked serious dissent. Earlier that spring a parliamentary commission led by General Bellonnet had studied the minister of war's request for a "crédit supplémentaire" of 7,673,859 francs to pay outstanding expenses in Algeria. The report Bellonnet returned to the Chamber of Deputies recommended the withholding of 10,000 francs as reprimand for Bugeaud's unauthorized decision to expand the southern bases. Bellonnet grasped the fact that Bugeaud was preparing a major move in the Sahara, raising the specter of a new round of warfare. Summarizing the report, one deputy noted: "These posts, these visits, or these establishments in the south, expose us to new conflicts, to troop increases and mounting costs, without any political or commercial gains."[70] Even in the northern Tell, "a land that France had watered with its purest blood," as another deputy remarked, the promises of colonization were far from realized.[71] This deputy invited his colleagues to take a close look at the statistics: rather than a prosperous agricultural colony, only a handful of European farmers actually tilled the land in Algeria. Moreover, they produced wheat, barley, and wine, crops that competed with those grown by rural constituents in the metropolis. Up until 1843 a steep tariff (law of 11 November 1835) had protected producers in France from having to compete with their counterparts in Algeria, even as it allowed French-produced goods to flow freely into the colony. However, in 1843 a new law reduced by half the duty paid on many Algerian exports (e.g., coral, wool, olive oil, hides, silk, and minerals) entering France, raising fears on the part of many French producers that future trade liberalization with the colony would threaten their profits.[72] Moreover, the deputy expressed his outrage at the costs incurred by the government and its failure to ensure the sort of basic security necessary for economic growth. There were more than 90,000 troops in Algeria to protect a mere 2,000 settlers engaged in farming (out of a total of 75,354 European civilians). In other words, forty-five soldiers protected each farmer in Algeria![73] Seen in this light, the plan to extend the colony's borders to the arid lands at the desert's edge seemed sheer folly.

TABLE 1.2 Troops and Settlers in Algeria, 1831–45

Year	European Civilians	French Troops
1831	3,228	17,190
1832	4,858	21,511
1833	7,812	26,681
1834	9,750	29,858
1835	11,221	29,485
1836	14,561	29,897
1837	16,770	40,147
1838	20,078	48,167
1839	25,000	50,367
1840	28,736	61,231
1841	35,727	72,000
1842	46,098	70,853
1843	58,985	75,034
1844	75,354	82,037
1845	99,800	95,000

Source: Ministère de la Guerre, *Tableau de la situation*, bk 9, 347.

The prospect of an invasion of the vast desert brought into clear focus an image of a war without end. As one deputy stated, "Our colleagues consider the little desert of the Algerian Sahara as a second field of *unlimited conquest*, where we will exhaust ourselves in sterile efforts that will compromise the occupation of the north."[74] While politicians accepted the costly conquest of the Tell, which gave France cultivable lands and naval ports, sending soldiers into the arid reaches of the Sahara, a land with no demonstrated economic or strategic value, was more than most had bargained for.

The penalty of ten thousand francs Bellonnet called for amounted to no more than a slap on the wrist, but the 5 June 1844 debate provided an occasion for hostile deputies to voice their opposition to the government. Deputy Jacques-François-Clair-Henri Joly proved to be a noteworthy critic. He used the expansion into Biskra "and a country called El-Agaat" (Laghouat) to place in doubt the previous fourteen-year effort. "War, always war," he complained, "expenses without results, a conquest without future, and most of all a colonization both exorbitant in cost and unpractical."[75] Given the lackluster results in the Tell, Joly questioned what might be achieved in the Sahara: "What are the goals of these expeditions? In order not to remain in a restricted occupation? I understood that with the Treaty of Tafna, but since it was broken, since we have arrived at the borders of the former Regency, you call that a restricted occupation? But where, then, do you want to stop?. . . . After having crossed Algeria, having arrived at the frontiers of the desert, is it the desert itself that you want to invade?. . . . But first [tell me] what right you have, and then I will ask you where your interest is."[76]

Joly was confident that his colleagues would share his dissatisfaction with the Saharan expansion's costs and its vague goals. Furthermore, he wished to draw attention to the fact that France had no legitimate claim to the lands of the Sahara. Joly continued by taking aim at the key argument justifying the Saharan expansion, namely, the alluring claim that the Sahara would be an easy, bloodless conquest. Joly did not accept this. Instead of the promised easy victories, he anticipated French troops being drawn into interminable conflicts not of their own devising and which they understood poorly.

> You had a quarrel with the dey of Algiers, you nobly and cruelly avenged yourself, you dethroned him, and you seized his states. Who told you that the inhabitants of the Sahara were the subjects of this same dey of Algiers? . . . You admit yourselves that there are oases that are inhabited by tribes that are not hostile; that, in addition, it is impossible that these tribes, geographically divided, could unite to attempt anything important against you; and you only want to import your government and your civilization.
>
> You say you are called by them, and that you respond to their appeal, and then this call is announced by cannon fire and battles.
>
> You say you are invited by the [local] populations. Yes, there is a leader, whose name I forget [Ben Salem], who came to Algiers to receive from us the investiture of his pashalik, and you received him, and you went forth to meet him, and you have overcome the difficulties of rule found around him. But he has a powerful neighbor living in another oasis, Aïn-Madi, with whom he is in open war, and he wants us to serve as an auxiliary to have the upper hand.
>
> Thus becoming auxiliaries, you become tributaries of indigenous leaders who, not recognizing any suzerain, are in feudal wars of neighbor against neighbor, and in this situation you think you show your dignity. Lo and behold, such are your expeditions. [77]

Having presented French troops serving as dupes, ignorant proxies in local "feudal wars," Joly continued his attack by taking aim at the overarching claim behind the French occupation, namely, the righteousness of the French cause embedded in claims of moral superiority. "I wonder," he mused, "if they don't have the force of justice and law with them when they ask: What do you want?

You had a quarrel with a prince who wasn't ours, with a sovereign of whom we were not subjects, and thus we shouldn't be the victims of a quarrel that should have ended with his fall and the taking of his states."[78] Having opened the proceedings to his vision of the vanquished, Joly narrowed his attack on French exceptionalism by pointing to Bugeaud's brutal tactics: "How do you expect to attract the sympathies of these peoples when they see around them their smoking fields, their harvests devastated, their houses burned, their *smalas* [families] carried off."

A strong opponent of French actions in Algeria, Joly (1790–1870) earned his law degree in Montpellier. He became active in the political life of the city during the Restoration and served as the head of Montpellier's democratic party. Elected deputy in 1831, Joly seated himself at the far left of the Chamber of Deputies, where he spent the next two decades in the opposition. He consistently expressed his disagreements with the government's Algerian policy and served as the opposition's most powerful voice of moral outrage. Joly's 1844 speech came a year before news of Pélissier's cruel "enfumades" at Dahra reached the capital, causing an outcry, but the level of violence visited upon Algerians already left many uneasy. Joly thought Bugeaud's practice of taking hostages was especially counterproductive and ill befitted the French army, accusing him of taking "three thousand women, old people and children" and then marching them hundreds of kilometers to hold them as prisoners. After being freed, they are sent, "naked, miserable, suffering," back to ruins of homes and fields. "And in this country we call that civilization, and we expect to be praised for it," he remarked sarcastically. "No, gentlemen, the Arabs cannot praise you because the war you make on them is not a fair and honest war; the war you make on them is a barbarous war. . . . This war is an atrocious war that represents neither the genius, the grandeur, nor the generosity of France."[79] In Joly's eyes the Algerian conquest risked condemning France's very identity—its manners, civility, and justice—to perdition. His colleagues in the opposition agreed: the transcript reporter noted that Joly's words brought hearty praise from the center and left of the Chamber of Deputies.

Bugeaud's turn south was shaping up to be a case of political overreach. All the frustrations—even shame—caused by the wars in the Tell came to a head with the Saharan expansion. Nevertheless, there were partisans of the policy among deputies. Struck by Joly's accusations of barbarism, they were at pains to insist that the French Sahara would not be a place of violence. "Our expeditions in the Sahara can only have a peaceful character," remarked M. de Corcelles. A deputy of the Orne and close friend of Alexis de Tocqueville, Claude François Philibert Tircuy de Corcelles (1802–1892) wholeheartedly supported the colonial project in Algeria, including the Saharan expansion. He assured his colleagues in the Chamber of Deputies that a serious study of the desert's history, geography, and economy revealed that violent resistance would not be encountered here. He argued that extending French power would be a relatively simple and inexpensive matter: "Two or three armed bases, two or three battalions of indigenous troops, entirely supported by the occupied country, will suffice. It never cost Abdelkader, or the Turks before him, any more," he promised. Citing a newly authored report by the Saharan specialist Ernest Carette, Corcelles asked, "Is it true that this is an unlimited desert, difficult to grasp, without any interest for us? Is it true that we could postpone our relations with it? No, gentlemen, it is a country that today we know, clearly delimited, inseparable from the Tell, populated by 7–800,000 inhabitants, where commerce is easy." Unlike the endless wasteland sketched by naysayers, the desert was, in fact, thickly populated and rich. Moreover, "all the masters of Algeria have possessed it without violence."[80]

Joly found Corcelles's vision entirely implausible, remarking caustically that this was "a Sahara desert that would no longer be a desert." Authors of the Chamber of Deputy's budget recommendations were equally unconvinced. Their report rejected any action undertaken with the aim of "vain domination" or "intimidation." "France bears with reluctant patriotism the burdens of this conquest," they wrote in a clear reprimand. The report suggested that only if Bugeaud could expand French influence without the use of weapons would support be forthcoming. The onus was on Bugeaud to live up to his promises and deliver a different—inexpensive and peaceful—conquest. The report admonished: "It is through negotiations and by the intermediary of indigenous leaders, facilitating communications and exchanges [and] establishing marketplaces, rather than by arms that we can complete the conquest." Parliamentary opinion had spoken and challenged those who dreamed of a Saharan empire to establish it by peaceful means.

THE CRISIS IN THE ARMY

Corcelles's accusations aside, the Chamber of Deputies's pessimism was not born of ignorance. Indeed, those most familiar with the Algerian situation knew that a critical situation was developing. France was at risk of losing its army in these colonial campaigns. By the mid 1840s mounting signs showed that it was not Algerians alone who were paying a heavy price for Bugeaud's war. While his razzias sapped Algerian resistance, they exacted an important, if disproportionate, toll on the French army. Military planners had known for some time that large numbers of troops committed to the Algerian campaigns left the army ill prepared to meet its continental defense needs. Those who looked across the Rhine were especially displeased by the Mediterranean expansion, arguing that France's destiny was European, not African.

The crisis arrived in several forms. The high mortality suffered by French troops in Algeria was already becoming a point of concern. (In 1848 it became known that the military's mortality rate was eight times higher for soldiers in Algeria than those in France.)[81] Others attacked the detrimental effects of Bugeaud's irregular tactics on the preparation and training of French soldiers; many of his troops showed more skill wielding an axe to cut down olive trees than marching in formation. Instead of the efficiency and rigor of modern soldiers who might stand up to Britain or Prussia, critics saw the army in Algeria turning into a ragtag bunch of marauders engaged in state-sanctioned banditry.[82] Another source of degradation of the army's integrity and morale were the effects of the constant campaigns, poor sanitary and living conditions, irregular and insufficient rations, and what was for some the psychologically exhausting work of repeated killings and wanton destruction.

Table 1.3, which draws on figures established by demographic historian Kamel Kateb, shows the heavy costs paid by the French army in Algeria. A careful look at the numbers of deaths dispels the myth of "long peace" of the nineteenth century. In the first five years under Bugeaud's command (1841–46), more than 35,935 French troops died in combat or from wounds and illness. These losses came at a time when people, weary of the high loss of life during Napoleon's wars, were particularly unwilling to support such costly conflicts.[83]

Algeria represented a crisis for the army not only in terms of resources but also morale. While the losses of their comrades weighed heavy on many soldiers, French deaths were not the only source of distress. The violence that soldiers unleashed upon Algerians—men, women, and children—was more than many had anticipated. The sheer scale of the killing was horrifying. Although the exact figures were not known at the time, historians have shown what many intuitively understood in the 1840s: the colonization of Algeria was preceded by a great bloodletting. Kateb, working from a conservative estimate of 10 Algerian deaths for every French soldier, concludes that 75,000 Algerians were struck down in battle during the forty-five-year period of the conquest (1830–75).[84] When he calculates the excess mortality due to the war, he estimates 825,000 Algerian losses in the same period. The number who fell victim to epidemics and hunger cannot be firmly established, but in the terrible famine of 1867–68 historians have concluded that some 800,000 died.[85] In all, the conquest of Algeria would claim the lives of roughly 1.6 million Algerians, making it among the most costly chapters in the history of modern European global expansion.[86] While many soldiers fighting for France undertook their murderous work without qualms—some even did so with zeal—others found the razzia and its deliberate attacks on women, children, and the aged morally troubling.

The best single collection of source material documenting this moral crisis is the series of letters written to General Castellane by a cadre of officers serving in Algeria between 1835 and 1848.[87] Esprit-Victor-Elisabeth-Boniface, comte de Castellane (1788–1862) was descended from one of the oldest noble families in

TABLE 1.3 Deaths in the French Army in Algeria, 1831–51

Year	French Soldiers in Algeria	Deaths in Hospital	Deaths in Combat	Total Killed
1830	37,000	Unknown	1,336	1,336
1831	17,190	1,005	55	1,060
1832	21,511	1,998	48	2,046
1833	26,681	2,512	64	2,576
1834	29,858	1,991	24	2,015
1835	29,485	2,335	310	2,645
1836	29,897	2,139	606	2,745
1837	40,147	4,502	121	4,623
1838	48,167	2,413	150	2,563
1839	50,367	3,600	163	3,763
1840	61,263	9,567	227	9,794
1841	72,000	7,802	349	8,151
1842	70,853	5,558	225	5,783
1843	75,053	4,809	84	4,893
1844	82,037	4,664	167	4,831
1845	95,000	4,694	605	5,299
1846	99,700	6,862	116	6,978
1847	92,413	4,437	77	4,514
1848	77,789	4,406	13	4,419
1850	71,496	4,098	Unknown	4,098
1851	65,598	3,193	Unknown	3,193
Total Deaths		82,585	4,740	87,325

Source: Kamel Kateb, *Européens, "Indigènes," et Juifs*, 38.

France. Skilled at riding the volatile political currents following the Revolution, Castellane went from military service in Napoleon's army to serving in some of the most powerful commands in the French army and in the parliamentary bodies of the Orléanist Monarchy and the Second Empire. During this period he commanded the Twenty-first Division at Perpignan. He served briefly in Algeria and visited the country only on occasion. A notable instance was his 1838 stay in the Constantine region, where the strict soldier was horrified by the army's lack of discipline and poor hygiene. He found the dress of special regiments, such as the Zouaves, ridiculous. Nevertheless, he had a strong interest in Algeria. Many of the officers who served here had previously passed through his command at Perpignan, and he had two sons who were serving in Algeria. Deeply distrustful of his rival Bugeaud and skeptical of his tactics, Castellane kept close tabs on affairs on the other side of the Mediterranean.[88] To this end, he maintained a correspondence with a group of trusted junior officers in Algeria. These men, in effect, served as Castellane's spies.[89] Their letters, which circulated outside the channels of official correspondence, where French violence remained unspoken, are rare in the candor and detail with which they describe Bugeaud's conquest. To consider their importance, it is worth investigating the source material. Official military reports drafted by officers in the field do not write with the frankness of the Castellane correspondence. The violence of the French razzia was collectively understood but almost never spoken of apart from body counts. Morally questionable acts—rapes, summary executions, killing of noncombatants, and looting—did not fit the norms of the field report. On the other hand, in their private correspondence officers recounted violence in explicit terms. And some published accounts even exaggerated the violence of French troops.[90] Sources from the Algerians are even rarer in the colonial archive. While the latter contains a good deal of intercepted material from Algerians involved in organizing military responses to the French army, few detail the devastation of the French raids.[91]

As author François Maspero has noted, Castellane served as an "occult confessor" to the French army in Algeria.[92] Letters addressed to him reveal an army sapped by casualties and illness, where low moral was typical and corruption and sadism ruled the day. Their authors explained the effects of the lack of discipline, inadequate supplies, and the irregular tactics of the razzia, which some denounced as more of a "large-scale hunting party" than warfare.[93] Not only did this manner of waging war bode ill for army discipline, but it was far from what many thought was their vocation as soldiers. As one infantry captain explained, "During the five months I have been in the country, I have spent four on expeditions. During this time, I sought in vain the opportunity to engage the enemy in combat. We have waged war only on herds, homes, harvests, and the weakest members of the population, who, without arms and prodded by hunger and misery, prefer to give up rather than engage in battle."[94]

Such campaigns did not crush the Algerian opposition, although many fled at the sight of French troops. Resistance and insecurity sprang up almost as soon as the French columns had passed through. Detailing operations near Collo in the spring of 1843, one military official wrote, "Up till now there have been few submissions; we shoot almost daily."[95] Thirty to forty French soldiers had been killed in this particular action and more than 150 wounded. He continued: "Despite the efforts and the courage of our brave troops, we gain little ground. The campaign continues, and we await with some anxiety the final result." Three years later a colonel in a mounted infantry group would express the same pessimism in terms that echoed some of the debates led by Joly and others in Paris. "Horses, cattle, and even sheep are going to disappear: war has destroyed the first and impeded their reproduction; the alternating razzias of the Arabs and our own have achieved the extinction of the bovine race." He concluded: "In sum, *we destroy the country that we claim to colonize and civilize.*"[96] This spirit of profound pessimism runs throughout the letters. Waging war on villagers and herders produced only easy victories, not decisive ones, and those who led the attack could only wonder when this all might end.

The crisis spread through the ranks. In April 1843 Lieutenant Colonel Forey had just returned from an extended razzia near Cherchell. His column left with the day's standard orders: "Ravage the countryside, carry off the maximum number of livestock possible and especially women and children; the governor-general wants to terrify the populations by sending them to France."[97] His troops fulfilled their orders to the letter. The five battalions led by Forey alone took six thousand head of livestock and "precious booty" consisting of arms and other unspecified wealth. They ensured future food insecurity and economic ruin by cutting over ten thousand olive and fruit trees. To spread fear, they abducted seventy women and children and took another two hundred "prisoner." (Algerian deaths are not mentioned.) The column's accomplishments, however, did not sit well with its commander. Forey traversed a region full of "natural beauty." Groves of ancient and immense olive trees punctuated the landscape, along with picturesque and populous villages. "But," he noted, "the orders were imperative" that these were to be leveled. Unnerved by the destruction, Forey considered his conduct: "I thought to have conscientiously fulfilled my mission in not leaving a single village standing, not one tree, not a field untouched. The harm that my column did on its passage is incalculable. Is it an evil? Is it a good? Or, rather, an evil for a good? That is what the future will decide."[98] Forey was a seasoned veteran of Algerian campaigns. He had arrived in Algeria in 1835 and had seen extensive action since then. But by 1843 his rationalizations were wearing thin. Only the month before this mission he had written, "This war, undertaken on such a vast scale, will never finish."[99]

It was not only officers who felt troubled by their actions. The commander of the Fifth Battalion of Chasseurs, Chef de Battalion Canrobert, observed the effects among the rank and file: "Actor or forced spectator in a multitude of these dramas, I have learned only too well the disastrous effects of this terrible and barbarous method. I have often been left aghast by the profound demoralization that it strikes into the heart of a soldier who slits throats, steals, rapes, and fights only for his own account, in front of his officers, who are often powerless to control him!"[100] Four years into Bugeaud's total conquest, the colonial idol of European superiority was tarnished, and the French army's purpose had become increasingly uncertain even to itself.

Henri Brunschwig, a historian of French colonialism, once argued, "In the eyes of its agents, imperialism . . . was a worthy thing. . . . Unwitting of [sic] the problems and evils they were engendering, they had clear consciences."[101] This sampling of the Castellane correspondence demonstrates that this was not the case in Algeria. It produced great political tensions and challenged the strategies of total conquest. High-level officials and specialists agreed that Algerians would submit only by force. Following from this opinion was the idea that the civilizing mission had to pass through the tempest of conquest.[102] However, the categories that underlay this rationale, "barbares" and "civilisés," strained under the burden of Bugeaud's war (just as they were redeployed to devastating political effect in the legislative debates). The radical discrepancy between the official version and the realities of campaigns in Algeria produced profound feelings of ambivalence among the actors on the front lines. The fact that experienced and talented officers with powerful political connections (many of whom later rose to become marshals) experienced such feelings boded serious trouble among the high echelons of command.

Nevertheless, the army in Algeria remained intact. Convinced that victory was just around the corner, Bugeaud kept his forces together as others had before and since. He employed a combination of draconian punishment for minor infractions combined with great indulgences after the hard work was over. While no evidence exists to suggest that soldiers who refused orders to kill, kidnap, or loot faced reprimands, those who stole or were insubordinate while in camp received the strictest chastisement, including beatings, long terms of solitary confinement, and physical torture.[103] On the other hand, those who saw a campaign through to successful completion were given free rein. Bugeaud himself was known to grant his soldiers the most license among commanders in Algeria. For example, having arrived at the port of Bougie after personally leading the famous "conquest" of the Kabylia in 1847 (it was conquered again in 1857), he let his troops run amok in the city. Although the French had had nominal control over Bougie since 1833, and its inhabitants had not raised arms against the French, they had to bear the brunt of the troops' riotous revels.[104] One colonel wrote:

Since we arrived on the 22nd [of May], there has been no reveille or retreat. They call it *days of rest:* in fact, these are *days of saturnalia.* The town of Bougie ... will long remember the passage of these undisciplined troops; one crosses only drunken men, wounded, with broken limbs; the inhabitants closed their doors and shutters; the gendarmes have been given a thrashing, women insulted, houses pillaged; all night long you hear only screams. Everything spreads disease and disorder. I can't wait to get out of this chaos. If this continues, there will no longer be an army.[105]

Fernand Braudel has written that "all conquests lead to exhaustion."[106] Algeria was no exception. As the French project in Algeria approached the end of its second decade, the actual costs France had paid for this colony came into sharper focus, including a skyrocketing budget, the commitment of massive numbers of troops, and the depletion of France's moral capital. The costs and violence of the conquest stretched the political will of important sections of French society, making Algeria a growing liability for the government. The colony's supporters could still argue that the price paid was worth it. Victory ensured France access to strategic Mediterranean ports as well as the agricultural lands of the Tell, future home to European settlers. The Sahara was an entirely different matter. Although Bugeaud insisted that French troops had to close the Sahara as a refuge to rebels, he left unsettled the important question of what place the desert might occupy in the colony and how he would avoid a replay of the failures of the Tell campaigns. If he hoped to rally the necessary political support for his ambitions, Bugeaud would have to offer up a new model of colonial conquest.

[2]

THEORIZING THE "PÉNÉTRATION PACIFIQUE"

La violence est l'argument du mensonge.
—Comte de Volney (1791)

Following his brilliant study of the French conquest of the Middle Niger region, historian A. S. Kanya-Forstner distanced himself from his earlier argument that ambition and administrative incoherence drove French expansion in Africa.[1] He now concluded that, "fascinated by the lure of the Sudanese interior, the French built an empire not on solid economic foundations but on a grand illusion."[2] It can similarly be said that the first generation of policy makers for the Algerian Sahara responded to a particular set of challenges with their own grand illusion. However, this illusion arose neither from the desert's heat nor from exotic European fantasies, any more than it drew the French to the Sahara or provided the foundation for their rule. The French were not, as some have argued, "hypnotized by the Sahara."[3] Inaccurate, unrealistic, at times even fantastical, their Saharan illusion was an instrumentalized representation formed in response to a specific set of political obstacles and possibilities rooted in the costs of the Algerian wars and the parliamentary politics of the Orléanist monarchy.

Three parties saw advantages in a Saharan expansion: the monarchy, which sought dynastic power and political legitimacy through colonial expansion; Governor-General Bugeaud, who strove to maintain his army as the principal source of power in the Algerian colony, thereby bolstering his already enormous personal power; and the Saint-Simonians, utopian social theorists who took special interest in Algeria as a place to realize their projects. Although these three parties were hardly political allies whose ideas were cut from the same ideological cloth, they collaborated to create the powerful idea that the Sahara would willingly become part of the French empire. This idea was offered up to counter that of a fourth player, the government's opposition in parliament, which was skeptical about colonial expansion. Many legislators had already turned against the whole Algerian project, and the idea of an empire of sand left them cold. Moreover, some hoped for political advantage by using setbacks in North Africa as leverage against the government. It was no secret that many deputies and some peers looked for better ways to claim the constitutional powers they felt they were entitled to. The left opposition in particular found a powerful tool in the charges of colonial barbarism, like that leveled by Deputy Joly in 1844, and conservatives could attack the Algerian enterprise as irresponsible adventurism that left France highly vulnerable on the Continent. Plans to push the frontiers of the unstable Algerian colony farther south opened the government up to further attacks.

The political opposition in Paris, combined with a looming crisis in the army, forced Bugeaud and like-minded policy makers to develop plans for a Saharan expansion that was inexpensive and required a minimum of force. In other words, the violence of Bugeaud's wars in the north of Algeria gave rise to the idea of a Saharan empire resulting from peaceful expansion, which became known as the "pénétration pacifique." This was not so much a strategy as a set of ideas that emphasized cooperation, commerce, and diplomacy rather than a head-on assault in the Sahara. Unfortunately, these ideas did not change the course of French expansion; the Sahara, like the Tell, was the scene of great violence. But the "pénétration pacifique" gave policy makers the much-needed illusion of control and helped respond to colonial critics by playing upon those values of French colonialism about which there was general consensus, such as trade and development. In particular, the "pénétration pacifique" presupposed an assumed ability to project French control and influence through inexpensive and bloodless means. This image emphasized both French power and its benevolence and thereby circumvented the problematic—and politically explosive—course of events in Algeria thus far.

As a policy, the "pénétration pacifique" was another matter. It would require a good deal of information about the economy, the political situation, and the geography of the Sahara. This desire to better understand the Sahara occupied the efforts of a diverse group of people.

KNOWLEDGE OF THE SAHARA PRIOR TO 1830

Before the French landed in Algeria, images of the Sahara resembled the distant oceans sketched in the atlases dating to the Middle Ages. Few dreamed that the desert, which was thought to be "entirely uninhabited and uninhabitable," might one day become a part of the French empire.[4] Indeed, in the eighteenth century, when empire was the stuff of sugar, slaves, and souls, few believed that the fate of France's Mediterranean aspirations might hinge on the Sahara. Thus, with no particular urgency and with little direct knowledge, early geographers filled these areas with hazy compositions of burning stretches of sand, home to mysterious and warlike "peuplades." Earlier Arab travelers and geographers such as Ibn Hawqal (tenth century) al-Bakri (eleventh), al-Idrisi (twelfth), Ibn Battuta (fourteenth), Ibn Khaldun (fourteenth), and al-Wazzan al-Fasi (a.k.a. Leo Africanus) (sixteenth) wrote descriptions of the Sahara, but only scattered parts of their work were available to French administrators in the 1830s and 1840s.[5] Analysts also read the accounts of the first generation of European explorers: Thomas Shaw (Algiers and Tunis, early eighteenth century),[6] Friedrich Hornemann (Cairo to Murzuq, 1797–98),[7] Mungo Park (Gambia River and Niger River, 1794–97, 1805–6),[8] Ritchie and Lyon (Tripoli to Fezzan, 1818–19),[9] Oudney, Clapperton, and Denham (Tripoli to Lake Chad, 1822–25),[10] Gordon Laing (Tripoli to Timbuktu 1825–26),[11] and René Caillé (Senegal to Morocco via Timbuktu, 1828–29). The accounts of sailors shipwrecked on the Sahara's Atlantic coast also provided glimpses of what to expect in the desert.

Although the writings of the Arab geographers were known to only a small group of orientalists, selective bits of their work circulated more widely and won them great authority. A figure such as al-Wazzan, who became famous to French readers as Léon l'Africain, is representative of this group. His writings remained rare until the government published a new edition of his work in 1830, translated and edited by Jean Temporal, to accompany the French landings in Algeria. Al-Wazzan's account of a prosperous trading center at Timbuktu contributed to the myth of the rich, unreachable, forbidden city on the Niger River, the "Nile of West Africa."[12] Although such talk elevated the hopes of those directly concerned (namely, merchants trading with the Maghreb) that they might one day see French caravans in the Sahara, they had to face the fact that arriving in Timbuktu from Algeria would be difficult if not impossible.

The first Frenchman to publish a firsthand account of the north-central Sahara was Jean André Peyssonnel (1694–1759), who traveled through the Maghreb in 1724–25. While some spoke of Saharan riches, looking south from the mountains south of Constantine he saw only a sea of sand devoid of life and most likely uninhabitable: "From these heights we saw the famous deserts of the Sahara. From this aspect there are neither trees nor date palms; at the foot of the mountains there are only salty lands that disappear into a sea of sand that has its own movements. Its waves are the mobile mountains that the wind forms, transports, and destroys capriciously."[13]

Peyssonnel's vision of a terrible land of shifting sands inspired few. The siren call of the sciences had only just begun to lure explorers like Peyssonnel to extreme climes.[14] Moreover, the desire to set foot in virgin lands as a form of adventure had not yet taken hold.[15] Only riches might have tempted Europeans to risk life and limb in such harsh lands, and according to Peyssonnel the possibility of finding them here was slim.

However, within a generation two French travelers wrote important accounts of the north-central Sahara. René Louiche Desfontaines (1750–1833) and Abbé Poiret (1757–1834) published studies that reaffirmed Peyssonnel's findings. Desfontaines spent five years in the Maghreb (1783–88) on a botanical and zoological mission for the Academy of Sciences.[16] His detailed account of the flora and fauna of North Africa reveal an affinity for the Mediterranean climate of the Tell. Like Peyssonnel, he found little in the Sahara that could be described as inviting.

> The desert, properly speaking, is only an immense sea of sand that tires and saddens the view by its uniformity; one sees neither greenness nor [signs] of human habitation. Nature appears dead in these sad lands; winds are frequent; and when they blow with impetuousness the whole atmosphere is blocked by clouds of flying sand; you can only see the sun as through a thick fog; travelers are obliged to stop and await the calm. In the summer you travel only at night; the burning heat of the sun, reflected by the sands, never fails to suffocate those who dare expose themselves during the day.[17]

This understanding of the Sahara as a wasteland of heat and sand, devoid of life, little inclined Desfontaines to spend much time in the desert. He did make it as far as Tozeur (in modern-day Tunisia), where he enjoyed the shade of an oasis's gardens, "forests of date palms, grape vines, orange and almond trees."[18] But he made no effort to see what lay farther afield. Abbé Poiret, for his part, traveled to the Constantine region, and the picture he sketched was equally bleak: "As soon as one traverses the chain of the Atlas, and progressively as one advances in these deserts, inhabitable and inhabited sites become ever rarer; one must travel one hundred leagues or more before finding the feeblest spring or the smallest plant." The challenges faced by those who ventured into these inhospitable lands were immense: "In addition to the elements, caravans have also to battle with the ferocious beasts and sometimes men. The inhabitants of these fiery countries are little known. They are almost entirely errant hordes, composed of un-subdued Arabs, the cruelest and bloodthirsty of men."[19]

Although he evoked a vivid, fear-inspiring image, Poiret never actually saw these lands nor met their inhabitants. He had hoped to visit the Sahara and accepted an invitation of his host, the bey of Constantine, to journey to the desert in February 1786.[20] However, an outbreak of the plague forced the cancellation of this journey. Lacking direct knowledge, Poiret had to construct his account from an amalgam of information gathered in discussions with people who had been to the desert and the testimony of his hosts in the Tell. When these sources fell short, Poiret likely relied on his own imagination to fill in the shades and contours of his Saharan tableau.

In the decade prior to the conquest of Algiers, new geographic institutions transformed the store of information about the Sahara. The year 1823 saw the founding of the Geographic Society of Paris. The first organization of its kind, it assembled some of France's top scientists.[21] From the beginning members of the society expressed their dissatisfaction with the current state of knowledge on the Maghreb, Sahara, and Central Africa. In the second issue of the society's journal François Jomard remarked on the "harvest for Geography!" that awaited the explorer who ventured into the lands of Central Africa.[22] Impatient for this hardy explorer to materialize and reap this field for science, in 1824 Conrad Malte-Brun, the society's secretary-general, wrote the Danish consul at Tripoli and his French counterpart at Bône with a list of questions.[23] Like his peers in other European capitals, Malte-Brun asked questions that exceeded the bounds of science.[24] In addition to information on terrain, climate, archeology, and ethnology, Malte-Brun wanted to know about the extent of the bey of Constantine's authority in the south and the prospect of setting up a commercial agent in the oases of Touggourt and Biskra. That he knew very little about the region can be gleaned from his questions: What is the difference between Arabs and Moors? Do the Moors predate the Arab conquest? Are they Asians? Persians? Who are the Berbers? Are they the same as the "Chowia"? The Kabyles? The "Neardie" tribe of the Aurès are said to be blond. Are they ancestors of the Vandals? Are they more favorable to Christians? Is the Greek cross that they tattoo on their forehead a Vandal vestige?

By 1825 these uncertain early efforts, together with reports from English explorers, produced some reliable information that countered the harsh picture sketched by eighteenth-century writers. For the first time geographers could look forward to the day when a European would traverse the great desert. Malte-Brun's own research efforts had revealed that the Sahara was not a wild and impassable Dantesque hell on earth, as Peyssonnel and others had earlier claimed, but a crossroads, intersected by the great arteries of trade linking sub-Saharan Africa and the Mediterranean.[25] This altered understanding prompted the society to create its first major monetary prize for a feat of exploration, a 9,000-franc award to the first Frenchman to reach Timbuktu from Saint Louis.[26]

Three years later, in December 1828, René Caillié claimed the prize for his 1827–28 trip from the African coast to Morocco via Timbuktu. The young, driven explorer made his voyage posing as an Egyptian, a Muslim who, having been captured by Napoleon and taken to France, was making his way back home on foot via Senegal. The story yielded Caillié the protection and assistance of the local people. Penniless and far from kin, Caillié was known to his

Muslim hosts as *miskīn* (poor, to be pitied); he owed his survival to the charity they bestowed on the destitute. As Jacques Berque has pointed out, Caillié was less "an advanced scout for Europe" than "a lost child, marginal in the eyes of Europeans, as in the eyes of the indigenous."[27] When he returned to France, Caillié discovered that he had many detractors who cast doubts upon his itinerary and found fault with the scientific value of his report.[28] Along with pure chauvinism (the strongest accusations came from Britain), Caillié's sober, no-nonsense account of Timbuktu motivated much of the criticism. Rather than the famed city of fabulous wealth—an African Eldorado—Caillié wrote tersely of Timbuktu. It "offers, at first view nothing but a mass of wretched-looking houses built of earth. In all directions one sees only immense plains of moving sand."[29] While Caillié was hardly pessimistic concerning the possibilities for European merchants—illustrated editions of his account included images of a great mosque and thriving city—he did not adequately respond to the mood of anticipation.[30] One critic writing in 1860 noted that Caillié's "affirmations, so different from the general opinion, threw into doubt the truthfulness of this traveler and brought upon him thousands of criticisms."[31] It was not until after his premature death in 1838 that a consensus formed in France concerning the authenticity and value of Caillié's work.[32]

The fact that a European, traveling alone and unarmed, could traverse the immense desert might have dispelled images of the Sahara as a perilous, fiery void. But even as he lived to tell his tale, Caillié did not like the Sahara. His reports, like those of Peyssonnel and Poiret, evoked a barren and lifeless land. He reminded his readers that they could not undertake travel here lightly: "I had great difficulties staying upright on my camel, such was my exhaustion. I kept on thinking that the only way to stay alive on this route was to quicken my pace; this idea bolstered my courage and gave me new strength. Still, I admit that I envied those who can make a name for themselves without having to buy it by such painful suffering and new perils."[33]

Caillié encountered hardships everywhere. In the long weeks it took to cross the desert, he sustained himself with two thoughts: leaving "these frightful deserts" and water.[34] As he wrote, "I thought of nothing but water—rivers, streams, rivulets, were the only ideas that presented themselves to my mind during this burning fever."[35] Although Caillié survived his crossing, his account did not inspire others to pack their bags and take off for the Sahara.

The Geographic Society of Paris did not try to follow up on Caillié's feat. With the major geographic questions of Central Africa "solved" (Timbuktu, the course of the Niger River), its concerns shifted. Having "discovered" Timbuktu, French efforts in the Sahara lagged. As was the case in Britain, "Exploration no longer had its old appeal."[36] Even in the early 1830s, after the French had arrived in Algeria, few thought of linking French holdings in North and West Africa across the desert. During this period the society's *Bulletin* published more articles on exploration in the United States and its western territories than on North Africa and the Sahara. As the sources reveal, the difficult questions encountered during the occupation of the Algerian Tell consumed the most attention of those thinking of Algeria's future. Moreover, the government had other concerns. The 1830s were troubling times. With insurrections, plots, coups, and assassination attempts at home, plus nationalist uprisings, social unrest, and diplomatic issues abroad—any one of which could lead to a general European war—the Sahara appeared distant and unimportant.

There were exceptions, of course. One was a pamphlet, addressed to the new king in September 1830, by Philippe Augier de La Sauzaie, son of a commercial family of the Charente region that had colonial interests.[37] A month after the dey of Algiers had capitulated to the French, Augier de La Sauzaie already saw France on the verge of a vast, profitable empire in Africa on a par with the British venture in India. He argued that the government only needed to exercise foresight and energy to realize its potential. The Sahara was key. Linking Algiers to Timbuktu would bring France's West African holdings into the orbit of Mediterranean trade. In a highly optimistic reading of Caillié's reports, Augier de La Sauzaie claimed that Saharan commerce involved a lucrative trade in ivory, gold, feathers, coral, arms, and textiles. The job of filling France's coffers with such profits was a simple matter of forging relations with the "Maures," who would bring their caravans to Algiers. Needless to say, Augier de La Sauzaie's offer was premature and did not move others, who were more preoccupied at the time by the basic question of how to hold on to the few French possessions in the Tell than setting off across the desert.

Interest in the Sahara did not entirely end at this time, however. For example, in the last years of Ottoman Algeria a young American conducted research from Algiers. Unknown to the Geographic Society of Paris, William Brown Hodgson (1800–71), a chargé d'affaires of the United States Consul to the Ottoman Regency, pursued his interest in the languages and peoples of the Maghreb southward with great passion. A combined geographic and ethnographic research project was initially proposed to Hodgson by James Cansham, the president of Princeton College, upon learning of Hodgson's appointment as the secretary to the American consul in Mexico. When this job fell through, Hodgson found Algiers to be an even more exciting terrain for research.[38] In Algiers both Hodgson and his superior, William Shaler, focused their research on linguistic and ethnographic questions.[39] Like their European counterparts— Venture de Paradis, Georges Hirt, and the French consul Chénier—the American diplomats were especially interested in Berber languages and Berberophone peoples.[40] After learning of Berberophone societies, like the Mzabis and the Tuareg, in the Sahara, the American showed an interest in the Sahara. Hodgson extended his research to include trade routes and the political situation at the southern terminuses of Mediterranean commerce. Like earlier students of the

Sahara, Hodgson made his explorations through proxies, but he differed from his predecessors by seeking firsthand accounts and providing full translations or summaries close to the original source.[41]

Hodgson's interviews in particular produced a different picture of the desert than those prevalent in the eighteenth century. Hodgson's research corroborated Caillié's findings that the Sahara could be crossed. But unlike the terrifying and lifeless void sketched by Caillié, Hodgson showed that the Sahara was inhabited and frequently traveled. Moreover, the American's research yielded detailed information on the desert directly south of Algiers that would become crucial after 1830. For example, in 1826 he asked a Saharan trader then in Algiers named el-Eghwati ("the Laghouati") to write a brief description of the Sahara near his hometown. His fourteen-page report provided numerous details on the region's trade and agriculture, as well as the political alignments and military capabilities of Algero-Saharan societies.[42] El-Eghwati reported that just across the arid stretches of the High Plateaux were wooded mountains where herds of camels and sheep grazed. Farther on the traveler encountered Laghouat, a large town with four mosques and abundant fruit trees. He reassured the reader that "trade is carried on here; and agriculture is attended to."[43] Nearby Aïn-Madi was home to the Ouled Tidjin (the Tijaniyya Sufi order), who owned hundreds of slaves and had a large library and a rich treasury, complete with gold-embroidered saddles. El-Eghwati sketched the same inviting picture of the market towns of the Wady Mezzab (Mzab), Wergelah (Ouargla), Caleah (In Salah), Timemoun (Timimoun), and Touggourt, "a town of wealth and abundance."[44] The country was nevertheless harsh. For example, el-Eghwati wrote that the route east from El Oued is "uninterrupted waste." "It is not frequented by Arabs," he continued, and "contains no village, affords no water, and is diversified by no hills nor stones. One expanse of sand everywhere meets the eye."[45] Nevertheless caravans regularly crossed these areas, and the Tuarychs (Tuareg), "a powerful people," routinely traveled to the Land of the Blacks (*bilād al-Sūdān*), where they undertook raids for slaves.[46]

In subsequent interviews with Mzabi migrants, Saharan merchants, and slaves, Hodgson assembled a sizable archive dealing with the Algerian Sahara and gathered information on the area as far south as the Niger River.[47] In 1829 he had collected enough material to draw a map of the region, "in which I have found populous oases, I believe heretofore unknown . . . described itineraries from the Atlantic to Fezzan . . . [and] traced the lines of march . . . through different sections of this vasty waste."[48] To the degree that Hodgson's boast is true (I have been unable to locate a copy of the map), such information was at least as good as—if not better than—that available to French administrators a decade later. Not until 1834 did Arnaud d'Avezac, a member of the Geographic Society of Paris, provide a French translation of el-Eghwati's description, thereby introducing the findings to French geographers.[49] Avezac's attentions earned him the friendship of Hodgson, who donated much of his archive to the Geographic Society of Paris in 1836.[50]

THE 1840s: THE SEARCH FOR A POLICY, A "PÉNÉTRATION PACIFIQUE"

When French administrators turned to the Sahara south of Algeria in the early 1840s, they had a meager and outdated list of sources. Few mentioned el-Eghwati's description, and for many the venerable "Léon l'Africain" remained the most authoritative source.[51] As one commentator retrospectively wrote in 1853, "We arrived at the limits of the Tell thinking we were already in the middle of the desert. . . . On this disinherited land one found neither mankind nor vegetation."[52] Responding to the poor state of general knowledge on Algeria, in 1837 the government established the Commission for the Scientific Exploration of Algeria. The goal of the commission was to study the soil, plants, and animals, and to map the terrain. Knowledge of the climate, health conditions, economy, and people of Algeria was also sought. Like its predecessor, Napoleon's famed scientific mission to Egypt, the commission would "prove that our engineers, our physicians, our naturalists, our scholars [can] rival the zeal and the ardor of the valiant soldiers of the army."[53] By 1840 the efforts of a select group of researchers began to produce solid information, with the Sahara being an important part of their work. Whereas earlier naturalists, such as Desfontaines, shied away from the desert, where "nature seemed dead," the generation of the 1840s responded to new expansionist demands and displayed a special zeal for the desert.

Ismayl Urbain: A New Look, New Frontiers, and Cost-Saving Control

For reasons that historians have yet fully to explain, Saint-Simonians and those sympathetic to the movement's principles figured prominently among members of the commission.[54] The Saint-Simonians' hopes for the Mediterranean and Africa dated back nearly a decade to their failed project to find a patron in Muhammad Ali, the "pacha industriel" of Egypt, but the branch led by Père Enfantin was not discouraged by this setback and looked to new opportunities in Algeria.[55] The commission provided the ideal occasion to showcase Saint-Simonian methods and discover regions where disciples might live in harmony with the laws of science and industry.

A young and enthusiastic Saint-Simonian named Ismayl Urbain (1812–1884) had responded to the call to Egypt and had converted to Islam there. Following the project's demise, in 1837 he disembarked in Algeria and worked as a military interpreter. Having learned to communicate in Egyptian dialect, Urbain's Arabic initially posed problems. But promotions came quickly, and three years following his arrival he was appointed to the commission, where he began work on the Sahara. Urbain did not undertake original research on the desert. His knowledge derived from his experiences as an interpreter on military campaigns and from conversations with fellow commission members. However, his work was noteworthy both for the fact that he was the first to synthesize early policy proposals and for the solutions he offered to the questions dogging the Saharan expansion.[56]

Urbain's 1843 report got off to an inauspicious start when he presented the social divisions in Algeria according to the standard ethnology of the day, which was based upon a bifurcation of the population into "Kabyles" and "Arabs." Kabyles live in the mountains "a terrain most appropriate for their habits," he wrote, while the Arabs live in the Sahara, "scorning the fertile plains of Africa for the arid solitudes that remind them of their homeland."[57] Ignoring the majority of Arabophone Algerians who lived in the Tell, Urbain's understanding was crude at best. But his commentary became more exact when he explained the forces that brought the French to the Sahara. "Since last year, the war has put us into contact with the population of the Saharah [sic]." This expansion "has opened to us political relations that are of a nature to profoundly alter the conditions and the difficulties of our establishment in Africa."[58] Urbain stressed that the challenge posed by the southern frontier should not be underestimated, arguing that a favorable outcome for France's project in the Tell depended upon a successful policy in the Sahara.

Mapping the Algerian Sahara represented the first order of business. Urbain solicited local understanding of Algeria's geography based on a division of the country between the Tell and the Sahara.[59] This allowed him to cut through much complexity with a simple formulation: "One calls desert (saharah) in Algeria the portion beyond the second chain of mountains [Saharan Atlas], situated thirty-five or forty leagues south of the coast. This zone extends from east to west the entire length of Algeria, to a depth of thirty to forty leagues from north to south."[60]

While Urbain talked in terms of geographic unity, he based his claim on a putative right of conquest. This area was part of the former Ottoman regencies and now belonged to France, Algeria's new master. To determine the eastern and western borders of the Algerian Sahara, Urbain simply extended the northern boundaries with Morocco and Tunisia. In the south Urbain cast his net over "wandering peoples whose constitution and importance we still do not know" and claimed not territory per se but the populations themselves that lived here. Wherever Saharan pastoralists—now French subjects—ranged in their search for pastureland was part of the Algerian colony.[61] This fuzzy thinking implied that French sovereignty extended to the pasturelands neighboring the Mzab, where the Larbaa and Ouled Naïl grazed in winter, with nothing preventing France from extending its claim to the lands as far south as Ouargla and beyond. Tracing a distinct political line on ethnographic frontiers, Urbain moved the limits of the French zone to a considerable extent. This became the Algerian Sahara, which Urbain pushed farther to the south than his contemporaries had done. Whereas others contemplated an Algerian Sahara that stretched from the High Plateaux to the Saharan Atlas Mountains, some three hundred kilometers from Algiers, Urbain proposed that the true zone of French authority already extended at least another six hundred kilometers south of the Mediterranean coast and could be extended even farther, depending on new discoveries, treaties, and capitulations. Obscuring the difference between the geographic, ethnographic, and the political, he cunningly left the southern frontier open and thus claimed a potentially immense hinterland for France.[62] Lest the timid recoil at the thought of managing this vast area, Urbain suggested that the Algerian Sahara did not have to be claimed as empire all at once but could be absorbed incrementally in accordance with France's capabilities and needs. (Bugeaud had used a similar formulation.) When the Convention of Lalla-Maghnia (18 March 1845) established the borders with Morocco, negotiators adopted Urbain's definition of the Sahara with few variations.[63] Article 4 specified: "In the Sahra [*sic*] there is no territorial limit to establish because the land is not cultivated and it serves the Arabs of the two empires. . . . The two sovereigns will exercise their full rights over their respective subjects in the Sahra [*sic*]."[64]

Having settled the boundaries of France's Saharan empire, Urbain undertook the equally important work of sketching the desert's characteristics. Though vast, it was not a wasteland, and he encouraged readers to abandon received opinion: "This Algerian Sahara in no way resembles the idea that we have made of the desert from geographic notions. One must not expect to find here these great solitudes of sand that the wind moves endlessly; nor is it this sea with storms far more terrible than those of the Ocean, and whose name alone awakens in the spirit grandiose thoughts, [where] fantastic images, the effects of the mirage, the tortures of thirst, all sorts of hazards and dangers, are mixed and confused."

These ideas were entirely wrongheaded. As Urbain stressed, "there is in all actuality water in this desert, and here they even speak of rivers." Such information certainly would have come as news to most readers, who were accustomed to understanding deserts as waterless, if not entirely barren. "This water brings life to the desert," he continued. "Everywhere it arrives grass grows; the soil, no matter how poor, is covered with precious vegetation." This was an important revision of eighteenth-century accounts. Urbain replaced oceans of sand, swept by burning winds, with flowing rivers and waves of lush grass. His words breathing life into the desert, this utopian thinker must have experienced no small amount of pleasure. He reclaimed this supposed damned land and made it available for productive work.

Nevertheless, Urbain had to admit that the climate was harsh. The desert was still a desert. When the summer heat begins, life becomes difficult and "populations flee with their herds and go toward the Tell to escape certain death."[65] This was an important point, for it threw into question the political and economic basis of French rule. The drive to establish agricultural settlements in Algeria's northern territories emanated as much from security concerns as from the search for economic prosperity. Policymakers believed that sedentary agricultural societies would displace "nomadic tribes," which were considered a source of disorder, revolt, and banditry. Urbain acknowledged that the harsh desert climate precluded this option for the Sahara. Nevertheless, he saw a solution. New research revealed a relationship of dependency existing between the southern peoples of the Sahara and those of the Tell. Although the oases held abundant date palms and some wheat and barley grew in their shade, the Sahara's arid climes left people unable to meet their food needs. The cereals cultivated in the Tell represented an essential part of the Saharan diet. Seen from the perspective of colonial policymaking, this offered a great opportunity to control the region effortlessly through grain embargoes. As Urbain wrote, "Our success freeing the limits of the Tell leaves us master of the situation. The nomadic tribes will come of their own initiative to offer their submission; because they now depend on us, according to our political needs, [we can] starve them by closing the marketplaces of the Tell."[66] The argument was seductive. Control of the Sahara followed from the fruits of victory in the Tell. With the grain supply in French hands, the Sahara lay at their mercy. Inasmuch as the most important conquests Urbain needed to make were political ones, the scenario of peaceful desert expansion was a supremely effective weapon.

Père Enfantin: The Saharan Mirages of Algerian Colonization

In his 1941 study of the Saint-Simonians in Algeria, historian Marcel Emerit noted, "We call utopia a doctrine that offers men a *mirage*."[67] Among the early theorists of the French Sahara, Barthelémy-Prosper "Père" Enfantin (1796–1864) saw some of the most elaborate and seductive mirages in the Sahara. In 1843, the same year that Urbain's article appeared, Enfantin, the head of the Saint-Simonian movement as well as Urbain's spiritual mentor and colleague on the commission, published his major work on Algeria entitled *Colonisation de l'Algérie*.[68] Unlike Urbain, Enfantin had little interest in Saharan trade or mapping trails. He came to Algeria to establish virtuous and productive settler colonies that would realize some of the dearest ideals of the movement. These included material progress, technical planning, rational spirituality, pacifism, and a society free of individualism and class conflict.[69] Settlements in Algeria represented the possibility to enact on a much larger scale the Saint-Simonian "Family," the communal society Enfantin had led at rue Ménilmontant in Paris, where members worked and lived in fraternal harmony so complete that they wore special clothing buttoned up the back to encourage the spirit of mutual help.[70] It is thus surprising that Enfantin took any interest in the lands of the Sahara, which—Urbain's tableau aside—were hardly suitable soils in which to plant European farmers. Yet in this desert Enfantin found the solution to some of the most pressing problems facing Algerian settlement. Here he resolved the contradictions that plagued his project for progressive colonization.

Colonisation de l'Algérie represented Enfantin's intervention in the debate between those, like himself, who favored civilian settlements and the military clique, represented by Bugeaud, who claimed that only military colonies founded on the Roman model would attract people who had the discipline and will to endure the harsh life in Algeria. Bugeaud's plan resurrected in Enfantin's mind the image of camps of military legions opening the path to modern-day latifundia in Algeria, leaving the utopian thinker aghast. Far from the entrenched interests that ruled France, the Algerian colony represented a rare—perhaps unique—opportunity to realize the dreams of the comte de Saint-Simon. In France progress had been slow, the bizarre twists of the Revolution indicating that the transformation of society would be a long, piecemeal process full of compromises and setbacks. Only in "new lands" like Algeria could Enfantin hope to realize his society of moral excellence. Enfantin feared that if Bugeaud had his way the new day of peace and progress would be deferred—perhaps forever. Enfantin stressed that in order to establish economic progress and virtue, the colonization of Algeria had to be a civilian affair. The very word "colonisation" meant the "transplantation of a *male* and *female* population, forming *families, villages, and towns*," not camps of soldiers.[71] Enfantin understood that he had a formidable foe in Bugeaud. While the Saint-Simonian movement could count on many sympathizers in Algeria, many of them part of the military administration, Bugeaud led the colonial administration, and as Algeria's governorgeneral he could block any or all of his rivals' projects.

The Sahara offered the perfect solution. Among the desert's riches, Enfantin claimed to see a vast supply of labor. This represented a solution to what, in many ways, lay at the heart of his conflict with Bugeaud, one as much about resources as ideals. If the Sahara had labor reserves in the form of a ready supply of cheap, healthy workers, then many different colonial projects could be accommodated in Algeria, a country where control of labor offered the most important variable to success. In Enfantin's view, the people of the Sahara represented its most important resource, which the harsh desert had molded into a robust, hard-working group. He noted that the coastal cities already teemed with men from the Sahara, who, like "Auvergnats, Limousins, and Savoyards [to Paris] came to earn a few sous in the city."[72] If properly exploited, this labor force offered the possibility of a dual colonization in Algeria. Saint-Simonian farms could claim some lands, while military colonies could be established elsewhere, worked by these hands from the Sahara. "Here, therefore, are the *laborers* of the military colonies, first for the foundational work, then for *interior services* (baths, mills, ovens, threshing, stores, transportation), and especially for *domestics* of the officers, so that every soldier-colonist will be *totally* liberated."[73]

Enfantin's argument is curious. While he freed soldiers from labor, he effectively rendered them idlers, extending and intensifying the military's tendency to live at the expense of others, a feature that consigned the army to perdition in Saint-Simonian doctrine. At the same time, Enfantin put the Saharan people into a position of perpetual servitude and subordination, a relation that does not reveal itself as conductive to the open-class system Saint-Simonians embraced. It may be that Enfantin was as sketchy a thinker as the comte de Saint-Simon, whose vision of the new society, despite its contradictions and flights of logic, inspired several generations of disciples even as it confounded those looking for a systematic program. Or it may be that Enfantin, like others in the 1840s (a decade when slavery remained legal in Algeria), hoped that Saharan labor—free, servile, or enslaved—would prove the decisive force to overcome the many obstacles confronting settler colonies in Algeria. These obstacles, as Enfantin well knew, were as formidable in the corridors of power as they were in the field.

If Enfantin had concerns about the compromised state of some of the most important values of his movement, he did not express them in print. Instead, he continued to run the Sahara question over in his mind, searching for ways it might help him respond to other worries. Among the most important of these for a Saint-Simonian was ending the violence of French colonialism, which was wasteful of resources and did not serve the goal of social reconstruction. The French had crossed the Mediterranean thirteen years earlier, Enfantin emphasized, "to civilize Africa."[74] Vanity and greed did not drive this project. It represented a noble endeavor, one that would disseminate the technological and scientific accomplishments of France, along with its high moral values born of reason. In Enfantin's view, this was not a civilizing mission of the normal sort advanced by proponents of the colonization of Algeria, who utilized the still polyvalent term "civilization" in condescending terms to speak about the domination of Algerians.[75] Enfantin did not simply wish to elevate the poor and the ignorant, who supposedly waited beyond Europe's borders. He wanted the colonial encounter to be a transformative one for both sides. In Algeria the elusive "Union of Orient and Occident," a key Saint-Simonian project, would occur. Won over through proximity and common interest ("becoming ours in living with us") Algerians and French would form an "association," the first step toward a world free of prejudice and guided by the spirit of progress.[76] In time this spiritual bond would produce a physical one, a mixed population of Algerians and French. And one day this *fusion* would form the avant-garde, leading to a new era when people coexisted beyond the petty boundaries of race and nation.

There were many stages on this road, and Enfantin acknowledged it would not be easy to overcome centuries of mistrust and conflict. The path had to be prepared by morally uplifting education along with collaborative work. Enfantin hoped that science, a universal project, would be an important common ground for fusion. And what better common scientific project existed than solving the enigmas of the Sahara. As he wrote, "We have not come to Africa to not know for several centuries that which we do not know today. For example: Where does the Great Desert begin? If there is actually a desert, that which is a desert, is it everywhere inhabited? Are there waters, lakes, a sea, perhaps? . . . [Are] there Touariks [*sic*]? . . . Where do the caravans travel? . . . And thousands of other questions important for the prosperous future of Algeria, science, and our honor as the missionaries of civilization."[77]

The French could not hope to resolve these important questions single-handedly. Enfantin noted that missions by European explorers, no matter how "courageous," had "nearly all been vain attempts."[78] If the Sahara were to be opened to science, Europeans and Algerians must work together: "Let us not harbor any illusions. Africa will not be known and open to us without the help of *Muslims*, converted to our *science* and our *habits*."[79]

There had been few examples of such associations since 1830, and throughout his work Enfantin demonstrated concern over the conflict that had marred French-Algerian relations. The extreme violence and injustice that had characterized so many aspects of French rule in Algeria forced Enfantin to emphasize that the French were not like the Romans, who conquered to win slaves and glory. "The word colonization," he wrote, "implies more today than the destruction or subjugation of conquered peoples."[80] Nevertheless, the history of French Algeria contradicted nearly every point of his hopes for association. To mask this fundamental problem, Enfantin, like many others, deployed racist formulations disguised as pragmatism: "They often say that the Arab loves force; this is true." He held this bellicose character responsible for the violence of colonization.[81] Placing the blame on those who resisted French expansion, Enfantin successfully negotiated some of the most fraught steps in his argument.[82] But resorting to a racist-cum-humanist argument only led to a new series of contradictions. How could a people so attached to force be won over to such unwarlike activities as scientific research and exploration? Moreover, the facts of recent history posed an overarching challenge to the Saint-Simonian "Union." This history consisted of nearly fifteen years of struggle, marked by unspeakable violence, devastation, and waste. Even if Algerians might find common points of interest with the French, how could they ever forget this past?

Again, the Sahara intervened. Enfantin reasoned that the peoples of the south were different from those who had stubbornly resisted the French in the Tell. Although "thieving and warlike," they could be transformed into "instruments of peace."[83] Two forces would advance the rapprochement. On the one hand,

French expansion would be of a different order. With the French coming as scientists, not settlers, a changed relation with the local population was now possible. As Enfantin noted, "The tribes little fear seeing us arrive in force to take their lands and govern them directly."[84] Not fearing the French, Saharans might recognize their shared interests and accept offers of trade, work, and scientific discovery. Second, Enfantin argued, desert peoples are outsiders to Algeria: "[The] whole population of the South has no relations of affection with the Kabiles [sic] of the North . . . [and they are] little esteemed by the nomadic Arabs."[85] Lacking affiliations of kinship, this "bastard population" would feel no solidarity with Algerians in the Tell and would be more readily won over to the French side.

That Enfantin worked with a profoundly flawed understanding of Algerian society—wistfully portraying people from the Sahara as outsiders to Algeria, who were, like the French, victims of the Algerian xenophobia and intolerance—hardly warrants mention. What is more interesting is the alternative history for French colonialism that Enfantin fashioned in the desert. Years of horrific conflict bred an intense longing for peace and cooperation in this utopian thinker. Rather than critically reassessing the colonial project itself, in which Enfantin was heavily invested—after all, it provided him the new lands necessary for his colonies—he fetishistically concealed the failings of one utopia with another.[86] The issues that made colonization in the Tell so difficult—expropriation, domination, and bloodshed—had no place in Enfantin's desert. Rather, he used the Sahara as a sort of philosopher's stone. Under Enfantin's pen the desert forged the elusive "Union of Orient and Occident." In its vast, arid stretches he found the space needed to circumvent history and the thorny contradictions embedded in his social projects. These included the expropriation of other's lands, the social destruction and proletarianization of Algeria's people, and—worst of all—his dependence on the military, a body that by his own admission consisted of the most archaic and wasteful debris of history. In this respect, Enfantin's project likely represents the first fully developed example of a French author using the Algerian Sahara as an *escape*, a trope that has proven so important in European relationships with these lands to this day.[87]

The Consensus: The "Sahara Algérien" of Carette and Daumas

The rivalry between the Saint-Simonians and Bugeaud is well known. The research of historian Michel Levallois has illuminated in detail the bitter struggles that animated policymaking in Algeria.[88] Nevertheless, the sources show that there was a remarkable consensus in the case of the Sahara.[89] This unity of opinion is demonstrated in the last two works of the early 1840s theorizing the "pénétration pacifique." The first is Ernest Carette's highly influential 1844 report on Saharan commerce.[90] The second is Eugène Daumas's famous 1845 book *Le Sahara algérien*.[91]

Ernest Carette (1808–1890) entered the Ecole Polytechnique in 1828. July 1830 found him, together with his fellow students, on the barricades of Paris fighting for the end of the Bourbon Restoration. (Like many others, Carette fought for a republic, not Louis Philippe's monarchial aspirations.)[92] He was sent to Algeria in 1840 as a military engineer to conduct research for the Scientific Commission. Here Carette developed ties with Urbain, Enfantin, and others in the country who were sympathetic to Saint-Simonian ideals.

Carette produced a wealth of studies in his work for the commission. One of its most productive members, he published new ethnographies, maps, and geographies. Among this work was a pathbreaking report on Saharan commerce. Based on six years of interviews in the "living libraries" (cafés and marketplaces) of Algeria, Carette confirmed the speculative views of Urbain and Enfantin by providing solid research. He wrote authoritatively on the importance of the Tell's cereals to the food supply of the Sahara and agreed with others that French control of grain markets gave France a powerful tool with which to force the submission of Saharans without engaging in costly battles.[93] Like his peers, Carette was dissatisfied with limiting Saharan policy to the establishment of a defensive buffer in the south. A bustling traffic in slaves, ostrich feathers, gold, ivory, textiles, leather, European manufactured goods, and other "objets de luxe" animated the economic life of the Sahara, which Carette thought would boost the faltering economic life of the Algerian colony. He avoided assessing the raw value of Saharan trade or making the case that a great El Dorado beckoned in the distant south. (He was also reluctant to comment on the issue of slavery at a time when slavery remained legal but abolition loomed.) Carette nevertheless made clear that he expected the Sahara to play a key role in the future development of Algeria's economy. Shortsighted policy makers, who thought about waging war rather than winning the peace, did not appreciate this richness, leaving the economic bonanza of Saharan trade unexploited. Indeed, Algeria's sizable portion of Saharan commerce, "having become less active following the state of war," had shifted to Morocco and Tunisia.[94] Having shown his partisan colors and made this oblique attack on Bugeaud, Carette appealed to his readers' nationalism, insisting that "it is insufferable that France remains a spectator to such a frustration of her rights."[95]

How to reassert Algeria's claim to Saharan commerce? Carette proposed a two-part plan. First, France needed to establish its presence in the northern oases. These should be selected less for their military value than their economic importance, a shift in strategic judgment that Carette hoped would mark a new, peaceful era for the colony. "When we begin to seek in Algeria something other than military positions," he reasoned, "[to] understand domination in forms other than razzias; when, to be master of the house, we try to hold its keys rather than break down the doors," the importance of the Saharan oases will become manifest.[96] The second part of Carette's plan consisted in establishing friendly relations with the Chaamba (*Sha'anba*) and Tuareg, who transported goods and controlled the southern routes. In Carette's understanding, the Chaamba confederation, based south of the Mzab, was the most obvious intermediary. Carette anticipated that the Chaamba "will be the most natural instruments and the most active agents of this undertaking."[97] His confidence in a peaceful expansion was such that he did not explain how French bases could be established in the oases without the use of force, nor how the Chaamba, who would be compelled to compete with French merchants, might be convinced to cooperate. Instead, he reiterated the advantages of the "pénétration pacifique": "This peaceful and modest intervention will in no way engage the warlike spirit [le géni belliqueux] of France. It is equally self-evident that it will not weigh heavily on the budget."[98]

Carette's report contained many errors and non sequiturs, as well as the fatal tendency to conjure allies in virtually unknown desert societies. But it responded particularly well to the contradictions, aspirations, and ambivalences of the colonial project. Carette gave policy makers from across the political spectrum a vision of the Sahara that precisely corresponded to what they needed to advance the cause of continued expansion in Algeria. Most important, he provided people who were frustrated with France's failed attempts to control the northern lands of Algeria with an image of new territory where they could expect the easy mastery that had hitherto proved so elusive.

Like others, Carette promised a painless and cost-free desert empire. Economic interest and ethnographic exceptionalism inclined Algero-Saharan people to welcome the French. With such friends, he argued, France's political and economic influence would increase steadily in the decades that lay ahead. Unlike others, however, Carette presented impeccable credentials, and his report had the hallmark of solid scientific work. As was previously mentioned, Carette's report forcefully responded to the naysayers during the 1844 parliamentary debates. As the expansionist deputy Corcelles put it, "No one in the army or the administration will disagree with me when I say that their science is equal to their modesty and the nobility of their character." Carette's work, the deputy continued "casts a bright light on the nature, the ensemble, and the limits of our possessions."[99]

The drive to reap the political windfalls of authoritative scholarship in pursuit of the Saharan empire appeared the following year when Eugène Daumas (1803–1871), who belonged to a totally different camp, published his highly influential work Le Sahara algérien. Having graduated from the newly opened cavalry school at Saumur, Daumas arrived in Algeria in 1835. After the French and Abdelkader had negotiated a peace treaty in 1837, Daumas served as the French consul to the emir at Mascara, where he put to use his growing command of the Algerian Arabic dialect.[100] These language skills, plus his loyalty to Bugeaud, earned Daumas a nomination in 1841 to head the reorganized Central Direction of Indigenous Affairs.[101]

In 1843 Daumas was ordered by Bugeaud to begin work on a project in the Sahara. This order reflected the governor-general's anxieties over the attention paid to the Saharan work of his rivals in the Scientific Commission and his hopes to move his troops southward. Two years later Daumas's work *Le Sahara algérien*, a 339-page book complete with a new map, appeared.[102] It generated great enthusiasm for the Sahara expansion and earned distinction for its author. Indeed, for the next fifty years Daumas was the most widely cited author on the Sahara.[103] Appearing after the less than fully successful opening round of Saharan expansion, Daumas's strategies effaced the failures at Biskra and Laghouat and reflected an optimistic belief—expressed dithyrambically at times—in France's future in the Sahara, one which outdid the Saint-Simonians.

Daumas's enthusiasm, as expressed in his book, partially accounts for the work's success. He dismissed the defeat at Biskra as an aberration, a small event overwhelmed by Daumas's larger story of a peaceful and prosperous French-controlled Sahara. Perhaps more important in terms of attracting the reader's attention was Daumas's decision to present his report as a travel itinerary, a seductive format. Daumas sketched a fascinating land, taking his readers from oasis to oasis on the caravan routes linking the Mediterranean coast to far-off cities like Timbuktu. Whereas a generation earlier Peyssonnel and Abbé Poiret saw only shifting sand dunes, Daumas saw an "ocean seeded with islands."[104] He wrote: "This famous desert, we have sounded its depths: and the more we advanced into its plains, [the more] its limits spread out. Everywhere, or nearly everywhere, towns and villages; everywhere tents, everywhere life; an exceptional life, it is true, but active and important to study for the common relations we have with it; curious for all that it reveals to science."[105]

Vibrant centers of commerce in the Mzab, at Ouargla, Ghadamès, and In Salah welcomed travelers. These rich islands linked currents of commerce upon which flowed goods both familiar and exotic. Dates, grains, livestock, shovels, plows, candles, and clothes were traded along with slaves, spices, dyes, perfumes, weapons, and jewelry. In these itineraries and lists the armchair imperialist saw a great and prosperous future.

Whereas the political authority of Carette's report derived from its sober style and claims to rigor, Daumas generated enthusiasm by embellishing his accounts of the economic resources of the desert with fanciful vignettes. For example, Daumas reported that a boy sultan ruled Touggourt and lived a life worthy of *A Thousand and One Nights*. Although only twelve or thirteen years old, he had four wives and a hundred women resided in his harem.[106] Lest the reader wonder to what levels the lust of the young sultan might sink, Daumas emphatically stated that it could be satiated by invoking his droit du seigneur. The protesting bridegroom faced hanging or crucifixion.

Just as tantalizing were Daumas's descriptions of the oasis of Ouargla. Here, during festivals local people strolled the streets dressed as European dandies,

FIGURE 1 Carnival at Ouargla.
Source: Pierre Christian, *L'Afrique française, l'empire de Maroc et les déserts du Sahara: conquêtes, victoires et découvertes des français, depuis la prise d'Alger jusqu'à nos jours* (Paris: A. Barbier, 1846), n.p.

and when the desert sun set, they passed the hours until dawn in saturnalian excesses.[107] Daumas provided many titillating scenes emphasizing licentious sexuality. He promised readers that beautiful women were to be found throughout the Sahara. Unlike their cousins in the cities, who, though rarely seen, were already the object of enormous fascination, Saharan women did not conceal their alluring features beneath a veil and many offered themselves up as prostitutes. So, too, did many boys: "In the town itself one finds handsome boys [des mignons] who openly practice their métier. . . . They are very young and live like women, tinting their hair, their nails, their eyebrows and lips."[108]

A colonial administrator, Daumas seemed to take his methodology from Balzac, who celebrated the imaginative abilities of the artist to render the truth of the world even if that truth derived more from the spirit than the senses. Writing in 1831, Balzac commented: "The warmest and most exact painter of Florence has never been to Florence; thus, such a writer was able to marvelously depict the desert, its sands, its mirages, its palms, having never gone from Dan to the Sahara."[109] Mixing fact and fiction, Daumas deployed his exotic scenes selectively. He spliced them between dense sections describing the desert's geography and politics. Though clearly aiming at a large public, Daumas saw his work as a tool for policymaking.[110] To establish his credentials, Daumas stressed that his research was exhaustive, his information coming "from the mouth of at least 2,000 Arabs," as he assured his readers.[111] Moreover, he did not neglect to offer details concerning the social and economic order of the Sahara of the sort necessary for future administrators. For example, he discussed the difference between nomadic and sedentary populations and highlighted the possibilities of exploiting their putative rivalries to benefit French interests. He drew attention to the commercial importance of the tribes of the Saharan Atlas, such as the Ouled Naïl and Larbaa, who merited special attention because they linked the Tell and Sahara thanks to their seasonal movements in search of pasturelands.

Daumas aimed to vindicate Bugeaud, specifically his patron's strategies in Algeria. Daumas argued that as a result of a long and hard but necessary fight in northern Algeria, Bugeaud had placed France at the threshold of a new era as an African power. He dedicated the book to the governor-general, writing, "The conquest of Algeria, *now achieved*, has victoriously resolved the question so long debated between the general occupation and the restricted occupation. You have won over everybody to the opinion that we must be everywhere or be secure nowhere."[112] Although victory came at great expense and loss of life, Bugeaud had established order in the Tell, Daumas argued, and this conquest had opened the doors to a prosperous and peaceful future in the Sahara. Nevertheless there were still overly timid people who fretted, "Might there not rise in the middle of them [the tribes of the Sahara] a fanatic, another Abdelkader . . .?" Daumas dismissed such worries. Bugeaud's "victory" in the Tell had already delivered the Sahara.[113] It was a simple question of food. Like the Saint-Simonians and Carette, Daumas offered up the foodstuffs-control strategy to silence those who opposed the Saharan expansion. "The Tell is the granary of the Sahara," he wrote unequivocally. "We hold the Saharans by famine; they know it well." To give his argument greater force, Daumas cited an anonymous Saharan voice, which reinforced his aura of mastery and authority: "'The land of the Tell is our mother,' say the Saharans. 'He who has married her is our father.'"[114] Lest his readers somehow fail to find this argument convincing—some might have reflected upon the fact that Daumas's own work had shown that the Sahara was an open, fluid territory, a land traversed by thousands of kilometers of routes and thus impossible to blockade—he backed up his thesis with the ethnographic argument that Algero-Saharan societies were somehow different and more receptive to peaceful relations with the French: "Saharans do not feel toward us this antipathy that we found among the mountain people and the inhabitants of the Tell. The appetite for gain dominates among them, and it silences the scruples of fanaticism."[115] Once hungry, now greedy, Daumas's Saharans were neither capable of nor interested in continued war against France.[116]

Despite their deep divisions and differing vision for the future of the Algerian colony, all these early authors agreed on the major outlines of Saharan policy.

First, the Sahara was of vital interest to French security in Algeria's northern Tell region. Second, Sahara was not the wasteland described in previous reports. While not suitable for European farmers, the Sahara supported large populations that had adapted to the harsh climate. Third, Algero-Saharan societies represented untapped wealth. Saharans were either the masters of a rich trans-Saharan trade or, conversely, they were a proletariat who might furnish valuable labor for the French colony. Fourth, and most important, these early authors all thought that French expansion into the Sahara would require little force and few resources. Either Saharans were ethnically different, friendlier, or they would recognize that Frenchmen did not come to exploit but rather to trade, explore, and learn. If this failed, planners built in a safeguard in the form of Saharan dependence on Mediterranean cereals, which ensured their docility: France could easily starve them into submission. These four points combined to create a powerful and convincing argument. Advantage and opportunity alone awaited in the Sahara. The fears generated by the accounts of eighteenth-century explorers like Caillé—which saw the Sahara as a hostile void—were dispelled by the commentators of the 1840s. Their words irrigated and populated the desert. The arguments of those who opposed the cost and violence of further conquests were neutralized by the promise of peaceful expansion.

The "pénétration pacifique" thus freed the *political* paths southward, those blocked by the opposition in Paris and the monarchy's fragility. It did not, however, open the desert to French empire, nor did it provide knowledge of the Sahara to advance French power. The salient features of the social, political, and economic realities of the Sahara remained concealed from French analysts for many years. With the exception of certain details on commerce or routes that might be gleaned from Carette and Daumas, little in this body of early work had great practical value to those who might be called upon to establish a Saharan empire. Moreover, none of the information produced by the discourses of "pénétration pacifique" provided a way to establish French influence without the use of force. Lasting alliances could not be made with fanciful boy sultans, any more than commercial accords could be negotiated with what were essentially phantom desert confederations. Even the seductive "blockade" strategy failed to account for the fundamental fluidity of desert trade. The latter, as the authors of "pénétration pacifique" themselves noted, possessed a resiliency and adaptability shaped by centuries of experience dealing with the vicissitudes of long-distance food provisioning.

[3]

THE "PÉNÉTRATION PACIFIQUE" IN PRACTICE, 1847–52

The number eight canon should suffice in any case because it was enough for Zaatcha.
—General Army Order, Algiers, 10 February 1850

Bugeaud resigned in June 1847. An unfavorable report by Alexis de Tocqueville, an increasingly powerful Saint-Simonian opposition, and a royal family that sought to place one of their own in the governor-general's seat combined to convince Bugeaud to try his fortune elsewhere. Thus, when General La Moricière captured Abdelkader on 23 December 1847, Bugeaud was not in Algeria to celebrate. Many felt that Bugeaud's departure and Abdelkader's defeat marked the beginning of a new chapter marked by peace and prosperity in Algeria.[1] These hopes were illusory. The war in Algeria did not end. In fact, the following years produced some the greatest revolts and witnessed some of the worst violence of the conquest. In a cruel parody of the "pénétration pacifique," the Sahara served as the theater for much of the drama.

CAVAIGNAC'S *"RECONNAISSANCE"* IN THE SOUTHWEST: THE KSOUR, 1847

A mission led by General Cavaignac to the region of Aïn Sefra in the last months of the emir's struggle to maintain control illustrates how difficult it would be to achieve a "pénétration pacifique." Before Louis-Eugène Cavaignac entered the history books for crushing the 1848 worker's revolt during the June Days, when he saved "France from all colors of socialists and anarchists," he spent much of his military career in Algeria.[2] This was, as historian Maurice Agulhon notes, "Cavaignac's homeland."[3] Cavaignac arrived in Algeria in 1832, about the time that the duc de Rovigo ordered the infamous massacre of the Ouffia, and fought with distinction in the wars of the 1840s. Well known for his republican sympathies, Cavaignac found that he was placed in an excellent position for high political office in Paris following the revolution of 1848.

Before this political ascendancy, Cavaignac led soldiers in the ongoing campaigns against Abdelkader, which drew French troops southward into the Sahara. Between 2 April and 22 May 1847 Cavaignac made the first tour of the ksour (ksūr; sing ksar), semifortified desert oases in the southwestern part of the country, 350 kilometers south of Tlemcen. His orders were simple: "Make us known to the populations . . . [and] prevent, if possible, Abdelkader's influence from establishing itself here."[4] Although the French column did not have an order to wage war, it made its way as if it did. Apart from special provisions in the marching orders to deal with scarce water, the column's composition was virtually identical to those operating on razzias in the Tell, with four infantry battalions, four cavalry squadrons, and a detachment of light artillery (3,037 men), accompanied by 1,945 camels and 197 mules.[5] Tactics bore no trace of the ideas of the "pénétration pacifique." Cavaignac's column was not preceded by diplomatic contacts or offers of trade. Not being at war with the people of the ksour, the French military did not consider a foodstuffs blockade.

Typical of the small urban centers at the desert's northern edge, the ksour had a diversified economy and held substantial wealth. The commerce that flowed through the area, peaking in the sixteenth and seventeenth centuries, remained important well into the nineteenth by virtue of the Mediterranean "arithmetic of distance."[6] Located between the dry expanses of the High Plateaux to the north and the next group of Saharan oases to the south at Timimoun, the ksour had strategic value as points of storage, distribution, and rest. Migrating pastoral groups like the Hamyan (Hamian), Trafi, and Ouled Sidi Cheikh (Awlad Sidi Shaykh) passed through the ksour twice a year, bringing herds of sheep and goats seeking seasonal pasturelands. They also loaded their camels with cereals, dates, and the various sundries that were at the heart of the region's economic life.[7] At the center of trade and transportation, the mountainous region was comparatively rich in water resources. Lying within a chain of mountains known as the Ksour Mountains (Jabal Ksur), the ksours enjoyed a reliable water supply. It served local people, who cultivated the lesser varieties of dates that grew in the region's cooler climate, along with garden legumes and fruits. The people of the ksour did much of this work as servile sharecroppers (khamamisa) tied in unequal economic and political relations to the more powerful pastoral groups.[8] The ksour were also home to industry. Dyers, spinners, and weavers produced carpets and clothing from the wool traded with local pastoralists and the dyes and chemicals (alum) that came from the south.[9]

All this wealth was not unknown to the French troops, who marched into the strategic region with Cavaignac in 1847. When the column arrived at the first ksar, the encounters were harsh. The fate of Moghrar-Tahtani on 27 April set the tone. The sixty-one families living in this ksar had advance notice of the approaching column, and they fled into the surrounding mountains. The ksar's leaders were not, however, ready to yield lightly, and when five French riders arrived outside the town walls, snipers shot down three. In reprisal Cavaignac shelled the ksar's mosque. When he saw the feeble effects of his light artillery, and the fact that there was no defending force behind the ksar's walls, he gave the order to enter and "demolish and devastate." Troops understood that such work would be preceded by looting. Knowing they would be the first French column to break into Moghrar-Tahtani's silos, Cavignac's men anticipated a great haul. They were not disappointed. Foodstuffs (dates, barley, jars of food preserves, ostrich eggs), woolen textiles and weaving materials (cloaks, burnouses, carpets, looms, carding and spinning devices), manuscripts, property deeds, religious amulets, ornamental weapons, and copper utensils all made their way into the looters' hands.[10]

The pillage caught the attention of the column's surgeon, Félix Jacquot (pseudonym of Joseph-Louis-Ernest Lapeyre),[11] who witnessed and reflected upon the scene from the minaret of the mosque.

> I do not know on which fatal slope was found he who began the work [oeuvre] of destruction: if the smell of powder invigorates, the furor of pillage transports and makes one mad. Look at this soldier, so peaceful and gentle a moment ago: fire is [now] in his eyes, his forehead is covered in sweat; panting, he seizes the pick and knocks down the walls, and upends everything, ransacking in all the corners. Shaking with excitement if he finds the smallest object, he yells out with childlike joy. If he finds nothing, he becomes vexed and despairing. Agitated and more and more excited, he breaks and destroys for the pleasure of destruction. It is no longer an intelligent being who thinks before acting; it is a spirit led astray by a short but furious madness.[12]

The looting was more than a source of destructive delight for these frenzied soldiers. While the luxury items represented bonuses to supplement the soldiers' pay, the foodstuffs were essential to the column's survival. Long-range operations in the dry and relatively barren Sahara presented formidable logistical challenges.

If one does the math, the problem becomes apparent.[13] The 3,037 men on the 50-day excursion needed 151,850 daily rations. Yet they carried only 25,000 rations of rice and vegetables and had another 25,000 rations of meat in a herd of cattle and sheep that followed the column. The only other foodstuffs for their consumption were 50,000 servings of coffee and sugar. In all, Cavaignac's column brought less than one third of the food it needed. Equally important was the need to feed the livestock, famished after the twenty-two-day march from Tlemcen. There was only enough barley for the cavalry's horses (571 rations consisting of 4 kilograms each). Provisioning the stock animals was impossible on this long trip. A loaded mule needed at least 3 kilograms of barley per day: on such a long expedition it would only be able to carry its own rations. (The maximum load for a strong, healthy mule is about 120 kilograms.) In all, the column had only 335 daily rations for their 197 mules. Finally, the most serious deficit was the food supplies for the column's 1,945 camels. The French had little experience with camels and grossly overestimated the camel's ability to go without food.[14] In all, the column brought only 33 daily rations (consisting of 2 kilograms of barley each) for the camels.[15] Although the long-term health of these requisitioned animals was of little importance to the French quartermaster, 60 kilograms of barley was hardly enough to keep 2,000 heavily loaded camels alive to complete the mission. By the time they arrived at Moghrar-Tahtani, it was clear that the animals were dangerously undernourished and would not survive the return trip. There was only meager forage available in surrounding areas and the ksar's crop of barley and stores of feed dates represented the only fodder in the area. All this should have come as no surprise. Only a year earlier, during an 1846 Saharan campaign, a French general lost half of his 800 horses because he had not taken enough grain to feed them.[16]

Cavaignac's column could certainly have traded with local people to get the food it needed, but looting easily solved the supply dilemma. Met with sniping and standing before what amounted to a large unguarded storehouse, Cavaignac never entertained the idea of negotiating with the people of Moghrar-Tahtani even though they had not fled far. Contrary to the project of peaceful penetration, the sack of the ksar represented what had become an undeclared standard operating procedure for the French army in Algeria. Moreover, officers and troops had grown accustomed to pillaging to supplement their pay.

Looting is not well documented in the official archive. Realizing that it amounted to theft, reporters kept these activities out of the written record. From the sketchy sources that exist it appears the loot taken on such expeditions was typically sold, either after the return of the column or to local people—or even back to the original owners.[17] The proceeds were then distributed among the troops according to rank. Soldiers might offer remarkable objects—such as the magnificent wool tent and carpet found at Moghrar-Tahtani—to a favorite officer as a token of admiration.[18] When relations in the ranks were not so cordial, the process did not go smoothly. At the 1852 sack of Laghouat, for example, Lieutenant-Colonel Cler found there was little honor among thieves. Général Pélissier threatened to court-martial him if he did not turn over several rifles, elaborately decorated with Mediterranean coral, that the superior officer coveted.[19]

Eager to locate more wealth, Cavaignac's troops quickly completed their destruction of Moghrar-Tahtani. The next day they followed the path leading to Moghrar-Foukani, a nearby, semifortified oasis consisting of 150 houses with some 750 inhabitants. Events followed a similar course here. After a brief engagement with a small defending force (20 defenders and 2 legionnaires were killed), Cavaignac's troops began looting and destroying. The soldiers, however, were disappointed. The stored wealth of the ksar was meager—or perhaps the inhabitants had already emptied their silos—and the anticipated haul came up short. Eager to pursue more lucrative prospects, Cavaignac ordered his men to speed up their destructive work. The violence meted out by the column at this point was not simply instrumental, part of an effort to feed the stock, make up for insufficient supplies, and rob. Finding little of value, Cavaignac meant to leave destruction in his wake as a sign of the French army's ferocity. According to this calculus, the date palms had to be destroyed, so Cavaignac sent his troops, wielding axes, into the gardens. When it became clear that it would take an inordinate amount of time to finish the job, Cavaignac ordered his troops to focus their labor on the male trees. Less spectacular than leaving a field of thousands of palm trunks, cutting all the male trees ensured the sterility of the grove and hunger and economic ruin for the ksar. In the village itself, fire could express French power with dramatic results and little effort. Although the ksar's walls were made of sun-baked brick, the floors, stairs, and roof beams were made of highly flammable, dry wood. Cavaignac instructed his troops to set fire to the buildings, certain that the ensuing inferno would leave little more than blackened walls. He was successful. When the main column left, smoke and flames from Moghrar-Foukani covered the sky like "a scene out of Rembrandt."[20]

Doctor Jacquot spoke unambiguously about the results of these actions. While the inhabitants of these two ksour escaped, Cavaignac's looting and systematic destruction of crops and date palms boded ill for the future:

> The misery of the Moghariens will be no less frightful: we have wrecked and toppled their town, emptied their silos of barley and wheat, cut their cereals in the fields, burned their looms, cut down their fruit trees, and taken the luxury goods that would have served them as a means of exchange to get what they needed to survive. Where will they plead for help? We will soon reduce all their neighbors to the same distress; the same denouement awaits them all. The wandering tribes, the marauders of the desert, will perhaps profit from these sad circumstances to complete our work. And who knows if the columns that visit this region in several years will find anything at Moghrar . . . other than a few ruined walls, blackened trunks, and the silence of the desert?[21]

A similar fate befell Thiout, a ksar to the east of Aïn Sefra. Most of the population had fled, but they did not fire upon the French. Nevertheless, Cavaignac made only halfhearted efforts to negotiate the surrender of the absent council (*jemā'a*). Keen to feed the column's stock on the ksar's maturing grain crop, Cavaignac turned the animals loose in the gardens. "Notwithstanding political concerns," the column's reporter wrote, this was necessary "to feed . . . our beasts of burden, which found nothing to eat."[22] His troops then entered the ksar and began breaking into buildings. They were disappointed a second time: the looting produced unimpressive riches. The solders, convinced they had missed a hidden booty, turned on the few remaining villagers to find the hidden silos.

These "interrogations" were brutal. In one case a woman who had failed to reveal the location of the silos was beaten and then raped by a dozen soldiers. The blows continued in the course of the sexual assault, and they proved fatal. Soldiers also beat the woman's child to death. A week later, in the village of S'fissia, soldiers fatally assaulted an elderly woman who refused to divulge the location of hidden silos. The victim was first thrown from a balcony and then stripped naked and subjected to threats before she died from her injuries. Jacquot described the scene as follows:

> Bent over with age, ruined by misery and time, stunned by her fall, besides being blinded and frozen with fear, she could not walk, nor even keep herself upright. A soldier held her by the arm. "Show us the silos!," they yelled at her. Trembling, half-dead, she tried to grasp anyone within reach to implore their mercy and kiss their clothing. She lavished kind names upon her young cavalier: "Sun of the days without fog, shadow near water, fountain of the desert" . . . — "Show us the silos!," they yelled even louder — "Flower of the sand, fertile palm," repeated the old lady. "All this gets us nowhere," said a soldier loading his rifle. When he cocked the weapon, the gun's springs emitted a click-clack sound that set the poor, sick woman to trembling.[23]

These acts were not committed by frustrated troops eager to avenge fallen comrades. Whatever appetite troops might have had to retaliate for the early sniping attacks was quenched in several skirmishes that left sixty-one ksourians dead for the six French soldiers killed in action. Such morbid calculations should have satisfied those who sought vengeance. How, then, to account for this violence in what was to be a simple reconnaissance mission of first contact?

Structural factors and habit certainly preordained the outcome of much of the conflict. Sending troops this far to the south depended on finding food and fodder, and force was the simplest and most familiar way to accomplish this task. Furthermore, given the circumstances it was easy enough to transform this tour into an extended razzia. Perfected in the Tell, the rules of the razzia suited Sahara expansion well irrespective of peaceful penetration. They served as an efficacious means of provisioning troops and produced devastating subsistence crises, which the French thought would put local people at their mercy.

The razzia were also lucrative—an added incentive. At the same time, the acts of Cavaignac's soldiers exceeded the boundaries of instrumental violence. The outstanding feature of the 1847 campaign was the troops' brutal excesses. As Jacquot described it, a sense of elation or ecstatic sadism motivated soldiers, and this clearly surpassed the violence needed to defeat enemies, fill panniers, and feed hungry mounts. Greed could account for some of the violence if one accepts the rationale that torturing people—like the old woman described by Jacquot—was simply about revealing the location of hidden silos, a motive that authors of several studies of recent torture might question.[24] In any case, means-ends rationality did not limit the soldiers' cruelty. For example, Doctor Jacquot was deliberately prevented from attending to a wounded villager in order to maximize this individual's suffering.[25] Cavaignac's troops look much less like rampaging looters than men purely devoted to violence: *Homo furens*, a man "exclusively devoted to the devastation of the natural and human soil on which he has hitherto been nourished."[26] While this person may lurk in everyone, he was immensely useful to the colonial state, which summoned him with various rites and rituals, perceptions and expectations.

Representing a terrible first round of peaceful penetration, Cavaignac's expedition to the ksour was nonetheless hailed as a great feat by contemporaries, who ignored its violence. Indeed, a Cavaignac biographer would later write, "The story of this hardy, advanced expedition, made so far into a country heretofore unknown, stands on its own next to a page torn from the history of Desaix's expeditions in Upper Egypt."[27]

ZAATCHA, 1849

Two years after Cavaignac's mission and five years after the first debacle at Biskra, the French again faced a serious challenge in the Ziban region. This time it centered on Zaatcha, a fortified oasis thirty kilometers southwest of Biskra. When trouble first started in early summer of 1849, it looked like an isolated tax revolt. But several months later the insurrection had spread across the Ziban and into the Aurès Mountains. By winter hundreds of French soldiers and thousands of Algerians lay dead.

Bou Ziyan (Bu Ziyan) led the rebels. He claimed to be the Mahdi, "the rightly guided one," a messianic figure who, according to popular Muslim tradition, would restore justice on earth, ending a period of oppression.[28] It was a claim that had to be proven, but Bou Ziyan's piety and miraculous powers convinced many that his cause was just and divinely inspired. In a letter confiscated by the French, one supporter wrote to Bou Ziyan, "Oh my lord I saw the Prophet [in a dream] just before the arrival of the infidels (against you) and [I saw] their flight. I saw him with the mujahideen and the Prophet of God, may grace and peace be upon him."[29] As word of the Mahdi's arrival at Zaatcha spread, people joined Bou Ziyan and took up arms, coming from throughout the region and, according to some reports, from as far as Tunis, Morocco, and Mecca.[30] Under Bou Ziyan's charismatic leadership, they dealt a stinging blow to the first French column sent to Zaatcha in July 1849, inflicting over two hundred casualties, which sent a shockwave through the high command. "This unexpected setback put everyone here into a state of crisis, even the governor-general," one officer reported.[31] The French command was intent on saving face: "The influence of the name of France depends on not leaving such an affront unpunished. If it is, our prestige in the eyes of Saharan populations will diminish."[32] According to this thinking, if there were to be a "pénétration pacifique" in the Ziban, it would have to wait until Bou Ziyan was crushed. In September 1849 the army assembled a column of nearly forty-five hundred men in Batna, commanded by Brig. Gen. Emile Herbillon. When it arrived at Zaatcha on 7 October 1849, all expected it would exact a quick and spectacular vengeance.[33]

This anticipated climax would not happen for another two months, and it would require an additional four thousand men. The sun-dried bricks that encircled Zaatcha stood up well against the French light artillery.[34] The walled plots, sunken gardens, and irrigation works that surrounded the oasis lent further protection to Bou Ziyan's highly motivated force. Moreover, the French had to deal with vulnerable supply lines and were inexperienced in the techniques of oasis warfare. Finally, according to the assessments written after the battle, they were handicapped by General Herbillon's altogether uninspiring command.[35]

The French did prevail, however, and the army had the vengeance it so desired. Following many weeks of deadly siege works (compared by participants to warfare during the Middle Ages), the French opened several holes in the oasis's walls and stormed inside the morning of 26 November 1849. The loss of life was heavy, with everyone inside Zaatcha slain. The official report cited some eight hundred dead found atop the ruins the day of the final battle. This number, which did "not account for those buried in the debris," included only a portion of those killed.[36]

The final combat was intense. Fearing ambushes in Zaatcha's narrow streets, French soldiers moved through the town on roofs and balconies. Bou Ziyan's men withdrew from their exposed positions and sought refuge in the darkened rooms at ground level. French reports note that they refused to surrender, and each building had to be stormed from the roof by descending poorly lit stairs or ladders.[37] This position heavily favored the defenders: "The room is large, and those who venture in immediately are shot at and have no idea where to return fire; the interior door is walled, and there are no other openings other than the crenel that pour out additional fire. This is another siege more deadly than the assault."[38] Failing to find an advantageous point of attack, Herbillon's men sent for sacks of powder to create bombs. As one officer reported, "Mines became the only way to bring down these fanatics, who continue to shoot from the rubble where they are buried."[39]

It took six hours before the French announced the fall of Zaatcha, and snipers continued to harass the soldiers until 3 p.m.[40] No exact count can be made of those who perished in this final stage of combat. However, it can be assumed that at least half—and perhaps many more—escaped the initial storming and the brief period of rooftop fighting and were buried in the rubble of the houses, or their bodies were left in the darkened rooms. This brought casualties to upwards of 1,600.[41] Herbillon's causalities were not light but disproportionate: 43 men lay dead and 175 more were wounded. This brought the total French losses to 320 killed in action and another 680 wounded.[42] (Another 250 soldiers died of cholera, which swept through the region in November.) To this loss of life should be added those killed in the preceding two months of fighting. The French archive contains no tally of those who perished in Zaatcha up to 26 November. Their numbers, however, were most likely high. Herbillon's men made several full-strength assaults on the oasis, and Bou Ziyan mounted repeated counterattacks. Moreover, on three separate occasions (31 October, 12 November, and 16 November), Herbillon's troops raided neighboring oases and attacked pastoralist groups heading south with their flocks for winter pastures. While the first raid was on a population that had rallied to support Bou Ziyan, the second and third raids targeted people who had not committed themselves to either side. Herbillon's men experienced supply shortages, their lines effectively cut off at al-Kantara gorges, and their morale was low. Opportunistic attacks on these lightly defended targets provided both food and an escape from the grueling siege works.

In all, the vengeance military leaders sought came at a cost of over twenty-two hundred lives. Intent on making Zaatcha a lasting symbol of the French army's omnipotence, Herbillon decided on a Carthaginian example. Its inhabitants slaughtered, the oasis was leveled. Troops destroyed what remained of the gardens (many palms had already been cut down to use in the siege works), as well as the buildings of the oasis. To ensure that his troops did a thorough job, he authorized them to use the column's remaining stocks of powder to bring down the buildings. Their work was efficient, leaving total devastation in their wake. As one observer wrote, "Today Zaatcha is only a mass of ruins and corpses."[43]

A special fate was reserved for the rebel leaders. Bou Ziyan put up a valiant final defense. Reports concur that it took the better part of a battalion of Zouaves, 50 of whom were killed or wounded, to take the house in which he took refuge with his family and close followers. Heavy rifle fire and artillery were trained on the stronghold. After a mine took down a section of the wall, Bou Ziyan emerged and was captured by French soldiers, who stripped him of his weapons. At the same time, soldiers stormed the house where his wife, two sons, daughter, and an infant child, along with a dozen women and 150 male followers, remained. "In an instant," the commanding officer wrote, "they were all massacred."[44] Herbil-lon personally ordered the execution of Bou Ziyan, who fell before the bullets of a firing squad. His head was severed, along with those of his seventeen-year-old son and Si Moussa al-Darqawi, a close lieutenant. As one eyewitness reported, "Bou Ziyan was decapitated and his head is perched on the end of a post in the middle of camp."[45] General Herbillon claimed that this would end rumors that the Mahdi had escaped, but it is more likely that he was trying to circulate news of another sort.[46] Several commentators agreed that the heads, looming over the ruins of the oasis, created an especially powerful effect.[47]

Many French officers were optimistic that these measures would serve to cow the local populations into submission. In a letter written in the midst of the battle, one soldier wrote, "The fall of Zaatcha will make the rest of our opera-tions in the Sahara go much quicker."[48] Another reporter agreed: "The taking and the sacking of Zaatcha changed instantaneously the hostile appearances of all the tribes that had defected or were ready to turn their arms against us. I say appearances because we cannot hide the fact that fear is the only thing that maintains French domination."[49]

In the ensuing months the French displayed the same murderous violence in suppressing neighboring groups that had joined the rebellion. For example, when French troops stormed the village of Nara (Aurès Mountains) on 5 Janu-ary 1850, they killed all the inhabitants and spent the next seven hours reducing their homes to rubble. The Ministry of War commented: "The effect of this example, similar to that of Zaatcha, was considerable and felt far away."[50]

The influence of the "pénétration pacifique" is nowhere present in these actions. Rather than mutual interest, blockades, and trade, the suppression of Bou Ziyan's revolt showed that French officers thought destruction and fear were the best tools to use with the people of the Sahara. In case there were any lingering doubts, three months later an order was circulated among the divisions specifying the lessons learned and announcing that "the siege of Zaatcha . . . must remain an exception."[51] Local commanders were called upon to collect detailed information on desert routes and oasis defenses. The order stated that the principal goal was not to ease French control into the Sahara through in-depth knowledge of the local situation but rather to "assure, in the event of an insurrection, the rapid success of our military operations." If resistance was encountered, the order concluded, "the number eight canon should suffice in any case, because it was enough for Zaatcha."[52]

LAGHOUAT, 1852

People in Laghouat today remember 1852 as the year of desolation ("sana al-khla").[53] Peace did not come to the Sahara following the destruction of Zaatcha.

It took only three years before another individual emerged to lead the northern Sahara in revolt. In the opening round of what became one of the most important rebellions in the Sahara, Muhammad ben Abdallah (Muhammad ibn 'Abd Allah), a Mahdi claimant, prepared for a showdown with the French at Laghouat.[54] Many in the region warmly welcomed ben Abdallah. Ouargla embraced him in 1851 and recognized him as a sharif. The people of Laghouat likewise joined his cause. Accepting ben Abdallah's Mahdist claims, his calls for resistance to the French struck a sympathetic chord in many, who also hoped he would rid them of Ahmed ben Salem, the French *khalifa*. The first French troops, which arrived on the scene in November 1852, feared another long and costly siege. As General Yusuf wrote in a letter to an unknown recipient, "Laghouat has become the boulevard of a resistance that will be determined and desperate." Already in the opening skirmishes the sharif's men had fought with "an incredible fury." "The Beni-Laghouat are so fanaticized," Yusuf continued, that "they responded to my offers of peace and safe quarter [*aman (amān,)*] by saying they have finally opened their eyes to the light and that they wanted to die for the Sacred Cause and arrive in paradise." Yusuf concluded his letter with an urgent appeal for reinforcements: "I implore you, do not delay."[55]

Yusuf's assessment of the danger represented by ben Abdallah was accurate enough, but his fears of a long and difficult siege were unfounded. When French reinforcements arrived, consisting of five quickly mobilized columns, they came with sufficient heavy artillery, including a powerful field howitzer.[56] When the barrage began the morning of 4 December 1852, it took only three hours before the gun knocked large holes in Laghouat's walls. At 11 a.m. French troops entered the breaches or availed themselves of ladders they had brought along to scale the walls. Once inside, they began the difficult work of rooting out resistance house by house. Here events followed the same course as at Zaatcha. Ben Abdallah's men took refuge in the rooms on the ground floor. French troops silenced each point of resistance by killing all inside. Unlike at Zaatcha, they achieved these actions with great speed. Pélissier stormed Laghouat from several points, and ben Abdallah's troops found several neighborhoods indefensible. Within three hours French soldiers had broken the major resistance. At 2 P.M. General Pélissier, joined by General Yusuf and Lieutenant Colonel Cler, celebrated their victory by dining together on the highest balcony of Laghouat's casbah.[57]

The officers' mission accomplished, the bloodshed continued. Although they crushed resistance quickly and suffered minimal losses, French troops continued killing throughout the day. Afterward, while visiting the newly conquered oasis, the artist Eugène Fromentin commented, "I would like to think, for their honor and for ours, that this great extermination [grande extermination] was the result of a tenacious resistance, because otherwise it would be a massacre."[58]

Laghouat was a populous oasis. About 4,000 people lived here in the 1840s, cultivating gardens along the Oued Mzi and participating in the trade that came through this strategic location. Before the battle the population increased thanks to people who responded to ben Abdallah's call. At day's end some 3,000 people lay dead. (The ratio of Algerian to French losses was 250 to 1.) [59] By campaign's end some 80 percent of the oasis's population had perished or fled. Many women and children were among the victims. Unlike Zaatcha, women, children, and the aged did not have the opportunity to leave the oasis before the final French assault; they were mowed down by French fire that did not discriminate between combatants and civilians. Even the wives and children of ben Salem's supporters, who were allied to France, did not escape. Prior to the assault ben Abdallah had assembled them in the former *khalifa*'s residence, perhaps to serve as hostages in negotiations. During the battle French soldiers received fire from the house's guards and immediately stormed the building. Shooting their way through the rooms, soldiers had killed some 40 women and children before an officer arrived, who, realizing the true identity of the victims, called a ceasefire. [60]

Historian Charles-André Julien caustically called the battle of Laghouat a "butchery." [61] Expressing Julien's outrage, the word well describes the intensity of the French soldiers' violence. This can be ascertained from the fact that at day's end there were few wounded among the people of Laghouat. Attacking soldiers had used their weapons to a deliberately murderous effect. [62] It was not indiscriminate firing into darkened rooms that claimed so many lives but rather the fact that soldiers "rushed inside and pitilessly stabbed everyone they found." [63] Even those who managed to flee to the gardens were not spared. The battle won and resistance stifled, in the afternoon French troops moved to Laghouat's outskirts to hunt down and kill those who had sought refuge there. (The more fortunate survivors slipped through the French dragnet and fled into the desert; ben Abdallah himself reputedly escaped in this manner.) As was the case in the ksour sacked by Cavaignac's men, a murderous fury animated soldiers at Laghouat. Officers placed few restrictions on them, so much a part of "African warfare" had this sort of violence become. Only the women and children of factions allied to the French were eventually spared, and even here protections were haphazard and incomplete.

In contrast to Zaatcha, the body count at Laghouat can be determined more accurately. The French were ready for a permanent base in the Sahara and Laghouat's dead had to be buried. (The decision came at the last minute. Pélissier wanted to level the oasis, like Zaatcha, but Governor-General Randon ordered him to spare its buildings and gardens.) It took several weeks before burial crews completed their work. In the first ten days Colonel Cler's crew alone burned or hastily buried 1,174 bodies. [64] In the next weeks crews dug large pits at the edge of the gardens and buried the dead pell-mell, along with the dead horses and mules. [65] The only care shown in the operation was the layer of quicklime thrown over the corpses to prevent disease. Soldiers found this to be difficult work. They had to descend into wells to retrieve corpses that had been thrown down them in the heat of battle but that now threatened the water supply. Moreover, Laghouat's narrow, labyrinthine streets made retrieving bodies from the interior of the city a slow process since each body had to be carried on the back of a mule. Faced with this gruesome corvée, soldiers' tempers flared. When Pélissier reproached the commander of one burial party for his crew's slowness, the junior officer retorted, "What do you want, sir? We can't bury the dead as fast as you kill them!"[66] Those soldiers who were assigned to shooting vultures in an effort to ward off the plague felt themselves lucky. After a few days Laghouat's survivors themselves were pressed into burial duties.

Unlike Zaatcha, the massacre of the population at Laghouat brought temporary peace to this part of the Algerian Sahara. The monthly reports that came from the new Saharan base rarely failed to laud the "profound peace and security" that had settled on the region.[67] Laghouat's new commander, Commandant Du Barail, celebrated this newfound order. "The current population can cause us no worry nor pose the least danger," he wrote in the spring.[68] As some would have it, fear inspired by the massacre ensured security. The military commentator Corneille Trumulet claimed that the massacre had instilled a "healthy terror" (une terreur salutaire) that dissuaded the desert people from further resistance.[69] Locals were so terrified of General Pélissier that they came to call him the devil (*Iblīs*; Arabic not having a phonetic equivalent for "p," Pélissier became *Blici*, a word sounding close to the proper Arabic word for the devil.) As Trumulet observed, "The similarity of this name with the terrible spirit of evil . . . later facilitated our entry into the ksour of our South. Their turbulent populations were able to appreciate, from the example of El-Ar'ouath [Laghouat], our procedures for entering towns that close their doors to us."[70]

Trumulet's claims notwithstanding, desolation as much as fear ensured the calm. In the following years reports from Laghouat showed the heavy price of this peace. Deep scars marked the oasis.[71] The economic and social effects of the massacre were the most difficult legacy, and even the hardened French commanders complained. They had established order, but trade caravans shunned the oasis well into the late 1850s, and the gardens remained uncultivated for years. Confiscated in retribution for their owners' support of ben Abdallah, the garden's absentee European owners proved to be dismal failures as date cultivators.[72] With little to tax, the costs of the occupation fell exclusively on the French state. The massacre left disturbing mementos as well. Perhaps the most troubling, in this regard, were the hundreds of orphans who roamed the streets. The governor-general's office had initially suggested that all the survivors of Laghouat should be deported and a new European population brought to replace them. But the survivors, most of whom were part of the ben Salem family and had been French allies, were allowed to stay, along with a ragtag bunch of orphans.[73] A haunting reminder of the violence dealt to their families, the orphans plagued even the hard-hearted with their constant thefts. Five years after the massacre, thirty orphans had learned to supplement begging with theft. Precursors to the ubiquitous "ya-oueds," the impoverished shoe shiners and paperboys who haunted the streets of northern cities, the orphans of Laghouat became so troublesome that the commandant sought a formal solution.[74] Seeing idle hands, he organized the orphans into a worker brigade.[75] These ragtag children were joined by some five hundred other survivors. They kept to themselves, "penned up" in an isolated section of town.[76] The French commandant called them a "trembling herd" and found their presence bothersome. "The fate that we subjected them to," he wrote, "became a burden [un embarras] for me, because they became my responsibility."[77]

Empty spaces within the oasis's walls served as further evidence of the devastation. As a permanent reminder of French omnipotence, Pélissier leveled prominent buildings in the rebels' neighborhood. To complete his symbolic victory, he destroyed four of Laghouat's six mosques.[78] The most impressive one, however, was spared and was converted into a church. Some six weeks after the oasis fell, Abbé Jacques Suchet came to Laghouat to deliver his first mass in the new church. Stirred by the spectacle of devastation yet bolstered by the fact of celebrating his faith here in this building, conquered from Islam, Suchet delivered a noteworthy sermon:

> The Francs and the Crusaders, our valiant fathers, did the work of God in memorable combat in the Occident and Orient. . . . Soldiers of France, you have not degenerated. In conquering Algeria, this new France, you also—do not doubt it—do *the work of God*. In pursuing the course of your victories over these proud children of Muhammad, masters of a large part of the globe, you extend Christian domination over the debris of Islamism, and even more than your fathers you accomplish here the work of God. . . . Yes, your invincible sword has hewn the cross that shines throughout this country like a radiant sun, which will shed light and fertilize it by banishing the crescent, the lugubrious sign of night and sleep, image of the Moor. By this victory at Laghouat, the Eagle of France has flown audaciously farther in these countries than the Roman eagles; and the cross, doubtless for the first time, is planted and radiates in the middle of this desert, which it will make flower again.[79]

As later events would demonstrate, although it established peace, the carnage at Laghouat only bought a temporary calm and starkly disproved everything that had been theorized in the 1840s. Indeed, Suchet's sermon ("Soldiers of France, you have not degenerated") demonstrates how far the French had deviated from the provisions of the "pénétration pacifique." Its ghastly failure was reflected in the starkest terms in Laghouat's deserted ruins. The project outlined by Urbain, Enfantin, Carette, and Daumas, while serving the political task of convincing leaders to embark upon a Saharan expansion, failed to curb French practices rooted in habits of brute force. The terms of the peaceful conquest were entirely inadequate to Suchet's project of picking up the pieces of the colonial idol. Even the orientalist terms of their plan ("bellicose Arabs," "Muslim fanaticism," "populations bâtardes," etc.) failed fully to account for the destruction French troops inflicted upon this oasis. Indeed, far from Saint-Simonian *progress* and Bugeaud's military *order*, Suchet's apocalyptic-redemptive paradigm more closely echoes the ultraconservative thinker Joseph de Maistre's exterminating angel, a figure with whom Suchet was undoubtedly familiar.[80] This trope alone, with its narrative of miraculous evil—devastation and apocalypse, purification and transcendence—was up to the task of explaining the destruction of the "pénétration pacifique."

PART 2

Exterminating the French
at Djelfa, 1861

When the lords of this world see their subjects perish en masse,
with God in their ranks, perhaps then you will obtain justice.
—Kateb Yacine, Nedjma (1957)

[4]

THE OULED NAÏL AND COLONIAL RULE

Although the history of nineteenth-century Algeria is marked by nearly unceasing outbreaks of sporadic, small-scale violence, researchers have privileged large-scale anticolonial movements, the struggles of Abdelkader, Ahmed Bey of Constantine, Mokrani (Muhammad al-hajj al-Muqrani, 1815–1871), and so forth.[1] These show the united face of Algerian resistance to best advantage — an expression important to previous historiography. But much armed anticolonial activity was more like the "varied and sometimes confused expressions of peasant discontent" typical of social movements elsewhere in colonial Africa.[2] It is difficult to render the political text contained within these episodes of anticolonial struggle. Often they contain a hidden second plot, marked by syncopation, displacement, and the echoes of other dramas. There is a pressing need to reexamine these sorts of events. The oblique angle offered by the Djelfa attack provides an especially helpful vantage point from which to rethink the national-resistance model of popular movements in the Middle East and to seek new ways to explain the dynamics of their violence.[3]

THE ATTACK ON DJELFA: THE REPORT
OF MARSHAL PÉLISSIER

In late April 1861 Marshal Pélissier, the governor-general of Algeria, wrote to the minister of war and informed him of an unfortunate incident that had recently occurred in Djelfa, one of the last military outposts in the south and the site of a small settlement of European colonists.[4] A group numbering fifty to sixty men and several boys, led by a reputed *mukaddam* (representative) of the Rahmaniyya Sufi order named Si Tayeb, had entered the village on the night of 14–15 April 1861. Armed with staffs, stones, and knives, the group slipped past the garrison and descended upon the village, where they raided five houses and a *café maure*, a local Arabic-style coffeehouse. They attacked with deadly intent, killing three Europeans (two men and a five-year-old girl) and critically wounded three settlers, two laborers from Laghouat, and three soldiers. The settlers, belatedly joined by French soldiers, killed four of their attackers, while the leader himself escaped.

In the days that followed, Louis Gaston de Sonis, the French commander at Laghouat, convened a military court to investigate the incident and punish the guilty. Fearing a major uprising, Sonis insisted that French justice be swift and harsh. After a two-day inquiry, the court arrived at its decision. On the morning of 19 April seven men were assembled, placed against the wall of the small French fort, and executed by firing squad.

Although the incident was not without precedent, it was embarrassing on several counts. These included both Sonis's inability to ensure the safety of European settlers and his draconian punishment, which went against the grain of Napoleon III's new liberal stance toward Algerians, his desire for an "Arab Kingdom," a confused and halfhearted project.[5] Pélissier tried to head off criticism by reporting that the attack was an isolated event and posed no threat to security in the southern territories. He insisted that Si Tayeb's poorly armed men were not the head of a major insurrection. Rather, they had fallen victim to the seductions of Si Tayeb: "This marabout [saintly individual], by means of the practices of his order, produced among those that participated a condition of abnormal nervous excitement, which brought these fifty or sixty fanatics to a state of near folly, after which he unleashed them upon the village."[6] This revolt was just another Algerian Jacquerie, the explanation posited.[7] The unpredictability, love of freedom, and religious zealotry of Algeria's rural people made stability in the colony elusive, if not impossible. Such thinking had become ingrained in the "colonial vulgate," punctuated by words like "fanatisme" (fanaticism), "belliqueux" (warlike), and "indomptable" (indomitable).[8] Taken together these words amounted to an argument, one that military officers used to explain their inability to establish order in the Algerian interior and their use of brute force to keep the peace.[9]

DJELFA'S PHYSICAL AND SOCIAL GEOGRAPHY

The territories of the Annex of Djelfa lay at the northern edge of the Algerian Sahara. The region was at the crossroads between the northern lands of the Tell and the Sahara. The High Plateaux comprised the region's northern borders and the south opened upon the Sahara desert at Laghouat. Located at a strategic passage through the Saharan Atlas Mountains, Djelfa was one of several points that have traditionally channeled travel between the Mediterranean world and sub-Saharan Africa. For centuries caravans large and small crossed here, along with herds of livestock and various types of travelers. Although great wealth passed through this region, the vicissitudes of climate ensured that life in the Djelfa region remained difficult. The climate's outstanding features are aridity and wildly fluctuating extremes in temperature. Historically precipitation is light, averaging 30–40 centimeters (11.7–15.6 inches) annually and severe drought occurs every seven to ten years, withering pastures and crops.[10] Rain can be just as damaging. Winter is the wet season, when rain and snow fall, replenishing groundwater and swelling streams. In the spring rain arrives in the form of sporadic, often violent storms that cause floods, damage pastures and crops, and erode precious topsoil. The temperatures are also severe. In winter a long, bitter cold descends on the Djelfa region, and from November to March heavy snows periodically fall on the mountaintops and descend into valleys, cutting off travel. Summers are no less harsh. Temperatures rival those of the oases deep in the Sahara, reaching 40–44 degrees Centigrade (104–11 degrees Fahrenheit). Summing up the effects of the climate, one French observer wrote, "Here are vast, windswept plateaux and immense plains burned and hardened by a relentless sun."[11]

Although this harsh climate makes life precarious, its extremes give the region considerable ecological diversity. In particular, variations in altitude help broaden the ecological range near Djelfa. The latter sits at the center of the Ouled-Naïl Mountains, a small, mountainous mass within the longer Saharan Atlas that itself stretches across Algeria from the Moroccan border to Biskra.[12] At the northern and southern ends of the Djelfa region are low-relief areas. Both are exceedingly dry. Arriving from the north by the Route nationale 1 today, the great trans-Saharan highway that (theoretically) links Algiers to Lagos, the traveler to Djelfa leaves the villages, orchards, and gardens of the comparatively humid Tell at Ksar el Boukhari and crosses the High Plateaux, which consist of over a hundred kilometers of barren, flat, windswept steppes. Another hundred kilometers to the south of Djelfa lies Laghouat, where one finds the terrain open to the rocky flats (ḥammāda-s) and sandy dunes characteristic of the Sahara. Separating these two regions, the mountains around Djelfa are high, with peaks reaching fifteen hundred meters. These mountains are the region's ecological lifeline, forcing precious precipitation to fall from passing clouds. (Indeed, the rainfall gradient is the only sure characteristic about this uncertain environment.) These waters feed the juniper and pine trees that dot the high ridges and, most important, nourish the region's rich spring pastures below. A variety of low shrubs and grasses grow here, and during wet cycles rich clusters of herbaceous plants ('ashāb) normally sprout.

Such diversity is well suited to pastoralism. This region has been dubbed the "Land of Sheep and Goats" (bilād al-ghunūm). Since the nineteenth century agricultural life has centered on raising these ruminants. Sheep are supremely well adapted to the climate, especially the Ouled Jellal and other breeds of the Algerian steppes.[13] Given their dexterous, narrow mouths and careful grazing, they do well in sparse pastures. Moreover, sheep drink sparingly and can go for relatively long periods without water. (Adult sheep remain healthy on as little as three liters a day and can endure several days without water.) Most important is their fecundity. When wet cycles produce rich pastures, well-nourished, healthy ewes are very prolific. This ensures quick herd recovery after periods of drought, a demographic elasticity essential to the variable climate.[14] Goats share many of the same adaptations. Moreover, when mixed in with the sheep, they help keep the herd moving at a good pace.

Lying just to the north of Djelfa, where the mountains give way to the steppes, are two seasonal marshes (sebkha), and adjacent pastures (shaṭṭ), known locally as the Zahrez-Rharbi and Zahrez-Chergui. These flat, enclosed depressions collect the water that flows out of the mountains.[15] Here may be found some of the richest pastures in the region; their regularly watered grasses are high in salt content and extremely nourishing. The Zahrez has been an excellent stopping point for pastoralists for centuries. They put their animals out to graze here and watch as their herds put on weight and gain strength before beginning the summer transhumance ('ashāba) north across the sparsely foddered trails of the High Plateaux, or the winter migration ('azīb) south to pastures in the Sahara.[16] On these heavily traveled routes there is little for animals to eat along the way; even today herders must make sure that their livestock are in excellent condition before leaving the Zahrez pastures.[17]

Long frequented by pastoralists, the varied lands of Djelfa were home to several groups in the nineteenth century. The dominant population consisted of four major groups of the Ouled Naïl (Awlad Na'il): the Ouled 'Isa, Ouled Khalid, Ouled Zekriof, and Ouled Si Mhammad. These factions were part of the Ouled Naïl, a large agnatic group that claimed descent from Si Naïl ben Naïl (ca. 1500–1594) and saw themselves a part of the same tribe (ḳabīla or 'ashīra). Arabophone, the Ouled Naïl were pastoralists who frequented the region roughly centered at Djelfa and Bou-Saada. This area was their homeland (waṭan), the place where they were born and where their ancestors were buried.

The rearing of livestock, the regional foodstuffs trade, and some grain cultivation determined the seasonal rhythms of the Ouled Naïl well into the period of French occupation. They subsisted on the products produced by their herds and traded the surpluses—primarily raw wool—for dates on their migrations to their winter pastures in the northern Sahara. (The Naïli herds frequented Saharan pastures along the Oued Rhir, near the Mzab, and the region near Ouargla.) It was essential to pass the winter in the Sahara to protect herds from the dangerous epidemics that struck livestock in the north during the winter.[18] In the summer the Ouled Naïl traveled to the mountainous area near Tiaret in the Tell. Here, in camps of distinctive red and black tents, the Ouled Naïl passed the summer near their herds, while individual Naïli merchants traveled north to trade dates, raw wool, and wool textiles for wheat and barley. The Ouled Naïl also planted cereals on the rare lands of the region that received enough water. Harvests from these fields varied widely from year to year, but a good crop could provide an extra margin of food security and reduce grain purchases.

When delving further into the social organization of the Ouled Naïl in the 1860s, social scientists encounter the thorny problem of colonial sources and the question of social organization in the Middle East, which has long dogged the study of agnatic kinship groups organized in a tribe. Focusing on the pastoral communities of Algeria, sociologist M'hamed Boukhobza long ago recognized that researchers must cease "looking for a stable organizing principal for the tribe," such as the segmentary model. He concluded that the tribe is simply "a community of interests" that shifts in terms of composition and orientation as these interests themselves shift.[19] With this caveat in mind, one can examine the French sources on the Ouled Naïl of Djelfa. The most important are by Marc-Antoine Arnaud, the French interpreter at Djelfa. Born in Algiers in 1835, Arnaud mastered Arabic while growing up in Algeria and moved on from his career as a military interpreter to work as a translator for the official journal *Le Mobacher,* in addition to translating several important manuscripts and books from Arabic into French.[20] At Djelfa he crossed over into ethnography and conducted interviews with the Ouled Naïl in the 1850s and 1860s. He published his findings in a series of articles for the *Revue africaine* based on "what our Saharans tell about themselves."[21] Like most French analysts at the time, Arnaud saw the Ouled Naïl made up of factions, distinct and separate social and political units—each a sort of principality—ruled by a single leader or council. Despite his flawed understanding, his conversations with local sources were thorough and are useful to the historian not so much for what they tell us about social reality, narrowly understood, but for revealing certain "social facts" that animated Naïli society.

Most of those involved in the Djelfa attack were members of the Ouled Si Mhammad, a powerful Naïli group.[22] As they recounted to Arnaud, the Ouled Si Mhammad came from illustrious ancestry. Their eponym, Si Mhammad, was reputed to be the only son of Abd al-Rahman ibn Salim ibn Malik ibn Na'il, the great grandson of the founder of the Ouled Naïl.[23] Before Abd al-Rahman died, he passed his *baraka* (God's blessing, beneficent force) to Mhammad, telling his son on his deathbed: "God will make you great among men. Alone among all the Ouled Naïl, your descendents will have the right of the *a'yān.*" This was the right to protect, denoting their notable status. According to oral tradition, this secured the ascendancy of the Ouled Si Mhammad. "Following these words, the children of Mhammad have not ceased to command respect. All the Ouled Naïl were at their feet, submissive and obedient. The others saw them as their natural tutors and turned toward them, without hate or jealousy, to take care of all their problems."[24] It was not, however, a prestigious genealogy alone that secured the Ouled Si Mhammad's power. Their founder had the foresight to seek a solid material footing for his people in the Zahrez pastures.

The late seventeenth and eighteenth centuries were a time of social unrest in the Ottoman regencies of Algeria. At this time another powerful tribe, the Sahari, was already engaged in a struggle to claim the Zahrez.[25] The Sahari sought to dislodge the region's inhabitants and claim the lands as their own. According to oral tradition, Mhammad recognized the advantages of patience and let the Sahari continue their attack. He reasoned that the combatants would exhaust themselves, enabling his people to defeat whoever came out on top more easily. It was a wise decision. The Sahari triumphed, and as Mhammad anticipated, he was able to take the fertile lands from them with little effort. The Ouled Si Mhammad grew rich and powerful here, which was recognized by the Ottoman bey of Titteri, who invited them to join his government (*Makhzan*).[26]

A COLONIAL SPRING IN THE ALGERIAN STEPPES

From 1845 on, it was no longer a state but a society that was being destroyed.
— Abdallah Laroui, *The History of the Maghrib: An Interpretive Essay*

In a recent radio interview historian Daniel Rivet called for a reconsideration of the "fait colonial" (colonial fact).[27] Lingering passions, he said, have burdened historians with facile categories of colonizer and colonized, bad and good. To underscore his point, Rivet pointed to a map of Algeria and asked: "Where is colonialism?" It was certainly found in the port cities—for example, in the workshop of Albert Camus's uncle—but he argued that much of rural Algeria, like the Aurès Mountains, did not see "the face of Europeans" until French soldiers arrived during the Algerian war of 1954–62. In fact, French colonialism had many "faces." One of the most insidious, a hidden face, was its destructive economic and social effects. The fraying of traditional ways of life and the breakdown of the social order all contributed to the crisis of rural Algerian society. For tens of thousands of people this crisis had a fatal outcome, occurring long before the arrival of settlers.

Djelfa has been defined by its geographic constraints, slow tempo, and sense of permanence. Indeed, at first sight the Djelfa region seems a quintessential land of the longue durée. Home to some of the most advanced military bases and nuclear research stations in Algeria today, Djelfa's timeless character can be seen in the traditions of longtime residents—especially their proud stoicism—

and in the landscape itself, so much so that in the 1950s Emile Dermenghem, a French specialist of the Algerian steppes, called it the "Land of Abel," harking back to the origins of monotheism.[28] However, the French occupation of the region after 1852 set into motion profound social, ecological, and economic transformations, which rapidly led to the unraveling of life in the area. In terms of colonial time, the longue durée at Djelfa lasted a mere decade.

The attack on Djelfa took place just after Ramadan had ended. In 1861 Ramadan fell in the spring (spanning March and April). Known among Arabic-speaking pastoralists as *rabī'* (the season when greenness comes), spring was a tense season in the Algerian steppes. Those who cultivated wheat and barley watched nervously as their crops matured through their most vulnerable stage in one of the most unpredictable seasons. If the severe desert winds (*sharkī* or *keblī*) that swept through the region from May to September arrived early, they would rapidly dry out the soil just as cereals were maturing.[29] Just as worrisome was the tendency of locusts to travel on these winds. If a swarm blew in from the south, it might consume an entire harvest and decimate pastures in a few days. Although sufficient rainfall was a constant worry in these rocky lands, spring rains often fell too heavily. Always happy to see the skies darken with rain clouds, people experienced a mixed sense of joy and apprehension after the spring downpours, in anticipation of the flash floods that would rage down from the mountains.[30] Even worse, these storms might bring hail pounding upon fields and pastures.

Although they focused upon their animals, there were few families of herders (*rahhala*, drivers of the herds) who did not have some lands seeded in grain. Grain cultivation in the Djelfa region followed traditional techniques until well into the twentieth century.[31] The fields were first scattered with seed, after which a light wooden plow, pulled by various types of draft animals, tilled the soil, turning up only a few centimeters of the surface. This tilling mixed the seed in deep enough so that germination could occur. The grain grew throughout the winter months. There was little need for labor at this point: winter rains watered plants and the protection of the crops from predation was entrusted to family members, allied sedentary groups, or placed under the influence of a saintly personage.

The rhythms and light rigors involved in growing grain fit in well with the cycles of the pastoralists of Djelfa. Grain was a good absentee crop, allowing most families to spend the winter with their flocks in the Sahara as the grain matured. The harvest likewise coincided with the movements of the herds, returning in the spring on their way north to summer pastures. Harvest generally began in May with the more precocious barley. The cultivators at Djelfa cut their grains with a sickle. (Later, under pressure from the administration, farmers began to use scythes to produce the longer straw the French garrisons wanted for their stock.[32]) Afterward herds grazed the stubble and fertilized the fields, many of which lay fallow the next season. The harvest was threshed by a variety of methods, an efficient one being tromping by animals. What happened next to the grains depended on the size of the harvest and the political dispositions and economic resources of the respective cultivators. Generally a portion would be stored in a silo or *matmūra*. In the Annex of Djelfa most silos were subterranean pits. The farmer would fill them, then seal and conceal the entrance. Secrecy helped protect their contents during the owner's migrations. Other pastoral tribes with sedentary clients stored provisions in the ksour, semifortified villages scattered throughout the region.[33] These food reserves formed an essential part of the economic security of pastoralists.

Although yields were low, traditional techniques were well suited to the dry region. For example, the light plow ensured stability for the fragile soils that more intensive cultivation would have left vulnerable to wind and water erosion. Most important, these techniques required little investment, a key consideration for cultivators who could not count on consistent returns from these marginal lands and focused their main attentions on their herds. As Dermenghem wrote of the Naïli farmer, "The grain that he confides to the soil is less a capital that he lends than a bet that he wagers."[34]

The demands of the herds were heaviest in the spring. Most important were the shearing and marketing of the raw wool. This commerce had become more complicated recently due to the fact that the French had enacted a variety of measures designed to concentrate the wool trade in the marketplaces under French control. By 1860 these efforts had succeeded in forcing some sellers to abandon their habitual wool markets in the Mzab (which had remained beyond direct French control until 1882) and conduct their trade at Djelfa under the eyes of colonial authority. Forced integration into a market economy was a deliberate strategy on the part of the French administration to gain control over Algerian pastoralists and neutralize their military capacity. It was given early articulation in parliamentary debates on custom duties. For example, when the duty on Algerian wools was debated in Parliament in 1851, one member claimed that a wool trade subject to the rules of the free market would earn the French "considerable authority over the Arab nomads."[35] Another member, M. Duraure, concurred and explained the operation in detail. Encouraged by the promise of high prices for quality wools, Algerian pastoralists would seek to maximize their interests and produce as much of the marketable wool as possible. In order to do this and ensure the required quality, they would have to adopt the practices of sedentary grazing used by European farmers. Soon, Duraure promised, "instead of being a pastoral people the Arabs will become a sedentary and cultivating people; instead of a tent, they will have a house; for their sheep, they will have a shed; around the shed they will have fields, cultivated fields fertilized by the manure of the sheep."[36] This social transformation of the Algerian pastoralists would serve two functions in colonial society. Economically it would better integrate pastoralists into an economy favorable to powerful interests in France, namely, French mill owners, who would be provided with the inexpensive raw wool and affordable meat to keep their workers satisfied from a social stand-point. Politically, sedentarization would resolve the security problem. Duraure concluded, "Instead of being obliged to have 75,000 men to guard us from their attacks . . . we will have a people perfectly subjected [*soumis*] to our laws."[37]

A decade later the successes of this policy were widely lauded. An 1863 com-mission explained how well the French-dominated market economy had pen-etrated the wool trade. Reported at the American consulate, this transformation was translated into the triumphalist terms of economic liberalism: "[Before] when the Arabs could not sell the wool, their sheep, nor their lambs at a profit, they had no interest in increasing their production beyond their own needs. But now that the markets are opened to them and commercial relations established, the natives, enlightened by the examples which surround them, by the facts to which they testify, can augment their flocks under the common stimulant of profit assured by the sale of their products."[38] Although it introduced new elements of risk, this commitment to a market economy was shared all the way down the line of command to the military commanders at far-off Djelfa. For example, the annual report of 1860 speaks optimistically about how well the French commercial policy had worked. The nomads who used to travel to the Mzab in annual caravans to trade their wool were now selling to buyers from the Tell at Djelfa, many of whom were French.[39]

In addition to the shearing and selling of wool, spring was the time when pas-toralists prepared for the *'ashāba*, the great migrations to their summer pastures in the Tell, an activity that had recently become more troublesome. Negotiating the grazing fee with their summer hosts was a traditional but often complex affair for the Ouled Naïl. In times of drought it was doubly so because herders were forced out of their customary ranges and had to compete with their neighbors for the few green pastures available.[40] The arrival of the French further compli-cated matters. Pastoralists now had to obtain a permit from the Bureau Arabe in Laghouat or Djelfa before moving their herds. The application had to include precise information on the destination, herd size, number of tents, names of leaders, and number of weapons. These requests had to travel up the chain of command for approval by the subdivision commander in Médéa, a process that could take weeks or even longer. This new effort to control the movement of the herds, an example of "rationalal policy" in French eyes, was supremely opaque and unintelligible to Algerian pastoralists themselves. In dry years, when rapid responses were critical, they were forced to wait for the French reply, a delay that sent tensions soaring as herders saw the health of their livestock deteriorate. Decisions concerning permits rarely considered the needs of the herds or the conditions of pastures but instead were based on the strategic interests of the colonial administration. This fact added yet another layer of uncertainty to an already unpredictable environment and way of life.

Finally, spring was a season when all felt the burdens of taxation. Although not all the contributions were collected in the spring, it was the time of the dreaded fiscal assessment. The process unfolded as follows.[41] First, the French-named head and representative of each faction, the caid (*kā'id*, or governor), would draw up a list of "matière imposable." This inventory was then turned over to the officer at the local Bureau Arabe, who would make a tour to verify the caid's figures. Depending on the officer's disposition, this was not a full accounting but rather an informal inventory. From the Bureau Arabe the fiscal census went to the Consultative Commission, which would use the reports—the only documentation of the tribe's wealth—to determine that year's taxes. For the *'achour*, a tax in kind or in coin on the grain harvest, the tour served primarily as an estimate. Although the *'achour* was based on cultivated terrain (one measure of wheat and barley for each *zouja* or *djebda* [7–10 hectares] cultivated), yields figured in the calculation and the collection came after the harvest. But springtime was when the *zekat* (*zakāt*) tax on livestock was both assessed and collected. The administration wanted to synchronize taxation with the transhumance, when the herds passed through the territory. In principle, the *zekat* was fixed at 1 percent (1 head of sheep for every 100 owned) and it had to be paid either in kind—live sheep or wool—or coin, depending on the preference of the colonial authorities.

Although much was at stake in the tax appraisal, it was hardly a regular process. It was effectively in the hands of the French-appointed caids, who were not disinterested parties to the process. Part of the caid's revenues came from the 10 percent he could collect from the tax receipts.[42] He also drew up first estimates of taxable wealth. This gave the caids much power. Depending on their disposition, they could work for or against local people. An individual caid might reduce tax burdens by underrepresenting wealth, or he could do the same in order to enrich himself. In terms of pure interest, the caid seeking economic advantage had every incentive to make sure the tax survey yielded high figures.[43] Other forms of corruption occurred as well. The archives for Djelfa contain many cases of caids who required full payment from taxpayers and then gave the colonial authorities lesser amounts, based on deflated estimates, and pocketed the difference. In particular, the 1850s witnessed a host of scandals relating to tax collection. For example, after making his springtime assessment tour for the *zekat* of 1857, the Bureau Arabe officer disciplined the caids of the Ouled 'Isa and the Ouled Zmissa for underrepresenting herd sizes. He fined them 100 francs apiece for their deceit.[44] It is not possible to determine whether these caids falsified the assessment in order to shield taxpayers or for personal gain. However, in the autumn of the same year caid Chérif ben El Khebeïzi of the Ouled Bou Abdallah was accused of embezzling eight thousand francs of the *'achour* receipts.[45] The same occurred with the *zekat* of 1860, when Lakdar ben Belkassem, the caid of the Ouled Abdelkader, embezzled three thousand francs by misrepresenting the herd size.[46] Thus, at every level—between the caid and taxpayers and between the caid and colonial authorities—the system produced corruption, mistrust, and conflict.

A self-proclaimed hallmark of French authorities was their fairness. Colonial planners thought that a just rule would rally Algerians to the French cause. Although Algerians resented serving Christian masters, it was thought they had suffered the despotism of Ottoman rule and would appreciate a new regime based on the rule of law. Exemplifying this opinion, in 1841 Alexis de Tocqueville wrote, "It is by justice alone that we will be able to excuse our religion."[47] His thoughts were widely shared. For example, in 1856 Auguste Margueritte, the commander at Laghouat, reflected at length on how successful French efforts had been among the local populations.

The submission of the indigenous populations of the Circle is now as complete as one could hope for. In the character of this submission there is more than passive obedience; in fact, one clearly observes a great satisfaction resulting from (1) a peaceful existence unknown to the Arabs before our domination; (2) a more just and equitable administration that works for all equally; (3) access to facilities [wells, corrals, marketplaces] which help commercial relations; (4) increased individual wealth. . . . We must add to these causes of satisfaction those resulting from the modification of the false ideas that the Arabs had of our character, our manner of behaving, which they thought must be against their interests, their morals, their religion. Certainly the Arab character is very versatile; it seeks novelty [changement], the marvelous, but it will transform itself under the influence of our domination and contact with our ideas. This transformation seems to us to have already begun, and we bring it to your attention in the anticipation and hope that it will increase daily.[48]

Few who lived under French command, however, found much in the way of fairness and justice at tax time, and whatever transparency existed revealed only graft. With few checks, little central oversight, and almost no accountability, the system was a structural invitation to caids to abuse their authority for personal profit.[49] Although the archives do not easily reveal such fraud to the historian, few at the time missed the fact that taxation was highly irregular and could be a source of great wealth to dishonest caids. One caid, Larby Mamelouk, an Italian-born convert to Islam, amassed a personal fortune of over one hundred thousand francs during his three-year tenure. His corruption was no secret, attracting the attention of thieves in 1874, who robbed him.[50]

COLONIZATION AND THE LOSS OF ECONOMIC RESILIENCE

Having been doctored, the tax records are also incomplete. Consequently they are an imperfect source for the historian trying to understand the economy of the Annex of Djelfa and the material state of Naïli society a decade into the

French occupation. Nevertheless, the alarm shown by French officers at tax-collection time testifies to the growing problem of poverty. Beginning in the late 1850s, French commanders regularly returned from their assessment tours and filed reports indicating that many families were destitute and that tax collection would be difficult. In 1860 the material situation had deteriorated so much that the local commander was granted a rare tax reprieve for his jurisdiction, much to his relief. As he wrote, "We needed a little time to obtain the money [to pay the tax] from selling of wool and grain."[51] He was less pleased when he received orders six months later (just four months before the Djelfa attack) to immediately collect the full tax.

Relief from the colonial tax burden was infrequent.[52] Instead of looking critically at the causes of immiserization, colonial observers blamed the ongoing drought. They argued that a dry spell had placed the people of the steppes in dire straits. While the sporadic data available confirms that Djelfa was in the midst of a cyclical drought, local people had experienced this many times. That people like the Ouled Naïl were in a critical situation this time around stemmed as much from changing socioeconomic patterns as from environmental factors. Whereas the colonial economy sought to create actors who would *specialize* and produce single nonfood products like wool, the vitality of the precolonial economy depended upon *diversity*, highly varied actors, and, in particular, the mobility of local people in terms of their ability to travel and trade with other regions. Like everywhere in the Mediterranean, the Algerian steppes were an aleatory environment where economic security depended upon people's ability to diversify, store, and redistribute.[53]

For pastoralists mobility and connectivity were the only sure ways to obtain a margin of security. Thus, groups like the Ouled Naïl were far from autarchic. Contrary to the first French reports, they did not live solely off their herds.[54] Instead, the pastoralists' livelihood was ensured by their central position in a network of trade that linked the date-growing oases of the Sahara with the cereal-producing regions of the Tell. The trade in Saharan dates for the grain grown in the Tell was at the center of the economy, linking the Sahara and sub-Saharan Africa with the Mediterranean world. A brief sketch of this rich commerce can help illustrate the nature of the crisis facing the people of Djelfa. Although primarily pastoralists, the Ouled Naïl were also merchants and colporteurs, serving as a primary link between the Tell and the Sahara. This made them major economic agents. The twice-yearly migration of herds was the motor of this trade. The Ouled Naïl planned their movements to coincide with the harvests of dates and grain, as well as the greening of pastures. In the late spring they were to be found in the mountains around Djelfa and the Zahrez, where they could harvest grain fields. In the summer they were in the Tell, where they could make grain provisions from the northern harvest. In the late fall and early winter (roughly November) they were in the Sahara, where they could buy newly harvested dates (making their purchases at Touggourt, the Mzab, and at Ouargla).[55] Although sheep and goats were the primary livestock, camels and horses ensured the Ouled Naïl's place in the regional economy.[56] Camels transported trade goods, while their horses provided a strong defense. This combined strength in the material of mobility and war guaranteed the pastoralists of Djelfa control of the north-south trade routes in and out of the Sahara.

Although exact sources are lacking, extant documents suggest that the Ouled Naïl participated in foodstuffs commerce in two ways. First, some took part directly. They purchased foodstuffs and other items with their own capital and transported the goods on their camels to the markets at the northern and southern terminals. Here they bartered for food staples, livestock, manufactured goods, and the products of local artisanal production. To the Tell they brought dates, along with woolen textiles, henna from In Salah, cotton textiles from the sub-Saharan producers, and occasionally slaves. To the south they brought barley and wheat, along with a long list of manufactured goods, plus sugar, coffee, and tea. Other capital-rich investors, like those in the Mzab, often made loans for such trade, or joint ventures might be established between the Mzabis and pastoralists like the Ouled Naïl.[57] Only powerful groups like the Ouled Naïl, who had sufficient resources and a wide range of influence, could participate in this trade, investing in large quantities and journeying to the markets with the best prices. Their profits could reach as much as 50 percent on the foodstuffs trade.[58] Second, the Ouled Naïl contracted their transportation and protection services. Danger abounded on Saharan trails, and caravans invited raids by rival tribes or bands of independent marauders. Success depended on a strong deterrent force, the protection of religious and military allies (negotiated through paid-protection institutions like the *qafāra*), as well as an intimate knowledge of the constantly shifting political terrain of the Sahara. Merchants paid handsomely for these services.

The arrival of the French in Algeria disrupted this commerce. The Ouled Naïl in particular saw their role diminish as early as the 1840s, only a decade after the French had arrived in Algeria.[59] The deadly and destructive wars of the first stage of French conquest were the most important factor. The razzias succeeded in severely disrupting Algeria's economy. The heavy loss of life in itself ensured that the economic effects of the wars spread far across the region. Moreover, the destruction of crops and confiscation of food reserves, along with losses of livestock, dealt a fatal blow to many Algerians. Even those who had never picked up arms against the French suffered as a result of the general crisis.

Following the occupation of Laghouat in 1852, a tense calm descended on the Djelfa region, yet the Ouled Naïl did not enjoy peace. They faced policies deliberately calculated to prostrate them.[60] As early as 1847 General Marey-Monge wrote, "A population located so far from our posts that is so numerous and so rich merits serious attention."[61] Marey-Monge suggested breaking the

Ouled Naïl materially ("to keep them from getting too rich [we must] take a lot of their grain" [along with an annual tax of 20,000 francs]) and politically ("we must divide this mass between many outside leaders"). Governor-General Bugeaud agreed and split the Ouled Naïl into three parts "in order not to leave 10–12,000 infantrymen in the hands of one man."[62]

When they established the Annex of Djelfa in 1852, leaders at the Division of Algiers were mindful of Marey-Monge's counsel. Eager to retain the upper hand, the Division of Algiers sent its new commandant, General du Barail, a list of projects to consolidate French power. They corresponded exactly to the terms outlined by Marey-Monge five years earlier. In addition to the taxes, requisitions, and political dismemberment, the French forbade the Ouled Naïl from storing grains. This was a particularly well-placed blow. Recognizing the importance of reserve cereals to the Ouled Naïl's economic independence, not to mention basic protection in years of dearth, colonial authorities insisted that after each harvest local populations sell or store their grains at the French-controlled market towns of Laghouat, Djelfa, or el-Hamman.[63] The Ouled Naïl could keep only enough for the winter. As was mentioned in previous chapters, policy makers of the 1840s saw food insecurity as one of their most important weapons for a "pénétration pacifique." Despite the dramatic failure of this policy by 1852, they clung to the idea that controlling the food supply would seal French hegemony. Whereas planners in the metropolis had long looked to establish social peace with a state-guaranteed supply of cereals and reasonably priced quality bread, in Algeria order was sought by means of the threat of famine.[64] Moreover, French control of the foodstuffs trade would integrate pastoralists into the colonial economy.

The cumulative effects of the new economic order combined with the ongoing drought to produce a catastrophe. Between 1867 and 1868 a terrible famine struck Algeria. Throughout the country some eight hundred thousand Algerians died, and in the Division of Algiers more than two hundred thousand succumbed to hunger and hunger-related illness.[65] While drought certainly played an important role in triggering this catastrophe, the victims of hunger died as a consequence of history rather than climate, which is proven by the fact that the European community in Algeria remained unaffected by the food shortages.[66] The famine hit the Ouled Naïl especially hard, claiming thousands of lives. Less than two decades after the French established direct rule, the tragic results of their policies manifest themselves during these years. When famine first hit Djelfa in the fall of 1867, the local commandant described the scene with equal parts disgust and horror: "Herds of women on their knees beg public charity in the street, and they force the town's inhabitants to witness their poor, starving children."[67] Five months later the situation had hardly improved: "Djelfa is still congested [encombré] by a mass of people dying of hunger."[68] Hoping to control the threat of disease these starving people posed for his troops and European settlers, in April 1868 the local commandant moved them to an improvised camp ten kilometers outside of town. The relief effort could only accommodate from two hundred to four hundred people, of which about seventy to a hundred died each month.[69] The deaths of those who were turned away and perished went uncounted. (Although hunger remained endemic through the summer and the following winter, relief funds ran out and the camp was closed on 15 June 1868.) The social and physical destruction resulting from the famine confirmed the view of some local commanders that this was what was needed to maintain order. For example, in March 1868 the commandant of Laghouat observed that "the Ouled Nayls [*sic*] have fallen into absolute stagnation [marasme] and we will not have to worry about them politically for a long time."[70] In addition, the social distribution of famine in these years testifies to the malevolent effects of colonial rule. As an illustration, the Ouled Naïl and the Larbaa (al-Arba'a), pastoralists centered at nearby Laghouat, felt the famine's impact in radically different ways. Both communities lived virtually identical lives as herders and traders between the steppes and the Sahara. However, the Larbaa escaped the famine's worst effects. The French in Laghouat depended upon Larbaa cavalrymen and allowed them to maintain larger herds of camels and horses than those of the Ouled Naïl. With their traditional mobility intact, the Larbaa traveled throughout Algeria, where they found markets selling grain at reasonable prices.

ECONOMIC DECLINE AND SEDENTARIZATION

Nevertheless, compared with Algerians living in the Tell, the people of Djelfa escaped some of the most harmful French policies. These included the various land ordinances, judicial condemnations, sequestrations, *cantonnements*, and outright confiscations that wrested lands away from Algerians in the Tell.[71] For example, Djelfa was spared the most nefarious of these measures, the Sénatus-Consulte of 22 April 1863, which individuated land titles and liberalized their sale, creating what one observer called "the most efficient war mechanism that one could invent against the native social structures."[72] The agriculturally marginal lands of the southern steppes did not attract covetous eyes seeking to dispossess Algerians and create "empty lands."

However, it did not take legions of settlers for French colonialism to alter societies like the Ouled Naïl. As early as 1850 witnesses reported on the crisis facing the region. During the winter of 1850–51, Adrien Berbrugger made one of the first trips by a European to the Algerian oases. He undertook the mission on behalf of the bey of Tunis, who asked him to study the wool trade. Traveling south from Tunis, Berbrugger visited the oases of at El Oued and Touggourt before reaching the Mzab. He found turmoil in the oases in the French zone of influence. The French policy of playing factions against each other created disorder, crippling the society. As Berbrugger wrote, "The ancient hatreds, the mutual grievances, have not yet fallen before our flag. Although recognizing our hegemony [soumises à la France] the people of the Sahara preserve their enmities. They proclaim loudly their loyalty [to France] and then turn around and rob all those who they call their enemies [who now become enemies of France]."[73] This insecurity harmed the economy. The premiums paid by merchants to protect their goods increased, and rising losses resulting from theft further cut into their bottom line. Just as damaging were the effects on agriculture. "The country is becoming depopulated," Berbrugger warned. "Cultivation is breaking up, and the oases are falling into [decline]. It takes an incessant struggle of man against nature to hold back the desiccating desert and the invading sands. The [situation is weighted against the cultivator] and this struggle becomes all the more dissymmetric when the cultivator cannot sell his products because of the insecurity of the routes."[74] He warned that without changes oasis societies might collapse, bringing ruin to the entire regional economy.

Insecurity in the Saharan oases directly affected the Oulad Naïl. For example, entire Naïli families no longer undertook the seasonal migrations. The great transhumance which put entire tribes in motion was disappearing. Small groups of armed shepherds assumed responsibility for the herds on increasingly short migrations, while the rest of the family stayed near cultivated fields. Given the dangers of moving whole families and herds into volatile regions, as well as their growing inability to meet the material needs of transhumance (which demanded a great deal of wealth, tents, weapons, and mounts), many Naïli families had to seek their livelihood through semi-sedentary agriculture.[75] Many in the French administration hoped that these first "indigenous colonists" would transform Algeria by settling on the land.[76] The author of the monthly reports at Djelfa was only too pleased to relate these facts to his superiors. In 1857 he wrote, "Already some factions have abandoned the tent to establish themselves in the ksour, where they are exclusively farmers."[77] The trend continued the succeeding year. The positive report for 1858 mentioned how the Naïli had opened new lands to cultivation and practiced European methods of animal husbandry, keeping herds close to home. The annual report the following year (1859) boasted about the same pattern.[78] In January 1861 the reporter provided the first figures to actually measure the phenomena: the previous year local farmers had opened up an additional 4,630 hectares (11,440 acres) of land to cultivation.[79] The reporter claimed that these families chose to settle voluntarily, seeking a better life as farmers, which seems dubious. Pastoralism in Algeria was an entrenched way of life, as well as a source of pride and part of the collective identity. Pastoralists, the *rahhala*, were esteemed and ranked high on the social ladder. Moreover, from a purely materialistic perspective, pastoralism was the means of production that best suited the local ecology, one that ensured the greatest economic security and sense of well-being.

The social transformations put into motion by the French administration disrupted the traditional economy and placed new burdens on the resources of the Annex. Since scarce rainfall strictly limited the latter, conflicts over land use intensified. The extension of cultivated lands necessarily reduced the area available for grazing and resulted in problems. French archives have little to say about land tenure in the Djelfa region, but they do reveal the tensions produced by different types of land use. The lands increasingly farmed by semi-settled families were not just there for the taking; and the new mode of production that arrived with French rule intensified internal conflicts in the local society. Wherever the soil promised to yield a crop, former pastoralists who had converted to farming would be tempted to clear and farm the land. When herders came to graze their animals in an area with newly cultivated fields, they were left with the job of keeping their animals away from the crops, a task made doubly difficult because small parcels of tilled land suddenly intersected a whole pasture. If these cases made it to French adjudication, the local administrators invariably favored the farmers over the herders. This intensified long-standing rivalries and created new social cleavages that compromised the feelings of solidarity that unified the society.[80]

Conflicts over land use begin to make their appearance in the reports of the Annex of Djelfa in the mid-1850s. People clashed over the same parcels of lands, and there were numerous complaints involving herds damaging crops in planted fields. For example, in the spring of 1861 a violent fight broke out between the Sahari al- Atiyya and the Ouled Bou Charega (Ouled Naïl) over land.[81] It will be recalled that the Sahari and the Ouled Naïl were old rivals. The competition for arable land intensified their conflict, adversely affecting regional stability. The caid of the Sahari al- Atiyya had to intervene to restore order. The standard solution to conflicts between herders and farmers was to make the former pay indemnities, but this did not always calm tempers, with many disputes ending in violence.[82] In March 1861, just prior to the attack on Djelfa, one such incident ended in a brawl between old rivals, the Sahari and the Ouled Bou Abdallah, a Naïli group.[83] Surprisingly, the French administrator was not alarmed. Rather, he saw in these incidents an indication of the "progress" that was being made in the area of settled agriculture.[84] In December 1858, after detailing a particularly bitter land dispute, the commander at Djelfa wrote, "[This] marks the progressive and favorable situation in which they find themselves."[85]

Just prior to the 1861 attack, a decision made at Médéa magnified these tensions and created a critical situation for herders at Djelfa. In the spring of 1860 the French command refused to issue to the Larbaa confederation the permit necessary to travel to their traditional summer ranges in the Tell. The subdivision commander did not give his exact reasons. His refusal may have been related to Larbaa reluctance to pay the right of passage to their hosts in the Tell, or he may have sought to keep the Larbaa together and preserve their military capacities through the summer. (It could take more than a month to assemble the Larbaa cavalry members once they were dispersed on their summer pastures.)[86] In either case the Larbaa pastured their animals on the Zahrez, the traditional range of the Naïli group, the Ouled Si Mhammad. Already depleted by a long drought, these pastures could not support so many animals. Local commanders were not blind to the problem and tried to impress upon their superiors the detrimental effects of the order. In August 1860 the commander at Laghouat expressed his concern. He shrewdly began his letter with flattery by expressing his agreement that the Larbaa had to accept French authority. This measure would convince them that summer grazing in the Tell was "a privilege" rather than "a natural right." But, he asked, "Is it not [right] to fear that now [that the Larbaa are] kept in the limits of the Circle, there will not result for them and the Ouled Naïl, on the territory where they are often camped, serious disadvantages and major difficulties for the nourishment of the herds?"[87] This plea went unanswered. In January 1861, just months before the attack on Djelfa, Larbaa herds competed directly with those of the Ouled Naïl for the little fodder that remained in the Zahrez.[88]

THE MONTHLY REPORTS

By the end of the century, French observers reported that colonial policies had fatally compromised the ecology of the steppes. In 1906 a detailed investigation concluded that intense market-driven exploitation, overgrazing, and farming had "transformed part of these lands into a new desert."[89] It might prove useful to review some of the monthly reports from the Annex of Djelfa and the Circle of Laghouat to gauge the situation at Djelfa. Read across the grain of their contradictions (either laconic observations of crisis or verbosely optimistic forecasts), these documents provide dramatic testimony of the cumulative effects of less than a decade of French rule. Shepherds watched their livestock steadily decline in health and number during this time: ewes lost weight, aborted, or gave birth to weak lambs unable to resist the trials of their first few weeks of life. A strange illness, the *bedrouna*, swept through the herds, further decimating their numbers.[90]

In July 1857 the reporter at Djelfa wrote that drought and poor pastures had decimated the herds of the Ouled Saad ben Salem. The following month the same conditions forced the Ouled Bou Abdallah out of their traditional ranges.[91] The ensuing years (1859–60) witnessed the same trend: "pastures are in poor condition, the herders left early for their winter pastures in the desert, high mortality among herds, and the animals on the market are poorly nourished";[92] "a great mortality" among herds;[93] "mortality in alarming proportions";[94] "the misery of the people has been high this year."[95] These trends reached their climax in 1861, when the Ouled Naïl lost 50 percent of their ewes to disease.[96]

Cultivated agriculture did not fare much better. The cutting of barley had just begun in early June 1857 when hail pounded the fields. In the Djebel Sahari north of Djelfa the grain harvest was a complete failure.[97] The following year farmers narrowly escaped the same fate when a hailstorm struck the Annex right after the harvest.[98] Even so, the year's harvest was poor and many farmers had to travel to the Tell to purchase seed for the following year.[99] The year 1859 opened with much optimism, but the crops withered under the effects of the drought. By summer the administrator noted pessimistically that grain fields would "not give the results that we expected." At harvest time farmers had barely enough for next year's seed.[100] The following year they were cruelly deceived again when spring storms devastated the fields. As one report noted, "Certain localities have been hit by large balls of hail, which have seriously damaged the harvests. In others floods came down from the mountains and carried away all the crops lying in their path. In short, the harvest of 1860, which opened under such ideal conditions, will not be as brilliant as one would have hoped."[101] It was, in fact, a total failure. For the third year in a row farmers would recover only seed from their devastated fields.[102] This brought some families to a crisis point. With the 1860 harvest decimated and the price of cereals skyrocketing, many requested permission to travel to the Tell and find work, hoping to earn enough to nourish themselves through the year.[103]

Food prices remained high across Algeria during these years, especially in Djelfa. Some petitioned the Bureau Arabe to travel to Sétif and the Hodna to find better prices, but their efforts produced little relief. In August 1860 barley sold for 80–90 francs for a *karubia* (an unspecified local unit of measure) and the price of wheat went up to 100–120 francs. In September the monthly reporter minced few words: the cereals available "are insufficient to meet the needs of the population and their prices are rising to high levels."[104]

As if all this was not enough, a few months before Ramadan 1861 a new menace appeared in the Annex. As one monthly report stated, "The wheat had barely sprouted when it became prey to an unusual enemy: large herds of gazelle driven out of the South by the lack of water."[105] In February 1861. when de Sonis, the commandant of Laghouat, came north for a tour of the Djelfa region, he saw how poorly people were faring and wrote in the margin of his monthly report, "There is reason to have little hope in the products of our lands this year."[106]

Throughout the colonial period, French administrators rarely failed to praise Algerians for their courage in the face of natural hardships. Rather than rebelling against man or cursing God, Algerians reputedly accepted setbacks with a fatalistic attitude. For the French this was an example of the Algerian belief in *Mektoub* (a French transcription of the Arabic *maktūb*, "it is written"). For colonial authors this was "a résumé of Moslem fatalism."[107] However, the people of Djelfa were showing signs of something other than resignation in the years leading up to the April 1861 attack. One of the first incidents took place in October

1859, when an unnamed "Chérif" came to the attention of the administration for proclaiming that England had united with the Algerian people against the French.[108] Whoever joined him in rebellion, he said, could count on a constant supply of arms supplied by the British navy. His arrest and imprisonment did not quell tensions. The same month another agitator appeared among the Sahari al-'Atiyya. This man, Rabah ben Frouk, gained attention by announcing that a republic had been declared in Paris.[109] The sources do not say exactly what hopes Rabah ben Frouk placed in a republican form of government, but he was in the mood to celebrate. To mark the occasion, he ignited a straw stack belonging to the caid.[110]

By 1861 the people of Djelfa faced a critical economic situation. Many observers in the administration wanted to locate the cause of the crisis in the ongoing drought. Certainly the impact of the harsh climate was not negligible. Drought, floods, hail, and insects devastated the crops and herds of Djelfa like so many biblical plagues. Leading up to the April 1861 attack, the region had endured six years of poor rainfall; the winter pastures of the Sahara had not seen a drop of rain all winter, which was normally the wettest season.[111] Nonetheless, the Ouled Naïl had long survived nature's deluges, the "misfortunes of the age."[112] People living at the edge of the Sahara had developed agricultural techniques and economic strategies that allowed them to weather the periods of dearth thanks to the resources amassed during good years. These included stores of grains and dates and healthy herds. In addition, their horses and camels enabled the Ouled Naïl to trade far and wide, from the Sahara to the Mediterranean Sea. When the harvest failed in one area, this high degree of mobility ensured that they could travel elsewhere to find affordable foodstuffs.

Historian Lucette Valensi has shown that French colonization changed the balance in North Africa from a sluggish economic equilibrium of subsistence agriculture to a volatile and ultimately disastrous disequilibrium.[113] This change occurred with great speed in the Algerian steppes, even though they were far from the centers of colonial power. Camels and horses were lost to wars and requisitions, and families could no longer travel with their herds, which were already dwindling. With the loss of mobility, the economic options of people narrowed. Moreover, the intensifying political volatility and violence in the Sahara made trade precarious and dangerous, impacting the all-important foodstuffs commerce and the transhumance. By the twentieth century people, not sheep, migrated from Djelfa to the Tell, a rural proletariat seeking work.[114] In the 1860s these changes that resulted from colonial rule compromised some of the most important safeguards that had given local people a margin of economic security, setting in motion forces that would fatally compromise pastoral society for the thousands of victims of the famine of 1867–68. In sum, this was a period when the Ouled Naïl entered what, in tribute to the work of the late M'hamed Boukhobza, I call a "nomadism of despair."[115]

THE LEADERSHIP CRISIS
AND RURAL MARABOUTS

Historian Charles André Julien once noted, "The conflicts between the tribes and French troops . . . had primary economic causes."[1] If he was correct, then the Ouled Naïl had sufficient cause to rise up against the French in 1861. But other troubles weighed on the people of Djelfa that were perhaps more disconcerting than their material impoverishment or the French occupation. The great living saint and leader of the Saharan branch of the Rahmaniyya Sufi order, Si Mokhtar ben Khalifa (Si Muhammad ibn al-Shaykh al-Mukhtar 'Abd al-Rahman ibn Khalifa, 1788–1860), had passed away the previous autumn (between September and December 1860), and his death spread grief and fear throughout the region. Mokhtar had been a student of the Rahmaniyya sheikh Muhammad ben Azzuz, and he represented the Rahmaniyya Sufi order in the Sahara from the *zāwiya* (Sufi center) he had founded in 1815 at Ouled-Djellal, 150 kilometers to the southeast of Djelfa.[2]

Mokhtar was not the first holy personage the Ouled Naïl had lost, and they hoped that his *baraka* (blessing) would continue to radiate from his richly decorated tomb in the *zawiya* at Ouled-Djellal.[3] Nevertheless his death left a void. The Ouled Naïl revered Mokhtar. He was an intimate of God, a *walī* (saint), and he embodied perfection. He knew well the difficult path toward God that confronted the Sufi novice. The *khouans* (*ikhwān*, "aspirants on the way") looked to Si Mokhtar for his education, or *tarbiyya*, and all the faithful solicited his *baraka*.[4] Mokhtar was well placed to advise the Ouled Naïl in temporal matters as well. His close relationship with God and his clarity of thought placed this saint in a unique position to counsel the Ouled Naïl. He had helped them through one of the most traumatic episodes of recent memory, namely, the French conquest. They sought his advice regarding how to protect themselves from the worst defeats suffered by their neighbors. As hopes for a military solution to the French occupation faded, he expressed his thoughts on how to live with Algeria's new rulers in a religiously orthodox and permissible fashion.[5] His responses to the French varied according to the possibilities of the day. When French power first manifested itself in the steppes, Si Mokhtar supported armed resistance. On four separate occasions he threw his weight behind those taking up arms against the French, aligning himself with Abdelkader in 1837, Bou Maza (Bū Maza)in 1847, and giving discreet aid to Bou Ziyan in 1849 (discreet inasmuch as many French analysts at the time thought he had remained neutral), and Muhammad ben Abdallah in the early 1850s.[6] After 1852 a grid of permanent French bases covered the region, and it would be a decade before local people again raised the banner of armed revolt. During this time, Mokhtar withdrew from politics and accepted only minimal contact with the French. He died before the Ouled Sidi Cheikh rallied the people of Djelfa in revolt in 1864.[7]

Adding to the anxiety surrounding Mokhtar's death was the fact that the question of his succession had not been arranged to the satisfaction of all concerned. Mokhtar had fathered six sons, but none was old enough to head the *zawiya*.[8] The official successor was his most devoted student, Si Muhammad ben Belkacem (Muhammad ibn Abi al-Qasim). Reputedly he had been hand-picked by Mokhtar and enjoyed the support of Muhammad ben Azzuz, the leader of the powerful Rahmaniyya *zawiya* at Nefta (Tunisia). Yet Belkacem did not enjoy the trust of the local population, which caused lasting problems for the local Rahmaniyya that continued into the twentieth century with respect to the *zawiya* at El-Hamel and the succession of Belkacem's daughter, Lalla Zaynab.[9] "In spite of his great qualities," a French analyst observed, "he has not managed to obtain the locals' loyalty. Sheikh Mokhtar from his tomb remains the true and only marabout."[10]

DISMANTLING TRADITIONAL AUTHORITY

Immensely important, the Sufi orders were not the only structure of authority among the Ouled Naïl. Secular notables, the *a'yān*, wielded power based upon their personal prestige, courage, and liberality, as well as such factors as *nasab* and *hasab* (ancestry), *khalīka mahmūda* (good character), *sabr* (patience), and *'akl* (intelligence).[11] While the French administration at Djelfa held a mixed opinion of the local Sufi sheikhs, commanders worked hard to undermine the secular leadership of the Ouled Naïl, whom they viewed as dangerous rivals.[12] Overall the administration of Algerians in the interior of the country went through many stages as policy makers sought to rule the country in a way that ensured stability at minimum cost. By 1852, when direct rule had been established at Djelfa, certain ideas had emerged concerning how to deal with local leaders and the tribes. The goal, according to historian Annie Rey-Goldzeiguer, was not to abolish traditional society entirely but rather to change its political structure by "creating a new structure of authority within it that better responded to French interests.[13] On this count, what the French knew as the *tribu*, or tribe, was a useful institution, one that gave the French a point of contact within local society, with its established structures and organizations. The *tribu* gave administrators a way to map the social and political geography of rural Algeria. Moreover, it offered one of the only institutions through which French power might flow into Algeria's vast interior, where 95 percent of Algeria's precolonial population lived. Inasmuch as they served as vehicles of alliance, the *tribus* even promised to endow a stable political personality to whole groups.[14]

Of course, the tribe was also the social institution that channeled armed resistance against the French. French commanders hoped that the terror generated by the army's campaigns and razzias would weaken its social bonds. The tribe was thus something that had to be contained and controlled. In times of peace, the most important goal was to transform it so that it would be more receptive to the French will. One way of doing this was to dismantle traditional structures of authority and target secular notables. A colonial myth grew up around Algerian notables during this period, presenting them as both self-serving schemers and supremely courageous warriors. As the influential colonial administrator Augustin Berque put it rather absurdly, they were "Machiavelli in a turban, Roland in a crimson burnous."[15] The French considered notables locally omnipotent, mini-despots, people useful in certain circumstances but generally dangerous and in need of control. Thus, whenever feasible the French tried to bypass the traditional leadership and select people as caids who, although Algerian, were outsiders to the tribe they were to administer. As sociologist Mhfoud Smati has observed, this was done in the belief that caids who were "strangers to the population that they were called upon to administer . . . [would] not share [their] views."[16] Not benefiting from tribal solidarity, the thinking went, outside caids would be dependent on the French, and consequently vulnerable and more responsive. With the Ouled Naïl, this policy began early. Already in 1849 the French decapitated the Ouled Si Ahmed in a raid that killed ten of their leaders and captured another forty.[17] In 1855 another purge further depleted the ranks of notables. The commandant at Laghouat wrote, "Some of the leaders of the Ouled Naïl seek to exercise an influence on the populations that is contrary to our interests. We had to change them, and they were replaced by devoted men, strangers to this region and thus outside of tribal intrigues."[18] This officer went on to outline his theory in candid terms: "We have succeeded in substituting our direct authority for that of the great indigenous chiefs, who formed an invisible barrier between the administered and us. The populations, under less pressure [from their own leaders], take heart in the justice and impartiality of our government, relations grow, and the racial antipathies disappear."[19] Rarely, however, did this direct authority achieve the desired results. The policy was at odds with the ways that power, leadership, and legitimacy worked in Algerian society. But it was part of a long-term process by which the relationship between French administrators and the Algerian caids transformed the basis of authority in the society at large. This process included substituting an impersonal, rule-based control, for the traditional face-to-face relations, which privileged the personal and affective.[20]

In the short term, the policy left local society without effective voices of direction and authority. As one French informer put it in 1873, "Men without personal influence can exercise power behind our bayonets, but they do not have the power to attach the populations to us."[21] At Djelfa the caids of the Annex were fined (*limogés*) and subjected to various symbolic abasements that marked them as lackeys of the administration. In one case a caid of the Ouled Naïl carried the most visible signs of his subordination to the French: he was missing both ears, cut off by French troops in 1852 (to collect the bounty that the army paid on Algerian ears). Carrying the scars of his humiliation, he was nonetheless described by a French commentator as "one of our most faithful servants."[22]

This policy was not without its critics in the administration. Colonel de Colomb, the commandant at Géryville, loudly criticized it after the Ouled Sidi Cheikh took up arms against the French in 1864.[23] Twelve years earlier Si Hamza ibn Abi Bakr (ca. 1810–1861), the leader of this powerful tribe, had agreed under duress to become the French *khalifa* of the Sahara.[24] This relationship greatly expanded the reach of the Ouled Sidi Cheikh, but it may also have cost Si Hamza himself much of his legitimacy. Even within his family opposition developed in reaction to the demands made on him. A series of mysterious deaths among family members who were close to the French provided proof to critics like Colomb that this policy was fraught with danger. Three years later, when his successors rose up in rebellion, many in Algiers and Paris sounded the tocsin of Muslim "fanaticism," whereas Colomb placed the blame on the effects of French treatment of their intermediaries: "The tendency of our policy to diminish [the powers] of our great indigenous leaders . . . was felt even here, where we had an interest in caressing and maintaining the family (by giving them great advantages), which was the key to our Saharan edifice."[25] In other words, respected and legitimate leadership was less dangerous than the power vacuums created by French policy.

Within the Ouled Naïl the *bach agha*, Si Chérif ben el-Ahrach, was in a similar predicament. He had to walk a fine line in order to preserve his standing among the Ouled Naïl and his political clout with the French. Unlike many lesser caids, Si Chérif was a Naïli, descended from a prestigious and esteemed family, and enjoyed respect. His family included many religious personages with close ties to the *zawiya* of Si Mokthar at Ouled-Djellel, where Si Chérif himself spent much of his youth. Prior to the arrival of the French, he had joined Abdelkader's struggle (part of the caidship the emir had organized in the region in 1836 under Si Chérif's uncle), and he had fought with the emir in his campaigns (1845–46) in the Saharan Atlas and the Kabylie.[26] Later, however, Si Chérif sided with the French against Muhammad ben Abdallah and led Naïli cavalry against the rebel in 1852 despite the fact that many Ouled Naïl answered Muhammad ben Abdallah's call to arms.[27] Si Chérif's accommodation with the French, and the fact that he now ruled in the invader's name, eroded much of his support and irked many. Maintaining the confidence of both the Ouled Naïl and the French was a difficult if not impossible task. Si Chérif had a European wife, a Spaniard named María Dolores, and he made sure to make the appropriate symbolic gestures to French colonialism, such as contributing to the construction of Djelfa's first church.[28] But being too close to the French made him suspect in the eyes of the Ouled Naïl. Contrary to his orders, in 1864 many Naïl groups joined the Ouled Sidi Cheikh in revolt. He was killed that same year in a confrontation with the rebels.[29]

Although they had eliminated potential rivals for power, French efforts had not succeeded in a clean sweep of Naïli society. There were still a host of lesser notables who enjoyed the esteem of their peers. Nevertheless, the growing power of the French over daily life, and the lack of influence such men had with the colonial administration, made them increasingly irrelevant. They had little voice in the outcome of such critical questions as taxation, property rights, trade, and food supply. Commanding the respect of the Naïli, they were ignored by those who now called the shots at Djelfa. In sum, by the 1860s colonial rule had bypassed the traditional secular leaders at Djelfa. The men the French chose were unable and often unwilling to represent and protect the interests of local people.

RAMADAN, 1861 (1277 A.H.):
THE ARRIVAL OF SI TAYEB BEN BOU CHANDOUGHA

"General disarray favors the man of God," anthropologist Abdellah Hammoudi has observed.[30] Quite so. The arrival of Si Tayeb ben Bou Chandougha (Si Tayyib ibn Bu Shandugha) supports Hammoudi's contention that the living saints of the Maghreb have been produced by and, in turn, often reproduce crises.[31] Si Tayeb appeared in the camps in the Zahrez pastures a week before the beginning of Ramadan. According to most witnesses, he was a stranger to the Ouled Si Ahmed, the Naïli group that first extended him hospitality. But it did not take long before his exceptional piety made him a figure of renown. "He prayed louder than the others," witnesses noted, "and took control of the *ḥaḍra* [Sufi sessions] by the intensity and elation of his piety." Others observed, "He projected an aura of seriousness and importance, and he furiously beat the *bendir* [drum]. Soon the most earnestly pronounced *halḳa* and the most pious meetings were those where he was in attendance."[32] After his stay with the Ouled Si Ahmed, Si Tayeb visited all the Ouled Si Mhammad. And it was not long before Tayeb's arrival made something of a sensation in the Annex: "His reputation extended to all the neighboring areas and soon one spoke of nothing save Si Tayeb ben Chandougha."[33]

It is unlikely that all the details of Si Tayeb's life story will ever be known, but French investigators recorded some important information. According to the interpreter Arnaud, Si Tayeb was a dashing personality. About thirty-five years of age, he is described as "tall, with a light brown beard and a pale, bony face. His high cheekbones are enflamed by the fatigue of his long and passionate prayers, and his eyes shine with a dark glare. He has no education and barely knows how to read. He is of less than illustrious origins. Before being the *One inspired by the Prophet*, he was happy to be able to call himself the *sekhar* [servant] of a spahis. However, the most exalted figures came to call him *Si* Tayeb [an honorific form of address] and to kiss his hands."[34]

Arnaud based his account on the testimony of those interrogated following the attack. A close examination of the transcripts of these interviews reveals other details about Si Tayeb. Like most itinerant holy men and aspirants to sainthood, Si Tayeb was regarded as an outsider by the people among whom he proselytized. Nearly all those interviewed insisted that Si Tayeb was a stranger to the Ouled Si Mhammad, claiming they had not known him before the spring of 1861. Only one member of the Ouled Si Ahmed, Abderrahman ben Dekcha, professed an acquaintance with him dating back several years. Dekcha was a herder in the service of Muhammad ben Aziez, the agha of the Ouled Si Mhammad, and Dekcha claimed he had known the future saint from the time (1856) when he was in the service of the agha's son, a spahis.[35] The veracity of this story is supported by the fact that at the beginning of Ramadan, Si Tayeb stayed with the Aziez family. Of obscure origin although perhaps not a total stranger to the Ouled Naïl, Si Tayeb was surrounded by an aura of mystery.

Although French investigators worked hard to determine who he met, as well as when and where, they did not succeed in fully documenting Tayeb's movements in their reports. The shepherd Dekcha testified that on the third day of Ramadan Si Tayeb was with the Ouled Si Mhammad, where he began to "cast his spells on many individuals among the *khouans* and others camped with Muhammad ben Aziez."[36] Afterward he sped throughout the local camps. Arnaud mentioned that Si Tayeb "visited all the tribes of the Ouled Oum Hani,

Ouled el-Ghouini, Ouled Abd el-Kader, [and the] Ouled Bou Abdallah [all of the Ouled Si Mhammad]."[37] The speed with which he traversed the Annex on these visits stunned all and further testified to his saintliness; only the gossip about Tayeb's magical deeds traveled as fast. Appearing far and wide, Si Tayeb defied the rules governing space and time. In Tayeb's celerity the Ouled Si Mhammad saw the saintly gift of ubiquity.

He also convinced many of his supernatural powers. Before the beginning of Ramadan one witness reported that Si Tayeb appeared normal, "like all of us," but during the month his piety became intense and his powers over others grew.[38] He soon gained a reputation for magic, or what the French reporter called "sorcellerie" (the original Arabic term is not given). Messaoud ben Mohad, a fifteen-year-old youth, reported that "people began speaking of [Si Tayeb] because by means of his signs and words he was able to put many in a state of ecstasy that rendered him all-powerful over them and left them entirely under his domination."[39] How was Si Tayeb able to exercise this power over others? Ali ben Mokhtar (a.k.a. Mohad) ben Fodail said: "Si Tayeb approached us and murmured in our ears words that we did not understand. He blew on our faces and swept his arms over us. He spit in our mouths. After this, we fell to the ground wailing. He would then hit us repeatedly with his staff. We felt as if flames shot through our chests, and we suffered great pains in our heads. We didn't have the strength to resist the will of the *mukaddam* any longer, and the ground gave way under our feet. We hastened to follow him everywhere."[40] Through his breath, voice, gestures, and saliva—as well as beatings—Tayeb's followers experienced the imposition of the new saint's will. Another witness reported the same scene: "He took their heads between his two hands and murmured in their ears words they didn't understand. They would then faint and fall, and when they woke up, they started to dance."[41]

THE MARABOUTS OF ALGERIA

A solitary and uneducated outsider who professed a special relationship with the supernatural and the sacred, Si Tayeb belonged to the highly diverse class of saintly individuals who populate the pantheon of the Maghreb. Popular beliefs have given rise to a profuse number of holy personalities. Perhaps the most ubiquitous is the itinerant holy man (*suwwāh*).[42] Belonging to what colonial authorities knew as "marabouts"[43] (from the Arabic *murābiṭ*), they comprised a diverse group of persons of local importance who, by virtue of outward piety, supernatural abilities, and other qualities, demonstrated a close relationship with God and an ability to mediate between the natural and supernatural worlds.[44] There are multiple dimensions to understanding the marabouts of Algeria. In some ways they can be seen as analogues to other Mediterranean social actors who achieved standing by exploiting gaps within seemingly immobile institutions for their own purposes. Like the unsophisticated seventeenth-century priest and exorcist Giovan Battista, studied by historian Giovanni Levi, marabouts functioned as local political entrepreneurs, people who amassed wealth and power from networks of social relations based on reciprocal solidarity, dependence, and inequality.[45] Certain values and norms specific to Muslim societies differentiated the marabouts. Orthodox theologians identified four sources of saintliness: genealogy (*nasab*); asceticism (*khalwa*); excellence in defense of Islam against aggression (jihad, *ribāṭ*); and miracles (*karāmāt*).[46] Recognized ties to the Sufi orders (*ṭarīka*) and education (including studies with renowned masters and involvement with the scriptural and philosophical traditions of Islam) also figured in the ranking of religious elites. Although marabouts might possess some of these qualities, they generally lacked the more formal signs of saintliness, such as genealogy and education. However, it was not the theologians who judged marabouts but the common believers. They expected marabouts to respond to different concerns than learned sheikhs and were less attentive to orthodox markers of saintliness.[47] People decided sainthood in terms of their patronage, alms, hospitality, and fidelity. Popular religiosity privileged the immediate and the local over the hierarchical and the scriptural in a way that favored holy men like Si Tayeb. Thaumaturgy and miraculous gifts were especially powerful markers of holiness.[48] Miracles generally responded to the needs of rural people, who suffered from devastating outbreaks of disease, common illnesses, and an unpredictable and harsh climate. Therefore, the most important miracles included locating springs, returning wayward livestock, protecting crops and pastures, and resuscitating dead palms—what historical anthropologist Houari Touati has called "a sacred of agricultural efficiency."[49] These spectacular and visible manifestations of power were a privileged marker of the divinely inspired marabouts and helped people judge the worthiness of possible candidates: "Here was irrefutable proof of the distinction between the true saint and the imposter. . . . The maraboutic saints presented themselves as the genuine holders of *karāmāt* ["marvels" or miracles] by showing themselves imaginative in their gestures and their intentions, to surprise their audience and preserve their hold on the masses."[50]

Possession of the resource of *baraka* was another marker. Literally meaning "blessing," *baraka* is a beneficent force that comes from God, who invests it in certain beings and things.[51] It is difficult to grasp the full social import of *baraka*, a word Clifford Geertz has said "is better to talk about than to define."[52] Those touched by *baraka* enjoy "superabundance in the physical sphere and prosperity and happiness in the psychic order."[53] A man or woman who was instilled with *baraka* could cure the sick and bring the fertility and good fortune that all sought in this difficult region. Individuals who claimed control over these forces could expect people to offer their patronage in return. Like the healing touch of medieval European monarchs, *baraka* nourished secular power.[54] However, those who sought to convert it into political power found it difficult to establish lasting power. *Baraka* "can increase or decrease according to the circumstances or the beings with which it comes into contact."[55] Its vectors were diffuse and it tended to be disputed and in need of reaffirmation.[56] In short, *baraka* could be a fickle ally.

THE CONFLICT AMONG THE *MUKADDAMS*

In theory the "path to sainthood" was open to all.[57] Its access was not barred by formal or institutional obstacles. As Houari Touati has written, "Anyone who knew how to exploit their personal talent and luck could follow, without too many difficulties, a saintly career."[58] However, it was a path that had many steps and detours. Si Tayeb had earned the confidence of the Ouled Si Mhammad by means of his piety and supernatural powers, and his influence had grown rapidly among other Naïli groups. While the paths to religious authority were democratic, those who traveled them could be expected to have their candidacy challenged and contested. Inspired individuals might earn a following and make themselves useful to the people who offered their patronage, but they had to contend with others who already held positions of religious influence. These positions might involve political power and considerable wealth, and those who held them could be expected to vigorously guard their assets. Moreover, there were more than material matters at stake in the rise of new saints. Religious elites had to be concerned with charlatans, *dajjāl* (imposters), and the *majnūn* (psychotics), who might deceive the faithful and misrepresent the sources of their power (e.g., black magic, or those who trafficked with malevolent spirits, the *jinn*).[59] For these two reasons, when new marabouts came onto the scene they could expect that their claims would be regarded with suspicion.

In the specific case under discussion, Tayeb's bid to religious authority was fueled by the volatile forces of magic, devotion, and belief. His rapid rise impinged upon the domains of several established interests. These were represented by Si Sadoq ben Sifer, a respected *mukaddam* of the Rahmaniyya who lived with the Ouled Naïl.[60] He had close ties to the caid of the Ouled Si Mhammad and the powerful bach agha of the Ouled Naïl confederacy, Si Chérif ben el-Ahrach, who was himself a *mukaddam* of Si Mokhtar.[61] Si Sadoq also enjoyed the restrained confidence of the French administration at Djelfa.[62] The newcomer Tayeb's ascendancy directly impinged upon Si Sadoq's position. Although the latter had little to say to the French investigators—his testimony is disappointingly laconic—his actions betrayed the fact that he regarded the rising fame of Si Tayeb with a good deal of uncertainty, if not outright mistrust. In his account Arnaud reports that there was a full-blown rivalry between the two:

"[Si Tayeb] had frequent meetings with the *mukaddams*. [They were obliged] to tolerate his fits in order to conserve their popularity among the brothers. Everywhere they kissed the tails of his spattered burnous and they all called him Monsignor [i.e., Si] Tayeb."[63] Si Sadoq was worried that "the best pronounced prayers were those where [Si Tayeb] was present. He became the true leader of all the meetings."[64] Si Sadoq may not have been involved in a bitter power struggle, as Arnaud suggests, but he would have wanted more time to judge the veracity of Tayeb's claims and measure the depths of popular devotion to the newcomer.[65] Popular fidelity to saints was notoriously capricious, and already some were saying that Si Tayeb was not Si Mokhtar's chosen *mukaddam* but rather a simple *khouan* like many others.[66] Clear answers to these questions were important and essential to sort out the validity of Tayeb's claim. Under normal circumstances time might have revealed Si Tayeb as a true saint or an imposter. But his arrival occurred at a particularly delicate and urgent moment. Who would succeed Si Mokhtar at Ouled-Djellel? Even if Si Tayeb himself had pronounced nothing on the subject, his growing influence among the Ouled Si Mhammad faction—the most powerful Naïli group in the area—would give him an important role in determining the future of the *zawiya*.

[6]

A HOLIDAY GONE WRONG
The Attack on Djelfa

The French investigative team worked like police detectives in the days following the attack. They convened hearings, conducted interrogations, performed autopsies, and established a chronology for the events leading up to the assault. The goal was to discover the motive behind the crime and establish the identity of the perpetrators, as well as to assess the political ramifications. These efforts resulted in an archive detailed enough to provide a narrative reconstruction of the days leading up to the attack.

THE END OF RAMADAN AND THE *ZIYARA*

On 12 April the festival marking the end of Ramadan, 'īd al-fiṭr, was an occasion for public prayer, family gatherings, and celebrations. The French assigned the beginning of the attack to this day. Si Tayeb celebrated īd with the Ouled el-Ghouini. He also visited the Ouled Oum Hani and the Ouled Chérif (of the Ouled Si Ahmed).[1] Among the latter, the caid Ben Slim ben Fedaïl offered him hospitality.[2] It was here that Si Tayeb held a large meeting that was attended by roughly thirty *khouans* from all the groups of the Ouled Si Mhammad, plus three individuals from the Sahari Khubaïza, their traditional rivals.[3] Here Si Tayeb announced that he would be leading the *ziyara* (ziyāra), a "visit" or pilgrimage to the *zawiya* of Si Mokhtar at Ouled-Djellal and to the tomb of Abd al-Rahman ibn Salam ibn Malik ibn Na'il (the eponym of the Ouled Naïl) at Aïn-Riche, on the path to Ouled-Djellal.[4] In the early afternoon on 12 April 1861 Si Tayeb assembled his followers and departed.

Si Sadoq, for his part, celebrated the end of Ramadan with Si Chérif ben el-Ahrach, the bach agha of the Ouled Naïl confederacy. Here he learned of the *ziyara* of Si Tayeb and the news worried him. The fact that a group of more than fifty people followed Si Tayeb on the highly symbolic route to Ouled-Djellal showed him how much influence the newcomer had gained in just one month. Concerned about his intentions, Si Sadoq immediately sent a messenger to tell Si Tayeb to return. Si Tayeb did not delay in sending back his refusal. Faced with this crisis, Si Sadoq immediately set off after the *ziyara* party.[5] The following day (13 April) he caught up with the group. There are no details of what, if anything, passed between the two, but one witness reported that Si Tayeb's followers showed no signs of partisanship. As this person testified, Sadoq enjoyed a warm welcome: the women let out joyous ululant cries and the men "ran forth to meet him, beating on their drums," before setting off.[6]

The party was large. About eighty people—mostly men but a handful of women and boys—participated. They led some sixty sheep and goats and carried a quantity of butter, intended as an offering.[7] Si Sadoq left his rival behind and took a place ahead of the main party together with a few faithful men and the women and children who herded the livestock. At midday (14 April) the pilgrims arrived at Mouilah, a place situated to the east of Djelfa, intersecting the path to Bou-Saada and Ouled-Djellal. Here Si Tayeb served his followers their meal. As one witness reported, "He spread out two burnouses and called everyone around him to form a circle. He distributed to each one *rouina* and *ka'bouche* [a paste of water and flour ground from grilled grain; a loaf of ground dates and butter]." Shortly after distributing the food, Si Tayeb unexpectedly exploded in anger and attacked his followers: "Si Tayeb took his staff in one hand and beat the *khouans* with it. In the other hand he held a knife, which he used to menace them."[8] In the midst of kicking, beating, and threats, Si Tayeb announced a change in plans. "We are going to return!" he cried out.[9] This statement, which seemed to announce the cancellation of the *ziyara*, spread confusion through the ranks. Unsure and fearful, some looked to Si Sadoq for leadership. "One *khouan* broke away from the band to alert Si Sadoq. [Sadoq] returned but did not speak with Si Tayeb. [He] stopped several feet from the troop [and] then retook the same path by which [we] had arrived."[10] Fearful of Si Tayeb's course of action yet wishing to avoid a direct confrontation, Si Sadoq chose to break with the upstart, calling upon the women and children to follow him back to camp.

The others—some fifty men and older boys—turned back west on a separate trail. The mood among the pilgrims had changed from joy to confusion. To keep them on track, Si Tayeb followed closely behind and, according to one witness, "pushed them before him like a flock of sheep."[11] By nightfall they had reached Bou Trifis, an hour and a half from Djelfa. Here Si Tayeb announced his plan to attack the European village and the French army base. "We are going to Djelfa," he cried. "You will only have to watch. With the tip of my finger I alone will exterminate Djelfa. The Christians' powder will not speak against you."[12] Looking into the astonished faces around him, Si Tayeb insisted, "I need do no more than blow on the French to make them disappear."[13] For some this was convincing. One follower reported, "We believed him and began marching, God wanted it thus."[14] Others remained doubtful. They had started out on a peaceful trip to demonstrate their devotion to a beloved saint, but the radical change in plans—from *ziyara* to revolt—had caught them off guard. Moreover, even though many had already raised arms against the French and would soon do so again, they were not prepared for an attack. Only a half dozen men had knives, and others had nothing more deadly than their staffs. However, Si Tayeb's claims that he could use magic to defeat the French were a powerful incentive. Popular lore provided many examples of saintly individuals who had decided the outcome of a battle thanks to their supernatural powers. But even on this count Si Tayeb was unprepared, and he could not even produce the prophylactic talismans used by saints to protect their followers from the enemy's arms.[15]

Not sharing the aspiring saint's view of things, a sizable group of his followers decided to take their leave. Si Tayeb immediately rained a shower of blows upon the dissidents. He attacked them with his staff, continued to kick those who fell to the ground, and brandished—but did not use—his knife. The beatings some received were severe. Ahmed ben Kouider ben Ahmed was struck with such force that he lost consciousness.[16] Others reported that Si Tayeb used magic to force them to follow him. A twelve-year-old boy testified, "I followed Si Tayeb along with many individuals, among whom were several children. He would take us by the neck, lift us off the ground, and blow on our faces. Then we started yelling and followed him wherever he wanted."[17] Faced with such powers, many felt themselves totally helpless. According to Arnaud's summary of their testimony, "Some had the intention to defend themselves and leave, but they could not lift their arms, their tongues would not speak, and their legs carried them back against their will near Si Tayeb. The ground itself opened up under their steps."[18] Si Tayeb's powers were less potent for others. A young man from the Ouled Chérif who claimed not to have heard his plans to attack Djelfa was "fearful that he would beat me like he beat the others" and fled into the night.[19]

Putting the Garrison to Sleep

Having thus rallied his party, Si Tayeb set off for the French village. It did not take long for the group to cover the last ground that separated them from Djelfa.

The *bordj* (fort) that housed the French garrison of Djelfa was on the outskirts of the village, and the party approached it cautiously and quietly under the cover of darkness. First they arrived at the house of the troop's gardener, located fifty meters from the bordj. As his followers stayed back, Si Tayeb approached and knocked on the door. No answer came and Si Tayeb continued on to the fort. It was a menacing structure, a foreign and foreboding building of ramparts and gun slits designed to project French power and permanency. Si Tayeb was undaunted, and he boldly broke the silence of the night by knocking on the door with his staff. To the great relief of all, this call also went unanswered. Whispers circulated the news that Si Tayeb had put the garrison to sleep with his magic. This settled the doubts of skeptics. Si Tayeb had visibly demonstrated the strength of his power. Buoyed with confidence, the group followed their leader into the village.[20]

The Fournier House

The European village of Djelfa was typical of many of the civilian settlements that grew up near the military bases in the steppes, where the monotony of daily life persisted at the edge of the extreme. The first building dated to 1852 and housed the French command. The *bordj* was erected shortly thereafter. Djelfa's distance from the main French base in the Sahara at Laghouat and its nearby forests and springs (forming the headwaters of the Oued El-Melah) earned the settlement the ironic nickname of "Versailles."[21] There was, of course, nothing splendid about this isolated village. Its inhabitants had to reconcile themselves to the heat, cold, wind, and sun of the place, as well as its isolation. The European settlers and several families of Algerian Jews who lived here worked as laborers or teamsters and participated in local commerce, like Djelfa's newly built flour mill, which animated local economic life. Some sought opportunities in the region's developing wool and livestock market. The government had high hopes of attracting European farmers to Djelfa. In 1856 it surveyed a nearby site to serve as a possible colonization center for fifty families cultivating a thousand hectares of land.[22] Not surprisingly, the response was unenthusiastic.

The night of 14 April Djelfa's *infra-ordinaire* became "extra-ordinary."[23] Si Tayeb's men launched their raid with an attack on the house of the baker Jean Fournier. Fate alone determined this choice. Fournier's house was the first the group encountered on their entrance into the village. This was a Sunday. Inside the house three men were engaged in a game of cards: Félix Bazan, a soldier; Philibert Fournier, a construction worker; and Jean Fournier, his brother and the host of the card party. They were accompanied by the baker's two-year-old son Henri, who played among the men, and his five-year-old daughter Emilie, who slept in an adjacent room. (The children's mother was not in the house at the time.) Around 10 p.m. their game was disturbed by sounds coming from the Bou-Saada road, the main thoroughfare through town. "Soon the noise got closer," reported Bazan. "In the midst of the cries we could perfectly distinguish that of 'Allah.'"[24] Going to the window to investigate, the men were met by a hail of stones. Jean Fournier quickly put out the lamp, while the soldier Bazan hid under the table with the boy. Even if they had tried to barricade the door, it would have done them little good. Within minutes a group of assailants had entered the house. Bazan received several violent blows from staffs, which sent him fleeing out the front door. His retreat was cut off by a volley of stones thrown by the rest of Si Tayeb's group, which had remained in the street. Running back into the house, he saw that twenty individuals had stormed inside. One of them grabbed Bazan by the throat and thrust a knife at his head, sending him reeling to the floor, where he received a beating from those armed with staffs, before being stabbed several times. Taking advantage of a moment of distraction among the attackers, the soldier picked himself up and left by the back door.

Philibert Fournier furnished investigators with few details, but it appears that his flight from his brother's home was swift and immediate, for he escaped serious injury. His brother Jean, on the other hand, was brutally attacked. He was hit in the eye with a stone that left him dazed and partially blinded. He was then attacked by a man with a knife, who stabbed him in the neck, inflicting a deep wound. He collapsed and was left for dead.[25]

The attackers did not spare Jean Fournier's two children. His son was hit several times in the head and arms with staffs. Having initially been protected by Bazan, he appears to have been abandoned to his fate when Bazan fled. The toddler narrowly escaped fatal injuries: his wounds consisted of a serious contusion to the left part of the head the size of a two-franc coin and bruises to the arm.[26] The blow to the head likely left the child unconscious; appearing dead, he was spared further assault. Fournier's daughter was less fortunate. She was asleep when Si Tayeb's followers entered the house. Finding the child in her bed, several assailants attacked the girl simultaneously with knives, staffs, and stones. The autopsy report gives some idea of the intensity of the violence to which she was subjected. After unfolding the bed sheet wrapped around her body, which was riddled with holes, the investigating doctor found the following physical traumas: three stab wounds to the legs and feet and a stab wound to the left shoulder administered with such force that it completely traversed her body. The report continued, "On the left anterior and lateral [side] of the head [is] a depression of the skull of 6 cm long and 3 cm wide. We see a cut of the lower lip and cheek of the same side, [also] a stab wound of the left chest just below the shoulder." The report concluded that the "death of this child was produced by the blow that she received to the head, which caused a fracture of the skull. Her death must have been quick; in actuality she was probably dead a few moments after the Arabs stormed the house."[27]

Who were the killers? Ali ben Mokhtar was among the group that surrounded the Fournier house. "I don't know who killed the child or who wounded the
people in the house," he confessed, but he was able to positively identify two
men, Si Tayeb and Mustapha ben Djerid of the Ouled Slim (a faction of the
Ouled Si Ahmed), as having gone inside. "As for me, I threw stones like the others, without really knowing what I was doing."[28] Other witnesses corroborated
Mokhtar's story, adding more names to the group of men who entered the house
with Si Tayeb. "Arriving at the house of Mr. Fournier," recounted one witness,
"they forced open the doors. Then Si Tayeb, still holding his staff and his knife,
entered, followed by Lakhdeur ben El Far armed with a staff, Hachmi ben
Ameuer with a knife and a staff, and Mustapha ben Ali ben Djerid also holding
a knife and a staff.... Leaving this house, the *khouans* fell upon another. Fearing the arrival of the soldiers, I fled and was already outside the village when I
heard two shots."[29]

Into the Village

The attack on the Fournier house may have lasted half an hour. By 10:30 p.m.
word of the attack had circulated further into the settlement. The butcher
Antoine Lesbre was at the café and dry goods store of Philippe Riaux when his
wife arrived with the frightening news of having heard loud noises. To reassure
her, Riaux "told her that it was probably just some drunk soldiers fighting."[30]
Shortly thereafter Bazan arrived, his clothes drenched in blood. The appearance of the soldier appeared to confirm Riaux's thesis of a brawl.[31] Bazan, however, quickly revealed the true nature of the disturbance. His story was broken
off by noise of an attack on the nearby home of the merchant François Carréga.
The attackers pelted Carréga's house with stones but did not immediately storm
inside. This gave the merchant time to find his shotgun, and he dispersed Si
Tayeb's men by firing on them from the second-floor window.[32] Seeking cover
and new targets, the attackers moved on to the center of town, where they found
Philippe Riaux, Antoine Lesbre, the carpenter Joseph Léo, and several other
settlers who had assembled in the street to investigate the noise. Once again Si
Tayeb's men launched their assault with a volley of stones that sent the settlers
fleeing back to a café owned by Riaux. Here they regrouped and trained their
firearms on Si Tayeb's men, dispersing them with scattered fire.

At the *Café Maure*

The attackers moved on to storm the *café maure*. The owner, Embarek ben
Mouley, reported that "upon hearing the cries 'Allah! Allah!' I thought that it
was people of the Rissaouas, who go through the streets and take whatever falls
into their hands. I therefore closed the door of my café."[33] Inside were Hamou

ben Abdallah, described in the reports as a "nègre" of Djelfa, El Khouini Bel Hussein, a construction worker from Laghouat, and another Laghouati, Abd el Kader ben Zamoun, a trader who had come to Djelfa to buy wool from the spring shearing. Théodore Papy, a European who had armed himself with a shotgun, also sought refuge in the café at the last moment.

Zamoun had just returned from dining with the *khodja* (secretary) of the Bureau Arabe in the fort and was preparing to turn in at the café when roughly twenty men arrived in the street and began to pelt the building with stones. They apparently showed some reluctance to enter and attack the café's occupants. Seeing this and interpreting it as hesitation to attack fellow Algerians, Si Tayeb called out, "They are worse than the Christians because they live among them!"[34] Having classed these Algerians as enemies, Si Tayeb led the attack against them. Although the door of the café held for a moment, the windows were broken and five individuals armed with knives entered and attacked the men inside. Among the defenders, only Hamou ben Abdallah and Théodore Papy escaped serious injury. Mouley received six stab wounds to his chest, arms, and buttocks. Bel Hussein was similarly stabbed in the upper back, shoulder, cheek, and neck. Zamoun, the wool merchant, received the most severe injuries, with four serious wounds to his hands, back, and shoulders. The doctor estimated that his recovery would necessitate at least thirty days in the hospital.[35] The assailants robbed both Laghouati men, taking the 82 francs that Bel Hussein had on his person and the 695 francs that Zamoun had brought with him to buy wool. Zamoun said that it was Si Tayeb himself who stole the money. He reported that while he was trying to hold the door closed, Si Tayeb entered through the window and stabbed him from behind, while at the same time another man, Mustapha ben Ali, stabbed him twice in the arm. In a state of shock, Zamoun fell to the ground. Si Tayeb searched the merchant, discovered the money (which was hidden in Zamoun's hat), and left him bleeding on the floor.

Final Attacks

With only a thin crescent moon that night, the town was veiled in darkness. Nevertheless the attackers managed to navigate their way through town and ransack the houses and businesses of Théodore Papy, Isaac el-Gouzi, Philippe Riaux, and Antoine Lesbre, all of whom had fled with their families into the safety of the night. At this last stage of the attack two more Europeans were killed. Jacques Drouin, a stable boy forty-five years of age, heard the noise and ran confusedly into the street, where Tayeb's men set upon him with knives. They inflicted a fatal stabbing, with the autopsy revealing fourteen separate knife wounds to Drouin's head, shoulders, face, and neck.[36] The final victim was a fifty-year-old man named Fourès. The noise from the street woke Fourès from his sleep and, still in his nightclothes, he ran out to investigate. He was first pelted with stones and then assailed by men with knives. Reeling from his wounds but still able to break away, Fourès sought shelter in Riaux's café. Bleeding profusely, he was unable to escape a second time when Si Tayeb's men entered. They stabbed him repeatedly in the back, chest, head, and legs. The chest wound proved fatal and he was found lifeless seated at a table.[37]

At some point Philibert Fournier, upon fleeing his brother's house, where his niece had been killed, found himself in the street and was assaulted a second time. This time he was confronted directly by Si Tayeb. "He is a tall man, and at that moment he was wearing a very white burnous."[38] Si Tayeb stabbed Fournier in the neck and the Frenchman fell to the ground, where he was stabbed several more times in the back and face. This second bout with Si Tayeb's men left him in critical condition. He was the most seriously injured of all the survivors, and the doctor estimated a fifty-day recovery.[39] Lastly, the carpenter Joseph Léo was stabbed twice in the chest and face while attempting to flee to safety.[40]

The French Repression

Si Tayeb's men suffered casualties as well. Although the French archives provide fewer details, they specify that two attackers fell victim to buckshot wounds. They were no doubt felled by the fire of those settlers armed with shotguns. The conical bullet of a military rifle killed a third.[41] He was the last to die that night. A small contingent of seven or eight soldiers had finally assembled at the *bordj* and descended into the village, where they engaged the attacking force in the main street.[42] Si Tayeb's forces met the soldiers with an initial pelting of stones, inflicting two light wounds. But the first shots from the army rifles caused heavy casualties. One man was killed instantly and four were left wounded in the street, some with their legs broken by the bullets and others with serious gunshot wounds, which proved fatal in three cases . The other assailants and their leader disappeared into the darkness.

PATTERNS OF VIOLENCE

The sun's first light the next morning revealed a frightful scene of devastation:

> The next morning the deserted village offered a gloomy spectacle. The inhabitants had fled to the *bordj*... . [Some of] the windows hung on their hinges; [others were] ripped off their [frames]. Broken glass was strewn across the ground. Enormous stones filled the stores, and the furniture of the houses was tipped over and broken. Long streaks of blood covered the streets of the village. A woman mad with grief searched in the houses for her murdered daughter, asking [the few] people she met what they had done with her.[43]

Violence consists not of concepts and theories but practices. It is therefore useful to subject the Djelfa attack to a close reading, examining these violent practices as a text that might reveal its logic. Although the French archives are silent on important details, the sources permit us to make several observations. Possibly the most salient feature of the attack is the marked division within the ranks of Si Tayeb's men between those who acted in a support position and those who actually did the killing. Only a handful participated alongside Si Tayeb in his murderous activities. The vast majority remained in the street and threw rocks or sang and chanted. This is confirmed by the autopsy reports, which reveal that fatal injuries were inflicted with knives. There were only two cases in which staffs and stones accounted for serious injury (the Fournier brothers), and only one death (Emilie Fournier). Although she was stabbed repeatedly, Emilie's fatal head wound was most likely inflicted by someone who pummeled her with a fist-sized rock. Assailants armed with knives were responsible for the remaining casualties. There were few knives among Si Tayeb's group: a careful sifting through all the documentation reveals no more than fifteen individuals who carried knives. The other forty-five or so men and boys had a few staffs between them. To the extent that they participated in acts of force, most did so from a distance with stones gathered from the rocky ground.

The absence of weapons certainly supports the French investigation's conclusion that the attack was not premeditated, but this evidence raises other questions. Was it the fact that they lacked efficient arms that discouraged most from homicide? Or did their reluctance to confront their enemies directly and seek to kill them result from differing conceptions of the attack, or simply a lack of motivation? The testimony of participants interviewed by the French investigators certainly supports the latter conclusion. As Khadir ben Djemal, a twelve-year-old boy said, "I entered the village behind Si Tayeb, but personally I did nothing, only clap my hands and shout."[44] Another, Kouider ben Mohad, said, "As for me, I didn't throw stones. I didn't have a staff. I only had my prayer beads in my hands."[45] Djemal and Mohad certainly hoped that these declarations would clear them. Few who were brought before the investigating officers had any illusions about French justice and most feared the worst. Djemal himself was told by a friend's father not to tell the French anything lest he be beheaded.[46] It is therefore to be expected that they would downplay their role in the attack or lie in a bid for clemency. However, other available evidence tends to support the veracity of their statements.

The accounts of witnesses from both sides agree that most of Si Tayeb's men stayed in the street and threw stones: they did not break down the doors, enter through windows, or engage in hand-to-hand combat. At the *café maure* only half a dozen assailants were involved; and at the Fournier house no more than twenty assailants gained entrance. This evidence suggests that among the sixty or so men and boys who attacked the village, at most twenty actually participated in murderous actions. This evidence refutes Governor-General Pélissier's suggestion that a horde of fanatical killers descended on Djelfa that night. Instead, the archives reveal a core group of assailants, surrounded by a larger crowd, who chose to engage in stone throwing, destruction of buildings, and singing rather than participate directly in Si Tayeb's mission to annihilate Djelfa's inhabitants.

Among the small cadre of followers who did turn their efforts to murder, their violence was intense, indiscriminate, and merciless. Victims who tried to defend themselves by covering their faces with their hands were met with a series of slashing blows that did not stop when they turned their backs to flee. The attack on Drouin exemplifies the ferocity of the assailants. They stabbed the Frenchman no less than fourteen times. Even those victims who mounted no defense, such as the sleeping girl, received the full force of the attack: the killers flailed at her in the darkened room with such force that their knives completely passed through her body. Not satisfied with the job, one attacker smashed in the girl's head with a rock. The violence was as indiscriminate as it was intense. All those who fell in the path of the attackers—child and adult; Muslim, Christian, and Jew—were targeted. The wounds suffered by Mouley, the owner of the *café maure*, show that he was attacked with as much ferocity as the soldier Bazan. Nor can any discernable difference be seen in the nature of the individual victim's wounds. Knives, clubs, and stones can be used to inflict injuries in several different ways, but the variations in the wounds appear to be a function of the circumstances of the attack (i.e., a child sleeping in a dark room versus a grown man defending himself in a lighted café), not a differentiated attack based on the victim's identity. Finally, the wounds fail to show any signs of ritual or sacrificial violence. No throats were slit and bodies were not mutilated or otherwise marked in a distinctive fashion.

THE COLONIAL CRISIS AT DJELFA, ISLAM, AND POPULAR RESISTANCE

What does this case tell us about the types of popular resistance in colonial Algeria? Every conflict has its particular causes and logic, and explaining spontaneous popular revolts is a notoriously difficult task in any historical setting. Colonial situations pose particular challenges. Political relations are invariably highly unequal and marked by extremes of cultural discontinuity. Moreover, colonialism brought a rapid restructuring of people's lives in cases like Algeria. Here the causes of revolts were always overdetermined; economic, social, and ideological factors overlapped, making explanations difficult. Added to this general challenge is the particular question of sources. The pastoralists of the Algerian steppes did not leave a large archive, and much of their history has to be written based on French documents.

In the case of the 1861 attack on Djelfa, the local administration's focus on socioeconomic issues yielded an impressive body of data even if, as I have pointed out, it remains problematic at times. I have previously surveyed the material causes for local discontent. Herd losses, disastrous harvests, rising food prices, and ongoing drought hit the Ouled Naïl hard. Figuring into the agrarian crisis were the fiscal charges of the colonial regime. French taxes were a burden that few Ouled Naïl could bear in 1861. Finally, there were the conflicts over changing patterns of land use and modes of production—perhaps the most cataclysmic of the social transformations brought about by the French occupation of Djelfa. These increased intracommunal tensions, on the one hand, and were totally unsuited to the local environment, on the other, leaving people at considerable risk.

The attack occurred at the moment when the people near Djelfa were beginning to feel the full negative effects of French colonialism. The forced transition from one socioeconomic system to another produced ruptures within pastoral society. The abandonment of traditional ways of life created economic insecurity and, with it, social anomie, a volatile transformation of the social bond and weakening of norms. Seen in this light, the attack on Djelfa emerges as comparable to what René Girard has called a "holiday-gone-wrong," the deritualized festival typical of societies in crisis.[47] The violence of Si Tayeb and his men was not sacrificial any more than it had a clear political purpose. Moreover, the violence of the attack can hardly be classified as reciprocal, a settling of scores or cycles of vengeance, which rely on more intimate circumstances. Instead, the attack began with a traditional festival that degenerated into a massacre, a single explosion of chaotic, undifferentiated violence. This confused, reckless armed struggle appears as both an expression of frustration and a desperate attempt to reverse the status quo. The fury of popular revolts the world over has been born of such despair and anger, such fear and hope.[48]

Forces emanating from the particular culture and social order of the Ouled Naïl also need to be considered even if the sources are imprecise. The crisis in traditional structures of authority is an important part of this question. Here the death of Si Mokhtar provides a rich field of analysis where popular religion, authority, and political legitimacy in Algerian society intersect. The death of this powerful and esteemed saint fueled anxieties. Did his disappearance mean that the Ouled Naïl no longer had a privileged intermediary to communicate with God on their behalf? To people whose everyday life was structured in terms of the supernatural and the sacred, and who were now facing the French occupation— one of the most challenging and traumatic periods in recent memory— the death of such an important leader cannot be underestimated. The visit to the saint's tomb was one way to demonstrate their continuing devotion and remain in contact with Si Mokhtar, to feel his benevolence and *baraka*. However, great efforts were now necessary to hear the sheikh's voice, and those with urgent questions found equivocal answers, the succession crisis at the *zawiya* at Ouled-Djellal being but one example. Without the divinely inspired guidance of Si Mokhtar, it was difficult to sort out with any degree of clarity the challenges presented by colonial rule.

There were many religiously sanctioned ways for Muslims to respond to the French occupation, including armed resistance, emigration, and dissemblance.[49] Many looked to them to fashion ways to accommodate themselves to the colonial regime. This took many forms, including political alliances and commercial agreements. The research undertaken by historian Julia Clancy-Smith on the Rahmaniyya shows that accommodation represented not an embrace of the colonial order per se but was rather an expression of pragmatism.[50] Nearing the end of his life a Sufi notable like Si Mokhtar simply removed himself from the politics of colonialism, an act that probably signaled neither his submission to the French nor his acceptance of the occupation but rather his forbearance. For their part many Ouled Naïl in 1861 were deeply dissatisfied with their accommodation to French rule. The submission to French authority brought with it the rites and rituals of the new regime, which rarely failed to highlight the inequalities of the new order, sometimes in humiliating fashion. Some Ouled Naïl had even donned the "burnous rouge" of the French (the uniform of Algerian auxiliaries in the French army) and fought alongside them. For this their neighbors called them the "red dogs" and heaped scorn and accusations upon them.[51] This illustrates how difficult it was for those seeking accommodation to assert themselves as autonomous actors, striving to reduce their risks or maximize their personal interests and those of the group they represented. Invariably the needs and values of the social world shaped such choices. In some cases self-interest was better served by the path of confrontation—even reckless violence—rather than accommodation. Whatever potential advantages those who sought rapprochement with the colonial regime might have enjoyed were compromised by the dishonor and humiliation (*dhilla*) that accompanied it, and which, in the end, balanced the scales of moral economy in the Algerian steppes.

Accommodation thus had its limits, which were fairly inelastic. Armed revolt provided another response to French rule. Here Islam offered up a specific set of political options to those living under colonial rule, including emigration and armed struggle, among other choices.[52] The history of the region up to 1861 shows that the eschatological traditions of Islam in particular were an influential way that the pastoralists of the steppes understood their historical condition and place in the world. On separate occasions local people had rallied to support two Mahdi pretenders (Bou Ziyan and Muhammad ben Abdallah), and they had previously extended hospitality to another (Bou Maza). These individuals tapped into the apocalyptic hopes of many Algerians that an armed uprising led by a divinely inspired leader, the Mahdi, would result in the annihilation of the invaders and miraculously usher in an era of perfection. As historian Peter von

Sivers has written, "In this vision, with its emphasis on revolutionary action, all other options are discarded as inferior and despicable."[53]

Si Tayeb never claimed to be the Mahdi, nor do the French records show that he expressed his mission within the orthodox terms of armed struggle in defense of Islam. While the attack on Djelfa shows many of the signs of an apocalyptic revolt (e.g., unconcern for pragmatic issues, an undifferentiated enemy, and confidence in divine intervention), seeing it as a uniquely religiously motivated struggle poses several risks. First, there is a lack of sources. Although rich in the testimony of firsthand witnesses, French reports reflected their authors' concern to identify culprits and measure the revolt's political significance. French interrogators did not pose the types of questions that might have confirmed the finer points concerning the motivation of the attackers. On the whole, the French listened to the testimony of the accused with a tin ear. Moreover, even if those investigating the attack had sought to understand their role, the fact remains that religious *doctrines* have generally proven to be a poor guide to understanding *practices* in Muslim societies, as in many others. In the end, they better illuminate how people understand and express their situation than explain what they do.[54]

In short, the attack on Djelfa poses serious interpretative challenges. It neither fits neatly into a story of Islamic revolt nor one of colonial accommodation, and it does not match the paradigm presented in studies of national resistance. For these reasons I am prompted to seek answers elsewhere. The anthropologist Fanny Colonna has suggested one way of understanding the role of religion and violence in colonial situations. She has argued that scholars who attempt to understand the role of Islam in fomenting resistance to colonialism miss the "real question," namely, "the effects of the colonial situation on the relationship of various religious forces *to each other* and to political forces."[55] She has suggested that this line of analysis avoids the problems of those who idealize the political value of Islamic religious thought, opening the way to a more nuanced and critical interrogation of Islam's social and political role in Muslim societies.

Refocusing on social and political questions rather than theological or ideological ones necessitates a closer examination of the figure of Si Tayeb and the effects of this newcomer's bid for religious authority. Si Tayeb had only fleeting contact with the French. He may have gained a certain familiarity with the administration's operations during his service as the domestic servant in the family of the French-named agha—if indeed he ever actually did this work. Yet his influence and power, unlike that of many others in the Annex, in no way emanated from the colonial regime. He came from the outside (or so the people believed), and it was the hand of God that brought him to the Ouled Naïl, not the French. His authority was founded on his piety and supernatural powers, as well as his relationship to Si Mokhtar and the Rahmaniyya. These qualities favored a meteoric rise on the path to sainthood. However, Si Tayeb

lacked important markers of power. Although they won him a large popular following, his spontaneous acts did not provide the same guarantees of influence
enjoyed by the established religious notables of the Ouled Naïl. Prominent figures remained cautious and avoided direct confrontations, but they manifestly
did not defer to the newcomer except in staged, obsequious displays (if we are to
believe the account by Arnaud, the military interpreter). This put Si Tayeb in a
delicate position. An inspired but upstart holy man might inspire fidelity among
those who felt that their French-appointed caids and surviving traditional elites
could not help them weather the crisis of the 1860s, but he could not count
on their endless devotion. Lacking genealogical legitimacy, and with volatile
magic and *baraka* serving as his primary source of authority, Si Tayeb had to
prove to his followers that he continually partook of God's favor.

Here events leading up to the attack—our best source—are revealing.
Departing on a journey of religious devotion, the *ziyara*, with only his most
faithful followers, Si Tayeb may have been reassured. First of all, the aspiring
saint could put some distance between himself and his detractors. Moreover,
he could demonstrate publicly the fruits of his proselytizing by claiming that
he had earned the fidelity of at least fifty followers. Not only had they ceded to
his authority during the religious ceremonies of Ramadan, but they were ready
to follow him on the highly symbolic local pilgrimage route and make the first
visit to the tomb of Si Mokhtar. The ultimate success of this *ziyara* would be a
feat that would not go unnoticed, and Si Tayeb could count on the rapid dis-
semination of information along the trade routes to spread word of his influence
throughout the Algerian Sahara, and as far as the powerful Rahmaniyya *zawiya*
at Nefta, Tunisia.

Si Tayeb faced a serious threat when Si Sadoq, the rival *mukaddam*, intercepted his group on 13 April. Even though he had successfully challenged Si
Sadoq's influence the previous month, Si Tayeb had to face the fact that his
rival was better known and more established. No doubt he was also troubled by
Si Sadoq's presence in the *ziyara* party. This situation was intolerable. At the
midday meal the following day, Si Tayeb exploded, demanding that his followers choose sides. Announcing that "we are going to return!," he used threats and
violence to ensure that the largest part of his group went with him. Confused
and shocked by their leader's sudden about-face, the pilgrims paraded before Si
Tayeb "like a flock of sheep."

This act set Si Tayeb on an especially precarious path. He would have to
account for his actions to his followers and, eventually, to the leadership of the
Rahmaniyya. When Si Tayeb announced at nightfall on 14 April that he would
"exterminate Djelfa," I suspect that this radical and dangerous decision was
driven, in part, by his transgression. Reversals and challenges to the status quo
were a necessary part of his bid for religious authority, but they bred anxiety and
begged higher confirmation. Fearing the results of his defiance while at the same

time remaining supremely confident, Si Tayeb sought to prove his legitimacy in a spectacular and decisive display of his power. Seen in this light, events help us to understand an important aspect of what was undoubtedly a complex tapestry of factors that motivated Si Tayeb's sudden decision to attack Djelfa. Striking a blow to the French at Djelfa would be the ultimate test of his legitimacy. The French had proven their ability to wield superior power — especially violent power — and nothing short of God's omnipotence itself could reverse the situation in favor of Tayeb's poorly armed group. That Si Tayeb could himself channel this power would demonstrate his ascendancy over his rivals. Moreover, his future esteem would be that much higher because his miraculous display would rid the area of a source of misfortune.

Bringing Algerian pastoralists to the brink of subsistence crises and leaving them in a chronic state of economic insecurity was the way French planners sought to create order in the 1840s. Twenty years later, following the defeat of Abdelkader and the putting down of the Saharan revolts, conditions had changed. However, the paradoxical tendency of colonial policy makers to find order in economic insecurity remained. This policy eventually won the French a shaky hegemony in the steppes and mountains of the northern Sahara. However, in the short run it was profoundly flawed. Economic insecurity unleashed a host of social tensions and crises that created conditions for conflict rather than assuring a *Pax Francus*. With daily existence having become precarious, and the fabric of the social order having frayed, the people of Algeria sought solutions by following increasingly dangerous paths.

PART 3

Slavery in the Algerian Sahara Following Abolition

*Labour and sorrow will be her lot and her cheeks
will grow thin with pining.*
—*The Odyssey*, book 8

SAABA'S JOURNEY TO ALGERIAN SLAVERY

In the summer of 1877 a Fula-speaking youth known as Saaba arrived in the remote and forsaken oasis of Ouargla. The journey north from her home on the Niger River to this settlement in the Algerian Sahara had taken over six months. During that time she had witnessed the killing of all the male members of her family. Her fellow captives had been beaten, and some had succumbed to sickness, hunger, and thirst. Saaba's mother, who had been captured with her, simply disappeared somewhere along the route. Traveling thousands of kilometers, Saaba had crossed one of the most hostile deserts of the world, a journey made entirely on foot. Suffering from exhaustion and exposure, she squatted amid the dust and flies at Ouargla, the southernmost French outpost in the Sahara. Together with a dozen young women and as many children, Saaba was put up for sale at the slave market at Ouargla.

THE SALE OF SLAVES AT OUARGLA, JULY 1877

To the south of Wergelah (Ouargla) the country is an uninterrupted expanse of sand, extending to Ber el Abid, the land of slaves.
—el-Eghwati, *Notes of a Journey into the Interior of Northern Africa* (1830)

Ouargla had once been a major hub of commerce between the Mediterranean and what Arab geographers called the "bilād al-Sūdān" (Land of the Blacks) and the French called the "Soudan," a broad stretch of land south of the Sahara that traversed the African continent, extending from the Atlantic coast in the west to the mountains of Ethiopia in the east.[1] Geography privileged the oasis for trade: it was strategically situated between the Niger River (at least 2,000 km to the south) and the Mediterranean Sea (800 km to the north). It was also on the east-west cross routes that linked Morocco and Tunis, and the trails farther east to Tripolitania and Cyrenaica (in modern-day Libya). Traders stopped here to exchange, store, and distribute their goods. It was also an important way station for the camels that carried the loads: after the long trek from the Tidikelt and Gourara regions to the south, or Ghat to the east, the decision to drive the exhausted animals farther north was made at their owner's peril.

Ouargla was also an important rest station for those who trafficked in slaves. The trans-Saharan was the primary route traveled by African slaves destined for the eastern and southern Mediterranean world. Traversing the desert was difficult and dangerous under the best of circumstances, and most slaves (like Saaba) had to do it entirely on foot. Many did not survive the journey, and those who did were fatigued, malnourished, and sick by the time they reached oases such as Ouargla. Jean Lethielleux, author of a history of Ouargla, has written, "The slaves brought from the Sudan stayed here several months to recuperate physically after a hard crossing, during which many of their fellow captives left their bones along the trail."[2] Moreover, slave traders took advantage of the stopover to add value to their charges. They instructed their captives in the rudimentary Arabic they would need to communicate with their future masters, and some may have encouraged non-Muslim captives to convert to Islam.

An important center of commerce up to the sixteenth century, Ouargla fell on hard times during the nineteenth century. The decline was slow, part of the waning of the Mediterranean world following the economic shift to the Atlantic. The arrival in 1830 of the French in Algiers and the ensuing wars in the northern lands of the Algerian Tell exacerbated the oasis's decline. Commercial traffic declined and that which remained (e.g., commerce in textiles, foodstuffs, slaves, dyes, medicine, beads, spices, and weapons)—along with "intellectual caravans" of pilgrims, saints, and scholars[3]—shifted from the routes leading to Ouargla to the eastern ones ending in Tunis and Tripoli or the western ones leading directly to Morocco.[4]

Ouargla's remote location—four hundred arid and desolate kilometers south of Biskra helped protect the oasis from the worst effects of French rule, like those witnessed at Djelfa. However, Ouargla's inhabitants, and the pastoralists that depended upon this oasis, did not escape the cycles of wars and unrest the occupation produced. In 1849 a local leader first recognized French sovereignty over the oasis and ruled the area as the French *khalifa*, or governor. His rule was cut short by Muhammad ben Abdallah, who took control of Ouargla in 1851. Ben Abdallah having been turned back at Laghouat in 1852, Ouargla felt the direct impact of the occupation when Si Hamza, of the Ouled Sidi Cheikh, came to Ouargla as the French *khalifa* in the Sahara. Establishing a base here, Si Hamza punished those who had supported Ben Abdallah's rebellion by confiscating their property. His rule became so oppressive that within the first decade as many as two hundred families had fled to Tunisia.[5] When the Ouled Sidi Cheikh themselves rebelled against the French in 1864, the French army retaliated by confiscating their property holdings in Ouargla. This caused further economic problems when the French again sequestered palm gardens, leaving them with uncertain title. Wary of taking up work in such conditions, no one emerged to make productive use of the palms, and many gardens went unattended for years.[6] The latest round of troubles occurred in 1871, when a new leader, Bou Choucha, led another round of anti-French resistance.[7] He managed to rally a formidable force of Chaamba (Sha'anba) to his cause, and at Ouargla the Beni Sisin threw in their support and helped Bou Choucha gain control of the oasis. When the French column sent to put down the uprising arrived, its leader, General de Lacroix, retaliated by destroying large sections of the Beni Sisin neighborhood and building a square over the ruins.[8] Just as devastating was Lacroix's confiscation of the Beni Sisin's date palms, which left their owners without any means of support. To escape French repression, another group of emigrants set out for Tunisia.[9] In addition to the ruinous effects of the first twenty years of French authority, nature had recently dealt the oasis several blows. A severe drought in the early 1870s scorched pastures and made irrigation of the date palm gardens a burdensome affair. When the rains finally arrived, locusts devoured the clusters of ripening dates and laid bare the garden vegetables.[10] A French report dating from June 1873 concluded that Ouargla was in "a state of misery."[11]

It was into this oasis that Saaba arrived and awaited her fate. Unlike the public slave markets in other oases—like Timimoun to the west (in the Gourara agglomeration), which still escaped French control—slaves at Ouargla were sold in the inner courtyard of a tumbledown residence in the Beni Sisin quarter. Abandoned by its owner at the time of the Bou Choucha uprising, five years of neglect had left the house in an advanced stages of disrepair by the time Saaba's group arrived. Walls had collapsed, the palm trunks that served as ceiling beams had broken, and debris filled the filthy rooms. The house was favored by slave traders because it was nondescript. Tucked away amid the ruins of the Beni Sisin neighborhood, the residence provided a location where slave traders could conduct their commerce without drawing too much unwanted attention. In 1848 the Second Republic had abolished slavery in all French-controlled territories. Slave trading was therefore illegal at Ouargla. The oasis was under French authority, represented by a French-named agha who received his orders from a military commander. Slave traders also wished to maintain a low profile for another reason. Many of the young people for sale at Ouargla, like Saaba, were born free Muslims. Although Islamic law permitted slavery and slave sales, it strictly forbid the sale of freeborn Muslims.

On the afternoon of 8 July 1877 a French explorer named Victor Largeau came to the slave market in search of someone to relieve his servant of the arduous task of cooking in the scorching summer heat. He had already gone through two cooks: he had fired the first for her "uncleanliness" while the second, a local woman from Ouargla, quit after "the neighbor women heckled her because she cooked in the home of a *Naçari* (Christian)."[12] Learning that a group of slaves had just arrived from In Salah, and knowing that slaves were fairly cheap, Largeau reckoned that it would be easier to buy a slave than to hire someone to cook for him.

He described the scene in the house as follows: "In the courtyard of this old house, a dozen young black girls, clothed in blue cotton robes, stood or crouched against the walls, their eyes lowered and full of tears; in the corner a group of fifteen children swarmed about, several of whom were not quite five years old. Squatting in the middle, a few Arabs chatted with the marabout slave trader." Following a physical inspection, Largeau decided on "a young girl of about 16 years of age (the eldest was not quite 18). She had a nice figure and a distinguished look that attracted my attention and her tears moved me to pity. Her name was Saaba."[13] After negotiating, the parties agreed upon a price of 650 francs.

Largeau could not directly hand over the money. Even before the French arrived in Algeria, local traditions generally prevented Christians and Jews in Algeria from purchasing slaves or participating in the trade.[14] As one observer remarked, "It goes without saying that there has never been a single slave in a Christian house."[15] In a report on slavery in the Médéa region, another commentator confirmed this practice: "The Jews never meddle in the buying of slaves. Any such presumption would be rejected by the most avid Muslim slaver."[16] All the same, before the French came the slaves had worked in the households of the foreign consuls in Algiers, including the American consulate, which contracted with Muslim masters for the services of Christian slaves, paying the equivalent of three dollars a month.[17] Nevertheless, even before the 1848 abolition laws officially forbade slavery in Algeria, there were few reports of the European community in Algeria buying slaves under French rule. As another observer commented, "The European, convinced that a Negro slave [*nègre*] becomes free solely due to his acquisition by him, never gets involved in this type of commerce."[18]

For his part Largeau had few qualms about slavery itself. Two years before buying Saaba, he had written a letter to a senior member of the governor-general's office recommending the administration take a hands-off approach to slavery in the Sahara. "Can we *close our eyes* a little about what happens among the Soufa and the Chaamba, and even let this sort of commerce take a certain development on condition that things take place quietly outside the towns?"[19]

FIGURE 2   Saaba, 1877. Photo by Victor Largeau.
Source: BNF-R Colis 6 bis N. 32 bis. Collection de la Société de Géographie–Clichés B.N.F.

This summed up several decades of practices whereby local French commanders and slave-holding notables had found accommodation concerning the question of slavery and the slave trade, as we shall see. Nevertheless, Largeau found
it expedient not to buy a slave himself. Before coming to the market, he worked
out a deal with a notable of Ouargla who sought a slave but could not afford
to buy one in the summer months, when commerce was at a standstill and

money was scarce. According to the arrangement, Largeau put up the money for the purchase price, while his partner acted as a proxy in the actual sale. Saaba would work and live with Largeau during his stay, and the notable would use funds from the date harvest in October to repay the Frenchman and take possession of her.

When the purchase was complete, Saaba was shaken by the news that she would be obliged to leave her companions. "When it came time to leave the market," Largeau related, "poor Saaba began to sob violently." Nevertheless he insisted that she faced her fate stoically: "Pulling herself together, she bid farewell to her companions and followed me with a firm step."[20]

THE VIOLENCE OF SAHARAN SLAVERY

The Sahara was one of the main routes to the Mediterranean world of the African slave trade, which spanned ancient times to the colonial period. Between the eighth and twentieth centuries some six million people bound for lives of servitude crossed the Sahara west of Egypt, and in the nineteenth century about six thousand slaves made the crossing annually.[21] As historian John Wright has concluded, this made the trans-Saharan slave trade "a mainstay of Maghrebi economies for over a thousand years."[22] Beyond the slave trade, the institution of slavery itself was the bedrock of the Sahara's socioeconomic order. Working alongside servile laborers of color, known as Haratin (Ḥarāṭn), African slaves dug and repaired wells, drew water from them, and did most of the agricultural work (e.g., tending to herds; fertilizing and tilling the gardens; pollinating, pruning, and harvesting the date palms) that made settled life in the Sahara possible. Marked by gender divisions, Saharan slavery included more women than men. Domestically the toil of enslaved women ensured the viability of Saharan households. Young slave women and girls were at the center of an equally important system of gift exchange, serving as tribute to foreign leaders and local notables, who derived no small part of their political capital from the control of the labor and sexuality of slaves.

The attack on Djefla and the conquests of the "pénétration pacifique" provided examples of a "spectacular" form of violence, meaning that perpetrators sought to amplify the political effects of physical force in visually overwhelming displays that communicated their omnipotence. Smoldering ruins, decimated crops, dead bodies, and physically scarred survivors served as politically symbolic texts or proclamations of power. Ostensibly intended to break the spirit of the enemy and pave the way for submission, they likewise impressed their authors.

The violence of slavery and the slave trade, on the other hand, was less visible. It responded to a different logic, one that tried to conceal its existence to outsiders. This was generally successful. Slave traders and masters kept their ownership and sale of people discreet and cloaked its true nature in the idioms of paternalism. Many of the French commanders who were responsible for implementing the abolition of slavery collaborated in this effort by presenting indigenous slavery as benign. If confronted with slavery's inherent violence, they presented it as "nobody's fault," a tough life in a tough land.[23]

While the violence of slavery might have been considered quotidian and banal, it was hardly inoffensive. It included psychosocial debasement, physical assault, and denying slaves a modicum of control over the fruits of their labor and their reproductive capacities. These practices degraded individual lives and — especially during the dangerous period between the capture and transport of slaves to the final point of sale — often destroyed them. Local forms of race thinking also buttressed slavery. These amounted to a "religious ethnography" specific to Muslim slave societies, which equated skin color with unbelief, thereby deploying symbolic violence to legitimate the exploitation of people of color.[24] In some cases, as I will argue, this intensified the social marginalization of people of color by suspending the inalienable freedom promised to all freeborn Muslims. The same attitudes compromised the protections Islamic law provided to Muslim slaves, such as spiritual equality, and encouragements for their emancipation and good treatment.

The ubiquity of such forms of violence helped mask their existence. While sources in the colonial archive that document Saharan slavery are considerable, extant documents are fragmentary and dispersed.[25] This fact underscores the problem of historical sources. My goal in the next three chapters is to use the story of Saaba to examine the larger macrostructural forces and events that uprooted thousands of people in sub-Saharan Africa and forced them to trek across the desert to a future of enslavement in colonial Algeria. This approach involves certain risks, the most pressing of which is the fact that the sources relating to Saaba herself are slim. A photograph, several paragraphs of text from a chance interview, and an offhand passage in a monthly report written by a French officer are all that remain of Saaba's story. This penury of sources proves Carlo Ginzburg's point that "the conditions of access to the production of documentation are tied to a situation of power and thus create an inherent imbalance."[26] As a result, I have been unable to provide much ethnographic detail in the story that follows, a story in which Saaba herself often disappears. Nevertheless, her "petite histoire" offers its own useful insights into the grander order of things.

This order involved a system of colonial accommodation with the precolonial institution of slavery. Following the seizure of Laghouat in 1852, it took several decades for the French to gain hegemony in the southernmost lands that now make up the Algerian Sahara. Beyond a line of outposts at the desert's northern edge — from Géryville in the west to Biskra in the east — French power depended on a complex and constantly changing system of alliances with local elites (a system quite different from that at Djelfa). The latter were deeply ambivalent about joining their interests with Algeria's new masters. In particular, they were concerned about preserving their property and status in the new regime. Slavery was an important indicator of status and source of wealth. It was also an institution that produced significant conflict within desert societies themselves, tensions that were exacerbated by the abolition legislation of 1848 and the French presence itself. Such tensions provided fertile ground for rapprochement between the French administration and Saharan notables.

A highly injurious form of accommodation emerged from all this, one often ignored by colonial historians. The latter have regarded accommodation in colonial situations as more or less a positive thing, a means whereby colonized people could minimize their risks in a dangerous new regime and—wielding what James Scott has called the "weapons of the weak"—manage to find some degree of agency and control over their lives while struggling for survival.[27] At the same time, there were losers in this colonial economy of accommodation. In the Algerian Sahara, slaves like Saaba numbered themselves among them.

SAABA'S HOME ON THE NIGER RIVER

As an explorer Largeau's interests in the Sahara ranged from natural phenomena, such as temperature and geography, to economic and political issues, history, and ethnography. With respect to the latter, Largeau paid attention to Saaba. He noticed that she followed Muslim customs, saying a short prayer in Arabic before eating ("Bismillah") and after finishing her meal ("Alhamdulillah"). At Largeau's prompting she recited the profession of faith (*shahāda*). Saaba was a Muslim. This raised questions for Largeau, who knew something of Islamic law concerning slavery. How had a Muslim woman arrived in Ouargla as a slave? Had she been illegally enslaved? Where did she come from? Saaba knew little Arabic, so Largeau sent for a local woman who spoke Fula to act as a translator.

"I am Fulani," Saaba confirmed, a freeborn Muslim from a wealthy family.[28] In the winter of 1876–77 she was abducted from her home in the middle Niger River region. Stretching roughly between Bamako and Timbuktu, this region was wealthy, and Saaba spoke about it with evident pride: "My country is very fertile; there is a lot of water and tall trees. The people are not poor, like they are here." At this point she interrupted her description to recount events leading up to her capture.

> One day we were at war with the Arabs, although I do not recall why. The Arabs arrived in great numbers at a time when the Fulani didn't expect them. They killed all the men and all the boys. I saw my father fall in a battle against ten of the whites; although my father was very strong; the Arabs killed him with their

guns. After all the men and young people were dead, the Arabs rounded up the young girls and those young children who could walk and placed us in their midst to take us along with them.[29]

Such was the beginning of a long and dangerous journey into slavery.

The Umarian Wars and Slave Raiding in the Middle Niger River Region

It is difficult to reconstruct the circumstances surrounding Saaba's capture and enslavement, especially given the social and political complexity of the middle Niger River region in the nineteenth century. Nevertheless the decades of war that ravaged the area at the time slave raiders attacked Saaba's home have been well documented by historians, whose information bears on her case.[30] These wars began in the 1850s, around the time Saaba was born, when Umar Tal (a.k.a. al-Hajj 'Umar ibn Sa'id 'Uthman Tal, ca. 1797–1864) turned his army against the Bambara monarchs of Ségou as part of his effort to control the strategic middle Niger River region. The war began as a jihad against non-Muslim states but lost much of its religious justification when Umar Tal attacked the caliphate of Hamdullahi (Masina), which Umar Tal claimed was led by apostates. He faced strong opposition, whose members succeeded in defeating and killing him in 1864. Violence remained endemic into the 1890s. The wars of the Umarian expansion made the second half of the nineteenth century one of the most violent periods in the region's history. Hundreds of thousands lost their lives in combat and an equal number succumbed to hunger and disease or fled their homes.[31] Slave raiding became a regular seasonal practice—with devastating results. As historian David Robinson has remarked, "The pattern of annual expeditions eventually exhausted the inland delta. Massina increasingly resembled a devastated march caught between forces which had made warfare into a way of life."[32] These conditions produced thousands of captives for the slave markets. According to anthropologist Claude Meillassoux, "The most immediate result of his [Umar Tal's] military action was filling the markets with a considerable quantity of slaves, especially women and children."[33] While Saaba's capture and enslavement grew out of these well-documented historical events, untangling who was responsible for her abduction remains a difficult task. The widespread wars and the constantly shifting political alliances make it likely that the exact circumstances surrounding the attack on her village or camp will never be known. Saaba only identified the attackers as "Arabs" and "Whites," designations that could have referred to several different groups. Although hard sources illustrating Saaba's particular history do not exist, there are some documents that help us understand in a general way how slave traders took people like Saaba from their homes and forced them across the Sahara.

Decades before Saaba's abduction, French officers in Algeria conducted inqui-
ries to better understand where the slaves brought to their jurisdiction came from.
An 1845 report written by Captain Durrieu, commander of the Subdivision of
Médéa, sheds some light on this activity.[34] In interviews with slave traders and the
captives sold in his jurisdiction, Durrieu put together an outline of slave-procure-
ment practices in the middle Niger River region. At midcentury he reported that
various Tuareg groups of the west-central Sahara played a major role in supplying
the Algerian markets with slaves and ran a sophisticated raiding network. First
Tuareg raiders would send out messengers from their camps near the desert's edge
to meet with local leaders. "The Tuareg camps that wanted to trade for blacks,"
Durrieu wrote, "first inform the leaders of the towns or the chiefs of the tribes
that they have arrived in their territory and let them know their intentions. Armed
with this news, "every leader, after having made guaranties for his own safety,
hastens to bring to the Tuareg the prisoners that he has taken in disputes with
his neighbors." The Tuareg then exchange woolen textiles and leather products
for the captives. The prices are low. "The Tuareg can buy one slave for one *cha-
chia* [red wool hat], a pair of *belgha* [leather shoes], and 10 or 15 *oudah* ["wada',"
cowrie shells]."[35] In addition to acting as intermediaries, the Tuareg made direct
raids against the populations of the Sahel in coordination with local allies. Saaba
makes no mention of her transfer to intermediaries, suggesting that slave raiders
with trans-Saharan capabilities, like the Tuareg, attacked her home.

TO TIMBUKTU

Saaba's captors followed the Niger River north through its inland delta, northeast of Ségou, toward Timbuktu. This first stage of travel, from the scene of
abduction to the marketplace, was only slightly less dangerous for slaves than
the initial capture. The large groups of slaves amassed following battles were
difficult to manage, and their slow travel made caravans vulnerable to counterattacks. In response, some slave raiders practiced a process of selection during
these forced marches. The first to be eliminated were captives who made signs
of resistance. They would be killed by the armed guards. Next the slave traders
identified and isolated older women and grown men. The latter were known to
be difficult to control, and the former had little market value. Such may have
been the case with Saaba's mother: "My mother followed me for a long time,
wailing and crying, but all of a sudden I did not hear her anymore. I think the
Arabs killed her."[36] Given the older woman's questionable worth at the marketplace, it is likely that Saaba's abductors found it expedient to kill or abandon her
mother. On the other hand, although they were difficult to care for and transport, children fetched high prices and slavers gave them special attention. If
they were too young to walk or when they collapsed from fatigue, slavers placed

children in baskets tied to horses or camels. The children in Saaba's caravan traveled in this manner: "We ended up putting all the little ones on the camels; otherwise they would have all died."[37]

At this stage the captives were tethered or chained together. Constant harassment, intimidation, and beatings served to further weaken resistance. A scene narrated by a French officer, Lieutenant Vallière, in his account of a slave caravan he met southwest of Bamako in the late 1870s gives an impression of this activity. The caravan's leader, fearful of bandits, sought to attach his group to the army column on their trip to Ségou. Vallière accepted his proposal and only later took note of the commerce to which he had lent his hand: "The poor captives, consisting mostly of women and children, were tethered together as they dragged themselves along painfully, while two or three blacks, who appeared to be the leader's servants, ran up and down the caravan with long whips, striking these poor people."[38]

ISLAMIC SLAVERY, THE ENSLAVEMENT OF MUSLIMS, AND AHMAD BABA'S *MI'RAJ*

When Saaba arrived at Timbuktu, her fortunes took a momentary turn for the better. As she related to Largeau, "They wanted to sell us at Timbuktu, but they were not allowed because we are Muslims."[39] It is simple enough to mark the legal prohibition of the enslavement of freeborn Muslims to explain this event. Islamic law allowed for slaves to come from only two sources: non-Muslims captured from populations within the *dār al-ḥarb* (land of war) and children born to a slave father. The law was unambiguous: slavery was an exception to the normal human condition, which was freedom, and under no circumstances could Muslims be reduced to slavery.[40] It nevertheless proved difficult to enforce the law in practice, and adjudicating disputes between masters and those who claimed to have been wrongly enslaved was a knotty process. What the law permitted was clear, as was what it forbade, but there was a yawning gap in social practice separating the two. This space was generally dominated by masters and slave merchants. They tried to establish gray areas based on physical characteristics and religion—what historian John Hunwick has called a "religious ethnography," wherein color became a marker of belief.[41] They suggested that Africans of color were not Muslims and thus could legitimately be enslaved. These strategies aimed to preserve and expand the capital of slave owners and were widely used. Examples of such abuse go back centuries. In the Songhay empire, Sunni 'Ali (1464–1492) conducted numerous raids and indiscriminately enslaved his neighbors.[42] Later Sultan Mulay Ismael (1672–1727) of Morocco egregiously violated the law when he formed a standing slave army.[43] His troops were impressed into service from among the Haratin (Ḥarāṭīn, sing. Ḥarṭānī), the servile people of color who lived in the Sahara.[44] Although the Haratin were legally free, Mulay Ismael chose physical characteristics as the basic criteria of slavery and ordered the Haratin enslaved and conscripted.[45] (The ulema of Fez protested and opposed this policy.)[46]

The question of legitimate enslavement prompted debate among jurists long before Saaba's capture. The best known intervention is the seventeenth-century fatwa entitled *"Mi'rāj al-Ṣu'ūd,"* authored by Ahmad Baba (Abu al-'Abbas Ahmad Baba al-Tinbukti, 1556–1627), a jurist from Timbuktu.[47] Literally translated in full as "The Ladder of Ascent Towards Grasping the Law Concerning Transported Blacks," the 1615 fatwa provides a fascinating look at how Muslim jurists in Africa viewed the question of enslavement and the social categories through which they adjudicated disputes.[48] Written more than two centuries before Saaba, historians are not sure how widely the fatwa was known or how centrally it figured in subsequent legal deliberations. But up to the late nineteenth century it was cited by authorities at Sokoto and in the middle Niger River region. The detail with which Ahmad Baba parses the question of lawful enslavement alone makes this document worthy of attention.[49]

Ahmad Baba issued his fatwa in reply to a request from those residing in the Tohat, an oasis agglomeration centered at Timimoun, who sought guidance concerning how to determine what was considered lawful enslavement. In particular, they wished Ahmad Baba to clarify how they should respond to captives' claims that they were freeborn Muslims and thus entitled to their freedom. "What do you say," they asked, "concerning slaves brought from the lands whose people have been established to be Muslims?"[50] The Tohati petitioners knew the basic elements of the law, namely, that "the reason why it is allowed to own [others] is [their] unbelief," and that a slave's conversion to Islam following enslavement did not automatically result in freedom. However, they had no way of determining if the claims of slaves that they had been captured as free Muslims were true or not. The Tohati petitioners posed three series of questions to the jurist. First, they appealed to him to provide reliable ethnic categories for the people of the Land of the Blacks. Believing that certain people were believers and thus free, while others were unbelievers subject to enslavement, they wanted to be able to differentiate between the two. This conceptualization ignored some of the most important aspects of the law, which relied on an individual rather than a collective determination of religious belief, but it appears that such categories were widely accepted at the time.[51] Second, they wanted to know what to do in cases where an individual's origins could not be determined. Should the slave's word be believed? Finally, they wanted Baba to respond to the Hamitic myth, the popular belief that the blackness of sub-Saharan Africans derived from the curse of Noah upon his son Ham, and that color was therefore a prima facie indicator of those who could be enslaved.[52]

Ahmad Baba replied unambiguously to all three questions. He gave the Tohati a list of lands where the people were known to be free Muslims, "who may not be enslaved under any circumstance," and a list of those who came from lands of unbelievers, where "there is no harm in possessing them without posing questions."[53] In cases where the land of origin could not be determined, the burden of proof fell on the owner. Citing a reliable jurist, Ahmad Baba wrote, "Whoever seeks salvation for himself should not purchase any of them except [in cases where] someone names his land and it is determined whether or not he is from that land, that is to say from a land of Islam or a land of unbelievers."[54] Ahmad Baba concluded that if the proof was not forthcoming, the slave's own declaration must be given priority.

The final question concerning the Hamitic myth was most important and held the widest ramifications. While the law addressed only questions of belief and disbelief in determining legal enslavement, a point that Ahmad Baba was ready to extend to a religious ethnography of the region, the final question went much deeper. Could physical characteristics be considered a factor of enslavement? Specifically, could skin color, understood as the result of Noah's curse upon Ham, mark the divide between free and enslaved? Were all black Africans not subject to enslavement by the light-skinned descendants of Noah?[55] As John Hunwick has noted, this question reveals "an underlying presumption by Arabo-Berbers that black Africans are inherently deserving of being enslaved by non-black peoples."[56] For his part, Ahmad Baba rejected the Ham fable as spurious. Quoting a respected authority, he wrote: "This is something not proven and is not correct."[57] Ahmad Baba then cited a text recounting the Prophet's explanation of physical difference among people: "Adam was created from a handful [of earth] which [God] took from all parts of the world. Hence his offspring turned out according to the earth [they were created from]; some came out red, others white, others black; some were easygoing, others downcast; some were evil and others good."[58]

Ahmad Baba shared this authority's opinion that "this is a sound Hadith . . . and it is to be relied upon in [the matter of] the blackness of their color, for it is a reversion to the clay from which they were created."[59] Ahmad Baba concluded with a categorical rejection of skin color as grounds for enslavement. "This is not a peculiarity of theirs [Ham's children]. Indeed, any unbeliever among the children of Ham or anyone else may be possessed [as a slave] if he remains attached to his original unbelief. There is no difference between one race and another."[60]

Hunwick has remarked that although Ahmad Baba's "legal mind rejected the simple equivalence of blackness with slavery," his thinking about black Africans was "affected by notions of the inferiority and enslavability of black Africans."[61] Such prejudicial beliefs were powerful and widespread. If a careful legal thinker like Ahmad Baba shared them, one can appreciate their importance in the slave societies of the Maghreb. Physical characteristics were a simple and efficacious way for slave traders and owners to distinguish between free and enslaved. More important, this distinction further legitimated the highly unequal and irregular social relations imbedded in slavery and justified the racial divides of Saharan society.

Slave owners throughout the Maghreb used the Hamitic myth to legitimate the enslavement of Africans of color well into the nineteenth century and afterward. One example of its importance in colonial Algeria is an 1840 letter written by a slave owner named Mustapha ben Ismaël. He wrote the letter to protest the decision by the Procureur général of the city of Oran to emancipate slaves owned by the Algerians under French authority. (Although the exact circumstances surrounding this court decision are not known, the fact that it was handed down eight years before the 1848 decree points up the importance of abolitionist sympathies among some in the French judiciary in Algeria and their willingness to act against slavery in major French-controlled cities like Oran.) Ismaël was outraged by this decision and claimed that it violated the premises of Islamic law, which the French had promised to respect in 1830. Although making a legal claim, he did not cite fatwa or treaties but rather the Hamitic myth.

> It is recognized in Islam by all the prophets that God sent Noah . . . [whose] children are Shem, Ham, and Japheth. One day, while Noah was sleeping naked, his son Ham saw him in this state and laughed and made fun of his father. Shem saw this and it angered him. Now, the *blacks* are the children of Ham and *Muslims* are the children of Shem. When Noah awoke, he learned of the conduct of Ham and the good heart of Shem. Then he said to Shem: "God gives you the descendents of Ham for slaves and so it will be for you and for your descendants to the Day of Judgment." The laugh of Ham was the cause of all that. The word of Noah is law for us, as long as there is not another law that contradicts it. God, his Prophet, and our law said in the Holy Book that it is permitted for the children of Shem to have the children of Ham for our slaves.[62]

The Hamitic myth allowed this slave owner to ignore questions of belief and unbelief and assert a primordial right of light-skinned people to own dark-skinned Africans. According to his reasoning, the children of Ham are blacks *and* unbelievers, their skin color serving as a marker of this unbelief. Like the Tohati merchants who petitioned Ahmad Baba, this Algerian slave owner sought to map a transgenerational curse onto physical differences and thereby provide a ready model to divide slaves from freeborn. Moreover, he was willing to take his racist logic so far as to exclude "blacks" from the community of believers, concluding: "The *blacks* are the children of Ham and *Muslims* are the children of Shem."

Unsurprisingly, Muslim people of color in the Maghreb, like the Haratin, opposed such prejudice. Some responded with countermyths. For example, a version of the Ham myth popular among Haratin communities in Mauritania held that all the sons of Noah were born light-skinned.[63] According to this version, one day Ham was walking while carrying the Holy Koran on his head.

Suddenly the heavens opened with a violent downpour and Ham was drenched. When he arrived at his destination, Ham noticed that rain had bled some of the ink out of the pages of the Koran and had impregnated his skin. In this version these "descendents of Ham" saw their dark skin not as a curse but rather as a blessing, a sign of God's favor and their special relationship to the revelations.

The question of race in Algerian history is complex and not fully understood. The boundaries separating "white" and "black," "free" and "servile" in Algeria were contested, fragile, and occasionally permeable. The institution of slavery ensured that they were further obscured and instrumentalized. Processes of social stratification and differentiation reflected a host of categories, including (real and imagined) kinship relations, gender, language, political alliances (*Saff*), religious affiliation (Muslims, Jews, Christians, polytheists), Sufi association, genealogy (*Shurfā*), age, and, of course, economic differences. Moreover, Islamic law's primacy of patrilineal descent ensured that many children of African slave mothers, like those born to Sufi Cheikhs, followed their fathers into the ranks of the elite. Thus, physical characteristics were only one aspect of the complex calculus that resulted in a stratified society. Nevertheless, the fact that so many people of color arrived in the Algerian Sahara in a state of total abjection after having been captured in raids and wars that confused origin and religious profession—a confusion magnified and manipulated by slave traders and owners—had major ramifications with respect to how people understood physical difference and social hierarchy.

The idea that black Africans and their descendents were inherently enslavable or somehow more servile than others continued to exercise a strong hold on Algerian beliefs throughout the colonial period.[64] Moreover, as the colonial regime grew in strength in the Algerian Sahara, a complex dialogue between Algero-Saharan and French views of race further shifted categories, complicating matters during this period. For example, one officer who was asked about the suitability of incorporating black Africans troops among the ranks of the French army in Algeria responded: "The man of the black race is considered by the Muslim populations as belonging to an inferior race, whether he was born free or slave. The military value of our troops might fall in discredit in our new conquest by virtue of the fact of having seen blacks among their ranks."[65] Such exchanges of views had important repercussions both in terms of colonial policy and social categories like race.

Anticipating these abuses, Ahmad Baba concluded the *Mi'rāj al-Ṣu'ūd* with a warning concerning the social hierarchies produced by slavery, namely, that those who owned other humans should not be carried away by their power. To lend authority to his views, Ahmad Baba cited a portion of the Prophet's chastisement of the slave owner: "God caused you to own him, and had He wished, He would have caused him to own you."[66] Ahmad Baba advised that although the master's power is great, there is nothing preordained or natural about the social hierarchies inscribed in the master-slave relationship. They were not legitimated by physical difference or by spurious traditions of transgenerational curses that so many supposed were at the root of these differences. Enslavement was solely a reflection of God's will, which was as omnipotent as it was ultimately unknowable. Those who chose to ignore this fact and deny slaves the fundamental humanity they shared in common with everyone were on a perilous course. "All men are the sons of Adam," Ahmad Baba concluded.[67]

THE TRANS-SAHARAN CROSSING

The fact that Saaba was a freeborn Muslim and deserving of her freedom was recognized by authorities in Timbuktu. Her sale, which was determined to be illegal, was forbidden. However, Saaba did not regain her freedom. The protections authorities extended were limited and did not extend much past the city's limits. Her captors, intent on realizing a profit from their raid, simply left Timbuktu and sought markets farther afield, where officials would be less intent on enforcing the letter of the law.

Leaving Timbuktu, Saaba went north across the Sahara, a place popularly known as the *bilād al-athūsh* (the land of thirst). The hardships and dangers Saaba endured during the trip along the Niger River to Timbuktu paled in comparison with the difficulties of this desert crossing. Whatever chances she might have had to return home vanished the moment she journeyed north. She provided the following laconic account to Largeau: "Then we crossed horrible deserts on foot, where there was neither water nor vegetation; many of us died on the journey. . . . We arrived at In Salah, where they sold us. Then we were brought here. We traveled only at night because of the heat."[68]

Travel was quite dangerous even between the oases of the northern Algerian Sahara, like Biskra and El Oued, which were separated by only 230 kilometers. The far-off central desert between Timbuktu and In Salah was especially difficult to cross.[69] The route was long—at least 1,500 kilometers—and points of water were few and far between. Moreover, political upheavals had added to the route's inherent dangers.[70] The two Tuareg confederations that controlled most of this region, the Ajjer and Ahaggar Tuareg, had been at war since 1873. Moreover, in 1876 Ottoman leaders in Tripoli began to occupy oases along the well-established Tripoli-Ghadamès-Ghat-Agadez-Kano route, a move that the Tuareg resisted, leading to further instability and risk. The caravans that frequented the route to Tripoli had to detour farther west to In Salah. This resulted in overcrowded camps, polluted water sources, and increased demand for scarce resources along the trail.

A caravan's success depended on a combination of experienced leadership and good fortune. The desert's harsh geography allowed for few mistakes, and its risks were shared unequally. When accidents occurred, it was the most vulnerable in the party—slaves—who first suffered the consequences. An 1875 report from British authorities in Bingazi provides some idea of the hardships captives endured during the crossing. While touring the main entrepôt at the Jalu oasis, south of Bingazi, one observer noted that the slaves who arrived here were in the last stages of exhaustion and malnourishment.[71] "They were emaciated to the point of mere skeletons, their long, thin legs and arms and the apparently unnatural size and prominence of their knees, elbows, hands, and feet giving them a most repulsive and shocking appearance."[72]

Deaths were common. Saaba reported that in her group many perished, but she provided no further details. The trans-Saharan route was among the most dangerous traveled by Africans bound for slavery. Historians Ralph Austen and Dennis Cordell concluded that "[trans-Saharan] death rates were significantly higher than on the Atlantic crossing."[73] Austen's 1992 figures on the trans-Saharan slave trade provide the best estimate of casualties.[74] Examining the records of the British vice-consul in the Fezzan region (in modern-day Libya), Austen found that in 1847 a caravan of 1,281 captives arriving in Murzuq experienced "huge deaths" as a result of a smallpox outbreak. The following year the same consul reported that 1,600 captives—the entire caravan—had died of thirst. In 1849 he reported that 834 slaves out of a total of 3,218 (26%) had died on the way to the Fezzan. In the Mediterranean port of Bingazi European consular officials also noted the elevated mortality rates. The Sardinian consul at Tripoli mentioned in 1850 that of the 2,400 slaves who had arrived at Bingazi from Wadai (Muslim monarchy whose territory is today part of Chad), another 2,500 to 3,000 slaves (over 50%) had died. That same year the British vice-consul at Bingazi reported that of 1,200 slaves traveling the same route, only 770 arrived (64%). Accounting for the fact that these central Saharan routes through modern-day Libya were among the most dangerous, Austen concluded that captives suffered losses averaging 20 percent. To the west Austen estimated a lower mortality rate of 15 percent to Tunisia, 10 percent to Algeria, and 6 percent to Morocco.[75]

Anecdotal accounts, filtered through popular memory, emphasize the tragic episodes, providing an additional illustration of how crossings could go disastrously wrong. For example, Fulgence Fresnel, writing from Bingazi in 1846, recounted the story of a man he named Scheheymak, a trader from the Jalu oasis, who in 1810 charted a new direct Wadai-Bingazi route that passed through the region of Al Khofra and the oasis agglomeration at Awila (a.k.a Augila) and Jalu (Libya).[76] This route, which crossed one of the fiercest and most arid stretches of the desert, was difficult even by Saharan standards. Scheheymak's first attempt involved a caravan of five hundred camels and an unspecified number of slaves. Fresnel reported that Scheheymak's guides betrayed him at a critical intersection, bypassing the only well within several days' journey. Thirty-five years later, the people in Bingazi still recalled that "most of the slaves and camels died of thirst." Scheheymak, however, was not discouraged. He made large profits on

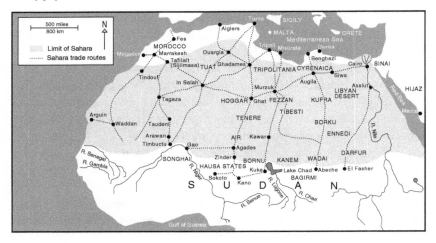

FIGURE 3 Trade routes of North Africa.
Source: John Wright, *The Trans-Saharan Slave Trade* (London: Routledge, 2007), n.p.

the survivors: a slave purchased for 7–8 thalers sold for 40 in Bingazi. "Despite
the losses suffered, the return of this caravan caused a great sensation . . . [and]
excited the greed of the merchants." Other examples include the Chaamba
trader Sid el Hadj Mohamed, who was interviewed by Eugène Daumas in 1845.
He confessed to making one particularly deadly mistake: on a trip from Zinder
to the Fezzan he lost four thousand of his five thousand captives.[77] Even if the
numbers are exaggerated (a single caravan that size would be exceptional),
the proportions of those who died are frightful enough in themselves. Another
example, dating from 1805, concerns Ouargla, where, according to Jean Lethielleux, a catastrophe befell a caravan that departed Timbuktu enroute to the salt
mines at Taoudenni. The leader missed a critical well, a mistake that reputedly
cost the lives of two thousand people.[78]

Fifty years later, when it began producing detailed records on Saharan trade,
the French administration avoided mentioning mortality rates of slaves during
desert crossings, but they occasionally made their way into reports.[79] This data
supports the belief that the Saharan crossing to Algerian oases was particularly
dangerous and deadly for slaves. For example, a September 1891 report from
Ouargla documented the deaths of forty captives enroute to In Salah from Timbuktu.[80] Another report spoke of the terrible fate of over three hundred slaves
traveling north from Timbuktu in April 1890. Raiders attacked the caravan and
left the captives to their own devices. "As a result," the report concluded, "a
considerable number of Negroes in this caravan died of hunger. According to
the natives, only one in twenty survived."[81]

[8]

THE SAHARAN SLAVE TRADE AND ABOLITION

In order to understand how Saaba arrived in French-controlled Ouargla in the period when slavery was officially abolished, it is necessary to interrupt her story to examine the world of the slave trade as it relates to colonial Algeria after 1848. The rise of modern European empires in the Mediterranean and the changing political scene in the region ultimately threatened this business in the nineteenth century. This was partly due to the abolition efforts of the British, who, beginning in 1807, attempted to halt the African slave trade, but they were not alone. By 1846 the bey of Tunis had officially abolished the trade and slaveholding in his domain.[1] Ottoman rulers in Tripoli took similar steps to abolish slave trading. Beginning in the 1850s, the bey in Tripoli issued a series of decrees to reduce the violence of the trade. In 1857 there was an official Ottoman move to abolish the trade in slaves as part of the Tanzimat reforms.[2]

ABOLITION IN ALGERIA: EUGÈNE SUBTIL'S PLANS
TO REVIVE THE TRADE

When its neighbors to the east abolished slavery, pressure progressively increased to curtail the trade in Algeria. Historically slavery had been an important institution here, and it continued to be so during the colonial era. Although there were no longer any Christian slaves—people abducted in Mediterranean raids, forced to work, and held for ransom—African slaves of color nevertheless remained. In the northern Tell notables owned slaves of color and exploited them for domestic help and as concubines. In the Sahara slave and servile labor was the basis of settled life in the oases. Throughout Algeria slaves constituted an important part of the elites' social and cultural capital: the ownership and control of others' bodies was a marker of social status. Even before the passage of the abolition law in 1848, French colonialism had altered these relations as part of the social mutations that accompanied French rule. However, slavery maintained its importance in Algeria well into the nineteenth century.[3] Although exact figures are lacking, French estimates in the 1840s mentioned some ten thousand slaves in the parts of Algeria under their control, and it is likely there were thousands more.[4]

By the 1840s there was talk of abolishing slavery throughout the French colonies. In Algeria, however, few colonial administrators were willing to devote the resources necessary to end slavery and slave sales, scoffing at the idealism of abolitionists. For his part, Governor-General Bugeaud found the whole project a waste of effort at a time when French attention needed to be focused on more urgent matters, such as defeating Abdelkader. An 1844 call for abolition from the African Institute in Paris provoked the following sharp retort: "It would be impossible to ask of such a government as ours the vigilant surveillance that it would take to stop the arrival of Negroes [nègres] by desert caravans and their sale in the markets of Algeria. To obtain that, it would take more than this grand army of bureaucrats, large and small, that you have in France, and even then I would ask you who will pay for it?"[5]

Bugeaud expressed his opposition to abolition by utilizing his standard rhetoric, a sardonic retort that masked its cunning with the logic of cost and utility. Assuming the mantle of a pragmatist, Bugeaud argued that it was too difficult to enforce abolition in Algeria and refused to take abolitionists seriously, disdainfully referring to them as "philanthropists." Bugeaud argued that the civilizing mission in Algeria was too challenging a task, and that however much one might want to liberate slaves, it would bring more pain and suffering than good. Others adopted the same argument, insisting that the indemnities to be paid to masters (envisioned as part of an abolition decree concerned mainly with French slave owners in the Caribbean and Indian Ocean) would be burdensome, contributing to the already high price of the Algerian occupation.

European colonial officials used the same argument, couched in terms of pragmatism and unintended consequences, throughout Africa, where slavery died "a slow death."[6] They subordinated the moral considerations of abolition to the practical issues of colonial rule, preferring to compromise the law in order to accommodate slaveholding elites and thereby achieve social order. Bugeaud's case is noteworthy. Although in 1844 he claimed to be overstretched and lacking necessary resources to abolish slavery, only four years earlier, when he was positioning himself to be named governor-general, he did not see slavery in terms of accommodation with the status quo, that is, a necessary evil. In fact, in 1840 he considered ways to purchase thousands of African slaves from Saharan traders. His goal was to boost Saharan commerce and use the slaves to meet the Algerian colony's growing labor needs.

The catalyst for these plans was a two-month voyage to the Fezzan between October and December 1839 by an obscure individual named Eugène Mathieu Subtil. The historical record has little to say about Subtil, including where he came from and what he was doing in the central Sahara at this time. Although it seems likely, there is no evidence to suggest that Subtil undertook this trip on the initiative of the government. Apparently he went as a private individual in search of mineral wealth.[7] What is known is that Subtil was ambitious and had a keen eye for opportunity. Also self-evident is the fact that the French government saw his proposals as both haphazard—his notes were undated, lacked an addressee, and remained unsigned—and politically sensitive. Policymakers took care to keep their distance in their correspondence.

The Fezzan, part of present-day Libya, was an important Saharan crossroads linking the Chad basin with the Mediterranean Sea. Located south of Tripoli, this strategic region experienced a long period of political turmoil after Ottomans seized Tripoli from Qaramanli rulers in 1835 and attempted to wrest control of trans-Saharan trade from autonomous Saharan groups.[8] This struggle provided opportunities for European powers. Subtil—who belonged to that shady class of informal agents, adventurers, and opportunists who played such an important role in shaping colonial policy in Africa and the Middle East—saw advantages for himself and for France. When he returned to Paris in late December 1839 or January 1840, Subtil established contact with officials at the War Ministry and presented a project to expand French influence far into the desert. He assured them that the conflict between Ottoman leaders in Tripoli and the Awlad Sulayman of the Fezzan, led by Abd al-Jalil, offered great opportunities for France and the Algerian colony.[9] Inasmuch as he considered the Ottomans his rivals, Abd al-Jalil was an attractive ally to the French. Subtil claimed that Abd al-Jalil headed a military force of fifty thousand men and that his influence ranged as far east as Egypt and as far south as the Hausa states. Pressed by wars with Ottoman authorities, Abd al-Jalil sought help from France and was prepared to enter into an alliance that would open routes into central Africa. Although Subtil provided many, often conflicting, details about the struggle between Abd al-Jalil and Tripoli, he insisted that French intervention on Abd al-Jalil's side would yield a large bounty. At stake was the commerce that traveled back and forth between the ports at Tripoli and Bingazi and the markets across the Sahara. If a deal could be struck, Abd al-Jalil promised to divert this trade to French merchants in Algeria. Moreover, Subtil promised the French that if British influence in Egypt ever posed a threat, Abd al-Jalil could harass the British and their allies along the desert frontier.[10]

It is unknown who Subtil first approached with this project when he returned to Paris in late December 1839 or January 1840.[11] Bugeaud, striving to replace Governor-General Valée in Algeria, learned of it and found it appealing. A letter Subtil wrote to the prime minister confirmed that he had contacted Bugeaud, who supported the proposed alliance with Abd al-Jalil.[12] The initial response from the Ministry of War was late in coming, but when it arrived in November 1840 it bespoke the same enthusiasm. The ministry found Subtil well suited for this type of diplomacy: "The man is enterprising and courageous, who, alone and without protection, was able to penetrate an unknown country and meet a leader whose name was unknown. Such a man deserves the encouragement of the government of his country, to which his efforts may one day bring profit."[13] Plans went forward and Subtil received instructions to collect samples of trade goods while in France and prepare for a return trip to close the deal with Abd al-Jalil the following winter.

There were many reasons why the French government found the alliance so attractive. This was a period of tension in the Mediterranean, when the "Eastern Question" posed by Egypt and the Ottoman Empire became the "Eastern Crisis," threatening conflict between Great Britain and France. Projecting French influence eastward toward Egypt through armed allies like Abd al-Jalil was a seductive proposition. The Ministry of War was especially happy to work with informal agents like Subtil, who provided it with a safe margin of deniability and secrecy, both valuable tools in the tangled diplomatic maneuvers of the great powers.[14] Seen from the perspective of the Algerian colony, Subtil's venture also had strong merits. The economy in eastern Algeria was stagnant. Its capital, Constantine, had still not recovered from the 1837 sack by French troops.[15] Looking forward to his tenure as governor-general, Bugeaud hoped to reinvigorate commerce in the Constantine region with Saharan caravans.[16]

As a political alliance, the plan with Abd al-Jalil was straightforward, but its economic aspects were unclear. In particular, the question loomed concerning what goods the caravans might bring to Algeria. French merchants were sure to be enthused by the prospect of new markets in central Africa, but what would they receive in exchange? At this early point, nothing much was known about the details of Saharan commerce and only dates seemed to be of any value. Here the negotiations took a curious twist. Subtil suggested that slaves could be imported to Algeria, where they might be freed and provide labor and military service. Citing Muhammad Ali's efforts to raise an army of slaves in Egypt, Subtil argued that African slaves would make excellent soldiers and workers in Algeria. The Ministry of War took this proposal seriously: "If the caravan brings Negro slaves from the Sudan—young, healthy, and in a state to carry arms—these blacks will be bought by the administration to be liberated."[17] The report further stated that the price must not exceed two hundred francs a head, and that they should include few women and children and no one over thirty-five years of age. The scale of the project was important: the Ministry of War was ready to purchase up to forty-five hundred men and five hundred women and children in the first order alone. "If the blacks delivered and bought back seem to be capable of [providing] good military service, one could accept another larger delivery."[18] This was a huge order, representing a figure just shy of the entire annual traffic across the entire Sahara at this time.[19] Subtil remained undaunted. At two hundred francs a head, he assured the French, "Abd al-Jalil will be able to furnish us with as many as we request."[20]

The plan was good news to many. "At the end of two or three years," Subtil promised, "we will have a well-trained, armed troop."[21] Bugeaud himself shared this enthusiasm. His bid for the governor-general's position was based on his promise to come up with fresh solutions to the intractable problems in Algeria. Along with robust military efforts, his plans included developing new forms of settlements, such as military colonies. Inspired by the Roman model, Bugeaud envisioned a system of militarized agricultural settlements as the backbone of French Algeria.[22] They alone could bring order to the troubled colony by establishing a permanent military grid across the interior. The costs were formidable, and even more daunting were the labor requirements of this project. Soldiers could not build the settlements by themselves, and the travails of agricultural work threatened to compromise their security and policing duties. The army in Algeria, over 70,000 men strong in 1840, was already stretched thin. Anticipating this problem, in 1840 Bugeaud entreated Parliament: "Look for colonists everywhere; take them at all costs—take them in the cities, in the countryside, from your neighbors—because we will need 150,000 in a few years."[23] The tone of this comment makes it clear that Bugeaud did not count on fulfilling his labor needs through a patriotic "levée en masse." Irrespective of military colonies, European settlements in general raised the suspicions of the army leaders who controlled Algeria. Could French civilians, descendents of the 1789 generation—many of whom had taken to the streets in 1830—be counted on in Algeria?

Thus, extending over and above specific problems in Algeria was France's "social question." Bugeaud had utter contempt for the urban poor and saw them as unsuitable candidates for the work of colonization: "I do not know what we might hope from this part of the European population, which flees to Africa to escape the misery that weighs on them in their country. If these men are poor, it is probably because they are lazy or vicious."[24] He was generally more at ease with rural people and held a conservative vision of a French peasantry that was stalwart and apolitical. Nevertheless, the Great Fear of the summer of 1789 was still a living memory for Bugeaud. Later in 1848 he would narrowly escape the wrath of enraged French peasants when they cornered him at his estate in the Dordogne region.[25] As early as 1837 Bugeaud had expressed his doubts concerning French colonists, maintaining that Algeria needed "a warrior population

used to work in the fields and organized along the lines of the Arab tribes, cultivating and defending the soil."[26] French soldiers might be able endure this hardship and discipline, but then they could hardly fight and French civilians plainly could not be counted on in any role, in Bugeaud's opinion. African slaves,
on the other hand, fit the profile. They offered a much-needed source of labor
and might even provide military service. The five thousand being considered by
the Ministry of War promised a good first start to meet Bugeaud's needs. At two
hundred francs apiece, they were inexpensive and, as Subtil noted, "This small
price will soon be paid back to the state."[27]

Abolition was still eight years away, but the question of slavery in Algeria was
already a sensitive matter. Plans to bring thousands of slaves to Algeria were sure
to encounter stiff opposition from reformers in Paris. Moreover, such a project would likely raise the ire of the British and lead to diplomatic problems.[28]
Anticipating all this, Subtil stressed that his project could be presented as one
of enfranchisement. After all, the slaves would be emancipated upon arrival in
Algeria. What philanthropist could possibly object to bringing people into the
fold of civilization and freeing them from the archaic burdens of African slavery? However, he reminded the officials at the Ministry of War that although the
slaves would be emancipated, they would not be free. The French state could
count on many years of labor because each slave would have to pay back his or
her purchase price. Subtil reasoned that "this sum will be considered the price
of engagement for life and from it will derive their liberty."[29] In his opinion, this
approach "avoids the question of the slave trade."

As hopeful as planners were, this first project came to naught. Subtil disappeared after returning to Libya in 1841, and when he resurfaced three years later
'Abd al-Jalil was dead, effectively ending plans for a Saharan alliance. Nevertheless Subtil persisted. In 1844 he sent the Ministry of War a revised project. As
was the case in 1840, unfree labor was still central to his schemes, but now he
recast the terms of servitude. Rather than encouraging the French state to purchase slaves outright, Subtil argued that the slave trade per se no longer existed
since, as he insisted, British efforts had brought it to an end. In effect, those who
crossed the Sahara were not captives bound for slavery but refugees fleeing wars
in their homelands. As he wrote to the minister of war, "Following these wars, it
often happens that persecuted families or even entire tribes not strong enough
to resist their enemies emigrate under the protection of the large caravans and
come to the Barbary States, which offer them guarantees of security and liberty,
and [here they] establish small colonies."[30]

Thus, people who had been slaves in 1840 became settlers. In addition to
living in settlements outside Tripoli and Tunis, they founded some twenty villages in the desert of Cyrenaica, and, according to Subtil, some remote provinces are "nearly entirely inhabited by them." These settlers were an important
economic resource for Ottoman authorities. "The Pachas have always favored

the establishment on their territory of these calm and laborious people," Subtil wrote. "They gave them lands that the settlers cultivate carefully and on which they pay the tithe without failure." Moreover, these communities farmed, did domestic work, and labored on special corvées for the state. Although "long and difficult," such work was performed consistently, with "a docility and resignation that contrasts sharply with the turbulent and unsubmissive character of the Arab tribes."[31]

"What has happened in Tripoli can occur in Algeria," Subtil promised. "Settlers" from the south of the Sahara could be relocated to the rural interior and placed in fortified villages to guard the frontiers with Morocco, Tunisia, and the Sahara. "Recognizing the mildness and fairness of our domination," more "migrants" from the south would soon start north and settle in these villages. One day "we will have faithful and devoted allies and intrepid and courageous guardians, for these men, mild and pacifistic in their relations, defend their territories with a heroic stubbornness when they are attacked." "The free Negro," Subtil continued, "is naturally good, faithful, devoted, and grateful to his benefactor." In short, they were everything the Algerians were not. This was an important point, which Subtil stressed in order to tap into fears about security in Algeria and the indigenous question. Subtil concluded: "If we want to contain these fanatic populations [of Algerians], we must act continually on them, make them feel our force and authority at every moment, for only the fear of an immediate punishment will keep them respectful and obedient."[32]

FREED SLAVES AND ARAB EXTERMINATION: EUGÈNE BODICHON

Subtil's second plan to solve Algeria's labor problem with a workforce of African "settlers" went nowhere, and on 29 June 1844 the project was officially rejected.[33] Whereas in 1840 the government approved the plan to open Algeria to slave caravans, four years later abolition was clearly on the horizon. Colonial officials like Saharan specialist Ernest Carette, who reviewed Subtil's project, were not duped by the real status of most people traveling north across the Sahara, who, although forced to move because of war, were hardly refugees.[34] Nevertheless, colonial planners faced the same problems—namely, labor and security—as they had before. Subtil's words underscoring the "devotion" of African slaves of color contrasted with Algerian combativeness and resonated strongly in the mid-1840s as the wars with Abdelkader reached their climax..

Nearly fifteen years in the making, the French colony in Algeria had seen little peace and had involved enormous sums. Between 1831 and 1840 France had spent a total of 341,221,125 francs in Algeria (see table 1.1), and by 1845 the military was spending nearly 8,000,000 francs annually for military fortifications and buildings alone.[35] Added to this was the fact that by 1845 it took nearly 100,000 soldiers garrisoned in Algeria to keep the peace, and that nearly 74,000 of them had lost their lives since 1830 (see table 1.2). When Subtil's project finally came to light in 1844 and appeared in the *Revue de l'Orient*, it struck a chord among readers intrigued by the thought of settling the most difficult and insecure parts of the Algerian interior with the sort of loyal and hardworking people Subtil described.[36]

As the war with Abdelkader and others dragged on, there were many individuals in Algeria who contemplated the colony's problems with growing frustration and rancor. Eugène Bodichon, for one, was inspired by Subtil's vision of docile human traffic crossing the desert, prompting him to consider the most violent solutions to the problems of colonization in Algeria. Bodichon, a doctor by profession, was born into a noble Breton family in 1810. After finishing medical studies in Paris in 1835, he came to Algeria and set up a medical practice in Algiers. Bodichon was a committed Republican, and during his student days he was close to militant Republican figures like François Guépin and Louis Blanc. In Algeria he earned a reputation for charity by offering his services gratis to the poor. In 1857 he married Barbara Leigh Smith, the famous British feminist and cousin of Florence Nightingale. The couple spent their honeymoon in North America, where they participated in important political debates involving slavery and American racial theories.[37] A Republican committed to helping the poor, furthering women's rights, and opposing slavery, Bodichon was among the most politically progressive figures among his peers in Algiers. He was not, however, a friend of the Algerians.

Bodichon frequently offered his thoughts on colonization in Algeria in the local press. Many of his efforts centered upon what since the 1830s had been called the indigenous question, the fundamental dilemma of creating a settler colony in a land that was already settled. Initially Bodichon presented favorable portraits of Algerians, which he collectively called "Moghrébins," and expressed an optimistic vision of Franco-Algerian relations.[38] Bodichon met Abdelkader in 1838 while on a mission with Charles Garavini, the U.S. consul in Algiers, and the scholar Adrien Berbrugger. The doctor was struck by the emir's intelligence and foresight and predicted that the French and the Algerians would have a prosperous future together. However, when hostilities recommenced in 1839 Bodichon turned definitively against the emir. He rallied in support of the harsh rhetoric of people like General Bugeaud, defending the conservative general's belief that force alone could bring peace. If the Algerian colony was to survive, extreme solutions to the indigenous question would have to be found.

Bodichon's thought radicalized rapidly in the following decade. In the 1840s he began a prolific period of writing, producing a series of articles that delved into nascent theories of scientific racism and arguments anticipating the die off of "primitive races."[39] Known to researchers today as the theory of autogenocide, these discourses envisioned the eventual die-off or "disappearance" of colonized peoples.[40] Pushed to the margins by European global expansion, they would suffer a demographic catastrophe. While Bodichon was intrigued by the way these theories resolved the indigenous question, they left him contemplating the prospect of an empty wasteland in Algeria. Compounding the problem was the fact that the same ideas that slated colonized peoples for destruction reappeared in the guise of acclimatization theory, which posited that Europeans were unsuited to inhabit certain environments, like the "African" climate of Algeria.[41] Bodichon's medical experience, for example, led him to conclude that for Europeans settlers "death comes quickly in Algeria."[42]

Faced with these concerns, Bodichon considered Subtil's project. The explorer was correct in assuming that only people who were acclimated to the climate would take root as settlers in Algeria. Bodichon also agreed that such colonists could best be found by diverting captives from the Saharan slave trade and directing them toward Algeria, where they would be legally emancipated and put to work on the land: "They will give us the hands that we lack in undertaking agricultural works."[43] Unlike European colonists, who might be expected to become ill at alarming rates, slaves lived in the harshest of African climates and would thus easily acclimatize to Algeria's comparatively clement weather. Once established, they would form a core of hearty, productive, and tireless colonists. Moreover, Bodichon believed that these former slaves, grateful for their freedom, would embrace Christianity and French ways and become enduring allies of France's cause in Africa: "Fifty years from now, more than 100,000 blacks, Christian and Frenchified [francisés], solidly planted in Africa, will aid us to establish an equilibrium with the Arabic race."[44]

Bodichon was so confident about the project that he speculated Algeria might prove to be a lure for enslaved Africans around the world, with slaves from as far away as the United States and South America seeking their freedom in Algeria: "If the Negro villages succeed, free blacks—men of color from the American states—will adopt Algeria as their homeland. Because here, where slavery does not exist and Europe is so close, they will not have to worry about being treated as *minors* [social underclasses] because of the color of their skin."[45] The hand of friendship Bodichon extended to the enslaved peoples of the world was part of his country's larger "revolutionary and democratic mandate," as he wrote.

The rhetoric of freedom and liberation for slaves developed in conjunction with a frankly murderous one for Algerians. This was partially expressed in terms of autogenocide. Bodichon cited the case of American Indians to make his point concerning Algerians. Although in Bodichon's opinion American Indians had been approached by Europeans benevolently, "they ran quickly toward the extinction of their race." Of a population that once numbered sixteen million, Bodichon counted only two million surviving in all of North America.[46] The same thing was happening "in Tahiti, New Holland, New Zealand, and on other islands of Australia and Polynesia."[47] Bodichon understood this demographic collapse as an ethnobiological fact, and it would produce the same results in Algeria, where the French were like "the pioneers in America, the English in Oceania and in southern Africa."[48] However, unlike some theories of autogenocide applied to North America, such as James Fenimore Cooper's *Last of the Mohicans* (1826) or François-René de Chateaubriand's *Atala* (1801) — both of which were wildly popular in France — Bodichon had no interest in constructing heroic, if archaic, virtues for the "last of" the Algerians.[49] He gave credence to his exterminationist arguments by means of the crudest caricatures of Algerians: "The *Moghrébins* are dominated only by terror. End it and they abandon themselves to the natural impulses: insurrections and plundering will multiply."[50] Algerians also blocked progress: "They remain stationary in the face of civilization and live in a state of perpetual hostility against all who are not part of their race."[51]

All this prompted Bodichon to ask his readers to reflect on what, in the end, is an "Arab":

He is the law of the strongest and the law of retaliation (lex talionis), of religious intolerance and the isolation of his coreligionists. He sanctions slavery, polygamy, castration, infibulations of women, despotism, servility within and hostility without. That is why we must combat him, we Christians who represent the preponderance of morality, who reject eunuchs and harems, and who carry with us the spirit of fraternity among all people, liberty for the strong and the weak, and universal benevolence.[52]

Borrowing freely from old discourses of oriental despotism, these arguments were pushed even further. In this passage Bodichon effectively created an exclusionary category to determine who is human and divided people into distinct communities represented, on the one hand, by Europeans and those (like African slaves) who fit into what Bodichon saw as the subject race to be liberated and, on the other, by the frightful "Arab" or archaic and violent "*Moghrébin*." Never departing from the terms of Republican humanism as he understood them, Bodichon effectively stripped Algerians of their humanity.

Moreover, Bodichon's writings were couched in the developing grammar of pseudoscientific racism, claiming that there was an essential racial incompatibility between the French and Algerians. He rejected the Saint-Simonian "fusion of the races" as absurd yet also found to be unworkable the assimilation of Algerians, based on their resignation and fatalism, proposed by military leaders like General Bugeaud and Eugène Daumas, who thought that in accepting their defeat Algerians would agree to assimilate as subaltern subjects. For Bodichon coexistence was impossible. Indeed, the mere physical proximity of Algerians would compromise France's future in North Africa. They were like a "gnawing worm" (un ver rongeur) that invaded the fragile roots of the civilization France had planted in Algeria and impeded its growth. As he put it, "The tree of European civilization needs lands vast enough where it can develop despite tempests; where it can then extend its branches into the depths of barbarous Africa. But if we are not careful, the Arab element, like a gnawing worm, will invade this tree, and although it has been well watered with sweat and blood, it will remain stunted and infertile."[53]

At the heart of the problem was an unalterable racial divide separating the Algerians from the French, barbarians from the civilized. Bodichon sketched it in zoological terms,

> In the state of nature, the wild dog, horse, and cow are instinctively the enemies of the domesticated dog, horse, and cow. This is a truth that is proven by numerous observations. It is such for the savage man and the civilized man. The first feels when in the company of the second, or even in the sight of the second, an instinctive antipathy, a natural aversion that sooner or later degenerates into hatred.
>
> Thus, the *Moghrébins* are our *natural enemies* because they will be barbarians and we will be civilized.[54]

The contrast Bodichon drew between, on the one hand, the barrier that separated the Algerians from the French and, on the other, the "grateful" slave-colonist could hardly be more striking. He used it to ease his readers into a consideration of extermination. Given the intractability of the Algerians, peace would come to the country only when "there would be no more Arabs on the surface of the Tell."[55] As he wrote: "If, instead of eight hundred thousand Arabs who in Algeria murder, pillage, kill prisoners, the shipwrecked, practice perpetual brigandage on the routes, sodomize, produce nothing, allow the plains to turn into pestilential marshes; . . . if, instead of this race, which is an affront to nature and humanity by its social state; if, instead of this eight hundred thousand, there were not one, in truth, nature and civilization would be the winners."[56] Or, as he put it in a blunt expression of his chilling vision, "Here their extinction is, therefore, for the general good."[57]

Fully disentangling the web of Bodichon's racism, accounting for its impact, and tracing its influence is beyond the scope of this chapter. I have found no trace of Bodichon in the archives of the governor-general's office, and his political activities as a student did not produce a police file on him in Paris. This makes judging the significance of his thoughts on colony policymaking difficult. Nevertheless, he did introduce dangerous new terms and ideas into the debate about slavery and abolition in Algeria. Most important, he brought the idea of extermination into questions that most pundits considered only in terms of the alternatives of pragmatism and idealism. In particular, Bodichon used his imaginary African "settlers"—essentially slaves brought across the Sahara for a life of servitude in Algeria—to keep his values of progress and civilization untarnished in the midst of the violence he projected for Algerians. If African slaves could be brought to Algeria, liberated from their shackles, and made free men and women, and if the labor of these people made the colony blossom, would not the "extinction" of Algeria's people be for the "general good," their extermination viewed as part of the civilizing mission?

Bodichon's fantasy of servile African people of color coming to Algeria made possible this extermination and situated it within the project of civilization. Whereas Subtil peddled his own project to the government in the standard colonial triad of order, authority, and economy—villages of "calm" taxpayers and military recruits—Bodichon saw in enslaved Africans a sort of human flood that would drive Algerians out of the French colony. He insisted that this was morally correct and useful and, in any case, was an inevitable aspect of the march of human progress. Like the original inhabitants of the Americas, Australia, and the Pacific islands, Bodichon reasoned that in Algeria as well "the natives melt like snow in the sun."[58]

RECEPTION OF THE 1848 ABOLITION IN ALGERIA

The Ministry of War and the governor-general of Algeria were unable to follow through on their offer to buy five thousand slaves from Subtil in 1840. Bodichon's project to annihilate Algerians and replace them with liberated slaves similarly came to naught. These schemes ended on 27 April 1848 when the Second Republic abolished slavery. The efforts of activists like Victor Schoelcher succeeded in outlawing the traffic in and ownership of human beings in all French-controlled territories.[59] Nevertheless, the abolition of slavery in Algeria was a long-drawn-out affair that did not end until the twentieth century.[60] Slavery in Algeria sustained itself through a variety of forces, including the resilience of precolonial institutions, clandestine practices adopted by slave traders and slaveowners (especially their ability to exploit ambiguities in the personal status of slaves by presenting them as free but servile), and, finally, a singular lack of will on the part of the colonial administration to enforce the letter of the law. French administrators accommodated slavery in many parts of the country, most notably in remote areas of the Algerian interior. It was not until 1905 that a concerted effort was made to abolish slavery throughout the colony.[61] In the interim French administrators concentrated on practical issues of colonial rule and downplayed the moral considerations embedded in the abolition legislation by emphasizing the benevolence ("douceur") of local conditions of enslavement. This translated into tolerance for slavery as part of larger efforts to accommodate local elites and avoid social unrest. Yet the position of colonial administrators toward slavery and abolition could swing in the opposite direction as well. In cases where administrators deemed that accommodation with local elites did not serve French interests, they could use the abolition legislation to punish masters by emancipating their slaves or protecting fugitives. In the end, slavery in Algeria was hardly "abolished" but waned only gradually.

In the first decades following abolition, the colonial administration's response was characterized by periodic and erratic enforcement and an overall "politique de l'autruche," or "see no evil, hear no evil, speak no evil." At the local level — especially among the commanders in the south, where slavery and the slave trade were most important — administrators were reluctant to enforce abolition. They feared jeopardizing alliances with the local elites, upon which their power depended. Sensing the apathy of their superiors, they ignored infractions. Moreover, both the governor-general's office and the local administration found that the abolition law could be an effective policy tool when used selectively to punish and reward.

Most colonial administrators had known that abolition was imminent since the passage of the law of 18 July 1845. This law marked the beginning of the end of legal slavery in the French colonies. It established the conditions of "rachat forcé" (self-purchase/manumission) and gave slaves a civil status.[62] Nevertheless, in the spring of 1848 news that the provisional government in Paris had actually decreed the total abolition of slavery caught the governor-general's office off guard. The revolution of 1848 already brought with it a host of dizzying changes, including the decree of 4 March 1848, which declared that Algeria was an integral part of the metropolis and called for the complete restructuring of the colony's administration.[63] (The changes of the revolution occurred with such speed that even stationery could not keep up: secretaries had to cross out the old letterhead and substitute "République française.") In response to abolition, colonial administrators sent out a flurry of correspondence to commanders of the three military divisions (Oran, Algiers, and Constantine), sounding the law's implications for the security and economic well-being of the colony. The division of Algiers responded that the application of the abolition decree would be problematic: "It raises thousands of difficulties and troubles for the administrators of our tribes in the interior. These difficulties are of such a nature that they risk serious consequences and can compromise the tranquility of Algeria." Moreover, the analyst continued, "the abolition of slavery in Algeria brings with it a deep disturbance of the interior economy of the family; it threatens their mores, their prejudices, and in some ways it puts an end to the household because the Negro is the only person that our natives consider admitting into the heart of the family, to reside within it, to come close to the women and serve them."[64] What this analyst failed to mention was the fact that the French feared not only insurrections and the disruption of Algerian households but the high cost of reparation. The reimbursement of slaveowners in the division of Oran alone was set at over 2.5 million francs.[65] To avoid this expensive option, the governor-general's office equivocated. Lacking a clear strategy, it simply did not distribute the text of the abolition law for the next four months.

In some circulars the governor-general's office announced a serious effort to end slavery. The correspondence cited by historian Dennis Cordell, in one of the first studies of abolition in Algeria, shows that Governor-General Randon demanded vigilance. For example, in 1857 Randon wrote to the Subdivision of Mascara, "Slaves have recently been sold in certain markets of Algeria. I do not need to remind you that this commerce is against the law, but I must recommend that you take great care to assure that the letter of this law is respected. Black men and women brought into Algeria to be sold must be liberated immediately without allowing the traders to claim any indemnity whatsoever."[66]

Randon followed up his abolitionist stance the following year with another reminder to "leave no stone unturned" in investigating reports of slave trading.[67] Nevertheless, Cordell suspects that Randon's orders do not reflect actual practices. As he notes, "the law and the circulars abolishing slavery and the slave trade were clear, but the ambiguity in attitudes persisted until the end of the century and beyond."[68]

THE EYES-CLOSED POLICY ON SLAVERY AND ABOLITION

The researcher's task in documenting such ambiguities is a difficult one. Military administrators avoided discussing questions of slave owning and slave sales in official correspondence. There are, however, some surviving traces in the archives. One such document is an order circulated by the commandant of Constantine specifying how he wanted his local commanders to proceed concerning abolition. It was joined to a copy of the abolition decree, which was first circulated in Algeria on 13 July 1848. The order included the following warning:

> This instruction included herein takes into account the fact that an immediate revelation of this decree to the natives could have grave consequences. Being myself persuaded of this gravity, I think that *we must not display this law in public places, but let it be known by an incessant but discerning effort.* If some educated slave becomes aware of the generosity of the government toward him and comes forward to claim the benefits of the decree that frees him, you must aid him with all your power to enjoy his liberty and let it be known that he was the victim of violence on the part of his master.[69]

This order effectively sought to delay the implementation of abolition without explicitly ordering subordinates to violate the law: one could simply remain mum about the law. The commander anticipated that only in rare instances would the slave learn of his or her freedom. Recrimination from slave owners and the thorny problem of reparations could thus be avoided. This way of proceeding also shielded the high command from the illegal activity. Local commanders could determine at their own discretion which slaves would go free and which owners would suffer the loss.

Other sources shed light on the colonial administration's murky solution to abolition. The letters contained in the "Affaires arabes, correspondance politique, confidentielle" of the governor-general's archive are a valuable source of information.[70] This correspondence documents a quasi-official policy of tolerance toward slavery and the slave trade, especially when it occurred far from the centers of French power. Particularly revealing are the letters generated by the 1856 case of Colonel Naigeon, the commander of Tiaret, a Tell region linked to the Sahara by pastoralists, like the Ouled Naïl, who spent the summer here. While searching for contraband gunpowder, Naigeon discovered three slaves (two men and one woman) recently purchased by those under his authority. He immediately seized and freed the slaves in compliance with the 1848 law. However, the commandant's zeal little pleased his superiors in Oran. In a letter to the governor-general's office, the director of the Affaires arabes for the division of Oran wrote, "I regret that we reacted in this manner due to the fact that we must not tolerate publicly in our markets, but on which it is good to *close our eyes* when it happens far from us in the interests of our commerce with the south, a commerce that we seek to encourage."[71] The central command in Algiers concurred: "I think along the same lines as you that we must in no case go too far in the application of the order of 1848 on the abolition of slavery, only ensuring that it is aimed at those who claim its benefits."[72] In effect, these letters state that French administrators should enforce the law only if and when slaves presented themselves and demanded their freedom. In all other cases officers agreed to "close our eyes."

A year after the Naigeon incident—and only one month after he spoke out so forcefully in favor of immediate abolition to the commandant of Mascara— Governor-General Randon stressed tolerance in the Sahara. In a cabinet note he wrote that "all introductions [of slaves] into the Tell will be met with the liberation of the slaves and the imprisonment of the buyer and seller." However, he also suggested that "we can very well close our eyes to what happens in the south, among the Beni Mzab, for example."[73] Legally slavery in the Mzab posed no problems at this time. Under the terms of an 1853 protectorate, the five cities preserved their autonomy. Randon knew this, but the special case of the Mzab allowed him to create an exception for other parts of the Algerian Sahara under French control, which were subject to the terms of the abolition law. Because these territories were far off, Randon suggested that slavery could be tolerated when it was discreet and served the larger commercial or political interests of colonial rule. This toleration of slavery colored French attitudes toward slavery and abolition in the Sahara for most of the nineteenth century. Some forty years later this policy had changed little. For example, in 1896 Governor-General Jules Cambon was confronted by demands from a group in the Tidikelt sympathetic to France—an oasis group that still evaded French control—to return their runaway slaves. He responded in terms nearly identical to those of his predecessor. In order to foster friendly relations, Cambon counseled leniency. "Can we not," he wrote, "without failing [to give] the blacks the protection that we owe to slaves in general, send back these Negroes?" This particular demand came from the Ouled Dahou, who had promised to help the French expand their influence at In Salah, an oasis group that still evaded French control.[74] In the governor-general's view, cementing relations with local notables was more important than respecting the law. "This sort of extradition," Cambon continued, "will ensure the gratitude of the populations of the Tidikelt and will provide an opportunity for talks that will put us into close contact with these regions."[75]

In cases where the political situation was different, however, administrators might rigorously enforce the abolition law. For example, in 1893 French officer Colonel Didier, commander of Ghardaïa, rejected the demand of masters in the independent oasis agglomeration at Gourara to return three of their slaves who had fled to French-controlled territories. (Especially vexing was the fact that one of the slaves had not been freed but taken into the service of the French caid. In retaliation Gourara merchants cut trade with French oases and stole two camels to make up for the slaves' loss.) Although the incident threatened trade between the French zone and the Gourara, the governor-general's office seconded Didier's decision to reject the demands of the slave owners.[76] It concurred with Didier's reasoning that providing safe haven to escaped slaves, who "form the large majority of the population," would win their brethren over to the French side. "Given that they are more or less oppressed, [they] cannot see in other than a good light the support that we give to the weak, support that they can solicit for themselves if we come among them."[77] Some fifty years earlier a similar situation motivated Lt. Col. Auguste Margueritte, the commander of Laghouat, to shelter slaves who had fled their masters in the Mzab. During his tenure at Laghouat (1855–60) Margueritte pursued a vigorous expansion policy, which included fomenting internal conflict within the five Mzabi cities. Margueritte hoped that this internal discord would eventually provoke a crisis, compromising the protectorate relationship, and justify French intervention and annexation. Welcoming fugitive slaves was an important part of this strategy. It served as notice to the Mzab that French power was just on the horizon and could make itself felt not only in the form of taxes but could also enter into intimate social relationships within the family, property, and the labor regime, all of which were intertwined with slavery. After Margueritte left Laghouat, his successor, Alexis Labrousse, initially supported plans for an occupation and continued Margueritte's policies on slavery and abolition. After realizing that support for an expensive military occupation of the Mzab would not be forthcoming, he changed direction and curried favor with the friendly factions in the Mzab.[78] These efforts included closing Laghout as a haven for runaway slaves. As Labrousse wrote in 1862, "The Negroes who escape from the Beni-Mzab and who arrive at Laghouat are often reclaimed by their masters. Until now they have never been returned, but this fact has drawn much protest. Laghouat is now full of black men and women without any means of subsistence."[79]

To summarize, the pattern found in the sources is threefold. The governor-general's office advocated a forceful policy against slavery in compliance with the 1848 abolition law. However, this did not prevent the same administration from counseling leniency to their subordinates in low-profile cases or where larger strategic interests were at stake. This created a situation where the colonial administration could discreetly tolerate slavery in Algeria. Finally, the bulk of enforcement powers remained in the hands of local commanders, who, with the tacit acquiescence of their superiors, selectively enforced abolition laws to either reward loyal Algerian elites or punish those who became troublesome. This three-tiered response to abolition produced the eyes-closed policy, the uneven and instrumental application of the 1848 law.

THE UNEVEN APPLICATION OF ABOLITION

Some commanders who personally opposed slavery did not hide their efforts to abolish the institution. For example, Victor Colonieu, the commander of Géryville, voiced his uncompromising opposition to slavery. An 1847 Polytechnic graduate, Colonieu was appointed to head Géryville in 1860. He took the opportunity offered by a report on trans-Saharan commerce to introduce his personal abhorrence of slavery. He rejected any plans to allow slaves to enter Algeria—even if they were manumitted or if the projects promised economic benefits: "Without doubt, allowing the sale of Negroes in Algeria will greatly increase our commercial relations with the Gourara, the Tohat, and the Tidikelt. However, we must not transgress the noble principles of humanity that have made our flag the symbol of individual liberty and the guarantor of the rights of man."

Referencing a conception of France's civilizing mission, as opposed to slavery, Colonieu continued his argument by clarifying the status of the slaves who might enter Algeria. The promises previously made by people like Subtil and Bodichon—namely, that slaves would be liberated—were unfounded. They relied on a false distinction between slave and indentured laborer. As Colonieu explained, one is "forced labor in perpetuity, [the other] is a term of forced labor—that is the difference. Only the length of time varies."[80] Such straightforward criticism of the eyes-closed policy was uncommon, but his superiors said nothing. This silence speaks both to the sensitive nature of the topic and the fact that he was a talented officer whose star was rising.

In the other military commands where slavery was an issue, officers freely pursued different policies. In some cases they revived the sort of projects to bring slaves into Algeria and use them in state service that Colonieu had forcefully condemned. The case of Paul Flatters, commander of Laghouat in 1877, provides a good example. Flatters is best known for the eponymous 1881 massacre, which involved a group of Tuareg who ambushed an exploration party headed by Flatters. In the spring of 1877 Flatters was an ambitious officer who sought recognition by proposing projects that might revive commerce between Algeria and the Sahara. He was not particularly upbeat about French prospects.[81] Even though the French had a strategic advantage in terms of controlling access to the Algerian Sahara from the north, the British dominated the trade in manufactured goods in the Sahara, with shipments from Morocco, Tunis, and Tripoli. Because France could not compete with these inexpensive products, Flatters suggested reevaluating how France might participate in Saharan trade. To this end, he urged officials to take a closer look at the makeup of Saharan commerce. The principal item of trade was still slaves. All the sources "are unanimous on this point," he wrote. Saharan trade "essentially consists in the traffic of Negro slaves." Although many of them went to other destinations in the Maghreb, Flatters argued that more than a thousand slaves secretly entered Algeria each year. Although abolition had done little to curb this traffic, it had the negative effect of closing the desert off to French merchants. Saharan traders would not deal with them for fear of losing their slaves. At the same time, Saharan merchants transformed themselves into smugglers, creating a black market economy beyond the reach of regular French businessmen and the fiscal arm of the state. Ignoring the fact that exorbitant French customs duties were the true cause of the Sahara's thriving black market, Flatters pulled out the anti-abolitionist trope of pragmatism. Pretending to be a realist, Flatters recommended that France lift its abolitionist restrictions: "The surest method of creating regular relations with the independent Sahara consists in opening the slave trade, or at least tolerating it in one form or another." He argued that until French troops occupied the lands of the Sahel, where the slave caravans originated, "the Arabs, the Tuareg, and the Negroes" would continue to smuggle slaves northward. "The practical side of things naturally insists upon a compromise. Instead of having to operate clandestinely, as is the practice today, if the merchants from the far south, coming to Algeria with their blacks, no longer feared the application of our abolitionist principles, they would soon flood our markets." The toleration Flatters proposed included direct French involvement in the slave trade. He had contacted the chamber of commerce in Algiers, which promised to deal with the slaves, placing the women and children in homes as domestic servants and finding work for the men on state projects. "Certainly this system is a thinly disguised slave trade," he admitted. However, "without wanting to defend the morality of the policy, we must admit that in practice the adoption of the indicated measure seems preferable to maintaining the current state of affairs."[82] At least one reviewer of Flatters's report supported it. Although this person agreed that the proposal was illegal, he suggested giving in to reality. Flatters offered "a slave trade with a bit of humanity."[83]

Although it was favorably reviewed, the office of indigenous affairs in Algiers ultimately rejected Flatters's proposal.[84] His report is further proof of how abolition varied from one military jurisdiction to another. Local commanders held vastly differing opinions concerning slavery, and the fact that the eyes-closed policy allowed these minor agents of the state to decide policy meant that abolition was a highly subjective affair. This had implications for the trade and shaped relations between slave owners and the colonial administration. Slave traders were confronted with an irregular "map" in Algeria. For example, the slave merchant who passed through Flatters's jurisdiction ran few risks—and he might even receive a hearty welcome.

THE REACTION OF SLAVE TRADERS

The uneven application of the abolition decree produced confusion among slaves, slave owners, and traders. Viewed objectively, abolition was arbitrary and irregular. Slaves who sought freedom might find aid from a commander like Colonieu, while others might be sent back to masters by an officer like Flatters or Labrousse. Slave merchants faced a reverse image of the same set of problems. Knowing which commanders tolerated slave commerce and under what conditions captives could be sold spelled the difference between attractive profits and financial ruin.

The criminal penalties slave traders and owners faced were few. The abolition law of 1848 was intended for other contexts and had few coercive measures to deter Algerians from participating in slavery. The law's main strength was the revocation of citizenship of those holding slaves. This meant little to Algerians. Although the Senatus Consulte of 14 July 1863 conferred a status of "sujet français" on Algerians, they conserved their "statut personnel," which barred them from gaining the rights of citizens.[85] (The only protection the 1863 subject status afforded Algerians was the right to live in Algeria; foreigners could be deported.)[86] When, beginning in 1905, the colonial administration finally decided to adopt an aggressive stance and abolish slavery, administrators were baffled as to what punishments they might apply. In the 1880s judges in Oran occasionally succeeded in fining slaveholders up to two hundred francs.[87] However, the main risk slave owners and traders faced was the liberation of their slaves.

Although slave prices were not extravagant, the prospect of losing their slaves was a sufficient deterrent for many. This led to intensified efforts on the part of those who dealt in slaves to determine the dispositions of the local commanders. In 1858 two men representing merchants operating near Ghadamès, south of Tripoli, traveled to the French base at Laghouat to get the local commander's views on the slave trade. Ghadamès was the main hub of the important central Saharan route that passed through present-day Libya. The talks represented the second meeting with the French commander at Laghouat, Lieutenant Colonel Margueritte. Undertaken by a Ghadamèsi trader named al-hajj Ali, who was joined by the respected Tuareg saint Si Othman (Si 'Uthman ag al-hajj al-Bakri, ca. 1790–ca. 1870), the talks were marked by considerable urgency. In 1857 Ottoman authorities in Tripoli had committed themselves to abolishing slavery in the territories under their control. Merchants dealing in slaves had to face the prospect that someday one of the most important ports in the Mediterranean slave trade would be closed to them. According to Margueritte, Si Othman told the French commander that slaves used to be sold in Tunis and Tripoli, but "recently restrictions have been enacted by the two regencies acting on newfound philanthropic scruples inspired by the European consuls."[88] The French officer reported that this alarmed the Saharan merchants, adding that "this is not a small part of the reason why they have visited Laghouat." Si Othman hoped to strike a deal with Margueritte, an Arabophone officer he had grown to trust. "If you continue to close your eyes on the sale of slaves from our land for another one or two years," Si Othman promised, "you will have all the commerce from the Sudan and Timbuktu." Othman continued, "the merchants who trade in slaves—and they all do—have not found outlets on the markets of the Fezzan, Tripoli, and the Tohat. They will be only too happy to come and sell them with their other merchandise in Algeria."[89]

Margueritte was unlike Flatters and the others, who proposed opening Algeria to large numbers of slaves. Although he was eager to see the caravan traffic shift to Laghouat and make Algeria the most important northern outlet of the trans-Sahara trade, he could not give Si Othman and al-hajj Ali the type of assurances they wanted. As one commenter on Margueritte's report glumly concluded, "Only one thing makes them hesitate [from trading at Laghouat]: the difficulties with the distribution and sales of their Negroes."[90] Margueritte could only offer equivocations on this question, which did not impress his audience. When Si Othman himself saw two of his slaves flee to a French zone the following year—a loss that remained uncompensated—the question of rerouting slave traffic to Algeria appeared closed.[91]

While Algeria could not become a major destination for slave caravans, a small trade into Algeria continued throughout the nineteenth century. This was a lesser trade, an intricate sort of smuggling that supplied people like Saaba to the northern oases of the Algerian Sahara and occasionally into the homes of Algerians in northern cities, where they served as concubines and domestic servants. Sources documenting this clandestine trade remain sketchy and incomplete, but there is enough evidence to permit one to examine the route traveled by Saaba north from In Salah.

COLONIAL ACCOMMODATION

Major trafficking in slaves from the middle Niger region to the Tidikelt region and its main oasis groups at In Salah and nearby Foggâret ez Zoûa continued throughout the second half of the nineteenth century. Explorer Paul Soleillet, who traveled to In Salah in 1875, reported that "the trade in Negro slaves is undertaken on a large scale throughout the Sahara. In Salah, like the other oases, receives and buys a large quantity of slaves."[1] Periodic reports from French outposts emphasized the significance of this traffic throughout the succeeding decades. For example, in April 1890 it was learned that a caravan left Timbuktu for In Salah with three hundred slaves for sale.[2] In September 1891 the commander of Ouargla noted, "The annual caravans from Timbuktu and the Sudan arrived at In Salah at the beginning of summer and have brought with them a considerable quantity of slaves."[3] A report from 1893 noted that the large annual caravan arrived in the Tidikelt from Timbuktu on 10 May with four hundred slaves who were sold for anywhere from four to five hundred francs apiece.[4] In that same year another caravan brought six hundred captives to the Tidikelt, along with large herds of cattle and sheep raided in the Sahel.[5] Undertaking his own research on Saharan slavery in 1953, one French administrator estimated that some twelve hundred captives arrived in the Tidikelt annually in the nineteenth century.[6] These slaves might be sent to any of several destinations. Most went west to the Moroccan oases in the Tafilalt region, while others traveled east to Ghat or Ghadamès, joining the trail north to Tripoli. Some might simply stay in the Tidikelt, where they were purchased by local masters who sought replacements for slaves who had died, escaped, or been freed. Still others, like Saaba, traveled north to French-controlled territories like Ouargla. This oasis served as a central location for networks that smuggled slaves into the Algerian oases, like Touggourt and El Oued (located 160 kilometers to the northeast), Biskra (an additional 250 kilometers farther north), or the Mzab (along a frequently traveled 200-kilometer path to the east).

THE ANNEXATION OF THE MZAB:
NEW FORMS OF ACCOMMODATION, 1882

The five oasis cities of the Mzab (Ghardaïa, Melika, El-Ateuf, Beni-Isguen, and Bou Noura) enjoyed a special status for the first four decades of French rule in the Sahara. Wishing to avoid further commitments following the occupation of Laghouat, Governor-General Randon negotiated a protectorate with the Mzabi pentapolis in May 1853. The terms included a formal gesture of submission and an annual tribute of forty-five thousand francs. In exchange the Mzabis retained control of their internal affairs and enjoyed free access to French-controlled territories.[7] The protectorate, in part, recognized the distinctness of the Mzab, which had been settled by Berberophone followers of the Ibadite sect in the eleventh century. They came to this remote desert location not because of its rich natural resources but rather to avoid persecution. Like other religious minorities in the Mediterranean, they became skilled merchants, establishing communities scattered throughout Algeria.[8] Life at home nevertheless remained hard. About twenty-five thousand people lived in the Mzab in the mid nineteenth century. Their activities centered on the Mzab's agricultural base, including date palms and horticulture, which required large amounts of water and unceasing labor.[9] The date palm gardens alone numbered nearly two hundred thousand trees, each one needing 150–200 liters of water a day.[10] Tapping ground reserves of water meant digging exceptionally deep wells (up to 100 meters deep) through limestone, while the exploitation of surface water necessitated an elaborate system of dams, reservoirs, and canals to capture the waters of the Oued M'Zab at rare moments when desert rains flooded the area. Mzabi families themselves provided much of the labor necessary for this system. Small landholding was encouraged by the egalitarian traditions of Ibadism and the social rigor of the Mzabis, whom the French dubbed the "Puritans of the Desert."[11] Although culturally exceptional, like other people in the Sahara the Mzabi used slaves to meet part of their labor needs.

For nearly thirty years questions of slavery and abolition in the Mzab were foreclosed by the fact that these five cities were governed according to their own laws. This changed in 1882 when the French occupied and annexed the Mzab and established a base at Ghardaïa, the principal city of the pentapolis. Suddenly colonial administrators faced thorny questions about slavery and abolition.[12] At first they showed little concern about slavery: the eyes-closed policy that had guided actions since 1848 seemed to be exportable to new Saharan territories. However, the enslaved people of the Mzab themselves challenged the status quo and forced an important reevaluation of policy. Immediately following the 1882 occupation, slaves presented themselves in large numbers to the new French commander at Ghardaïa. They were eager to claim their rights under French law, which they already knew a great deal about. This was due to earlier efforts by people like Margueritte in Laghouat, who, as was previously mentioned, had spread word of France's abolition in order to foment social discord in the Mzab. Slaves in the Mzab were thus better informed than slaves in the areas under French control. The promise of freedom had indeed rallied Mzabi slaves to the French side, and they were eager to enjoy their new freedom. Unfortunately they met with disappointment. When French troops occupied the Mzab, they faced new challenges, and encouraging master-slave conflict was not on the agenda. Quite the opposite. The success of the 1882 annexation depended upon quickly finding a modus vivendi vis-à-vis Mzabi notables, who were split between those adopting a pragmatic wait-and-see attitude and elements that strongly opposed the occupation. The action of the slaves threatened to turn this volatile political situation against the French.

It was a delicate state of affairs for French policymakers. It would be difficult for commanders to return slaves forcibly to their masters. The large numbers who demanded freedom made it difficult to maintain the open secret of the eyes-closed policy. Conversely, it was impossible to liberate the slaves of the Mzab en masse because this risked turning the wavering Mzab elites decisively against the French. A new policy had to be forged that could both silence slaves' demands for emancipation and protect the interests of Mzabi elites. There was also the troubling question of the abolition decree itself: How could colonial administrators compromise with slavery and still give their policies a veneer of legality that would satisfy critics? Immediately following the occupation the governor-general's office and the Ministry of Justice hammered out a compromise, the beginnings of a tortuous policy that sought to give slavery in the Mzab the appearance of a type of servile status.[13] The provisions of this arrangement included requiring Mzabi councils to publicly announce the abolition of slavery. At the same time, French officials warned slave masters that they would be subject to fines if they mistreated their slaves, the idea being that if they had tolerable relations with their masters, slaves would choose to remain with them.

On the surface this appeared to satisfy both the letter and spirit of the law, while also providing an incentive for slaves to remain with their masters. The latter eventuality was the one the French administrator most hoped for. They thought that French guarantees of protection from physical abuse would convince slaves to remain in unspecified relations of servility and bondage. However, the compromises worked out by the French never seriously delved into the actual legal status of such individuals. For example, they did not enter into the all-important question of the property rights of slaves and servile people. Documents suggest that the French assumed that slaves would technically be free yet still remain subject to the master's will, like all minor members of the family. From the slave owner's perspective, this arrangement appeared to protect their interests. The household already represented a formidable system of social hierarchy that could control female slaves living under the master's roof. Most of the male slaves who worked in the gardens had come as children and were presumably assimilated into the system of subordination and domination that characterized relations between Saharan elites and the servile classes. But slavery carried strong social stigmas, including the ethnography of unbelief (see chapter 7). These motivated slaves to flee their masters in order to seek their fortunes elsewhere even if such flight did not offer better material conditions.

In the end, this first attempt at accommodation did not afford the sort of protections vis-à-vis their property and status that that Mzabi slave owners demanded. To buttress the position of slave owners, French administrators added an inherently illogical set of rules to the policy, a Catch-22 that effectively ruled out freedom for most slaves and openly placed the policing powers of the French administration on the side of slave owners. Much like the British system of self-purchase implemented in northern Nigeria in the first decades of the twentieth century, this early French policy put a financial obstacle between slaves and their freedom.[14] Slaves who sought emancipation and presented themselves to the French for protection had to prove that they had the necessary means to support themselves.[15] Those who could not had to return to their masters. The authors of this policy made no mention of the source of this means of support, even though they were not ignorant of the fact that slaves enjoyed limited opportunities to accumulate capital and had few legal protections to safeguard their property. In the Mzab, as elsewhere in the Algerian oases, the rule seems to have been "that which is property cannot be proprietor" (al-memluk ma imleksha).[16] French commanders at Ghardaïa and Mzabi slave owners both embraced this new policy. It provided a quasi-legal veneer for slave ownership by blurring the personal status of slaves, presenting them as legally free but voluntarily servile. It also gave French administrators the political cover they needed to fend off public criticisms of military rule. (The settler press in particular did not miss an opportunity to embarrass the military for their archaic and "feudal" authority in Algeria.) As one officer commented, "These measures sufficed to discourage the Mzabis from committing acts of cruelty that push the Negroes to flee their masters and that seem to have caused the flight that occurred upon the arrival of our troops."[17] Later administrators in the Mzab justified the continuation of slavery by boasting how well slaves in the Mzab lived, invoking the old myth of the benevolence of slavery in Muslim societies. Typical of such beliefs are the following commentaries: "They openly embrace their duty to forever remain with their owner." "They are without a doubt the happiest people of the Annex [of Ghardaïa]."[18] One commander went so far as to write that "the Negro population is perhaps happier than the Mzabi himself. Supported by their masters, they live without worry, assured of tomorrow's meal, blissfully asleep in a servile indifference. Thus, they mock the liberty that we brought with us and never seek to escape this dependence that ensures their means of existence."[19]

In the end, the fact that slaves stayed with their masters had little to do with their good treatment or their unconcern for political values like "liberty." Slaves had few options. The colonial administration, which had promised slaves in the Mzab their freedom in the 1850s, now turned back those who fled their masters, providing the legal prop and coercive force of the state necessary to preserve slavery.[20] This left "freed" slaves with nowhere to go and little or no means of subsistence. Most had come to the Mzab as children; crossing the desert to return to their homeland and families was impossible. Some might go farther north to find work in the cities. Sizable populations of Africans of color had left the oases and migrated north to the cities, where they worked as house painters, porters, laborers, and garbage collectors (vidangeurs).[21] Most of these were of the servile Haratin class, but there were probably fugitive slaves mixed in with these communities. However, such movement was not easy and finding regular remunerated work remained uncertain.[22] For slave women this was doubly true. In sum, although abolition was the law of the land, slaves who sought their freedom became vagrants and were effectively transformed into de facto fugitives. Escaping the stigma of slavery and enjoying a minimum of control over the fruits of one's labor and reproduction — the freedom all slaves sought — remained just as elusive as it had following the French occupation of the Mzab.

THE SLAVE TRADE TO THE ALGERIAN SAHARA FOLLOWING ABOLITION

While the slave initiative in the Mzab revealed the weakness of previous modes of accommodation with slavery, the eyes-closed policy worked fairly well in dealing with the slave trade itself. Once again the Mzab provides an illustrative case, revealing the type of networks that brought people like Saaba to Algeria as slaves. It also contains the best documents on this generally undocumented activity.

The Mzab carried on an active commerce with the Tidikelt throughout the period under consideration. This trade primarily consisted in donkeys, minerals, dyes, and medicines, along with hides and ostrich feathers intended for the Mzab. These were traded for European manufactured goods, textiles, tea, and coffee, which went south to the Tidikelt. Prior to the French occupation, the Mzab was also a center for the smuggling of firearms and ammunition, an experience that sharpened merchants' skills in the contraband trade. For its part the Tidikelt served both as a link between the central Sahara and the Mediterranean and as a main hub for slave caravans traveling north from Timbuktu. Most slaves went from the Tidikelt either to Ghadamès in the east or west to Morocco, which in the era of abolition became the "last great slave market" of the Maghreb, where laws to end the slave trade were not enacted until 1922.[23] Although subject to French laws outlawing slavery, Algerians still sought slaves throughout the second half of the nineteenth century. These ranged from wealthy urban notables, who could hide female slaves by presenting them to French authorities as wives, to people in isolated rural areas, who understood the eyes-closed policy and had confidence they would be left alone. As late as 1906 one French civil administrator who visited Ksar Chellala (located in the High Plateaux, between Djelfa and Tiaret) found widespread slavery: "All the well-off indigenous families have one or several male or female slaves that they buy without difficulty on what one can almost call the [slave] market of Ksar Chellala."[24] Although the eyes-closed policy assured slave traders a good margin of security, they still ran certain risks. Above all they had to ensure that their activities remained discreet if not invisible to the authorities. For example, slave caravans entering Ksar Challala had to travel by night and disguise the slaves as free domestic servants or minor members of the trader's family. Running these risks drove slave prices up in Algeria: in Ksar Chellala traders could expect anywhere from four hundred to six hundred francs for young adult slaves—almost double the price paid in Morocco. This made Algeria a risky but attractive market.

EVIDENCE OF THE CLANDESTINE TRADE TO THE MZAB

Some of the slaves sold in Algeria after 1848 came from Morocco, crossing the porous border into the French colony. Others came from the old routes directly south of Laghouat, converging on Ouargla and the Mzab. The evidence for traffic into the central Algerian Sahara is slim, as is to be expected. The eyes-closed policy necessarily ruled out keeping statistics on slaves entering a given jurisdiction even if the local administrator learned of such movements. For example, in an 1876 report on commerce Said ben Driss, the French-appointed commander at Ouargla, broke the unspoken rule and mentioned the arrival of eighteen slaves in his oasis. Horrified, his superior wrote in the margin of the report: "Do not put this passage in the copy."[25] Only after 1905 did administrators—anticipating a more vigorous abolitionist policy from the central authorities—begin to write candidly about the clandestine slave trade. In the period under discussion few reporters provided precise information. For their part, colonial administrators mentioned slavery and the slave trade only under five circumstances: (1) when slave trading occurred outside French-controlled territories (e.g., among the still independent oases south of Ouargla); (2) when they intercepted caravans from regions not under French authority; (3) in detailed reports of events where slaves were participants; (4) in reports that claimed the slaves were happy; and (5) in indirect formulations, like those lamenting how abolition had ruined the economy of the Algerian Sahara.

The most likely place for French administrators to note figures on slave trafficking would have been in the economic reports on Saharan commerce they began compiling in the second half of the nineteenth century. Contemplating a great economic future across the Sahara, the upper echelons of the colonial administration placed special importance on these documents and made concerted efforts to get the most up-to-date and accurate information as possible. In the Mzab prior to 1882, the data is scattered, but because the Mzab was still independent, there was a willingness to talk about slave imports. For example, in 1880 a military mission that toured the area southeast of the Mzab reported that at least a hundred slaves entered the Mzab annually from the still independent southern oases of the Gourara, Tohat, and Tidikelt, along with the four hundred camel loads of goods involving "legitimate" commerce.[26] After the French extended direct rule to the Mzab in 1882, their reports became much more complete on trade in general but fell silent on the specific question of the slave trade. Nevertheless the impressive detail concerning legitimate trade in the commercial records is worth studying. For example, table 9.1 documents commerce between the French-controlled Mzab and the "extreme south," the oases of the Tohat, Gourara, and Tidikelt. While these data include nothing on the illegal traffic in slaves, they give us a general idea of the character and importance of this trade, which totaled more than 300,000 francs a year in goods and 150,000 francs in loans.

In the early 1890s Colonel Didier, the commander at Ghardaïa, kept precise records. He knew the Sahara well, having headed the Bureau arabe at Bou-Saada before arriving in the Mzab. Although hardly complete, his records are invaluable because he not only detailed the content of the trade but also indicated precisely how many *people* came north with each caravan. His figures for 1892 are worth scrutinizing. In March of this year a caravan arrived in Ghardaïa from the Aoulef (Tidikelt) with twenty-nine people and five camels; another that same month arrived from In Salah with six people and two camels; and one arriving from Timimoun consisted of twelve people and an equal number of camels.[27] In April traders from the *zawiya* at al-Kahala (Tidikelt) arrived with twelve people and four camels;[28] and a caravan from Aoulef came with twen-

TABLE 9.1 Trade Between the Extreme South and the Mzab, 1890

Imports (francs)		Exports (francs)	
Donkeys	60,000	Cotton textiles and scarves	60,000
Alunite	20,000	Sugar and coffee	30,000
Saltpeter	5,000	Soap	12,000
Feathers	25,000	Glass jewelry	30,000
Hides	30,000	Hardware	20,000
Tuareg arms and crafts	20,000	Iron bars	10,000
		(Loans from Mzabi lenders	150,000)
Total	160,000	Total	162,000

Source: Victor Deporter, "Mouvement commercial entre le Mzab et l'extrême sud pendant l'année 1890," *Alger*, 27 June 1891. CAOM 22 H 33.

ty-three people and five camels.[29] In all, the data Didier recorded for 1891–92 reveals ratios ranging from one person for every two camels to six people for each camel.

The proportion of people to camels in these caravans is suspect. Some travelers made the voyage on foot, which was typical, but they could not carry items of value to the legitimate trade. Camels alone had commercial value in this sense. In terms of the caravan's labor needs, one person could oversee and lead many camels laden with goods. Thus, caravan leaders generally tried to keep the size of their parties to the minimum necessary to look after the livestock and provide adequate defense. The more people came along, the more food would have to be carried, taking up loads that were better given over to lucrative goods.

The Mzabi figures can be compared against those of other regions. Administrators in the southern Oranais also compiled fairly complete figures in their attempt to measure the value of trade with the Sahara.[30] Historian Hélène Chevaldonné has compiled this data to facilitate comparison.[31] Looking at the movements of large caravans numbering thousands of camels, the average ratios she finds are one person for every three to seven camels—the exact opposite of Didier's numbers for the Mzab. The nature and scale of this western trade (primarily in foodstuffs) was substantially different from the Mzab's trade with the far south. Nevertheless, the caravans in the west included substantial numbers of women and children, suggesting that in some cases entire families made the trip. This unavoidably increased the overall number of people traveling in a given caravan relative to the number of camels. Even admitting that particular fact, the figures for the western routes never show a caravan with more people than camels.

There is the possibility that the people making the voyage to the Mzab were free travelers. The early 1890s was a period of crisis in the Tidikelt region. The French move down the Niger River to Timbuktu (occupied in 1893–94) disrupted the trade upon which the oases depended. In addition, the repeated failures of the local date harvest caused much hardship.[32] Migration was the typical response to such circumstances. However, given the body of evidence (plus the 1889 incident discussed in the next section), it is likely that some of the numbers listed by Didier represent traffic in people destined for slavery.

SAABA'S GROUP, THE ZAWIYA AL-KAHALA, AND THE DEPORTER RAID OF 1889

Having examined the clandestine slave trade and the colonial accommodation of slavery, I now wish to return to our original story. Saaba did not tell Largeau who had purchased her group at In Salah or how she managed to get to Ouargla. However, in a rare breach of the eyes-closed policy, a monthly report from Laghouat dated July 1877 mentions the passage of her group. The entry was made by Paul Flatters, an officer who, as we have seen, openly advocated lifting the ban on slavery. According to his account, on 8 July 1877 a caravan consisting of nineteen slaves traveling from the zawiya al-Kahala in the Tidikelt region passed Ouargla on its way to El Oued.[33] This was the same day that Largeau reported buying Saaba. If Flatters's dates are correct, the caravan most likely first stopped in Ouargla. Assuming that only Largeau had enough money to purchase a slave, its leader pressed northward with the rest of the young women and children.

In reconstructing the route Saaba followed to slavery in the Algerian Sahara, we progress from the accommodations made to slavery in parts of Algeria under French control to the oasis agglomerations in the Tidikelt, which the French did not capture until the turn of the century. The zawiya al-Kahala was located in the ksar of Foggâret ez Zoûa, located northeast of In Salah in the Tidikelt region.[34] In the eighteenth century Foggâret ez Zoûa (a.k.a. Foggaret al-Kahala and Kasbet Foukania) was settled by the Zoua (a.k.a. Ouled Sidi al-hajj Muhammad), an Arabophone group related to the Ouled Sidi Cheikh. Si al-hajj Muhammad, the Zoua's founder, was the son of Si al-hajj Bu Hafs (d. 1660), the founder of the eastern branch of the Ouled Sidi Cheikh.[35] Although a lesser part of this preeminent Saharan tribe, the Zoua enjoyed considerable prestige and influence in religious circles throughout the strategic region. Indeed, their name is derived from "people of the zawiya," reflecting a close attachment to religion, piety, and learning.[36] Their zawiya was founded in 1799 by the grandson of the Zoua's founder.[37] In addition to their kinship ties to the Ouled Sidi Cheikh, the Zoua were related to the Chaamba of El Goléa, the most important oasis group straddling the trail north from the Tidikelt to Ouargla and the Mzab. In short, their kinship relations and religious capital made the Zoua important figures in the trade that linked the Tidikelt with its northern neighbors.[38]

The total population of the Tidikelt region numbered roughly eleven thousand people living in dozens of separate ksour.[39] Four different kinship groups accounted for most of the eastern Tidikelt's population: the Ouled Ba Hamou, the Ouled el Mokhtar, the Ouled Zenan, and the Zoua. Their economy centered on both agriculture (based on pastoralism and the date palm) and regional and trans-Saharan trade. The Ouled Ba Hamou were a pastoralist people and the most powerful group in the Tidikelt. They excelled in trade and benefited from their strong ties to the Tuareg, who knew them as the Aït Ba Khamu or Dag Ba Judda.[40] According to one French observer, they were "an incontestable and even formidable power" and controlled much of the transport of livestock and the routes that linked the Tidikelt to the south.[41] Their main rivals, the Ouled el Mokhtar, were primarily involved in commerce. They tried to offset the dominance of the Ouled Ba Hamou through an alliance with the Zoua, benefiting from their religious influence and ties to the northern tribes. This gave the Ouled el Mokhtar a considerable advantage in the northern end of the Tidikelt's trade.

These commercial rivalries inevitably affected politics, which were contentious and divisive. In the 1880s and 1890s, as the Sahara became enmeshed in the larger struggle that divided up Africa among major state powers, rival groups in the Tidikelt weighed their options vis-à-vis the powerful forces to the north, namely, Morocco and France. Each country represented both a threat and a potential ally who might help shift the balance of power in the oases in the favor of a particular faction. Morocco, a Muslim power and traditional trading partner, was the more likely ally. The Sharifian monarchy had already aided people like the famed Saharan rebel Bou Amama (Bu 'Amama), who, beginning in 1881, fought the French in a revolt that tied up much of the south. Moreover, Morocco had a special interest in these oases. The Convention of Lalla-Maghnia (18 March 1845), which established the boundaries between Algeria and Morocco, did not specify their southern limits beyond Teniet el Sassi.[42] Moreover, Morocco had long claimed sovereignty in the oases of the Gourara, Tohat, and Tidikelt. In 1887 Sultan Mulay Hassan appointed Abd el Kader Badjouda ('Abd al-Qadir Si al-hajj Muhammad Awlad Ba Judda al-Amri) of the Ouled Ba Hamou as governor ('Amel) of the Tidikelt.[43] The Badjouda clan had a reputation for opposing French influence in the Sahara, one that dated back to the rebel Muhammad ben Abdallah's welcome in the Tidikelt after his 1852 failure at Laghouat. In response to the Moroccan maneuver, in 1890 Governor-General Tirman considered sending troops to crush the Badjouda and occupy the southwest oases.[44] Finding this option unrealistic, Jules Cambon, Tirman's successor, instead sought to play his own hand at oasis politics. He named Muhammad ibn al-hajj Ahmad ibn Muhammad (a.k.a. Gaga) of the Ouled el Mokhtar as their own governor.[45] In the next decade French authorities tried to use the factional politics (Ṣaff), which overlaid kinship divisions, along with divisions within the tribes themselves to break apart the Moroccan system of caids, naming their own set of rival leaders as heads of the Tidikelt.[46] The plan even included successful attempts to lure members of the Ouled Ba Hamou to the French side—including Badjouda's own son.[47] The game was complicated, however, and it quickly fell out of French control. While Saharan notables felt that a French occupation was inevitable, many failed to find concrete advantages in a rapprochement with the French, relations that, as I have previously argued, always carried inherent liabilities.

All of this political complexity and struggle figured into the practices of slavery and the slave trade. The Tidikelt was home to significant numbers of enslaved people at the end of the nineteenth century. Here lived nearly fifteen hundred slaves, comprising about 13 percent of the total population.[48] Another nineteen hundred servile people of color, the Haratin, supplied the rest of the labor. The slave trade itself represented a source of considerable wealth and an important part of the region's economy. All things considered, finding accommodation with slavery in the Tidikelt was of primary concern to all parties. For example, before accepting the position of French governor of the Tidikelt, Ahmad ben Muhammad traveled to Touggourt in May 1894 to meet with General de La Roque, commander of the division of Constantine.[49] He wanted to secure French guarantees that they would respect property in the Tidikelt—in particular, that the French would not "alter our relations with our servants."[50] General de La Roque worked out an unspecified deal with the future governor, telling Governor-General Cambon, "Don't worry about the slavery question; it won't give us any problems."[51] Two years later (1896) another notable from the Tidikelt, Abd el Kader ben Kouider of the Ouled Dahan (part of the Ouled Ba Hamou), came to Constantine to again seek assurances from the French regarding the question of slavery. Ben Koudier was even more emphatic about the importance of resolving the issue. The Badjouda family had rallied opposition forces to resist the French by invoking the question of slavery, planting fear in the minds of slave owners and traders. Ben Kouider wanted a categorical response from the French on the question of slavery. If the matter was not settled, he warned, he would turn the whole region against the French.[52] He told the French general, "In the Tidikelt Negroes [nègres] alone work; to emancipate them would mean the ruin of the country. Your plans on this subject are not known to us, and we would like to be able to reassure our people on your intensions."[53] Like many slave owners facing European attempts at abolition, Ben Kouider blurred the line between slaves and servile people in an effort to gain La Roque's support.[54] As he stated, "We have no slave markets: the Negroes I'm talking about are nearly all born in the area. They have houses, villages. They work for us—we do not sell them—and it seems to me that they do not fall under the interdiction imposed upon all French subjects against owning Negroes."[55]

This group Ben Kouider referred to belonged not to the servile but to the free Haratin, who were always denoted by their common name in colonial documents. The word Ben Kouider used was translated as "nègre," which colonial translators invariably used for *abd* (slave) or any of the various euphemisms that existed in the local vocabularies to denote slaves or those associated with the slave class (e.g., emancipated slaves or their immediate descendants). Implying that the servitude of these "Negroes" was not harsh, Ben Kouider successfully assuaged whatever concerns the French general might have had. La Roque could report to his superiors in Algiers that there were no slaves per se in the Tidikelt, only a laboring group of "Negroes."

In this case, the French administration's colonial *mal de voir* responded to the interests of Saharan slave owners, who had devised strategies to protect their social position and property in the emerging new regime dominated by France.[56] These included exploiting French ambivalences concerning abolition and redeploying the colonial vocabulary of mutual economic interest and its rhetoric of order to maximum effect. In fact, the distinction between slave and servile was fuzzy only to those who wished to close their eyes to the institution of slavery. The divide that separated free (*ahrār*) from servile was arguably the most important social marker in the oases and well known to the social actors themselves. The Haratin helped draw the line within the servile category itself because they strongly rejected the taint of slavery or slave origin, while slave masters could be counted on to keep track of those who were their legal property. In Ben Kouider's case, the image he presented of free servants is undermined by the fact that his meeting with General de La Roque was actually prompted by the flight of several "negros" whom he wished to have returned. These individuals had stolen camels and fled their masters on a dangerous trip north where they hoped to find refuge in French territories. Eager to prove his good intentions, Governor-General Cambon ignored the abolition law and personally ordered the fugitives returned.[57]

The slave trade itself offered similar ground for accommodation between French administrators and Saharan notables. However, it was more difficult to blur the true nature of a slave's status in this case, especially at the point of sale. Unable to exploit social ambiguities to make slaves "disappear," parties seeking accommodation to the slave trade faced certain risks. The weakest links were the informal agreements negotiated between local French commanders and Saharan notables, which included protection for slave traders who ventured into French-controlled territories. These were part of the game of pitting oasis factions against one another, which stretched the abilities of French officers. In many cases French commanders saw their alliance networks fall apart, undercut by poor intelligence and shifting allegiances. When they did, French officers suspended the guarantees they had made to slave traders and used the abolition law to punish people they considered their enemies. For their part notables had to face a similar set of challenges when negotiating deals with the French. The military command had its own factions, which were as divided and mutually hostile as those found in the oases.

The "scramble for Africa" did not just pit France against Morocco—or France against Britain and Germany, for that matter. Plucking the last prizes in the Sahara also pit French military commands in Algeria against each other. Officers in Géryville, Laghouat, Ghardaïa, and Biskra all had their sights set on the last groups of oases to the south of Algeria. The divisions of Oran and Constantine had advantages over those in the division of Algiers. For example, their commands received the first rail lines into the Sahara, which reached Aïn-Sefra (1887) and Biskra (1888). In the end, whoever finally planted the French flag in the Tohat, Gourara, and Tidikelt would garner the most fame. These rivalries provoked bitter and complex struggles within the French army. An illustrative case is provided by the Mzab, which was under the authority of the division of Algiers. Colonel Alphonse Ferjeux Didier, who commanded Ghardaïa from 1883 to 1886 and again from 1890 to 1895, involved himself deeply in the factional politics of the Mzab and the oases farther south. Overall, he was a fairly skilled player. He had been in Algeria since 1864 and had a good understanding of how to manipulate the local political scene to his advantage. From Ghardaïa Didier had established a good system of relations in the far south. He even succeeded in getting the head of the hostile Badjouda clan to send him routine updates on Tidikelt politics, while at the same time remaining close to the Badjouda's rivals, the Zoua and the *zawiya* al-Kahala.[58] Didier showed himself equally skilled at playing off the factional struggles within the French military. In 1892, for example, he compromised the network of alliances that rival commanders in the division of Constantine had established by trying to arrest one of their key Saharan allies, Kouider ben Younès, on slave-trafficking charges.[59] Inevitably Didier made enemies along the way, and the deals he brokered often soured. In 1890 notables in Beni Isguen (Mzab) lodged a formal complaint against him, casting a shadow over his command, and four years later an anonymous charge of racketeering led to a rare internal investigation of Didier's actions.[60] (Although he was exonerated, Didier was never subsequently promoted and ended his career as a colonel.)

Commander Victor Deporter, who led the circle of Ghardaïa from 1886 to 1890, also tried his hand at making special deals and playing factions off against each other. Born into a family of French settlers located in the Constantine region, he spoke fluent Arabic and, like Didier, possessed substantial experience in the Sahara. Many of his early efforts focused on winning Ghardaïa control of the Chaamba groups centered in El Oued, thus taking them away from the division of Constantine.[61] He also promoted the Qadiriyya Sufi order, whose sheikhs hoped to expand farther into the Sahara from their new *zawiya* at Rouis-sat (Ouargla).[62] Deporter hoped that the Qadiriyya would counterbalance the benefits supposedly enjoyed as a result of Constantine's ties to the Tijaniyya Sufi order at Temacine (Touggourt).[63] However, Deporter recognized that the main prize remained the oases immediately to the south. He became involved here during the investigation of the 1885 murder of a French explorer, Marcel Palat, who was shot in the head by his guide while enroute to the Tidikelt. According to most accounts, Palat's assassin came from the Ouled Ba Hamou of In Salah.[64] Oddly, Deporter did little to bring those responsible for Palat's death to justice. Instead he used the incident as a point of leverage in his dealings with the Badjouda clan, hoping to develop closer relations and increased trade with the Tidikelt.[65] After an exchange of letters, Deporter viewed the Badjouda as his closest allies and recommended favoring this faction in future relations with the Tidikelt.[66] At the same time, Deporter shifted the blame for Palat's murder away from the Ouled Ba Hamou (to which the Badjouda belonged) and onto the Ouled Sidi Cheikh, who had served as the dead explorer's initial guides and protectors. The fact that the Ouled Sidi Cheikh were kin to the rebel Bou Amama—whose Saharan raids were a continual source of problems for French commanders—gave added credibility to the accusations.[67] The division of Oran, which administered the Ouled Sidi Cheikh, was at pains to prove its innocence in the affair, a setback to its own plans to use the tribe as a proxy force in the oases.[68]

Like Didier, the game Deporter played was a complicated one involving high stakes, and his intrigues earned him the enmity of many. He ran into trouble when the issue of the role of the slave trade fell into public view. On 4 June 1889 Deporter ordered the interception of a caravan traveling north from the Tidikelt with thirty slaves, including nineteen girls between the ages of eight and sixteen and eleven boys between the ages of six and twelve. (Deporter took a photograph to document the event; see fig. 4.) They originally came from Timbuktu and were destined for buyers at Beni-Isguen (Mzab).[69] The raid violated the eyes-closed policy and the governor-general's office was little pleased by the announcement. Governor-General Tirman noted, "It is regrettable that slaves were brought into our territory and [we believe] that this fact is without doubt due to the complicity of our natives."[70] Reading between the lines of the administrative vernacular, one learns that the governor-general's office was most unhappy that Deporter had publicly unveiled the continued existence of the slave trade in French-controlled territories. The fact that the incident made it into the press when *Le Petit Colon* published an account entitled "The Slave Market" on 25 June 1889 compounded the anger and embarrassment of the governor-general. The article suggested the slave trade benefited from the acquiescence, if not the active participation, of the French administration.

FIGURE 4 Group of captured young blacks in a slave caravan coming from In Salah.
Photo by Victor Deporter.
Source: BNF-R Cartes et Plans, We 138. notice no. FRBNF38640919. Collection de la
Société de Géographie–Clichés B.N.F.

Deporter did not have altruistic motives when he ordered the caravan intercepted. It had been sent by the *zawiya* al-Kahala. Although the Zoua were not
known to be especially hostile to the French, they were rivals of the Badjouda
and thus prospective enemies of Deporter in his new system of alignments.
Moreover, their links to the volatile Chaamba made them suspect in Deporter's
eyes.[71] We do not know the exact circumstances leading up to Deporter's decision to intercept the caravan, but its leader, Sayyid 'Abd al-Qadir ibn Sayyid
al-Shaykh, cried foul. Sayyid al-Shaykh lived at the Foggâret ez Zoûa with his
wife and two children. He was a powerful notable with ties to the sultan of
Morocco and close relations with the Tuareg and notables in the oases of the
Gourara.[72] When Deporter distributed the slaves to families in the Mzab and
to French missionaries (Pères Blancs), Sayyid al-Shaykh suffered a loss totaling nearly 15,000 francs — an enormous sum.[73] Seeking redress, he first took his
complaint to his kin, Si Eddin, the influential agha of the Ouled Sidi Cheikh,
and with Si Eddin's support he presented his case directly to the French commander of Géryville.

Sayyid al-Shaykh's letter of protest was written in Arabic by a Taitoq Tuareg
notable (Shaykh Sayyid ibn Guerraj al-Tariq) who was most likely a partner in
the slave caravan.[74] It vaguely outlined the arrangement the slave trader had

made with Deporter, suggesting that Sayyid al-Shaykh had made a payment in order to earn the right of free passage with his slaves.[75] However, the letter was frank in denouncing Deporter's betrayal: "The commandant (*hākim*) in Ghardaïa has deceived him, he has released the slaves, one after another." The letter created a troublesome situation for Deporter's superiors in Algiers, one that the Division of Oran eventually made good use of, accusing Deporter of having "tacitly authorized the sale of slaves."[76] Most worrisome was the public attention and embarrassment suffered by the governor-general's office. In March 1890 Governor-General Tirman wrote to the minister of war asking that Deporter be relieved of his command, and the rogue officer was called back to Algiers.[77] This did not mollify Sayyid al-Shaykh. He went from Géryville to Morocco, where he asked Sultan Mouley al-Hasan to intervene on his behalf.[78]

My findings on abolition in Algeria hold few surprises for the historian of slavery and abolition elsewhere in Africa. As Martin Klein and other historians have shown, throughout French-controlled Africa administrators showed a singular lack of enthusiasm for enforcing the abolition dictated by Paris. Abolition became less a question of enforcing norms than achieving goals. In Algeria top officials pronounced strict enforcement in public orders, while instructing local commandants to be "discerning" and to be especially tolerant in the southern territories in order to avoid disrupting Saharan trade. This mixed message produced a de facto policy of toleration, namely, the eyes-closed policy, which lasted until the first decade of the twentieth century. Entrusted with an open secret, local commanders found that they enjoyed near unilateral power to make decisions on abolition and slavery. A few, like Victor Colonieu, who had a special abhorrence of slavery, were no doubt vigilant in enforcing abolition. The majority—men like Flatters, Deporter, and Didier—either encouraged the slave trade in an effort to boost trade or selectively enforced abolition as part of a wider system of rewards and punishments designed to advance their influence with local notables. Slave traders responded by remaining discreet, while at the same time aggressively cultivating ties with the local administrators to discover the terms of quid pro quo under which they might trade slaves in French zones. In the case of the *zawiya* al-Kahala, this meant providing special services for the local commander, who was expected to close his eyes to their slave trading. This system was part of the double bind of French colonialism, which entrapped Saaba and thousands of others like her. While promising individual emancipation and liberating change, the agents of French colonialism made accommodation with the status quo. In the Sahara, this status quo depended upon slavery.

Only the most general remarks can be offered in considering the end of Saaba's story. The archives are silent on her fate, and we learn nothing of her after Victor Largeau left Ouargla in October 1877. Her last words, recorded by the explorer, are worth considering. Her narrative ends thusly: "This country is ugly and those who live here are poor and wretched. The Arabs told us that farther on there are the French, who eat blacks."[79] Among the ruined, facing the barbarians.

PART 4

Imagining France's Saharan Empire

Whence the birth of ideologies, doctrines, bloody farces.
—E. M. Cioran, *Précis de décomposition* (1949)

[10]

ROMANTICISM AND THE SAHARAN SUBLIME

French expansion in the Sahara did not sustain itself, as it were, through materi-al interests alone. A rich body of aspirations, myths, and fantasies accompanied economic and geostrategic concerns and formed a part of the complex matrix that drove the Saharan conquest and shaped its violence. In the early chapters I showed how the "pénétration pacifique" facilitated the first stage of French pen-etration in northern parts of the Sahara, making continued expansion—marked by violence and cost overruns—palpable by concealing its brutal realities. This was a process of deception and self-deception where, in the memorable phrase of Marx and Engels, the world was made to appear "auf den Kopf" (on its head). Later other intellectual and cultural forces impinged upon events. Ideas did not simply alter or mask realities in a way that suited the interests of colonial con-quest. Rather, they forged what French historians of European expansion have called a colonial "imaginary."[1] Made up of various hopes, utopias, and inchoate longings, this imaginary shell reflected rather than concealed the social and cultural tensions that were at the heart of the colonial project in Algeria.

In this and the succeeding chapter I return to France's project in the Sahara during the 1850s and 1860s. In the present chapter I focus on French colonial ideology and the ways it became bound up in a particularly violent aesthet-ics of the sublime in the Sahara. A part of European thought since the seven-teenth century, the sublime entered colonial discourse thanks to the Romantics and people like Edmund Burke, who gave the sublime its modern form in the decades leading up to the French Revolution, a supremely terrifying and grand event. Later French actors involved in the Sahara adapted the sublime to colonial conquest. In chapter 11 I examine one of the most influential yarns spun by French pundits about Saharan people, namely, the Tuareg myth. This myth centered on the "discovery" of the Tuareg, a Saharan peoples lost to time. My analysis illustrates how this "mirage" created a climate of complacency, which ultimately plunged the French on a disastrous course in the Sahara.

The ideas examined in these final two chapters were born of the paradoxes, contradictions, and general cultural malaise—the "mal du siècle"—that affected postrevolutionary France. As Alfred de Musset famously wrote of his generation in *The Confession of a Child of the Century* (1836), "All the evils of the present come from two causes: the people who have passed through 1793 and 1814, nurse wounds in their hearts. That which was is no more; what will be, is not yet."[2] As I will shortly argue, far from resulting in a withdrawal from politics, the moody pessimism that supposedly characterized this generation coincided with strategic colonial interests. In Algeria it motivated those who were involved in the Saharan expansion to see their project through the prism of the Romantic spirit, which championed excess and risk, freedom and transgression. The ideas of Romanticism were thus constitutive in their own right of colonial policy in the Algerian Sahara. My argument in these sections does not rely on a clear-cut distinction between reality or the imaginary, nor do I provide a microsocial study of violent practices or an analysis of colonial violence's macropolitical causes, as in the previous chapters. My goal here is simply to identify a specific imaginary construction of the Sahara—as both a place of extremes (including extreme violence) and, at the other end of the spectrum, a place of nostalgic escape—in a way that sheds light on particular dimensions of violent events that other studies have ignored. The French understandings of the Sahara, each in their own way, took the experience of colonial expansion—marked by trauma, disruption, and discontinuity—and gave it coherence, renegotiating colonialism in the Sahara to produce a narrative of fulfillment or even redemption. In the case of the myths surrounding the Tuareg, these stories lulled colonial actors into forgetting that, according to the very rules they had written, colonialism in the desert, as elsewhere, was always about force.

THE RESTRICTED OCCUPATION OF THE SAHARA AND THE REORIENTATION OF SAHARAN POLICY

French policymaking in the Sahara was never univocal. While there was an enthusiastic drive for commercial expansion in the Sahara that gained momentum among certain factions, other parts of the government sounded a more cautious note. For example, the Ministries of Commerce and Education eagerly signed on to expansionist projects for central Africa, but the Ministry of War—the most important single ministry for Algeria, responsible for the administration of most parts of the colony until 1858—quietly held back ambitious plans for the Sahara.[3] Ironically, the most important figure in this move was Eugène Daumas, who single-handedly had done the most to inspire Saharan expansion in the 1840s. In the decade after he wrote *Le Sahara algérien*, Daumas had taken a decidedly conservative turn in his view of things, a change of opinion that coincided with his nomination to the Ministry of War in 1852. Although he had been dismissed from his position in Affaires indigènes in 1847 following Bugeaud's fall, Daumas's fortunes improved following Louis-Napoléon's coup d'état (2 December 1851). In January 1852 he was appointed to head the Office of Algerian Affairs at the Ministry of War. He held this position until July 1858, when he took up work in the new Ministry of Algeria and the Colonies. Once in Paris, Daumas found that he had different powers to serve, and he abandoned his expansionist proposals developed during his time with Bugeaud. In a decade dominated by wars in the Crimea and Italy, his superiors had little interest tying up their military resources in Africa. Daumas carefully tailored his response by proposing new goals in Algeria. Thus, even as Daumas's 1840s works on the wealth and potential of the Sahara won him public acclaim and went into multiple editions, as a policymaker in the 1850s he practiced restraint.

Daumas voiced his cautions with discretion. He not only had to contend with his own reputation as a visionary of Saharan expansion but also with many interests that nourished their own Saharan aspirations. As a result, he articulated a policy that made concessions to the sweeping rhetoric of Saharan destiny while simultaneously rejecting the many projects for continued conquests from such ambitious local commanders as Lieutenant Colonel Margueritte at Laghouat. For example, Daumas blocked repeated plans to occupy the Mzab and thwarted Margueritte's efforts to embroil France in the internal disputes of Saharan populations then beyond French control. Margueritte was quietly restrained, however, and Daumas saw to it that the minister of war's office avoided pessimistic statements on Saharan policy. An exception, a rare document that articulated the ministry's doubts in clear terms, is a report written by A. de Cavergna, of the minister of war's Office of Algerian Affairs, in the summer of 1854.[4] Most likely written at Daumas's request, the report responded to news from Tripoli that the Ottomans had established a small garrison at Ghat, the strategic oasis south of Tripoli, a move that inflamed local tensions and provided a ripe moment for France to intervene. Cavergna rejected this reasoning and wrote a document that strongly admonished those calling for aggressive expansion. Whereas promoters of Saharan expansion like Ludovic de Polignac, Léon Roches, and Sautter de Beauregard wrote of wealth and adventure in the desert, the Algerian Affairs officer reported that thousands of kilometers of difficult routes had to be crossed just to arrive at Ghat, and most of the region was in the hands of dangerous bandits and rebels. This threw a sharply critical light on the plans for French caravans and challenged the vision of those who saw a vast trading empire in Africa, France's "African Indies."[5] Moreover, while France might have been the preeminent military power in the Maghreb, realizing French designs on the Sahara could provoke a confrontation with the Ottoman Empire, a conflict France did not seek at this time. To attack the Ottomans in the Sahara while French troops fought alongside them against Russia in the Crimea was out of the question. Finally, Cavergna called for a realistic appraisal of French power. He insisted that they were far from enjoying military hegemony in the region. While more optimistic eyes saw a map redrawn to French advantage, Cavergna wrote, "Our domination does not extend far beyond Biskra. We hold Ouargla only nominally and wait to learn with each letter that it has fallen to the Chérif, Muhammad ben Abdallah."[6]

The problem of continued armed resistance was a grave one and imposed real limits to the type of facile economic plans hatched by many pundits. Although turned back at Laghouat and driven out of Ouargla, Muhammad ben Abdallah remained a major obstacle.[7] He nearly succeeded in seizing control of Touggourt in 1853,[8] and since then he had rallied a sizable force of Chaamba, who were impressed by the Sharif's religious credentials and ability to lead them on profitable raids.[9] Further limiting French options were worries about the loyalty of Si Hamza, the French *khalifa* of the Sahara. The French feared he might use the sheer vastness of the region—"such an impressive distance between Géryville and the oasis of Ouargla"—to chart an independent course of action.[10] Indeed, Governor-General Randon suspected that "far from trying, as I have asked, to put the inhabitants of the Tohat and Tidikelt in contact with us, I think he is turning them away from us."[11] These problems forced the French to devise new tactics. By the fall of 1854 some local commanders openly expressed their pessimism and worried that they might never gain the upper hand in the Sahara. For example, the commander of Bou-Saada, facing another winter of long and costly patrols in the northern Sahara against a highly mobile enemy, expressed his impatience as follows: "This type of war, of raids and marauders, is the most tiring, if it is not the most terrible." With such elusive enemies, he feared it might last "a long little while."[12]

NINETEENTH-CENTURY FRENCH EXPLORERS OF THE SAHARA

An aggressive Saharan policy involving large columns of troops and permanent bases deep in the Sahara was not an option. These tactics had won control of the northern oases, but France was in no position to field troops farther into the desert and could not practice gunboat diplomacy in the Sahara. The need for information and contacts remained high, however. The British had recently enjoyed several successes south of Tripoli, and with their intentions in central Africa far from certain, Paris feared that they might outflank the French. These worries increased the need for reliable political intelligence. Such information had to be gathered with discretion to avoid alarming the Ottomans or galvanizing Saharan antipathy toward Algeria's new masters. Moreover, these efforts also had to respond to the perennial concerns over expense.

Colonial administrators used a variety of means to meet these needs. Many sought to establish contacts with local notables, who would act as French intermediaries. A variety of partners had been used thus far, including the Ben Ghana family in the southern Constantinois, the Ben Salem at Laghouat, the Ouled Sidi Cheikh for the remote central Sahara, and various notables in the Tidikelt. The range of cooperation varied greatly, but none of these relationships had proven to be particularly successful. Ahmed ben Salem was weak and ineffective, and although Si Hamza of the Ouled Sidi Cheikh was powerful, he proved to be a difficult partner who valued his independence more than the French alliance. The Sufi orders presented another possibility. The Tijaniyya, for example, had *zawiyas* at Aïn Madi and Temacine (near Touggourt) and commanded much esteem among Saharan societies, including the Tuareg Kel Ajjer confederation, which controlled some of the most strategic trade routes in the Sahara.[13] Expressing this opinion, the commandant of Constantine concluded that the influence and power of Sheikh Muhammad al-Aïd (Temacine) "is uncontested in the desert."[14] Unlike the Ouled Sidi Cheikh, the Tijaniyya *zawiya* had no military force, but in their 1838 struggle against Abdelkader the *zawiya* at Aïn Madi had shown its ability to rally loyal followers into effective militias. Many in the colonial administration hoped that they could use the Tijaniyya's Saharan influence to advance French projects. Yet relations with the Tijaniyya sheikhs yielded mixed results. Like Si Hamza, they had their own interests to protect, and over time hopes faded that the Sufi orders would spearhead French influence.[15]

A second possibility was to use individuals recruited among the various Saharan groups living in the Tell and get them to return to the Sahara, gather information, and establish contacts. Access to potential candidates was easy since there were thousands of people originally from the Sahara living in the French-controlled cities. Yet while some might serve as "living libraries" and share information with researchers, like Ernest Carette, few candidates had the resources and influence necessary to travel all the way across the Sahara—many were simple laborers—and those who did proved untrustworthy. For example, in 1854 Governor-General Randon approached Muhammad ben Ahmad al-Ouezzani, the son of an influential Saharan family, and asked him to travel to Timbuktu.[16] He agreed and departed under great secrecy. When Al-Ouezzani returned, claiming to have succeeded, the governor-general expected a wealth of intelligence. He soon learned that the trip was a fraud. Al-Ouezzani had traveled no farther than the oases of southern Morocco, where he safely passed a suitable amount of time among family and clients before returning to collect his payment.[17]

Colonial administrators did not give up on the quest to find reliable indigenous agents. As I will demonstrate in the next chapter, the French fascination with the Tuareg was first born of these political interests. However, the initial setbacks encouraged planners to consider using French agents. Sending individual Frenchmen, whether civilian or military, carried certain risks. Most, of course, were borne by the explorers themselves: solitary travel was extremely dangerous and individual explorers had few defenses against bandits and the harsh Saharan climate. However, inasmuch as they were expendable and operated independently or under the auspices of nongovernmental institutions, like the Geographic Society of Paris, the administration's officials had little to worry about. They might reap the rewards in the event that the explorers' travels met with success, but they were not responsible for the explorers' welfare. Some local commanders, conversely, expressed their reluctance to send explorers to those areas beyond their immediate control. They felt a personal responsibility for the explorers' safety and worried that recriminations might follow if they were harmed. Moreover, local administrators generally spent many years at a given command and jealously guarded their jurisdictions. They worried that outside explorers would compromise the relations they had developed with Saharan contacts. For example, the explorer Paul Soleillet accrued debts totaling thousands of francs among Mzabi lenders, who clamored to be repaid by the governor-general, causing the local administration decades of headaches.[18] Higher up the chain of command, officers feared that explorers' deaths could reveal French vulnerability and compromise the image of omnipotence they had so carefully cultivated. Undoing the damage from a single explorer's death might involve the army in exactly the sort of costly military campaigns they sought to avoid. Nevertheless, the example of René Caillé's solitary, incognito crossing of the Sahara at the beginning of the century still loomed large, and Jean Prax and Adrien Berbrugger had recently shown that even those who did not hide their origins but who possessed the right credentials and skills could travel safely. (Prax's conversion to Islam was thought to have contributed to his success.)

The ranks of military men with this type of know-how were small but growing. By the 1850s some soldiers had spent decades in Algeria. For example, an officer like Auguste Margueritte had spent most of his life in North Africa, possessed a working knowledge of Arabic, and claimed great insight into local customs and mores. Even more attractive were candidates who bore a physical resemblance to the local populations. However rudimentary their language skills, it was thought that being able to pass as a local would ensure their safety in dangerous situations. (Despite the obvious fact that the people of Algeria were endlessly diverse in their physical appearance, the French thought there was a "type arabe.") In the early 1850s several men reputedly having such physical qualities were slated to travel south and discreetly "raise the veil" on the region.[19] They included Jean Dastuge, a lieutenant in a Spahis regiment, and Charles Cusson, aka Muhammad ben Chérif, a former legionnaire, convert to Islam, and onetime secretary to the emir Abdel Kader. Later soldiers with long experience in Algeria led two of the most successful Saharan missions of the 1850s. In 1856 Captain Bonnemain, an officer who had led a "near legendary" life among Algerians, became the first Frenchman to visit Ghadamès.[20] In 1858 Ismaël Bouderba, son of Ahmed Bouderba, who served as an interpreter in the French army, traveled over twenty-four hundred kilometers to Ghat, accompanied by Tuareg guides.[21] Their success provided support for the project of sending Frenchmen into the Sahara, and by the end of the decade planners believed a lone French explorer might safely travel to regions beyond French military control.

The move to individual French explorers was given further momentum by forces outside the colonial administration. Most notable in this respect was the Geographic Society of Paris's 1855 announcement of a cash prize for the first explorer to cross the Sahara from Algeria to Senegal via Timbuktu (or vice versa).[22] The society had raised its own monies and combined them with contributions from the Ministries of Education, Agriculture and Commerce, plus Public Works and private contributions, to offer an 8,320-franc prize.[23]

The prize gave Saharan exploration a publicity boost and lent it new urgency and impetus. It also swelled the ranks of potential explorers with an ever more diverse cast of characters. Whereas would-be explorers in the 1840s and 1850s were military men (like Bonnemain and Bouderba) or scientists (like Prax, Berbrugger, and MacCarthy), after 1855 people came to the Sahara with a host of inchoate goals. Many looked to success in the Sahara to escape failed careers, debts, or personal grief. Like Michel Leiris, who traversed Africa from Senegal to Djibouti nearly a hundred years later, they left Europe on vague projects to discover themselves or find their "heart" in Africa.[24] Examples include Paul Soleillet (b. 1842), the scion of a wealthy textile family from Nimes. Having lost his wife in childbirth, he had failed as a revolutionary in Poland and had gone through a humiliating bankruptcy before setting his sights on the Sahara.[25] In 1874 he made a now famous trip to In Salah, where he huddled all night outside the ksar with his terrified guides before acceding to the demand that he return north or face execution.[26] Another was Camille Douls (b. 1864), a young student from Rodez, who contracted "le spleen" of the Romantics while studying in Paris. Seeking a cure in the Sahara, and inspired by Jules Verne's writings, he was especially eager to discover the desert's fantastic wonders. In 1887 Douls, posing as an Arab traveler, disembarked on the Sahara's Atlantic coast, near Cape Juby, single-handedly to face the desert's "barbarism, with its stream of evils and atrocities."[27] Having survived this mission, he sat for a stunning photographic portrait by Nadar in full "Arab" garb. He subsequently made a name for himself in Paris as a dashing figure known for his daring and adventure. (He was strangled two years later en route to Timbuktu.[28]) The writer Isabelle Eberhardt also chose the Sahara for her particular romantic quest.[29] Born in Geneva in 1877 to a family of destitute Russian nobles, Eberhardt first traveled to the Sahara in 1899, where, finding a refuge from the "lugubrious" European society of the Tell, she decided to continue her unique Orientalist writings and study of Sufi mysticism. As she wrote, "I love my Sahara with an obscure love, mysterious, profound, inexplicable, but real and indestructible. . . . My life is forever linked to this land, which I can never leave."[30] She traveled widely in the Algerian Sahara before perishing in a desert flash flood in 1904.

Others, like Norbert Dournaux-Dupéré, sought modest economic gain in the Sahara.[31] Born in Point-à-Pitre in 1845, he was the illegitimate son of a Creole woman. Although his natural father, a Frenchman, raised his son while posing as his godfather, Dournaux-Dupéré was left with his mother's name and no inheritance when his father died.[32] He made a living as a soldier in Mexico, a colonial administrator in Senegal, and a schoolteacher in Algeria before deciding that "a little [economic] independence is a nice thing, and I would be happy if I can find some in a few years."[33] Saharan exploration was his chosen path to wealth—a particularly ill-fated one, as it turned out. Dounaux-Dupéré died near Ghadamès in 1874, having been murdered by thieves. Fame was as important as fortune for others. Marcel Palat (b. 1856), for one, counted on the publicity of a successful Saharan crossing to save his military career. A cavalry lieutenant and an aspiring novelist,[34] Palat was expelled from the Bureaux arabes in 1881 for taking an Algerian woman as his concubine.[35] In all likelihood this relationship did not shock his superiors, but it did not sit well with the local population. They might have tolerated discreet carnal relations between a Christian and Muslim woman of ill repute, but they bristled when Palat had the poor taste to make inspection tours in her company. In the winter of 1885–86 he sought to repair this damage with a bold solitary trek to Timbuktu dashingly dressed as an Arab.[36] However, his attempt to travel "in the skin of an Oriental, abdicating all my repugnance and sensitivity to become a sort of savage," convinced no one in the Sahara and put him at great risk.[37] His fate was sealed when he clashed with his hosts, the Ouled Sidi Cheikh, over the terms of their hospitality. After they made it known that he no longer enjoyed their protection, it was only a short time before this persona non grata was killed south of El Goléa.[38] Similarly, the marquis de Morès, a rich adventurer, traveled to the Sahara in 1896 in the hopes of reaching Ghat and forging an anticapitalist, anti-Jewish alliance with the "warrior tribes" of the Sahara.[39] This project was to be the climax of a checkered career. After a failed stint as a rancher in North Dakota, Morès returned to France during the Dreyfus affair and became the darling of the extreme right by challenging Dreyfusards to duels and writing seething anti-Semitic pieces for *Le Libre Parole* and *L'Assaut*.[40] Morès hoped his exploits in the Sahara would continue this momentum and earn him a lasting reputation as a dashing figure in the struggle for empire. His fame was great but posthumous. Although he had proved himself an excellent gunfighter, Morès spurned the colonial administration and the protection it represented. Not benefiting from their patronage and contacts, he attracted the attention of raiders, who killed him north of Ghadamès.[41]

Other Saharan explorers suffered from mental instability. Such was the case with Gaston Méry, who received a commission in 1892 from the Syndicat d'Ouargla au Soudan to explore the region south of Touggourt. He was born in Algeria in 1843, spoke Arabic, and had explored the Patagonian region of Argentina — on paper seemingly an ideal candidate.[42] However, his mental state was volatile and quickly unraveled in the Sahara. In addition to many "acts of violence and brutality" against his fellow travelers, Méry argued with a guide and shot him in the arm, killed his interpreter's dog after it failed to attack a gazelle on command, and, in a fit of rage, threatened to blow up his entire party with several boxes of blasting powder.[43]

This colorful cast of misfits, opportunists, and psychopaths was ill-suited to perform the delicate work the colonial administration needed. Anticipating the problems caused by opening the floodgates to travelers of all sorts, the minister of war first announced the Geographical Society's award to the governor-general's office in a note that bespoke apprehension.[44] However, many officials responsible for Saharan policy recognized that solitary French explorers suited the flexible approach the situation demanded. Even if they never returned, huge windfalls of information could be expected. The investigations that followed explorers' deaths produced thousands of pages of intelligence and had the effect of pushing events forward, thereby breaking up stalemates and standoffs. Old enemies had to restate their positions and would-be neutral parties were forced to choose sides. In some cases new allies presented themselves in the hope of gaining an advantage by cooperating with investigators.[45]

LITERARY AND ADMINISTRATIVE REPRESENTATIONS OF THE DESERT

As I previously argued (see chapter 2), in the 1840s the language of the "pénétration pacifique" ensured that the Sahara was represented within the conventions of the pastoral and the picturesque. The Sahara was calm, a place of rest — strikingly unlike the ravaged martial landscapes of the Tell. It was distinguished by its visual beauty — drifting dunes, swaying palms, and bubbling oasis springs — bathed in a glorious luminosity that few regions could rival. A land of opportunity for merchants and scientists, the Sahara was especially suited to artists. Even as the French empire expanded through military conquest—the violence in the ksour, the bloodshed at Zaatcha, and the massacre at Laghouat—these original pastoral terms were little disturbed by events. The stench of death still lingered in Laghouat when Louis de Baudicour wrote that the oases were "earthly paradises" where at nightfall cool temperatures brought the locals out, who "give themselves over to all sorts of entertainment while swarms of doves flutter above them, from palm to palm, singing melodious songs." [46] Likewise, when the young explorer Henri Duveyrier first visited the Sahara in 1857, he hardly noticed the vast cemetery on the outskirts of Laghouat; instead, he was swept away by the beauty of the oasis: "The gardens were covered with apricot and peach trees and many flowering trees. Only the melancholy yet harmonious song of the *chouath*, which rolled from tree to tree, disturbed the solemn silence of the night." [47] This idyllic image endured throughout the nineteenth century. Paul Soleillet described Ouargla in 1874 in terms that recalled Virgil's Elysian Fields: "Everything is green, nothing but green, yet the light is so beautiful, so white, so pure that objects stand out in such sharp and arresting forms. The colors are so true and everything offers itself in a manner so rigorous that one must have a soul completely impervious to nature's beauties not to admire such things." [48]

This pastoral Sahara lured dozens of talented artists—among them Eugène Fromentin, Gustave Guillaumet, and Etienne Dinet (a.k.a. Nasr ad Dine)—to the Algerian oases to seek the Sahara's beautiful light and colors. [49] At the turn of the century images of desert palms and dunes became stock "images d'Epinal," filling tourist brochures that lured travelers to oases like Biskra and Touggourt. [50] André Gide, for example, was just one among many Europeans to undertake the Saharan tourist circuit, where he was seduced by the "softness of the clear shadows, murmurs of the gardens, [and] sweet odors" found in the Algerian oases. [51]

Nevertheless, representations of the Sahara began to change. While the oases have remained within a pastoral aesthetic to the present day, in the 1850s the long tracts of desert between settlements emerged under a different, more forbidding light. [52] This was the first time that the Algerian Sahara became accessible to Europeans. Seeing the desert for the first time with their own eyes, the experience shocked many. Like René Caillé, who found the Sahara "suffocating," these travelers wrote of an unforgiving land of shifting dunes, blinding heat, and agonizing thirst. [53] Félix Jacquot found "absolute sterility" in the High Plateaux, leaving him with "a sad impression and a painful tightening of my heart." [54] In 1872 an officer on the first military mission to El Goléa wrote that the desert "opens up to the eye like an incomparable chaos." [55] And as late as 1893 Fernand Foureau, a seasoned desert traveler, wrote that "the traveler feels drowned in this boundless immensity, and it seems that he will never arrive at a port in this sea without limits." [56]

In part these new views of the desert originated in the changing realities of the occupation and the shifting needs of the French administration. Policy-makers were no longer interested in seductive reports aimed at winning over political support for Saharan expansion. With bases at Laghouat, Biskra, and Bou-Saada, the French Sahara was a reality, and the days when authors might use Leo Africanus as a primary source were coming to an end (see chapter 2). For example, in 1862 Colonel Trumelet disparaged the fact that the Sahara was known only through "a few novels full of conventional orientalist jargon."[57] Planners were hungry for firsthand accounts that mentioned more than vague "mœurs et coutumes." The importance of empirical observation was spread-ing even to orientalist circles in Paris. When William MacGuckin de Slane, a military interpreter and one of the foremost orientalists in Paris, undertook a new translation of al-Bakri's *Description of North Africa* (1068), he not only used multiple manuscripts to check its accuracy but traveled to the Maghreb to deter-mine the exact name and location of geographic references. His project was not only to render a truthful translation but to correct the "errors" of the original and make al-Bakri's text useful to the French empire.[58]

Rarely, however, did authors stick to the empirical facts. Just as Daumas had interspersed his account of trade and trails with folkloric vignettes and stories of sexual licentiousness, the reports of the 1850s were not the purely descriptive documents one might have anticipated. While many continued to supply anec-dotes to give added oriental color to their reports, there was a noticeable attempt to raise or shift the level of writing to achieve a more elevated, poetic diction, to the point where the language and devices common to Romantic writers infil-trated administrative reports and expedition logs. These deviated significantly from the usual military-administrative reports, which stressed sobriety, accuracy, and matter-of-fact observation.[59]

Many of these stylistic traits used to describe the Sahara had their origins in the texts written by the new generation of explorers, who had arrived in the desert at this time. Civilian explorers like Camille Douls excelled in this genre, but often it was the soldiers who went the furthest in borrowing from the literary field. For example, Bonnemain's 1857 report on Ghadamès was narrated entirely through the first person. Although it included useful details on politics, commerce, and geography, its most outstanding feature involved lengthy aesthetic descriptions of the desert.[60] Even when Bonnemain concentrated on descriptions of the route, he spent as much time talking about his personal psychological reactions and existential states of mind as he did about distances, sources of water, and land-marks. Likewise, Ismaël Bouderba's report describing his twenty-four-hundred-kilometer journey to Ghat dwelt at length on his affective reactions to the des-ert.[61] As his guide reminded him, this was "al-bilād al-khawf" (the land of fear). Bouderba stressed the landscape's hostility and monotony as well as his feeling of hopelessness. He also gave voice to its otherworldly, fantastical features, such as the rocky mass known as the "ksar al-jenūn" (Citadel of the Demons), which inspired "a profound terror," according to Bouderba.[62] None of this information was particularly helpful to future travelers, and it did not respond to Trumelet's demand for pragmatic information. However, it made for a particularly gripping read and marked a distinctive Saharan genre of administrative reports.

In order to better understand these texts, it is useful to situate them within the broader military-administrative culture in Algeria. The figure of the French commander in Algeria has been held up as the epitome of self-control and prudence, a person strictly bound by wise decision making and rational behavior. Writing in 1927, André Chevrillon of the Académie française noted that the military administrator worked "in an unquestionable and precise system, in a hierarchy of command and obedience to the idea of order and duty."[63] Such officers, he continued, "pursued, in a primitive or half-civilized country, their assigned task of governing to achieve practical ends." If this were indeed the case, the writing they produced—the monthly reviews, journals, and reports—might be expected to be bound by the strict rules of pragmatism, documents that favored utility over style.

Such, indeed, was the stereotype of the written work of bureaucrats. Balzac once wrote disparagingly that the administrative report was the epitome of banal prose, which reflected the larger bureaucratic climate of caution and stagnation. According to Balzac, it expressed only the "power of inertia."[64] Certainly the administrative report was fully instrumental and structured around a carefully designed formula. As Max Horkheimer and Theodor Adorno noted, it was "firmly directed toward its end."[65] Nevertheless, there were important ways in which colonial administrators authored texts that aspired to much more than a calculated articulation of knowledge in the service of colonial power. Indeed, had Balzac lived to read certain reports that circulated within the colonial administration in the 1850s and thereafter, he might have recognized a little of his own influence in their carefully crafted pages.

Even before the heyday of Saharan expansion, soldiers wrote highly literary accounts of their life and adventures in Algeria. In what may be the first example of this trend in Algeria, J.-L. Lugan, an artillery captain, wrote about an 1830 military expedition to Médéa (the same one that devastated Blida) with such elegance and refined style that the editors of the prestigious literary periodical *La Revue de Paris* selected it for publication in 1832.[66] Lugan's piece consisted of a narrative of the column's march and military encounters—the standard information included in a military report—and its length was only slightly longer than the typical handwritten notebooks that fill the military archives today. However, even if Lugan's account was probably drawn from an official report, it departed considerably from the norm in tone and language. It was written with care and showed attention to literary conventions. Lugan included something of a dramatic plot, arousing feelings of excitement and concern, character development and psychology, and detailed descriptions of the setting. Many of Lugan's passages consciously strove toward a distinct literary lyricism. For example, in his opening lines Lugan carefully drafted a mise en scène that alerted the reader that this was no mere chronicle: "The distribution of the flags was done on one of those days with the African sun blazing. The army was lined up in battle formation on the beach, the calm sea resembling a glowing mirror. A religious silence reigned; the only sound was the murmur of the tide. Yet in the midst of this calm, in this solemn wait, the spirit, the élan of the soldiers' hearts, showed through in their eyes, in their tanned faces."[67]

Later Lugan provided novelistic descriptions of the landscape and people he met en route. In one passage Lugan described the encounter between an Algerian emissary sent to meet the column and the French commander. "The sight of this man," Lugan wrote of the emissary, "made a strong impression on us. All his features breathed audacity and fanaticism. He had a lean face, a short, thin beard, black, sparkling eyes, and dry, nervous hands." This man had been sent to negotiate with the French, to tell them that although he did not consider the French enemies, they were unwelcome in his town and should remain on the outskirts. This provoked a strong reaction from the French commander. Lugan wrote a dramatic account of the standoff between these two men: "'Arab,' the officer said, 'your proposition is strange. This land is ours, I am your master, and I will enter your town if it pleases me.'" A look of shock spread across the face of the emissary. Lugan continued, "He had the exact appearance of one of these fanatics who, to gain eternal life, commit themselves . . . to *sacred combat.*"[68] Fourth-rate writing, perhaps, but Lugan's story was intended for first-rate readers, or so the editors of the *Revue de Paris* thought. They published Lugan's story alongside some of the greatest authors of the day, such as Stendhal, Scott, Hugo, Dumas père, and Sue.

Such publications soon proliferated, with accounts of soldiers' Algerian experiences becoming best-sellers. One of the most famous soldier-writers was Jacques Leroy de Saint-Arnaud, who led troops through the bloody campaigns of the 1840s. Having begun his military career by suppressing a royalist uprising in the Vendée (1832) and having also fought alongside Greek nationalists, he was eager to share his African experiences. He wrote richly descriptive letters to his family, which stressed his complete and total freedom in Algeria in a way that mirrored the calls for artistic freedom that rang through the pages of literary revues back home.[69] In Africa, however, it was not art for art's sake but a sort of cult of violence that Saint-Arnaud celebrated. He suggested that his work in Algeria represented the soldier's true purpose and highest calling. In an age when military men openly questioned their future in a Europe bound by "pacifistic tendencies" and resented their transformation into "bureaucrat soldiers," Saint-Arnaud—who had added "Achilles" to his given names—reveled in the violence of the conquest.[70] While the administrative reports of battles were expected to reflect the sort of "bureaucratic" norms disparaged by Balzac—which carefully elided violent excesses—soldiers such as Saint-Arnaud developed a literary cult of colonial violence. They reflected upon actual practices, such as the scorched-earth tactics deployed to subdue Algerian resistance, but adapted their particular set of goals and rules from the literary field. Reflecting on Saint-Arnaud's description of the sack of Constantine in 1837, the critic François Maspero commented: "The words that he uses to describe the terrifying scenes that followed the explosion—body parts, clothes torn to rags, bits of flesh, heads dripping blood, a red mire trampled underfoot—strangely recalls Racine."[71] Writing in the immediate aftermath of the Algerian revolution, another commentator located the root of such narrative choices not in French Classicism but in Romanticism. Mostefa Lacheraf found that a "lyrical sadism" ran throughout the French accounts of the conquest, which reflected not only shifting literary conventions and new markets for hybrid soldier-writers but was part of a new and disturbing relationship between aesthetics and politics. As Lacheraf commented,

> Many superior officers of the Conquest—thrown as youngsters into a war far from Europe, where certain humanitarian conventions were respected on the field of battle, against a people that they had to crush—found that they were liberated, so to speak, of any sorts of moral hindrances. They returned to the most absolute form of the warrior vocation and publicly announced their violence, practicing it as a means of escape or relief. One is even tempted to think that this generation of officers, who knew Romanticism, . . . fashioned themselves . . . under the African sky, in the face of a resolute enemy, into both the organ and the instrument of another Romantic psychosis [that was] cruel, animated by a feeling of adventure . . . It was, so to speak, another aspect, that of a warrior Romanticism that historians and psychologists will one day study.[72]

In other words, Lacharef invites us to see how Shelley's "tempestuous loveliness of terror" served the soldier as it had the poet.

Lacharef's argument is suggestive of the way that a military mystique of violence coincided with the forces generated by an increasingly militant literary field intent on charting new social functions for art, and how the two were driven closer together at this historical juncture by the imperial needs of the French state.[73] In France the sorts of transgressions valorized by soldiers and writers were dangerous—especially once they made claims on political and social action in postrevolutionary France. As historian Raoul Girardet has written, "Neutrality or, more precisely, political passivity became one of the essential dogmas of the new military morality."[74] In the barracks of France the various civilizing processes were in full swing, and transgressions would not be tolerated. However, the government found it useful for its armed agents in Algeria to have free rein.

This intensified the violence of French troops, sanctioning transgressions that were anathema in the metropolis, while at the same legitimating such violence within the rules of an artistic field that enjoyed widespread esteem. Romanticism's emphasis on freedom and energy, the sensual and exotic, maximized the military effectiveness of the army in the irregular, brutal, and faraway wars of colonial conquest. Soldiers who sought to follow Baudelaire and give aesthetics priority over politics consequently found their vocation sanctioned and supported. In Algeria soldiers were free to fashion a social and political reality—with violence at its center—out of Romantic discourses and the realities of colonial warfare. Here they had the liberty to situate themselves among the esteemed ranks of modern French writers, the "sacré de l'écrivain," as long as Algerians bore the cost of such fantasies and posed no political risks. A latter-day Achilles was a welcome agent of colonialism, whereas a latter-day Bonaparte was not.[75]

THE SAHARAN SUBLIME: FROM AESTHETICS TO POLITICS

Du sublime au ridicule il n'y a souvent qu'un pas.
—*Nouveau dictionnaire universel* (1870)

Romantic idioms and perhaps even a "Romantic psychosis" infiltrated French texts of the Sahara, and these had an important impact on the outcome of policymaking, including the introduction of a cult of violence. In the following section, which deals with the impact of European Romanticism on French imperialism, I will concentrate on one specific and particularly important component of the Romantic aesthetic, namely, the sublime.[76]

The sublime was a central concept for the Romantics, who learned of it from Nicolas Boileau's seventeenth-century translation of the classical Greek treatise *On the Sublime*.[77] The sublime reflected the irresistible power of language—the "marvelous in speech"—to ravish, transport, and radically imbue the reader with awe, reverence, and lofty emotion.[78] The term encompassed a considerable semantic range, which was enlarged in the late eighteenth and early nineteenth centuries by Romantic writers. Some, struggling with the problem of a *Deus absconditus* (hidden God), avoided the "vision tragique" by seeking links between the spiritual and physical worlds.[79] They looked to extreme phenomena in nature and read them as divine catastrophes, or tangible and incontrovertible proof of God's presence and omnipotence.[80] Edmund Burke, one of the most influential theorists of the sublime, used it as a tool to attack the intellectualism of his age as well as the "beautiful," the privileged category of the Classicists. In his treatise on aesthetic theory entitled *Philosophical Enquiry into the Origin of our Ideas of the Sublime and the Beautiful* (1757), the horror and wonder of human experience that had been banished by cold rationalism was reinstated. Burke produced a set of terms for those considering extreme phenomena *tout court* and their psychological effects, the states of stupefaction, terror, and, ultimately, pleasurable submission.[81] Following the French Revolution, the sublime was well suited to make sense of such forces of modernity as urbanization, industrialization, and secularization, which gripped people and transformed their lives with disorienting and often traumatic results. "It provided a language," Thomas Weiskel writes, for these "urgent and apparently novel experiences of anxiety and excitement."[82] This was important in bringing the sublime out of the realm of aesthetics and making it useful for politics.[83]

Arduous and desolate, the Algerian Sahara was initially not a landscape that might readily provoke the type of affective reaction that Burke had described. For example, when the colonial scholar Emile Masqueray first spied the desert north of Laghouat in 1875, he exclaimed, "Great God, what an ugly land." Masqueray expected to see magnificent dunes and picturesque vistas such as those sketched by Fromentin. Instead, he found a banal, dreary, colorless country: "It is chalk-white, of a dull gray or a dirty white, furrowed and crisscrossed with deep wrinkles, deformed by enormous hillocks, and it fades into the distance—a great distance—ever more monotonous and banal."[84] This place had nothing uplifting or awesome about it. The Sahara was, however, far from the everyday experience of most, and numerous locales featured the disorienting characteristics that Burke associated with the sublime. While many would write that the desert was a singularly ugly and hostile place, they stressed the landscape's wild disorder, desolation, and radical alterity. For example, Louis de Colomb, the commander of Géryville, warned European travelers "used to the rich crops, the prairies, forests, and large rivers of their native land" to be prepared for a rude experience. "Indeed, nothing lives here," he wrote, "neither plant, nor insect, nor bird," and traveling in the desert amounted to a "long journey into death."[85] Even geologists and geographers, who came to the Sahara armed with a technical vocabulary and a sober scientific mission, expressed their difficulty in coming to terms with the landscape. The reporter for an 1873 mission, unable to account for a particular rock formation, at first thought that glaciers must have existed in the Sahara. Confronted with that absurdity, he concluded that the desert landscape was "a chaos that is impossible to compare to anything."[86] Likewise, ten years later a member of the trans-Saharan railway survey team wrote, "It is difficult to sort out the chaos that country presents."[87] Geographers eventually borrowed from the Arabic language to find the necessary words to give form to the desert, suggesting that the Sahara, with its complex and extreme phenomena, tested the representational limits of both ordinary and scientific language.[88]

Some reacted to the Sahara's radical discontinuity with confusion and depression. Many desert travelers encountered problems of disorientation and experienced a breakdown of their cognitive abilities. The desert's unlimited horizons destabilized the mind, produced vertigo, and invited madness. In the 1850s Pierre Henri Stanislas d'Escayrac de Lauture published an article warning travelers of the risk of desert madness. Having explored the deserts farther east, on several occasions Lauture had fallen victim to disorientation, hallucinations, and crises of mania. This was not the mirage or *sarāb*, something he thought originated in atmospheric conditions, but a more profound psychological problem unique to the desert. He proposed that the Arabic word *raql* be employed in technical definitions.[89]

These mental breakdowns and liminal states provided material for many fantastical passages in writings on the Sahara. Masqueray described in detail his hallucinations involving cool lakes, sumptuous palaces, lush forests, and the siren calls of beautiful music.[90] Others wrote refined interior monologues that gave voice to their awe and wonder. Finding himself in the Sahara's Atlantic coast in 1887, Camille Douls wrote,

> I sat down on these rocks that jut out over the sea, and in front of these two immensities that are most striking to the heart of man—the Ocean and the Desert—I remained thinking and dreaming for a moment. I was in one of those solemn moments in human existence that are signaled by a white or black stone. . . . seeing myself alone on this rock dominating the sea, my initial impression was not fear [la crainte]; it was more like astonishment. It was impossible to analyze my feelings, and yet I felt that bittersweet sensation, that sort of intoxication [ivresse], both enjoyable and painful, that one feels during the great shocks of the soul.[91]

Douls's comments might be understood as the expression of a sort of attraction-repulsion. At the beginning of a venture into a hostile country involving extreme personal risk, he did not feel fear but rather a disorienting mental ambivalence, a voluptuous panic. Roger Caillois, sociologist and fellow traveler of Georges Bataille, called this sensation of vertigo "ilinx." He proposed that it stemmed from a repressed desire for moral disequilibrium, "a desire for disorder and destruction," rather than a physiological imbalance.[92] Douls suggested that his own intoxication was provoked by the radical asymmetry between his small and mortal self and the great and spectacular natural scenes spread out before his eyes, namely, the desert and the ocean. Stripped of science, reason, and the tools of technology, Douls felt the powerful simplicity of existence and found pleasure in contemplating his insignificant place in an all-powerful natural world.

Some writers used these moments of contemplation to speculate upon modern life and the conditions of belief. For Louis de Colomb the omnipotence of nature, a landscape untouched by human hands, allowed him to reflect freely upon humanity's place in the world:

Man, who lives in large cities, who sees only human works, who hears only human cries and songs, of which every sense experiences the emanations and the noise of a compact humanity, can forget God, or at least stop thinking about him for some time. He who traverses the Saharan deserts, who walks without noise on these piles of sands, during weeks on end, without meeting anything that reminds him of man and his ephemeral presence; this man understands how small he is before the master of masters; this man understands how brief are his few minutes of eternity that he must spend on this planet, where he tramples through the most desolate part; this man prostrates himself and prays.[93]

Like Douls, Colomb found that the inhuman features of the desert marked a portal leading from the world of man to the world of God. The former was a mundane place—noisy, crowded, and full of "works"—while the latter was silent, open, and free. Here Colomb found himself presented with the profound truths that remained hidden in the everyday world. Like the mystic who sounded his or her "ephemeral presence" in solitary contemplation, Colomb's recognition of his fragility put him in contact with the outer limits of a vast and powerful universe—the sacred—before which he prostrated himself in a moment of terror and joy. He did not see a mirage in the desert but rather a miracle.

Another particularly poignant account of this experience was the product of Dr. Félix Jacquot's 1847 trip with Cavaignac to raid the ksour. After several days his mind began to slip. As he wrote, "The sight of the dunes caused a sad impression. . . . Here the image of man—face to face with this ungrateful nature—seems small, isolated, without options and without courage."[94] He continued to reflect on this spectacle by inscribing it within a larger narrative of natural disaster: "Then one thinks of the desert tempests that shake these masses [the dunes]: they lift up and march ahead in silence, terrible and pitiless like death. Nothing can resist their slow yet always steady invasion: trees dry out, rivers fill in, springs cease to flow; soon palms, homes, the oases—all are in covered by the common shroud. . . . And when the calm returns, the traveler seeks in vain the shade of the trees and the wells where he drank earlier." Such thoughts brought feelings of dizziness and disorientation to the doctor: "Certainly you have had occasion unwisely to sound an abyss with your eye. Vertigo seized you, but you remained fixed, not daring to pull yourself away from this spectacle. Such was my imagination, filled with sinister and dark images of the dunes, held fatally in the sands, and I was left helpless, as in a dream [un songe]."[95]

Jacquot's vision of a northward march of the desert, consuming all in its path, paralyzed him with its horror. Its force was such that he claimed to lose all agency and watched helplessly as his own annihilation unfolded before his eyes: springs dried up, billowing clouds of sand moved in, and a deadly shroud of dust settled upon the now lifeless and forever sterile landscape. Spellbound, Jacquot could not begin to fathom the reasons for such a catastrophe, and he could only stand transfixed before the fantasy of his own annihilation.

In the ensuing decades many writers echoed this description of an apocalyptic landscape. For example, when Victor Largeau traveled through the vast dunes of the Great Eastern Erg to Ghadamès in 1875 (prior to his sojourn in Ouargla, where he bought Saaba), he wrote of the extreme physical hardships and mental "chaos" experienced here. A foreboding land's "mal" became Largeau's "malheur," a fatigue that gave way to feelings of hopelessness and "general malaise." Like Jacquot, Largeau tried to understand the origins and deeper meanings of such a landscape. In 1876 he published an account in which he described how he climbed a large mountain of sand, the ghourd el-Nacer, to better survey the full scene:

> The sight is horrible and grandiose: everywhere, from all sides, as far as the eye can see, there are crests of dunes succeeded by crests of dunes. . . . The masses of sand take all sorts of forms. . . . The deep valleys, which wind between these masses, appear strewn with small lakes filled with clear water: they are tight tufts of *helma* or even the white calcareous stretches stripped naked by the sweeps of gray that produce this curious effect. . . . These somber *oughroud*, which everywhere display their bare crests like granite peaks, are like so many giant tombs covering lands that were once pleasant and fertile.
>
> And now, over this buried nature, hovers a deathly silence; only the lugubrious cawing of a few crows, flying from crest to crest, occasionally breaks the silence.
>
> It is impossible to render what one feels upon witnessing such a strange spectacle.[96]

Such encounters led Largeau to the problem of theodicy. In a report from the same mission submitted to the governor-general's office, Largeau wrote that the dunes were a positive "revolution" that revealed the power and "infinite wisdom of He who presides over the laws of nature."[97] However, in the published version Largeau chose to shatter God's beatitude and to describe the scene not as theological discovery but as a cosmological disaster: "If I did not fear blasphemy in attributing to the one and perfect God the passions of men, I would say that the Master of the Worlds resolved one day to *annihilate a nation corrupted* by some foul vice, and decided that by throwing into this country the transformed soil of another country, equally accursed, he would leave to future generations the spectacle of desolation that we have before our eyes."[98]

Louis de Colomb likewise found the hand of the same punishing God in the desert, as evidenced by notes taken on a trip near Géryville in January 1857:

> It would be difficult, I think, to resist the emotion that seizes the heart at the sight of this spectacle of a wild and desolate nature. It is a sort of *religious terror* that

invades, little by little, the farther one goes into this terrifying chaos. There is no longer any sign of man here: it is God, God alone, but probably an irritated God who buried this corner of the world under his disapproval, and he has not yet pulled it out of the abyss. . . .

If Dante Alighieri had known this country, he would have made it his entry to hell and then he would have been able to say with more confidence: "If bitter he was, hardly less so is death."[99]

The debts of colonial writers like Jacquot, Largeau, and Colomb to Romantic authors were substantial. They narrated their travels and experiences utilizing terms freely borrowed from the Romantics, who had spent much ink pondering the powerful and infinite qualities of nature. Balzac himself had written about the Sahara in an 1832 short story entitled "Une passion dans le désert," which described the landscape with the same terms later employed by these explorer-writers: "Here the sky was on fire, the silence was awful in its terrible and wild grandeur. Everywhere the infinite, the immensity, weighed on the soul."[100]

While French explorer-writers shared a common idiom, their paths differed from the "circuitous journey" of canonical Romantic writers like Wordsworth or Coleridge. Wordsworth, for example, would find that the scenery at the Simplon Pass was every bit as awesome and terrible as the Saharan dunes, and like them it revealed "characters of the great Apocalypse."[101] However, this did not lead him to the radically negative conclusions of Largeau and Colomb—at least according to certain commentators. Rather than a vengeful God, Wordsworth wrote of the chance for reconciliation, "the features of the same face, blossoms upon one tree." As literary critic M. H. Abrams has noted, these writers tried "to naturalize the supernatural and to humanize the divine."[102] Their nature was sublime, and although its apocalypse included violent catastrophe, this disaster was purposeful, dialectical, and, ultimately, humanistic. The devastating energy that produced nature's terrible fury was needed to immediately and finally transform a world sacrificed to evil and corruption. However, it would not leave a lifeless ruin in its wake: an earthly paradise, free of suffering and injustice, was to follow these terrible moments of revolution. There is no such promise evident in the devastation written into the Sahara by the French explorer-authors. Their Saharan apocalypse was not redemptive but punitive. Enraged by the transgression of His commands, God annihilated the civilizations whose ashes were scattered among the dunes. Afterward He retreated into a silence broken only by the desert wind and (as Largeau described it) the hoarse, raucous cries of passing crows. Claiming to seek in the desert the same dramatic solutions to the alienation and fragmentation typical of modernity, these authors found only waste and ruin.

As such, these writers might be ranked as minor nineteenth-century prophets of despair.[103] However, as was stated earlier, my purpose is to understand their contribution to the violent culture of French empire in the Sahara by imagining the Sahara as a land of extremes. The political implication of their project can be glimpsed in several areas. First, there is the privileged position they assumed in the Sahara. Although they took great physical risks in the desert, these Saharan travelers tended to downplay their own vulnerability. For example, unlike modern mountain climbers, who base their whole project on the metaphysics of danger,[104] Saharan explorers rarely probed their worries, fears, or moments of doubt, instead choosing to describe them in fetishistic ways, which denied expressions of weakness and insecurity. For example, while concern and anxiety are frequent emotions (e.g., apprehensions about sufficient water and bandits are ubiquitous), they are rarely given the same attention as the "intoxication" provoked by the terrifying landscape. Camille Douls was typical when he wrote that he did not feel fear but rather astonishment when he faced the desert alone.[105] Ismaël Bouderba supplied another oft-repeated model when he displaced fear onto other characters in his narrative. This occurred at the point in his account where his party approached what they thought was an armed raiding party. Whereas most of Bouderba's narrative was told in the first person, when fear gripped the party, he abstracted himself out of the group and described the panic of others as an omniscient narrator: "Each rider was plunged into his own thoughts, which were more or less gloomy, and they maintained a profound silence; only the sound of the camels' steps seemed to reveal the presence of animated beings. Suddenly one of the men of the Gourara, who was likely consumed by gnawing fear, yelled out, 'The Razzia, there are many of them!' At this word panic [erupted]." The panic that seized the party did not rattle Bouderba, and he resumed the first person to express how he restored "a little calm" among the others.[106]

Historian Saul Friedlander has commented on the tendency of many nineteenth-century writers to produce apocalyptic interpretations of the forces then transforming European society (e.g., technology, industrialization, urbanization), while at the same time carving out a voyeuristic space that protected them from the forces of annihilation.[107] Among twentieth-century writers, Ernst Jünger is perhaps most famous for his apocalyptic descriptions of the trenches of the First World War, and for his belief in the ecstatic truths revealed by the "Fronterlebnis." While others were consumed by the hellish, industrial inferno of the trenches, Jünger claimed to possess a supernatural ability to exist here unscathed, which he used to articulate a type of "armored" subjectivity that later proved important to Nazi ideology.[108] The explorer-writers of the Sahara likewise gave themselves a special status. While the doleful environment provoked crises of depression and melancholy, these states revealed sacred truths that empowered their beholders. None of these writer-explorers felt threatened by the Saharan catastrophe: their disaster was in the past. They could contemplate the ultimate truths inscribed in the desert landscape, while others were subjected to its apocalyptic laws. The terrible violence that was the motor of their revelation and enchantment had been visited upon those whose ashes comprised this "African graveyard."

This cult of transgression without risks contributed to feelings of omnipotence among many of these writers. They witnessed the apocalypse without fear of personal harm. They could claim that they did not partake of the ordinary and were thus not subject to the rules of the everyday. For Corneille Trumelet, a French officer with a long Saharan record, this meant the acquisition of superhuman powers: "The desert—I've already experienced it—transformed me. After a few days the sights and sounds I took in acquired a rare power: I could glimpse extraordinary distances, or, rather, for me there were no longer any distances. Across this pure and thin air of the Sahara, I felt that I could touch with my finger mountains that were leagues away. I perceived sounds, noises, with an extreme clarity. With a little effort I'm sure I would have been able to hear the conversations of ants." Trumelet went on to describe how such amazing sensory powers and the ability to cross great distances inspired him to act imperiously: "Under these influences—which I experienced with a sort of exquisite pleasure a thousand times during our preceding march—I felt the desire, when we passed near a *douar* [village], to camp the column there and go and seek hospitality as a guest of God."[109] Trumelet wrote as if he were the master of the supernatural world he encountered in the Sahara, as if all of its strange power, energy, and otherworldly knowledge became invested in him. Animated by this newfound strength, he could not only hear the ants talk but could rule over local people like a bygone seignorial lord.

The same tendencies appeared in Emile Masqueray's account of his 1875 trip. Although his ethnographic and linguistic studies were marked by their unflagging devotion to seriousness and accuracy, in the Sahara Masqueray was inspired to write frankly imperialist, violent fantasies. For example, while strolling through the narrow streets of Laghouat, the scene of such bloodshed in 1852, Masqueray reflected upon his ascendancy over the locals and fantasized about the raw strength and power that he possessed: "I entered boldly into the courtyard of a home . . . and took all the straw and feed I needed for my mount without a thought of the owner. All the strength that had welled up in my lungs, my veins, and my muscles released itself in brusque movements and short commands. I was afraid of nothing, and these beings that fled the daylight seemed to have been made to obey me."[110] Resembling not a "chivalrous knight" but later stereotypes of the "Nordic barbarian" or "Hun," Masqueray fantasized about using his supernatural powers, the strength that surged through his robotic body, to rule over the seeming subhuman and fragile inhabitants of the oasis. Everything fled before Masqueray's omnipotent and fearless being.

In the classic text on the sublime Longinus wrote that "our soul is uplifted by the true sublime; it takes a proud flight, and is filled with joy and vaunting, as though it had itself produced what it has heard."[111] The sublime contributed to the larger strategies of colonial expansion in Algeria and shaped practices. One of the most important examples was the emergence of a cult of violence in the 1840s, when French authors routinely postulated a division between the rules of war that applied in Europe and those necessary for "African warfare." This was the foundation for the regime of exception that legitimated the terrible violence agents of French empire visited upon Algerians. French military leaders and politicians considered such attacks against defenseless populations as a necessary step to achieve victory and peace. Such individuals claimed that the cruelty of these encounters was a normal feature of armed conflict in Algeria. This led to horrifying events like the "enfumades" at Dahra (1845) and helped mitigate the controversy afterward, shielding its perpetrators from political repercussions and allowing them to continue their grisly work.

The Saharan sublime further contributed to normalizing violence, with its glorification of the colonial agent, and provided a particularly brutal reading of the desert. The writers of the Saharan sublime interpreted the desert as a landscape of destruction. The dunes were ruins of an apocalyptic disaster visited upon a decadent society by an omnipotent and punishing God. The revelation of such sacred power seemed to give these writers pleasure on a par with that of Romantic writers by restoring the *Deus absconditus* to this world. Theirs, however, was a negative theodicy, and their pleasures were not those of the pious. Although Colomb prostrated himself, simulating submission and humility, before the Saharan God he claimed to see in the dunes, others writers of the Saharan sublime identified themselves with this idol, which they characterized as an omnipotent agent motivated by rage and disgust, and even identified with the harsh and inhuman Saharan landscape itself. This identification displaced their roles from subjects to agents. The desert's harsh rules did not apply to them, and they took pleasure in contemplating the annihilation of others. Such an understanding furthered their megalomaniac and narcissistic fantasies of colonial power. The most extreme articulations (Masqueray and Trumelet) conferred a godlike character upon colonial agents in the desert. The political repercussions of such a reading of the landscape were not negligible. The Saharan sublime exalted the ecstatic qualities of the desert's imagined violence while simultaneously normalizing and glorifying the actual violence of the French conquest. Terror and violence figured as part of the terrible, divine order of things—an order beyond human norms—and the select Europeans who entered here would experience the intoxicating pleasures of a secular sacred, its "succor and success."[112]

THE "BLUE LEGEND"
Henri Duveyrier and the Tuareg

Although unique, the Saharan sublime's cult of personal power shares certain traits with other discourses of European expansion that insist upon a highly aesthetic response to the landscape. For example, literary critic Bruce Greenfield has shown how Meriwether Lewis and William Clark's account of their survey mission of the North American Great Plains and Rocky Mountains (1804–6) privileged an aesthetic response to the landscape to particular political effect.[1] While performing their work as official agents of the state, dispassionately mapping the paths to American empire, Lewis and Clark simultaneously cast themselves as Argonauts engaged in a dangerous quest of discovery in a wondrous and otherworldly land. Like French explorers in the Sahara, they communicated their personal responses to the region's scenic wonders in terms loosely borrowed from the arts and philosophy. This had the effect of eliminating Native Americans from the landscape, creating a discursive "empty lands." In their place rose the West, a landscape that entranced the beholder with visual wonders and metaphysical challenges. The implications was that only those with the requisite civility and culture could fully appreciate its value. This legitimated claims of "entitlement" necessary to Jeffersonian expansion, or, as Greenfield has stated, it gave a "transcendent authority for claims to the land."[2]

Similar strands run through French writings on the Sahara in the nineteenth century and reappear well into the twentieth. Most famous is the case of Ernest Renan's grandson, Ernest Psichari (1883–1914), who served in the French army in Mauritania. His writings on violence and the Sahara were an important influence on right-wing thinkers in the 1930s.[3] Less obvious figures include the naturalist Théodore Monod (1902–2000), who used a blankly harsh Saharan canvas to sketch his influential and pessimistic version of environmentalism and atomic-age humanism.[4] Although the apocalyptic elements of the Saharan sublime certainly favored this negative relation to nature, unlike Lewis and Clark French explorers could not write native Saharans out of the desert. Notwithstanding their fantasies of omnipotence, it was not until the close of the nineteenth century that the French had the political and technological wherewithal single-handedly to achieve hegemony in the desert. At that time breech- or magazine-loaded rifles, a new corps of specialized indigenous troops, and an advanced line of southern bases — matched by advances toward Timbuktu from the south — put the French in a situation where they might consider subduing the last islands of resistance in the Tohat, Tidikelt, and Gourara.[5] Until then they were confronted with the task of finding allies and intermediaries who might be enlisted in the French cause.[6]

The project of finding suitable allies involved many obstacles. There were, of course, the interests of Algero-Saharan societies themselves, which, as I previously demonstrated, rarely corresponded to those of the French in a way that would produce a stable alliance. On the French side there was the question of stereotypes. The French began their drive for empire in the Mediterranean world with a largely negative view of the people who lived there.[7] As both Edward Said and Henry Laurens have argued, there was, of course, the imagery produced by Napoleon's Egyptian campaign, which redeployed stereotypes to find positive images that would support the French claim that the expedition was one of liberation, helping the freedom-loving Egyptian people throw off the Mameluke "yoke" (le joug).[8] However, the reader of the *Description de l'Egypte* (1809–28) saw the same Egyptians represented in a less positive light in illustrations produced after the fact. In these plates Egyptians were generally depicted as crouching on the ground, with a pipe stuck in their mouth, either scheming or passively observing events unfold around them. In Algeria stereotypes reappeared with variations that reflected the different goals of French Empire. Negative representations dominated the first two decades of the occupation, providing a backdrop to the "indigenous question" and the extreme violence of the razzia. However, circumstances also ensured that much of the iconography presented positive images. These visual texts showed viewers that France's Algerian enemies were, in fact, valiant warriors, a strategy that expressed the army's bid to represent its military campaigns as an epic struggle. Inasmuch as French generals posed as modern Alexanders, they needed their Dariuses. For example, in Pierre Christian's richly illustrated text *L'Afrique française*[9] the plates representing Algerians show ranks of well-armed cavalry and foot soldiers whose resolve is engraved on their faces.

FIGURE 5 El-Hadji-Abd-El-Kader.
Source: Pierre Christian, *L'Afrique française, l'empire de Maroc, et les déserts de Sahara: conquêtes, victoires et découvertes des français, depuis la prise d'Alger jusqu'à nos jours* (Paris: A. Barbier, 1846), n.p.

The emir Abdelkader, France's most formidable enemy, was glorified in text and image as a great hero. For example, an artist for *L'Afrique française* sketched Abdelkader atop a powerful black steed. Although he is shown surrounded by determined and fear-inspiring foot soldiers, the emir himself is given the contemplative look of a man of learning. His links to Sufism and its meditative religious traditions are illustrated by the prayer beads the emir holds in his right hand. Published in 1846, this image appeared at a time when the emir, although at war with France, represented values with which French audiences somehow identified.

This tendency reached its apogee in Louis-Jean Delton's magnificent photographic portrait of the emir, which was taken in Paris in 1865.[10] In this famous photograph Abdelkader, wearing the sash of the Legion of Honor, sits astride a large white horse against a painted backdrop of palm trees. This portrait documented the evolving relationship with the emir, including his intervention on behalf of Christians menaced by violence in Damascus in 1860. It also presented the French with an image of a man who had been a worthy adversary in Algeria, thereby increasing the stature of the army that had defeated him. Thus, the figure of Abdelkader reveals the complexity of pictorial representations, a case that demonstrates the limits of bifurcated analytic categories and the danger of writing the history of orientalism as one of negative representations.[11]

Nevertheless, the particular force of settler colonialism—the need to degrade deposed people and transform them into useful and docile subaltern auxiliaries to colonialism—ensured that negative images of Algerians remained deeply embedded in the thoughts of many. These are expressed most clearly in the newspapers and reviews representing settler opinion, like *Le Cri d'Alger* and *L'Evolution algérienne et tunisienne,* which spewed some of the most hateful rhetoric toward Algerians in the first decades of the twentieth century. Well before a large European community existed in Algeria, however, particularly hostile representations of Algerians—many of them sketched by military administrators who, according to some historians, were sympathetic to the plight of Algerians—circulated widely. Claiming to know Algerians by virtue of long experience and daily encounters, they wrote of a morally bankrupt population that responded only to base needs, greed, and the tocsin of "Muslim hate" toward Christians. For example, Ferdinand Lapasset, a French officer serving in the Bureaux arabes of the northern Constantine region (Cercle de Philippeville)—who has been characterized by scholars as an "arabophile" with "humanitarian instincts"—provided his own crude example of this line of thought in an inspection report for 1858.[12] He wrote that the mounted cavalryman did indeed cut a dashing figure. Atop a beautiful steed, clutching a richly decorated rifle, a saber dangling at his side, "the Arab" was a sight to spark the imagination. However, he stressed that this was only a superficial view of the Arab, one fashioned by outsiders:

Many see only his exterior, and in seeing an indigenous chief pass by, on a magnificent horse with elegant clothing, they say: What a handsome and elegant man! Wait a minute: take this handsome man down from his horse, strip him of the clothes, which are the source of your admiration, and you will see a body degraded by vice and by a syphilitic character, by a diseased skin—such is Arab society. The external appearances of this population inspire the imagination of simple and patriarchal manners—but if one has the patience and the time to penetrate, intimately, their inner lives, one can appreciate to what point of debasement they have fallen.[13]

By stripping the Arab of his burnous (an action structurally similar to lifting the veil of Muslim women), Lapasset hoped to impress upon his reader the "true" nature of the Arab. His body was not sinewy and muscular, like that of the warrior of classical times, but undernourished, diseased, and covered in syphilitic sores, a reflection of his overall moral, physical, and sexual corruption. This officer's "patience" and desire to "penetrate" the intimacy of Arab society, along with his eagerness to strip naked the Algerian, permitted him to entertain not only fantasies of physical domination but to indulge his desire to humiliate and debase, leaving no space where positive representations might take root. (Coming on the cusp of Napoleon III's so-called Arab Kingdom policy, such comments reflect the entrenched racism of officers who were expected to liberalize colonial rule. They also serve as a warning to those who might give structural determinacy to a field suffused with indecision.)

In the Sahara a different set of representations emerged. Authors like Père Enfantin saw partners in the Sahara in the person of healthy workers, guides, and fellow explorers. These largely disappeared in the northern oases as soon as the victories at Zaatcha and Laghouat resulted in French military dominance. However, the frontier of the Saharan imagination merely receded and did not end. Farther south French military power was forced to acknowledge its limitations, which expressed themselves in struggles over various representations. The Tuareg emerged as the most important figures. Confederations of pastoral Tuareg lived throughout the central Sahara beyond In Salah, an extremely dry place lacking the sort of pastureland enjoyed by the Ouled Naïl farther north. Despite the harsh climate, the Tuareg raised camels, sheep, and goats. Like other desert societies, they lived off trade, mastering the waterless expanses thanks to their geographic knowledge, commercial skills, military strength, and diplomacy. Most consequential to the Algerian colony were the Kel Ahaggar Tuareg, centered in the Hoggar Mountains (near the modern city of Tamanghasset), and the Kel Ajjer Tuareg, immediately to the northeast. They participated in trade between the Mediterranean and Central and West Africa, making the Ajjer and the Ahaggar essential links across the desert. Reflecting French hopes for the Tuareg, colonial ethnographic studies stressed that they were open, honest, free of "fanaticism," and respectful of the "liberty" of women. Moreover, the Tuareg were rumored to be numerous and powerful, which prompted the French to seek a good relationship, one that advanced their plans. In addition, unlike other Muslim people, Tuareg men, not women, veiled themselves, a fact that further fueled the French imagination. In one of the first colonial articles on the Tuareg, Oscar MacCarthy emphasized their military qualities: "Mounted on swift camels, which permit them to travel vast distances in a few hours, covered in clothing that aids their movement and clings to their body, armed with lances and light javelins, veiled and hidden from all eyes, they will soon become, under the name of the *Moletsnine* (the veiled ones), the terror of all neighboring peoples."[14] Having such a formidable force fighting on the French side was an idea that appealed to many planners. Henri Aucapitain, an officer in the Affaires arabes and an aspiring ethnographer, echoed MacCarthy and stressed the future military role of the Tuareg: "The Tuareg, who lead an exceptional life and are natural observers, will become the most active instrument of civilization in the Sudan. Less religious than the nomads of the Tell, it seems that their customs, like their manners and their geographic position, make them destined for this mission."[15]

The first meeting with Tuareg representatives took place in 1855 when Si Othman (Si 'Uthman ag al-hajj al-Bakri, ca. 1790–ca. 1870) accepted an invitation to travel to Algiers and meet with Governor-General Randon.[16] Si Othman was a sheikh of the Ifogas (N'Fughas), an important Tuareg faction with religious influence and considerable political clout. He was an initiate of the Tijaniyya Sufi order and served as the Tijaniyya representative among the people of the central Sahara. This first visit went well and was followed by a series of meetings and trade initiatives. The latter raised French hopes that a people had been found who could open the path to the Sahara for them. Over the course of the next few decades these aspirations congealed into the "Tuareg exception." As explained by ethnologist Paul Pandolfi, this stereotype held that "the Tuareg are strange and mysterious (dress, veil, geographic location); they are Berbers of the 'white' race, nomads and warriors. Their Islamization is held to be superficial and women play a powerful role in their society."[17] In short, the French saw the Tuareg as representing everything that other people in the Maghreb lacked and, as such, the perfect ally.

HENRI DUVEYRIER, THE SAHARAN HAMLET

As this stereotype was taking shape within the colonial administration, Henri Duveyrier, a wide-eyed seventeen-year-old youth, arrived at Laghouat on 27 March 1857.[18] Having just finished his studies, he arrived in Algeria ready to try his hand as an explorer. This choice of career and the trip to the Sahara represented something of an adolescent revolt. Duveyrier had spent the previous two years in boarding schools in Germany (specifically Lautrach and Leipzig), where his father had sent him in preparation for a career in commerce. Duveyrier's father, a well-known and celebrated Saint-Simonian playwright and political essayist, hoped his eldest son would ensure the family's financial well-being with a career in business rather than the path of intellectual enrichment that he himself had followed. Henri Duveyrier's adolescence in Germany represented an especially difficult period in his life. He had just lost his beloved mother to tuberculosis when he departed in 1854 at age fourteen. Under the dark Northern

European sky, where winter lagged well into spring ("the weather is depressing"), Duveyrier grieved over the loss of his mother and the pain of separation from his father, brother, and younger sister. He kept a journal in order to share his experiences with his brother, Pierre, who was in Naples, and he corresponded frequently with his father, Charles, in Paris. A particularly welcome letter Henri received from his father was an 1855 New Year's greeting that included a lock of his dead mother's hair.[19] News of German explorer Heinrich Barth's travels in Africa also reached him about this time and lifted the young boy's spirits. Celebrated by his teachers, Barth's adventures—five years of travel (1850–1855) through most of West and Central Africa—turned Duveyrier's thoughts toward exploration. In far-off Africa Duveyrier could escape the confining atmosphere imposed upon him by his father, as well as the grief young Duveyrier felt for his mother. Acting on these aspirations, he recorded the weather in a journal, collected plant specimens, and made observations on the plight of "exotic" local populations—German Jews.[20]

Although his time spent in Germany made Duveyrier moody and difficult, as soon as he arrived in Algeria he made every effort to turn the page on the past. This included digging into the emerging tropes of European orientalism to fashion a new identity for himself. The work began as soon as he sighted the Algerian coast from his ship, but the first night in the Sahara at Laghouat completed his transformation. When his guide and hosts retired after dinner to partake of the social pleasures reserved for older men, namely, tobacco and conversation, Duveyrier went back to his room, where he gazed out the window onto the gardens and the night. The soft light of the starry desert sky, with its strange and wondrous beauty, transported the young man far from his past: "The sky was pure and covered with stars that seemed to emerge from the velvety firmament. A delicious scent drifted up to me from the gardens, and I wondered if I shouldn't believe my senses and conclude that I was transported by the beauty of the spectacle. I no longer knew myself. I, who up until now had been so impervious to the beautiful aspects of nature, had never experienced a feeling of ecstasy."[21]

In this nighttime rapture Duveyrier claimed to have found an opening onto a new self. "I was not the same person as in Leipzig," he wrote. Africa had "changed my entire character."[22] Although attentive historians might debate the extent to which this claim is true—and the student of literature will surely find his attempt to imitate the wonderstruck poet hackneyed—this moment of desert "ecstasy" launched Duveyrier down a path that took him from the future in commerce envisioned by his father and led him deep into the desert, where he became one the most important and controversial figures in the history of the colonial Sahara.

Following this short trip to Algeria, Duveyrier spent two years (1857–59) preparing for a more ambitious expedition. He embarked upon a crash course, working with the top names of the French academy. He studied linguistics with Ernest Renan, geology with Armand Dufrénoy, biology with Constant Duméril, astronomy with A. J. F. Yvon Villarceau, and meteorology with Emilien Renou. He learned the art of preparing specimens at the Musée d'histoire naturelle. Arabic also figured in his curriculum. His first Arabic professor, Herr Fleischer of Leipzig, had been a student of Sylvestre de Sacy, and in Paris he studied with Armand Caussin de Perceval at the Collège Impérial de France. Duveyrier also traveled to London to seek the advice of master explorer Heinrich Barth. This impressive list reveals his father's powerful connections and the scope of his own ambition.[23]

In 1859 Duveyrier returned to Algeria and spent 1859–61 deep within the Sahara. Although he did not make it to Timbuktu as planned, Duveyrier traveled as far south as Ghat and roamed widely throughout the lands south of Algeria and Tripoli. This secured Duveyrier's reputation as an African explorer. When his 499-page account entitled *L'Exploration du Sahara: Les Touâreg du Nord* appeared on booksellers' shelves in 1864,[24] he was crowned the foremost expert on the Sahara.[25] Although doubts would later be cast upon the paternity of this book,[26] it surpassed all other European texts on the Sahara and guided French policymakers for the next twenty years.[27]

However, Duveyrier was never able to outdo this first success. The trip ruined his health (he nearly died from illness in 1861) and he only returned to the Sahara for brief visits thereafter. In different times Duveyrier's reputation alone might have earned him a place in the academy or colonial administration, and he eagerly aspired to "make a name for myself and a modest position" in either of these institutions.[28] Nevertheless, having been a rising star at age twenty-four, by thirty Duveyrier's expectations for his future had faded. He remained an important figure at the Société de géographie de Paris but was passed over for an opening as director of the Bibliothèque d'Alger in 1869,[29] a humiliating experience that was compounded when he learned that he would have to work his way up the ranks as a military interpreter or a teacher in a secondary school (collège) if he hoped to have a future in Algeria.[30] He refused both options. When his father died in 1869, Duveyrier became embittered and retreated from society. His ill temper even caused him to sever relations with his once beloved brother and sister. Thirty years after his monumental Saharan voyage, Duveyrier still suffered from "difficulties reintegrating himself after his return."[31] On 25 April 1892 he took his own life.

Duveyrier's biography is complex: it is marked by his mother's death, close but difficult relations with his father, a precocious drive to become an explorer, unimagined success on his Saharan exploration, and an acclaimed book. This was followed by a stalled career, growing acrimony, and suicide. But Duveyrier was no Julien Sorel: his life was also quite straightforward. Born to privilege, he achieved his early fame less through original actions and ideas than ambition and connections. His father's friends opened the doors to the knowledge, influence, and funding that contributed to the success of his travels. Moreover, despite the claims of some scholars, his "brand of colonialism" differed little from that of his peers.[32] Duveyrier was resolutely imperious in his outlook and actions. For example, he beat his local servants and showed contempt for his guides and hosts. "I was forced to thrash my servants with a stick," he complained in 1860. "They are true savages and have a hard head!"[33] Although remembered today as a great friend of the Tuareg, a precursor to Charles de Foucauld, in private letters this "fou du désert" contemptuously wrote that they were greedy, crude, and infantile.[34] When he encountered setbacks, Duveyrier spun vast webs of conspiracy, and when he met success, he saw this as the result of finally finding people with enough intelligence to appreciate his vision and foresight.

On the whole, Duveyrier's work might have remained on the shelves alongside the large corpus of texts by European explorers of the nineteenth century. However, his writings were widely read by policymakers, and he had considerable influence over the course of events. This is particularly true in terms of representing Saharan societies. Historian Jean-Louis Triaud has uncovered Duveyrier's role in the construction of the "Black Legend" of the Sahara, a paranoid view of the Sanusiyya Sufi order that held that they were a secret association of religious fanatics—Duveyrier compared them to the Jesuits—who would oppose every French move from their secret base deep in the desert.[35] Just as important but less well documented by historians is Duveyrier's contribution to what might be called the "Blue Legend" of the Tuareg. Whereas he cast the Sanusiyya as the villains of the Saharan drama, Duveyrier billed the Tuareg as its heroes. They were an honorable society of warriors who harked back to the nobility of France's distant past. Disdaining physical labor yet honest, powerful, and bound by a sense of noblesse oblige, the Tuareg represented the Sahara's upper class and France's natural partner.

THE INVENTION OF THE TUAREG

Duveyrier had written that if the Tuareg did not exist they "would have to be invented." Such an ally was necessary to fulfill French goals in the Sahara, for "without them the deserts they inhabit and that separate the white race from the black race would be impassible."[36] In the pages that followed, Duveyrier proceeded to do perform the sort of "invention" necessary to create this ally. Duveyrier evoked an impressive physical image of the Tuareg, describing them as tall—some were "real giants"—and strong, "thin, hard, nervous; their muscles [were] like steel springs."[37] Robust, they faced the hardships of the desert stoically and with perseverance. Duveyrier continued by remarking that the

FIGURE 6 Touâreg men.
Source: Henri Duveyrier, *L'Exploration du Sahara: les Touâreg du nord* (Paris: Challamel Ainé, 1864), 382.

Tuareg were born with light skin, but that the use of indigo on hands, arms, and face had given them a bluish tint: "Although white, the Tuareg appear blue."[38] They had other European features, including a small nose, round face, fine lips, and straight hair; some even had blue eyes. The beautiful features of Tuareg women, in particular, showed how much closer they were to "European women than Arab women." Another noteworthy physical characteristic was the Tuareg's dignified and noble gait, which Duveyrier described as "slow and clipped, made with large strides and with the head held high."[39]

However, the most striking visual aspect of the Tuareg was the fact that the men veiled their faces. Although the Tuareg call themselves *Imajaghen*, Arabic speakers call them *Tawarik*, a word adapted from the Berber *Twareg*. French and

English writers used Tuareg and *Touareg*, respectively. But Duveyrier reported that they were known among the Arabs as the *"Molâthemîn,"* the "veiled," an appellation that permitted Duveyrier to emphasize the distinctive facial covering (*tăgulmust*) worn by Tuareg men. Duveyrier stressed that they never lifted their head veil—neither in combat, in transit, or while resting. This gave Tuareg men an especially mysterious appearance: only their eyes peered out from behind the veil. Duveyrier refashioned the cultural meaning of the veil for the Tuareg. It was not a sign of deceit or concealment, nor did it feminize Tuareg men. Rather, Duveyrier saw in it a symbol from Europe's past, when knights peered out at their enemies from behind an armored visor. The physical qualities of the Tuareg were mirrored in their moral character. They were honest, generous, independent, and impervious to the lure of religious fanaticism. Most important was their trustworthiness and fidelity: "The protection of their guests and clients remains the virtue par excellence of the Tuareg." Not only did this make them especially estimable, but this quality proved to be the bedrock of Saharan trade and society. As Duveyrier remarked, "If it were not elevated among them to the status of a religion, commerce across the desert would be impossible."[40]

Duveyrier speculated that the Tuareg were once a Christian peoples. He found evidence for this in the ubiquitous Tuareg cross, a pattern formed by the intersection of two lines of equal length, which decorated Tuareg saddle horns, shields, weapons, clothing, and even bodies. Gender relations also testified to Christian vestiges. Tuareg society was matrilineal and monogamous. Duveyrier found that women enjoyed an impressive degree of freedom. He reasoned that the origins of such equality must be in Christian doctrine since to his mind Islam was an essentially misogynistic religion. Finally, Duveyrier attributed the Tuareg abhorrence of theft and deceit to Christian influences.[41]

Even before Duveyrier had published his work on the Tuareg, French writers had commented upon their unique social structure, which was based upon a separation between servile and noble classes. According to these first studies, there were two ranks of Tuareg: a mounted warrior elite whose "feet never touch the ground" and sedentary slaves and serfs who worked the land and tended herds for their absentee masters.[42] The warriors were an especially proud group: "Avoiding civilized lands, they were used to isolation; as brave as they were ferocious, they never fell under the yoke of foreign domination."[43] Duveyrier subscribed to these beliefs. Long before he had met a Tuareg notable, he observed that the nomads lived "under an aristocratic regime."[44] Writing to his father in 1861, he commented: "The Tuareg are aristocrats; their republic is an aristocratic republic."[45]

In his work Duveyrier built upon this understanding and fashioned the Tuareg into remnants of a bygone European age, a sort of ancien régime that had survived deep in the desert. According to Duveyrier's social portrait of the Tuareg, they were divided into five hierarchical orders. First were the rulers, the "amanôka" (amănokal) and "amghâr" (amghar) that Duveyrier assumed were a hereditary class. In theory they enjoyed absolute political authority and were not bound by any constitution. However, in reality Duveyrier acknowledged that they had to answer to the political will of the second order, the nobility. The nobles, or "ihaggaâren" (ihăggarăn), were a nobility of the sword who, mounted on swift camels (mehari), guarded caravan routes and routed enemies. Although they disdained work and even rejected learning, their military duties ensured that their life was "far from inactive."[46] In the event of war, they mobilized Tuareg society in armed struggle. Their military role and birth earned them their elite status. Moreover, as Duveyrier wrote, nobles alone were "in possession of political rights."[47] The third order was comprised of religious elites, whom he called "marabouts" or "inislimîn" (ineslemăn). These were former members of the nobility whose ancestors had devoted themselves to God's work. In a society dominated by martial values, the religious elites prevented "disorder and anarchy."[48] They were responsible for justice, education, and diplomacy, in addition to attending to the spiritual needs of the Tuareg. Unlike other Muslim religious elites, the Tuareg marabouts were tolerant and had a great respect for Christian civilization and values.

These ruling classes despised physical labor since "all manual work is considered unworthy."[49] Such labor was performed by two servile groups, namely, serfs and slaves. The serfs, or "irahâd" (imghad), worked the land in a seignorial relationship with the nobility. In addition to paying the latter an annual tithe, they provided labor, hospitality, and in some cases, military service. Unlike other subject peoples in the Arab world, Tuareg serfs had no property rights. Nobles had absolute control of all "irahâd" possessions. Seemingly exploitive, Duveyrier explained that this was, in fact, a reciprocal relationship closely related to the classic feudal model inasmuch as the noble protected his serfs and assured their subsistence in times of need. Like Europe's medieval society, Duveyrier contended that Tuareg serfdom developed because "in this land the authority of the sword often replaces that of the law."[50] At the bottom of the social ladder were slaves (eklan), who, as "children of the house," served as domestics and concubines. Duveyrier assured his readers that Tuareg slavery had nothing in common with the harsh institution of the New World plantations and was comparable to that of the ancient Greeks, who chose not to kill captives taken in warfare but rather to keep them in the household. As Fustel de Coulanges explained in his text *La Cité antique* (which appeared in 1864, the same year as Duveyrier's work), this ancient institution was based on a "reciprocal need that the poor has of the rich and the rich has of the poor."[51] Just as the Tuareg master assured his slave of a good life, so slaves brought great benefits to Tuareg society. In particular, they contributed to the liberation of Tuareg women. "A slave girl in the tent," Duveyrier wrote, "allowed mistresses of a good family to attend to their pleasures with a freedom that is unknown to Arab women."[52]

Duveyrier stressed that this was a stable social order. Although a type of *fronde* had rocked the northern Tuareg in the seventeenth century, when nobles had overthrown "imanân" rule, revolutions were unknown.[53] Each order knew its place and strove to advance the interests of all. As Duveyrier commented, "The nobles do not abuse the serfs" and the services and tithes serfs owed the nobility "do not exceed their abilities." As Duveyrier saw it, the nobles did their best to care for the hen that laid the golden eggs.[54] Such social wisdom on the part of the elites, together with the recognition on the part of the lesser orders that social harmony served the common interest, ensured order. The nobles had so little to fear from below that they even armed their serfs. "To defend the honor of their name," Duveyrier wrote, "[serfs] do marvelously when they are called to combat, especially when they fight against the Arabs."[55] This was a rare quality. In an age of upheavals, the harmonious social order of the Tuareg protected them against the ravages of revolution: "Alone, from the heights of their mountains, they were able to contemplate all the revolutions that had so often shattered West Africa without ever being touched by them."[56]

Such stability preserved Tuareg values. Among these the most important was what Duveyrier called Tuareg "chivalry," meaning their bravery, honor, courtesy, and gallantry. Manifestations of such qualities could be seen throughout their society. Hospitality was one example. The protection of travelers was regarded as a duty, and a promise was binding and sacred to Tuareg nobles and serfs alike. Ikhenukhen, the leader of the Kel Ajjer, embodied these principles. Duveyrier wrote that he possessed "a great solidity of principles, devotion without limits to that which he sees as his duty, and an inalterable respect for a sworn promise."[57] Warfare was also bound by the rules of honor and tradition. Firearms were commonly available in the Sahara, and Tuareg warriors esteemed fine rifles and pistols. But in combat they chose "armes blanches," such as lances, swords, and daggers.[58] The Tuareg rejected firearms, "which they call weapons of treachery, considering *armes blanches* the only honorable way to fight."[59] Moreover, Tuareg nobles did not seek combat for combat's sake. Armed encounters were limited, purposeful, and showed all the restraint of a well-disciplined police force. The "great occupation" of a noble "meharist," Duveyrier wrote, "is to assure the security of the routes in favor of commerce."[60] Chivalry was also present in relations between men and women. Duveyrier repeatedly stressed that relations between the sexes had nothing in common with the position of women in Arab society. Tuareg women enjoyed personal freedom, profited from education, and made their voices heard in politics. Moreover, men and women could openly demonstrate their affection without fear. "A woman can embroider on the veil or write on the shield of her knight [chevalier] verses of homage and wishes for prosperity; the knight can inscribe on the rocks the name of his beloved, sing her virtues, and no one sees anything wrong."[61]

THE NOBLE SAHARAN SAVAGE

If Duveyrier's view of the Tuareg as a stalwart people of considerable military strength grew out of a need to "invent" a Saharan ally, his writings, which sketched the Tuareg as the embodiment of chivalrous qualities harking back to the European Middle Ages, were based on an entirely different motivation. Strategic interests alone cannot account for why Duveyrier chose to idealize the Tuareg as a lost society of desert knights.

Saint-Simonian ideas certainly shaped Duveyrier's particular view of Tuareg society.[62] This was so despite the fact that he had severed his filiations with the Saint-Simonian movement in a letter to Père Enfantin written some six months into his 1859 journey.[63] "One *père* is enough," he later explained to his father.[64] Nevertheless, Duveyrier's Tuareg possessed many features the Saint-Simonians idealized.[65] They were orderly and efficient, their social relations were free of strife and conflict, and their actions were oriented toward productive activities, such as commerce and agriculture. Moreover, although Tuareg society was rigidly hierarchical, it was a hierarchy based on virtue, not birth. Like the governing class of engineers and technocrats Saint-Simon and his disciples had envisioned for Europe, Tuareg nobles were placed at the top of the social ladder to better guide the work of slaves and serfs toward a common good in the form of material prosperity and social stability. Moreover, like the Saint-Simonians, the Tuareg were not soulless, being pragmatic yet deeply spiritual. The class of religious elites represented by Si Othman preserved the moral fiber of Tuareg society, while at the same time channeling belief away from the fanaticism Duveyrier thought typical of other Muslims. Wise and forward-looking men like Si Othman led Tuareg faith toward openness, tolerance, and generosity. Finally, as Saint-Simon had hoped—and as Duveyrier saw it—relations between men and women were based on mutual respect, voluntary consent, emotional affection, and intellectual affinity.

On the other hand, Duveyrier's Tuareg represented not a utopia of the future but one belonging to the past. They did not know key Saint-Simonian values like progress, science, and industry. In addition, planning did not figure into their thinking. Duveyrier could not find any interest on the part of the Tuareg in increasing production or rationalizing economic efforts. Indeed, the values of the warriors that Duveyrier idolized the most were hardly different from those professed by the European military elites that Saint-Simonians thoroughly despised. Saint-Simon himself had envisioned the disappearance of wasteful and regressive military classes, to be replaced by those who were guided by positive laws. Therefore, in a strange twist, Duveyrier made the Tuareg the very people that his father and Saint-Simonian friends anticipated would soon be lost to history. Nowhere does Duveyrier seem troubled by this disjunctive element in his Tuareg, nor did he enlist the "Last of" narratives embraced by advocates of extermination and theorists of autogenocide. Rather, he trumped it by celebrating the Tuareg's inviolate chivalry. In an age of revolution, transformation, and change, these "children lost in the desert" enjoyed an age-old permanence.[66] Thus, at the heart of Duveyrier's "Blue Legend" was a noble savage who represented eternity in an age of change. They helped the young Duveyrier simulate mourning for the old values of the ancien régime and its aristocratic primitives, which he had never known.

Duveyrier's Tuareg represent one aspect of a larger phenomenon of cultural investments French authors made in the Sahara. According to Jean-Robert Henry, a specialist of colonial literature, "The desert aids in the mythic return to origins, to the 'before' civilization." It has served as a sort of "antidote to modernity."[67] This tendency emerges most clearly in the popular Saharan adventure stories of the 1920s and 1930s, along with fantastical literature like Pierre Benoit's 1919 novel *Atlantide*, a popular tale of magic and desire that figured the Tuareg as the descendants of citizens of Atlantis who were protected by the Sahara from incursions by the outside world.[68] An early author like Duveyrier shows the antecedents of such thinking. The desert was the "refuge of [Tuareg] independence and home to their liberty," according to Duveyrier, and protected a people and culture otherwise lost to time.[69] With their feudal society, archaic weapons, and outmoded chivalry, the Tuareg were the perfect "antidote" to the emerging forms of modernity in Europe. France had already experienced the leveling impact of mass politics, and the revolution of 1848 had recently indicated the path democratic political values might take. Both were threats to an elitist like Duveyrier, who viewed them in terms of the ugly face of industrial society and class conflict. By traveling to the Sahara, Duveyrier assumed that he had escaped these historical forces, which were irreversibly transforming France. For him the permanence of Tuareg society proved that the ravages of time might be transcended thanks to the temporal and social displacements made possible by French colonialism.

In this chapter I have argued that Henri Duveyrier fashioned his Tuareg in a way that corresponded to what I have loosely called a "colonial imagination." It concentrated on two forces acting upon Duveyrier's particular imagination. The first concerned the strategic interests of the French state and its need to find or "invent" suitable Saharan allies. The second was Duveyrier's nostalgia for a European past that had been destroyed in the upheavals of revolution, urbanization, and industrialization. This gave rise to the "Blue Legend," a stereotype that saw the Tuareg as living in a timeless past, sheltered by the desert from the forces of change. Although bearing the marks of Duveyrier's idiosyncratic personality and his Saint-Simonian upbringing, this nostalgic view of the Tuareg had wide appeal and formed part of a long-standing French fascination with indigenous societies in the Americas, the Pacific islands, and elsewhere.[70] (In the case of the Tuareg, this fascination continues to dominate popular French views of the Sahara.) Although the harsh realities of colonial expansion challenged this positive stereotype in Algeria, the old belief in the "recovery of a lost world" retained its appeal for decades.[71]

Although there was a good deal of ambivalence in Duveyrier's lived relationships with his Tuareg hosts and guides (as reveled in his letters back home), the political needs of French empire ensured that the positive stereotype dominated in his published work. This "Blue Legend," in turn, shaped colonial policy. In 1862 an official mission, led by Colonel Mircher, traveled from Tripoli to Ghadamès in order to sign an agreement with Si Othman (dated 26 November 1862). This was to be the bedrock of the Franco-Tuareg alliance, whereby the Tuareg would extend the putatively inviolable terms of hospitality identified by Duveyrier to French travelers. In addition, with their help France could expand its influence. Under Tuareg protection, French merchants could cross the desert to trade with cities like Kano, which was viewed as an African Birmingham, the "emporium of the Sudan."[72] Unfortunately, the alliance went nowhere. After Duveyrier returned home, the Ouled Sidi Cheikh rebelled in 1864, resulting in decades of insecurity that closed the Algerian Sahara to the French. Following the 1870 French debacle against the Prussians and the Mokrani rebellion, which tied up forces in the north, the Sahara remained low on the government's list of priorities. During this period contacts with the Tuareg nearly ceased. It was not until 1880 that Republican politicians acted on the old dream of Saharan empire as part of a general enthusiasm for imperial conquest in Africa. Although the "Blue Legend" was twenty years old, its dossiers were dusted off and its programs put into practice, as if the Tuareg truly represented permanence, stability, and honor. Duveyrier had taught planners that the Tuareg were, after all, a people of culture, not politics.

CONCLUSION

*It has been said that men "make a waste land and call it peace"; and the
desert is not simply that of a savaged landscape but of a tortured mind.*
—Richard Slotkin, *Regeneration through Violence* (1973)

The denouement of French expansion in the Algerian Sahara occurred in two
stages. The first came in 1881 when the "Blue Legend" reached a dramatic climax and resolution in the massacre of the Flatters Mission. The second followed twenty-one years later, in 1902, when the French spilled much Tuareg
blood in the "battle" of Tit, which was fought to promulgate the myth of their
own superiority.

On 16 February 1881 a military survey mission for the trans-Saharan railway,
led by Colonel Paul Flatters, approached a remote point of water named In-
Uhawen (a.k.a. the wells of Tadjenout), representing the southernmost point
ever visited by a French military column. Flatters's troops, consisting of a caravan of tired camels and men (the majority were Algerian riders recruited near
Laghouat and Ouargla), straggled out over eighteen kilometers leading up to
the well.[1] This did not make for the best defense posture, but Flatters felt sure
that his troops were completely safe. This was, after all, his second mission to
scout the trans-Saharan route, and he had exchanged letters with Ahitagel ag
Muhammad Biska, the Amenūkal of the Kel Ahaggar, whom Flatters considered one of the greatest of the "native chiefs," an all-powerful leader sure to
honor his word and protect the safety of French travelers in his lands.[2] Moreover, there were practical concerns. No one knew the exact location of the well,
and it might prove difficult to reconnoiter the area with the full column. Flatters therefore decided to leave the heavy baggage and half of his troops behind

while he departed with the ranking officers and scientific personnel, followed by the camels, to find the well. "We have nothing to fear," Flatters reportedly said to one guide who had counseled caution. To prove his point he traveled armed only with a revolver.[3]

This remark surely ranks near the top of a long list of famous last words uttered by travelers to the Sahara. Less than half an hour after they found the well, a sizable Tuareg force descended upon Flatters and his men.[4] Armed only with lances and a few muzzle-loading firearms, the Tuareg quickly subdued the French mission. Forced to dismounted and spread pell-mell around the well, they were no match for the swift and well-organized Tuareg party. Flatters and his officers were killed within minutes. Those few men who were able to jump on a camel in hopes of fleeing found that their animals would not budge: the thirsty animals had the smell of water in their nostrils. Despite being whipped repeatedly, they rounded back to the well, where the Tuareg killed their riders. By nightfall the fighting had ended. Among the 50-odd men with Flatters, only 10 escaped, and the Tuareg succeeded in taking nearly all the mission's 250 camels. When the party guarding the baggage—some 40 Chaamba, Larbaa and Ouled Naïl, along with 4 Frenchmen—learned of the disaster, their mood became grim. Although well armed and capable of repulsing an attack, they had almost no water and, worst of all, no transportation. The nearest point of safety was Ouargla, which involved a journey of two to three months on foot. With few options and in desperate need of water, they decided to set off the same night. They burned all their supplies except for arms and ammunition, and, carrying the entirety of the mission's cashbox (102,000 francs, divided evenly among them),[5] the 56 survivors started out on the 1,500-kilometer journey, described in the official report as "the most extraordinary and painful march that man has ever made."[6]

Within five days the food supply had dwindled, and by 22 February 1881, as they contemplated tracing their tracks back across the arid plain of Amadghor, little remained to eat. Within days they were reduced to ingesting grass. Some lost hope and attempted suicide, while the strongest marched ahead of the main party hoping to find game or a herd to raid. Just as they seemed certain to die of starvation, fortune smiled on them: a group of Tuareg riders approached the survivors and offered to sell them food. The men were as hungry as they were rich and thought little of paying the high prices for meat, milk, and dates. However, their hopes were short-lived. The dates were tainted with a poison that produced dizziness and psychosis, and this poisoning was followed by another Tuareg attack that killed twenty-two. This sealed the fate of the survivors. Within a week the chain of command had broken down and "general disorder" reigned. The formation of small groups led to mistrust among and within them. Thefts and accusations of hoarding further divided the men and increased the level of discontent. The only surviving Frenchman, a noncommissioned officer named Joseph Pobéguin, joined the struggle.

On the night of 23 March 1881 social relations completely broke down. A "tirailleur Algérien," part of a small group that included Pobéguin, was ambushed and killed by another group. According to the description contained in the official report, "Shots were heard near the area where several other men had gone hunting. From afar they could be seen building a big fire. When they returned, they brought with them some meat that they offered to Pobéguin, telling him it was mutton. He saw that it was human flesh and rejected it."[7]

In the days that followed, fights, assassinations, and cannibalism continued. Petty disputes resulted in shots being fired, with the victim rapidly cut up and consumed. After a week, Pobéguin was again offered human flesh. Although he "had first shown the greatest repugnance," now, the investigative report noted, "he ate it like the others." Having overcome his aversion, Pobéguin distinguished himself in the days that followed by the vigor with which he participated in these grisly efforts to stay alive. At one meal, as his group was breaking bones to get at the marrow, Pobéguin asked that the victim's heart and liver be set aside for him. By the end of the month, Pobéguin was killed and consumed by the others.

This terrible ordeal ended in the final weeks of April, when just over a dozen survivors straggled into Ouargla. Over the next few days the shock of the defeat was redoubled as stories of theft, murder, and cannibalism slipped out.[8] Some tried to forge a heroic narrative out of this disaster by fabricating images of Flatters mounting a vigorous last stand.[9] Other responses were typified by the horror expressed by one general, who simply wanted to forget the matter and "throw a veil over these deplorable events."[10] Still others—the majority—felt an overwhelming desire to find fault and extract vengeance. Commissions of inquiry were formed, survivors interviewed, archives reviewed, hypotheses formed, and accusations made.

No firm answers emerged. "The appetite for pillage and hate for the Christian name" provided a satisfactory answer for some, who could dust off the old terms of the colonial vulgate.[11] Others thought the defeat was due to the treachery of Flatters's Chaamba guides.[12] The most important body of opinion blamed the decades of Saharan mythmaking that had preceded the trans-Saharan project. According to this scenario, poor intelligence and faulty military tactics fell by the wayside. The Flatters massacre was the result of a naïve sense of French humanism that was inappropriate for the Sahara. As Louis Rinn, head of the Affaires arabes in Algiers, wrote, "Flatters paid with his life for an error that he was forced to commit, so to speak. He followed a course of conduct based on our European ideas, on our principles of civilization, which could be of no aid in the country he had to cross."[13]

"European ideas" and "principles of civilization," which had no place in Africa, were responsible for the disaster. Rinn suggested it was time to stop trying to see oneself in the other; only a policy based on realism—on the harsh rules of the Sahara—was appropriate.[14] This explanation drew on a now familiar refrain. Africa was fundamentally different from Europe, and the principles that guided thought and policies in France would have unanticipated and self-defeating results in Algeria. In part this argument was appealing to the French because of its racist simplicity, which held that the minds of the "indigènes" (Arabs, Berbers, Tuaregs—it did not matter in this case) were simple and superstitious. They grasped only the rules of violence and greed. Military thinkers found this explanation satisfying and used it to hollow out what remained of the "philanthropic" presuppositions informing French Saharan policy.

A clumsy leader, Flatters was no dupe to the "Blue Legend." On the contrary, he had nourished great contempt for the Tuareg and their French friends during the time he had spent in Algeria. It was only when the project for the trans-Saharan exploration took shape that he became a proponent of the Franco-Tuareg alliance, seeing in it the prospects for promotion and perhaps even fame. However, only those who took the time to consult Flatters's personal file and his archived reports dating from his tenure at Laghouat in the 1870s knew this fact.[15] Most analysts found Rinn's explanation more satisfying. According to one Saharan officer, "We are generally overly ready to judge these people based on ourselves. As a result, we are almost always the fools of our generosity."[16]

Understood in these terms, the debacle called for a "sensational vengeance."[17] Only a spectacular punishment, on a par with those meted out in the days of Bugeaud, would right the balance of power and restore France's prestige. However, it would take twenty-one years before the French would be in a position to act. In 1881 the army was tied down in Tunisia, and no one could guarantee that even a burial party could reach the remote location in safety. Indeed, the Tuareg victory forced the government to take stock of its interests in the Sahara, and in the weeks that followed French leaders abandoned plans for the trans-Saharan railway and strictly curtailed their list of Saharan objectives.[18] In the meantime, Governor-General Tirman dreamed of when he might achieve a grim vengeance in the form of the "complete destruction of several million" Ahaggar Tuareg.[19] Forced to wait for this day, he satisfied himself by paying a bounty for the severed heads of Ahitaghel's kin and encouraging the Chaamba to conduct bloody raids against the Tuareg.[20]

For his part, Henri Duveyrier subscribed to the logic of vengeance while insisting that French interests would not be served by "annihilating the entire Tuareg race."[21] Once the "oracle" of the Sahara, the Flatters debacle forever tarnished his reputation.[22] Duveyrier's initial response, in the form of a lecture to the Geographic Society of Paris in 1881, was a confused one.[23] Later he refined his argument by suggesting that only a portion of the Tuareg could be held accountable and that the Ouled Sidi Cheikh might be the true authors of the crime.[24] Finally, three years later Duveyrier placed responsibility for the Flatters debacle upon the shoulders of his bête noire, the Sanusiyya.[25] He insisted that it was only one event in a long list of attacks by this "secret armed society," which counted thousands of fanatical adherents in the Sahara, all of whom hungered to take up arms against the French.[26]

Nevertheless, the paranoia of the "Black Legend" could not save Duveyrier's "Blue Legend." The Tuareg metamorphosed from Duveyrier's noble warriors into a treacherous, barbaric peoples. They were distinguished by an "intractable and ferocious character" and used cunning and deceit to lure Flatters's unsuspecting party, a "mission pacifique," to their doom.[27] Although commanders in the field continued to conduct relations with the Tuareg, and those with sufficient experience sought to exploit the myriad divisions within Tuareg society — the same internal rivalries that likely produced the attack in the first place — to seek out French allies, the Flatters debacle forced them to treat the Tuareg with suspicion as hostile enemies. Moreover, the public call for vengeance never ceased. A decade after the disaster, a journalist was still insisting that the "blood debt" owed the French must never be forgotten: "The dignity and the interests of France unquestionably demand reparation."[28] Further fueling demands for reprisal were the articles being written at this time by Messouad Djebari, an Algerian military interpreter serving in Tunisia, who claimed that several Frenchmen, including Colonel Flatters himself, had been captured, not killed, by the Tuareg. According to Djebari's sources, they were missing in action and were being held as captive slaves in the remotest oases.[29] Adding to the scandal were accusations that the French government was responsible for their continued internment. Djebari argued that Paris needed victims and martyrs for the Saharan cause in order to conceal the fact that the desert empire profited only a small group of capitalists.

The fury of the Dreyfus affair inevitably contributed energy to the revanchist mood. Its web of conspiracy theories spilled over directly into the Sahara in 1897 when a Tuareg force ambushed the marquis de Morès, the darling of the anti-Dreyfusards, in the desert south of Tunisia. Although de Morès intended to rally the support of the Tuareg against the Jews, his death consolidated the extreme right against the Tuareg, who now became actors in a vast Judeo–Anglo-Saxon conspiracy. The *Dépêche algérien* proclaimed, "Look [at Morès's dead body] — it is the result of the theories of the Polignacs and the Duveyriers concerning the honor, honesty, and loyalty of the Tuareg."[30] The article insisted that these desert people must be hunted down: "Punish them as they deserve; chase them into their hideouts; make them pay [expier] for all the blood shed."[31] Another anti-Dreyfusard Algerian paper wrote that the Tuareg were like other "Semitic pirates, politicians, and financiers" and ought to be outlawed.[32]

Events speeded up the process concerning when this might happen. On 5 August 1890 a written agreement with Britain recognized French control of the lands south of Algeria.[33] This provided the diplomatic open door for French troops from West Africa to occupy Timbuktu in 1893, while in Algeria Jules

Cambon, the energetic new governor general (1891–97), incrementally extended his control southward with a row of forts south of Ouargla and Touggourt.[34]
Finally, in the winter of 1898–99 the Foureau-Lamy mission crossed through the
region where Flatters had been killed while en route to Lake Chad, an event
that showed that a well-armed, vigilant force could successfully travel through
the Tuareg territories. Events finally came to a head in the winter of 1899–1900.
A skirmish between a French expedition and militias from In Salah provided
the justification for what many officers had been waiting to do for a decade.
Taking advantage of ambiguous commands from Algiers, Captain Louis Pein
launched a full-scale attack against the In Salah agglomeration and neighboring ksour.[35] Pein's victory was stunning and his well-armed troops slaughtered
their enemies. At the fortified oasis of In Rhar French troops killed six hundred,
while only losing nine men.[36] At In Salah the French claimed to have killed
every male member of the Badjouda clan, the family whose members had led
the resistance.[37]

Although the French flag flew at In Salah, the Tuareg remained unscathed,
safe in the inaccessible Hoggar Mountains, and the memory of Flatters remained
unavenged. Even as the conquest of the Algerian Sahara seemed complete, the
calls that reverberated throughout the previous decades to extract vengeance
against "Flatters's killers" went unanswered. Commanders in the new desert
posts had more urgent concerns than a twenty-year-old vendetta. The tasks of
ensuring sufficient food and supplies and establishing some modicum of reg-
ularity in communications more than consumed their time in the first years.
Henry Laperrine, the commander of the newly organized Territories of the
Oases, noted that Flatters was a closed book for him. "For me it is pretty much
ancient history. I took 16 or 17 rifles from them and had the heads cut off of
those who were involved more than five years ago. . . . As far as I'm concerned,
that's vengeance enough."[38] Others, however, thought differently, especially
young, ambitious officers like Lieutenant Cottenest, at In Salah, who was eager
for his share of glory and sought promotion. Cottenest must indeed have set his
sights high if he wanted to advance his career because his immediate superiors
were thoroughly unimpressed by his intellectual pretensions and tendency to
"beat up on inoffensive poor herders while being quite nice toward people who
stood up to him."[39] In short, they saw him as a bully, someone not up to the
task of constructing useful relations with local people. He was, however, just
as ambitious as Flatters and would make his case on a national stage by giving
France its vengeance for the events of 1881. When Cottenest left In Salah on a
counter-razzia against the Kel Ahaggar in March 1902, he took it as his chance
to earn notoriety by "avenging the massacre of the Flatters mission on the very
site where it occurred."[40] Accordingly, he left a trail of devastation behind his
column of 130 troops, who had been recruited among the people of the Tidikelt
(Ouled el Mokhtar, Zoua, and elements of the Ouled Ba Hamou).[41] His attacks

against the villages of servile classes of Tuareg went unopposed, and he soon racked up an impressive list of torched homes and booty. Near the ashes of one settlement Cottenest fashioned a crude monument and warning by nailing a Tuareg shield to the trunk of a cut palm tree inscribed "Mission Flatters, 1881–1902."[42]

The crowning battle he craved occurred on 7 May 1902, when a force of some 250 mounted Tuareg presented themselves to Cottenest's column. They had shadowed the French force for more than a week as it burned villages, cut down palms, and destroyed gardens. They might have been hoping to avoid a direct encounter or looking for an opportune moment to attack. In any case, as Cottenest's correspondence makes clear, they hoped to negotiate an end to the destruction rather than engage the better-armed French force in battle. "[They] assembled to make their submission if I did not attack them," Cottenest wrote.[43] He refused the offer. The attempted surrender of the Kel Ahaggar Tuareg never made it into the official history. Three days later Cottenest cornered the Tuareg force near a village named Tit (just north of the modern city of Tamanrasset). Cottenest's men soundly defeated them.

In November 1903 another French column visited the area and did its part to continue Cottenest's project of disseminating fear. Led by Lieutenant Guillo-Lohan, these troops killed individuals who fled, kidnapped servile Tuareg women of "a certain allure,"[44] and impressed each other with their skills as marksmen by shooting people who had fled and thought themselves beyond the reach of French weapons. Guillo-Lohan found that the "Flatters memorial" Cottenest had fashioned in the ruins of the Tuareg village had fallen down. In retaliation he sacked the remaining homes. At Tit he came across a macabre scene: the unburied corpses of more than a hundred Tuareg had been scattered among the desiccated bodies of the camels and horses that had fallen in the skirmish. It was a rewarding sight for Guillo-Lohan. He wrote that the noble factions of the Kel Ahaggar could not hold out much longer. Concluding with cruel but unintentional irony, he wrote that peace would not be long in following—having become "a question of life or death."[45]

In the first part of this study I described how the initial stage of France's "pénétration pacifique" of the Algerian Sahara began in the late 1840s with the plundering of the ksours, the brutal Carthaginian peace visited upon Zaatcha, and the massacre at Laghouat. At this time the area farther south was protected from such destruction by its vast spaces and inhospitable climate, which made the maintenance of large military forces costly and dangerous. By the end of the nineteenth century the Sahara no longer provided the same buffer. France was finally in a position to complete its desert empire, which it did by utilizing the same strategies predicated on violence and fear. Although the idea of a "pénétration pacifique" long outlived its original moment in the 1840s and continued to inform metaphors of conquest to the end of this period, brute force and terror remained the tools of expansion. In the case of the contest between Cottenest and the Kel Ahaggar Tuareg, this reflected the convergence of a public ready to avenge Flatters, on the one hand, and ambitious junior officers seeking fame as a way to advance their careers, on the other, rather than any officially approved policy. As one analyst noted, given the fact that it took as much time to travel from the last train stop in Algeria to the Tidikelt as it did to take a steamer from Marseille to Madagascar, "it is not too surprising that a center independent of the administration's will occasionally tended to create itself down there."[46]

Although most people who lived in the Algerian Sahara had never seen the face of a European, the weight of French colonialism was felt everywhere. In the second part of this book we saw how French policies disrupted the region's fragile political ecology, producing hitherto unimagined strains on the local society. This inevitably affected political relations and the social dynamic by which power and authority flowed. The discontent and anxiety produced by the French occupation congealed in the minds of local Algerian leaders, who promised to defeat the French through spectacular feats of armed resistance.

Other Saharans searched for ways to adapt to the new colonial presence and preserve their social status. In the third part of this study we looked at one important point where the interests of colonizer and colonized found a site of accommodation, namely, slavery. Here the colonial divide became less clear as elite merchants and slave owners collaborated with local French commanders to establish a modus vivendi and seek ways to continue the slave trade following its abolition. Between 1848 and 1906 thousands of slaves—mainly young women, boys, and girls—were smuggled across the Sahara to live out lives of illegal servitude under the cover of these informal agreements. The slave Saaba was caught up in this trade. Her biography reflects the larger forces of victimization and violence that formed part of the project of French empire in the Sahara.

The French spun many myths in the Sahara, most of which were related to their own supremacy. As we saw in the concluding chapters, some of these myths fulfilled certain dreams and aspirations. A diverse group of explorers and would-be poets translated the literary flights of the Romantics and the "mal du siècle" into the Sahara. Here, amid the brutal, inhuman desert, they saw the hand of an omnipotent and destructive god. Under the force of their imagination the Sahara was transformed into an apocalyptic land, where unlimited violence was written into every dune and every rocky plain. While some felt overpowered by the desert's scale and desolation, others claimed this terrible power as their own. In this way the Saharan sublime augmented and reinforced the colonial ideology of European omnipotence. Finally, there was the "Blue Legend" of the Tuareg. Forged in the imagination of Henri Duveyrier, the Tuareg of the central Sahara fulfilled his longing for moral value, order, and stability. Situating these concepts in a far-off European past, he embodied this bygone moment in the Tuareg. Isolated by thousands of kilometers of desert, they remained unaffected by the upheavals of the modern era, representing for Duveyrier the veiled ghosts of history. It was these people, he claimed, who would lead and protect the apostles of French science and commerce, the pathfinders of French empire, across the Sahara and into the unknown regions of Africa.

Preface

1. Roger Cohen, "News Analysis: Algeria Fails to Curb Killings," *New York Times*, 9 January 1998.

2. State torture was documented by the Algerian League for the Defense of Human Rights, by Middle East Watch/Human Rights Watch (HRW), and by Amnesty International. See HRW reports at http://www.hrw.org/doc?t = mideast&c = algeri. Accessed April 2008.

3. Tragically announcing this shift was the cruel assassination in 1995 of Hocine Dihimi ("Yamaha"), beloved mascot of a popular Algiers soccer team (Belcourt). For a fictionalized account see Vincent Colonna, *Yamaha d'Alger: roman* (Auch, France: Tristram, 1999).

4. Juan Goytisolo, *Landscapes of War: From Sarajevo to Chechnya*, trans. Peter Bush (San Francisco: City Lights Books, 2000), 88.

5. Jean-François Lyotard, *The Differend: Phrases in Dispute*, trans. G. Van Den Abbeele (Minneapolis: University of Minnesota Press, 1988).

6. Many of the problems were already known. See Lahouari Addi, *L'Algérie et la démocratie: pouvoir et crise du politique dans l'Algérie contemporaine* (Paris: La Découverte, 1994). Algerian journalists and activists worked tirelessly to get the story out, as did many foreigners. A notable effort to shine light on the violence as it unfolded is Youcef Bedjaoui, Abbas Aroua, and Méziane Aït-Larbi eds., *An Inquiry into the Algerian Massacres* (Plan-les-Ouates [Geneva, Switzerland]: Hoggar, 1999). For the work of photographers, see Ghania Mouffok, ed., *Algérie: une saison en enfer* (Paris: Parangon-Aventurine, 2003); and Akram Belkaid-Ellyas and Jean-Pierre Peyroulou, *L'Algérie en guerre civile* (Paris: Calmann-Lévy,

2002). Foreign photographers working in Algeria at the time included the Iranian Abbas (*Allah O Akbar: A Journey through Militant Islam*, [London: Phaidon, 1994]) and the Swiss Michael von Graffenried (*Inside Algeria* [New York: Aperture, 1998]).

7. Bernard-Henri Lévy, "Le Jasmin et le sang,"*Le Monde*, 8 January 1998; Robert Young Pelton, *The World's Most Dangerous Places*, 4th ed. (New York: Harper Resource, 2000). The *Guardian* called *Pelton's* book "a gem." See David Rowan, "Be Afraid, Be Very Afraid," *Guardian* (London), 2 August 1997.

8. Paul A. Silverstein, "Regimes of (Un)Truth: Conspiracy Theory and the Transnationalization of the Algerian Civil War," *Middle East Report* 214 (spring 2000): 6–10.

9. Discussion with residents of El Attaf, Rouina, and El Abadia (wilāya of Aïn Defla), and Oued Rhiou (wilāya of Relizane), November 2004 and March 2007.

10. Habib Souaïdia, *La Sale Guerre: le témoignage d'un ancien officier des forces de l'armée algérienne* (Paris: Découverte, 2001). The human rights group Algeria Watch archives relevant debates on its Internet site, www.algeria-watch.org/index_en.htm.

11. Marc Bloch, *French Rural History: An Essay on Its Basic Characteristics*, trans. Janet Sondheimer (Berkeley: University of California Press, 1966), xxiii.

12. The conference, organized by Anne Berger, was entitled "Algeria: In and Out of French," and was held 3–5 October 1996. See Anne-Emmanuelle Berger, ed., *Algeria in Others' Languages* (Ithaca, N.Y.: Cornell University Press, 2002).

13. S. Ghellab, "La Tragédie persiste," *El Watan*, 6 June 2007; Salima Tlemçani, "Dix ans après le massacre de Bentalha," *El Watan*, 24 September 2007. For a discussion of the psychological trauma, see Mostéfa Khiati, *Algérie: l'enfance blessée; les enfants de Bentalha racontent* (Algiers: Editions Barzakh, 2002); see also Gadhila Choutri, ed., *Violence, trauma, et mémoire* (Algiers: Casbah éditions, 2001).

Introduction

1. Guy de Maupassant, *Complete Works*, vol. 12, *Au soleil; or, African Wanderings. La Vie errante; or, In Vagabondia*, trans. Paul Bourget (Akron, Ohio: St. Dunstan Society, 1903), 14; subsequent references to this edition are acknowledged in the text. Translation modified; checked against Guy de Maupassant, *Ecrits sur le Maghreb. Au soleil, La Vie errante*, ed. Denise Brahimi (Paris: Minerve, 1988).

2. Margueritte, "Suite de l'Exposé," Laghouat, 10 March 1860. Centre des archives d'outre mer (hereafter CAOM) 79 I 4.

3. Dossier personnel, "Flatters." CAOM 18 H 61.

4. Sven Lindqvist, *Exterminate All the Brutes*, trans. Joan Tate (New York: New Press, 1996); Isabel V. Hull, *Absolute Destruction: Military Culture and the Practices of War in Imperial Germany* (Ithaca, N.Y.: Cornell University Press, 2005); Caroline Elkins, *Imperial Reckoning: The Untold Story of Britain's Gulag in Kenya* (New York: Henry Holt, 2005); Priya Satia, "The Defense of Inhumanity: Air Control and the British Idea of Arabia," *American Historical Review* 111, no.1 (February 2006): 16–51.

5. Elkins, *Imperial Reckoning*, xv.

6. Kamel Kateb, *Européens, "indigènes," et juifs en Algérie, 1830–1962* (Paris: Editions de l'Institut national d'études démographiques, 2001), 47, 67; Djillali Sari, *Le Désastre*

démographique de 1867–1868 en Algérie (Algiers: Société nationale d'édition et de diffusion, 1982).

7. Kateb, *Européens, "indigènes," et juifs*, 16, 30.

8. Ibid., 39.

9. For example, *L'Espace français*, the first of the five-volume *Histoire de la France*, ed. André Burguière and Jacques Revel (Paris: Seuil, 2000), does not mention French colonies or Algeria despite the fact that in 1870 Algeria legally became part of "l'espace français," as three departments.

10. Among the exceptions is Christophe Charle, an influential French historian who has published an important book on European colonialism entitled *La Crise des sociétés impériales: Allemagne, France, Grande-Bretagne, 1900–1940; essai d'histoire sociale comparée* (Paris: Seuil, 2001).

11. Caroline Douki and Philippe Minard, "Histoire globale, histoires connectées: un changement d'échelle historiographique?" *Revue d'histoire moderne et contemporaine* 54, no. 4 bis (January 2008): 7–21.

12. Benjamin Stora, *La Gangrène et l'oubli: la mémoire de la guerre d'Algérie* (Paris: La Découverte, 1991).

13. Mohammed Harbi, "L'Algérie en perspectives," in Benjamin Stora and Mohammed Harbi, eds., *La Guerre de l'Algérie, 1954–2004: la fin de l'amnésie* (Paris: Robert Laffont, 2004), 27.

14. Loi n° 2005–158. See full text in *Journal officiel* at http://admi.net/jo/textes/ld.html. Accessed February 2008. The Conseil constitutionnel has subsequently suppressed this part of the law.

15. Claude Liauzu, "Une loi contre l'histoire," *Le Monde diplomatique* 52, no. 613 (April 2005): 28.

16. Ruggiero Romano, *Les Conquistadores: les mécanismes de la conquête coloniale* (Paris: Flammarion, 1972), 73.

17. *Genocide in Algeria* (Cairo: Front of National Liberation, 1957) [anonymous brochure at the Bibliothèque nationale d'Algérie, el-Hamma branch, Algiers]; Pierre Vidal-Naquet, *Les Crimes de l'armée française, Algérie 1954–1962* (Paris: François Maspero, 1975); Yves Bénot, *Massacres coloniaux, 1944–1950: la IVe république et la mise au pas des colonies françaises* (Paris: La Découverte, 1994); Amar Belkhodja, *Barbarie coloniale en Afrique* (Algiers: Editions ANEP, 2002); Olivier Le Cour Grandmaison, *Coloniser, exterminer: sur la guerre et l'état colonial* (Paris: Fayard, 2005).

18. David L. Minter, *William Faulkner: His Life and Work* (Baltimore, Md.: Johns Hopkins University Press, 1997), 95.

19. My choice of the terms "colonial" and "imperial" follows a historical logic and reflects the language used in my sources. Positing a divide between colonial settlements and imperial political and economic domination is not a particularly helpful analytical move for Algeria and does little to sort out historical complexity. I share Ann Laura Stoler's belief that the best theoretical observation to be made, one that typifies the forms of rule used by modern expanding states—whether British "indirect rule," the heavy presence of the French colony in Algeria, or American "empire lite" today—is how all rely on the production of states of exception that "vigilantly produce exceptions to their principles and

exceptions to their laws." Ann Laura Stoler, "On Degrees of Imperial Sovereignty," *Public Culture* 18, no. 1 (winter 2006): 140.

20. Frantz Fanon, *The Wretched of the Earth*, trans. Richard Philcox (New York: Grove Press, 2004), 1–51. Novelist Mouloud Feraoun's wartime journal describes the effects of this violence. See Mouloud Feraoun, *Journal, 1955–1962: Reflections on the French-Algerian War*, ed. James D. Le Sueur; trans. Mary Ellen Wolf and Claude Fouillade (Lincoln: University of Nebraska Press, 2000).

21. Charles Tilly, Louise Tilly, and Richard Tilly, *The Rebellious Century, 1830–1930* (Cambridge, Mass.: Harvard University Press, 1975).

22. Etienne Balibar, *Politics and the Other Scene*, trans. Christine Jones, James Swenson, and Chris Turner (London: Verso, 2002), 135.

23. Lila Abu-Lughod, "The Romance of Resistance: Tracing Transformations of Power through Bedouin Women," *American Ethnologist* 17, no. 1 (February 1990): 52.

24. Julius R. Ruff, *Violence in Early Modern Europe, 1500–1800* (Cambridge: Cambridge University Press, 2001).

25. Cécile Dauphin and Arlette Farge, *De la violence et des femmes* (Paris: Albin Michel, 1997); Georges Vigarello, *A History of Rape: Sexual Violence in France from the 16th to the 20th Centuries*, trans. Jean Birrell (Cambridge: Polity Press, 2001).

26. Fernand Braudel, *The Mediterranean and the Mediterranean World in the Age of Philip II*, trans. Siân Reynolds, 2 vols. (Berkeley: University of California Press, 1995); Samir Khalaf, *Civil and Uncivil Violence in Lebanon: A History of the Internationalization of Communal Conflict* (New York: Columbia University Press, 2002).

27. Balibar, *Politics and the Other Scene*; see also Jacques Derrida, *Force de loi: le "fondement mystique de l'autorité"* (Paris: Galilée, 1994).

28. Nancy Scheper-Hughes and Philippe Bourgois, "Making Sense of Violence," in Nancy Scheper-Hughes and Philippe Bourgois, eds., *Violence in War and Peace* (Malden, Mass.: Blackwell, 2004), 1.

29. Jean-Philippe Cazier, ed., *Abécédaire de Pierre Bourdieu* (Mons, Belgium: Sils Maria, 2006), 205–7; Pierre Bourdieu, *Masculine Domination*, trans. Richard Nice (Stanford, Calif.: Stanford University Press, 2001), 33–42; Pierre Bourdieu and Loïc J. D. Wacquant, *An Invitation to Reflexive Sociology* (Chicago: University of Chicago Press, 1992), 162–72.

30. Paul Farmer, "An Anthropology of Structural Violence," *Current Anthropology* 45, no. 3 (June 2004): 315.

31. Mansour Ahmed Abou-Khamseen, "The First French-Algerian War (1830–1848)" (Ph.D. diss., University of California, Berkeley, 1983).

32. Steven L. Kaplan, *Farewell, Revolution: Disputed Legacies; France, 1789/1989* (Ithaca, N.Y.: Cornell University Press, 1995).

33. Anatole France, *The Gods Will Have Blood*, trans. Frederick Davies (London: Penguin, 1979), 77.

34. Aimé-Marie-Gaspard Clermont-Tonnerre, "Le Rapport du marquis de Clermont-Tonnerre, ministre de la guerre, sur une expédition à Alger (1827)," ed. Paul Azan, *Revue africaine* 70 (1929): 216.

35. Arlette Farge, *Subversive Words: Public Opinion in Eighteenth-Century France*, trans. Rosemary Morris (University Park: Pennsylvania State University Press, 1995).

36. Roger Caillois, "Guerre et sacré," *Revue de Paris* 57 (October 1950): 110.

37. In 1808 Napoleon sent the engineer Vincent-Yves Boutin to make a reconnaissance of Algiers's defenses. See Auriant, "Notes et documents d'histoire: sur la piste du mystérieux Boutin," *Mercure de France* 177 (1925): 231–42.

38. Arno J. Mayer, *The Persistence of the Old Regime* (New York: Pantheon, 1981).

39. Jean-Baptiste-Joseph Fourier, "Préface historique," *Description de l'Egypte*, vol. 1 (Paris: Imprimerie impériale, 1809), v.

40. Henry Laurens, *Le Royaume impossible, la France et la genèse du monde arabe* (Paris: Armand Colin, 1990), 16; Henry Laurens, *L'Expédition d'Egypte* (Paris: Armand Colin, 1989).

41. Perry Anderson, "Internationalism: A Breviary," *New Left Review* 14 (March–April 2002): 5–25.

42. Fourier, "Préface historique," xcii.

43. Mona Ozouf, *Festivals and the French Revolution*, trans. Alan Sheridan (Cambridge, Mass.: Harvard University Press, 1988).

44. Laurens, *Le Royaume impossible*, 18.

45. "Proclamation en arabe adressée par le général de Bourmont aux habitants de la ville d'Alger et des tribus, en juin 1830," trans. M. Bresnier, in A. Berbrugger, ed., "La Première Proclamation adressée par les Français aux Algériens, 1830," *Revue africaine* 6 (1862): 151 (French), 154 (Arabic); Arabic text with a French translation made in 1862.

46. Clermont-Tonnerre, "Le Rapport . . . sur une expédition à Alger (1827)," 239–41. See also Wendy Brown, "Tolerance as Discourse of Power," in *Regulating Aversion: Tolerance in the Age of Identity and Empire* (Princeton, N.J.: Princeton University Press, 2006), 25–47.

47. Ministre des Affaires étrangères, traités, Alger 18300005, Microfilm n° TR117. An image of the convention is available at https://pastel.diplomatie.gouv.fr/choiseul/ressource/pdf/D18300005.pdf.

48. Marshal Soult, "Rapport soumis au Roi par le Président du Conseil, Ministre Secrétaire d'Etat de la Guerre sur les mesures à prendre pour assurer l'avenir de l'occupation et de l'administration de l'ancienne Régence d'Alger," July 1834. CAOM F80 1671.

49. Gabriel Esquer, *La Prise d'Alger 1830* (Paris: Larose, 1929), 75.

50. Eugène Pellissier, *Annales algériennes*, vol. 1 (Paris: J. Dumaine; Algiers: Bastide, 1854), 75.

51. Alfred Nettement, *Histoire de la conquête d'Alger, écrite sur des documents inédits et authentiques, suivie du tableau de la conquête de l'Algérie* (Paris: J. Lecoffre, 1856), 540.

52. Abdelkader Djeghloul, *Eléments d'histoire culturelle algérienne* (Algiers: ENAL, 1984).

53. Albert Hourani, *Arabic Thought in the Liberal Age, 1798–1939* (Cambridge: Cambridge University Press, 1983), vi.

54. Following the Treaty of Tafna (1837), Bouderba presented Abdelkader as the Algerian Muhammad Ali. Ahmed Bouderba, "Observations sur la traite de 30 mai avec Abd el Kader et les avantages immenses qui peuvent résulter pour la France et l'Afrique, la civilisation et l'humanité," 3 November 1837. CAOM F80 1672.

55. Adrien Berbrugger, "Voyage d'Alger à Nougha après des Bibans, dans la province de Constantine, 28 décembre 1837–4 janvier 1838." CAOM F80 1672; Hamdan Khodja, *Le Miroir: Aperçu historique et statistique sur la Régence d'Alger* (Arles: Actes Sud, 1985), 155.

56. Marwan R. Buheiry, "Anti-Colonial Sentiment in France During the July Monarchy:

The Algerian Case" (Ph.D. diss., Princeton University, 1973). As Buheiry notes, the term "décolonisation" was not a neologism of the 1950s but first appeared in a newspaper article of 1836 entitled "De la décolonisation d'Alger" (108).

57. Amédée Desjobert, *La Question en Algérie* (Paris: Duprat, 1837), quoted in Buheiry, "Anti-Colonial Sentiment," 173.

58. "Rapport soumis au Roi par le Président du Conseil, Ministre Secrétaire d'Etat de la Guerre sur les mesures à prendre pour assurer l'avenir de l'occupation et de l'administration de l'ancienne Régence d'Alger," June 1834. CAOM F80 1671.

59. Note addressed to Parliament by the Chamber of Commerce of Algiers, 26 February 1835. CAOM F80 1671.

60. Claude Collot, *Les Institutions de l'Algérie durant la période coloniale, 1830–1962* (Paris: Editions du CNRS; Algiers: OPU, 1987), 47.

61. Mahfoud Kaddache, *L'Algérie des Algériens: Histoire d'Algérie, 1830–1954* (Algiers: Rocher Noir, 1998), 7–19.

62. Hadji-Ahmed-Efendi, *La Prise d'Alger racontée par un Algérien*, trans. M. Ottocar de Schlechta (Paris: Imprimerie impériale, 1863), 14.

63. Si Abbas Bendjelloul, "La Prise d'Alger en 1830, d'après un écrivain musulman," trans. Laurent-Charles Féraud, in *Recueil des notices et mémoires de la Société archéologique de la Province de Constantine* (1865): 67–79.

64. Suraiya Faroqhi, *The Ottoman Empire and the World Around It* (London: I. B. Tauris, 2004), 75–97.

65. Abdeljelil Temimi, *Le Beylik de Constantine et hadj 'Ahmed Bey, 1830–37* (Tunis: Presses de la Société tunisienne des arts graphiques, 1978); E. Vayssettes, "Histoire de Constantine, sous la domination turque" in *Recueil des notices et mémoires de la Société archéologique de la Province de Constantine*. Published in 3 parts: vol. 11 (1867): 241–352; vol. 12 (1868): 255–392; vol. 13 (1869): 453–620.

66. Smaïl Aouli, Ramdane Redjala, and Philippe Zoummeroff, *Abd El-Kader* (Paris: Fayard, 1994).

67. René Gallissot, *Maghreb-Algérie: classe et nation*, 2 vols. (Paris: Arcantère, 1987).

68. Bernard Lewis, "The Roots of Muslim Rage," *Atlantic Monthly* 266, no. 3 (September 1990): 47–60. Long before Lewis Joseph Desparmet had related this story for Algeria in "Les Réactions nationalitaires en Algérie," *Bulletin de la Société de géographie d'Alger et de l'Afrique du Nord* 132 (1932): 437–56.

69. Jean-Baptiste Flandin, *Prise de possession des trésors d'Alger* (Paris: Féret, 1835); idem, *Notice sur la prise de possession des trésors de la régence d'Alger* (Paris: Chassaignon, 1848).

70. Esquer, *La Prise d'Alger*, 382.

71. Pierre Berthezène, *Dix-huit mois à Alger* (Montpellier: Richard, 1834), 130–31.

72. A. Berenguer, "Documents suédois sur la prise d'Alger (1830)," *Revue d'histoire et de civilisation du Maghreb* 4 (1968): 42.

73. Walter Benjamin, "Critique of Violence," in *Selected Writings*, vol. 1, *1913–1926*, ed. Marcus Bullock and Michael W. Jennings (Cambridge, Mass.: Harvard University Press, 1996), 236–52; Judith Butler, "Critique, Coercion, and Sacred Life in Benjamin's 'Critique of Violence,'" in Hent De Vries and Lawrence E. Sullivan, eds., *Political Theologies: Public Religions in a Post-Secular World* (New York: Fordham University Press, 2006), 201–19.

74. Nabila Oulebsir, *Les Usages du patrimoine: monuments, musées et politique colo-niale en Algérie, 1830–1930* (Paris: Editions de la Maison des sciences de l'homme, 2004).

75. René Lespès, *Alger: esquisse de géographie urbaine* (Algiers: Carbonel, 1925), 110.

76. See inventory in P. Genty de Bussy, *De l'établissement des Français dans la Régence d'Alger* (Algiers: Imprimerie du gouvernement, 1833), 401–2. By 1832 the army occupied eight mosques, and by 1837 French engineers had destroyed seven mosques. The most noto-rious case occurred later, when the duc de Rovigo converted the Djamaa Ketchaoua, one of the most prominent mosques of Algiers, into a Catholic church. Led by Ahmed Bouderba, the people of Algiers strongly resisted this move. See Oulebsir, *Les Usages du patrimoine*, 88.

77. Larbi Ichboubene, *Alger: Histoire et capitale de destin national* (Algiers: Casbah Editions, 1997), 126.

78. Ibid., 130.

79. The religious institutions of Algerian Jews—who in a city like Algiers made up about 10 percent of the population—seem not to have attracted the attention of French planners. See M. Eisenbeth, "Les Juifs en Algérie et en Tunisie à l'époque turque (1516–1830)," *Revue africaine* 95 (1951): 114–87; 96 (1952): 343–84.

80. P. Rozet, *Relation de la guerre d'Afrique pendant les années 1830 et 1831*, vol. 2 (Paris: Firmin-Didot, 1832), 81.

81. "Expédition de l'Armée française en Afrique contre Blédéah et Médéah," *Le Specta-teur militaire* 10 (1831): 384.

82. Apologetic accounts of the sack of Blida include those by Rozet, *Relation de la guerre d'Afrique*, 132–40; and J.-L. Lugan, "Relation de l'expédition de l'Atlas," *Revue de Paris* 39 (1832): 1–19, 116–24.

83. Lugan, "Relation de l'expédition," 121.

84. "Expédition de l'Armée française," 384.

85. Ibid.

86. Pellissier, *Annales algériennes*, 151.

87. Quoted in Charles-Robert Ageron, *Le Gouvernement du général Berthezène à Alger en 1831* (Saint-Denis: Bouchène, 2005), 88.

88. Pierre Berthezène, *Dix-huit mois à Alger* (Montpellier: Richard, 1834), 190.

89. Rovigo's order of the day, 7 April 1832, quoted in Louis-André Pichon, *Alger sous la domination française* (Paris: Barrois et Duprat, 1833), 401.

90. Ronald B. Asch, "Warfare in the Age of the Thirty Years' War," in Jeremy Black, ed., *European Warfare, 1453–1815* (New York: Palgrave, 1999), 45–68.

91. Pichon, *Alger sous la domination française*, 108.

92. Duc de Rovigo to Ministre de la Guerre, 9 April 1832, quoted in Gabriel Esquer, ed., *Correspondance du duc de Rovigo, 1831–1833*, vol. 1 (Algiers: Jourdan, 1914), 396–99.

93. Michel Foucault, *History of Sexuality*, vol. 1, *An Introduction*, trans. Robert Hurley (New York: Vintage Books, 1990), 136.

94. Ibid., 142.

95. Alexis de Tocqueville, "Rapports sur l'Algérie (1847),"in *Œuvres complètes*, vol. 1, ed. André Jardin (Paris: Gallimard, 1991), 798.

96. Jean-Louis Planche, *Sétif 1945: histoire d'un massacre annoncé* (Paris: Perrin; Algiers: Chihab, 2006).

97. Timothy Mitchell, *Colonising Egypt* (Berkeley: University of California Press, 1991).

98. See the case of Charles Cusson, aka Muhammad ben Sharif, in A. Berbrugger, "Nécrologie," *Revue africaine* 11 (1867): 494–96.

99. Charles-André Julien, *Histoire de l'Algérie contemporaine*, vol. 1: *La conquête et les débuts de la colonisation, 1827–1871* (Paris: PUF, 1979), 210–69, 406–9.

100. Colonel Didier, Cercle de Ghardaïa, to Commandant de Laghouat, 26 January 1897. CAOM 1 P 16.

101. Genty de Bussy, *De l'établissement*, 276.

102. Charles-Robert Ageron, *Les Algériens musulmans et la France (1871–1919)*, 2 vols. (Paris: PUF, 1968).

103. Aimé Dupuy, "Remarques sur le sens et l'évolution du mot: 'indigène,'" *Informations historiques* 3 (1963): 152–57. My thanks to Bouabdallah Kouidmi for this reference.

104. *Trésor de la langue française*, vol. 10 (Paris: Editions du CNRS, 1983), 96–97.

105. Guillaume-Thomas Raynal, *Histoire philosophique et politique des établissements et du commerce des Européens dans les deux Indes* (Amsterdam: n.p., 1770), 125.

106. Patrick Brantlinger, *Dark Vanishings: Discourse on the Extinction of Primitive Races, 1800–1930* (Ithaca, N.Y.: Cornell University Press, 1993).

107. François Furet, "Ancien Régime," in François Furet and Mona Ozouf, eds., *A Critical Dictionary of the French Revolution*, trans. Arthur Goldhammer (Cambridge, Mass.: Harvard University Press, 1989), 604–15.

108. Taher-Pacha to Polignac, 27 May 1830; quoted in E. le Marchand, *L'Europe et la conquête d'Alger, d'après des documents originaux tirés des archives de l'Etat* (Paris: Perrin et cie., 1913), 247; Vincent-Yves Boutin, *Aperçu historique, statistique et topographique sur l'état d'Alger, à l'usage de l'armée expéditionnaire d'Afrique: avec plans, vues et costumes, publié par ordre de Son Excellence le ministre de la guerre* (Paris: Picquet, 1830).

109. "Proclamation en arabe adressée par le général de Bourmont," 150 (French), 153 (Arabic). This was an improvised expression that later confused the French translator working from the original document, who rendered it as "Marocains" (Moroccans).

110. The people of Algiers did not become known as "Algérois" until the 1890s, when most of them were of European origin. See Paul Guérin ed., *Lettres, sciences, arts, encyclopédie universelle, dictionnaire des dictionnaires* (Paris: Librairies-imprimeries réunies, 1892).

111. "Note du 1er novembre 1831," in Ageron, *Le Gouvernement du général Berthezène*, 162; Genty de Bussy, *De l'établissement*, 19.

112. The terms appeared in the following works: Boutin, *Aperçu historique*; and William Shaler, *Esquisse de l'État d'Alger, considéré sous les rapports politique, historique et civil*, trans. X. Bianchi (Paris: Ladvocat, 1830). Other texts available in the first year of the conquest included the anonymous *Relation d'un séjour à Alger* (Paris: Le Normant, 1820); Louis Liskenne, *Coup d'œil sur la ville d'Alger* (Paris: Guyonnet, 1830); Jean-André Peyssonnel's accounts in the *Revue trimestrielle* (see Peyssonnel, *Voyage dans les régences de Tunis et d'Alger*, ed. Lucette Valensi (Paris: La Découverte, 1986); Abbé Poiret, *Voyage en Barbarie* (Paris: Rochelle, 1789); and Thomas Shaw, *Voyage dans la régence d'Alger* (Paris: Marlin, 1830; reprint, Tunis: Bouslama, 1980). Finally, there were the reports in governmental archives, including de Loverdo "De la régence d'Alger et des avantages que la possession

de ce pays peut procurer à la France" (1827), published in *Le Spectateur militaire* 15 (1833): 137–69, as welll as the reports of Jean-Michel Venture de Paradis.

113. Joseph Nil Robin, *La Grande Kabylie sous le régime Turc* (Saint-Denis: Bouchène, 1998). The literature on Berber-speaking peoples under colonial rule is large and continues to grow. See Patricia M. E. Lorcin, *Imperial Identities: Stereotyping, Prejudice, and Race in Colonial Algeria* (London: I. B. Tauris, 1995); Alain Mahé, *Historie de la Grande Kabylie, XIXe-XXe siècles* (Paris: Bouchène, 2001).

114. *Procès-verbaux et rapports de la commission nommée par le Roi, le 7 juillet 1833* (Paris: L'imprimerie royale, juin 1834), 86.

115. This was the term used by the minister of war in instructions to the first Commission d'Afrique. *Procès-verbaux et rapports*, 8.

116. De Peyerimhoff; quoted in Jacques Alaude, *La Question indigène dans l'Afrique du Nord* (Paris: n.p., [1913]), 10.

117. Aristide Michel Perrot, *Alger: esquisse topographique et historique* (Paris: Ladvocat, 1830), 94.

118. For example, Sous-intendant civil Barrachin proposed "un refoulement lent et progressif des indigènes par une population importée"; see report of 5 September 1831. SHAT 1 H 9.

119. Le maréchal Clauzel, *Nouvelles observations sur la colonisation d'Alger* (Paris: Selligue, 1833), 26.

120. Pichon, *Alger sous la domination française*, 99.

121. Ibid.

122. Proclamation of Governor-General Bugeaud to the "Habitants de l'Algérie," 22 February 1841, published in [*Le*] *Moniteur algérien* 424 (23 February 1841).

123. Christian Schefer, "La 'conquête totale' de l'Algérie (1839–43)," *Revue de l'histoire des colonies françaises* 4 (1916): 22–49.

124. Marwan R. Buheiry, *The Formation and Perception of the Modern Arab World*, ed. Lawrence I. Conrad (Princeton, N.J.: Darwin Press, 1989), 13–32; Jennifer Elson Sessions, "Making Colonial France: Culture, National Identity, and the Colonization of Algeria, 1830–1851" (Ph.D. diss., University of Pennsylvania, 2005), 129–36.

125. Lucien-François de Montagnac, *Lettres d'un soldat: Neuf années de campagnes en Afrique* (Paris: Plon, 1885), 299.

126. Jean-Clément Martin, *La Vendée et la France* (Paris: Seuil, 1987).

127. Raoul Busquet, "L'Affaire des grottes du Dahra (19–20 juin 1845)," *Revue africaine* 51 (1907): 116–68; Emile-Félix Gautier, *L'Algérie et la métropole* (Paris: Payot, 1920), 11–54.

128. Bugeaud to Saint-Arnaud, 24 juin 1845. CAOM 2 EE 11.

129. Baron de Jomini, *Précis de l'art de la guerre*, vol. 1 (Paris: Anselin, 1838), 157; John Shy, "Jomini," in Peter Paret, ed., *Makers of Modern Strategy* (Princeton, N.J.: Princeton University Press, 1986), 143–85.

130. Martin, *La Vendée et la France*, 206–46.

131. Busquet, "L'Affaire des grottes du Dahra," 129.

132. Notes of discussion, *Bulletin de la société d'anthropologie de Paris* 2 (1861): 484.

133. "Mohamed grelotte!" *Le Cri d'Alger*, 4th ser., no. 223 (1909).

134. James Fenimore Cooper, *Le Dernier des Mohicans, histoire de 1757*, trans. A.-J.-B. Defauconpret (Paris: C. Gosselin; Mame et Delaunay-Vallée, 1826).

135. Mark Wolff, "Western Novels as Children's Literature in Nineteenth-Century France," *Mosaic* 34, no. 2 (June 2001): 87–102; René Rémond, *Les États-Unis devant l'opinion française, 1815–1852*, vol. 1 (Paris: Librairie Armand Colin, 1962), 293. Examples of military authors referencing Cooper in Algeria include Docteur Félix Jacquot, *Expédition du Général Cavaignac dans le Sahara algérien en avril et mai 1847* (Paris: Gide et J. Baudry, 1849), 10; Général Daumas, *Les Chevaux du Sahara et les mœurs du désert*, 3rd ed. (Paris: Michel Levy, 1855), 422; and A. Margueritte, *Chasses de l'Algérie et notes sur les Arabes du sud*, 3rd ed. (Paris: Jouvet, 1884), 72.

136. James Fenimore Cooper, *The Last of the Mohicans*, ed. John McWilliams (Oxford: Oxford University Press, 1994), 9. See also John McWilliams, *The Last of the Mohicans: Civil Savagery and Savage Civility* (New York: Twayne, 1994).

137. James Fenimore Cooper, *Œuvres complètes de J. Fenimore Cooper*, vol. 5, *Le Dernier des Mohicans*, trans. A.-J.-B. Defauconpret (Paris: Furne et Cie, Charles Gosselin, 1846), 4; italics added.

138. George Dekker and John P. McWillians, eds., *Fenimore Cooper: The Critical Heritage* (London: Routledge and Kegan Paul, 1973), 267.

139. Eric L. Santner, "History Beyond the Pleasure Principle: Some Thoughts on the Representation of Trauma," in Saul Friedlander, ed., *Probing the Limits of Representation: Nazism and the "Final Solution"* (Cambridge, Mass.: Harvard University Press, 1992), 144.

140. Ricardo Cicerchia, "Journey to the Center of the Earth: Domingo Faustino Sarmiento, a Man of Letters in Algeria," *Journal of Latin American Studies* 36, no. 4 (November 2004): 670.

141. Federico Finchelstein, *Transatlantic Fascism: Ideology, Violence and the Sacred in Argentina and Italy, 1919–1945* (Durham, N.C.: Duke University Press, forthcoming.

142. Enzo Traverso, *La Violence nazie: une généalogie européenne* (Paris: La Fabrique éditions, 2002); *The Origins of Nazi Violence*. trans. Janet Lloyd (New York: New Press, 2003). See also Le Cour Grandmaison, *Coloniser, exterminer*.

143. André Nouschi, *Enquête sur le niveau de vie des populations rurales constantinoises de la conquête jusqu'en 1919* (Paris: PUF, 1961); John Ruedy, *Modern Algeria: The Origins and Development of a Nation* (Bloomington: University of Indiana Press, 1992), 68–100.

144. Auguste Warnier, *Le Lieutenant-Général baron de Létang; Des moyens d'assurer la domination française en Algérie; Examen par M. le docteur Warnier* (Paris: Imprimeur du roi, A. Guyot, 1846).

145. Jacques Frémeaux, *Les Bureaux arabes dans l'Algérie de la conquête* (Paris: Denoël, 1993).

146. Ferdinand Hugonnet, *Souvenirs d'un chef de bureau arabe* (Paris: Michel Lévy frères, 1858).

147. Général Daumas, *Mœurs et coutumes de l'Algérie: Tell, Kabylie, Sahara* (Paris: Hachette, 1853), n.p.

148. Antony Thrall Sullivan, *Thomas-Robert Bugeaud, France and Algeria, 1784–1849: Politics, Power, and the Good Society* (Hamden, Conn: Archon Books, 1983); Jean-Pierre Bois, *Bugeaud* (Paris: Fayard, 1997); Barnett Singer and John Langdon, *Cultured Force: Makers and Defenders of the French Colonial Empire* (Madison: University of Wisconsin Press, 2004).

149. Speech by General Bugeaud to the Chamber of Deputies, [debate of "crédits sup-plémentaires," 1839–40], meeting of 14 May, *Le Moniteur universel*, 15 May 1840. An excerpt is in Thomas Robert Bugeaud, *Par l'épée et par la charrue: écrits et discours de Bugeaud*, ed. Paul Azan (Paris: PUF, 1948), 78.

150. For Bugeaud's efforts to cover up the Dahra mass murder, see Bugeaud to Pélissier dans le Dahara, Algiers, 1 July 1845. CAOM 2 EE 11.

151. Roger Germain, *La Politique indigène de Bugeaud* (Paris: Larose, 1953). For an explanation of "indigenous" settlements see Ferdinand Lapasset, *Mémoire sur la colonisation indigène et la colonisation européenne* (Algiers: Dubos Frères et Bastide, 1848).

152. Bugeaud to Général de La Rue, Bivouac of Fondouk, 5 March 1846. CAOM 2 EE 12.

153. Ibid.

1. The Peaceful Expansion of Total Conquest

1. The column's size and composition were typical of Bugeaud's light, rapid forces. It was composed of 2,400 infantry (2nd Régiment de ligne, elements from the Foreign Legion and the Tirailleurs indigènes), 600 cavalry (3rd Chasseurs and 3rd Spahis), and 6 pieces of field artillery (4 light mountain pieces and 2 field cannons). Joseph-Adrien Seroka, "Le Sud Constantinois de 1830 à 1855," *Revue africaine* 56 (1912): 428–29. General Aumale stocked supplies in Batna and his troops raided neighboring villages and camps for food before departing. For example, a raiding party led by Commander Thomas stole 2,000 sheep, 350 goats, and 48 cattle from the Ouled Mohboub. Commandant Thomas, Bou Sebââ, 13 February 1844. Centre des archives d'outre-mer (hereafter CAOM) 2 H 22.

2. François Furet, *Revolutionary France, 1770–1880*, trans. Antonia Nevill (Oxford: Blackwell, 1992), 326. However, my argument is contra Furet at the point where he downplays the links between Orléansim and Bonapartism (387).

3. Led by Bou Aziz Belhadj ben Bou Lakhraz ben El Hadj, the Ben Ganah family had ruled the region since 1826. Following the fall of Constantine in 1837, they aspired to keep their traditional position, ruling the region for the French as the "Cheikh el-Arab." See *Les Ben-Gana depuis la conquête française* (Paris: E. Dentu, 1879); B. Bengana, *Une famille de grands chef sahariens: les Bengaga* (Algiers: Soubiron, 1930); Edmond et Marthe Gouvion, *Kitab Aayane el-Marharibe* (Algiers: Imprimerie Orientale Fontana Frères, 1920). See also Direction des Territoires du Sud, Affaires indigènes, "Notice biographique sur le Bachagha Bou Aziz ben Gana," n.d.; and "Notice sur Si Bouaziz ben M'hamed ben Gana, Bachagha des Ziban et Arab Cheraga, de l'Annexe de Biskra," Biskra, 27 December 1926 (both in CAOM 16 H 41). On the struggle between the Ben Ganah and the Bou Akkaz (Bu Ukkaz) families to control Biskra see Abdelhamid Zouzou, *L'Aurès au temps de la France coloniale: évolution politique, économique et sociale, 1837–1939*, 2nd ed. (Algiers: Houma, 2002).

4. Several historians have dealt with this expedition. See Julia A. Clancy-Smith, *Rebel and Saint: Muslim Notables, Populist Protest, Colonial Encounters; Algeria and Tunisia, 1800–1904* (Berkeley: University of California Press, 1997), 80–82; Peter von Sivers, "Insurrection and Accommodation: Indigenous Leadership in Eastern Algeria, 1840–1900," *International Journal of Middle East Studies* 6 (1975): 259–75; Michel Levallois, *Ismaÿl Urbain, 1812–1884: une autre conquête de l'Algérie* (Paris: Maisonneuve et Larose, 2001), 423–33; and

Zouzou, *L'Aurès au temps de la France coloniale*, 186–88. Primary accounts include: Seroka, "Le Sud constantinois"; idem, "Historique de Biskra," 1855. CAOM 10 H 76. Also helpful are the letters of Dagnan, the "intendant militaire de la province de Constantine," and Dussert, the "sous-directeur de la province de Philippeville et Constantine," published in *Campagnes d'Afrique, 1835–1848: lettres adressées au Maréchal de Castellane* (Paris: Librairie Plon, 1898), 341–46, 358–60. See also Ismayl Urbain's account in *Le Journal des débats*, 22 October 1844; and the mission's reports published in *Le Moniteur universel*, 6 April 1844. The original copy of Aumale's report to Bugeaud, dated 22 March 1844, can be found in Service historique de l'Armée de terre (hereafter SHAT) 1 H 95. Information on the political situation in the Ziban is contained in an anonymous, untitled, undated report [ca. 1845] in SHAT 1 H 229; see also J. Maguelonne, "Monographie historique et géographique de la tribu des Ziban," *Recueil des notices et mémoires de la société archéologique du Département de Constantine* 44 (1910): 213–304.

5. Report of Aumale to Bugeaud, Batna, 22 March 1844, *Le Moniteur universel*, 6 April 1844 (also SHAT 1 H 95).

6. Report of Gouverneur Général de l'Algérie (hereafter GGA) to Ministre de la Guerre, Algiers, 29 March 1844, *Le Moniteur universel*, 6 April 1844.

7. Report of Aumale to Bugeaud, Batna, 22 March 1844, *Le Moniteur universel*, 6 April 1844.

8. De Larcy, meeting of 15 January, *Le Moniteur universel*, 16 January 1840.

9. Jean-Baptiste Duvergier, *Collection complète des lois, décrets, ordonnances et avis du Conseil d'État* (Paris: A. Guyot et Scribe, 1834).

10. Christian Schefer, *L'Algérie et l'évolution de la colonisation française* (Paris: Honoré Champion, 1928), 169; Eugène Pellissier, *Annales algériennes*, vol. 1 (Paris: Librairie militaire; Algiers: Librairie Bastide, 1854), 407–28; Louis Milliot, *Le Gouvernement de l'Algérie* ([Algiers]: Publications du comité national métropolitain du centenaire de l'Algérie, [1930]), 8–14; Albert Duchêne, *La Politique colonial de la France: le Ministère des colonies depuis Richelieu* (Paris: Payot, 1928).

11. Jean Despois, *L'Afrique du nord*, 3rd ed. (Paris: PUF, 1964), 103.

12. See Schefer, *L'Algérie et l'évolution*, 154–81; and Claude Collot, *Les institutions de l'Algérie durant la période coloniale (1830–1962)* (Paris: Éditions du CNRS; Algiers: Office des publications universitaires, 1987).

13. Peregrine Horden and Nicholas Purcell, *The Corrupting Sea: A Study of Mediterranean History* (Oxford: Blackwell, 2000), 396–97.

14. Patricia M. E. Lorcin, "Rome and France in Africa: Recovering Algeria's Latin Past," *French Historical Studies* 25, no. 2 (2002): 295–329; Jacques Frémeaux, "Souvenirs de Rome et présence française au Maghreb: essai d'investigation," in Jean-Claude Vatin, ed. *Connaissances du Maghreb* (Paris: Editions du CNRS, 1984), 29–46.

15. Jacques Ladreit de Lacharrière, "Un essai de pénétration pacifique en Algérie: les négociations du Général Clauzel avec le bey de Tunis (1830–1831)," *Revue diplomatique* 23 (1909): 240–70, 439–68.

16. Frederick Cooper, *Decolonization and African Society: The Labor Question in French and British Africa* (Cambridge: Cambridge University Press, 1996), xii.

17. Abdeljelil Temimi, *Le Beylik de Constantine et hadj 'Ahmed Bey, 1830–37* (Tunis: Presses de la Société tunisienne des arts graphiques, 1978); Eugène Vayssettes, *His-*

toire de Constantine sous la domination turque de 1517 à 1837 (Saint-Denis: Bouchène, 2002).

18. Smaïl Aouli, Ramdane Redjala, and Philippe Zoummeroff, *Abd El-Kader* (Paris: Fayard, 1994).

19. René Gallissot, *Maghreb-Algérie: classe et nation*, 2 vols. (Paris: Arcantère, 1987).

20. Quoted in Charles-André Julien, *Histoire de l'Algérie contemporaine*, vol.1, *La Conquête et les débuts de la colonisation, 1827–1871*, 2nd ed. (Paris: PUF, 1979), 153.

21. See the comments of the minister of war at the Chamber of Deputies, meeting of 15 January, *Le Moniteur universel*, 16 January 1840; and "Rapport du Ministre de la Guerre," presented to the Chambre des députés, séance de 29 avril 1840, *Le Moniteur universel*, 30 April 1840.

22. M. Sabry, *L'Empire égyptien sous Mohamed-Ali et la question d'Orient, 1811–1849* (Paris: Librairie Orientaliste Paul Geuthner, 1930). See also Ussama Makdisi, *The Culture of Sectarianism: Community, History, and Violence in Nineteenth-Century Ottoman Lebanon* (Berkeley: University of California Press, 2000).

23. Christian Schefer, "La 'conquête totale' de l'Algérie, 1839–43," *Revue de l'histoire des colonies françaises* 4 (1916): 22–29.

24. Speech of 15 January 1840, quoted in H. d'Ideville, *Memoirs of Marshal Bugeaud*, trans. Charlotte M. Yonge, vol. 1 (London: Hurst and Blackett, 1884), 299.

25. Jean-Pierre Bois, *Bugeaud* (Paris: Fayard, 1997); Antony Thrall Sullivan, *Thomas-Robert Bugeaud, France and Algeria, 1784–1849: Politics, Power, and the Good Society* (Hamden, Conn.: Archon Books, 1983); Joseph Valynseele, *Les Maréchaux de la Restauration et de la Monarchie de Juillet* (Paris: n.p., 1962), 375–86.

26. André Jardin and André-Jean Tudesq, *Restoration and Reaction, 1815–1848*, trans. Elborg Forster (Cambridge: Cambridge University Press; Paris: Editions de la Maison des sciences de l'homme, 1983).

27. Thomas-Robert Bugeaud, *Veillées d'une chaumière de la Vendée* (Paris: Ledoyen, 1849), 5.

28. Marc Bloch, *French Rural History; An Essay on Its Basic Characteristics*, trans. Janet Sondheimer (Berkeley: University of California Press, 1966), 215.

29. Bois, *Bugeaud*, 465.

30. Thomas-Robert Bugeaud, *Œuvres militaires du Maréchal Bugeaud duc d'Isly*, ed. Maurice-Henri Weil (1883; reprint, Paris: Trois Hussards, 1982).

31. Bois, *Bugeaud*, 73–95.

32. Bugeaud, "Ordre général au quartier-général à Alger," 22 February 1841, [*Le*] *Moniteur algérien*, 23 February 1841.

33. *Procès-Verbaux et rapports de la commission nommée par le Roi, le 7 juillet 1833, pour aller recueillir en Afrique tous les faits propres à éclairer le gouvernement sur l'état du pays et sur les mesures que réclame son avenir* (Paris : L'imprimerie royale, juin 1834), 86.

34. Address of Guilhem, Chamber of Deputies, meeting of 14 January, *Le Moniteur universel*, 15 January 1840.

35. The word "razzia" came into French usage at this time. An entry in the national dictionary of 1856 reflects its clear origin in the Algerian wars: "Mot d'origine arabe, et qui est employé, depuis très-peu d'années, pour désigner les invasions faites par des soldats sur le territoire étranger ou ennemi, dans le but d'enlever les troupeaux, les grains, etc.

Ce mot entraîne toujours avec lui l'idée de pillage. Une razzia n'est au fond qu'un pillage exécuté sur des peuples nomades qu'il est impossible d'atteindre autrement que par la destruction de leurs récoltes et de leurs troupeaux." Louis-Nicolas Bescherelle, *Dictionnaire national ou Dictionnaire universel de la langue française*, vol. 2 (Paris: Garnier frères, 1856), 1095.

36. "Proclamation du Général Bugeaud aux tribus insoumises de la province d'Oran," 29 Apriil 1837, quoted in Sullivan, *Thomas-Robert Bugeaud*, 88.

37. Ibid.; translation modified.

38. T. M. Johnstone, "Ghazw," *Encyclopaedia of Islam*, vol. 2 (Leiden: Brill, 1966), 1055a. See also Général Daumas, *Les Chevaux du Sahara et les mœurs du désert*, 3rd ed. (Paris: Michel Lévy, 1855).

39. Thomas-Robert Bugeaud, "Quelques réflexions sur Trois Questions fondamentales de notre établissement en Afrique," report distributed in the Chamber of Deputies in 1846; quoted in Thomas Robert Bugeaud, *De la colonisation de l'Algérie* (Paris: Guyot, imprimeur du Roi, 1847), 87.

40. See Bugeaud, "Quelques réflexions sur Trois Questions" and "L'Algérie des moyens de conserver et d'utiliser cette conquête," in Weil, ed., *Oeuvres militaires du Maréchal Bugeaud*, 259–320.

41. Bugeaud, *De la colonisation de l'Algérie*, 7.

42. Sakina Drihem, "Les Beni Toufout de Collo, une tribu algérienne face à la conquête" (master's thesis, Université de Provence, 1988).

43. Louis Veuillot, *Les Français en Algérie: souvenirs d'un voyage fait en 1841* (Tours: A. Mame & cie, 1857), 132.

44. Louis de Baudicour, *La Guerre et le gouvernement de l'Algérie* (Paris: Librairie du Centre algérien, 1853), 391.

45. Letter of Bugeaud to A. Thiers, Algiers, 5 April 1843, quoted in Paul Azan, ed., *Par l'épée et par la charrue: écrits et discours de Bugeaud* (Paris: PUF, 1948), 140.

46. Bugeaud to M. de Beaumont, 4 March 1844, quoted in Roger Germain, *La Politique indigène de Bugeaud* (Paris: Larose, 1953), 146.

47. GGA to Ministre de la Guerre, Algiers, 10 April 1844. CAOM 2 EE 5.

48. This understanding of the extent of French sovereignty dates back to the first year of the conquest. In a dispatch of 5 June 1831 the prime minister and the minster of the interior, Casimir-Périer, claimed that France's North African possessions included all the territories of the conquered Ottoman regency. See Christian Schefer, *L'Algérie et l'évolution de la colonisation française* (Paris: Honoré Champion, 1928), 77. See also Roger Germain, *La Politique indigène de Bugeaud* (Paris: Larose, 1953), 139.

49. GGA to Ministre de la Guerre, Algiers, 10 April 1844. CAOM 2 EE 5.

50. Commandant de la Sous-division of Médéa to Commandant de la Division d'Alger, Médéah, 1 September 1847. CAOM 10 H 78.

51. The best source of Laghouat's history, which makes extensive use of Arabic letters and manuscripts then housed in the Algiers Library, is E. Mangin, *Notes sur l'histoire de Laghouat* (Algiers: Adolphe Jourdan, 1895). See also Roger Le Tourneau, "Occupation de Laghouat par les Français, 1844–1852," in *Etudes maghrébines: mélanges Charles-André Julien* (Paris: PUF, 1964), 111–36; "Notice biographique sur les principales familles indigènes de la Division qui ont exercé ou qui exercent encore des commandements," Division

d'Alger, Algiers, 1 September 1859. CAOM F80 1677; "Historique du Cercle de Laghouat," ca. 1865. CAOM 10 H 78.

52. Quoted in Mangin, *Notes sur l'histoire de Laghouat*, 54.

53. GGA to Ministre de la Guerre, Algiers, 13 April 1844. CAOM 2 EE 5.

54. Schefer, "La 'conquête totale' de l'Algérie, 1839–43," 40.

55. Germain, *La Politique indigène de Bugeaud*, 147.

56. Bugeaud to Ministre de la Guerre, 1 August 1841, in Marcel Emerit, "La Légende de Léon Roches," *Revue africaine* 92 (1947): 89–90.

57. His authority encompassed Laghouat and five neighboring fortified villages, plus the pastoralist tribes the Larbaa and Harazlia. See Général Marey [Monge], *Expédition de Laghouat* (Algiers: A. Bourget, [1846]), 52–55; and Marey to [GGA?], n.d. CAOM 1 HH 28.

58. General Marey, Tiaret, 20 June 1844. Marey, *Expédition de Laghouat*, 64. General Marey Monge's column numbered 2,800 men (including 1,700 infantry, 140 regular cavalry, 400 mounted Algerian auxiliaries, 300 "chameliers"), plus 1,400 camels and mules (7–8).

59. Ibid., 65.

60. The colonial Spahis were inspired by the Ottoman regencies' *sipāhī*-s, a corps of mounted gendarmerie, generally recruited locally for short-term police duties and military campaigns. See A. Temimi's entry in the *Encyclopaedia of Islam*, vol. 9, 656a.

61. Bugeaud to Pierre Genty de Bussy, Algiers, 17 November 1843, quoted in Capitaine Tattet et Féray-Bugeaud d'Isly, ed., *Lettres inédites de Maréchal Bugeaud duc d'Isly, 1808–1849* (Paris: Émile-Paul Frères, 1923), 266.

62. Thomas, "Rapport concernant l'évènement qui eu lieu le 12 mai dans la kasbah de Biskra," 21 May 1844. CAOM 10 H 76.

63. Survivors included the commander of Biskra, Lieutenant de Tirailleurs Petitgaud, Sous-lieutenant Crochard, and the surgeon, Aide-major Arcelin.

64. Anonymous report, Constantine, 24 May 1844, cited in Maurice d'Irisson, comte d'Hérisson, *La Chasse à l'homme: guerres d'Algérie* (Paris: Paul Ollendorff, 1891), 120–23.

65. GGA to Ministre de la Guerre, Algiers, 9 and 24 April 1845. CAOM 2 EE 6.

66. Commandant Supérieur de Constantine, Henri d'Orléans to Bugeaud, 2 June 1844, *Le Moniteur universel*, 18 June 1844.

67. Furet, *Revolutionary France*.

68. Piscatory, meeting of 14 May (debate of "crédits supplémentaires," 1839–40), *Le Moniteur universel*, 15 May 1840.

69. The fact that Bugeaud and Guizot were friends did not weaken the unfavorable comparison. See Jean Baillou et al., *Les Affaires étrangères et le corps diplomatique français*, vol. 1, *De l'Ancien régime au Second Empire* (Paris: Éditions du CNRS, 1984), 573–635.

70. De Corcelles, meeting of 5 June, "Débat sur les dépenses imprévues de l'Algérie, crédit extraordinaire," *Le Moniteur universel*, 6 June 1844. As will become apparent, Corcelles was a proponent of expansion.

71. Emmanuel Poulle, meeting of 5 June, "Débat sur les dépenses imprévues de l'Algérie, crédit extraordinaire," *Le Moniteur universel*, 6 June 1844.

72. Block et Guillaumin, *Annuaire de l'économie politique et de la statistique pour 1857* (Paris: Buillaumin, 1857), 98–114.

73. Ministère de la Guerre, *Tableau de la situation des établissements français dans l'Algérie, 1845–46*, vol. 9 (Paris: Imprimerie royale, [April] 1846), 347.

74. De Corcelles, "Débat," *Le Moniteur universel*, 6 June 1844; emphasis added.

75. Joly, meeting of 5 June, "Débat sur les dépenses imprévues de l'Algérie, crédit extraordinaire," *Le Moniteur universel*, 6 June 1844.

76. Ibid.

77. Ibid. The last two paragraphs speak to the relations between the Tijaniyya Sufi order at Aïn-Madi and the Ben Salem family at Laghouat. Joly overstated the tensions for rhetorical effect.

78. Ibid.

79. Ibid.

80. De Corcelles, "Débat," *Le Moniteur universel*, 6 June 1844.

81. See the J.-C. Boudin article in *L'Echo d'Oran*, 10 June 1848, cited in Kamel Kateb, *Européens, "Indigènes," et Juifs en Algérie, 1830–1962* (Paris: Éditions de l'Institut national d'études démographiques, 2001), 37.

82. Charles Antoine Thoumas, *Les Transformations de l'armée française: essais d'histoire et de critique sur l'état militaire de la France*, vol. 2 (Paris: Berger-Levrault, 1887), 632–33.

83. Jacques Houdaille, "Le Problème des pertes de guerre," *Revue d'histoire moderne et contemporaine* 17 (1970): 418.

84. Kateb, *Européens, "Indigènes," et Juifs*, 47. Given the ratios of casualties discussed in chapter 3, this low figure probably does not represent the true scale of Algerian losses in combat.

85. Djillali Sari, *Le Désastre démographique de 1867–1868 en Algérie* (Algiers: Société nationale d'édition et de diffusion, 1982).

86. Bouda Etemad, *Possessing the World: Taking the Measurements of Colonisation from the 18th to the 20th Century*, trans. Andrene Everson (New York: Berghahn, 2007), 94.

87. *Campagnes d'Afrique, 1835–1848: lettres adressées au Maréchal de Castellane* (Paris: Librairie Plon, 1898).

88. Castellane's mistrust of Bugeaud dated from the Brossard trial held in Perpignan in August 1838. See Bois, *Bugeaud*, 295–99.

89. In 1858 Generals Angenoust and Courtigis officially protested Castellane's espionage in their commands. See William Serman, *Les Officiers français dans la nation, 1848–1914* (Paris: Aubier, 1982), 42.

90. Charles Bocher, "Siège de Zaatcha, souvenirs de l'expédition dans les Ziban en 1849," *Revue des deux mondes* 10 (1851): 70–100.

91. An exception are the oral interviews included in J. Desparmet, "Les Réactions nationalitaires en Algérie," *Bulletin de la Société de Géographie d'Alger et de l'Afrique du Nord* 37, nos. 130–31 (1932): 171–84; 437–56.

92. François Maspero, *L'Honneur de Saint-Arnaud* (Paris: Plon, 1993), 129.

93. De Lioux, camp of Tixeraïm, 11 February 1841, cited in Castellane, *Campagnes d'Afrique*, 221.

94. Cler, Cherchell, 1 July 1842; ibid., 274.

95. Daganan, Constantine, 24 April 1843; ibid., 314.

96. Dubern, Arzew, 4 March 1846; ibid., 476 (emphasis added).

97. Forey, Milianah, 26 April 1843; ibid., 310.

98. Ibid., 311.

99. Forey, camp at Kouba, 3 March 1843; ibid., 301.

100. Canrobert, Tenès, 18 July 1845; ibid., 413.

101. Henri Brunschwig, *French Colonialism, 1871–1914: Myths and Realities*, trans. William Glanville Brown (London: Pall Mall Press, 1964), 167.

102. An example of this thinking is Alexis de Tocqueville, "Travail sur l'Algérie (octobre 1841)," in *Œuvres complètes*, vol. 1, ed. André Jardin (Paris: Gallimard, 1991), 691–759.

103. Pierre Guiral, "Observations et réflexions sur les sévices dans l'Armée d'Afrique," *Revue de l'occident musulman et de la Méditerranée* 15–16 (1973): 15–20. Gurial names two of the most feared punishments. The first, the "silo," consisted of packing deep, narrow trenches with wrongdoers, generally stripped naked, who could not sit or recline. Insects and the elements did the rest. The other, more severe, was known as the "clou." The condemned had his hands and feet bound together and was suspended face down from his tethers. The position produced a circulatory imbalance resulting in severe pain and, ultimately, unconsciousness. See also William Serman, "Denfert-Rochereau et la discipline dans l'armée française entre 1845 et 1874," *Revue d'histoire moderne et contemporaine* 20 (January–March 1973): 95–103.

104. Madjid Chemirou, "L'Histoire de Bejaia et de sa région de 1833 à 1880" (master's thesis, Université Denis Diderot, Paris VII, 2002). See also Laurent-Charles Féraud, *Histoire de Bougie* ([Saint-Denis]: Bouchène, 2001).

105. De Mirbeck, bivouac at Bougie, 24 May 1847; cited in Castellane, *Campagnes d'Afrique*, 513–14.

106. Fernand Braudel, *The Mediterranean and the Mediterranean World in the Age of Philip II*, vol. 1, trans. Siân Reynolds (Berkeley: University of California Press, 1995), 166.

2. Theorizing the "Pénétration Pacifique"

1. A. S. Kanya-Forstner, *The Conquest of the Western Sudan: A Study in French Military Imperialism* (Cambridge: Cambridge University Press, 1969).

2. A. S. Kanya-Forstner, "French Expansion in Africa: The Mythical Theory," in Roger Owen and Bob Sutcliffe, eds., *Studies in the Theory of Imperialism* (London: Longman, 1972), 281.

3. Jacques Frémeaux, "La Mise en place d'une administration aux marges sahariennes de l'A.O.F. (1891–1930)," in Edmond Bernus et al., eds., *Nomades et commandants: administration et sociétés nomades dans l'ancienne A.O.F.* (Paris: Karthala, 1993), 23.

4. Augustin Bernard and Napoléon Lacroix, *Historique de la pénétration saharienne* (Algiers: Giralt, 1900), 7.

5. The following list of of Arab geographers whose works were published in France is partially based on Armand d'Avezac et al., *Afrique: esquisse général de l'Afrique et Afrique ancienne* (Paris: Firmin Didot Frères, 1844), 34–35.

   Muhammad ibn 'Ali al-Nasibi Abu al-Qasim Ibn Hawqal (d. 977). The first passages in French were included in Charles-Athanase Walckenaer, *Recherches géographiques sur l'intérieur de l'Afrique septentrionale* (Paris: F. Didot, 1821). The first full translation was undertaken by William Mac Guckin de Slane (a military interpreter and one of the foremost French [Irish-born] Arabists of his generation) and published as *Description de l'Afrique par Ibn Haucal* (Paris: Imprimerie royale, 1842). A much earlier English translation circulated in Paris and was entitled *The Oriental geography of Ebn Haukal, an Arabian* traveler of the Xth century, translated from a manuscript in his own possession by Sir William Ouseley (London: T. Cadell and W. Davies, 1800).

'Abd Allah ibn 'Abd al-'Aziz Abu 'Ubayd al-Bakrī (ca. 1040–1094). An incomplete and flawed French translation of *Description of North Africa* (1068) was published by Etienne Quatremère in 1831 ("Notice d'un manuscrit arabe contenant la description de l'Afrique," *Notices et extraits des manuscrits de la bibliothèque du Roi et autres bibliothèques publiés par l'Institut Royal de France*, vol. 12 [Paris: Imprimerie royale, 1831], 437–664.) Later Mac Guckin de Slane produced a corrected translation based on a comparative reading of four different manuscripts. See "Description de l'Afrique septentrionale," trans. Mac Guckin de Slane, *Journal asiatique*, 5th ser., vol. 12 (1858): 412–92, 497–533; vol. 13: 58–80, 97–194, 310–416, 467–519; vol. 14: 117–52. See also Mac Guckin de Slane, *Description de l'Afrique septentrionale par Abou-Obeid-el-Bekri* (Algiers: Imprimerie du Gouvernement, 1857).

Muhammad ibn Muhammad al-Sharif Abu 'Abd Allah al-Idrisi (ca. 1100–ca. 1165). First latin edition, *De Geographia universäli. Hortus cultissimus, mire orbis regions, provincias, insulas, urbes, earumque dimensiones et orizonta describens* (Rome: Typ. Medicea, 1592); first publication in France, *Geographia nubiensis* (Paris: H. Blageart, 1619); first French translation, *Géographie d'Edrisi, traduite de l'arabe en français, d'après deux manuscrits de la Bibliothèque du Roi et accompagnée de notes par P. Amédée Jaubert*, 2 vols. (Paris: Imprimerie royale, 1836–40).

Muhammad ibn 'Abd Allah Ibn Battuta (1304–ca. 1369), *Voyage dans le Soudan, traduit sur les manuscrits de la Bibliothèque du Roi par M. Mac Guckin de Slane* (Paris: Imprimerie royale, 1843).

'Abd al-Rahman ibn Muhammad Ibn Khaldun (1332–1406). The first mention of the manuscript housed in the Royal Library is in d'Herbelot, *Bibliothèque orientale* (Paris: n.p., 1697). Etienne Quatremère began editing the *Muqaddimah* manuscript following the fall of Algiers; the Arabic text was not published until 1858. "Prolégomènes d'Ebn-Khaldoun," in *Notices et extraits des manuscrits de la bibliothèque du Roi et autres bibliothèques publié par l'Institut Royal de France* 16 (1858): 1–422; 17 (1858): 1–407; 18 (1858): 1–434. After Quatremère's death, Mac Guckin de Slane translated and anonymously published the first French version of the *Muqaddimah* during the Second Empire. "Prolégomènes historiques d'Ibn-Khaldoun," in *Notices et extraits des manuscrits de la bibliothèque du Roi et autres bibliothèques publié par l'Institut Royal de France* 19 (1862): 1–486; 20 (1865): 1–93; 21 (1868): 1–573. For an analysis of the colonial politics of translation, see Abdelmajid Hannoum, "Translation and the Colonial Imaginary: Ibn Khaldun Orientalist," *History and Theory* 42, no. 1 (2003): 61–82.

Al-Hasan ibn Muhammad al-Zayyati al-Fasi al-Wazzan (ca. 1496–1548) (a.k.a. Léon l'Africain and Leo Africanus). The first French publication of his description of Africa appeared in the sixteenth century. See Jean Léon, Africain, *Historiale description de l'Afrique Tierce partie du monde* (Antwerp: Imprimerie de Christophe Planin, 1556). The version used in the modern period was a new translation published in 1830. See Léon l'Africain, *De l'Afrique, concernant la description de ce pays*, 4 vols., trans. Jean Temporal (Paris: n.p. ["Imprimé aux frais du gouvernement"], 1830). My thanks to Oumelbanine Zhiri, author of *L'Afrique au miroir de l'Europe: fortunes de Jean Léon l'Africain à la Renaissance* (Geneva: Droz, 1991), for her help in establishing this information. See also

Natalie Zemon Davis, *Trickster Travels: A Sixteenth-Century Muslim between Worlds* (New York: Hill and Wang, 2006).

Other original sources were located by French researchers. The most important for the Algerian Sahara are: "Kitab-el-Adouani, ou le Sahara de Constantine et de Tunis," trans. and ed. Laurent-Charles Féraud, in *Recueil des notices et mémoires de la Société archéologique de la Province de Constantine* 12 (1868): 1–208 (translation of a ninth–tenth century A.D. manuscript found at Touggourt); and Abu Salim al-Ayya 'Abd Allah ibn Muhammad (ca. 1629–ca. 1679) and Abu Salim al-'Aiyashi 'Abd Allah ibn Muhammad, *Voyage dans le sud de l'Algérie et des états barbaresques de l'ouest et de l'est, par El-Aïachi et Moul-Ah'med traduits sur deux manuscrits de la bibliothèque d'Alger par Adrien Berbrugger* (Paris: Imprimerie royale, 1846). The trip made by al-Sid el-hajj Salem from Fez to Timbuktu in 1787 was published and made available to French readers before the conquest. See Assid el-Hadj Salam Chabigny, "Relation d'un voyage de Fez à Timbouctou, fait vers l'année 1787," *Nouvelles annales des voyages, de la géographie et de l'histoire* 7 (1820): 5–51.

6. Thomas Shaw, *Travels, or observations relating to several parts of Barbary and the Levant* (Oxford: Printed at the Theatre, 1738); first French edition: *Voyages de M. Shaw dans plusieurs provinces de la Barbarie et du Levant, traduit de l'anglais* (The Hague: J. Nmeaume, 1743); and the widely read 1830 edition: *Voyage dans la régence d'Alger: ou description géographique, physique, philologique, etc. de cet état, traduit avec nombreuses augmentations par J. Mac Carthy* (1830; reprint, Tunis: Bouslama, 1980).

7. Frédéric Horneman, *Voyages dans l'intérieur de l'Afrique pendant les années 1797 et 1798*, trans. F. Sovlès (Paris: André, an XI [1802]).

8. Mungo Park, *Voyages dans l'intérieur de l'Afrique, fait en 1795, 1796, et 1797 par M. Mungo Park, avec des éclaircissements sur la géographie de l'intérieur de l'Afrique, par le major Rennel*, trans. J. Castéra (Paris: Dentu, an VIII [1799]).

9. George Francis Lyon, *Voyage dans l'intérieur de l'Afrique septentrionale en 1818, 1819 et 1820*, trans A.-J.-B. Defauconpret (Paris: Gide, 1822).

10. Dixon Denham, *Voyages et découvertes dans le nord et dans les parties centrales de l'Afrique . . . exécutés pendant les années 1822, 1823 et 1824, par le major Denham, le capitaine Clapperton et le doctor Oudney*, trans. Eyriès and de Larenaudière (Paris: A. Bertrand, 1826).

11. Gordon Laing's much sought after notes were lost, but some of his correspondence appeared in the *Quarterly Review* (1828).

12. Catherine Coquery, *La Découverte de l'Afrique: l'Afrique noire atlantique des origines au XVIIIe siècle* (Paris: René Julliard, 1965), 11; Charles Germain Marie Bourel de La Roncière, *La Découverte de l'Afrique au moyen âge* (Cairo: Société royale de géographie d'Egypte, 1924–27), vol. 1: 121–63; vol. 3: 27–31.

13. Jean André Peyssonnel and René Louiche Desfontaines, *Voyages dans les régences de Tunis et d'Alger*, vol. 1: Peyssonnel, *Relation d'un voyage sur les cotes de Barbarie fait par ordre du Roi en 1724 et 1725* (Paris: Librairie de Gide, 1838), 357–58.

14. Lucette Valensi, "Introduction," in Peyssonnel, *Voyage dans les régences de Tunis et d'Alger*, ed. Lucette Valensi (Paris: La Découverte, 1987), 15.

15. Philippe Joutard, ed., *L'Invention du Mont Blanc* (Paris: Gallimard, 1986).

16. René Louiche Desfontaines, *Flora atlantica, sive Historia plantarum, quae in Atlante, agro tunetano et algeriensi crescunt* (Paris: Blanchon, 1800).

17. René Louich Desfontaines, *Fragmens d'un voyage dans les régences de Tunis et d'Alger fait de 1783 à 1788,*" vol. 2 of Peyssonnel et Desfontaines, *Voyages dans les régences de Tunis et Alger* (Paris: Librairie de Gide, 1838), 71–72.

18. Ibid., 73.

19. Abbé Poiret, *Voyage en Barbarie, ou lettres écrites de l'ancienne Numidie pendant les années 1785 et 1786,* vol. 1 (Paris: Rochelle, 1789), v.

20. Denise Brahimi, "Voyageurs français du XVIIIe siècle en Barbarie" (Ph.D. diss., Université de Paris III, 1976), 101.

21. Alfred Fierro, *La Société de géographie, 1821–1946* (Geneva: Droz, 1983); Dominique Lejeune, *Les Sociétés de géographie en France et l'expansion coloniale au XIXe siècle* (Paris: A. Michel, 1993).

22. François Jomard, "Coup-d'œil rapide sur le progrès et l'état actuel des découvertes dans l'intérieur de l'Afrique," *Bulletin de la Société de géographie* 2 (1824): 249. For an understanding of Africa and the Sahara prior to the founding the Geographic Society, see Malte-Brun [né Malthe Conrad Bruun], "Coup d'œil sur les découvertes géographiques qu'il reste à faire et sur les meilleurs moyens de les effectuer," *Nouvelles annales de voyages de la géographie et de l'histoire* 1 (1819): 1–104.

23. "Questions de MM. Malte-Brun et Jomard sur l'Afrique pour M. Knudsen, consul de Danemark à Tripoli et M. Dupré V, consul de France à Bône" [ca. 1824] Bibliothèque nationale-Richelieu, Département des cartes et plans, Société de géographie (hereafter BNF-R SG) Colis 3 bis. n° 1625. Knudson's response provided few details on the Sahara. Dated "Tripoli, le 4 novembre 1824," it was published in the *Bulletin de la Société de géographie* 24 (April 1825): 262–63.

24. Dominique Lejeune and Maxine F. Taylor, "Nascent Expansionism in the Geographical Society of Paris, 1821–1848," *Proceedings, Western Society for French History* 7 (1979): 229–38. See also Michael Heffernan, "The Science of Empire: The French Geographical Movement and the Forms of French Imperialism, 1870–1920" (92–114) and Oliver Soubeyran, "Imperialism and Colonialism Versus Disciplinarity in French Geography" (244–64), both in Anne Godlewska and Neil Smith, eds., *Geography and Empire* (Oxford: Blackwell, 1994). Of interest for the later period is Michael Heffernan, "The Spoils of War: The Société de géographie de Paris and the French Empire, 1914–1919," in Morag Bell, Robin Butlin, and Michael Heffernan, eds., *Geography and Imperialism, 1820–1940* (Manchester, Engl.: Manchester University Press, 1995), 221–64. Lastly, see Yves Lacoste's seminal work *La Géographie, ça sert d'abord à faire la guerre* (Paris: Maspero, 1981).

25. Malte-Brun to Président de la Société de géographie, Paris, 15 July 1825. BNF-R SG Colis 3 bis. n° 3079. According to his unnamed sources, the caravans departed every year from Oran to Timbuktu. He also reported that the "Beni Mozab" of "Gardeia" speak a Berber language and trade with the far south.

26. The prize monies came from the minister of the Navy and the Colonies, who matched the society's 2,000-franc contribution. Other funding came from the minister of Foreign Affairs (2,000 francs), the minister of the Interior (1,000 francs), and two individual donors, Count d'Orloff and an anonymous enthusiast (1,000 francs each). See "Comte de Chabrol, Ministre Secrétaire d'État de la Marine et des Colonies, à M. le Président de la Commission Centrale de la Société de géographie, 3 January 1825," in *Bulletin de la Société de géographie de Paris* 23 (March 1825): 166–67; Fierro, *La Société de géographie,* 210; and

Jomard, "Notice historique sur la vie et les voyages de René Caillié: Discours lu à la séance publique de la Société de géographie du 10 décembre 1838," *Bulletin de la Société de géographie de Paris* 10, no. 60 (December 1838): 330–59.

27. Jacques Berque, preface to *Voyage à Tombouctou*, by René Caillié (Paris: Maspero, 1979), 6.

28. J.-R. Pitté, "Les Controverses autour de la découverte de Tombouctou au début du XIXe siècle," *Revue historique* 515 (1973): 81–104; Isabelle Surun, "La Découverte de Tombouctou: déconstruction et reconstruction d'un mythe géographique," *L'Espace géographique* 32, no. 2 (2003): 131–44; "Considérations critiques sur l'Afrique intérieur occidentale et analyse comparée du voyage de Caillié et des autres itinéraires connus," *Revue des deux mondes* 2 (April 1830): 117–43; and "Réponse aux objections élevées en Angleterre contre l'authenticité de voyage de Caillié à Ten-Boktoue," *Revue des deux mondes* 2 (April 1830): 144–65.

29. René Caillié, *Travels through Central Africa to Timbuctoo and across the Great Desert, to Morocco*, vol. 2 (London: Franck Cass, 1968), 49; translation modified.

30. M. Jomard and René Caillié, "Esquisse de la grande mosquée de Temboctou" and "Vue d'une partie de la ville de Temboctou," in *Voyage à Temboctou et à Jenné, dans l'Afrique Centrale, précédé d'observations faites chez les Maures Braknas, les Nalous et d'autre peuples, pendant les années 1824, 1825, 1826, 1827, 1828*, vol. 2 (Paris: Imprimerie royale, 1830), n.p.

31. "Notes sur le commerce de l'Afrique centrale," *Revue algérienne et coloniale*, 1e semestre (1860): 418.

32. The Geographic Society of Paris accepted Caillé's account as bona fide soon after his arrival in Paris. See "Rapport de la Commission Spéciale chargée de rendre compte du voyage de M. Auguste [*sic*] Caillé," *Bulletin de la Société de géographie de Paris* 68 (December 1828): 245–56. However, the cloud of suspicion that surrounded the trip was such that Caillé could not secure funding for a subsequent voyage to Bamako, where he hoped to be named a French consul. See M. Jomard, "Notice historique sur la vie et les voyages de René Caillié: Discours lu à la séance publique de la Société de géographie du 10 décembre 1838," *Bulletin de la Société de géographie* 60 (December 1838): 330–59. The definitive moment in the rehabilitation of Caillié's reputation came in 1855, when Heinrich Barth—having just returned to Europe from five years in west-central Africa, including seven months at Timbuktu—wrote the president of the Society of Geography that "M. René Caillié [était] un des plus sincères voyageurs." "Extrait d'une lettre de M. Barth à M. Jomard, Londres, le 21 septembre 1855," in *Bulletin de la Société de géographie de Paris*, 4th ser., vol. 10 (October and November 1855): 302.

33. Caillié, *Travels through Central Africa*, 133; translation modified.

34. Ibid., 132.

35. Ibid., 110.

36. Philip D. Curtin, *The Image of Africa: British Ideas and Action, 1780–1850* (Madison: University of Wisconsin Press, 1964), 318.

37. Philippe Augier de La Sauzaie, *Mémoire au Roi (sur la possibilité de mettre les établissements français de la côte septentrionale de l'Afrique en rapport avec ceux de la côte occidentale, en leur donnant, pour point de raccord, la ville centrale et commerciale de Tumbuctou)* ([Paris]: Porthmann, [1830]).

38. Letter of Cansham to Hodgson, Princeton, 15 March 1824, National Archives, College Park, Md. (hereafter NARA), RG 84 Vol. 005.

39. William Shaler, "On the Language, Manners, and Customs of the Berbers, or Brebers, of Africa Communicated by William Shaler, Consul of the United States at Algiers, in a Series of Letters to Peter S. Du Ponceau, and by the latter to the Society," *Transactions of the American Philosophical Society*, vol. 2 (Philadelphia: Abraham Small, 1825), 438–65.

40. Henri Aucapitaine, "Études récentes sur les dialectes berbères de l'Algérie," *Nouvelles annales des voyages, de la géographie et de l'histoire*, vol. 163 (1859): 170–92.

41. These informants doubtlessly revealed information about their homeland with much discretion. On this question, it is useful to recall David Robinson's recent analysis of how West African elites helped the French construct their colonial archive. "They knew what kind of information was sought, needed, and believed, and how to integrate their own interests with that information." *Paths of Accommodation: Muslims Societies and French Colonial Authorities in Senegal and Mauritania, 1880–1920* (Athens: Ohio University Press; Oxford: James Currey, 2000), 4.

42. El-Eghwati, *Notes of a journey into the Interior of Northern Africa, translated from the Arabic by William Brown Hodgson* (Washington, D.C. [?]: n.p., 1830), 31 pp. The report was dated "Rebia el Tseni" (Rabī' II) 1242 A.H. (November 1826).

43. Ibid., 6.

44. Ibid., 21.

45. Ibid., 17.

46. Ibid., 19.

47. William Brown Hodgson, "Grammatical Sketch and Specimens of the Berber Language: preceded by four Letters on Berber Etymologies, addressed to the President of the Society by William B. Hodgson, Esq. Read October 2d, 1829," in *Transactions of the American Philosophical Society*, vol. 4 (Philadelphia: James Kay, Jun. & Co., 1834), 1–48; idem, *The Foulahs of Central Africa, and the African Slave Trade* ([New York?], n.p., 1843); idem, *Notes on Northern Africa, The Sahara and Soudan in Relation to the Ethnography, Languages, History, Political and Social Condition, of the Nations of Those Countries* (New York: Wiley and Putnam, 1844). Hodgson continued his "exploration" of Africa by interviewing Africans in the United States. See Wiiliam Brown Hodgson, *The Gospels Written in the Negro Patois of English with Arabic Characters by a Mandingo Slave in Georgia* (New York: n.p., 1857).

48. Hodgson, "Grammatical Sketch," 28. The standard map used by the French at the time was produced in 1790 (revised 1803) by the British geographer Major James Rennell. It was based on information from the first generation of European explorers in Central Africa. It reveals the lack of knowledge of the Algerian Sahara under the broad banners "Beni Mezzab," and "Pays des Dattes ou Wergela." In the area to the south is a much larger blank space entitled "Toùâryk, Ssahharâ ou Grand Désert;" which is color-coded "Inconnu." The map is reproduced in Augustin Bernard and Napoléon Lacroix, *La Pénétration saharienne, 1830–1906* (Algiers: Challamel, 1906; reprint, Calvission: Editions Jacques Gandini, 1993). A copy of the original English version is in Curtin, *The Image of Africa*, 204. In 1828 Colonel Lapie issued a new map based on information from Thomas Shaw. See Pierre Lapie, *Carte comparée des Régences d'Alger et de Tunis* (Paris: Picquet, 1828); idem, *Carte topographique et spéciale du royaume d'Alger, du littoral des côtes dans une étendue de plus de 300 lieues*

d'après Lapie et sur les dessins inédits du l'interprète Cheik Joussouf (Paris: Houzé, n.d.). A ministerial decision dated 24 July 1838 created the first topographic service for Algeria. It employed a handful of surveyors who devoted most of their early work to delimiting property boundaries. See Ministère de la Guerre, *Tableau de la situation des établissements français dans l'Algérie, 1845–46*, vol. 9 (Paris: Imprimerie royale, [April] 1846), 502–4.

49. Marie Arnaud Pascal d'Avezac (1800–1875) published his translation in the *Bulletin de la Société de Géographie de Paris*, 2nd ser., 2, no. 5 (May 1834): 277–96. In a series of four subsequent articles published in the same journal, Avezac undertook a critical analysis of el-Eghwati's description: 2, no. 8 (August 1834): 81–115; 2, no. 9 (September 1834): 145–76; 4, no. 24 (December 1835): 349–87; 5, no. 25 (January 1836): 5–38. Avezac concluded this lengthy project by admitting at the end of the fourth article that he had produced only "une œuvre incomplète, souvent conjecturale, qui n'aurait prétendre à une exactitude rigoureuse" (38). An anonymous letter [Malte-Brun?] from the Geographic Society of Paris asks for information on the dialects of the Mzab and details on Saharan caravans, indicating that the writer had no knowledge of Hodgson's work. See "Questions sur l'Afrique pour M. le Comte d'Esterno (M. Biouichi)," 22 March 1833 (BNF-R SG Colis 3 bis. n° 1625).

50. "Lettre de M. William B. Hodgson à M. d'Avezac, Paris, le 29 septembre 1836," in *Bulletin de la Société de géographie de Paris*, 2nd ser., 4, no. 31 (October 1836): 247–50. The fact of Hodgson's close ties to the French policymaking elites is revealed a decade later by the dedication to General Daumas in a copy of his 1844 work *Northern Africa, the Sahara and Soudan* (New York: Wiley and Putnam, 1844). Copy located in CAOM 4 H 22–23.

51. See, e.g., Shaw's description.

52. Commandant d'Oran to GGA, Oran, 8 September 1853. CAOM 4 H 22–23.

53. "Rapport de la Commission chargée de rédiger les instructions pour l'exploration scientifique de l'Algérie" (Extrait des Comptes rendus des Séances de l'Académie des Sciences, séance du 23 juillet 1838) (N.p: n.p., [1838]), 94.

54. There is little scholarship currently available concerning the Commission Scientifique. See the general treatment by Monique Dondin-Payre, *La Commission d'exploration scientifique d'Algérie: une héritière méconnue de la Commission d'Égypte* (Abbeville: F. Paillart, 1994). Also of interest is François Leimdorfer, *Discours académique et colonisation: thèmes de recherche sur l'Algérie pendant la période coloniale* (Paris: Publisud, 1992). More generally see M. Collinet, "Le Saint-simonisme et l'armée," *Revue français de sociologie* 2, no. 2 (1961): 38–47.

55. Antoine Picon, *Les Saint-Simoniens: raison, imaginaire et utopie* (Paris: Belin, 2002), 131–64; Philippe Régnier, "Le Mythe oriental des Saint-Simoniens," in *Les Saint-Simoniens et l'Orient: vers la modernité*, ed. Magali Morsy (Aix-en-Provence: Edisud, 1989), 29–52; Philippe Régnier, *Les Saint-Simoniens en Égypte, 1833–1851* (Cairo: Banque de l'Union Européenne, 1989).

56. Ismayl Urbain, "Le Sahara algérien," *La Revue de l'Orient* (1843): 148–53; also published under the title "Le Désert de l'Algérie," *Le Journal des débats*, 27 September 1843. See also Ismayl Urbain, "Les Zibans, oasis du Sahara algérien," *La Revue de l'Orient* 5 (1844): 316–19.

57. Urbain, "Le Sahara algérien," 149.

58. Ibid., 149.

59. Jean Despois, *L'Afrique du nord*, 3rd ed. (Paris: PUF, 1964), 103.

60. Urbain, "Le Sahara algérien," 149.

61. Ibid., 150.

62. The same strategy was followed by Adrien Berbrugger. He claimed that the natural southern frontier of Algeria was south of Ouargla, where his sources (Carette, Daumas, Ibn Khaldun) mentioned a large zone of dunes marking the beginning of Tuareg territory. However, he left open the possibility of extending the borders farther south, the question being whether trade and agriculture "changeront peut-être un jour" the frontier. Adrien Berbrugger, "Des frontières de l'Algérie," *Revue africaine* 4 (October 1860): 406 (first published in *Akhbar* in 1852).

63. J. Cambon, "Avertissement," in N. Lacroix H.-M. P. de La Martinière, *Documents pour servir a l'étude du nord-ouest Africain. Réunis et rédigés par ordre de Jules Cambon*, vol. 3, *Les Oasis de l'extrême sud algérien* (Algiers: Gouverneur général de l'Algérie, 1897).

64. Émilien Jean Renou, *Description géographique de l'empire du Maroc suivie d'Itinéraires et renseignements sur le pays de Sous et autres parties méridionales du Maroc, recueillis par M. Adrien Berbrugger* (Paris: Imprimerie royale, 1846), 462. See also Napoléon Lacroix and Henri Poisson de La Martinière, *Documents pour servir à l'étude du nord-ouest Africain*, vol. 2, *Le Sud-ouest et les régions limitrophes, Figuig, l'Oued Guir, l'Oued Saoura* (Algiers: Gouvernement général de l'Algérie, service des affaires indigènes, 1896), 1–72.

65. Urbain, "Le Sahara algérien," 150.

66. Ibid., 153.

67. Marcel Emerit, *Les Saint-Simoniens en Algérie* (Paris: Les Belles Lettres, 1941), 35; emphisis added.

68. Barthelémy-Prosper Enfantin, *Colonisation de l'Algérie* (Paris: P. Bertrand, 1843).

69. See Barthelémy-Prosper Enfantin et. al., *Doctrine de Saint-Simon*, 2 vols. (Paris: Au Bureau de l'Organisateur, 1830).

70. The Ménilmontant retreat collapsed after Enfantin and other leaders were condemned to a year in prison for exceeding the limits of public assembly.

71. Enfantin, *Colonisation*, 10.

72. Ibid., 410.

73. Ibid., 410.

74. Ibid., 418.

75. For example, see, "Rapport sur la colonisation de l'ex-Régense d'Alger, par M. de la Pinsonnière," *Procès-verbaux et rapports de la commission nommée par le Roi, le 7 juillet 1833, pour aller recueillir en Afrique tous les faits propres à éclairer le gouvernement sur l'état du pays et sur les mesures que réclame son avenir* (Paris: Imprimerie royale, juin 1834), 329.

76. Emerit, *Les Saint-Simoniens*, 201.

77. Enfantin, *Colonisation*, 419; repunctuated for sense.

78. Ibid., 420.

79. Ibid., 419.

80. Ibid., 32.

81. Ibid., 35.

82. Enfantin subscribed to the comte de Saint-Simon's theory of history, which explained history as a series of stages and struggles between the forces of reaction and modernity. Adapting this model to Algeria, Enfantin viewed military leaders on opposite sides of the

war—specifically Abdelkader and Bugeaud—as atavistic remnants of the same feudal and theological stage, their conflict marking the death rattle of the past. On Saint-Simon and history, see Emile Durkheim, *Socialism and Saint-Simon (Le Socialisme)*, ed. Alvin W. Gouldner, trans. Charlotte Sattler (Yellow Springs, Ohio: Antioch Press, 1958). See also Frank E. Manuel, *The New World of Henri Saint-Simon* (Notre Dame, Ind.: University of Notre Dame Press, 1963). On the religious and racial elements of Saint-Simonian thought, see Youngsoo Yook, "Continuity and Transformation: Emile Barrault and Saint-Simonianism, 1828–1865" (Ph.D. diss., University of Washington, 1995).

83. Enfantin, *Colonisation*, 418.

84. Ibid., 408.

85. Ibid., 411.

86. My argument here is informed by Eric Santner, "History Beyond the Pleasure Principle: Some Thoughts on the Representation of Trauma," in Saul Friedlander, ed., *Probing the Limits of Representation: Nazism and the "Final Solution"* (Cambridge, Mass.: Harvard University Press, 1992), 143–54.

87. Jean-Claude Vatin, "Désert construit et inventé, Sahara perdu ou retrouvé: le jeu des imaginaires," in Jean-Robert Henry, ed., *Le Maghreb dans l'imaginaire français: la colonie, le désert, l'exil* (n.p.: Edisud, 1986), 107–31. Novelists have used irony to engage this trope; see Paul Bowles, *The Sheltering Sky* (New York: Vintage Books, 1990); Rachid Boudjedra, *Timimoun: Roman* (Algiers: Editions Anep, 2002).

88. Michel Levallois, *Ismaÿl Urbain, 1812–1884: une autre conquête de l'Algérie* (Paris: Maisonneuve et Larose, 2001).

89. Michel Collinet, "Le Saint-Simonisme et l'armée," *Revue française de sociologie* 2 (1961): 38–47.

90. Ernest Carette, *Du commerce de l'Algérie avec l'Afrique centrale et les états barbaresques* (Paris: Guyot, 1844). Carette's other works on Saharan commerce include: "Etudes sur le Sahara," 1839, SHAT 1 H 227; *Etude sur les routes suivies par les Arabes dans la partie méridionale de l'Algérie et de la Régence de Tunis* (Paris: Imprimerie royale, 1844); *Recherches sur la géographie et le commerce de l'Algérie méridionale* (Paris: Imprimerie royale, 1844); "Mémoire sur les caravanes africaines que parcourent l'espace compris entre l'oasis de Touat et les frontières occidentales de l'Egypte et du Dar-Four ou Renseignements sur la partie du Désert située entre 0 degrés et 25 degrés de longitude oriental de Paris," Benghazi, 1 September 1846. CAOM 4 H 28.

91. Lieutenant Colonel Daumas, *Le Sahara algérien: Etudes géographiques, statistiques et historiques sur la région au sud des établissements français en Algérie* (Paris: Fortin, Masson et Cie, 1845).

92. Ernest Carette, *Couplets chantés au nom des élèves de l'Ecole polytechnique au banquet qui leur fut offert par les anciens élèves de cette École, le 16 août 1830* (Paris: Imprimerie de J. Tastu, n.d.).

93. Carette, *Du commerce*, 18.

94. Ibid., 32.

95. Ibid., 33.

96. Ibid., 21.

97. Ibid., 35.

98. Ibid., 36.

99. M. de Corcelles, meeting of 5 June, "Débat sur les dépenses imprévues de l'Algérie, crédit extraordinaire," *Le Moniteur universel*, 6 June 1844.

100. E. Daumas, *Correspondance du Capitaine Daumas, consul à Mascara (1837–1839)*, ed. Georges Yver (Algiers: Adolphe Jourdan, 1912).

101. Daumas's ties to Bugeaud cost him his job in 1847 when the latter was dismissed. He made a comeback in the Second Empire and was promoted to Directeur des affaires de l'Algérie at the Ministère de la Guerre.

102. E. Daumas, *Le Sahara algérien: études géographiques, statistiques et historiques sur la région au sud des établissements français en Algérie* (Paris: Fortin, Masson et Cie., 1845). The map, drawn by Captain Gaboriaud, indicated trade routes linking Tripoli, Tunis, Algeria, and Morocco to Timbuktu, Kano, Bernou, and Ouadaï.

103. Daumas's other book, coauthored with Ausone de Chancel, was entitled *Le Grand Désert: itinéraire d'une caravane du Sahara au pays des nègres, Royaume de Haoussa* (Paris: N. Chaix, 1848).

104. Daumas, *Le Sahara algérien*, 4.

105. Ibid., vi.

106. Ibid., 130.

107. Ouargla was home to a sort of popular commedia dell'arte, with some skits involving lewd scenes. It could be that Daumas provided an exaggerated account of this street theater. See I. Bouderba, "Voyage à R'at," *Revue algérienne et coloniale* 1 (December 1859): 247.

108. Daumas, *Le Sahara algérien*, 79.

109. Honoré de Balzac, preface to, *La Peau de chagrin* (1831), cited in Jean-Marie Seillan, *Aux sources du roman colonial (1863–1914): l'Afrique à la fin du XIXe siècle* (Paris: Karthala, 2006), 13.

110. He would later write: "Mon but, en effet, était de faire connaître un pays ignoré, les tribus qui l'habitaient, leur force numérique, leurs mœurs, les chefs qui exerçaient sur elles le plus d'empire, leur géographie physique et politique. . . . Je prévoyais le moment où nous allions nous trouver en contact immédiat avec une région inconnue et qu'il ne nous état plus permis de considérer comme une vaste solitude et d'appeler le Désert." Le Général Daumas et Ausone de Chancel, *Le Grand Désert: itinéraire d'une caravane du Sahara au pays des nègres, Royaume de Haoussa*, 2nd ed. (Paris: Michel Lévy Frères, 1856), vi.

111. Ibid., 12. In fact, he presented little new material. Levallois accuses Daumas of plagiarizing Urbain: "Daumas publiera plusieurs ouvrages sur l'Algérie en utilisant les travaux d'Urbain, sans jamais lui reconnaître le moindre emprunt." Levallois, *Ismaÿl Urbain*, 415. It is more likely that he borrowed from Carette.

112. Daumas, *Le Sahara algérien*, v; emphasis added.

113. Ibid., vii.

114. Ibid., 10–11; emphasis added.

115. Ibid., 109.

116. Bugeaud had said as much three years earlier: "C'est l'alcool qui a vaincu les Indiens [of North America]; c'est le commerce qui soumettra les Arabes." Thomas-Robert Bugeaud, *L'Algérie, des moyens de conserver et d'utiliser cette conquête* (Paris: Dentu, 1842), 110.

3. The "Pénétration Pacifique" in Practice, 1847–52

1. This narrative was offered retrospectively in "Rapport à l'Empereur, Paris, le 21 mai 1853." CAOM 1 H 10.

2. Letter of Bugeaud to Genty [de Bussy], La Durantie, 8 August 1848, in *Lettres inédites du maréchal Bugeaud, duc d'Isly (1808–1849)*, ed. Eugène Tattet (Tours: Deslis; Paris: Emile-Paul, 1923), 317.

3. Maurice Agulhon, *The Republican Experiment, 1848–1852*, trans. Janet Lloyd (New York: Cambridge University Press; Paris: Editions de la Maison des sciences de l'homme, 1983), 61.

4. Capitaine [Friedrich A. L. Bartholomé] Anselme, "Journal des opérations militaires, 1847." SHAT 1 H 213.

5. Ibid. See also Lieutenant Nicolas, "Itinéraire suivi en avril et mai 1847 par le Général Cavaignac de Tlemcen jusqu'aux Kçours en passant par le Djebel Antar," Tlemcen, 1 June 1847. SHAT 1 H 213.

6. Braudel, *The Mediterranean and the Mediterranean World*, vol. 1, 282.

7. Mougin, "Caravanes du Sud-Oranais, déc. 1901–jan. 1902," Oran, 20 February 1902, 19e corps d'armée, Division d'Oran. CAOM 11 APOM 5; Chanzy, "Les Hamyane," 19 June 1870. CAOM 10 H 44.

8. Despois, *L'Afrique du nord*, 219.

9. Emile Gautier, *L'Industrie des tentures dites "Dokkali" au Gourara et au Touat* (Algiers: Jourdan, 1913). See also "Travail et emploi des laines par les indigènes," in E. Du Champ et al., *Le Pays du mouton: des conditions d'existence des troupeaux sur les hauts-plateaux et dans le sud de l'Algérie* (Algiers: Giralt, 1893), 529–33.

10. Du Champ et al., *Le Pays du mouton*. See also Docteur Félix Jacquot, *Expédition du Général Cavaignac dans le Sahara algérien en avril et mai 1847* (Paris: Gide et J. Baudry, 1849).

11. Lapeyre, a "chirurgien aide major de première classe" stationed at Tlemcen, wrote under the pseudonym Félix Jacquot. It is unclear why he made this choice. Accounts critical of the army's actions in Algeria were rarely sanctioned during the July Monarchy or Second Empire. In fact, this type of writing flourished and provides the historian with a rich supplement to the government's archives. Reflecting on this phenomenon during the Algerian war (1954–62), a period of severe repression, Charles André Julien noted with sarcasm, "Il est incontestable que la Monarchie de Juillet et le Second Empire laissèrent aux écrivains qui critiquaient la guerre d'Algérie une liberté qui paraîtrait séditieuse aux autorités de la IVe République." "La Question algérienne," in *Nationalisme et guerre coloniale* (N.p.: n.p., [1958]), 17. This pamphlet is located in CAOM B 3502.

12. Jacquot, *Expédition du Général Cavaignac*, 161.

13. The following information is derived from Anselem, untitled, undated report. SHAT 1 H 213.

14. The first use of camels by the French army dates to Napoleon's Egyptian campaigns. In 1799 he formed the Régiment des dromadaires (eight companies of mounted infantry). Disbanded two years later, little practical knowledge of the experience entered into military theory and practice. In anticipation of a Saharan campaign, in 1843 Bugeaud charged

Commandant Carbuccia to consider the possibility of using camels in Algeria. In 1844 one such company of mounted infantry was ready for service. They departed for Laghouat with Marey's column. The experience was a total disaster: after five days of travel, the disorganized company had to return. In subsequent attempts more than half the camels died at the hands of their inexperienced French handlers. See Pierre Denis, *L'Armée française au Sahara, de Bonaparte à 1990* (Paris: Harmattan, 1991), 65–70; J. L. Carbuccia, *Du dromadaire comme bête de somme et comme animal de guerre* (Paris: Dumaine, 1853); C. Massoutier, *Etude sur l'organisation et la conduite des convois des colonnes opérant dans le sud de l'Algérie* (Algiers: Jourdan, 1882).

15. Anselme, untitled, undated report. SHAT 1 H 213.

16. Bugeaud to Aumale, Algiers, 6 April 1846, in H. d'Ideville, *Memoirs of Marshal Bugeaud*, vol. 1, trans. Charlotte M. Yonge (London: Hurst and Blackett, 1884), 215.

17. General Yusuf, *De la guerre en Afrique*, 2nd ed. (Paris: J. Dumaine, 1851).

18. Jacques Leroy de Saint-Arnaud, *Lettres du maréchal Saint-Arnaud*, vol. 1 (Paris: Michel Lévy frères, 1855), 141.

19. Pierre Braud, *Général Cler: un oublié de l'histoire* (n.p.: Cercle généalogique du Haut-Berry, 1995), 82.

20. Jacquot, *Expédition du Général Cavaignac*, 171. Cavaignac left a group of snipers hidden in the gardens to inflict further casualties on the Aït Foukania. Two were shot down as they approached. "Les Berbers, croyant que toute la colonne s'était retirée, descendirent la montagne pour arrêter l'incendie qui continuait sa marche envahissante" (173). See also Anselme, "Journal des opérations militaires 1847." SHAT 1 H 213.

21. Jacquot, *Expédition du Général Cavaignac*, 174–75.

22. Anselme, "Journal des opérations militaires 1847." SHAT 1 H 213.

23. Jacquot, *Expédition du Général Cavaignac*, 255.

24. Henri Alleg, *The Question*, trans. John Calder (Lincoln, Nebr.: Bison Books, 2006); Elaine Scarry, *The Body in Pain: The Making and Unmaking of The World* (New York: Oxford University Press, 1985); and Marnia Lazreg, *Torture and the Twilight of Empire: From Algiers to Baghdad* (Princeton, N.J.: Princeton University Press, 2008). French torture techniques to find hidden caches is detailed in Maurice d'Irisson, comte d'Hérisson, *La Chasse à l'homme*, 65.

25. Jacquot, *Expédition du Général Cavaignac*, 234.

26. J. Glenn Gray, *The Warriors: Reflections on Men in Battle* (Lincoln: University of Nebraska Press, 1998), 212. See also the discussion of Rausch (intoxication or ecstasy) in Saul Friedlander, *History, Memory, and the Extermination of the Jews of Europe* (Bloomington: Indiana University Press, 1993), 106–11; and Dominick LaCapra, *History and Memory after Auschwitz* (Ithaca, N.Y.: Cornell University Press, 1998), 26–40.

27. *Biographie du Général Cavaignac* (Paris: Plon frères, [1848]), 20.

28. The Muslim apocalypse would be preceded by a time of chaos when the "deceiver" (*al-Dajāl*) would descend to earth and spread strife and oppression. When this time of troubles reached its climax, a liberator, "the rightly guided one" (*al-Madī*) would appear and defeat the deceiver. The Mahdi's victory would mark the beginning of a realm of hitherto unknown justice that would continue until the Last Judgment. See Mercedes Garcia-Arenal, ed., *Mahdisme et millénarisme en Islam* (Aix-en-Provence: Edisud, 2000). Colonial understandings of Mahdism can be found in Charles Richard, *Etude sur l'insurrection du Dhara* [sic] (Algiers: Besancenez, 1846), 85–126.

29. Dossier of letters found in the ruins of Zaatcha, French translation no. 7, unsigned, undated. CAOM 15 K 25.

30. Général Herbillon, *Insurrection survenue dans le sud de la province de Constantine en 1849: Relation du siège de Zaatcha* (Paris: J. Dumaine, 1863).

31. Letter of Colonel Beauchamps, Algiers, 17 August 1849, in Ruth Charlotte Sophie Beaulaincourt-Marles, ed., *Campagnes de Crimée d'Italie, d'Afrique, de Chine et de Syrie 1849–1862: lettres adressées au Maréchal de Castellane* (Paris: Plon, 1898), 20.

32. [Réné-Louis] Borel de Bretizel, Annexe de Biskra, "Archives Journaux de marche de la colonne de Zaatcha, sept.–nov. 1849" (typed copy), Constantine, 14 December 1849, in "Journal des opérations de la colonne expéditionnaire des Zibanes, siège de Zaatcha." CAOM 10 H 76.

33. It comprised elements of the Eighth and Forty-third Infantry Regiments, the Fifth Battalion of Chasseurs, a battalion-strength force of Tirailleurs indigènes, the Third Regiment of Chasseurs and Third Regiment of Spahis. See "Journal des opérations de la colonne expéditionnaire des Zibanes, Siège de Zaatcha." CAOM 10 H 76.

34. Thirty-five hundred rounds of artillery were fired on Zaatcha to little effect. When heavier pieces were used, they easily brought down the exterior walls, but these gave way to interior constructions that offered no point of entry. See "Note sommaire sur l'emploi de l'artillerie au siège de Zaatcha"; "Résultat Obtenu"; "Journal des opérations de l'artillerie au siège de Zaatcha." CAOM 10 H 76. Jean Lethielleux discusses the defensive qualities of adobe bricks in *Ouargla, cité saharienne: des origines au début du XXe siècle* (Paris: Geuthner, 1983), 123.

35. "Journal des opérations de l'artillerie au siège de Zaatcha." CAOM 10 H 76.

36. Most historians nevertheless cite this figure as the total killed. "Journal des opérations de la colonne expéditionnaire des Zibanes, Siège de Zaatcha." CAOM 10 H 76. This figure is also cited in a letter by Colonel Dumontet, Constantine, 14 December 1849, in Castellane, *Campagnes d'Afrique*, 24. A lesser figure of five hundred of the enemy killed is mentioned by Brasdefer to Général Pélissier, Zaatcha, 26 November 1849. CARAN 235 AP 2.

37. Lettre of Colonel Dumontet, Constantine, 14 December 1849, in Castellane, *Campagnes d'Afrique*, 24.

38. "Journal des opérations de la colonne expéditionnaire des Zibanes, Siège de Zaatcha." CAOM 10 H 76.

39. Ibid.

40. Ibid.

41. Multiple sources concur that few women and children were among the victims that final day. Although many women fought in the first six weeks of the siege, they took advantage of a respite on 16 November and left.

42. Settar Outmani, "La Prise et la destruction de Zaatcha: épisode clé de l'insurrection des Ziban en 1849," *Annuaire de l'Afrique du nord* 36 (1997): 164.

43. Lettre of Colonel Dumontet, Constantine, 14 December 1849, in Castellane, *Campagnes d'Afrique*, 24.

44. Commandant Lavarande, 27 November 1849. SHAT 1 H 131. Cited in Outmani, "La Prise et la destruction de Zaatcha," 163. See also Charles Bocher, "Siège de Zaatcha: souvenirs de l'expédition dans les Ziban en 1849," *Revue des deux mondes* 10 (1851): 98; Eugène

Fieffé, *Histoire des troupes étrangères au service de France depuis leur origine jusqu'à nos jours* (Paris: Libraire militaire, Dumaine, 1854); E.-Ch. Bourseul, *Souvenirs de la guerre d'Afrique: insurrection des Zibans, Zaatcha* (Metz: Imprimerie de Verronnais, 1851).

45. Brasdefer to Général Pélissier, Zaatcha, 26 November 1849. CARAN 235 AP 2.

46. Herbillon, *Insurrection*, 195. The heads were later displayed at the Biskra market, before entering a museum collection in Constantine and, later, Paris. Ouatmani, "La Prise et la destruction de Zaatcha," 163.

47. Zaatcha was an important part of local memory and remains so today. The Rahmaniyya zawiya at Ouled-Djellal proudly marks the graves of adherents who fell with Bou Ziyan and are now buried in the courtyard near the mosque (author's visit, November 2004). Zaatcha also became an important historical event for Algerian nationalism. The government commemorated the 1849 events in street names and postage stamps. (A five-dinar stamp entitled "Resistance of Zaatcha" was issued in 1998.) For the French the destruction visited upon Zaatcha has also reverberated. The fact that there was a "rue Zaatcha" in colonial-era Algiers belies a more profound ambivalence about the battle. For example, although Zaatcha is located not far from Biskra, the center of Saharan tourism during the French period, there are few reports of visitors coming to the site. One of the rare bits of evidence is a photo of the eerie ruins taken in the late 1850s by Félix Jacques Antoine Moulin (now owned by Vintage Work, Ltd., Fine Photography, located in Chalfont, Pa.). Describing the fall of the barricade at the Faubourg du Temple during the June Days of 1848 in *Les Misérables*, Victor Hugo noted how soldiers massacred revolutionaries in Paris "as they did in Zaatcha." And some seventy years after the battle an anonymous traveler to the site wrote hauntingly that all that remained were a "few sterile palms" and some "mounds of dirt." "Monographie de Biskra et du Sahara de Constantine," *Bulletin de la société de géographie d'Alger* 22, nos. 83–86 (1921): 591; quoted in Outmani, "La Prise et la destruction de Zaatcha," 165.

48. Letter of Lieutenant Colonel Borel de Bretizel, bivouac at Zaatcha, 24 October 1849, in Castellane, *Campagnes d'Afrique*, 22.

49. "Journal des opérations de la colonne expéditionnaire des Zibanes, siège de Zaatcha." CAOM 10 H 76.

50. Ministère de la Guerre, *Tableau de la situation des établissements français dans l'Algérie, 1846–1847–1848–1849*, vol. 9 (Paris: Imprimerie nationale, [November] 1851), 11.

51. Circulaire, Armée d'Algérie, Affaires arabes, Algiers, 10 February 1850, n° 2. CAOM 22 H 1.

52. "Opinion de M. le Général Commandant de la Division et les Commandants des Subdivisions au sujet de la propagation de la religion catholique dans les tribus," 30 novembre 1850, n° 1501. CAOM 16 H 114. One thing that did change was the special attention paid to Mahdism and the political force of Islam. Commanders received orders to avoid provoking religious discontent and to ban Christian missionaries from the region. Suddenly "La GUERRE SAINTE" was the main fear.

53. Lazhari Labter, *Retour a` Laghouat mille ans après Beni Hilel* (Algiers: Editions El ikhtilef, 2002), 30. Expressed in local dialect, "sana al-khla" refers to the "emptiness" of this year, devastated like pastures without rain. My thanks to Bouabdallah Khouidmi for help in translating this experession.

54. Annie Rey-Goldzeiguer, "Mohammed ben 'Abdallâh," in *Les Africains*, vol. 12 (Paris: Editions Jeune Afrique, 1978), 199–201; Julia A. Clancy-Smith, *Rebel and Saint: Muslim*

Notables, Populist Protest, Colonial Encounters; Algeria and Tunisia, 1800–1904 (Berkeley: University of California Press, 1997), 176–88.

55. Général Yusuf to ?, Laghouat, 21 November 1852, n° 24. CAOM 8 X 417.

56. In all, General Pélissier led 2,500 infantry, 500 regular French cavalry, and 1,200 Algerian cavalry auxiliaries (Goums). Units came from the Fiftieth and Sixtieth de ligne, First Chasseurs d'Afrique, First Battalion d'infanterie légère d'Afrique, Second Chasseurs d'Afrique, Second Zouaves, the Spahis, Goums, and Tirailleurs indigènes of Oran and Constantine.

57. Jean Joseph Gustave Cler, *Reminiscences of an Officer of Zouaves* (New York: D. Appleton, 1860), 121.

58. Eugène Fromentin, *Un été dans le Sahara*, ed. Anne-Marie Christin (Paris: Le Sycomore, 1981), 150 n. This comment remained unpublished in earlier editions of his famous travel account.

59. Théodore Pein, *Lettres familières sur l'Algérie, un petit Royaume arabe* (Algiers: Jourdan, 1893), 293 (2,300 victims); E. Mangin, *Notes sur l'histoire de Laghouat* (Algiers: Adolphe Jourdan, 1895), 126 (2,500 victims); Général Cler, *Souvenirs d'un officier du 2e de zouaves* (Paris: Michel Lévy frères, 1859); Georges Hirtz, "Laghouat, les Larbaa, les Mekhalif, la Zaouia Tidjania: essai sur l'évolution sociale et politique de la région de Laghouat depuis 1830," Laghouat, 1 March 1950, "Confidentiel." CAOM 8 X 192; Marie France Dedieu, "Le Bureau arabe de Laghouat, 1859–60" (master's thesis, Université de Toulouse–Le Mirial, 1971); Colonel C. Trumelet, *Histoire de l'insurrection dans le Sud de la Province d'Alger en 1864* (Algiers: Adolphe Jourdan, 1879).

60. Cler, *Reminiscences of an Officer*, 52–53.

61. Julien, *Histoire de l'Algérie*, 392.

62. Pein, *Lettres familières sur l'Algérie*, 293.

63. Ibid., 293.

64. Letter of Lieutenant Colonel Cler, bivouac at Aïn Madi, 17 December 1852, in Castellane, *Campagnes d'Afrique*, 56.

65. Anonymous letter addressed to Adrien Bruberger, quoted in Julien, *Histoire de l'Algérie*, 391.

66. Mangin, *Notes sur l'histoire de Laghouat*, 127.

67. Biweekly Report, Commandant supérieur de Laghouat, Auguste Margueritte, to GGA, 15 March 1855. CAOM 79 I 3.

68. Du Barail to GGA, 4 May 1853. CAOM 1 H 10.

69. Colonel C. Trumelet, *Les Français dans le désert: journal historique, militaire et descriptif d'une expédition aux limites du Sahara Algérien*, 2nd ed. (Paris: Challamel, 1885), 75.

70. Ibid.

71. In a commissioned mural decorating one of Laghouat's many new neighborhoods, a contemporary artist chose to paint a vast panoramic scene from the 1852 battle (author's visit, November 2004). Although it provides a moving view of the action, the mural bizarrely reverses the protagonists: Algerian cavalrymen are shown mowing down terror-stricken French infantrymen. Such representations speak to the ambivalences of memory of the early colonial period in contemporary Algeria.

72. Efforts to turn the palm gardens over to Europeans proved disastrous. The few

Europeans who came to Laghouat fled when confronted with the difficulties of realizing a profit in the date business. Troubled by the economic stagnation of the oasis, the French commandant sold the gardens back to the Laghouati or Mzabi investors. The process was done haphazardly, without establishing clear titles for the new owners, creating long-lasting problems involving property tenure at Laghouat. See Gaston, "Journal de Route pendant ma tournée dans la subdivision du 27 avril au 11 mars 1856," Médéa, 12 May 1856. CAOM 1 H 13; and General Yusuf to GGA, 14 June 1855. CAOM 1 HH 53.

73. Roger Le Tourneau, "Occupation de Laghouat par les Français (1844–1852)," in *Etudes maghrébines: mélanges Charles-André Julien* (Paris: PUF, 1964), 128.

74. Bruno de Rotalier, "Les *yaouleds* (enfants des rues) de Casablanca et leur participation aux émeutes de décembre 1951," *Revue d'histoire de l'enfance irrégulière* 4 (2002), http://rhei.revues.org/document61.html (accessed 12 December 2007).

75. Biweekly Report, Commandant de Laghouat to Commandant de Médéa, Laghouat, February 1857. CAOM 79 I 3.

76. I have not been able to identify this population from extant sources. It is probable that they were members of the Ahlaf Ṣaff (faction), formerly allied with France.

77. Général du Barail, *Mes souvenirs*, vol. 2 (Paris: Plon, 1896), 58.

78. Margueritte, "Renseignements historiques, géographiques, géologiques, politiques et administratifs," [Laghouat], 1 March 1860. CAOM 79 I 4.

79. [Jacques] Suchet, vicaire général, to Monseigneur l'Evêque d'Algérie, Algiers, 17 February 1853. CAOM 1 H 10.

80. Louis-Marie Rapine-Dumezet de Sainte-Marie, *Essais historiques sur l'effusion du sang humain par la guerre* (Paris: Buisson, 1807); Louis Veuillot, *La Guerre et l'homme de guerre*, 2nd ed. (Paris: Victor Palmé, 1870).

4. The Ouled Naïl and Colonial Rule

1. André Nouschi, *Enquête sur le niveau de vie des populations rurales constantinoises de la conquête jusqu'en 1919* (Paris: PUF, 1961); Abdeljelil Temimi, *Le Beylik de Constantine et Hâdj 'Ahmed Bey, 1830–1837* (Tunis: Presses de la Société tunisienne des arts graphiques, 1978); Yahya Bu Aziz, *Thawrat 1871: dawr a'ilatay Muqrani wa-al-Haddad* (Algiers: al-Shari-kah al-Wataniyah lil-Nashr wa-al-Tawzi, 1978); Adib Harb, *al-Tarikh al-'askari wa-al-idari lil-Amir 'Abd al-Qadir al-Jazairi, 1808–1847* (Algiers: al-Sharikah al-Wataniyah lil-Nashr wa-al-Tawzi, 1983); Louis Lataillade, *Abd el-Kader: adversaire et ami de la France* (Paris: Pygmalion, 1984); Mohamed Chérif Sahli, *L'Emir Abdelkader: mythes français et réalités algériennes* (Algiers: Entreprise algérienne de presse, [1988]); Abdelkader Boutaleb, *L'Emir Abd-el-Kader et la formation de la nation algérienne: de l'émir Abd-el-Kader à la guerre de libération* (Algiers: Editions Dahlab, 1990); Smaïl Aouli, Randame Redjala, and Philippe Zoummeroff, *Abd el-Kader* (Paris: Fayard, 1994); Bruno Etienne, *Abdelkader: isthme des isthmes (Barzakh al-barazikh)* (Paris: Hachette, 1994); Mahfoud Kaddache, *L'Algérie des algériens: histoire d'Algérie, 1830–1954* (Algiers: Editions Rocher noir, 1998); Abdelhamid Zouzou, *L'Aurès au temps de la France coloniale: évolution politique, économique et sociale, 1837–1939*, 2nd ed. (Algiers: Houma, 2002).

2. Catherine Coquery-Vidrovitch, *Africa: Endurance and Change South of the Sahara*, trans. David Maisel (Berkeley: University of California Press, 1988), 168.

3. Edmund Burke III, "Islam and Social Movements: Methodological Reflections," Edmund Burke III and Ira M. Lapidus eds., *Islam, Politics, and Social Movements* (Berkeley and Los Angeles: University of California Press, 1988), 17–35.

4. GGA to Ministre de la Guerre, 25 April 1861. CAOM 16 H 1.

5. Annie Rey-Goldzeiguer, *Le Royaume arabe: la politique algérienne de Napoléon III, 1861–1870* (Algiers: SNED, 1977).

6. GGA to Ministre de la Guerre, 25 April 1861. CAOM 16 H 1.

7. Redouane Ainad-Tabet, "Le 8 mai 1945: jacquerie ou revendication agraire?," *Revue des sciences juridiques, économiques, et politiques* 9, no. 4 (December 1972): 1007–16.

8. Dale Eickelman, "New Directions in Interpreting North African Society," in Jean-Claude Vatin, ed., *Connaissances du Maghreb* (Paris: CNRS, 1984), 280.

9. Benjamin Claude Brower, "Lutte mystique: un nouveau regard sur les Soufis sahariens dans le XIXème siècle," in Zaïm Khenchelaoui, ed., *Des voies et des voix* (Algiers: Editions du CNRPAH, 2007), 59–74.

10. Climate data was first recorded systematically in the late nineteenth and early twentieth centuries. For a general overview, see Jean Despois, *L'Afrique du Nord*, 3rd ed. (Paris: PUF, 1964); and Rabah Chellig, *Les Races ovines algériennes* (Algiers: Office des publications universitaires, 1992). For a detailed breakdown of the region's microclimates, see François de Villaret, *Siècles de steppe: jalons pour l'histoire de Djelfa; Deuxième partie: les Oulad Naïl* (Ghardaïa: Centre de documentation saharienne, 1995), x–xiii. I wish to express my thanks to Naas Djemoui for bringing this source to my attention.

11. Léon Lehuraux, *Le Nomadisme et la colonisation dans les hauts plateaux de l'Algérie* (Paris: Editions du Comité de l'Afrique française, 1931), 2.

12. René Maire, *Carte phytogéographique de l'Algérie et de la Tunisie* (Algiers: Baconnier, 1926).

13. I. L. Mason, *A World Dictionary of Livestock Breeds, Types and Varieties*, 4th ed. (Wallingford, Oxon, Engl.: CAB International, 1996).

14. Albert Geoffroy Saint-Hilaire, *Rapport sur les races ovines et caprines de l'Algérie* (Paris: Au siège de la société, 1857).

15. Villaret, *Siècles de steppe*, iii.

16. Chellig, *Les races ovines algériennes*.

17. Interview with Lahaoul Ben Ziane Barraka, pastoralist of Aïn Ma'abed (Wilāya of Djelfa), Roché de Sel, 25 November 2004.

18. M'hamed Boukhobza, *L'Agro-pastoralisme traditionnel en Algérie: de l'ordre tribal au désordre colonial* (Algiers: Office des publications universitaires, 1982), 52–53. Winter diseases included the "riya," or pulmonary strongylosis, a particularly deadly infection that could decimate entire herds. The dry, warm winter climate of the Sahara provided the only protection.

19. Ibid., 67.

20. Arnaud's translations include: *Les Roueries de Dalila: conte traduit des Mille et une Nuits* (Algiers: n.p., 1879); Mohammad Abou Ras al-Nasri, *Voyages extraordinaires et nouvelles agréables: récits historiques sur l'Afrique septentrionale par Mohammed Abou Ras ben Ahmed ben Abd el-Kader en-Nasri*, trans. M. A. Arnaud (Algiers: A. Jourdan, 1885); Cheikh Abd Al Hadi ibn Ridouan, *Etude sur le soufisme*, trans. M. Arnaud (Algiers: A. Jourdan, 1888); Ahmad Faris al-Sidyaq, *Sa Majesté Bakchiche, ou Monsieur Pourboire par Ahmed-Farès*, trans. M. Arnaud (Algiers: Fontana, 1893).

21. M. Arnaud, "Notice sur les Sahari, les Ouled ben Aliya, les Ouled Naïl et sur l'origine des tribus cheurfa," *Revue africaine* 8 (1864): 104–17 and 10 (1866), 17–35; Arnaud "Histoire des Ouled Naïl, faisant suite à celle des Sahari," *Revue africaine* 16 (1872): 327–35, and 17 (1873): 300–312 and 374–90. See also Louis Rinn, "Le Royaume d'Alger sous le dernier dey," *Revue africaine* 41 (1897): 347.

22. At the time of the Djelfa attack, the Ouled Si Mhammad faction had grouped itself loosely into the following sub-units. Claiming descent from the sons of Si Mhammad's wife Dia came the Ouled Abdelkader and the Ouled Bou Abdallah; from the sons of his wife Cheliha came the Ouled Si Ahmed and the Ouled el-Ghouini; from the sons of his wife Hani came the Ouled Oum Hani and the Tameur. Arnaud, "Notice sur les Sahari"; Anonymous, "Historique du Cercle de Laghouat" ca. 1865. CAOM 10 H 78.

23. Villaret, *Siècles de steppe*, 76–85; Emile Dermenghem, *Le Pays d'Abel: le Sahara des Ouled-Naïl, des Larbaa et des Amour* (Paris: Gallimard, 1960), 35.

24. Arnaud, "Histoire des Ouled Naïl," 335.

25. Villaret, *Siècles de steppe*, 56–70.

26. The region was annexed to the Beylik of Titteri ca. 1725 and the Ouled Si Mhammad joined the bey's *Makhzan* toward the end of the eighteenth century. Ibid., 104–9.

27. "Colonialisme et post-colonialisme en Méditerranée," *Les Matins de France Culture*, 5 November 2003.

28. Dermenghem, *Le Pays d'Abel*.

29. According to Victor Demontès, "L'évaporation est intense; les plantes souffrent et se dessèchent. . . . On se croirait devant la bouche d'un four." *L'Algérie économique* (Algiers: Imprimerie algérienne, 1922), 193–94. The temperatures of the dry winds could rise as high as forty degrees Centigrade.

30. Demontès, *L'Algérie économique*, 245; "La Météorologie générale et la climatologie algérienne," *Bulletin de la Société de géographie d'Alger* 5 (1900): 410–21.

31. My information is based on conversations with: Bou Abdallah Khouidmi, Aix-en-Provence, September 2001; El-Attaf, November–December 2004; El-Attaf, March 2007; and the Djemoui family of Djelfa, November 2004. See also Dermenghem, *Le Pays d'Abel*, 32–33; Robert Capot-Rey and Philippe Marçais, "La Charrue au Sahara," *Travaux de l'Institut des recherches sahariennes* 10 (1953): 39–69; Marc Côte, *L'Algérie: espace et société* (Paris: Armand Colin, 1996); J. Erroux, *Les Blés des oasis sahariennes* (Algiers: Institut de recherches sahariennes, n.d.); Napoléon Lacroix and Augustin Bernard, *Evolution du nomadisme en Algérie* (Paris: Challamel; Algiers: Jourdan, 1906); Mathéa Gaudry, *La Femme Chaouia de l'Aurès: étude de sociologie berbère* (Paris: Geuthner, 1929), 155–62; Emile Laoust, *Mots et choses Berbères: notes de linguistique et d'ethnographie* (Paris: Challamel, 1920; reprint, Rabat: Société marocaine d'édition, 1983), 299–59; Michel Launay, *Paysans Algériens: la terre, la vigne et les hommes* (Paris: Seuil, 1963); André Nouschi, *Enquête sur le niveau de vie des populations rurales constantinoises de la conquête jusqu'en 1919* (Paris: PUF, 1961), 63–66; Nacereddine Saidouni, *L'Algérois rural à la fin de l'époque ottomane, 1791–1830* (Beirut: Dar al-Gharb al-Islami, 2001), 202–83; Lucette Valensi, *On the Eve of Colonialism: North Africa Before the French Conquest*, trans. Kenneth J. Perkins (New York: Africana Publishing Co., 1977), 27–31; Lucette Valensi, *Tunisian Peasants in the Eighteenth and Nineteenth Centuries*, trans. Beth Archer (Cambridge: Cambridge University Press, 1985), 110–60. Lastly, see the periodic reports of the Annex of Djelfa: CAOM 75 I 4; 75 I 10; 75 I 13.

32. "Tableaux de Renseignements," 15 September 1855, Cercle de Biskra. CAOM 15 K 25.

33. Laoust, *Mots et choses berbers*, 403–5; Robert Capot-Rey, "Greniers domestiques et greniers fortifiés au Sahara: le cas du Gourara," *Extrait des travaux de l'Institut de recherches sahariennes* 14 (1956): 139–58; Jean Despois, "Les Greniers fortifiés de l'Afrique du Nord," *Cahiers de Tunisie* 1 (1953): 38–62; Auguste Geoffroy, "Les Arabes pasteurs et nomades de la tribu des Larbaa (Région saharienne de l'Algérie)," in *Les Ouvriers des deux mondes: études sur les travaux, la vie domestique et la condition morale des populations ouvrières des diverses contrées* (Paris: Librairie de Firmin-Didot et cie., 1887), 414; Charles Pellat "Matmura," *Encyclopaedia of Islam*, vol. 6 (Leiden: Brill, 1963), 842a. See also François Sigaut, *Les Réserves des grains à long terme: techniques de conservation et fonctions sociales dans l'histoire* (Lille: Editions de la Maison des sciences de l'homme, 1978).

34. Dermenghem, *Le Pays d'Abel*, 33.

35. Debate recorded in *Le Moniteur universel*, 2–3 January 1851.

36. Ibid.

37. Ibid.

38. Undated report on the commercial situation of Algeria. Translation and summary of a commercial commission convened by Governor-General Pélissier, 23 March 1863. National Archives, College Park, Md., NARA RG 84, Volume 01; translation modified.

39. Annual Reports, Annexe de Djelfa, 17 December 1859 and 17 December 1860. CAOM 75 I 13.

40. N. Lacroix et Augustin Bernard, *Evolution du nomadisme en Algérie* (Paris: Challamel; Algiers: Jourdan, 1906), 36; Ernest Gellner, *Saints of the Atlas* (Chicago: University of Chicago Press, 1969), 169–72. There was also the *eussa*, a fee that was in principle paid to Ottoman authorities for access to northern grain markets. After the French conquest, tribes in the Tell continued to collect it. See Lieut. Col. Daumas, *Le Sahara Algérien: études géographiques, statistiques et historiques sur la région au sud des établissements français en Algérie* (Paris: Fortin, Masson et Cie, 1845), 9.

41. Jacques Frémeaux, "Les Bureaux Arabes dans la province d'Alger, 1844–1856" (Ph.D. diss., Université de Toulouse–Le Mirail, 1976); Ministère de la Guerre, *Tableau de la situation des établissements français dans l'Algérie, 1846–1847–1848–1849*, vol. 9 (Paris: Imprimerie nationale, [November] 1851), 716–19. Compare this with the collection system of the Ottomans described in Nouschi, *Enquête sur le niveau de vie*, 95–102; P. Boyer, *L'Evolution de l'Algérie médiane, ancien département d'Alger de 1830 à 1956* (Paris: Adrien-Maisonneuve, 1960), 37–41.

42. Colette Establet, *Etre caïd dans l'Algérie coloniale* (Paris: Editions du CNRS, 1991), 271.

43. Ibid., 283.

44. Monthly Report, Annexe de Djelfa, 1 May 1857. CAOM 75 I 4.

45. Ibid, November 1857.

46. Ibid, April 1860. The following year another caid of the Annex of Djelfa, El Hadraini ben Sahraoui, of the Ouled 'Isa, was fined one hundred francs for bad conduct: "Sous prétexte de se faire donner le diffa [*diyāfa*, an honorary meal for guests], lors de ses tournées beaucoup trop répétés, et dans lesquelles il a toujours une suite fort considérable, il se faire livrer par ses administrés des quantités exagéré de vivres (orge et moutons)." Ibid., February 1861.

47. Alexis de Tocqueville, entry for 27 May 1841, "Notes du voyage en Algérie de 1841," in Alexis de Tocqueville, *Œuvres*, ed. André Jardin (Paris: Gallimard, 1991), 680.

48. Monthly Report, Cercle de Laghouat, November–December 1856. CAOM 79 I 3.

49. Establet, *Etre caïd dans l'Algérie coloniale*, 301–7.

50. The money was stolen from him while returning to Biskra. Commandant Colomb to Henri Duveyrier, Biskra, 8 May 1874. CARAN 47 AP 4.

51. Monthly Report, Annexe de Djelfa, 1 June 1860, December 1860. CAOM 75 I 4

52. Even during the terrible famine of 1866–67 few tax reprieves were given. Zouzou, *L'Aurès au temps de la France coloniale*, 503.

53. Peregrine Horden and Nicholas Purcell, *The Corrupting Sea: A Study of Mediterranean History* (Oxford: Blackwell, 2000), 123–70.

54. E. du Champ et al., *Le Pays du mouton: des conditions d'existence des troupeaux sur les hauts-plateaux et dans le sud de l'Algérie* (Algiers: Giralt, 1893), 112.

55. Donald C. Holsinger, "Trade Routes of the Algerian Sahara in the Nineteenth Century," *Revue de l'occident musulman et de la Méditerranée* 30 (1980): 57–70.

56. The Saharan steppes marked the northern limit of the camel. Although they could spend short amounts of time in the Tell, camels faired poorly for longer periods. The Ouled Naïl reared the smaller, surefooted breeds of camel suited to carrying loads; they conducted military operations on horseback. See Général Daumas, *Mœurs et coutumes de l'Algérie: Tell, Kabylie, Sahara* (Paris: Hachette, 1853), 352–59; and Commandant [Gaston] Cauvet, *Le Chameau* (Paris: J. B. Baillière,1925).

57. See Annual Report 1899, Ghardaia. CAOM 63 I 1. See also Donald Charles Holsinger, "Migration, Commerce and Community: The Mizabis in Nineteenth-Century Algeria" (Ph.D. diss., Northwestern University, 1979), 64, 83, 102–21, 125–45. An important colonial-era study is Ernest Carette, *Recherche sur les origines et les migrations des principales tribus de l'Afrique septentrionale et particulièrement de l'Algérie* (Paris: Imprimerie nationale, 1953).

58. Boukhobza, *L'Agro-pastoralisme traditionnel en Algérie*, 49.

59. Nouschi, *Enquête sur le niveau de vie*; C.-R. Ageron, *Les Algériens musulmans et la France, 1871–1919* (Paris: PUF, 1968); and Tony Smith, "Muslim Impoverishment in Colonial Algeria," *Revue de l'occident musulman et de la Méditerranée* 17 (1974): 139–62.

60. The best study of sedentarization during the nineteenth century is N. Lacroix and Augustin Bernard, *Evolution du nomadisme en Algérie* (Paris: Challamel; Algiers: Jourdan, 1906). Much research was also conducted in the twentieth century; some of which is useful for our purposes. See C. Bataillon, *Le Souf: étude de géographie humaine* (Algiers: Institut de recherches sahariennes, 1955); M. Brigol, "L'Habitat des nomades sédentarisés à Ouargla," *Travaux de l'Institut de recherches sahariennes* 16, no. 2 (1957): 181–97; A. Cauneille, *Les Chaanba (Leur nomadisme): évolution de la tribu durant l'administration française* (Paris: CNRS, 1968); Robert Capot-Rey, "Le Nomadisme pastoral dans le Sahara français," *Travaux de l'Institut de recherches sahariennes* 1 (1942): 63–86; idem, "Transformations récentes dans une tribu du Sud oranais," *Annales de géographie* 324 (1952): 138–42; Jean Despois, "L'Economie pastorale saharienne," in G. Salvy, ed., *Le Sahara des nomades* (Paris: Présidence du Conseil, 1953); Colonel de Fraguier, "La Crise du nomadisme et de l'élevage sur les hauts plateaux algériens," *Travaux de l'Institut de recherches sahariennes* 9, no. 1 (1953): 71–97; idem, *Les Problèmes humains du Sahara sud-oranais* (Paris: Comité d'action scien-

tifique de la défense nationale, 1959); V. Monteil, "L'Evolution et la sédentarisation des nomades sahariens," *Revue internationale des sciences sociales* 11, no. 4 (1959): 599–612; Y. Regnier, *Le Petit-fils de Touameur: les Chaâmba sous le régime français; leur transformation* (Paris: Domat-Montchrestien, 1939); Alain Romey, *Les Sa'id 'Atba de N'Goussa: histoire et état actuel de leur nomadisme* (Paris: Harmattan, 1983); G. Salvy, *La crise du nomadisme dans le Sud marocain* (Paris: Centre de hautes études administratives sur l'Afrique et l'Asie moderne, n.d.).

61. Général Marey-Monge, "Note sur les Ouled Naïl et l'organisation à donner," Médéah, 9 March 1847, CAOM 10 H 78.

62. Bugeaud to Ministre de la Guerre, 20 March 1847. CAOM 2 EE 7. Quoted in Roger Germain, *La Politique indigène de Bugeaud* (Paris: Larose, 1953), 161.

63. Général Camou, Division d'Alger, to Commandant du Barail of Laghouat, January 1854. Quoted in E. Mangin, *Notes sur l'histoire de Laghouat* (Algiers: Jourdan, 1895), 137. See also Georges Hirtz, "Laghouat, les Larbaa, les Mekhalif, la Zaouia Tidjania: essai sur l'évolution sociale et politique de la région de Laghouat depuis 1830," 1 March 1950, marked "Confidentiel." CAOM 8 X 192.

64. Steven L. Kaplan, *Provisioning Paris: Merchants and Millers in the Grain and Flour Trade During the Eighteenth Century* (Ithaca, N.Y.: Cornell University Press, 1984).

65. Djillali Sari, *Le Désastre démographique de 1867–1868 en Algérie* (Algiers: SNED, 1982).

66. Michael Watts, *Silent Violence: Food, Famine and Peasantry in Northern Nigeria* (Berkeley: University of California Press, 1983).

67. Monthly Report, Cercle de Laghouat, November 1867. CAOM 79 I 4.

68. Ibid., March 1868.

69. Compiled from the Monthly Reports of the Cercle de Laghouat, 1867–68. CAOM 79 I 4.

70. Monthly Report, Cercle de Laghouat, March 1868. CAOM 79 I 4.

71. Nouschi, *Enquête sur le niveau de vie*; John Ruedy, *Modern Algeria: The Origins and Development of a Nation* (Bloomington: University of Indiana Press, 1992), 68–100; idem, *Land Policy in Colonial Algeria: The Origins of the Rural Public Domain* (Berkeley: University of California Press, 1967).

72. Quoted in Mahfoud Bennoune, *The Making of Contemporary Algeria, 1830–1987* (Cambridge: Cambridge University Press, 1988), 45. See also Nouschi, *Enquête sur le niveau de vie*, 303–22.

73. Berbrugger to GGA, Tenacub, 27 January 1851; see also Berbrugger to Division de Constantine, Touggourt, 17 December 1850. CAOM 4 H 22–23.

74. Berbrugger to GGA, 27 January 1851. CAOM 4 H 22–23.

75. Général Daumas, *Les Chevaux du Sahara et les mœurs du désert*, avec commentaires par l'Emir Abd-el-Kader (Paris: Michel Lévy, 1855), 364; Geoffroy, "Arabes pasteurs nomades de la tribu des Larbas," 409–64; Dermenghem, *Le Pays d'Abel*, 33.

76. Commandant Margueritte coined this term in the Saharan case in his report dated November–December 1856. CAOM 79 I 3. See also Ferdinand Lapasset, *Mémoire sur la colonisation indigène et la colonisation européenne* (Algiers: Dubos Frères et Bastide, 1848).

77. Annual report, Annexe de Djelfa, 1857. CAOM 75 I 13.

78. Ibid., 25 December 1858 and 17 December 1859. CAOM 75 I 13.

79. Monthly Report, Annexe de Djelfa, 1 January 1861. CAOM 75 I 4. By 1930 the process of sedentarization of the Ouled Si Mhammad and the Sahari was complete. See Léon Lehuraux, *Le Nomadisme et la colonisation dans les hauts plateaux de l'Algérie* (Paris: Editions du Comité de l'Afrique française, 1931), 68.

80. Lacroix and Bernard, *Evolution du nomadisme en Algérie*, 53.

81. Monthly Report, Annexe de Djelfa. CAOM 75 I 4. See also Allan Christelow's comments on the "judicial void" in Algeria in *Muslim Law Courts and the French Colonial State in Algeria* (Princeton, N.J.: Princeton University Press, 1985), 170–79.

82. See, e.g., Monthly Report, Annexe de Djelfa, January and February 1861. CAOM 75 I 4.

83. Ibid., March 1861.

84. Ibid.

85. Ibid., December 1858. Two years later the same logic is expressed. "La possession revendiquée par différents individuels de certaines parcelles de terre labourable prouvent en somme que malgré la mauvaise récolte de cette année nos indigènes se préparent avec ardeur aux travaux agricole, espérant meilleur résultat pour la prochaine campagne agricole" (ibid., September 1860).

86. Marie-France Dedieu, "Le Bureau Arabe de Laghouat, 1859–60" (master's thesis, Université de Toulouse–Le Mirail, 1971). For the record of an attempt to find the Larbaa pastures close to Laghouat, see Cercle de Laghouat, Biweekly Report, 30 June 1855. CAOM 79 I 3.

87. Monthly Report, Cercle de Laghouat, August 1860. CAOM 79 I 4.

88. Ibid., January 1861. The pastures of the Zahrez were especially resistant to drought. For example, when below-average rainfalls devastated the pastures of the region in 1919–20, the Zahrez still had sufficient fodder. Whereas the herds just to the north suffered 65 percent losses, those in the Zahrez had a mortality rate of only 30 percent. GGA, *Les Territoires du sud de l'Algérie*, vol. 2, *L'Œuvre accompli, 1903–1929* (Algiers: Imprimerie algérienne, 1929), 122.

89. Couput, "Rapport à M. le Gouverneur général sur l'amélioration des parcours et l'augmentation des points d'eau," Algiers, 28 November 1906. CAOM 24 H 109. See also "Station d'élevage ovin de Tadmit," n.d., ANA [Archives nationales d'Algérie], série Agriculture, boite 006.

90. *Bedrouna,* or "disease," generally takes the form of a gastrointestinal disorder. It decimates sheep forced to eat less nourishing drought-resistant plants. It was especially detrimental to ewes with young: the only treatment available to shepherds was to slaughter the nursing lambs and thereby save their mothers the physical stress of lactation. Economically this was a bitter pill, but for pastoralists, known for their pride in their herds, it was an especially heartbreaking option. See Abu Salim al-Ayya Abd Allah ibn Muhammad and Abu Salim es-Sid ibn 'Abd Allah ben Muhammad ben Abu Beker el Aäci, *Voyage dans le sud de l'Algérie et des états barbaresques de l'ouest et de l'est par El-Aïachi et Moul-Ah'med; traduction sur deux manuscrits de la bibliothèque d'Alger par Adrien Berbrugger* (Paris: Imprimerie royale, 1846), 315; Général Yusuf, Commandant of the Division of Alger, "Rapport à Son Excellence le Ministre de l'Algérie et des Colonies sur la question ovine dans la Division d'Alger," in Gouvernement Général de l'Algérie, *Tableau de la situation des établissements françaises dans l'Algérie, 1859–1861* (Paris: Imprimerie impériale, 1862), 299. See also

A. Railliet, "Maladies parasitaires les plus graves du mouton algérien," in Du Champ et al., *Le Pays du mouton*, 515–28. For a contemporary study of diseases and affliction of Maghrebi sheep, see A. Kabbali and Y. M. Bergers, eds., *L'Elevage du mouton dans un pays à climat méditerranéen* (Rabat: Actes Editions, 1990), 213–30.

91. Monthly Report, Annexe de Djelfa, July and August 1857. CAOM 75 I 4.

92. Ibid., November 1859.

93. Ibid., December 1859.

94. Ibid., April 1860.

95. Ibid., June 1860.

96. Yusuf, "Rapport à Son Excellence le Ministre de l'Algérie et des Colonies," 300.

97. Monthly Report, June 1857. CAOM 75 I 4.

98. Ibid., July 1858. It hit with such violence that it caused injuries among livestock.

99. Ibid., October 1859.

100. Trimestrial Report, Annexe de Djelfa, 3rd trimester. CAOM 75 I 10.

101. Monthly Report, Annexe de Djelfa, June 1860. CAOM 75 I 4.

102. Ibid., August 1860.

103. Ibid., July 1860.

104. Ibid., September 1860. A note on sources: the prices for foodstuffs sold on the market at Djelfa were recorded in the Rapports trimestriels (CAOM 75 I 10). These prices do not reflect the spikes in prices that are noted, but not systematically specified numerically, in the monthly reports. I cannot fully account for the discrepancy but have chosen to privilege the monthly reports for the following reasons. First, I suspect that some of the trade in grain at this time still took place outside the French marketplace in direct transactions between the trading partners. The *official* prices recorded for the market place of Djelfa may therefore not represent *actual* prices, which were probably higher in these periods of dearth. In the trimestrial report prices may, in fact, be part of a scheme to conceal local problems through a statistical Potemkin village. Second, I have detected a Pollyannaish tendency whenever a greater period of time is covered in the report. Whereas the monthly reports often express a certain alarm, the trimonthly and annual reports, which were read at the highest levels of the administration, are uniformly optimistic and speak glowingly of the possibilities for the future. Third, André Nouschi's thorough research shows that grain prices rose throughout Algeria at this time. See his *Enquête sur le niveau de* vie, 256–57, 295.

105. Monthly Report, Annexe de Djelfa, February 1861. CAOM 75 I 4.

106. Ibid.

107. William Leonard Schwartz, "A Glossary of Franco-Arabic Words," *French Review* 12, no. 2 (December 1938): 139.

108. Monthly Report, Annexe de Djelfa, October 1859. CAOM 75 I 4.

109. Ibid.

110. Ibid. He, too, was arrested.

111. The monthly report for October 1856 noted that the drought was "grave." Monthly Report, Annexe de Djelfa, October 1856. CAOM 75 I 4. See also Monthly Report, Cercle de Laghouat, December 1860. CAOM 79 I 4.

112. Yves-Marie Bercé, *History of Peasant Revolts: The Social Origins of Rebellion in Early Modern France*, trans. Amanda Whitmore (Ithaca, N.Y.: Cornell University Press, 1990).

113. Valensi, *On the Eve of Colonialism*.

114. Dermenghem, *Le Pays d'Abel*, 32.

115. Boukhobza, *L'Agro-pastoralisme traditionnel en Algérie*. This work grew out of Boukhobza's doctoral dissertation, which was directed by Pierre Bourdieu and Abdelmalek Sayed. In 1993 Boukhobza was brutally murdered by a team of armed men in his Algiers home.

5. The Leadership Crisis and Rural Marabouts

1. Charles-André Julien, *Histoire de l'Algérie contemporaine*, vol. 1, *La Conquête et les débuts de la colonisation, 1827–1871* (Paris: PUF, 1964), 418.

2. Ahmad Badawi, *al-Zawiya mukhtariya Awlad Djilal* [guidebook published by the Zawiyya of Ouled-Djellal] (N.p.: n.p., n.d. [ca. 2003]); Julia Clancy-Smith, *Rebel and Saint: Muslim Notables, Populist Protest, Colonial Encounters (Algeria and Tunisia, 1800–1904)* (Berkeley: University of California Press, 1997); Youssef Nacib, *Cultures oasiennes: essai d'histoire sociale de l'oasis de Bou Saâda* (Algiers: ENAL, 1986); Kamel Filali, *L'Algérie mystique des marabouts fondateurs aux khwans insurgés XVe–XIXe siècles* (Paris: Publisud, 2002). Reputedly one of the best studies of the Rahmaniyya, the doctoral dissertation of Mohamed-Brahim Salhi remains unpublished and is unavailable in the United States. See "Etude d'une confrérie religieuse algérienne: la Rahmania à la fin du XIXe siècle et dans la première moitié du XXe siècle" (Ph.D. diss, EHESS, 1979). Among colonial works, see Louis Rinn, *Marabouts et khouan: étude sur l'islam en Algérie avec une carte indiquant la marche, la situation et l'importance des ordres religieux musulmans* (Algiers: A. Jourdan, 1884); Octave Depont and Xavier Coppolani, *Les Confréries religieuses musulmanes* (Paris: Maisonneuve and Geuthner, 1897); Adrien Delpêche, "Un diplôme de mokadem de la confrérie religieuse Rahmaniya," *Revue africaine* 18 (1874): 418–22.

3. Edmond Doutté, *Magie et religion dans l'Afrique du nord* (Algiers: Jourdan, 1908; reprint, Paris: Geuthner/Maisonneuve, 1983).

4. Gerhard Böwering, "Règles et rituels soufis," in Alexandre Popovic and Gilles Veinstein, eds., *Les Voies d'Allah: les ordres mystiques dans l'islam des origines à aujourd'hui* (Paris: Fayard, 1996), 140; E. Geoffroy, "Shaykh," *Encyclopaedia of Islam*, vol. 9 (Leiden: Brill, 1966), 397a.

5. For the controversial strategies of another important Sufi order, the Tijaniyya, see Jillali el-Adnani, *La Tijâniyya, 1781–1881: les origines d'une confrérie religieuse au Maghreb* (Rabat: Editions Marsam, 2007).

6. François de Villaret, *Siècles de steppe: jalons pour l'histoire de Djelfa; deuxième partie: les Oulad Naïl* (Ghardaïa: Centre de documentation saharienne, 1995), 111; Clancy-Smith, *Rebel and Saint*, 58, 195; Joseph-Adrien Séroka, "Le Sud Constantinois de 1830 à 1855," *Revue africaine* 56 (1912): 444, 509; Marc-Antoine Arnaud, "Histoire des Ouled Naïl, faisant suite à celle des Sahari," *Revue africaine* 17 (1873): 379–80; *Les Ben-Gana depuis la conquête française* (Paris: E. Dentu, 1879), 12–13. Letter of Bou Bekeur ben Mohamed Ennekhi, Cheikh Messaoud, Mohamed ben Selama, and Moubarek ben al-Hamara of Ouled-Djellal to Bou Ziyan (translation; original letter not attached), no. 27. CAOM 15 K 25; Borel de Bretizel, "Archives Journal de marche de la colonne de Zaatcha, septembre–novembre 1849," Constantine, 14 December 1849. CAOM 10 H 76; Ministère de la Guerre, *Tableau*

de la situation des établissements français dans l'Algérie, 1846–1847–1848–1849, vol. 9 (Paris: Imprimerie nationale, [November] 1851), 10.

7. Malek Bahous, *L'Insurrection des Ouled Sidi Cheikh, Si Slimane Ben Hamza, 1864* (Oran: Dar El Gharb, 2001).

8. A report of 1908 names them as Si Mohamed Seghir ben Cheikh (the leader of the *zawiya* of Ouled-Djellal), Si Ahmed ben Cheikh residing at the *zawiya* of Ouled-Djellal, and Si Belkacem ben Cheikh (Captain de spahis at Bou-Saada), Si Mostefa ben Cheikh, Si Boulanouar ben Cheikh, and Si Mohamed el Kebir ben Cheikh. Annual Report, Cercle de Djelfa, 1908. CAOM OASIS 78.

9. In 1862 Belkacem left the *zawiya* at Ouled-Djellal to the young son of Mokhtar (Si Mohamed Seghir ben Cheikh Mokhtar) and returned to El-Hamel. The *zawiya* here flourished under his leadership, but many Naïli groups refused political counsel emanating from El-Hamel — most notably in 1864, when they joined the Ouled Sidi Cheikh in revolt against Belkacem's wishes. They also sent their offerings to Mokhtar's son at Ouled-Djellal. Division de Constantine, Affaires arabes, to GGA, 29 March 1865, no. 180. CAOM 16 H 1; Annual Report, Cercle de Djelfa, 1908. CAOM OASIS 78; Clancy-Smith, *Rebel and Saint*, 214–53; al-Hajd Mazari, *al-Hamil: markaz ish'a thaqafi wa qala'a lil-djhad wa al-thawra* (Algiers: Dar al-Hakuma, 1993); Nacib, *Cultures oasiennes*, 238–63; Ahmed Nadir, "La Fortune d'un ordre religieux algérien vers la fin du XIXe siècle," *Le Mouvement social* 89 (October–December 1974): 59–84.

10. Affaires indigènes, GGA to Commandant d'Alger, 27 February 1907, no. 660. CAOM 2 U 22.

11. Lilla Abu Lughod, *Veiled Sentiments: Honor and Poetry in a Bedouin Society* (Berkeley: University of California Press, 1999), 39–69, 78–117; Pierre Bourdieu, *Algeria 1960* (Cambridge: Cambridge University Press, 1979); Boukhobza, *L'Agro-pastoralisme traditionnel en Algérie*, 80; Eickelman, *Moroccan Islam*, 141.

12. A schematic of the "administration indigène" is included in "Appendice," Ministère de la Guerre, *Tableau de la situation des établissements français dans l'Algérie, 1846–1847–1848–1849*, vol. 9 (Paris: Imprimerie nationale, [November] 1851), 716–19.

13. Rey-Goldzeiguer, *Le Royaume arabe*, 32.

14. Auguste Warnier and Ernest Carette, *Description et division de l'Algérie* (Paris and Algiers: Hachette, 1847).

15. Augustin Berque, "Esquisse d'une histoire de la seigneurie algérienne," *Revue de la Méditerranée* 7, no. 1 (1949): 26.

16. Mhfoud Smati, *Les Elites algériennes sous la colonisation* (Algiers: Imprimerie d'Ahlab, 1998), 44. An especially dramatic example of the divide separating French-appointed caids and local elites occurred in 1906 at Gourara. The caid, Kaci ben Bouhoun, outraged local leaders and their wives, who had been invited to celebrate the marriage of his nephew. Just as the guests were assembling a group of prostitutes who worked at his nephew's brothel decided to join the celebration. Kaci ben Bouhoun had invited the women to humiliate those local leaders who had opposed the newly opened brothel. Letter addressed to GGA, 29 December 1906. CAOM 22 H 16.

17. Ministère de la Guerre, *Tableau de la situation des établissements français*, 10.

18. Biwekly Reports, Cercle de Laghouat, 15 January 1855. CAOM 79 I 3.

19. Ibid.

20. Establet, *Etre caïd dans l'Algérie coloniale.*

21. Charles Cusson to Ministre de l'Intérieur, "Voyage à Ghadamès," Paris, 7 April 1874. CAOM F80 1733.

22. Colonel C. Trumelet, *Histoire de l'insurrection dans le Sud de la Province d'Alger en 1864* (Algiers: Adolphe Jourdan, 1879), 199. The practice of collecting a bounty for ears is documented in Comte d'Hérisson, *La Chasse à l'homme: guerres d'Algérie* (Paris: Paul Ollendorff, 1891), 124, 129, 133, 349. Hérisson recounts that they were often cut from living prisoners. A bounty of ten francs per pair of ears collected in rebel territories was paid well into the Second Empire.

23. Colonel de Colomb, "Note sur les Ouled Sidi Cheikh et sur le Cercle de Géryville," n.d. [ca. 1866]. CAOM 22 H 9.

24. Hamza Boubakeur, *Un soufi algérien, Sidi Cheikh: sa vie, son oeuvre, son rôle historique, ses descendants* (Paris: Maisonneuve et Larose, 1999).

25. De Colomb "Note sur les Ouled Sidi Cheikh." CAOM 22 H 9.

26. Villaret, *Siècles de steppe,* 110–17.

27. After the defeat of Abdelkader, Si Chérif was imprisoned at Boghar until 1850. He played no role in Bou Ziyan's uprising. See Villaret, *Siècles de steppe,* 120–22.

28. Ibid., 122. See also Monthly Report, Annexe de Djelfa, August 1858. CAOM 75 I 4.

29. Villaret, *Siècles de steppe,* 127.

30. Abdellah Hammoudi, "Sainteté, pouvoir et société: Tamgrout aux XVIIe et XVIIIe siècles," *Annales, économies, sociétés, civilisations* 35, nos. 3–4 (1980): 617.

31. Abdellah Hammoudi, "Segmentarité, stratification sociale, pouvoir politique et sainteté : réflexions sur les thèses de Gellner," *Hespêris Tamuda* 15 (1974): 147–77; idem, "The Path of Sainthood: Structure and Danger," *Princeton Papers in Near Eastern Studies* 3 (1994): 71–88. See also Raymond Jamous, *Honneur et baraka: les structures sociales traditionnelles dans le Rif* (Paris: Maison des Sciences de l'Homme; Cambridge: Cambridge University Press, 1981).

32. Arnaud, "Attaque nocturne de Djelfa par des *khouans*," Djelfa, 9 May 1861. CAOM 16 H 1.

33. Ibid.

34. Ibid. In the article where this account was eventually published, Arnaud (or the editors) modified the text: "C'était un homme d'environ trente-cinq ans, d'une complexion frêle et délicate, à la barbe clair-semée. Il n'avait aucune espèce d'instruction, et, par son origine et sa position de fortune, appartenait à la dernière classe des gens de la tribu. Avant d'être *l'Inspiré du Prophète*, il s'estimait très-heureux de pouvoir s'attribuer la qualité d'homme de peine d'un spahis. Mais il était affilié à la confrérie des Rahmania, dont font partie la plupart des Ouled Naïl." Arnaud, "Histoire des Ouled Naïl," *Revue africaine* 17 (1873): 384.

35. "Procès-verbal d'information sur les meurtres commis dans la nuit du 14–15 avril lors de l'attaque du village de Djelfa. Interrogatoire des accusés," no. 2. Cercle de Laghouat. CAOM 16 H 1. This is confirmed by the Dursus Report, which dates this service to 1856 at Laghouat. See Dursus Report, 6 May 1861. CAOM 16 H 1.

36. "Procès-verbal d'information sur les meurtres," no. 2.

37. Arnaud, "Histoire des Ouled Naïl," 385.

38. Testimony of Ahmed ben Fereuch, "Procès-verbal d'information sur les meurtres," no. 2.

39. Testimony of Messaoud ben Mohad, "Procès-verbal d'information sur les meurtres," no. 2.

40. Testimony of Ali ben Mokhtar (brother of Caïd ben Slim ben Fedaïl des Ouled Si Ahmed), "Texte du procès-verbal de la commission de Comandant de Sonis," Djelfa, 18 April 1861. Copy forwarded by the Affaires arabes, Division d'Alger to GGA, Algiers, 30 April 1861, no. 268. CAOM 16 H 1. His testimony is discussed at length in the narrative report of Commandant Dursus, which quotes this passage virtually verbatim. See Dursus Report, 6 May 1861. CAOM 16 H 1

41. Testimony of Salem ben Mohad ben Bachir, "Procès-verbal d'information sur les meurtres," no. 2.

42. Kamel Filali, "Quelques modalités d'opposition entre marabouts: mystiques et élites du pouvoir, en Algérie, à l'époque ottomane," in Frederick de Jong and Bernd Radtke, eds., *Islamic Mysticism Contested: Thirteen Centuries of Controversies and Polemics* (Leiden: Brill, 1999), 248.

43. For most French observers "marabout" was a generic title for any personage of religious importance as well as for the tombs of saints.

44. Jacques Berque, *L'Intérieur du Maghreb* (Paris: Gallimard, 1978), 53–56, 410–28; Michael Brett, "Mufti, Mrabit, Marabout and Mahdi: Four Types in the Islamic History of North Africa," *Revue de l'occident musulman et de la Méditerranée* 29 (1980): 5–15; Allan Christelow, "Saintly Descent and Worldly Affairs in Mid-Nineteenth-Century Mascara, Algeria," *International Journal of Middle East Studies* 12 (1980): 129–55; Edmond Doutté, "Les Marabouts," *Revue de l'histoire des religions* 19, no. 39 (1899): 343–69 (article continued in 21, no. 41 [1900]: 22–66; 21, no. 41 [1900]: 289–336); Filali, *L'Algérie mystique*; Gellner, *Saints of the Atlas*; Abdellah Hammoudi, *The Victim and Its Masks: An Essay on Sacrifice and Masquerade in the Maghreb*, trans. Paula Wissing (Chicago: University of Chicago Press, 1993); Jonathan G. Katz, "Visionary Experience, Autobiography and Sainthood in North African Islam," *Princeton Papers in Near Eastern Studies* 1 (1992): 85–118; Nasser Rabbat, "Ribāt," *Encyclopaedia of Islam*, vol. 8 (Leiden: Brill, 1963), 439b; Pessah Shinar, "Note on the Socio-economic and Cultural Role of Sufi Brotherhoods and Marabutism in the Modern Maghrib," *Proceedings of the First International Congress of Africanists*, ed. Lalage Brown and Michael Crowder (London: Longmans, 1964), 275; and Houari Touati, *Entre dieu et les hommes: lettrés, saints, et sorciers au Maghreb, 17e siècle* (Paris: EHESS, 1994).

45. Giovanni Levi, *Inheriting Power: The Story of an Exorcist*, trans. Lydia G. Cochrane (Chicago: University of Chicago Press, 1988).

46. Touati, *Entre dieu et les hommes*, 193–223.

47. These categories are admittedly schematic. I am attentive to Houari Touati's warning against "decoupages commodes" of savant-popular, scriptural-extatique, urban-rural saints. See Touati, *Entre dieu et les hommes*, 12.

48. Filali, *L'Algérie mystique*, 14.

49. Touati, *Entre dieu et les hommes*, 139.

50. Filali, *L'Algérie mystique*, 14.

51. Joseph Chelhod, "La *baraka* chez les Arabes ou l'influence bienfaisante du sacré," *Revue de l'histoire des religions* 148 (1955): 67–88; Edmond Doutté, *Magie et religion dans l'Afrique du nord* (Algiers: Jourdan, 1908; reprint, Paris: Geuthner/Maisonneuve, 1983), 439–40; Jamous, *Honneur et baraka*, 207–10.

52. Clifford Geertz, *Islam Observed: Religious Development in Morocco and Indonesia* (Chicago: University of Chicago Press, 1968), 33.

53. G.. S. Colin, "*Baraka*," *Encyclopaedia of Islam*, vol. 1 (Leiden: Brill, 1963), 1032a; Edward Westermarck, *Ritual and Belief in Morocco* (New Hyde Park, N.Y.: University Books, 1926).

54. Marc Bloch, *Les Rois thaumaturges: étude sur le caractère surnaturel attribué à la puissance royale particulièrement en France et en Angleterre* (Paris: A. Colin, 1961). See also Clifford Geertz, *Local Knowledge: Further Essays in Interpretive Anthropology* (New York: Basic Books, 1983), 121–47.

55. Chelhod, "La *baraka* chez les Arabes," 70.

56. Geertz, *Islam Observed*, 43–46.

57. Hammoudi, "The Path of Sainthood."

58. Touati, *Entre dieu et les hommes*, 133.

59. Ibid., 134

60. Literally meaning "placed in front," a *mukaddam* was an individual "sent in advance" on the authority of the sheikh of the tarīka (i.e., his chosen lieutenant or representative).

61. Testimony of Kouider ben Mohad, "Procès-verbal d'information sur les meurtres," no. 2. The annual report for 1860 notes that Si Chérif organized Koranic instruction in a small *zawiya* on behalf of the Rahmaniyya, and that he made the *ziyāra* to Si Mokhtar at Ouled-Djellal. See Annual Reports, Annexe de Djelfa, 17 December 1860. CAOM 75 I 13.

62. It was Si Sadoq to whom Dursus granted the travel permit for the pilgrims to go to Ouled-Djellal.

63. Arnaud, "Histoire des Ouled Naïl," 385.

64. Ibid.

65. The relation seems to be close to the "concurrence sourde" that animated secular rivalries. See Boukhobza, *L'Agro-pastoralisme traditionnel en Algérie*, 75.

66. Testimony of Ahatah ben Mokhtar of the Ouled Si Ahmed, "Procès-verbal d'information sur les meurtres," no. 2.

6. A Holiday Gone Wrong

1. Testimony of Ali ben Mokhtar (brother of Caïd ben Slim ben Fedaïl des Ouled Si Ahmed), "Texte du procès-verbal de la commission du Commandant de Sonis, fait à Djelfa, 18 avril 1861." Copy forwarded by the Affaires arabes, Division d'Alger to GGA, Algiers, 30 April 1861, no. 268. CAOM 16 H 1.

2. Ben Slim ben Fedaïl was a spahis when he was named caid of the Ouled Si Ahmed in December 1856. Monthly Report, Annexe de Djelfa, October and December 1856. CAOM 75 I 4.

3. Attendance included three Ouled el-Ghouini (El Hachmi ben Mamar, Mohamed ben Saad [both killed in the attack], and Mohamed ben Said); twenty-seven individuals from the Ouled Bou Abdallah, Ouled Maileb, Ouled el Haki, and Ouled Slim; and three people from the Sahari. Ali ben Mokhtar, "Texte du procès-verbal de la commission de Commandant de Sonis, fait à Djelfa, 18 avril 1861." Division d'Alger to GGA, 30 April 1861, no. 268. CAOM 16 H 1.

4. Ibid.

5. Ibid.

6. Ibid.

7. Dursus Report, Djelfa, 6 May 1861. CAOM 16 H 1.

8. Testimony of Salem ben Mohad ben Bachir, "Procès-verbal d'information sur les meurtres commis dans la nuit du 14–15 avril lors de l'attaque du village de Djelfa, n° 2, interrogatoire des accusés," CAOM 16 H 1.

9. Ibid.

10. Ibid.

11. Ibid.

12. Testimony of Kouider ben Mohad, "Procès-verbal d'information sur les meurtres, no. 2." CAOM 16 H 1. See also Arnaud, "Attaque nocturne de Djelfa par des *khouans*," Djelfa, 9 May 1861. CAOM 16 H 1. There are other versions of Si Tayeb's words announcing the attack. In one he is quoted as saying: "Qu'importe [our lack of weapons]; la poudre des français ne partira pas; je soufflerai sur eux ou je présenterai mon doigt; il disparaîtront." Dursus Report, 6 May 1861. CAOM 16 H 1.

13. Attia ben Chourah ben Tsameur, "Procès-verbal d'information sur les meurtres commis dans la nuit du 14–15 avril lors de l'attaque du village de Djelfa, no. 1, déposition des témoins," Djelfa, 15 April 1861. CAOM 16 H 1.

14. Ibid.

15. Doutté, *Magie et religion dans l'Afrique du nord*, 239–42.

16. Testimony of Ben Ahmed, "Procès-verbal d'information sur les meurtres, no. 2." CAOM 16 H 1.

17. Testimony of Khadir ben Djemai, "Procès-verbal no. 268." CAOM 16 H 1.

18. Arnaud, "Attaque nocturne de Djelfa par des *khouans.*"

19. Testimony of Ahmed ben Kouider ben Amran, "Procès-verbal d'information sur les meurtres, no. 1." CAOM 16 H 1. The list of those leaving Si Tayeb before the attack includes:

Ahmed ben Kouider ben Amran: 18 years old; of the Ouled Slim

Salem ben Mohadben Bachir: 24 years old; of the Ouled Chérif

Ahmed ben Kouider ben Ahmed: 18–20 years old; the herder of Si Sadoq ben Sifer

Ahmed ben Si Tayeb: age unknown; of the Ouled Maileb.

Ahmed ben Touït: 22 years old; of the Ouled Abd el Kader.

Abdelkader ben Ahmed: 22 years old; of the Ouled Si Ahmed

Ahatah ben Mokhtar: 18 years old; of the Ouled Djaballah

"Procès-verbal d'information sur les meurtres, no. 1"; and "Procès-verbal d'information sur les meurtres, no. 2." CAOM 16 H 1.

20. Testimony of Kouider ben Mohad, "Procès-verbal d'information sur les meurtres, no. 2." CAOM 16 H 1. See also Arnaud, "Histoire des Ouled Naïl," 389.

21. Oscar MacCarthy, *Géographie physique, économique et politique de l'Algérie* (Algiers: Dubos frères, 1858), 363.

22. Monthly Report, Annexe de Djelfa, December 1856. CAOM 75 I 4.

23. Georges Perec, *L'Infra-ordinaire* (Paris: Seuil, 1989).

24. Testimony of Félix Bazan. "Procès-verbal d'information sur les meurtres, no. 1." CAOM 16 H 1.

25. Testimony of Jean Fournier, "Procès-verbal d'information sur les meurtres, no. 1."

CAOM 16 H 1; "Rapport sur les blessures des colons, soldats et indigènes attaqués pendant la nuit du 14 avril 1861 à Djelfa." CAOM 16 H 1.

26. "Rapport sur les blessures des colons soldats." CAOM 16 H 1.

27. "Rapport médico-légal sur la mort de nommés Fourés, Drouin et Fournier tués pendant la nuit de 14 avril 1861." CAOM 16 H 1.

28. "Texte du procès-verbal de la commission du Commandant de Sonis. CAOM 16 H 1. Mokhtar was executed.

29. Kouider ben Mohad, "Procès-verbal d'information sur les meurtres, no. 2." CAOM 16 H 1.

30. "Procès-verbal d'information sur les meurtres, no. 1." CAOM 16 H 1.

31. Ibid.

32. Ibid.

33. Ibid. The identity of the "Rissaouas" is uncertain.

34. Arnaud, "Attaque nocturne de Djelfa par des *khouans.*"

35. "Rapport sur les blessures des colons, soldats." CAOM 16 H 1.

36. "Rapport médico-légal sur la mort de nommés Fourés, Drouin et Fournier." CAOM 16 H 1.

37. Ibid.

38. "Procès-verbal d'information sur les meurtres, no. 1." CAOM 16 H 1.

39. "Rapport sur les blessures des colons, soldats." CAOM 16 H 1.

40. Ibid.

41. Dursus Report, Djelfa, 6 May 1861. CAOM 16 H 1.

42. Khadir ben Djemal, "Texte du procès-verbal de la commission du Commandant de Sonis"; and Arnaud, "Attaque nocturne de Djelfa."

43. Arnaud, "Attaque nocturne de Djelfa."

44. "Texte du procès-verbal de la commission du Commandant de Sonis." CAOM 16 H 1.

45. Ibid.

46. Ibid. Four of the ten accused—Embarek ben Abdelmalek, Bou Bakeur ben Ali, Yahia ben Taieb, and Belkassem ben Seddik—admitted to throwing stones but nothing more. Nevertheless, they were all executed by firing squad.

47. René Girard, *Violence and the Sacred*, trans. Patrick Gregory (Baltimore, Md.: Johns Hopkins University Press, 1977), 125.

48. Alain Corbin, *The Village of Cannibals: Rage and Murder in France, 1870*, trans. Arthur Goldhammer (Cambridge, Mass.: Harvard University Press, 1992); Georges Lefebvre, *The Great Fear of 1789: Rural Panic in Revolutionary France*, trans. Joan White (New York: Pantheon Books, 1973); Frantz Fanon, *The Wretched of the Earth*, trans. Richard Philcox (New York: Grove Press, 2004); Pierre Bourdieu and Abdelmalek Sayad, *Le Déracinement ou la crise de l'agriculture traditionnelle en Algérie* (Paris: Editions de minuit, 1964).

49. Rudolph Peters, *Islam and Colonialism* (The Hague: Mouton, 1980); Michael Bonner, *Jihad in Islamic History: Doctrines and Practice* (Princeton, N.J.: Princeton University Press, 2006).

50. Clancy-Smith, *Rebel and Saint*.

51. Report of Commandant Marguerite of Laghouat to GGA, 31 March 1855. CAOM 79 I 3.

52. Michael Bonner, *Jihad in Islamic History: Doctrines and Practice* (Princeton, N.J.: Princeton University Press, 2006).

53. Peter von Sivers, "The Realm of Justice: Apocalyptic Revolts in Algeria, 1849–1879," *Humaniora Islamica* 1 (1973): 48–49.

54. Mohammed Arkoun, *L'Islam, religion et société: interviews dirigées par Mario Arosio,* trans. Marucie Borrman (Paris: Editions du Cerf, 1982), 20. See also Mohammed Arkoun, *Essais sur la pensée islamique* (Paris: Maisonneuve et Larose, 1977); Olivier Roy, *Globalized Islam: The Search for a New Ummah* (New York: Columbia University Press, 2004).

55. Fanny Colonna, "Cultural Resistance and Religious Legitimacy in Colonial Algeria," *Economy and Society* 3, no. 3 (August 1974): 234; emphasis added.

7. Saaba's Journey to Algerian Slavery

1. Raymond Mauny, *Tableau géographique de l'ouest africaine au Moyen Age, d'après les sources écrites, la tradition, et l'archéologie* (Amsterdam: Swets & Zeitlinger N.V., 1967).

2. Jean Lethielleux, *Ouargla, cité saharienne: des origines au début du XXe siècle* (Paris: Geuthner, 1983), 161.

3. "Africa's Intellectual Caravans: *Bilad as Sudan* and *al Maghaarib*" was the full title of the inaugural symposium of the Sudanic Maghaarib Studies Unit in the Africana Studies Department at Vassar College, November 2002.

4. Lethielleux, *Ouargla, cité saharienne*. See also Abdoulhadi Hamit, *La Piste du commerce transsaharien: étude d'anthropologie économique et historique* (Villeneuve d'Ascq, France: Presses universitaires du septentrion, 1998); Jean-Louis Miège, *Le Maroc et l'Europe*, 4 vols. (Paris: PUF, 1962); John E. Lavers, "Trans-Saharan Trade before 1800: Towards Quantification," *Paideuma* 40 (1994): 243–78; Adu A. Boahen, "The Caravan Trade in the Nineteenth Century," *Journal of African History* 2 (1962): 349–59; André Martel, *Les Confines saharo-tripolitains de la Tunisie, 1881–1911* (Paris: PUF, 1965).

5. See "Rapport sur la question de commerce avec l'Afrique centrale." Laghouat, 10 March 1860. CAOM 22 H 26.

6. They lost a total of 5,872 date palms. Of these 2,347 were sold or rented to the new agha (Subdivision of Médéa to GGA, 17 February 1879, no. 137. CAOM 1 I 124). Another seven gardens consisting of 2,007 palms were sequestered in 1866 but remained under the care of four "nègres" (slaves or freed slaves) until the rebels received *aman* from the French in 1873. Gouverneur général civil, Secrétariat général des finances to Commandant Division d'Alger, Algiers, 28 March 1881, no. 1056. CAOM 1 I 124.

7. Lacroix, "Notice sur Bou Choucha," Algiers, 19 July 1873, and the anonymous entry "Note sur le faux chérif Bou Choucha," n.d. [1874]—both in CAOM 2 H 84. See also Monthly Report, Cercle de Laghouat, May 1874. CAOM 79 I 4.

8. Subdivision of Batna to Division of Constantine, Ouargla, 14 January 1872, no. 6. CAOM 10 H 76. A symbol of French power, the square also served military necessity: the labyrinth of winding alleys that made up urban Ouargla had no space large enough to assemble troops.

9. Norbert Dournaux-Dupere, "Voyage au Sahara, rédigé d'après son journal et ses notes, par Henri Duveyrier," *Bulletin de la Société de géographie de Paris* (August 1874): 113–70.

10. Monthly Report, Cercle de Laghouat, June 1874. CAOM 79 I 4.

11. Situation trimestrielle du 17 mars au 10 juin 1873, Annexe de Touggourt, no. 139. CAOM 18 K 4.

12. Victor Largeau, *Le Pays de Rirha–Ouargla–Voyage à Rhadamès* (Paris: Hachette, 1879), 224.

13. Ibid., 225.

14. Cabinet, Provence de Constantine, Armée d'Afrique to Ministre de la Guerre, 3 January 1845, no. 1. CAOM 12 X 19; Capitaine Durrieu, "Renseignements sur l'introduction et le commerce des nègres esclaves dans la subdivision de Médéa," Bureau arabe de Médéa, Médéa, 27 January 1845. CAOM 12 X 19.

15. P. Rozet et E. Carette, *Algérie* (1850; reprint, Paris: Bouslama, 1980), 109.

16. Durrieu, "Renseignements." CAOM 50 II 265.

17. Two dollars went toward food and clothing for the slave, with one dollar going to the master. See Tabias Lear to William Shaler, Washington, 23 April 1815. NARA College Park, RG 84, Vol. 01.

18. Durrieu, "Renseignements." CAOM 50 II 265. While this continued to be the norm, some Europeans did, in fact, purchase slaves after 1848. The last documented case I'm aware of is that of Alexandre Joly, who purchased a girl in 1900. Then an instructor at the madrasa of Algiers, in 1900 Joly returned home from the French conquest of In Salah with Berika, a ten-year-old girl originally from Timbuktu. Joly had paid 250 francs for her at the small oasis of Igli. A local Algerian woman complained of Joly's repeated beatings of the girl to the prefecture office in Algiers. The governor-general ordered her emancipation. See Préfet d'Alger to GGA, Algiers, 9 July 1900, no. 4769. CAOM 4 H 16.

19. Largeau to Commandant Aublin, chef des affaires politiques, to GGA, El Oued, 10 December 1875. CAOM 4 H 8–10; emphasis added.

20. Largeau, *Le Pays de Rirha*, 226.

21. John Wright, *The Trans-Saharan Slave Trade* (London: Routledge, 2007), 168.

22. Ibid., 167.

23. Paul Farmer, "An Anthropology of Structural Violence," *Current Anthropology* 45, no. 3 (June 2004): 307.

24. John O. Hunwick, "Islamic Law and Polemics over Race and Slavery in North and West Africa (16th–19th Centuries)," *Princeton Papers: Interdisciplinary Journal of Middle East Studies* 7 (2000): 43–68; Pierre Bourdieu, *Masculine Domination*, trans. Richard Nice (Stanford: Stanford University Press, 2001), 33–42; Pierre Bourdieu and Loïc J. D. Wacquant, *An Invitation to Reflexive Sociology* (Chicago: University of Chicago Press, 1992), 162–72.

25. One exception to this rule is CAOM 12 H 50, a carton that appears to have been assembled following a renewed effort (begun in 1905–6) by colonial officials to end slavery.

26. Carlo Ginzburg, "Microhistory: Two or Three Things That I Know about It," *Critical Inquiry* 20, no. 1 (autumn 1993): 21.

27. James C. Scott, *Weapons of the Weak: Everyday Forms of Peasant Resistance* (New Haven, Conn.: Yale University Press, 1985).

28. Largeau, *Le Pays de Rirha*, 228.

29. Ibid.

30. David Robinson, *The Holy War of Umar Tal: The Western Sudan in the Mid-Nineteenth Century* (Oxford: Clarendon Press, 1985); John H. Hanson and David Robinson, *After the Jihad: The Reign of Ahmad al-Kabir in the Western Sudan* (East Lansing: Michigan State University Press, 1991). See also John H. Hanson, *Migration, Jihad, and Muslim Authority in West Africa: The Futanke Colonies in Karta* (Bloomington: Indiana University Press, 1996); Richard Roberts, *Warriors, Merchants, and Slaves: The State and the Economy in the Middle Niger Valley, 1700–1914* (Stanford, Calif.: Stanford University Press, 1987); B. G. Martin, *Muslim Brotherhoods in Nineteenth-Century Africa* (Cambridge: Cambridge University Press, 1976); Bintou Sanankoua, *Un empire peul au XIXe siècle: la Diina du Maasina* (Paris: Karthala, 1990); Jean-Louis Triaud and David Robinson, eds., *La Tijaniya: une confrérie musulmane à la conquête de l'Afrique* (Paris: Karthala, 2000).

31. Robinson *The Holy War of Umar Tal*, 334.

32. Ibid., 313.

33. Claude Meillassoux, *L'Esclavage en Afrique précoloniale* (Paris: Maspero, 1975), 62.

34. Durrieu, "Renseignements." CAOM 50 II 265.

35. The Tuareg then returned north and sold the captives at Timimoun, Aoulef, and the Tidikelt. They traded captives for burnous, haiks, tobacco, dates, and henna.

36. Largeau, *Le Pays de Rirha*, 228.

37. Ibid., 229.

38. Joseph-Simon Gallieni, *Voyage au Soudan français (Haut Niger et pays de Ségou), 1878–1881* (Paris: Hachette, 1885), 317.

39. Largeau, *Le Pays de Rirha*, 229.

40. R. Brunschvig, "Abd," in *The Encyclopaedia of Islam*, vol. 1 (Leiden: Brill, 1960), 180a; "Code de l'esclavage chez les Musulmans," in Eugène Daumas and Ausone de Chancel, *Le Grand Désert ou l'itinéraire d'une caravane du Sahara au pays des nègres* (Paris: Napoléon Chaix et Cie, 1848), 419–43; David S. Powers, *Law, Society, and Culture in the Maghrib, 1300–1500* (Cambridge: Cambridge University Press, 2002), 23–52.

41. Hunwick, "Islamic Law and Polemics over Race and Slavery."

42. John O. Hunwick, "Notes on Slavery in the Songhay Empire," in John Ralph Willis, ed., *Slaves and Slavery in Muslim Africa*, vol. 2, *The Servile Estate* (London: Frank Cass, 1985), 19.

43. Wright, *The Trans-Saharan Slave Trade*, 50; Allan Richard Meyers, "The Abid l-Buhari: Slave Soldiers and Statecraft in Morocco" (Ph.D. diss., Cornell University, 1974).

44. Colin, "Hartani," *Encyclopaedia of Islam*.

45. Chouki El Hamel, "'Race,' Slavery and Islam in Maghrebi Mediterranean Thought: The Question of the *Haratin* in Morocco," *Journal of North African Studies* 7, no. 3 (2002): 29–52.

46. Majda Tangi, *Contribution à l'étude de l'histoire des "Sudan" au Maroc du début de l'islamisation jusqu'au début du XVIIIème siècle* (Villeneuve d'Ascq, France: Presse universitaires du septentrion, 1994), 49–51. See also Aziz Abdalla Batran, "The 'Ulama' of Fas, M. Isma'il and the Issue of the Haratin of Fas," in Willis, ed., *Slaves and Slavery in Muslim Africa*, vol. 2, 1–15.

47. Mahmoud Zouber, *Ahmad Baba de Tombouctou (1556–1627): sa vie et son oeuvre* (Paris: Maisonneuve et Larose, 1977).

48. Ahmad Baba, "Mi'rāj al-Ṣu'ūd, Aḥmad Bābā's Replies on Slavery," ed. and trans. John Hunwick and Fatima Harrack, *Textes et Documents* (University Mohammed V, Institute of African Studies) 7 (2000): 7–65.

49. Ibid., 7.

50. Ibid., 13.

51. Hunwick, "Islamic Law and Polemics over Race and Slavery."

52. David M. Goldenberg, *The Curse of Ham: Race and Slavery in Early Judaism, Christianity, and Islam* (Princeton, N.J.: Princeton University Press, 2003); Edith R. Sanders, "The Hamitic Hypothesis: Its Origins and Functions in Time Perspective," *Journal of African History* 10, no. 4 (1969): 521–32; Ephraim Isaac, "Genesis, Judaism, and the Sons of Ham," in Willis, ed., *Slaves and Slavery in Muslim Africa*, vol. 1, *Islam and the Ideology of Enslavement*, 75–91. See also Ephraim Isaac, "The Boast of Superiority of the Blacks over the Whites," excerpted in Bernard Lewis, *Islam from the Prophet Muhammad to the Capture of Constantinople* (London: Oxford University Press, 1987), 210–16.

53. Ahmad Baba, "Mi'rāj al-Ṣu'ūd," 27 and 40.

54. Ibid., 29.

55. For a discussion of physical differences and social categorization see Derrick J. Stenning, *Savannah Nomads: A Study of the Wodaabe Pastoral Fulani of Western Bornu Province Northern Region, Nigeria* (London: Oxford University Press, 1959), 17; and Jean-Pierre Olivier de Sardan, *Les sociétés Songhay-Zarma (Niger-Mali) Chefs, guerriers, esclaves, paysans* (Paris: Karthala, 1984), 38.

56. Hunwick, "Islamic Law and Polemics over Race and Slavery."

57. Ahmad Baba, "Mi'rāj al-Ṣu'ūd," 31. Ahmad Baba continued by recounting Ibn Khaldun's environmental explanations explaining skin color differences as a result of climate varieties. Ibn Khaldun, *The Muqaddimah: An Introduction to History*, vol. I., trans. Franz Rosenthal (New York: Pantheon, 1958), 169–170.

58. Ahmad Baba, "Mi'rāj al-Ṣu'ūd," 32.

59. Ibid.

60. Ibid., 34–35.

61. Hunwick, "Islamic Law and Polemics over Race and Slavery," 51.

62. Letter of 24 January 1840. Quoted in Marcel Emerit et al., *La Révolution de 1848 en Algérie* (Paris: Larose, 1949), 37; emphasis added.

63. A. Leriche, "Les Haratin (Mauritanie), Note ethnographique et linguistique," *Bulletin de liaison saharienne* 6 (octobre 1951): 24–29.

64. Louis Blinn, "Les Noirs dans l'Algérie contemporaine," *Politique africaine* 30 (June 1980): 22–31; Zygmunt Komorowski, "Les Descendants des Soudanais en Algérie et leurs traditions," *Africana Bulletin* (Warsaw) 15 (1971): 43–53.

65. "Rapport de Capitaine Jacques, Commandant la 2e Cie de Tirailleurs sahariens sur l'élément nègre de la Cie," El Goléa, 4 June 1900. SHAT 1 H 1032.

66. Ahmad Baba, "Mi'rāj al-Ṣu'ūd," 35.

67. Ibid.

68. Largeau, *Le Pays de Rirha*, 229.

69. Robert Capot-Rey, *Le Sahara français* (Paris: PUF, 1953).

70. Président de Chambre de Commerce d'Alger (signé Vallier), 13 July 1876. CAOM 22 H 26. Consulat français de Tripoli to GGA, 19 April 1876, no. 1; 30 June 1876, no. 4; 27

July 1876, no. 4. Consulat français de Tripoli to Affaires étrangères, 23 December 1874; 8 October 1876. CAOM 22 H 26.

71. Abolition efforts had forced slave traders to conduct their transactions in this location south of the main port city.

72. P. Henderson to the Earl of Derby, Benghazi, 24 December 1875. Quoted in Bernard Lewis, *Race and Slavery in the Middle East: An Historical Enquiry* (New York: Oxford University Press, 1990), 164.

73. Dennis D. Cordell and Ralph A. Austen, "Trade Transportation, and Expanding Economic Networks: Saharan Caravan Commerce in the Era of European Expansion, 1500–1900," in *Black Business and Economic Power*, ed. Alusine Jalloh and Toyin Falola (Rochester, N.Y.: University of Rochester Press, 2002), 92.

74. Table 2, "Slave Trade: 'Maghrib' and Sahara," in Ralph A. Austen, "The Mediterranean Islamic Slave Trade out of Africa: A Tentative Census," *Slavery and Abolition* 13, no. 1 (April 1992): 223–27.

75. Table 2, "Adjustments for Death Rates," in Austen, "The Mediterranean Islamic Slave Trade," 227.

76. Fulgence Fresnel, "Mémoire sur les caravanes africaines qui parcourent l'espace compris entre l'oasis de Touat et les frontières occidentales de l'Egypte et du Darfour," Benghazi, 1 September 1846. CAOM 1 E 182. See also John Wright, "The Wadi—Benghazi Slave Route," *Slavery and Abolition* 13, no.1 (April 1992): 174–84; idem, *The Trans-Saharan Slave Trade*, 103–13.

77. Daumas and Chancel, *Le Grand Désert*, xiii.

78. Lethielleux, *Ouargla, cité saharienne*, 163.

79. Benjamin Claude Brower, "The Servile Populations of the Algerian Sahara Seen Through the French Colonial Archive," in Paul Lovejoy, Ismael Montana, and Behnaz Mirzai, eds., *Slavery, Islam, and Diaspora* (Trenton, N.J.: Africa World Press, 2009).

80. Monthly Reports, September 1891, Annexe d'Ouargla. CAOM 78 I 1.

81. This story was confirmed by Brahim ben Teggai, who was from In Salah and brought the news to Ouargla after a visit home. Monthly Report, April 1890, Cercle de Ghardaïa. CAOM 76 I 3.

8. The Saharan Slave Trade and Abolition

1. Elisabeth C. Van Der Haven, "The Abolition of Slavery in Tunisia (1846)," *Revue d'histoire maghrébine* 27, nos. 99–100 (May 2000): 449–64; Abdelhamid Largueche, *L'Abolition de l'esclavage en Tunisie à travers les archives, 1841–46* (Tunis: Société tunisienne d'étude du XVIIIe siècle, 1990).

2. Wright, *The Trans-Saharan Slave Trade*; Ehud R. Toledano, *The Ottoman Slave Trade and Its Suppression, 1840–1890* (Princeton, N.J.: Princeton University Press, 1983); idem, *Slavery and Abolition in the Ottoman Middle East*.

3. Raëd Bader, "L'Esclavage dans l'Algérie coloniale, 1830–1870," *Revue d'histoire maghrébine* 26, nos. 93–94 (May 1999): 57–69.

4. "La Question de l'esclavage," signé Azessa de Montgravier, Capitaine d'artillerie, attachée aux Affaires arabes de la division d'Oran, n.d. [ca. 1848]. CAOM 12 H 50; Marcel

Emerit, "L'Abolition de l'esclavage," in Marcel.Emerit et al., *La Révolution de 1848 en Algérie* (Paris: Larose, 1949), 38.

5. Bugeaud to M. le Duc de Montmorency, président de l'Institut d'Afrique, Algiers, 4 October 1844. CAOM 2 EE 10.

6. Paul E. Lovejoy and Jan S. Hogendorn, *Slow Death for Slavery: The Course of Abolition in Northern Nigeria, 1897–1936* (Cambridge: Cambridge University Press, 1993); Roger Botte, "L'Esclavage africain après l'abolition de 1848," *Annales, histoire, sciences sociales* 5 (Sept.–Oct., 2000): 1009–37; Martin A. Klein, *Slavery and Colonial Rule in French West Africa* (Cambridge: Cambridge University Press, 1998); Martin A. Klein, ed., *Breaking the Chains: Slavery, Bondage, and Emancipation in Modern Africa and Asia* (Madison: University of Wisconsin Press, 1993); Suzanne Miers and Richard Roberts, eds., *The End of Slavery in Africa* (Madison: University of Wisconsin Press, 1988); Roberts, *Warriors, Merchants, and Slaves.*

7. He located sulfur deposits in the desert of Barkudota, or Cyrenaica, and made claim to them. The Pacha in Tripoli, apparently under pressure from the British consul, refused to recognize his rights. See Eugène Subtil, "Mémoire sur l'utilité d'établir des relations entre Abd el Gelill, chef du Fezzan, et la France," n.d. [ca. 1840]. CAOM 1 E 184.

8. Dennis D. Cordell, "The Awlad Sulayman of Libya and Chad: Power and Adaptation in the Sahara and Sahel," *Canadian Journal of African Studies* 19, no. 2 (1985): 319–43.

9. Subtil, "Mémoire sur l'utilité d'établir des relations entre Abd el Gelil, chef du Fezzan, et la France."

10. Ibid.

11. Who Subtil dealt with at the Ministry of War is unknown. This was a moment of rapidly changing ministries. Three men held the position of minister of war during this period: General Schneider (12 May 1839–1 March 1840), General Cubières (1 March 1840–29 October 1840), and Marshal Soult (29 October 1840–10 November 1845).

12. Subtil to M. le Ministère Soult, Président du Conseil, undated. CAOM 1 E 184. Soult served as prime minister from 12 May 1839 to 21 February 1840.

13. Anonymous analysis of Subtil's project dated 6 November 1840, letterhead of the Ministre de la Guerre, Direction des affaires d'Algérie, 1e bureau. CAOM 1 E 184. The same report recommends Subtil for the Legion of Honor, an award he received on 8 November 1840.

14. Ibid.

15. It took many years for Constantine to recover. Six years after the fall of the city to the French, the intendant militaire of the province of Constantine, M. Daganan, wrote, "Constantine est horrible à voir: toutes les constructions tombent en ruine, la moitié des maisons qui existaient il y a cinq ans se sont écroulées et les débris sont gisant sur place: la population indigène est dans un état affreux de misère et de privations: c'est un spectacle désolant qui navre le cœur." Constantine, 24 April 1843, in *Campagnes d'Afrique, 1835–1848: lettres adressées au Maréchal de Castellane* (Paris: Librairie Plon, 1898), 314

16. Undated, unaddressed note signed by Subtil. CAOM 1 E 184.

17. Unsigned, undated, unaddressed report on letterhead of the Ministre de la Guerre. CAOM 1 E 184.

18. Ibid.

19. In the nineteenth century about six thousand people crossed the Sahara as slaves annually. See Wright, *The Trans-Saharan Slave Trade*, 168.

20. Undated, unaddressed note signed Subtil. CAOM 1 E 184.

21. Ibid.

22. Thomas Robert Bugeaud, *De la colonisation de l'Algérie* (Paris: Guyot, imprimeur du Roi, 1847); idem, *L'Algérie des moyens de conserver et d'utiliser cette conquête* (Paris: Dentu, 1842), 49–50.

23. "Adresse de M. le Général Bugeaud, Chambre des députés [debate over "crédits supplémentaires," 1839–40], séance de 14 mai," in Thomas Robert Bugeaud, *Par l'épée et par la charrue: écrits et discours de Bugeaud*, ed. Paul Azan (Paris: PUF, 1948), 78; repunctuated for clarity.

24. Thomas Robert Bugeaud, "Mémoire sur notre établissement dans la province d'Oran par suite de la paix" (1837), in Maurice-Henri Weil, ed., *Œuvres militaires du Maréchal Bugeaud, Duc d'Isly* (Paris: Trois Hussards, 1982), 194.

25. Alain Corbin, *The Village of Cannibals: Rage and Murder in France, 1870*, trans. Arthur Goldhammer (Cambridge, Mass.: Harvard University Press, 1992), 9.

26. Ibid.

27. Undated, unaddressed note signed Subtil. CAOM 1 E 184.

28. A year later British authorities turned their abolition efforts from Tunis and Tripoli to Algeria. In April 1841 Lord Palmerston took up the matter of a French slave trader named Caracassone with the French minister of foreign affairs (Palmerston to M. le Baron Bougessey, Ministre des affaires étrangères, 19 April 1841. CAOM 1 E 181). Palmerston accused this individual of bringing slaves from Tripoli to Bône by boat and then overland to Constantine for the purpose of selling them and was prepared to back up his accusation with the names of the ships involved, among other details. Paris delayed its response until September, when pressure on the French chargé d'affaires in London prompted the foreign minister to demand an account from Bugeaud. Direction politique, Ministre des affaires étrangères, Paris, 2 September 1841; Secrétariat Général, Direction des affaires d'Algérie, 1e Bureau to Maréchal Bugeaud, Algiers, 27 September 1841, no. 300. CAOM 1 E 181.

29. Ibid.

30. Eugène Subtil, "Mémoire sur la marche des grandes caravanes de l'Afrique centrale, et sur les moyens à employer pour les faire arriver à Constantine, avec un supplément sur la colonisation de l'Algérie par les nègres libres de l'Afrique centrale," 15 June 1844. SHAT 1 H 229.

31. Ibid.

32. Ibid.

33. Subtil, "Mémoire sur la marche des grandes caravanes de l'Afrique centrale," marginal note signed [illegible], 29 June 1844. SHAT 1 H 229.

34. Capitaine E. Carette, "Rapport sur deux mémoires de M. Subtil relatifs au commerce de l'Afrique central," Paris, 13 September 1846. SHAT 1 H 229.

35. Ministère de la Guerre, *Tableau de la situation des établissements français dans l'Algérie, 1845–46*, vol. 9 (Paris: Imprimerie royale, 1846), 49.

36. Eugène Subtil, "Histoire d'Abd el Gelil, sultan du Fezzan, assassiné en 1842," *Revue de l'Orient: Bulletin de la Société oriental* 5, nos. 17–20 (1844): 3–30; idem, "Considérations politiques et commerciales sur Ghadamès: suivies d'un itinéraire de Tripoli à Ghadamès," *Revue de l'Orient: Bulletin de la Société oriental* 5, nos. 17–20 (1844): 97–123.

37. Barbara Leigh Smith Bodichon, *An American Diary, 1857–8*, ed. Joseph W. Reed, Jr.

(London: Routledge and Kegan Paul, 1972). For the role of Algeria in the feminist thinking of Barbara Leigh Smith Bodichon, see Deborah Cherry, "Earth into World, Land into Landscape: The 'Worlding' of Algeria in Nineteenth-Century British Feminism," in Jill Beaulieu and Mary Roberts, eds., *Orientalism's Interlocutors: Painting, Architecture, Photography* (Durham, N.C.: Duke University Press, 2002), 103–30.

38. Although Bodichon believed in an "Arab"-"Kabyle" divide, the positive characteristics of the Kabyle stereotype retreat in much of Bodichon's writing. When discussing extermination in Algeria, he slipped in between larger categories like "Moghrébin" and more specific ones like "Arabes." See Patricia M. E. Lorcin, *Imperial Identities: Stereotyping, Prejudice and Race in Colonial Algeria* (London: I. B. Tauris, 1995), 119–26.

39. Eugène Bodichon, *Etudes sur l'Algérie et l'Afrique* (Algiers: chez l'auteur [printed at Plon frères, Paris], 1847).

40. Patrick Brantlinger, *Dark Vanishings: Discourse on the Extinction of Primitive Races, 1800–1930* (Ithaca, N.Y.: Cornell University Press, 1993).

41. Jean-Christian-Marc Boudin, *Histoire statistique de la colonisation et de la population en Algérie* (Paris: J.-B. Baillère, 1853).

42. Eugène Bodichon, *Hygiène à suivre en Algérie: acclimatement des Européens* (Algiers: imprimerie de Rey, Delavigne et Cie, 1851). Bodichon became somewhat of an authority on this question and authors relied on his expertise. See Girard de Cailleux, "De l'acclimatation et particulièrement de son influence sur la constitution, la guérison et la mortalité des aliénés de la Seine transférés dans les asiles départementaux," *Journal d' hygiène mentale* 2 (1862): 125–34.

43. Bodichon, *Etudes sur l'Algérie et l'Afrique*, 124. This is from an article originally published in the *Réforme et courrier d'Afrique*.

44. Ibid., 128.

45. Ibid., 127.

46. Ibid., 145.

47. Ibid., 146.

48. Ibid., 151.

49. François-Auguste-René de Chateaubriand, *Atala, ou les amours de deux sauvages dans le désert* (Paris: Migneret, 1801; rev. ed. Paris: Le Normant, 1805); James Fenimore Cooper, *Le Dernier des Mohicans, histoire de 1757*, trans. A.-J.-B. Defauconpret (Paris: C. Gosselin; Mame et Delaunay-Vallée, 1826).

50. Bodichon, *Etudes sur l'Algérie et l'Afrique*, 133.

51. Ibid., 149.

52. Ibid., 142.

53. Ibid., 128–29.

54. Ibid., 132; emphasis added.

55. Ibid., 128.

56. Ibid., 150.

57. Ibid., 151.

58. Bodichon, *Etudes sur l'Algérie et l'Afrique*, 146.

59. Nelly Schmidt, *Victor Schœlcher et l'abolition de l'esclavage* (Paris: Fayard, 1994); Lawrence C. Jennings, *French Anti-Slavery: The Movement for the Abolition of Slavery in France, 1802–1848* (Cambridge: Cambridge University Press, 2000).

60. Johannes Nicolaisen and Ida Nicolaisen, *The Pastoral Tuareg: Ecology, Culture, and Society* (New York: Thames and Hudson, 1997), 597.

61. Renewed abolitionist efforts began with an anonymous 1905 report denouncing the widespread existence of slavery in Algeria, including slave sales in French marketplaces "400 kilomètres d'Alger," slave owning by Aurélie Picard-Tijani at the *zawiya* of Aïn Madi/ Kourdane, and the complicity of the French administration in returning and punishing fugitive slaves. See "Note," Cabinet, GGA, 2 June 1905. CAOM 12 H 50. In the newly formed Southern Territories this abolition effort was marked by the law of 15 July 1906 abolishing slave sales.

62. Gaston Martin, *Histoire de l'esclavage dans les colonies françaises* (Paris: PUF, 1948).

63. Claude Collot, *Les Institutions de l'Algérie durant la période coloniale, 1830–1962* (Paris: Editions du CNRS; Algiers: OPU, 1987).

64. Division d'Alger to GGA, 25 June 1848, no. 170. CAOM 1 H 1.

65. The reparation price of 428 francs per head was used by the analyst; the total number of slaves in the division was estimated at 6,277. See Montgravier, "La Question de l'esclavage." CAOM 12 H 50. Montgravier notes that children comprised two-thirds of the slave population.

66. GGA to subdivision de Mascara, 12 November 1857, no. 256. CAOM 20 J 42, cited in Dennis D. Cordell, "No Liberty, Not Much Equality, and Very Little Fraternity: The Mirage of Manumission in the Algerian Sahara in the Second Half of the Nineteenth Century," in *Slavery and Colonial Rule in Africa*, ed. Suzanne Miers and Martin Klein (London: Cass, 1999), 44; Cordell's translation.

67. GGA to Affaires arabes, division d'Oran, 15 August 1858, quoted in Cordell, "No Liberty, Not Much Equality, and Very Little Fraternity," 44.

68. Ibid., 45.

69. Captain Leselle found this in the archives during his research for his report; "Les Noirs du Souf," Manuscript, n.d. [1955], p. 21. CAOM 20 X 1; emphasis added.

70. CAOM 1 H 27, 1 H 28, 1 H 29.

71. "Confidentielle," division d'Oran, Affaires arabes to GGA, 2 August 1856, no. 290. CAOM 1 H 27.

72. "Confidentielle," Bureau Politique des Affaires indigènes, Algiers, 8 August 1856, no. 181. CAOM 1 H 27; emphasis added.

73. Bureau politique [des Affaires indigènes], "Minute," Algiers, 29 December 1857, no. 487. CAOM 12 H 50. This case involved the arrest of slave traders in the Cercle de Bordj bou Arreridj who arrived from Djelfa with ten slaves, one of whom, a woman, died during the journey.

74. In Salah was then dominated by the Ouled Badjouda, relatives of the Ouled Dahou.

75. GGA to division d'Alger, n.d. [ca. May 1896]. CAOM 22 H 54.

76. Les Affaires indigènes to GGA, 10 August 1893. CAOM 22 H 38.

77. Les Affaires indigènes to GGA, 7 July 1893, no. 576. CAOM 22 H 38.

78. Labrousse to division d'Alger, 2 January 1862. CAOM 22 H 14.

79. Unaddressed letter by Labrousse dated 3 January 1862. CAOM 22 H 14. For details on Labrousse's Mzab plan, see "Rapport sur l'organisation politique et administrative des Beni Mezabs et sur l'installation matérielle d'une annexe à Ghardaïa," 2 January 1862, no. 13. CAOM 22 H 13.

80. "Etude sur le commerce de l'Algérie avec l'Afrique centrale," signé Colonieu, n.d. CAOM 22 H 26.

81. Cercle de Laghouat to Médéa, 11 April 1877, no. 102. CAOM 22 H 26.

82. Cercle de Laghouat to subdivision de Médéa, 11 April 1877, no. 102. CAOM 22 H 26.

83. Anonymous marginal note. Ibid.

84. Affaires indigènes, division d'Alger, 22 June 1877, no. 458. CAOM 22 H 26.

85. GGA to Procureur général près du Cours d'Appel d'Alger, August 1905. CAOM 12 H 50. See Patrick Weil, *Qu'est-ce qu'un Français: histoire de la nationalité française depuis la révolution* (Paris: Grasset, 2002), 225–46.

86. "Note," n.d. (Response to the letter of August 1905, cited in previous note) CAOM 12 H 50.

87. Préfecture d'Oran to GGA, Oran, 22 February 1881, no. 1345. CAOM 12 H 50.

88. "Renseignements recueillis par le Bureau arabe de Laghouat par des Touaregs sur l'itinéraire de Ouargla à Rat et à Idelès," Laghouat, 28 October 1857. CAOM 22 H 26.

89. Biweekly Report, Laghouat, September 1857. CAOM 79 I 3.

90. Lieutenant [Charles-Germain] Marty, "Renseignements commerciaux sur le pays des Touaregs et le Soudan," Laghouat, 8 April 1858. CAOM 22 H 26.

91. In his comments forwarded to Paris, General Chadellemprey, commander of the division of Algiers, noted he could not reimburse Si Othman for his loss. However, "sans le lui dire positivement, je me borne à lui faire répondre que nous empêcherons tout ce qui pourrait encourager la venue des esclaves nègres chez nous." Division d'Alger to GGA, 7 August 1860. CAOM F80 1677.

9. Colonial Accommodation

1. Paul Soleillet, "Exploration du Sahara Central: voyage de M. Paul Soleillet d'Alger à l'Oasis d'In Çalah, Rapport adressé par le voyageur à M. le Ministre de l'instruction publique," Paris, 20 December 1875. CARAN F17 3002/2.

2. Monthly Report, April 1890, Cercle de Ghardaïa. CAOM 76 I 3.

3. Monthly Report, September 1891, Annexe d'Ouargla. CAOM 78 I 1. Note: only the reports of CAOM 76 I 1 and 76 I 3 provide a detailed breakdown.

4. Affaires indigènes, division d'Alger to GGA, Algiers, 15 June 1893, no. 500. CAOM 12 H 50.

5. GGA to Ministre des affaires étrangères, Algiers, [day left blank] June 1893, mention "non envoyé." CAOM 12 H 50.

6. Capitaine Le Prieur, "Les Populations des oasis sahariennes du Touat," December 1953. CAOM 10 APOM 1228.

7. Donald Charles Holsinger, "Migration, Commerce and Community: The Mizabis in Nineteenth-Century Algeria" (Ph.D. diss., Northwestern University, 1979).

8. Pierre Bourdieu, *Les Mozabites* (Paris: PUF, 1970).

9. Holsinger, "Migration, Commerce and Community," 77.

10. Ibid.

11. André Chevrillon, *Les Puritains du désert (sud-algérien)* (Paris: Plon, 1927).

12. Ostensibly to stop the bitter fighting between rival Mzabi factions, the occupation

was motivated by concerns to cut the flow of arms into the hands of rebels (Ouled Sidi Cheik, Chaamba of Metlili, Bou Amama, among others) in the Sahara. Monthly Report, June 1881, Cercle de Laghouat. CAOM 71 I 5. See also "Rapport sur l'Annexion du Mzab et sur l'organisation politique et administrative du cercle de Ghardaïa," Médéa, 26 January 1883. CAOM 50 II 264.

13. Letter of 7 November 1882, summarized in "Rapport sur l'Annexion du Mzab."

14. Lovejoy and Hogendorn, *Slow Death for Slavery.*

15. "Rapport sur l'Annexion du Mzab."

16. Leselle, "Les Noirs du Souf."

17. "Rapport sur l'Annexion du Mzab."

18. Annual Reports, Cercle de Ghardaïa, 1897. CAOM 63 I 1.

19. Ibid.

20. Klein, *Slavery and Colonial Rule in French West Africa*, 126–40.

21. An informal 1845 census counted 2,540 migrant African laborers of color in the major Algerian cities under French control. See "Etat du mouvement des corporations indigènes dans les territoires civils pendant l'année 1845," Ministère de la Guerre, *Tableau de la situation des établissements français dans l'Algérie, 1845–46*, vol. 9 (Paris: Imprimerie royale, 1846), 96–97.

22. F.-J.-G. Mercadier, *L'Esclave de Timimoun* (Paris: Editions France-Empire, 1971).

23. Wright, *The Trans-Saharan Slave Trade*, 137–52.

24. Préfecture d'Alger to Direction des Affaires indigènes, 5 October 1906, no. 20153. CAOM 12 H 50.

25. Biskra, 17 June 1876. CAOM 22 H 26.

26. "Relation sur une partie du voyage effectué par la Mission du transsaharien (Mission Choisy), du 17 janvier au 9 mars 1880, par M. Massontrer," 28 May 1880. CAOM 4 H 8–10.

27. They brought 150 meters of rope worth 280 francs and returned with cotton cloth, spices (muse), and burnous worth 320 francs. Monthly Report, March 1892, Cercle de Ghardaïa. CAOM 76 I 3

28. They carried 39 kilos of henna worth 270 francs. They returned with cotton cloth and locally woven wool burnous totaling 275 francs. Monthly Report, April 1892, Cercle de Ghardaïa. CAOM 76 I 3

29. They brought 69 kilos of henna worth 350 francs and 150 meters of palm fiber rope. They returned with cotton cloth, saffron, and burnous worth 350 francs. Monthly Report, 1st ser., Cercle de Ghardaïa. CAOM 76 I 3

30. CAOM 24 H 1.

31. Hélène Chevaldonné, "Le Bureau arabe de Méchéria (Sud-oranais), 1890–1905," D.E.A. thesis, Université de Provence, Aix Marseille 1, 1988–89.

32. Monthly Report, September 1892, Annexe d'Ouargla. CAOM 78 I 1.

33. Monthly Report, Cercle de Laghouat, July 1877. CAOM 79 I 5.

34. Affaires indigènes, division d'Oran to GGA, 2 November 1890, no. 1. CAOM 12 H 50.

35. "Généalogie des Oulad Sidi Cheikh, 3e partie," Napoléon Lacroix and Henri Poisson de La Martinière, *Documents pour servir à l'étude du nord-ouest Africain*, vol. 2, *Le Sud-ouest et les régions limitrophes, Figuig, l'Oued Guir, l'Oued Saoura* (Algiers: Gouvernement général de l'Algérie, service des affaires indigènes, 1896), unpaginated.

36. Ibid., 790.

37. "Monographie sur l'arrondissement de In Salah," Dossier 2: Population, 1963. SHAT 1 H 2107.

38. Interview with Mouleg Ahmed from In Salah, at Hassi Messeguem, 2 January 1881. "Mission Flatters, Journal de Route" (surviving manuscript of the mission's journal, n.d.). CAOM 4 H 11; Capitaine Chardenet "Rapport sur le mouvement commercial du Tidikelt," In Salah, 26 August 1900. CAOM 22 H 59; Victor Deporter, *A propos du Transsaharien. Extrême sud de l'Algérie: le Gourara, le Touat, In-Salah, le Tidikelt, les pays des Touareg-Hoggar, l'Adrar, Tin Bouctou, Agadès.* (Algiers: Fontana, 1890), 211.

39. François Godron, "Renseignements sur les populations du Gourara, Touat, Tidikelt: Zaouias, Ordres religieux, Soffs," El Goléa, 16 May 1894. CAOM 22 H 55. The accuracy of Godron's population figures are confirmed by the first official census undertaken in 1906 by the local djema'a under French supervision. See A.-G.-P. Martin, *A la frontière du Maroc: les oasis sahariennes* (Paris: Augustin Challamel, 1908).

40. Deporter, *A propos du Transsaharaien,* 210.

41. Godron, "Renseignements sur les populations du Gourara, Touat, Tidikelt," 16 May 1894. CAOM 22 H 55.

42. Lacroix and Poisson de La Martinière, *Documents pour servir à l'étude . . . ,* vol. 2, *Le Sud-ouest,* 1–72.

43. Deporter, *A propos du Transsaharaien,* 210.

44. GGA Tirman to Président du conseil, 12 October 1890. CAOM F80 1695.

45. Division de Constantine, Général de La Roque to Commandant de Tombouctou, 19 November 1894. F80 1695.

46. The documents mapping the divisions of the oases are found in the series of "Notices individuelles" compiled in the early 1890s. CAOM 22 H 36.

47. Al-hajj al-Mahdi al-hajj 'Abd al-Qadir Awlad Si al-hajj Muhammad Ba Judda succeeded his father upon his death in 1889. The French thought the son had submitted to their authority in 1891 (Ricaud to Commandant du cercle de Biskra, 15 March 1891, no. 131. CAOM F80 1695). The following year Governor-General Cambon planned to name Mahdi ben Badjouda the "Caïd des Caïds" of the Tidikelt. GGA to Président du Conseil, 26 July 1892. CAOM F80 1695.

48. Godron, "Renseignements sur les populations du Gourara, Touat, Tidikelt," 16 May 1894. CAOM 22 H 55.

49. GGA to Général de La Roque, 15 April 1894, no. 990. CAOM 22 H 54.

50. Ben Ahmed to GGA, 20 May 1894. CAOM 22 H 54.

51. Général de La Roque to GGA, 1 June 1894. CAOM 22 H 54.

52. Général de La Roque to GGA, 16 May 1896, marked "Confidentielle." CAOM 22 H 54.

53. "Renseignements fournis par Abd el Kader ben Ahmed ben Kouider du 10 au 15 mai 1896." CAOM 22 H 54.

54. On this blurring of status and the language of the French archive, see Benjamin Claude Brower, "The Servile Populations of the Algerian Sahara Seen Through the French Colonial Archives," in Paul Lovejoy, Ismael Montana, and Behnaz Mirzai, eds. *Slavery, Islam, and Diaspora* (Trenton, N.J.: Africa World Press, 2009).

55. Ibid.

56. Henri Moniot, ed., *Le Mal de voir: ethnologie et orientalisme; politique et épistémologie, critique et autocritique* (Paris: Union générale de l'édition, 1976).

57. "Note," GGA to Commandant de la division d'Alger, n.d. [ca. May–June 1896]. CAOM 22 H 54.

58. Colonel Didier to Subdivision de Médéah, Ghardaïa, 13 April 1886. CAOM 1 I 100

59. Division d'Alger to GGA, 30 June 1892. CAOM 22 H 32. The caravan was led by Kouider ben Younès, a major slave trader to Touggourt and El Oued. Général de La Roque, commander of the division of Constantine, personally intervened with the governor-general on Younès' behalf. Division d'Alger to GGA, Algiers, 13 July 1892, no. 608; Affaires indigènes, Division de Constantine to GGA, Constantine, 16 July 1892, no. 538; and "Minute," GGA, 24 August 1892, no. 2163. CAOM 12 H 50.

60. "Dossier personnel," Didier. CAOM 12 H 51.

61. Jacques Frémeaux, "Deporter" (biographical entry), in *Parcours* 10 (December 1988): 25–27.

62. Didier was an initiate of the Qadiriyya, apparently without having converted to Islam. See R. Peyronnet, *Livre d'or des officiers des Affaires indigènes, 1830–1930*, vol. 2 (Algiers: Gouvernement général de l'Algérie. Commissariat général du Centenaire, 1930), 391. See also "Fiche de renseignement individuel: Si Mohammed Tayeb ben Brahim, Naïb des Kadrya," El Goléa, 1 December 1898. CAOM 2 U 22; "Dossier: Mission de Si Mohammed Taïeb ben Brahim, Naïb des Qadiriya, 1897." CAOM 22 H 54; GGA to Ministre de l'intérieur, 16 May 1897. CAOM F80 1696.

63. Kamel Filali, "Le différend Qadiriyya-Tijaniyya en Algérie," *Revue d'histoire maghrébine* 24, nos. 87–88 (1997): 301–14.

64. Report of Mohammed ben Abderrahman, "juif marocain d'Insalah" (aka Yucef ben Attia), 31 August 1886. CAOM 4 H 13.

65. Division d'Alger to GGA, 27 December 1886; and Abd El Kader ben Badjouda to Commandant supérieur de Ghardaïa, 28 October 1886 (French translation; no Arabic original). CAOM 4 H 13.

66. Deporter to Subdivision de Médéa, Ghardaïa, n.d. CAOM 4 H 13.

67. Monthly Report, 1st ser., Cercle de Ghardaïa, November 1886. CAOM 76 I 3.

68. Division d'Oran, Affaires arabes, to GGA, Oran, 31 August 1886. CAOM 4 H 13.

69. Division d'Alger to GGA, 13 September 1889, no. 554. CAOM 12 H 50.

70. "Minute," GGA to division d'Alger, 27 June 1889, no. 3874. CAOM 12 H 50.

71. Monthly Report, 1st ser., Cercle de Ghardaïa, October 1886. CAOM 76 I 3.

72. Didier, "Notices individuelles," Cercle de Ghardaïa to GGA, Affaires indigènes, Ghardaïa, 20 December 1893. CAOM 22 H 36.

73. Division d'Alger to GGA, 20 June 1889, no. 340. CAOM 12 H 50.

74. With accompanying French translation. CAOM 12 H 50. I wish to express my thanks to David Powers for his help in translating this letter. I would also like to thank Hanan Almarzouqi and Sakina Drihem for checking the French translation against the original.

75. The payment might have been Tuareg crafts that Deporter sent to the 1889 Universal Exposition in Paris. See Division d'Alger to GGA, 22 November 1890, no. 534. CAOM 12 H 50.

76. Division d'Oran to GGA, 2 November 1890, no. 1. CAOM 12 H 50. Général Henri

Poisat, head of the division of Algiers, defended Deporter in a letter to the GGA, 22 November 1890, no. 534. CAOM 12 H 50.

77. GGA to Ministre de la Guerre, Algiers, 15 March 1890, no. 7. CAOM 18 H 49.

78. "Notices individuelles," Ghardaïa, 20 December 1893. CAOM 22 H 36.

79. Largeau, *Le Pays de Rirha*, 229.

10. Romanticism and the Saharan Sublime

1. Cornelius Castoriadis, *The Imaginary Institution of Society*, trans. Kathleen Blamey (Cambridge, Mass.: MIT Press, 1987).

2. Quoted in Richard Terdiman, *Present Past: Modernity and the Memory Crisis* (Ithaca, N.Y.: Cornell University Press, 1993), 4.

3. Claude Collot, *Les Institutions de l'Algérie durant la période coloniale, 1830–1962* (Paris: Editions du CNRS; Algiers: OPU, 1987).

4. Marginal note "vu [et] approuvé, Daumas." A. de Cavergna, "Note sur l'occupation de Ghat par les Turcs," Ministre de la Guerre, direction des affaires de l'Algérie, no. 978, n.d. CAOM 22 H 26.

5. "Note sur les intérêts politiques de la France au désert et au pays des Nègres," signé [Ludovic de] Polignac, 17 March 1854. CAOM 22 H 26. Polignac's project for Saharan expansion, along with like-minded plans authored by Swiss entrepreneur Sautter de Beauregard and Léon Rochas, the French consul in Tripoli, are addressed in Benjamin Claude Brower, "A Desert Named Peace: Violence and Empire in the Algerian Sahara, 1844–1902" (Ph.D. diss., Cornell University , 2005), 312–32.

6. Ibid.

7. N. Ney, "Les Relations de la France avec l'extrême sud de l'Algérie et les derniers voyages d'exploration," *Revue des deux mondes* 8 (1 April 1875): 617–32.

8. The French established indirect rule at Touggourt in January 1854. See the anonymous document entitled "Note sur la nécessité de l'expédition de Touggourt, 1853," no. 41, n.d. (ca. December 1853). CAOM 15 K 25..

9. Letter of Mohammed ben Abdallah to the people of el-Oued, the Achach, and the Ouled Ahmed (French translation; no original), no. 9. CAOM 15 K 25.

10. Armée d'Algérie, Etat-major général to Colonel Durrieu, Commandant de Mascara, Algiers, 6 January 1854. CAOM 2 H 22. As the head of the Ouled Sidi Cheikh, in 1852 Si Hamza was drafted into French service in the struggle against Mahammad ben Abdallah. Although he proved willing enough to attack the latter, who represented a serious rival, Si Hamza was leery of the French, which rankled them. As Colonel Trumelet wrote, "Si Hamza est une sorte de tirelire qui reçoit mais qui ne rend pas." Despite his recalcitrance, the French partnership cost Si Hamza much of his political capital among Saharan societies and even among his own kin. (See CARAN F17 3007 for descriptions of the insults suffered by Si Hamza.) When he died mysteriously in 1861, it was widely believed that he was the victim of a plot by family members who opposed the rapprochement. In 1864 the alliance collapsed and the Ouled Sidi Cheikh led a massive revolt that lasted nearly two decades. See Colonel C. Trumelet, *Les Français dans le désert: journal historique, militaire et descriptif d'une expédition aux limites du Sahara algérien*, 2nd ed. (Paris: Challamel, 1885), 99. See also Cheikh Si Hamza Bou Bakeur, *Un soufi algérien Sidi Cheikh: sa vie, son œuvre, son*

rôle historique, ses descendants (Oulad Sidi-Cheikh) (Paris: Maisonneuve et Larose, 1990), which suggests (on page 160) that the French were the authors of Si Hamza's death.

11. GGA to Commandant de la division d'Oran, 26 June 1858. Quoted in Augustin Bernard and Napoléon Lacroix, *Historique de la pénétration saharienne* (Algiers: Giralt, 1900), 34.

12. Commandant Pein to Colonel Liebert, Commandant de Biskra, Bou Saaada, 13 September 1854. CAOM 15 K 25.

13. Jillali el-Adnani, *La Tijâniyya, 1781–1881: les origines d'une confrérie religieuse au Maghreb* (Rabat: Editions Marsam, 2007).

14. Commandant de Constantine to GGA, 9 November 1873. CAOM 4 H 4–6.

15. Benjamin Claude Brower, "Lutte mystique: un nouveau regard sur les Soufis sahariens dans le XIXème siècle," in Zaïm Khenchelaoui, ed., *Des voies et des voix* (Algiers: Editions du CNRPAH, 2007), 59–74.

16. Ministre de la Guerre to GGA, 2 October 1855. CAOM 1 E 214; Bernard and Lacroix, *Historique de la pénétration saharienne.*

17. In subsequent decades local agents were recruited only for dangerous secret missions, such as spying on the Sanusiyya. See Jean-Louis Triaud, *La Légende noire de la Sanûsiyya: une confrérie musulmane saharienne sous le regard français, 1840–1930*, 2 vols. (Paris: Editions de la Maison des sciences de l'homme, 1995). Prestigious missions were reserved for Frenchmen. For example, Mardochée Aby Serour, a Jew from the Drâa valley (Morocco), was turned down for the trip to Timbuktu in 1872 because of protests against giving a Maghrebi Jew this high-level assignment. See Jacob Oliel, *De Jérusalem à Tombouctou: l'odyssée saharienne du rabbin Mardochée* (Paris: Olbia, 1998).

18. Loverdo, Affaires arabes, Médéa to Division d'Alger, Médéa, 15 June 1877; Commandant de Médéa to Commandant d'Alger, Médéa, 18 September 1886; GGA to Commandant d'Alger, 4 January 1887; Commandant de Médéa to Commandant d'Alger, Médéa, 23 May 1874. CAOM 4 H 7. Soleillet later gained a reputation for leaving his lodging debts unpaid with French hoteliers—or, as one investigator wrote who hoped to head him off when he arrived in Algiers in 1879, "de faire des dupes dans les hôtels où il descend." G. Thiriet to M. Blasselle, avocat défenseur à Alger, Paris, 19 May 1879. CAOM 12 X 271.

19. Commandant du Division d'Oran (par intérim) to GGA, Oran, 8 September 1853. CAOM 4 H 22–23.

20. Born in Corsica, François-Louis de Bonnemain settled with his family in Algiers soon after the French occupation. He grew up speaking Arabic in the streets with his Algerian friends, who called him "Moustapha." Never formally educated, Bonnemain joined an irregular Algerian cavalry unit before entering the Gendarmes maures and moving into the Affaires indigènes. For his Ghadamès report, see Bonnemain to Commandant de Constantine, "Rapport détaillé du Capitane adjudant major de Bonnemain, de 3e spahis, sur sa mission à Ghadamès." Constantine, 24 March 1857. CAOM 4 H 27–28. See also Bonnemain, "Voyage à R'adamès," *Revue algérienne et coloniale* 1 (October 1859): 116–32.

21. Ismaël Bouderba was sent by his father, Ahmed Bouderba, to the prestigious Collège Louis le Grand in Paris. Bilingual in French in Arabic, he began his military career as an interpreter for the French army. At this time, when belief in the so-called "union des races" was at its height, Bouderba was well situated to pursue a career in the French administration. For Bouderba's report, see Ismaël Bouderba, "Voyage a Rhat," *Revue algérienne et*

coloniale 1 (December 1859): 241–305; manuscript: "Relation d'un voyage à R'at entrepris en août 1858, par M. Ismaël Bouderbah, interprète au Bureau arabe de Laghouat, par ordre de monsieur le maréchal Randon, Gouverneur général de l'Algérie." CAOM F80 1677.

22. The prize was announced in the *Bulletin de la Société de géographie de Paris*, 4th ser., vol. 9 (May 1855): 318–19.

23. See correspondance in CAOM F80 1733.

24. Unlike these explorers, Leiris's quest was marked by irony. In the end he found only a "phantom Africa." See Michel Leiris, *L'Afrique fantôme* (Paris: Gallimard, 1934), 162. See also Phyllis Clarck-Taoua, "In Search of New Skin: Michel Leiris's *L'Afrique fantôme*," *Cahiers d'études africaines* 42, no. 167 (2002): 479–98.

25. J. Gros, *Les Voyages et découvertes de Paul Soleillet dans le Sahara et dans le Soudan en vue d'un projet d'un chemin de fer transsaharien: racontés par lui-même.* (Paris: Maurice Dreyfous, 1881). François Poulalion, *Expédition Paul Soleillet* (Algiers: Chambre de commerce d'Alger, 1938); J. Valette, "Pénétration française au Sahara, exploration: le cas de Paul Soleillet," *Revue française d'histoire d'Outre-mer* 67 (1980): 253–67; M. Chailley, "Paul Soleillet," *Encyclopédie mensuel d'Outre Mer* 1 (May 1952): 140–43.

26. Paul Soleillet, "Exploration du Sahara Central: voyage de M. Paul Soleillet d'Alger à l'Oasis d'In Çalah; Rapport adressé par le voyageur à M. le ministre de l'Instruction publique," Paris, 20 December 1875. CARAN F17 3007/2; idem, *Voyage de Paul Soleillet d'Alger à l'oasis d'In-Çalah: rapport présenté à la Chambre de commerce d'Alger* (Algiers: Jourdan, 1874).

27. Camille Douls, "Cinq mois chez les maures nomades du Sahara occidental," *Le Tour du monde* 1 (1888): 187.

28. Albert Roussanne, *L'Homme suiveur de nuages: Camille Douls, Saharien, 1864–1889* (Rodez, France: Editions du Rouergue, 1991).

29. Isabelle Eberhardt, *Ecrits sur le sable*, in *Œuvres complètes*, ed. Marie-Odile Delacour and Jean-René Huleu, 2 vols. (Paris: Grasset, 1988 and 1990).

30. Isabelle Eberhardt to Augustin de Moerder, El Oued, 18 January 1901, in Marie-Odile Delacour and Jean-René Huleu eds., *Ecrits intimes* (Paris: Payot, 1991).

31. Notes by Jacques Delair. Bibliothèque nationale de France-Arsenal (hereafter BNF-A) Ms 15.004/13; Paul Delair to N. Dournaux-Dupéré, 23 August 1872, BNF-A Ms 14.999/5.

32. Anonymous document to Joly, Paris, 24 July 1875. BNF-A Ms 15.003/1; Jacques Delair, "Dournaux-Dupéré (1845–1874)" a fifty-page biography in manuscript, BNF-A Ms 15.006. See also Henri Duveyrier, "Voyage au Sahara, par Norbert Dournaux-Dupéré: Rédigé d'après son journal et ses lettres," *Bulletin de la Société de géographie de Paris* 8 (August 1874): 113–70.

33. Norbert Dournaux-Dupéré to Paul Delair, Saint-Louis, 15 July 1870. BNF-A Ms 14.998/4.

34. A collection of Palat's short stories was published posthumously under the pseudonym Marcel Frescaly. See *Nouvelles algériennes* (Paris: Charpentier, 1888). See also the correspondence relating to the fatal 1885–86 trip in Frescaly, *Journal de route et correspondence* (Paris: Charpentier, 1886).

35. Division d'Oran, Affaires indigènes to GGA, Oran, 24 April 1881, no. 176; and Commandant du division d'Oran, "Rapport spécial concernant M. Palat," Oran, 24 April 1881. Dossier personnel, Palat. CAOM 18 H 110.

36. N. Fauçon, "Le lieutenant Palat, son exploration et sa mort tragique," *Nouvelle Revue* 42 (15 October 1886): 790–805.

37. Frescaly, *Journal de route*, 116.

38. The testimony of Salah ben Dissa on the turn of events that led to Palat's murder makes for interesting reading on the breakdown of relations. See Deporter Commandant de Ghardaïa to Médéa, Ghardaïa, May 1886, no. 258. CAOM 4 H 12–17.

39. Charles Droulers, *Le Marquis de Morès, 1858–1896* (Paris: Plon, 1932); Jules Delahaye, *Les Assassins et les vengeurs de Morès*, 3 vols. (Paris: Victor Retaux, 1905–7); Mohammed ben Otsmane El-Hachaichi, *Voyage au pays des Senoussia à travers la Tripolitaine et les territoires Touareg* (Paris: Challamel, 1903).

40. A full-length photograph of Morès in moccasins, cowboy hat, buckskin jacket and pants, and a revolver at the hip was found in Maurice Barrès's papers and is included in the fifth volume of *L'Œuvre de Maurice Barrès*, ed. Philippe Barrès (Paris: Club de l'honnête homme, 1966). Studies on Morès's time spent in the United States include: Jerome D. Tweton, *The Marquis de Morès: Dakota Capitalist, French Nationalist* (Fargo: North Dakota Institute for Regional Studies, 1972); Robert Francis Byrnes, *Morès, "The First National Socialist"* (Notre Dame, Ind.: University of Notre Dame Press, 1950); and Rabbi Steven S. Schwarzschild, "The Marquis de Morès: The Story of Failure, 1859–1896," *Jewish Social Studies* 22 (January 1960): 3–26. (Schwarzschild mounted a campaign in the 1950s to have the National Park Service and the State Historical Society reclassify their management of Morès's ranch home in Medora, North Dakota. My thanks to Eleanor Kaufman for sharing her research at the Institute for Regional Studies in Fargo.) The anti-Semitic career of Morès was highlighted in two obituaries published in *La Libre parole* on 19 June 1896 and 19 July 1896.

41. This produced a volley of attacks against the government and the military administration in Algeria, who were accused of orchestrating Morès's murder to serve Jewish interests. The Constantine paper *La Silhouette* (21 June 1896), headlined Morès's story "Joie d'Israël."

42. Méry's curriculum vitae was sent to the Sous-secrétaire d'Etat des Colonies on 4 July 1892. CAOM FM 2 Missions Méry.

43. Capitaine Ricaud, Commandant de Touggourt to Commandant de Batna, Touggourt, 6 April 1893, no. 100; ibid, 25 April 1893, no. 125. CAOM 4 H 18–19. Méry responded to these charges by slandering the local officers in newspapers hostile to the military. See *Le Petit Journal*, 14 May 1893, and *Dépêche algérienne*, no. 2779. See also his published report *Une mission chez les Touareg Azdjer: Conférence faite à la Société de géographie de Paris le 5 mai 1893* (Paris: Administration des deux revues, 1893).

44. Ministre de la Guerre to GGA, Paris, 10 September 1855, no. 586. CAOM 4 H 1–4.

45. Si el Hachemi ben Sidi Brahim, a representative (nāib) of the Qadiriyya Sufi order, personally assumed the role of police agent in investigating Morès's death and identified the killers in 1898. See Commandant de Batna to Division de Constantine, 23 May 1898, no. 1368. CAOM 4 H 29.

46. Louis de Baudicour, *La Guerre et le gouvernement de l'Algérie* (Paris: Librairie du Centre algérien, 1853), 55.

47. Henri Duveyrier, *Journal de route: Sahara algérien et tunisien*, ed. Ch. Maunoir and H. Schirmer (Paris: Augustin Challamel, 1905), ix-xxiii; idem, "Journal 1 août 1854 à 21 août 1855, Paris, Genève, Lautrach," manuscript. CARAN 47 AP 1.

48. Paul Soleillet, "Exploration du Sahara Central: Voyage de M. Paul Soleillet d'Alger à l'Oasis d'In Çalah: Rapport adressé par le voyageur à M. le ministre de l'Instruction publique," Paris, 20 December 1875. CARAN F17 3007/2.

49. Roger Benjamin, *Orientalist Aesthetics: Art, Colonialism, and French North Africa, 1880–1930* (Berkeley: University of California Press, 2003).

50. For a description of the standard fin de siècle itinerary, see the travel account written by British painter Frances E. Nesbitt, *Algeria and Tunis: Painted and Described* (London: Black, 1906).

51. André Gide, *Amyntas* (Paris: Gallimard, 1925), 121.

52. Michel Roux, *Le Désert de sable: le Sahara dans l'imaginaire des Français, 1900–1994* (Paris: Harmattan, 1996).

53. Réné Caillié, *Travels through Central Africa to Timbuctoo and across the Great Desert to Morocco*, vol. 2 (London: Franck Cass, 1968). See also Abdelaziz Alaoui Lahgazi, "L'Expérience du désert et de l'Islam chez René Caillé, Charles de Foucauld, Ernest Psichari et Saint-Exupéry" (Ph.D. diss., Université de Provence, 1989), 222.

54. Docteur Félix Jacquot, *Expédition du Général Cavaignac dans le Sahara algérien en avril et mai 1847* (Paris: Gide et J. Baudry, 1849), 91.

55. C. Parisot, "D'Ouargla à El Golea'a: extrait d'une lettre au secrétaire général," *Bulletin de la Société de géographie de Paris* 5 (January-June 1873): 322–25. Parisot was with the column of Général de Gallifet.

56. Fernand Foureau, "Rapport sur mes deux missions sahariennes de 1892 et 1893, adressé au Ministre de l'instruction publique et au Ministre des Affaires étrangères et au Sous-secrétaire de l'état des colonies," Paris, July 1893. BNF-R, SG Colis 18/2404.

57. Colonel C. Trumelet, *Les Français dans le désert: Journal historique, militaire et descriptif d'une expédition aux limites du Sahara Algérien*, 2nd ed. (Paris: Challamel, 1885), viii (preface to the first edition).

58. Al-Bakri, "Description de l'Afrique septentrionale," trans. M. de Slane, *Journal asiatique*, 5th ser., vol. 12 (1858): 412–14.

59. For an example of the classic military report, see Jus, "Notes sur le Sahara," *Revue algérienne et coloniale* 1 (October 1859): 49–60.

60. Bonnemain to Commandant de Constantine, "Rapport détaillé du Capitane adjudant major de Bonnemain, de 3e spahis, sur sa mission à R'damès," Constantine, 24 March 1857. CAOM 4 H 27–28.

61. "Relation d'un voyage à R'at entrepris en août 1858, par M. Ismaël Bouderba, Interprète au bureau Arabe de Laghouat, par ordre de Monsieur le Maréchal Randon, Gouverneur Général de l'Algérie." CAOM F80 1677.

62. Ismaël Bouderba, "Voyage à Rhat," *Revue algérienne et coloniale* 1 (December 1859): 280.

63. André Chevrillon, *Les Puritains du désert (sud-algérien)* (Paris: Plon, 1927), quoted by Léon Lehuraux in his necrology of Commandant Cauvet, *Travaux de l'institut de recherches sahariennes* 7 (1951): 7.

64. Honoré de Balzac, *Œuvres completes*, vol. 11, *Les Employés* (Paris: Calmann Lévy, 1892), 15.

65. Max Horkheimer and Theodor W. Adorno, *Dialectic of Enlightenment*, trans. John Cumming (1944; reprint, New York: Continuum, 1998), 30.

66. J.-L. Lugan, "Relation de l'expédition de l'Atlas," *La Revue de Paris* 39 (1832): 5–19, 116–24.

67. Ibid., 5.

68. Ibid, 9.

69. Jacques Leroy de Saint-Arnaud, *Lettres du maréchal Saint-Arnaud*, 2 vols. (Paris: M. Lévy frères, 1855). Saint-Arnaud's letters were a success and had gone into a third edition by 1864.

70. The first term is taken from Captain F. Durand, *Des tendances pacifiques de la société européenne et du rôle des armées dans l'avenir* (1841), quoted in Raoul Girardet, *La Société militaire de 1815 à nos jours* (Paris: Perrin, 1998), 16; the second citation is found on page 43.

71. François Maspero, *L'Honneur de Saint-Arnaud* (Paris: Plon, 1993), 114. Shocked by the violence, Maspero questioned the motivation for publication: "Ce qu'il y a de fascinant, dans sa correspondance, ce n'est pas tellement qu'il y raconte avec autant de naturel que de clarté et d'élégance toute une série d'actions qui peuvent difficilement être présentées comme des faits d'armes—cette interminable répétition de pays dévastés, de villages brûlés, de populations massacrées sans distinction d'age et de sexe. Il avait bien le droit de raconter sa vie à sa famille. Là où ça devient formidable, c'est quand on vit cette famille décider que le plus bel hommage à rendre au cher disparu est de publier ses lettres et que, tout en supprimant ou amputant, bien légitiment, un certain nombre, elle choisit délibérément de conserver l'essentiel de *ces lettres-là*. Il n'y a dans ce geste aucune hésitation, aucun doute: ces massacres font partie de la gloire militaire du maréchal" (16–17).

72. Mostefa Lacheraf, *L'Algérie: nation et société* (Paris: Maspero, 1965), 90.

73. Roger Caillois, *Le Mythe et l'homme* (Paris: Gallimard, 1938), 172.

74. Girardet, *La Société militaire*, 88.

75. Paul Bénichou, *Le Sacré de l'écrivain, 1750–1830* (Paris: Gallimard, 1973).

76. Dominick LaCapra, *History and Memory after Auschwitz* (Ithaca, N.Y.: Cornell University Press, 1998), 37.

77. Nicolas Boileau, *Œuvres diverses du sieur D— avec le Traité du sublime ou du merveilleux dans le discours (traduction du grec de Longin)* (Paris: Chez D. Thierry, 1674). See also *Longinus on the Sublime*, ed. and trans. William Rhys Roberts (Cambridge: Cambridge University Press, 1899); Samuel H. Monk, *The Sublime: A Study of Critical Theories in XVIII-Century England* (New York: Modern Language Association, 1935); Elder Olson, "The Art of Longinus' *On the Sublime*," in *Critics and Criticism, Ancient and Modern* (Chicago: University of Chicago Press, 1961), 232–59. More recent readings of "sublime subjectivity" that inform my argument include: Neil Hertz, "Lecture de Longin," *Poétique* 15 (1973): 292–306; and Suzanne Guerlac, "Longinus and the Subject of the Sublime," *New Literary History* 16, no. 2 (1985): 275–89.

78. *Dictionnaire universel françois et latin: contenant la signification et la définition tant des mots de l'une et de l'autre langue*, 3rd ed. (Paris: Chez Julien-Michel Gandouin, 1732).

79. Lucien Goldmann, *Le Dieu caché: étude sur la vision tragique dans les Pensées de Pascal et dans le théâtre de Racine* (Paris: Gallimard, 1959).

80. Alain Corbin, *The Lure of the Sea: The Discovery of the Seaside in the Western World, 1750–1840*, trans. Jocelyn Phelps (Berkeley: University of California Press, 1994). See also

David B. Morris, *The Religious Sublime: Christian Poetry and Critical Tradition* (Lexington: University Press of Kentucky, 1972).

81. Edmund Burke, *A Philosophical Enquiry into the Origin of Our Ideas of the Sublime and Beautiful*, ed. Adam Phillips (Oxford: Oxford University Press, 1990).

82. Thomas Weiskel, *The Romantic Sublime: Studies in the Structure and Psychology of Transcendence* (Baltimore, Md.: John Hopkins University Press, 1976), 4. See also Philippe Lacoue-Labarthe and Jean-Luc Nancy, *L'Absolu littéraire: théorie de la littérature du romantisme allemand* (Paris: Seuil, 1978).

83. David E. Nye, *American Technological Sublime* (Cambridge, Mass.: MIT Press, 1994); Harsha Ram, *The Imperial Sublime: A Russian Poetics of Empire* (Madison: University of Wisconsin Press, 2003).

84. Emile Masqueray, *Souvenirs et visions d'Afrique* (Paris: Dentu, 1894), 170.

85. Louis de Colomb, *Exploration des ksours et du Sahara de la Province d'Oran* (Algiers: Dubos; Imprimerie du Gouvernement; Paris: Challemel, 1858), 7.

86. Parisot, "D'Ouargla à El Golea'a: extrait d'une lettre au secrétaire général," 322–25.

87. "Relation sur une partie du voyage effectué par la Mission de trans-saharien, (Mission Choisy,) du 17 janvier au 9 mars 1880, par M. Massontrer, Sous Lieutenant au 38e de Ligne, adjoint de 1e classe au Bureau arabe de Laghouat, attaché à mission Choissy," 28 May 1880. CAOM 4 H 8–10.

88. Robert Capot-Rey, *Le Sahara français* (Paris: PUF, 1953).

89. Henri Stanislas d'Escayrac de Lauture, "Mémoire sur le ragle ou hallucination du désert," *Bulletin de la Société de géographie de Paris*, 4th ser. (March and April 1855): 121–39. Lauture, *Le Désert et le Soudan: Géographie naturelle et politique, histoire et ethnographie, moeurs et institutions de l'empire des Fellatas, du Bornou, du Baguermi du Waday, du Dar-Four* (Paris: A. Bertrand, J. Dumaine, F. Klinksiek, 1855). Leading up to the First World War, specialists attributed these mental imbalances to the "air électrisé du désert." See E. F. Gautier, *La Conquête du Sahara: Essai de psychologie politique* (Paris: Armand Colin, 1910), 31. With the discovery of petroleum reserves in the Algerian Sahara in the 1950s and the arrival of large numbers of European oil workers, it resurfaced as a problem. See G. L. Fessard and J. Lambert, "Les Problèmes d'adaptation psycho-sociologique en milieu industriel saharien," *Hygiène mentale* 3 (1960): 191–213.

90. Masqueray, *Souvenirs et visions*, 51.

91. Douls, "Cinq mois chez les maures nomades du Sahara occidental," 187.

92. Roger Caillois, *Man, Play, and Games*, trans. M. Barash (New York: Free Press of Glencoe, 1961), 24.

93. Louis de Colomb, "Notice sur les oasis du Sahara et les routes qui y conduisent," *Revue algérienne et colonial* (August–October 1860), 513. The original manuscript for this article, "Les Oasis du Sahara et les routes qui y conduisent, Gourara, Touat, Tidikelt" (1860) is located in CAOM 4 H 1.

94. Jacquot, *Expédition du général Cavaignac dans le Sahara algérien*, 91.

95. Ibid., 91–92

96. Victor Largeau, *Expédition de Rhadamès: extraits du journal de route de M. Largeau* (Algiers: Imprimerie de V. Aillaud et Cie, 1876), 39–40. The same passage appears in Victor Largeau, *Le Pays de Rirha, Ouargla: voyage a Rhadames* (Paris: Hachette, 1879), 379–80.

97. Victor Largeau, "Rapport à monsieur le général Chanzy, Gouverneur Général Civ-

il de l'Algérie, Commandant supérieur des forces de terre et de mer," Algiers, May 1875 (96pp., handwritten). CAOM 4 H 8–10.

98. Largeau, *Expédition de Rhadamès*, 39–40; emphasis added.

99. Colomb, "Notice sur les oasis," 523–24

100. Honoré de Balzac, *Oeuvres complètes de H. de Balzac*, vol. 12, *Les Chouans* et *Une passion dans le désert* (Paris: Calmann Lévy, 1892), 443.

101. William Wordsworth, *The Prelude; or, Growth of a Poet's Mind*, 2nd ed., ed. Ernest de Selincourt (Oxford: Clarendon Press, 1959), 211.

102. M. H. Abrams, *Natural Supernaturalism: Tradition and Revolution in Romantic Literature* (New York: Norton, 1971), 68.

103. Fritz Stern, *The Politics of Cultural Despair: A Study in the Rise of the Germanic Ideology* (Berkeley: University of California Press, 1963).

104. Chantal Maudit, *J'habite au Paradis* (Paris: J.-C. Lattès, 1997); Jon Krakauer, *Into Thin Air: A Personal Account of the Mount Everest Disaster* (New York: Villard, 1997); Reinhold Messner, *Solo Nanga Parbat*, trans. A. Salkeld (New York: Oxford University Press, 1980); Jean-Jacques Languepin, *Himalaya, passion cruelle: expédition française à la Nanda Devi, 1951* (Paris: Flammarion, 1955); Maurice Herzog, *Annapurna: First Conquest of an 8,000 Meter Peak*, trans. J. Morin and J. A. Smith (New York: Dutton, 1953).

105. Douls, "Cinq mois chez les maures."

106. Ismaël Bouderba, "Voyage à Rhat," *Revue algérienne et coloniale* 1 (December 1859): 261.

107. Saul Friedländer, introduction (3–17) and "Themes of Decline and End in Nineteenth-Century Western Imagination" (61–83), in Saul Friedländer et al., eds., *Visions of Apocalypse: End or Rebirth?* (New York: Holmes & Meier, 1985).

108. Andreas Huyssen, "Fortifying the Heart—Totally: Ernst Jünger's Armored Texts," *New German Critique* 59 (Spring–Summer, 1993): 3–23; see also Klaus Theweleit, *Male Fantasies*, trans. Stephen Conway (Minneapolis: University of Minnesota Press, 1987).

109. Trumelet, *Les Français dans le désert*, vii.

110. Masqueray, *Souvenirs et visions d'Afrique*, 201.

111. *Longinus on the Sublime*, 55.

112. Roger Caillois, *Man and the Sacred*, trans. M. Barash (New York: Free Press of Glencoe, 1959), 22.

11. The "Blue Legend"

1. Bruce Greenfield, "The Problem of the Discoverer's Authority in Lewis and Clark's *History*," in Jonathan Arac and Hariet Ritvo, eds., *Macropolitics of Nineteenth-Century Literature: Nationalism, Exoticism, Imperialism* (Philadelphia: University of Pennsylvania Press, 1991), 12–36.

2. Ibid., 24.

3. Ernest Psichari, *Terres de soleil et de sommeil* (Paris: Louis Conrad, 1945); idem, *Le Voyage du centurion* (Paris: Louis Conrad, 1916); idem, *L'Appel des armes* (1913; reprint, Paris: Edition de Paris, 2001). Henri Massis, *Notre ami Psichari* (Paris: Flammarion, 1944). See also Alec G. Hargreaves, *The Colonial Experience in French Fiction: A Study of Pierre Loti, Ernest Psichari, and Pierre Mille* (London: Macmillan, 1989).

4. Théodore Monod, *Le Chercheur d'absolu* (Paris: Gallimard, 1997), esp. 31–51; idem, *Méharées: Explorations au vrai Sahara* (1937; reprint, N.p.: Actes Sud, 1989).

5. Augustin Bernard and Napoléon Lacroix, *La Pénétration saharienne, 1830–1906* (Algiers: Imprimerie algérienne, 1906).

6. See, e.g., the project of Subtil and Abd al-Jalil presented in chapter 9.

7. Henry Laurens, "L'Islam dans la pensée française, des Lumières à la IIIe République," in Mohammed Arkoun, ed., *Histoire de l'islam et des musulmans en France du Moyen Age à nos jours* (Paris: Albin Michel, 2006), 483–99.

8. Edward Said, *Orientalism* (1978; reprint, New York: Vintage, 1994), 80–88; Henry Laurens, *L'Expédition d'Egypte* (Paris: Armand Colin, 1989); idem, *Les Origines intellectuelles de l'expédition d'Egypte: l'orientalisme islamisant en France, 1698–1798* (Istanbul: Editions Isis, 1987).

9. Pierre Christian, *L'Afrique française, l'empire de Maroc, et les déserts de Sahara: conquêtes, victoires et découvertes des français, depuis la prise d'Alger jusqu'à nos jours* (Paris: A. Barbier, 1846).

10. The photograph is presently in the collection of the Musée de l'Armée, Paris. It is reproduced in Malek Alloula, *Alger: photographiée au XIXe siècle* (Paris: Marval, 2001), 155.

11. On the risks involved in oversimplification, see Lucette Valensi, *The Birth of the Despot: Venice and the Sublime Porte*, trans. Arthur Denner. (Ithaca, N.Y.: Cornell University Press, 1993), 56–60.

12. Patricia M. E. Lorcin, *Imperial Identities: Stereotyping, Prejudice, and Race in Colonial Algeria*. London: I. B. Tauris, 1995), 91.

13. Ferdinand Lapasset, Lieutenant Colonel d'Etat major, Commandant supérieure du Cercle de Philippeville, Rapport d'Inspection générale, 1858, Philippeville, 25 October 1858. CAOM 56 K 2. My thanks to Sakina Drihem for alerting me to this source.

14. Oscar MacCarthy, "Les Touareg," *Revue de l'Orient* 3 (1856): 136.

15. B. Aucapitaine, "Sur les Toaregs Imouchar," *Revue orientale et américaine* 3 (1860): 73. Positive images of the Tuareg were expressed at the same time in Bouderba. CAOM F80 1677. See also Capitaine Bonnemain, "Voyage à Ghadamès." CAOM 4 H 28

16. General Martimprey to Henri Duveyrier, Algiers, 30 September 1860, n° 1393. CAOM 4 H 4–6. See also the interview with Polignac in *Le Temps* (Paris), 16 June 1893 (clipping in CAOM F80 1695).

17. Paul Pandolfi, "La Construction du mythe Touareg: quelques remarques et hypothèses," *Ethnologie comparée* 7 (spring 2004), n.p. Pandolfi notes that today the French postcolonial imaginary has reserved a preeminent place for the Tuareg, who have become so ubiquitous in representations of the Sahara that "comme la dune de sable, ils sont devenus une véritable métonymie du désert." Paul Pandolfi, "Avant propos, figures Saharaines," *Ethnologie comparée* 7 (spring 2004), n.p.

18. René Pottier, *Un prince saharien méconnu, Henri Duveyrier* (Paris: Plon, 1938); Emmanuelle Mambre, "Henri Duveyrier explorateur du Sahara (1840–1892)," (master's thesis, Université de Provence, 1991–92). The title of this section is a play on Pottier's "prince."

19. Henri Duveyrier, "Journal . . . Paris, Genève, Lautrach." CARAN 47 AP 1.

20. Bavarian anti-Semitism met with Duveyrier's disapproval: "C'est étonnant comme les Allemands portent une haine profonde pour ces pauvres peuples; ils les répugnent, se moquent de leur culte, les persécutent pour ainsi dire." Duveyrier, "Journal . . . Paris,

Genève, Lautrach." CARAN 47 AP 1. Duveyrier's botanical specimens, dried and crumbling, are assembled in a notebook entitled "Commentarii in faunam floramque pagi Lautrach locorumque circumjunctorum, Lautrach, MDCCCLV." CARAN 47 AP 1.

21. Henri Duveyrier, *Journal d'un voyage dans la province d'Alger* (Paris: A. Challamel, 1900).

22. Ibid.

23. Mambre, "Henri Duveyrier explorateur du Sahara," 18; Pottier, *Un prince saharien*, 35. See also the unbound notes written in Henri Duveyrier's hand in CARAN 47 AP 4.

24. Henri Duveyrier, *L'Exploration du Sahara: Les Touâreg du Nord* (Paris: Challamel Ainé, 1864). Conceived as the first of a two-volume work, the second volume was never published. According to a letter written by Charles Duveyrier, his son completed a manuscript of the second volume in 1866 and turned it over to Dr. Warnier for editing. This manuscript has disappeared, along with Duveyrier's field notes dating from 1860–61 and the manuscript of the first volume. See Charles Duveyrier to Ismayl Urbain, Vichy, 24 August 1866. BNF-A Ms 13739/152.

25. Duveyrier's vita is impressive. He served as the secretary and president of the Geographic Society of Paris and received numerous awards. These included the Ordre impérial de la Légion d'honneur (22 January 1862) and the Grand médaille d'or from the Geographic Society of Paris. He also received two medals at the 1867 Universal Exposition. The Commission impériale welcomed Duveyrier as a member in 1868, and he served on the education ministry's Commission des voyages et missions scientifiques et littéraires. In 1880 he was inducted into the Société archéologique de la province de Constantine and in 1888 he was admitted to the Società Africana d'Italia. CARAN 47 AP 3.

26. Emmanuelle Mambre, "Les Touareg du Nord d'Henri Duveyrier: éléments d'une controverse," *Les Cahiers de l'IREMAM* 4 (1993): 19–23.

27. Soon after its publication, the GGA took delivery of thirty copies of Duveyrier's book for distribution among its officers. See Gouverneur général to Ministre de la Guerre, 31 July 1865. CAOM F80 1733. The only work that rivaled the scope and detail of Duveyrier's opus was Gerhard Rohlfs's *Mein erster Aufenthalt in Marokko und Reise südlich vom Atlas durch die Oasen Draa und Tafilet* (Bremen: J. Kühtmann, 1873). Duveyrier's work was not surpassed in French until the publication of E. F. Gautier's study *Le Sahara algérien* (Paris: Armand Colin, 1908).

28. Henri Duveyrier to Charles Duveyrier, Biskra, 15 December 1859. CARAN 47 AP 1.

29. Ismayl Urbain, a close friend of Charles Duveyrier, was on the committee, and Henri enjoyed the backing of princesse Mathilde and the marquis de Chasseloup Laubat, onetime minister of Algeria (1859–60). Nevertheless the position went to Oscar MacCarthy, an engineer by training and Duveyrier's first guide in the Sahara. Duveyrier's difficult personality comes through in the arrogance and bitterness of his correspondence with Urbain soliciting his support. See the letter dated 7 July 1869, Saint Germain en Laye, 8 rue Napoleon. BNF-A Ms. 13739/155.

30. Duveyrier's Arabic skills were not excellent, and Urbain thought he would have to spend some time mastering the language before he could aspire to a university position. See Urbain to Henri Duveyrier, Algiers, 27 November 1869. CARAN 47 AP 6. The interpreter possibility was raised by Dr. Warnier. See Warnier to Charles Duveyrier, Abbéville, 23 August 1866. BNF-A Ms. 13739/152.

31. Mambre, "Henri Duveyrier explorateur du Sahara," 144.

32. Michael Heffernan, "The Limits of Utopia: Henri Duveyrier and the Exploration of the Sahara in the Nineteenth Century," *Geographical Journal* 155, no. 3 (1989): 349.

33. Entry for 25 August 1860 in page proofs for his "Journal de route." CARAN 47 AP 7.

34. *Fous du désert: les premiers explorateurs du Sahara, 1849–1887* [Heinrich Barth, Henri Duveyrier, and Camille Douls] (Paris: Phébus, 1991). Duveyrier exhibits negative feelings toward Saharans in the following documents: Bokhari (n.d. [ca. March 1857]), fragments of 1857 journal. CARAN 47 AP 1; Henri Duveyrier to Charles Duveyrier, puits de Zourèg, n.d. [ca. end June 1859]. CARAN 47 AP 1; 2 September 1860, page proofs for his "Journal de route." CARAN 47 AP 7; Forgemol to Commandant of Batna, Biskra, 24 December 1860. CAOM 4 H 4–6; Henri Duveyrier to Charles Duveyrier, Ouâdi Tikhammalt, 14 January 1861. CARAN 47 AP 1.

35. Jean-Louis Triaud, *La Légende noire de la Sanûsiyya: une confrérie musulmane saharienne sous le regard français, 1840–1930*, 2 vols. (Paris: Maison des sciences de l'homme, 1995).

36. Duveyrier, *L'Exploration du Sahara: Les Touâreg du Nord*, 373.

37. Ibid., 381.

38. Ibid., 432.

39. Ibid., 382.

40. Ibid., 383.

41. Ibid., 414.

42. Henri Aucapitaine, "Sur les Toaregs Imouchar," *Revue orientale et américaine* 3 (1860): 63.

43. Ibid, 61.

44. Henri Duveyrier, "Note sur un projet d'exploration d'une partie du Sahara et du Touat," Paris, 8 April 1859. BNF-A Fonds Enfantin, MS 7720/239.

45. Henri Duveyrier to Charles Duveyrier, 31 July 1861. CARAN 47 AP 1.

46. Duveyrier, *L'Exploration du Sahara: Les Touâreg du Nord*, 332.

47. Ibid., 331.

48. Ibid., 333.

49. Ibid., 332.

50. Ibid., 334.

51. Fustel de Coulanges, *La Cité antique: étude sur le culte, le droit, les institutions de la Grèce et de Rome* (Paris: Durand, 1864), 139.

52. Duveyrier, *L'Exploration du Sahara: Les Touâreg du Nord*, 338.

53. Ibid., 331.

54. Ibid., 335.

55. Ibid., 338.

56. Ibid., 381.

57. Ibid., 352.

58. In a letter to General Martimprey Ikhenoukhen requested a twin-barreled rifle. However, he specified that he wanted one decorated with inlays based on Islamic, not French, themes. See Mohammed Ikhenoukhen el-Haggari, 14 Doumade el-Aou 1277 (1861). CAOM 4 H 4–6.

59. Duveyrier, *L'Exploration du Sahara: Les Touâreg du Nord*, 392.

60. Ibid., 335.

61. Ibid., 429.

62. Dominique Casajus, "Henri Duveyrier et le désert des Saint-Simoniens," *Ethnologies comparées* 7 (spring 2004), n.p.

63. Duveyrier wrote the letter as soon as he arrived in Laghouat, the scene of his 1857 ecstasy. See Henri Duveyrier to Père Enfantin, Laghouat, 9 November 1859. BNF-A Ms 7720/236.

64. Henri Duveyrier to Charles Duveyrier, Biskra, 15 December 1859. CARAN 47 AP 1.

65. Antoine Picon, *Les Saint-simoniens: raison, imaginaire et utopie* (Paris: Belin, 2002).

66. Duveyrier, *L'Exploration du Sahara: Les Touâreg du Nord*, 387.

67. Jean-Robert Henry, "Romans sahariens et imaginaire français," *Centre de recherches et d'études sur les sociétés méditerranéennes* (1981): 423–40.

68. Pierre Benoit, *L'Atlantide: roman* (Paris: Albin Michel, 1919).

69. Duveyrier, *L'Exploration du Sahara: Les Touâreg du Nord*, 2.

70. Tzvetan Todorov, *On Human Diversity: Nationalism, Racism, and Exoticism in French Thought*, trans. Catherine Porter (Cambridge, Mass.: Harvard University Press, 1993).

71. Georges Bataille, "Nietzschean Chronicle," in *Visions of Excess: Selected Writings, 1927–1939*, trans. and ed. A. Stoekl (Minneapolis: University of Minnesota Press, 1985), 203.

72. Henri Aucapitaine, *Etude sur la caravane de la Mecque et le commerce de l'intérieur de l'Afrique* (Paris: Imprimerie de J. Claye, n.d. [ca. 1861]), 5; see also the anonymous article entitled "Notes sur le commerce de l'Afrique centrale," *Revue algérienne et coloniale*, 1st ser., vol. 2 (1860): 417–20 An excerpt was published in the *Monituer universel*, 30 June 1860: 772.

Conclusion

1. This description is taken from the published report of the official inquiry. See Gouvernement Général de l'Algérie, dressée par M. Bernard, *Deuxième mission Flatters: historique et rapport rédigé au Service central des Affaires indigènes* (Algiers: Jourdan, 1882).

2. The first Flatters mission left Biskra on 7 February 1880. A strike among the men forced Flatters to return after three months.

3. Bernard, *Deuxième mission Flatters*, 100.

4. The force was led by Atici and Anaba ag Chikat, the maternal nephews of Ahitagel ag Mohamed Biska. With them was a diverse group recruited from the Tégéhé Mellet and Kel Gela, along with other Tuareg fighters. See Paul Pandolfi, *Les Touaregs de l'Ahaggar, Sahara Algérien: parenté et résidence chez les Dag-Ghâli* (Paris: Karthala, 1998), 85–88.

5. Capitaine Rebillet, Chef du géni à Laghouat, to Directeur du génie à Alger. Mitili, 27 March 1881. CAOM 1 I 102. Only three thousand francs were recovered. See Mohamed ben Belkassen, Khalifa de l'Agha d'Ouargla to Commandant de Laghouat (Belin), Ouargla, 21 May 1881. CAOM 4 H 11.

6. Bernard, *Deuxième mission Flatters*, 106.

7. Ibid., 134.

8. This was first reported by the Commandant de Laghouat in a letter dated 21 April 1881. CAOM 4 H 11.

9. This version, written by Charles Féraud, included Flatters firing until his hand, still clutching a revolver, was cut off. Féraud to Ministre des Affaires étrangères, Tripoli, 10 May 1881. CAOM 4 H 11.

10. Commandant d'Alger to GGA, 5 October 1881. CAOM 4 H 11.

11. Commandant de Ghardaia (Didier) to Commandant de Laghouat, 18 March 1883. CAOM 4 H 11.

12. "Enquête sur le massacre de la Mission Flatters, Rapport établi par le Commandant Supérieur du Cercle de Laghouat," n.d. (1881). CAOM 4 H 11.

13. Louis Rinn, Chef de Service central des Affaires indigènes, "Résumé et Conclusion," Algiers, 1 June 1882, quoted in Bernard, *Deuxième mission Flatters*, 334.

14. Rinn, "Analyse d'un projet d'expédition saharienne," Algiers, June 1886. CAOM 4 H 22–23.

15. Commandant de Laghouat (Flatters) to Commandant de Médéa, 30 September 1876, n° 482. CAOM 1 I 101. See also Flatters "Dossier personnel." CAOM 18 H 61.

16. Capitaine (Charles) Massoutier, "Conférence sur les questions sahariennes," Laghouat, 17 March 1891. CAOM 22 H 35.

17. Capitaine Charles Massoutier, "Enquête sur le massacre de la mission Flatters," n.d. (ca 1881). CAOM 22 H 27.

18. Barthélemy Saint–Hilaire, Ministre des Affaires étrangères to Gouverneur Générale Albert Grévy, 18 May 1881, quoted in N. Lacroix and H. P. de La Martinière, *Documents pour servir à l'étude du Nord-Ouest africain*, vol. 3, *Les Oasis de l'extrême sud algérien* (Algiers: Gouverneur Général d'Algérie, 1897), 23–28.

19. Marginal note, signed [Governor-General Louis] Tirman. Service central des Affaires indigènes to Ministre de l'intérieur, Algiers, 26 April 1884, n° 93. CAOM 4 H 11.

20. Ibid. A bounty of two hundred francs was paid for three heads, which were preserved and given to the Ecole des sciences d'Alger.

21. Henri Duveyrier to Capitaine Bernard, Paris, 2 December 1881 (unsigned draft). CARAN 47 AP 4.

22. Triaud, *La Légende noire de la Sanûsiyya*, vol. 1, 310.

23. Henri Duveyrier, "Le Désastre de la mission Flatters," *Bulletin de la Société de géographie de Paris*, 7th ser., vol. 1 (1881): 364–74.

24. Henri Duveyrier to Capitaine Bernard, Paris, 2 December 1881. CARAN 47 AP 4.

25. Henri Duveyrier, "La Confrérie musulmane de Sidi Mohammed ben Ali es-Senouci et son domaine géographique en l'année 1300 de l'Hégire = 1883 de notre ère," *Bulletin de la Société de géographie de Paris*, 7th ser., vol. 5 (1884): 145–226.

26. Triaud, *La légende noire de la Sanûsiyya*, vol. 1, 310–46.

27. Ibid.

28. *Le Temps*, 15 December 1892. Clipping in CAOM F80 1695.

29. Messouad Djebari, *Les Survivants de la Mission Flatters* (Tunis: Imprimerie Brigol, 1895). Further details on Djebari can be found in A. S. Kanya-Forstner and Paul E. Lovejoy, *Pilgrims, Interpreters and Agents: French Reconnaissance Reports on the Sokoto Caliphate and Borno, 1891–1895* (Madison: African Studies Program, University of Wisconsin–Madison, 1997).

30. *La Dépêche algérienne*, 9 July 1896. Clipping in CAOM 4 H 29.

31. Ibid.

32. *Le Républicain de Constantine*, 21 June 1896. CAOM 4 H 29.

33. A. S. Kanya-Forstner, "French African Policy and the Anglo-French Agreement of 5 August 1890," *Historical Journal* 12, no. 4 (December 1969): 628–50.

34. Forts Miribel, Lallemand, and MacMahon. CAOM 22 H 47. Cambon was not working explicitly to avenge Flatters but was doing his part in the so-called scramble for Africa. More important, he wanted to expand the power of the military and the governor-general's office in an Algeria that was now dominated by civilian rule.

35. E.-F. Gautier, *La Conquête du Sahara: essai de psychologie politique* (Paris: Armand Colin, 1910).

36. Telegram from Lieutenant Colonel d'Eu to Division d'Alger, 29 March 1900. CAOM F80 1696.

37. Interview with Flamand, *La Dépêche algérienne*, 1 March 1900. Clipping in CAOM 22 H 59.

38. Chef d'escadron Laperrine to Capitaine Cauvet, Adrar, 24 March 1902. CAOM 14 X 2.

39. Chef d'escadron Laperrine to Capitaine Cauvet, Adrar, 14 April 1902. CAOM 14 X 2.

40. Monthly Report, Annexe d'In Salah, 21 April–20 May 1902. CAOM 66 I 3.

41. Jeremy Keenan, *The Lesser Gods of the Sahara: Social Change and Contested Terrain amongst the Tuareg of Algeria* (London: Frank Cass, 2004), 59, n. 16.

42. "Rapport de tournée de Lieutenant Guillo-Lohan," In Salah, 18 February 1903. CAOM 22 H 49.

43. Lieutenant Cottenest to Capitain Cauvet, In Amedjel, 10 May 1902. CAOM 14 X 3.

44. "Rapport de tournée de Lieutenant Guillo-Lohan." It should be noted that this report was edited with an eye toward publication. The passages referring to the most flagrant acts are crossed out in the original document. I have included them here.

45. This occurred several years later. See Paul Pandolfi, "In-Salah 1904 / Tamanrasset 1905: les deux soumission des Touaregs Kel-Ahaggar," *Cahiers d'études africaines* 38, no. 149 (1998): 41–83.

46. Gautier, *La Conquête du Sahara*, 38.

BIBLIOGRAPHY

RESEARCH AIDS AND ARCHIVAL INVENTORIES

Antoine, Marie-Elisabeth, and Suzanne Olivier. *Inventaire des papiers de la Division des Sciences et Lettres du ministère de l'Instruction publique et des services qui en sont issus (sous-série F)*. 2 vols. Paris: Archives nationales, 1975, 1981.

Bensussan, Gérard, and Georges Labica. *Dictionnaire critique du marxisme*. Paris: Presses Universitaires de France, 1982.

Bernard, Gildas. *Guide des recherches sur l'histoire des familles*. Paris: Archives nationales, 1981.

Bonté, Pierre, and Michel Izard, eds. *Dictionnaire de l'ethnologie et de l'anthropologie*. Paris: Presses Universitaires de France, 1991.

Broc, Numa. *Dictionnaire illustré des explorateurs et grands voyageurs français du XIXe siècle*. Vol. 1: *L'Afrique*. Paris: Comite des travaux historique et scientifiques, 1988.

Brochier, Jeanne André. *Livre d'or de l'Algérie: Dictionnaire des personnalités passés et contemporaines*. Algiers: Baconnier, 1937.

Boyer, Pierre. "Bref aperçu sur les archives sahariennes du dépôt des archives d'outre-mer." *Revue de l'Occident musulman et de la Méditerranée* 15 (1972): 181–85.

Cahen, Gilbert, Alexandre Labat, and Gabrielle Vilar-Berrogain. *Etat sommaire des versements faits aux archives nationales par les ministères et les administrations qui en dépendent (Série F)*. Paris: Imprimerie nationale, 1972.

Catalogue d'exposition: histoire de l'Algérie des origines à l'indépendance, 15 octobre 1994 à 15 novembre 1994. Algiers: Bibliothèque nationale de l'Algérie, 1994 (French and Arabic bilingual edition).

Cheurfy, Achou. *Mémoire algérienne: le dictionnaire biographique.* Algiers: Dahlab, 1996.

Chevaldonné, Hélène. *Répertoire numérique de la sous-série 2 U: culte musulman.* Aix-en-Provence: CAOM, 1988.

Duclos, France. "La Société de géographie: sa bibliothèque et ses collections photographiques." *Ethnographie* 87, no. 1 (1991): 179–84.

The Encyclopaedia of Islam. Rev. ed. Edited by P. J. Bearman et al. Leiden: Brill, 1960–2004.

Esquer, G., and E. Dermenghem. *Inventaire sommaire, Archives du Gouvernement Général de l'Algérie, Série E et EE (Correspondance politique générale).* Algiers: Ancienne imprimerie V. Heintz, 1949.

———. *Répertoire, Archives du Gouvernement Général de l'Algérie, Série X (Dons et acquisitions diverses).* Algiers: Imprimerie E. Imbert, 1954.

Fabre, Marc-André. *Inventaire des archives conservées au Service historique de l'Etat-major de l'Armée, Château de Vincennes.* 2nd ed. Paris: Ateliers d'impression de l'Armée, 1954.

Fagnan, E. *Catalogue général des manuscrits de la Bibliothèque nationale de l'Algérie.* Algiers: Bibliothèque nationale de l'Algérie, 1995.

Favier, Jean, ed. *Les Archives nationales: état des inventaires.* Vol. 2: *1789–1940.* Paris: Archives nationales, 1991.

Favier, Jean, and Rémi Mathieu, eds. *Les Archives nationales: état général des fonds.* Vol. 2: *1789–1940.* Paris: Archives nationales, 1978.

Favier, Jean, et al., eds. *Les Archives nationales: état général des fonds.* Vol. 3: *Marine et Outre-Mer.* Paris: Archives nationales, 1980.

Féraud, Laurent-Charles. *Les Interprètes de l'armée d'Afrique.* Algiers: Jourdan, 1876.

Fierro, Alfred. *Inventaire des manuscrits de la Société de géographie.* Paris: Bibliothèque nationale, 1984.

Furet, François, and Mona Ozouf, eds. *A Critical Dictionary of the French Revolution.* Translated by Arthur Goldhammer. Cambridge, Mass.: Harvard University Press, 1989.

Gouvernement Général de l'Algérie, Commissariat du Centenaire. *Les Territoires du sud de l'Algérie.* Vol. 3: *Essai de bibliographie.* Algiers: P. et G. Soubiron, 1930.

Gouvion, Edmond, and Marthe Gouvion. *Kitab aâyane el-marharibe.* Algiers: Imprimerie Orientale Fontana Frères, 1920.

Hachi, Moufida, and Fadéla Takour. *Répertoire numérique du fonds des Territoires du sud conservé au centre des Archives nationales, 1870–1962.* [Algiers: Archives nationales de l'Algérie,] 1999.

d'Huart, Suzanne, and Chantal de Tourtier-Bonazzi. *Archives privées: état des fonds de la série AP.* Paris: S.E.V.P.E.N., 1973.

d'Huart, Suzanne, Chantal de Tourtier-Bonazzi, and Claire Sibille. *État sommaire des fonds d'archives privées.* Paris: Centre historique des Archives nationales, 2004.

Inventaire: Fonds de la Bibliothèque nationale Franz Fanon, Histoire de l'Algérie (unbound inventory located at the Bibliothèque nationale de l'Algérie, El-Hamma).

Klein, Martin. *Historical Dictionary of Slavery and Abolition.* Lanham, Md.: Scarecrow Press, 2002.

Lamoussière, Christiane, and Patrick Laharie. *Le Personnel de l'administration préfectorale, 1881–1926.* Paris: Centre historique des Archives nationales, 2001.

Laplanche, Jean, and J. B. Pontalis. *The Language of Psycho-Analysis.* Translated by Donald Nicholson-Smith. New York: Norton, 1973.

Liauzu, Claude. *Dictionnaire de la colonisation française.* Paris: Larousse, 2007.

Maitron, Jean, ed. *Dictionnaire biographique du mouvement ouvrier français.* Paris: Editions ouvrières, 1964–.

Martin, Henry, and Frantz Funck-Brentano. *Catalogue des manuscrits de la Bibliothèque de l'Arsenal.* Paris: E. Plon, Nourrit et Cie., 1885–99 (Supplément: *Fonds Enfantin par Henry-René d'Allemagne,* 1903 [located at the Bibliothèque de l'Arsenal]).

Masse, Henri. "Les Etudes arabes en Algérie (1830–1930)." *Revue africaine* 74 (1933): 208–58, 458–505.

Maze-Sencier, Geneviève, ed. *Dictionnaire des maréchaux de France du Moyen Age à nos jours.* Paris: Perrin, 1988.

Merabet, Omar. *Bibliographie de l'Algérie du sud (Sahara) et des régions limitrophes.* Algiers: Service géologique de l'Algérie, 1968.

Mesure, Sylvie, and Patrick Savidan, eds. *Le Dictionnaire des sciences humaines.* Paris: Presses Universitaires de France, 2006.

Michelin Map: Africa North and West 741. St-Armand-Montrond [France]: Imprimerie Clerc, 2007.

Michelin Map: Algeria and Tunisia 743. St-Armand-Montrond [France]: Imprimerie Clerc, 2007.

Miller, Joseph C. "Muslim Slavery and Slaving: A Bibliography." *Slavery and Abolition* 13, no. 1 (April 1992): 249–71.

Ministère de la Guerre, *L'Afrique française du nord: bibliographie militaire des ouvrages français ou traduits en français et des articles des principales revues françaises relatifs à l'Algérie, à la Tunisie et au Maroc de 1830 à 1926.* 2 vols. Paris: Imprimerie nationale, 1930.

Nicot, Jean. *Inventaire des archives de l'Algérie.* Vincennes: Ministère de la Défense, Etat-major de l'Armée de terre, Service historique, 1994–.

Parcours (Recherches biographiques de l'Algérie, 1830–1962). Vols 1–18: 1985–93.

Pérès, Henri, and Paul Mangion. *Vocabulaire de base de l'Arabe dialectal algérien et saharien: ou, mille et un mots d'usage courant chez les arabophones de l'Algérie et du Sahara: mots-outils, glossaire français-arabe et glossaire arabe-français, en caractères arabes et en transcription.* Algiers: Maison des livres, 1961.

Peyronnet, Commandant R. *Livre d'or des officiers des Affaires indigènes, 1830–1930.* 2 vols. Algiers: Gouvernement général de l'Algérie, Commissariat général du Centenaire, 1930.

Playfair, R. Lambert. *A Bibliography of Algeria, from the Expedition of Charles V in 1541 to 1887.* London: Clowes, 1898.

Prevost, M., and Roman D'Amat, eds. *Dictionnaire de biographie française.* Paris: Librairie Letouzey et Ané, 1933–.

Reig, Daniel, ed. *Dictionnaire arabe-français, français-arabe.* Paris: Larousse, 1983.

Rey-Courtel, Anne-Lise, and E. Houriez. *Les Archives nationales: État des inventaires.* Vol. 3: *Marine et Outre-Mer.* Paris: Archives nationales, 2000.

Sills, David L., ed. *International Encyclopedia of the Social Sciences.* New York: Macmillan, 1968–.

Thé, Bernard Blaudin de. *Essai de bibliographie du Sahara français et des régions avoisinantes.* 2nd. ed.. Paris: Klincksieck, 1960.

Trésor de la langue française. Paris: Editions du Centre National de la Recherche Scientifique, 1983.

Tulard, Jean, ed. *Dictionnaire du Second Empire*. Paris: Fayard, 1995.

Utheza, Charles. *Archives centrales de l'Algérie, Bureaux arabes de la Division d'Oran, Série J (Archives), Répertoire numérique*. Direction des Archives de France, Annexe d'Aix-en-Provence, 1973 (located at CAOM).

————. *Archives centrales de l'Algérie, Bureaux arabes de la Division d'Alger, Série I (Archives), Répertoire numérique*. Direction des Archives de France, Annexe d'Aix-en-Provence, 1976. (located at CAOM)

————. *Gouvernement général de l'Algérie, Bureaux arabes du Constantinois, Série K (Dossiers), Répertoire numérique*. Aix-En-Provence: CAOM, 1991–1995 (located at CAOM).

Wehr, Hans. *A Dictionary of Modern Written Arabic*. 3rd ed. Edited by J. Milton Cowan. Ithaca, N.Y.: Spoken Language Series, 1976.

Yvert, Benoît. *Dictionnaire des ministres de 1789 à 1989*. Paris: Perrin, 1990.

ARCHIVAL SOURCES

Centre des Archives d'Outre-Mer (CAOM), Aix-en-Provence

Série E and EE: Gouvernement Général de l'Algérie, Correspondance Politique Générale (inventory by G. Esquer and E. Dermenghem, 1949)

1 E Gouverneur Général Correspondance (1840s)
1 EE Gouverneur Général Correspondance (1860s)
2 EE Gouverneur Général Correspondance (1840s)

Série H and HH: Gouvernement Général de l'Algérie, Affaires Indigènes (inventory by P. Boyer, n.d.)

1 H Correspondance politique
2 H Opérations militaires
3 H Questions militaires
4 H Explorations, voyages (mainly French explorers)
8 H Organization administrative
10 H Etudes, notices (In Salah, 1902; El Oued, 1908; Touggourt, 1903; Saharan tariffs, 1893; Saharan commerce, 1890s; Sufi orders; Hamyane; Ouled Naïl; Zaatcha, etc.)
12 H Réformes en faveur des indigènes (12 H 50 on slavery)
16 H Questions religieuses
18 H Dossiers personnels des officiers d'Affaires indigènes (biographical details)
20 H Affaires divers (confidential correspondence)
21 H Territoires du Sud: Chefs indigènes et questions militaires
22 H Territoires du Sud: Opérations militaires et pénétration saharienne
23 H Territoires du Sud: Rapports politiques périodiques
24 H Territoires du Sud: Questions administratives et économiques
27 H Islam: Documentation générale (Saharan forts, 1890s)
30 H Maroc: Correspondance politique et divers (French deserters to Morocco; Bou Amama; Aïn Sefra; border questions)

Serie I: Gouvernement Général de l'Algérie, Bureaux Arabes de la Division d'Alger
(inventory by Charles Utheza, 1976)

1 I Divison d'Alger
60 I Subdivision de Laghouat
61 I Cercle d'El Goléa
62 I Annexe d'Ouargla
63 I Annexe de Ghardaïa
64 I Cercle de Laghouat
66 I Oasis sahariennes
70 I Subdivision de Médéa
73 I Cercle de Bou Saada
75 I Cercle de Djelfa
76 I Cercle de Ghardaïa
77 I Cercle d'El Goléa
78 I Annexe d'Ouargla
79 I Cercle de Laghouat

Série J: Gouvernement Général de l'Algérie, Bureaux Arabes de la Division d'Oran
(inventory by Charles Utheza, 1973)

1 J Division d'Oran
10 J Subdivision d'Aïn-Sefra
11 J Cercle d'Aïn-Sefra
13 J Cercle de Geryville
22 J Cercle d'Aïn-Sefra
23 J Cercle de Geryville

Série K: Gouvernement Général de l'Algérie, Bureaux Arabes de la Division de
Constantine (inventory by Charles Utheza, 1991–95)

1 K Division de Constantine
4 K Cercle de Biskra
8 K Cercle de Touggourt
9 K Annexe d'El-Oued
10 K Subdivision de Batna
15 K Cercle de Biskra
17 K Poste de Touggourt
18 K Annexe de Touggourt
23 K Cercle de Touggourt
24 K Annexe d'El-Oued
44 K Cercle de Biskra
68 K Cercle de Bou-Saada

Sous-Série 2u Culte Musulman, Affaires Indigènes du Gouvernement Général de l'Algérie / Département d'Alger (inventory by Hélène Chevaldonne, 1988)

2 U 22 Zawiya El Hamel
2 U 24–25 Pèlerinages locaux

Série X: Dons et Acquisitions Diverses (inventory by G. Esquer and E. Dermenghem, 1954)

8 X Etudes et pièces diverses (studies by Hirtz, Dermenghem, "Etude sur l'histoire et les populations du Sahara"; "Monographie du poste d'El Goléa"; letter of Yusuf; prostitution)
9 X Coupures de presse et brochures diverses
11 X Papiers Motylinski
12 X Collections d'autographes, d'affiches, documents officiels hors série (slave traffic; abolition in Algeria; irrigation in the Sahara; Saharan commerce; Flatters; Margueritte; Soleillet; Sonis)
13 X Lettres de Lyautey
14 X Papiers Cauvet
18 X (Duveyrier, Laperrine on Saharan combat, 1887–88)
19 X Dossiers Urbanisme
20 X (Capitaine Leselle; Saharan commerce; slavery in Souf, 1957)
23 X Fonds Isabelle Eberhardt
31 X Papiers Dermenghem

Série Oasis

49 Oasis Ouargla
83 Oasis Djelfa
91 Oasis Tidikelt

Série F^{80}: Fonds Ministériels

F^{80} 10 Commission d'Afrique (1833–34)
F^{80} 1671 (Planning, 1830–35)
F^{80} 1672 (Planning, 1836–38)

Série APC: Archives Privées

23 APC Meynier
65 APC Flatters
75 APC Margueritte
83 APC Collection d'autographes (Foucauld letter)

Série APOM: Archives Privées d'Outre-Mer

10 APOM CHEAM (Centre des Hautes Études de l'Afrique et de l'Asie Moderne), Etudes et travaux d'auditeurs

11 APOM Mougin (caravan study, 1901)
26 APOM Trouillet (Rebillet letters)

Bibliothèque AOM

Assorted published documents and pamphlets

Centre des Archives Nationales (CARAN), Paris

Archives Privées

47 AP Papiers Henri Duveyrier
235 AP Papiers Maréchal Pélissier
F¹² Commerce et Industrie
F¹⁷ Instruction Publique

Bibliothèque Nationale de France, Arsenal (BNF-A), Paris

Ms. 14 Norbert Dournaux-Dupéré
Ms. 15 Henri Duveyrier
Ms. 7720 Charles Duveyrier (correspondence with Père Enfantin)
Ms. 13739 Charles Duveyrier (correspondence with Ismael Urbain)

Bibliothèque Nationale de France, Richelieu

Département des Cartes et Plans, Société de Géographie (BNF-R), Paris

Carton Du- Ey 372–406 (Duveyrier-Rohlfs correspondence)
Carton Foureau
Carton Mart-Me (E. Masqueray; Maulin, "Projet d'un voyage chez les Touaregs," 1862)
Carton Ta-Ve (Saharan exploration, 1885)
Colis 3 bis 1622–1632 (early letters of the Société de Géographie on Sahara; H. Duveyrier, "Le Progrès de nos connaissance sur l'Afrique," n.d.)
Colis 4 (Sahara, 1870s)
Colis 6 (Largeau)
Colis 15 (Flatters)
Colis 15 bis (Touareg, 1880s)
Colis 18 (Foureau)
Colis 19 (Sahara, 1820s)
Colis 27 (H. Duveyrier instruction to Soleillet, 1873)
Colis 33 (Douls, Flatters, 1880s)
Colis 35 (Besset, Tidikelt, 1905)
Ms in-4 3 (Flatters)
Ms in-4 18 (expedition to El Goléa, 1872)
Ms in-4 25 (Soleillet, 1874)

Ms in-8 4 (Foucauld, 1885)
Ms in-8 63 (Rohlfs, 1859)
Ms in-8 109 Algérie (Saharan routes, 1870s)
Ms in-8 110 (route to Laghouat, 1882)

Service Historique de l'Armée de Terre (SHAT), Vincennes

Série 1 K Algérie

Various Saharan reports

Série 1 H Algérie

1 H   90 Correspondance des trois provinces
1 H 208 Organisation des Spahis, 1834–45
1 H 211 Journal de marche, Oran 1847
1 H 213 Operations militaires, 1840s
1 H 229 Mémoires, Chefs indigènes
1 H 230 Mémoires
1 H 262 Oran, Cavaignac correspondance, 1847
1 H 263 Cavaignac correspondance, 1847
1 H 267 Yusuf correspondance, 1852
1 H 339 Situations générales, 1840–1850s
1 H 1032 Tidikelt, 1900s
1 H 2107 In Salah, 1963
1 K 563 Nomades

Archives de la Chambre de Commerce de Marseille (ACCM)

Mq 4 Banques coloniales
Mq 5 Commerce saharien (1870s)

Bibliothèque Nationale de l'Algérie, El-Hamma

Fonds Maghrébins

Archives Nationales de l'Algérie (ANA), Algiers

Territoires du Sud
Série Agriculture
Série Personnelle

National Archives, College Park, Maryland (NARA)

Record Group 84 (records of Foreign Service Posts, Consular Posts, Algiers, Algeria)
RG 84 Volume 001
RG 84 Volume 005
RG 84 Volume 009
RG 84 Volume 010
RG 84 Volume 011

PRIMARY SOURCES

'Abd Allah ibn Muhammad, abu Salim al-'Aiyashi. *Voyages dans le sud de l'Algérie et des états barbaresques de l'ouest et de l'est par El-'Aïachi et Moula-Ahmed, traduits sur deux manuscrits arabes de la Bibliothèque d'Alger par Adrien Berbrugger*. Paris: Imprimerie Royale, 1846.

Abd al-Qadir ibn Muhyi al-Din. *Lettre aux Français: notes brèves destinées à ceux qui comprennent pour attirer l'attention sur les problèmes essentiels*. Translated by René R. Khawan. Paris: Phébus, 1984.

Affaire de l'Oued Mahouine (Cercle de Tébessa): massacre d'une caravane (27 victimes). 2 vols. Constantine: Marle, 1870.

Ahmed-Efendi, Hadji. *La Prise d'Alger racontée par un Algérien*. Translated by M. Ottocar de Schlechta. Paris: Imprimerie Impériale, 1863.

Alaude, Jacques. *La Question indigène dans l'Afrique du Nord, son équivoque: une maladie de la pensée politique française, 1863–1912*. Paris: n.p., n.d. [ca. 1913].

Amat, Charles. *L'Esclavage au M'zab: étude anthropologique des nègres*. Paris: Imprimerie. de A. Hennuyer, [1885].

———. *Le M'zab et les M'zabites*. Paris: Challamel, 1888.

Amaury, A. *Colonisation de l'Algérie: Observations, par appendice et à l'appui d'un plan d'établissement en Algérie de colonies agricoles*. Paris: P.-F. Beaulé, 1842.

———. *Projet d'établissement de colonies agricoles à fonder en Algérie, proposé comme un des plus puissants moyens d'extinction de la mendicité et même du paupérisme en France*. Paris: Imprimerie de Pollet, 1842.

Amero. "Résultats économiques de l'émancipation commerciale des colonies anglaises." *Revue algérienne et coloniale*, 1st ser., vol. 2 (1860): 505–27.

André, Pierre Jean Daniel (pseud. Général Pierre Redan). *L'Islam et les races*. 2 vols. Paris: Geuthner, 1922.

Annuaire militaire de l'Empire français pour l'année 1861. Paris and Strasbourg: Veuve Berger-Levrault et Fils, 1861.

d'Armagnac, Lieutenant. *Le Mzab et les pays Chaamba*. Algiers: Baconnier, 1934.

———. *Le Sahara, carrefour des races*. Algiers: Baconnier, 1934.

Armieux, Louis Léon Cyrille. *Topographie médicale du Sahara de la province d'Oran, par le Docteur Armieux*. Algiers: F. Paysant, 1886.

Arnaud, Marc-Antoine. "Notice sur les Sahari, les Ouled ben Aliya, les Ouled Naïl et sur l'origine des tribus cheurfa," *Revue africaine* 8 (1864): 104–17; 10 (1866): 17–35.

———. "Histoire des Ouled Naïl, faisant suite à celle des Sahari." *Revue africaine* 16 (1872): 327–35; 17 (1873): 300–312 and 374–90.

——. *Les Roueries de Dalila: conte traduit des* Mille et une Nuits. Algiers: Aillaud, 1879.

——. *Voyages extraordinaires et nouvelles agréables: récits historiques sur l'Afrique septentrionale,* by Mohammad Abou Ras al Nasri. Algiers: A. Jourdan, 1885.

——. *Etude sur le soufisme,* by Cheikh Abd Al Hadi ibn Ridouan. Algiers: A. Jourdan, 1888.

——. *Sa Majesté Bakchiche, ou Monsieur Pourboire,* by Ahmed-Farēs. Algiers: Fontana, 1893.

——, trans. "Les Rius Cheurfa (Nobles): traduction d'un fragment du livre 'De la vérité,' par Mohamed ben Bou Zid des Ouled Khaled (Djebel Amour)." *Revue africaine* 17 (1873): 208.

Arnaud, Edouard Joseph, and Maurice Adrien Cortier. *Nos Confins sahariens: étude d'organisation militaire.* Paris: E. Larose, 1908.

Asse, René. *La Mission Flatters, poésie.* Paris: A. Tresse, 1881.

Attanoux, J. B. "C'est qu'il faut penser des Touareg." *Questions diplomaties et coloniales* 2 (1 August 1897): 33–38.

Aucapitaine, Marie Jean Charles Henri. *Voyage au Soudan oriental et dans l'Afrique septentrionale pendant les années 1847 et 1848: comprenant une exploration dans l'Algérie, la régence de Tunis, l'Egypte, la Nubie, les déserts, l'île de Méroé, le Sennaar, le Fa-Zoglo et les contrées inconnues de la Nigritie par M. Trémeaux.* Paris: Imprimerie de Lacour, 1853.

——. "Etudes sur le Sahara algérien." *Revue de l'Orient de l'Algérie et des colonies* 1 (1855): 60–69, 144–162.

——. *Les Confins militaires de la grande Kabylie sous la domination turque (Province d'Alger).* Paris: Moquet, 1857.

——. "Etudes récentes sur les dialectes berbères de l'Algérie." *Nouvelles annales des voyages, de la géographie et de l'histoire* 163 (1859): 170–92.

——. "Sur les Touaregs Imouchar." *Revue orientale et américaine* 3 (1860): 61–72.

——. "Notice sur la tribu des Ait Frqoucen." *Revue africaine* 4 (October 1860): 446–58.

——. *Etude sur la caravane de la Mecque et le commerce de l'intérieur de l'Afrique.* Paris: Imprimerie de J. Claye, n.d. [ca. 1861].

——. *Les Kabyles et la colonisation de l'Algérie: études sur le passé et l'avenir des Kabyles.* Paris: Challamel, 1864.

——. *Les Beni-Mezab: Sahara algérien.* Paris: Challamel Aîné, 1867.

——. *Nouvelles observations sur l'origine des Berbères-Thamou, à propos des lettres sur le Sahara, adressées par M. E. Besor à M. E. Liebig.* Paris: Challamel, 1867.

d'Avezac, Armand. *Afrique: esquisse général de l'Afrique et Afrique ancienne.* Paris: Firmin Didot Frères, 1844.

Baba, Ahmad. "Mi'rāj al-Ṣuʻād, Aḥmad Bābā's Replies on Slavery." Edited and Translated by John Hunwick and Fatima Harrack. *Textes et documents* (University Mohammed V, Institute of African Studies) 7 (2000): 7–65.

Bajolle, Léon Céline Marius. *Le Sahara d'Ouargla: de l'Oued Mia à l'Oued Igharghar.* Algiers: Imprimerie de l'Association Ouvrière, P. Fontana, 1887.

al-Bakri, ʻAbd Allah ibn ʻAbd al-ʻAziz Abu ʻUbayd. "Notice d'un manuscrit arabe contenant la description de l'Afrique." Translated by Etienne Quatremère. *Notices et extraits des manuscrits de la bibliothèque du Roi et autres bibliothèques publiées par l'Institut Royal de France* 12 (1831): 437–664.

——. *Description de l'Afrique septentrionale par Abou-Obeid-el-Bekri.* Translated by William MacGuckin de Slane. Algiers: Imprimerie du Gouvernement, 1857.

——. "Description de l'Afrique septentrionale." *Journal asiatique*, 5th ser., 12–14 (1858): (12): 412–92; 97–533; (13): 58–80; 97–194; 310–416; 67–519; (14): 117–52.

Balzac, Honoré de. *Œuvres complètes.* Vol. 12: *Les Chouans* et *Une passion dans le désert.* Paris: Calmann Lévy, 1892.

——. *Œuvres complètes.* Vol. 11: *Les Employés.* Paris: Calmann Lévy, 1892.

Du Barail, Général François-Charles. *Mes souvenirs.* 2 vols. Paris: Plon, 1894–96.

Barbier, Joseph-Victor. *A travers le Sahara: les missions du Colonel Flatters d'après des documents absolument inédits.* Paris: Téqui, 1895.

Barth, Henri (Heinrich). *Reisen un Entdeckungen in Nord- und Central-Afrika in den Jahren 1849 bis 1855.* 5 vols. Gotha: J. Perths, 1857.

——. *Travels and Discoveries in North and Central Africa.* 5 vols. London: Longman, Brown, Green, Longman and Roberts, 1857–58.

——. *Voyages et découverts dans l'Afrique septentrionale et centrale pendant les années 1849 à 1855.* Translated by Paul Ithier. 4 vols. Paris: A. Bohné, 1860–61.

——. "Sur les expéditions scientifiques en Afrique." *Bulletin de la Société de géographie de Paris*, 6th ser., vol. 4 (July–December 1872): 133–49.

von Bary, Erwin. *Le Dernier Rapport d'un Européen sur Ghât et les Touareg de l'Aïr.* Translated by Henri Schirmer. Paris: Fischbacher, 1898.

Bassenne, Marthe. *Aurèlie Tedjani, princesse des sables.* Paris: Plon, 1925.

ibn Battuta, Muhammad ibn 'Abd Allah. *Voyage dans le Soudan, traduit sur les manuscrits de la bibliothèque du roi par M. MacGuckin de Slane.* Paris: Imprimerie Royale, 1843.

Baudicour, Louis de. *La Guerre et le gouvernement de l'Algérie.* Paris: Librairie du Centre Algérien, 1853.

——. *La Colonisation de l'Algérie: ses éléments.* Paris: Jacques Lecoffre, 1856.

——. "La Culture du tabac en Algérie." *Revue contemporain* 18 (1860): 667–709.

——. *Histoire de la colonisation de l'Algérie.* Paris: Challamel Aîné, 1860.

Bendjelloul, Si Abbas. "La Prise d'Alger, en 1830 d'après un écrivain musulman." Translated by Laurent-Charles Féraud. *Recueil des notices et mémoires de la Société archéologique de la Province de Constantine* 9 (1865): 67–79.

Bengana, Bouaziz. *Une famille de grands chefs sahariens: les Benganga.* Algiers: Soubiron, 1930.

Les Ben-Gana depuis la conquête française. Paris: E. Dentu, 1879.

Benhazera, M. *Six mois chez les Touareg Ahaggar.* Algiers: Jourdan, 1908.

Benoit, Pierre. *L'Atlantide: roman.* Paris: Albin Michel, 1919.

Bentham-Edwards, Matilda. *Through Spain to the Sahara.* London: Hurst and Blackett, 1868.

Berbrugger, Adrien. *Voyage au camp d'Abd el-Kader à Hamzah et aux montagnes de Wannouhah (Province de Constantine), 1837–1838.* Toulouse: Imprimerie Eugène Aurel, 1839.

——. *Algérie: Historique, pittoresque et monumentale; recueil de vues, monuments, cérémonies, costumes dessinés d'après nature, avec texte descriptif des localités, mœurs, usages, jeux.* 3 vols. Paris: J. Delahaye, 1843.

——. *Négociations entre Monseigneur l'évêque d'Alger et Abd El Qader pour l'échange des prisonniers.* Paris: J. Delahaye, 1844.

——. *Le 48e de ligne en Afrique en 1830 et de 1837 à 1844*. Algiers: n.p., 1844.

——. *Le Pégnon d'Alger, ou Les origines du gouvernement Turc en Algérie*. Algiers: Imprimerie A. Bourget, 1847.

——. *Projet d'exploration de la deuxième ligne des oasis algériennes par Gabès, Souf, Touggourt, Ouargla, Goléa, Touat et retour par Metlili et le Ouadi Mzab*. [Paris]: Imprimerie de A. Bourget, [1850].

——. *Les Epoques militaires de la Grande Kabylie*. Algiers: Bastide, 1857.

——. *Géronimo le martyr du fort des Vingt quatre heures à Alger*. 2nd ed. Algiers: Bastide, 1859.

——. *Bibliothèque-Musée: Livret explicatif des collections diverses de ces deux établissements*. Algiers: Bastide, 1860.

——. "Des frontières de l'Algérie." *Revue africaine* 4 (1860): 401–17.

——. *Du meilleur système à suivre pour l'exploration de l'Afrique centrale*. Algiers: Publication Historique Algérienne, 1860.

——. *Les Puits artésiens des oasis méridionales de l'Algérie*. 2nd ed. Algiers: Bastide, 1860.

——. "Nécrologie [of Charles Cusson]." *Revue africaine* 11 (1867): 494–96.

——. "Les Anciens Etablissements religieux musulmans de Constantine." *Revue africaine* 12 (1868): 121–33.

Berbrugger, Adrien, and Jean André Napoléon Périer. *De l'hygiène en Algérie*. Paris: Imprimerie Royale, 1847.

Bernard, Augustin, and Napoléon Lacroix. *Historique de la pénétration saharienne*. Algiers-Mustapha: Giralt, 1900.

——. *Evolution du nomadisme en Algérie*. Paris: Challamel / Algiers: Jourdan, 1906.

——. *La Pénétration saharienne, 1830–1906*. Algiers: Imprimerie Algérienne, 1906.

Bernard, F. *Quatre mois dans le Sahara*. Paris: Delagrave, 1881.

——. *Deuxième mission Flatters: historique et rapport rédiges avec documents à l'appui et une carte adressée au service central des Affaires indigènes*. Algiers: Gouvernement Général de l'Algérie, 1882.

——. *Deux missions françaises chez les Touareg en 1880–81*. Algiers: Jordan, 1896.

Berthezène, Pierre. *Dix-huit mois à Alger*. Montpellier: Richard, 1834.

Bescherelle, Louis-Nicolas. *Dictionnaire national ou dictionnaire universel de la langue française*. Paris: Garnier Frères, 1856.

Besset, Lieutenant [G.], and Capitaine [Louis Auguste Théodore] Pein. *Reconnaissances au Sahara: D'In Salah à Amguid et à Tikhammar* [Besset]; *Chez les Touareg Azdjer: d'Ouargla à Tarat* [Pein]. Paris: Comité de l'Afrique Française, 1904.

Beuassier, [Marcelin]. "Notice sommaire sur le colonel Beauprêtre." *Revue africaine* 14 (1870): 441–44.

Biographie du Général Cavaignac. Paris: Plon Frères, n.d.

Bissuel, Henri. *Les Touareg de l'ouest*. Algiers: Jourdan, 1888.

——. *Le Sahara français: conférence sur les questions sahariennes, faite les 21 et 31 mars 1891 à MM. les officiers de la garnison de Médéa*. Algiers: A. Jourdan, 1891.

Bodichon, Barbara Leigh Smith. *An American Diary, 1857–8*. Edited by Joseph W. Reed Jr. London: Routledge & Kegan Paul, 1972.

Bodichon, (Dr.) Eugène. *Tableau synoptique représentant les noms, les émigrations, les filiations, l'origine des races de l'Afrique septentrionale*. Nantes: Imprimerie de Vve C. Mellinet, 1844.

——. *Considérations sur l'Algérie*. Paris: Comptoir Central de la Librairie, 1845.

——. *Etudes sur l'Algérie et l'Afrique*. Algiers: chez l'auteur [printed at Plon Frères, Paris], 1847.

——. *Projet d'une exploration politique, commerciale et scientifique d'Alger à Tombouctou par le Sahara*. Paris: L. Martinet, 1849.

——. *Hygiène à suivre en Algérie: acclimatement des Européens*. Algiers: Imprimerie de Rey, Delavigne et Cie, 1851.

——. *De l'humanité*. Brussels: A. Lacroix, Verboeckhoven et Cie, 1866.

——. *Le Vade-mecum de la politique française*. Algiers: Imprimerie de A. Bouyer, 1883.

——. *Œuvres diverses*. Paris: E. Leroux, 1886.

Boileau, Nicolas. *Oeuvres diverses du sieur D—— avec le Traité du sublime ou du merveilleux dans le discours (traduction du grec de Longin)*. Paris: Chez D. Thierry, 1674.

Bonnafont, Dr. [Jean-Pierre]. "Notice sur les trois chefs Touareg qui sont venus à Paris." *Bulletin de la Société d'anthropologie* 4 (1863): 104–17.

Bonnemain, Capitaine [François-Louis] de. "Voyage a R'adamès." *Revue algérienne et coloniale* 1 (novembre, 1859): 116–32.

Bouderba, Ismaël. "Voyage à R'at." *Revue algérienne et coloniale* 1 (December 1859): 241–305.

Boudin, Jean-Christian-Marc. *Histoire statistique de la colonisation et de la population en Algérie*. Paris: J.-B. Baillère, 1853.

Bourguignat, Jules-René. *Souvenirs d'une exploration scientifique dans le nord de l'Afrique*. Paris: Challamel Aîné, 1868–70.

Bourseul, E.-Ch. *Souvenirs de la guerre d'Afrique: insurrection des Zibans, Zaatcha*. Metz: Imprimerie de Verronnais, 1851.

Boutin, Vincent-Yves. *Aperçu historique, statistique et topographique sur l'état d'Alger, à l'usage de l'armée expéditionnaire d'Afrique: avec plans, vues et costumes, publié par ordre de Son Excellence le ministre de la guerre*. Paris: Picquet, 1830.

Brosselard, Charles. *Les Khouan: de la constitution des ordres religieux musulmans en Algérie*. Paris: Challamel, 1859.

Brosselard-Faidherbe, Henri François. *Les Deux Missions du colonel Flatters en Afrique: Récit historique et critique par un membre de la première mission, d'après ses notes de voyages, les journaux de route du colonel et les interrogatoires subis par les survivants de la deuxième mission*. Paris: M. Dreyfous, 1884.

Broussais, Emile. *De Paris au Soudan: Marseille-Alger-Transsaharien*. Algiers: Imprimerie Casabianca, 1891.

——. *Le Crime d'El-Ouatia. Assassinat du marquis de Morès. Chambre criminelle de Sousse, juillet 1902. Plaidoiries de Me de Las Cases et de Me Broussais pour Mme la marquise de Morès*. Paris: Imprimerie Plon-Nourrit et Cie, 1904.

Buchanan, Angus. *Sahara*. New York: D. Appleton, 1926.

Bugeaud, Thomas Robert. *Mémoire sur notre établissement dans la province d'Oran, par suite de la paix*. Paris: Gaultier-Laguionie, 1838.

——. *L'Algérie, des moyens de conserver et d'utiliser cette conquête*. Paris: Dentu, 1842.

——. *De la colonisation de l'Algérie*. Paris: Guyot, Imprimeur du Roi, 1847.

——. *Veillées d'une chaumière de la Vendée*. Paris: Ledoyen, 1849.

——. *Lettres inédites de Maréchal Bugeaud duc d'Isly, 1808–1849*. Edited by Capitaine Tattet et Féray-Bugeaud d'Isly. Paris: Emile-Paul Frères, 1923.

———. *Par l'épée et par la charrue: écrits et discours de Bugeaud*. Edited by Paul Azan. Paris: Presse Universitaires de France, 1948.

———. *Œuvres militaires du Maréchal Bugeaud, duc d'Isly*. Edited by Maurice-Henri Weil. Paris: Trois Hussards, 1982.

———. *La Guerre des rues et des maisons*. Edited by Maité Bouyssy. Paris: Jean-Paul Rocher, 1997.

———. *Le Peuplement français de l'Algérie par Bugeaud (d'après les écrits et discours du Maréchal)*. Tunis: Editions du Comité Bugeaud, n.d.

Burckardt, John Lewis. "Mœurs des brigands arabes." Translated by Stanislas Julien. *Revue des deux mondes* 3–4 (1831): 691–700.

Burke, Edmund. *A Philosophical Enquiry into the Origin of Our Ideas of the Sublime and Beautiful*. 1757. Edited by Adam Phillips. Oxford: Oxford University Press, 1990.

Burthe d'Annelet, André Joseph Victor de. *A travers l'Afrique française du Cameroun à Alger, par le Congo, le Haute-Oubanghi-Chari, le Ouadaï, l'Ennedi, le Borkou, le Tibesti, le Kaouar, le Zinder, l'Aïr, le Niger, le Ahaggar et le pays Ajjer (septembre 1928–juin 1931)*. Paris: P. Roger, 1932.

Caillié, Réné. *Voyage à Temboctou et à Jenné, dans l'Afrique Centrale, précédé d'observations faites chez les Maures Braknas, les Nalous et d'autre peuples, pendant les années 1824, 1825, 1826, 1827, 1828*. Paris: Imprimerie Royale, 1830.

———. "Discours lu à la séance publique de la Société de géographie du 10 décembre 1838." *Bulletin de la Société de géographie de Paris* 10 (December 1838): 330–59.

———. *Travels through Central Africa to Timbuctoo and across the Great Desert, to Morocco*. 2 vols. London: Frank Cass, 1968.

———. *Voyage à Tombouctou*. 2 vols. Paris: La Découverte, 1996.

Carbuccia, J. L. *Du dromadaire comme bête de somme et comme animal de guerre*. Paris: Dumaine, 1853.

Carette, Ernest. *Couplets chantés au nom des élèves de l'Ecole polytechnique au banquet qui leur fut offert par les anciens élèves de cette Ecole, le 16 août 1830*. Paris: Imprimerie de J. Tastu, n.d.

———. *Du commerce de l'Algérie avec l'Afrique centrale et les Etats Barbaresques: Réponse à la note de M. Jules de Lasteyrie sur le commerce du Soudan*. Paris: Guyot, 1844.

———. *Etude sur les routes suivies par les Arabes dans la partie méridionale de l'Algérie et de la Régence de Tunis pour servir à l'établissement du réseau géographique de ces contrées*. Paris: Imprimerie Royale, 1844.

———. *Recherches sur la géographie et le commerce de l'Algérie méridionale*. Paris: Imprimerie Royale, 1844.

———. *Etudes sur la Kabylie proprement dite*. 2 vols. Paris: Imprimerie Nationale, 1848.

———. *Recherches sur l'origine et les migrations des principales tribus de l'Afrique septentrionale et particulièrement de l'Algérie*. Paris: Imprimerie Nationale, 1853.

Carette, Ernest, and P. Rozet. *L'Algérie*. Paris: F. Didot, 1856.

Carette, Ernest, and Dr. Auguste-Hubert Warnier. *Description et division de l'Algérie*. Paris: Editions L. Hachette et Cie, 1847.

Castaing, Alphonse. "Souvenirs d'un indigène de la Nigritie." *Revue orientale et américaine* 3 (1860): 141–54.

Castellane, Esprit-Victor-Elisabeth-Boniface, comte de. *Journal du maréchal de Castellane, 1804–1862*. 5 vols. Paris: Plon, 1895–97.

———. *Campagnes d'Afrique, 1835–1848: lettres adressées au maréchal de Castellane*. Paris: Librairie Plon, 1898.

Castellane, Louis Charles Pierre, comte de. *Souvenirs de la vie militaire en Afrique*. Paris: V. Lecou, 1852.

Cat, E. *Biographies algériennes, 1830–1900*. N.p.: n.p., n.d.

Cauneille, A. (Cdt.). *Les Chaanba (leur nomadisme)*. Paris: Centre National de Recherche Scientifique, 1968.

Cauvet, Gaston. "La Culture du palmier dans le Sud Algérien." *Bulletin du Comité de l'Afrique française, renseignements coloniaux* 12 (1902): 137–43.

———. "L'Oasis d'El-Golea." *Bulletin de la Société de géographie d'Alger* 9 (1904): 17–60.

———. *Les marabouts: petits monuments funéraires et votifs du Nord de l'Afrique*. Algiers: J. Carbonel, 1923.

———. "L'Oasis ruinée de Sidi Bou Hania." *Bulletin de la Société de géographie d'Alger* 28 (1923): 145–68.

———. "Les noms des tribus Touareg." *Bulletin de la Société de géographie d'Alger* 29 (1924): 275–319.

———. "Les Origines caucasiennes des Touareg." *Bulletin de la Société de géographie d'Alger* 29 (1924): 419–444; 30 (1925): 1–38.

———. "La Formation celtique de la nation Targue." *Bulletin de la Société de géographie d'Alger* 30 (1925): 377–399; continued in 31 (1926): 60–95, and 183–205.

———. *Le Chameau: Anatomie, physiologie, races, extérieur, vie et mœurs, élevage, alimentation, maladies, rôle économique*. Paris: J. B. Baillière, 1925.

———. *Les Berbères en Amérique: essai d'éthnocinésie, préhistoire*. Algiers: J. Bringau, 1930.

———. *Notes sur le Souf et les Souafa*. Algiers: Imprimerie Baconnier, 1934.

———. *Le Raid du Lieutenant Cottenest au Hoggar*. Marseille: Brunon, 1945.

Cauvin, F. "Contribution à l'étude de la pathologie indigène dans l'annexe de Laghouat." *Archives de l'Institut Pasteur d'Algérie* 17, no. 2 (June 1939): 286–93.

Celarié, Henriette. *Nos sœurs musulmanes: scènes de la vie du désert*. [Paris]: Hachette, 1925.

Chabigny, Assid el-Hadj Salam. "Relation d'un voyage de Fez à Timbouctou, fait vers l'année 1787." *Nouvelles annales des voyages, de la géographie et de l'histoire* 7 (1820): 5–51.

du Champ, E., A., et al. *Le Pays du mouton: des conditions d'existence des troupeaux sur les hauts-plateaux et dans le sud de l'Algérie*. Algiers: Giralt, 1893.

Champeaux, Guillaume de. *A travers les oasis sahariennes: les spahis sahariens*. [Paris]: R. Chapelot, 1903.

Chanzy. "Du commerce de l'Algérie avec le Sahara et l'Afrique centrale et de son influence sur notre domination." *Journal des sciences militaires* 26 (1853): 264–88; 27 (1853): 111–46.

Chateaubriand, François-Auguste-René de. *Atala, ou les amours de deux sauvages dans le désert*. Paris: Migneret, 1801; rev. ed., Paris: Le Normant, 1805.

Cherbonneau, Auguste. *Précis historique de la dynastie des Benou-Djellab, princes de Tuggurt*. Paris: Imprimerie E. Thunot et Cie, 1851.

Chevrillon, André. *Les Puritains du désert*. Paris: Plon, 1927.

Choisy, Auguste. *Le Sahara: souvenirs d'une mission à Goléah*. Paris: E. Plon, 1881.

———. *Documents relatifs à la mission dirigée au sud de l'Algérie par M. Choisy*. Paris: Imprimerie Nationale, 1890.

Christian, Pierre. *L'Afrique française, l'empire de Maroc, et les déserts de Sahara: conquêtes, victoires et découvertes des français, depuis la prise d'Alger jusqu'à nos jours.* Paris: A. Barbier, 1846.

Clauzel, Le Maréchal Bertrand. *Nouvelles observations sur la colonisation d'Alger.* Paris: Selligue, 1833.

Cler, Jean-Joseph-Gustave. *Souvenirs d'un officier du 2ᵉ de zouaves.* ("Rédigé sur les notes du général Cler, par le Bon A. Du Casse," pseud. de le Bon Valois de Forville.) Paris: Michel Lévy Frères, 1859.

Clermont-Tonnerre, Aimé-Marie-Gaspard. "Le Rapport du marquis de Clermont-Tonnerre, ministre de la guerre, sur une expédition à Alger (1827)." Edited by Paul Azan. *Revue africaine* 70 (1929): 207–53.

Colomb, Louis Joseph Jean François de. *Exploration des ksours et du Sahara de la Province d'Oran.* Algiers: Imprimerie du Gouvernement. Paris: Challamel, 1858.

———. *Notice sur les oasis du Sahara et des routes qui y conduisent.* Paris: Charles Lahure, 1860.

"Considérations critiques sur l'Afrique intérieur occidentale et analyse comparée du voyage de Caillié et des autres itinéraires connus." *Revue des deux mondes* 2 (April 1830): 117–43.

Cooper, James Fenimore. *Le Dernier des Mohicans, histoire de 1757.* Translated by A.-J.-B. Defauconpret. Paris: C. Gosselin; Mame et Delaunay-Vallée, 1826.

———. *Œuvres complètes de J. Fenimore Cooper.* Volume V: *Le Dernier des Mohicans.* Translated by A.-J.-B. Defauconpret. Paris: Furne et Cie; Charles Gosselin, 1846.

———. *The Last of the Mohicans.* Edited by John McWilliams. Oxford: Oxford University Press, 1994.

Correch (de Lauzerte), Adolphe. *Désastre de Constantine et système de colonisation.* Paris: Dentu, 1837.

Corneille, Thomas. *Le Dictionnaire des arts et des sciences par M. D. C. de l'Académie françoise.* Paris: Chez la Veuve Jean-Baptiste Coignard, Imprimerie Ordinaire du Roy & de l'Académie françoise, 1694.

Cottenest. "Etude historique sur le service des affaires indigènes et la colonisation algérienne, 1830–1850." *Bulletin de la Société de géographie d'Alger* 11 (1906): 83–91.

Coudreau, Henri. *Le Pays de Wargla et les peuples de l'Afrique et Hartmann.* Paris: Viat, 1881.

Coulanges, Fustel de. *La Cité antique: étude sur le culte, le droit, les institutions de la Grèce et de Rome.* Paris: Durand, 1864.

Du Couret, Louis. *Mémoire à sa Majesté Napoléon III, empereur des Français, par le hadji Abd-el-Hamid Bey sur les résultats de la mission officielle que ce voyageur vient de remplir en Afrique.* Paris: Imprimerie de Pommeret et Moreau, 1853.

Coÿne, Abel Andri. *Une ghazzia dans le Grand-Sahara: Itinéraire de la ghazzia faite, en 1875, sur les Braber, par les Chambaa de Metlili et de Goléa.* Algiers: A. Jourdan, 1881.

Crosnier, Elise. *Aurèlie Picard, 1849–1933, première française au Sahara.* Algiers: Baconnier, n.d. [ca. 1947].

Dastuge, H. *Quelques mots au sujet de Tafilet et de Sidjilmassa.* Paris: Imprimerie E. Martinet, 1867.

Daubige, Charles. "Le Mozabite contre l'Arabe." *Revue des deux mondes* 53 (1 October 1882): 673–681.

Daudet, Alphonse. *Tartarin de Tarascon*. Paris: Flammarion, 1877.

Daumas, Général Melchior Joseph Eugène. *Exposé sur l'état actuel de la société arabe, du gouvernement et de la législation qui la régit*. Algiers: Imprimerie du Gouvernement, 1844.

———. *Le Sahara algérien: Etudes géographiques, statistiques et historiques sur la région au sud des établissements français en Algérie*. Paris: Fortin, Masson et Cie, 1845.

———. *Principes généraux du cavalier arabe*. Paris: Hachette, 1854.

———. *Les Chevaux du Sahara et les mœurs du désert*. 3rd ed. Paris: Michel Lévy, 1855.

———. *Mœurs et coutumes de l'Algérie: Tell, Kabylie, Sahara*. 2nd ed. Paris: Hachette, 1855.

———. *Correspondance du Capitaine Daumas, consul à Mascara, 1837–1839*. Edited by Georges Yver. Algiers: Adolphe Jourdan, 1912.

———. *La Femme arabe*. Algiers: Jourdan, 1912.

Daumas, Général Melchior Joseph Eugène, and Ausone de Chancel. *Le Grand désert: itinéraire d'une caravane du Sahara au pays des Nègres; royaume de Haoussa*. Paris: N. Chaix, 1848.

Delahaye, Jules. *Les Assassins et les vengeurs de Morès*. 3 vols. Paris: Victor Tetaux, 1905–7.

Delayen, Gaston. *Les Deux Affaires du capitaine Doineau: l'attaque de la diligence de Tlemcen (1856); l'évasion de Bazaine (1874), d'après des documents inédits*. La Chapelle-Montligeon (Orne): Imprimerie de Montligeon; Paris: Editions des Juris-classeurs, 1924.

Deloncle, Pierre Eugène Marie Joseph. *La Caravane aux éperons verts (Mission Alger-Niger)*. Paris: Plon, 1927.

Delpêche, Adrien. "Un diplôme de Mokadem de la confrérie religieuse Rahmaniya." *Revue africaine* 18 (1874): 418–22.

Demontès, Victor. *L'Algérie économique*. Algiers: Imprimerie Algérienne, 1922.

Denham, Dixon. *Voyages et découvertes dans le nord et dans les parties centrales de l'Afrique . . . exécutés pendant les années 1822, 1823 et 1824, par le major Denham, le capitaine Clapperton et le docteur Oudney*. Translated by MM. Eyriès et de Larenaudière. Paris: A. Bertrand, 1826.

Depont, Octave, and Xavier Coppolani. *Les Confréries musulmanes*. Algiers: A. Jourdan, 1897.

Deporter, Victor. *A propos du Transsaharien. Extrême sud de l'Algérie: le Gourara, le Touat, In-Salah, le Tidikelt, les pays des Touareg-Hoggar, l'Adrar, Tin bouctou, Agadès*. Algiers: P. Fontana et Cie, 1890.

———. *La Question du Touat. Sahara algérien: Gourara, Touat, Tidikelt, caravanes et Trans-saharien*. Algiers: P. Fontana et Cie, 1891.

Derrécagaix, Victor-Bernard (Général). *Le Sud de la province d'Oran*. Paris: Delagrave, 1873.

———. *Exploration au Sahara: les deux missions du colonel Flatters*. Paris: Société de Géographie, 1882.

———. *Récits d'Afrique, Yusuf*. Paris: R. Chapelot, 1907.

Desfontaines, René Louiche, and Jean-André Peyssonnel. *Flora Atlantica, Sive Historia Plantarum, Quae in Atlante, Agro Tunetano Et Algeriensi Crescunt*. Paris: Blanchon, 1800.

———. *Voyages dans les régences de Tunis et d'Alger*. Paris: Librairie de Gide, 1838.

Desjobert, Amédée. *L'Algérie en 1844*. Paris: Guillaumin, 1844.

Desparmet, Joseph. *Le Mal magique*. Paris: Geuthner, 1932.

——. "Les Réactions nationalitaires en Algérie." *Bulletin de la Société de géographie d'Alger* 37 (1932): 437–56.

——. *Coutumes, institutions, croyances des indigènes de l'Algérie*. Algiers: Carbonel, 1939.

Dickson, C. H. "Account of Ghadamis." *Journal of the Royal Geographical Society* 30 (1860): 255–60.

Dictionnaire universel françois et latin: contenant la signification et la définition tant des mots de l'une et l'autre langue. 3rd ed. 5 vols. Paris: Chez Julien-Michel Gandouin, 1732.

Djebari, Messouad. *Les Survivants de la mission Flatters*. Tunis: Imprimerie Brigol, 1895.

Douls, Camille. "Cinq mois chez les maures nomades du Sahara occidental." *Le Tour du monde* 1 (1888): 177–224.

——. "Le Sahara occidental." *Bulletin de la Société géographique et commerciale du Havre* (1888): 32–37.

——. "Voyage d'exploration à travers le Sahara occidental et le sud marocain." *Bulletin de la Société de géographie de Paris* 9 (1888): 437–79.

Dournaux-Dupéré, Norbert. "Le Rôle de la France dans l'Afrique septentrionale: le voyage de Timbouktou." *Bulletin de la Société de géographie de Paris* 6 (December 1873): 607–50.

——. "Voyage au Sahara, rédigé d'après son journal et ses notes, par Henri Duveyrier." *Bulletin de la Société de géographie de Paris* 8 (August 1874): 113–70.

Doutté, Edmond. "Les Marabouts." *Revue de l'histoire des religions* 19, no. 39 (1899): 343–69; 21, no. 41 (1900): 22–66 and 289–336.

——. *L'Islam algérien en 1900*. Algiers: Giralt, 1900.

——. *Magie et religion dans l'Afrique du nord*. Algiers: Jourdan, 1908. Reprint, Paris: Geuthner/Maisonneuve, 1983.

Dreyfus, A. I. "L'Hôpital militaire de Laghouat." *Bulletin de la Société de géographie d'Alger* 41 (1936): 93–110 and 193–216.

Droulers, Charles. *Le Marquis de Morès, 1858–1896*. Paris: Plon, 1932.

Dubois, Félix. *Timbuctoo the Mysterious*. Translated by Diana White. New York: Longmans, Green and Co., 1896.

Ducat, Auguste. *La Guerre en Afrique*. Paris: Dumaine, 1845.

Duchêne, Albert. *La Politique colonial de la France: le ministère des colonies depuis Richelieu*. Paris: Payot, 1928.

Duclos, Paul, and Léon Lehuraux. *Lettres d'un saharien (Commandant Paul Duclos)*. Algiers: P. & G. Soubiron, 1933.

Duponchel, Adolphe. *Le Chemin de fer trans-saharien, jonction coloniale entre l'Algérie et le Soudan: etudes préliminaires du projet et rapport de mission, avec cartes générale et géologique*. Paris: Hachette et Cie, 1879.

Durand, A. "Les Touareg." *Bulletin de la Société de géographie d'Alger* 9 (1904): 686–713.

Duvergier, Jean-Baptiste. *Collection complète des lois, décrets, ordonnances et avis du conseil d'état*. Paris: A. Guyot et Scribe, 1834.

Duvernois, C. "Le Commerce du sud de l'Algérie." *Revue de l'Orient, de l'Algérie et des colonies* 8 (1858): 269–73.

Duveyrier, Henri. "Coup d'œil sur le pays des Beni M'zab et sur celui des Chaanba occidentaux." *Revue algérienne et coloniale* 2 (January–February 1860): 125–41.

——. "Excursion dans le sud de la Tunisie." *Revue algérienne et coloniale* 2 (May 1860): 413–16.

——. "Excursion dans le Djerid ou pays des dattes (sud de la Tunisie)." *Revue algérienne et coloniale* 2 (June 1860): 542–59.

——. "Notice sur le commerce du Souf." *Revue algérienne et coloniale* 3 (November 1860): 637–49.

——. *Voyage dans le pays des Beni-Mezab (Algérie).* Paris: n.p., 1861.

——. *Exploration du Sahara: les Touâreg du nord.* Paris: Challamel Aîné, 1864.

——. "Historique des explorations au sud et au sud-ouest de Géryville." *Bulletin de la Société de géographie de Paris* 4 (1872): 225–61.

——. "Voyage du Dr. Nachtigal au Bahar El Ghazal." *Bulletin de la Société de géographie de Paris* 6 (December 1873): 651–56.

——. "L'Afrique nécrologique." *Bulletin de la Société de géographie de Paris* 8 (December 1874): 561–644.

——. *Voyage au Sahara.* Paris: Martinet, 1874.

——. "Le Désastre de la mission Flatters." *Bulletin de la Société de géographie de Paris,* 7th ser., vol. 1 (April 1881): 364–74.

——. *La Tunisie.* Paris: Hachette, 1881.

——. *La Confrérie musulmane de Sîdi Mohammed ben 'Alî es-Senoûsî et son domaine géographique en l'année 1300 de l'hégire, 1883 de notre ère.* Paris: Société de géographie, 1886.

——. *Journal d'un voyage dans la province d'Alger février, mars, avril 1857.* Paris: Augustin Challamel, 1900.

——. *Sahara algérien et tunisien: journal de route de Henri Duveyrier.* Edited by Charles Maunoir and Henri Schirmer. Paris: A. Challamel, 1905.

Eberhardt, Isabelle. *Ecrits sur le sable. Œuvres complètes.* Edited by Marie-Odilie Delacour and Jean-René Huleu. 2 vols. Paris: Grasset, 1988 and 1990.

——. *Ecrits intimes.* Edited by Marie-Odilie Delacour and Jean-René Huleu. Paris: Payot, 1991.

Edwards, Matilda Barbara Betham. *Through Spain to the Sahara.* London: Hurst and Blackett, 1868.

el-Eghwati. *Notes of a Journey to the Interior of Northern Africa.* Translated by William Brown Hodgson. Washington, D.C. [?]: n.p., 1830.

d'Eichthal, Gustave, and Ismayl Urbain. *Lettres sur la race noire et la race blanche.* Paris: Paulin, 1839.

Enfantin, Barthélémy-Prosper ["Père"]. *Colonisation de l'Algérie.* Paris: P. Bertrand, 1843.

Enquête sur le commerce et la navigation de l'Algérie. Algiers: Bastide, 1863.

Ernest-Picard, Paul. *La Monnaie et le crédit en Algérie depuis 1830.* Paris: J. Carbonnel; Librairie Plon, 1930.

Escayrac de Lauture, Pierre Henri Stanislas d'. *Le Désert et le Soudan: géographie naturelle et politique, histoire et ethnographie, mœurs et institutions de l'empire des Fellatas, du Bornou, du Baguermi du Waday, du Dar-Four.* Paris: A. Bertrand, J. Dumaine, F. Klinksiek, 1855.

——. "Mémoire sur le ragle ou hallucination du désert." *Bulletin de la Société de géographie de Paris,* 4th ser., vol. 9 (March–April 1855): 121–39.

Esterhazy, Walsin. *De la domination Turque dans l'ancienne régence d'Alger.* Paris: Gosselin, 1840.

Estève, Louis. *Une nouvelle psychologie de l'impérialisme: Ernest Seillière.* Paris: Félix Alcan, 1913.

Eu, Clément-Celestin d'. *In-Salah et le Tidikelt: Journal des opérations; suivi d'une instruction sur la conduite des colonnes dans les régions sahariennes.* Paris: R. Chapelot, 1903.

"Expédition de l'Armée française en Afrique contre Blédéah et Médéah." *Le Spectateur militaire* 10 (1831): 371–90.

Faidherbe, Louis. "L'Avenir du Sahara et du Soudan." *Revue maritime coloniale* 8 (June 1863): 221–48.

Fallet, C. *Conquête de l'Algérie.* Rouen: Hecard et Cie, 1856.

Faucon, Narcisse. "Le Lieutenant Palat, son exploration et sa mort tragique." *Nouvelle revue* 42 (October 1886): 790–805.

———. *Le Livre d'or de l'Algérie, 1840–1889: histoire politique, militaire, administrative, événements et faits principaux, biographie des hommes ayant marqué dans l'armée, les sciences, les lettres, etc. de 1830 à 1889.* Paris: Challamel, 1889.

Féraud, Laurent-Charles. *Kitab el Adouani ou le Sahara de Constantine et de Tunis.* Constantine: Arnolet, 1868.

———. *Notices historiques sur les tribus de la province de Constantine.* Constantine: L. Arnolet, 1869.

———. "Notes historiques sur la province de Constantine: les Beni Djellab, sultans de Touggourt." *Revue africaine* 25 (1881): 198–222.

———. *Histoire de Bougie.* Edited by Nedjma Abdelfettah Lalmi. [Saint-Denis]: Bouchène, 2001.

———. *Histoire des Sultans de Touggourt et du Sud Algérien.* 2 vols. 1878–86. Reprint, Algiers: Grand-Alger Livres (G.A.L.), 2006.

Fieffé, Eugène. *Histoire des troupes étrangères au service de France depuis leur origine jusqu'à nos jours.* Paris: Dumaine, 1854.

Fillias, Achille. *Géographie physique et politique de l'Algérie.* 2nd ed. Paris: Hachette, 1837.

———. *Histoire de la conquête et de la colonisation de l'Algérie, 1830–1860.* Paris: A. de Vresse, 1860.

———. *L'Insurrection des Oulad Sidi Cheikh (1864).* Algiers: Meyer, 1884.

Flamand, Georges-Barthélemy-Médéric. "La Traversée de l'erg occidental." *Annales de géographie* 39, no. 8 (15 May 1899): 231–41.

———. "Au Tidikelt: le programme saharien." *Questions diplomatiques et coloniales* 4, no. 9 (15 March 1900): 321–27.

———. *Recherches géologiques et géographiques sur le haut-pays de l'oranie et sur le Sahara (Algérie et territoires du sud).* Lyon: A. Rey & Cie, 1911.

Flandin, Jean-Baptiste. *Prise de possession des trésors d'Alger.* Paris: Féret, 1835.

———. *Notice sur la prise de possession des trésors de la régence d'Alger.* Paris: Chassaignon, 1848.

Flatters, Paul François Xavier. *Documents relatifs à la mission dirigée au sud de l'Algérie par le lieutenant-colonel Flatters.* Paris: Ministère des Travaux Publiques, 1884.

Fock, A. *Algérie, Sahara, Tchad: réponse à M. Camille Sabatier.* Paris: Challamel, 1891.

Follie, Adrien. *Voyage dans les déserts du Sahara contenant la relation de son naufrage et de ses aventures pendant son esclavage: un précis exact des mœurs, des usages et des opinions des habitants du Sahara.* Paris: Imprimerie du Cercle Social, 1792.

Foucauld, Charles de. *Esquisses sahariennes: trois carnets inédits de 1885.* Edited by Marc Franconie and Jacques Debetz. Paris: J. Maisonneuve, 1985.

——. *Correspondances sahariennes: lettres inédites aux Pères blancs et aux Sœurs blanches, 1901–1916.* Edited by Philippe Thiriez et Antoine Chatelard. Paris: Editions du Cerf, 1998.

——. *Reconnaissance au Maroc: journal de route.* 1888. Reprint, Clichy: Editions du Jasmin, 1999.

Foureau, Fernand. *Une mission au Tademayt (territoire d'In-Salah) en 1890: rapport à M. le Ministre de l'instruction publique et à M. le Sous-secrétaire d'état des colonies.* Paris: C. Schlaeber, 1890.

——. *Mon neuvième voyage au Sahara et au pays Touareg, mars-juin 1897: rapport adressé à monsieur le Ministre de l'instruction publique et à la Société de géographie.* Paris: A. Challamel, 1898.

——. *Mission saharienne Foureau-Lamy d'Alger au Congo par le Tchad.* Paris: Masson, 1902.

Fourier, Jean-Baptiste-Joseph. "Préface historique." *Description de l'Egypte.* vol. 1. Paris: Imprimerie Impériale, 1809. Pp. i–xcii.

Fous du désert: les premiers explorateurs du Sahara, 1849–1887 [Heinrich Barth, Henri Duveyrier, and Camille Douls]. Paris: Phébus, 1991.

France, Anatole. *The Gods Will Have Blood.* Translated by Frederick Davies. London: Penguin, 1979.

Fresnel, Fulgence. "Mémoire sur le Waday: notice historique et géographique sur le Waday et les relations de cet empire avec la côte septentrionale de l'Afrique." *Bulletin de la Société de géographie de Paris,* 3rd ser., vol. 11 (1849): 48–67 and 84–86.

Frison-Roche, Roger, *L'Appel du Hoggar.* [Paris]: Flammarion, 1936.

Fromentin, Eugène. *Un été dans le Sahara.* 1857. Edited by Anne-Marie Christin. Paris: Le Sycomore, 1981.

——. *Sahara et Sahel.* Paris: E. Plon, 1879.

Furlong, Charles Wellington. *The Gateway to the Sahara: Adventures and Observations in Tripoli.* 2nd ed. New York: Scribner's Sons, 1914.

Galibert, Léon. *Histoire de l'Algérie moderne depuis les premiers établissements des carthaginois jusque et y compris les dernières campagnes du général Bugeaud et une introduction sur les divers systèmes de colonisation qui ont précédé la conquête française.* Paris: Furne et Cie, 1843.

Gallieni, Joseph-Simon. *Voyage au Soudan français (Haut Niger et pays de Ségou), 1878–1881.* Paris: Hachette, 1885.

Ganzin, Eugène. *De la situation du crédit commercial, industriel et agricole en Algérie et de son organisation par la Banque de France.* Algiers: Imprimerie Algérienne de Dubos Frères, 1858.

Gautier, Emile-Félix. "Etudes d'ethnographie saharienne." *L'Anthropologie* 18 (1907): 37–68, 315–32.

——. *Sahara algérien.* Paris: Librairie Armand Colin, 1908.

——. *La Conquête du Sahara: essai de psychologie politique.* Paris: Armand Colin, 1910.

——. *L'Industrie des tentures dites "Dokkal" au Gourara et au Touat*. Algiers: Jourdan, 1913.

——. *L'Algérie et la métropole*. Paris: Payot, 1920.

——. *Les Territoires du sud de l'Algérie: description géographique*. Algiers: Imprimerie Algérienne, 1929.

——. *Le Passé de l'Afrique du nord*. Paris: Payot, 1964.

Gendre, F. "La Région des ksours du sud-oranais." *Revue tunisien* (1910): 16–36, 74–78, 118–34, 223–26, 322–29, 522–38.

Genty de Bussy, P. *De l'établissement des Français dans la Régence d'Alger*. Algiers: Imprimerie du Gouvernement, 1833.

Geoffroy, Auguste. *Etudes d'après Fromentin*. Paris: Challamel Aîné, 1882.

——. "Les Arabes pasteurs et nomades de la tribu des Larbaa (Région saharienne de l'Algérie)." In *Les Ouvriers des deux mondes: études sur les travaux, la vie domestique et la condition morale des populations ouvrières des diverses contrées*, 409–62. Paris: Librairie de Firmin-Didot et Cie, 1887.

Geoffroy Saint-Hilaire, Albert. *Rapport sur les races ovines et caprines de l'Algérie*. Paris: Au Siège de la Société, 1857.

Gessler. "La Colonisation du Sahara." *Revue du monde colonial* 8 (May 1863): 400–407.

Gide, André. *Amyntas*. Paris: Gallimard, 1925.

Girot, L. *Observations historiques, politiques et militaires sur l'Algérie et sur sa colonisation*. Paris: Mme Leneveu, 1840.

Gognalons, L. "Fêtes principales des sédentaires d'Ouargla (Rouagha)." *Revue africaine* 53 (1909): 85–100.

Goichon, Amelie-Marie. *La Vie féminine au Mzab: étude de sociologie musulmane*. 2 vols. Paris: Geuthner, 1927–31.

Gordon, Helen Cameron. *A Woman in the Sahara*. New York: Frederick A. Stokes, 1914.

Gouvernement Général de l'Algérie. *Situation générale des territoires du Sud de l'Algérie pendant les années 1914 et 1915: rapport d'ensemble présenté par M. Ch. Lutaud*. Algiers: Typographie Adolphe Jourdan, 1916.

——. *Les Territoires du sud de l'Algérie*. Vol. 2: *L'Œuvre accompli, 1903–1929*. Algiers: Imprimerie Algérienne, 1929.

Gouvion, Marthe, and Edmond Gouvion. *Le Kharedjisme: monographie du Mzab*. Casablanca: Imprimerie Réunies, 1926.

Graulle, E. *Insurrection de Bou-Amama (avril 1881)*. Paris: Charles-Lavauzelle, 1905.

Grevin, Emmanuel. *Voyage au Hoggar*. Paris: Librairie Stock, 1936.

Gros, Jules. *Les Voyages et découvertes de Paul Soleillet dans le Sahara et dans le Soudan en vue d'un projet d'un chemin de fer transsaharien: racontés par lui-même*. Paris: Maurice Dreyfous, 1881.

Guenard, Capitaine. "Les Oulad Sidi-Cheikh: résumé de leur histoire depuis leur origine jusqu'à leur révolte." *Bulletin de la Société géographique et archéologique d'Oran* 2 (1882): 328–45.

Guérin, Paul, ed. *Lettres, sciences, arts, encyclopédie universelle, dictionnaire des dictionnaires*. Paris: Librairies-Imprimeries Réunies, 1892.

Guillaumin, Mce., and Maurice Block. *Annuaire de l'économie politique et de la statistique pour 1857*. Paris: Guillaumin et Cie, 1857.

Guizot, F. *History of France from the Earliest Times to 1848*. 8 vols. Translated by Robert Black. New York: Hurst, 1869–78.

El-Hachaichi, Mohammed ben Otsmane. "Chez les Senoussis et les Touaregs." *Revue de Paris* 16, no. 15 (August 1901): 677–709.

———. *Voyage au pays des Senoussia à travers la Tripolitaine et les pays Touareg*. Translated by V. Serres and M. Lasram. Paris: Challamel, 1903.

Halleck, H. Wagner. *Elements of Military Art and Science*. New York: D. Appleton & Co., 1862.

Hanoteau, Adolphe. *Poésies populaires de la Kabylie du Jurjura*. Paris: Imprimerie Impériale, 1847.

Hanoteau, Adolphe, and A. Letourneux. *Les Kabyles et les coutumes kabyles*. 3 vols. Paris: Imprimerie Nationale, 1872–73.

d'Harcourt, B. "Une colonne d'expédition dans le désert." *Revue des deux mondes* 80 (1 March 1869): 5–35.

Hardy, Georges. "La Pénétration saharienne et la psychologie du nomade saharien d'après quelques ouvrages récentes." *Revue de l'histoire des colonies françaises* 17 (March–April 1929): 113–46.

Ibn Hawqal, Muhammad ibn 'Ali al-Nasibi Abu al-Qasim. *Description de l'Afrique par Ibn Haucal*. Translated by William MacGuckin de Slane. Paris: Imprimerie Royale, 1842.

Herbillon, Général Emile. *Insurrection survenue dans le sud de la Province de Constantine en 1849: relation du siège de Zaatcha*. Paris: J. Dumaine, 1863.

Hérisson, Maurice d'Irisson, comte d'. *La Chasse à l'homme: guerres d'Algérie*. Paris: Paul Ollendorff, 1891.

Hérisson, Robert. *Avec le Père de Foucauld et le général Laperrine: carnet d'un saharien, 1909–1911*. Paris: Plon, 1937.

Hodgson, William Brown. "Grammatical Sketch and Specimens of the Berber Language: preceded by Four Letters on Berber Etymologies, addressed to the President of the Society by William B. Hodgson, Esq. Read October 2d, 1829." *Transactions of the American Philosophical Society* 4, 1–48. Philadelphia: James Kay, Jun. & Co., 1834.

———. *The Foulahs of Central Africa and the African Slave Trade*. N.p.[New York?], n.p., 1843.

———. *Notes on Northern Africa, the Sahara and Soudan in Relation to the Ethnography, Languages, History, Political and Social Conditions, of the Nations of Those Countries*. New York: Wiley and Putnam, 1844.

———. *The Gospels Written in the Negro Patois of English with Arabic Characters by a Mandingo Slave in Georgia*. New York: n.p., n.d. [1857?].

———. *"Remarks on the Recent Travels of Dr. Barth in Central Africa or Soudan: A Paper Read Before the Ethnological Society of New York, November, 1858*. N.p.: n.p., n.d. [pamphlet housed in Olin Library, Cornell University].

Hornemann, Friedrich Conrad. *The Journal of Frederick Horneman's [sic] Travels, from Cairo to Mourzouk, the Capital of the Kingdom of Fezzan, in Africa, in the Years 1797–8*. London: G. and W. Nicol, 1802.

———. *Voyages dans l'intérieur de l'Afrique pendant les années 1797 et 1798*. Translated by F. Sovlès. Paris: André, an XI (1802).

Hugonnet, F. *Souvenirs d'un chef de bureau arabe*. Paris: Michel-Levy, 1858.

——. *Français et arabes en Algérie: Lamoricière, Daumas, Bugeaud, Abd el-Kader*. Paris: Challamel, 1860.

Huguet, (Dr.) J. "Les Juifs du Mzab." *Bulletin de la Société d'anthropologie de Paris* 3 (1902): 559–73.

——. "Sur les Touareg." *Bulletins et mémoires de la Société d'anthropologie de Paris* 3 (1902): 614–42.

——. *Les Soffs du Tell, du Sud et du Sahara, extrait de la Revue de l'Ecole d'anthropologie de Paris*. [Paris]: Félix Alcan, 1907.

——. "Les Sofs chez les Abadhites et notamment chez les Beni Mzab." *L'Anthropologie* 21 (1910): 151–84.

Humphreys, Rachel. *Algiers, the Sahara and the Nile*. London: W. J. Ham-Smith, 1912.

Hurlaux, E. "Quelques mots sur le Rocher de sel du Djebel Sahari." *Bulletin de la Société de géographie d'Alger* 9 (1904): 738–40.

Hyam, Joseph C. *Biskra, Sidi-Okba and the Desert: A Practical Handbook for Travelers*. 2nd ed. Algiers: Hyam and Co., 1913.

d'Ideville, H. *Memoirs of Marshal Bugeaud*. Translated by Charlotte M. Yonge. 2 vols. London: Hurst and Blackett, 1884.

al-Idrisi, Muhammad ibn Muhammad al-Sharif Abu 'Abd Allah. *De Geographia Universäli: Hortus Cultissimus, Mire Orbis Regions, Provincias, Insulas, Urbes, Earumque Dimensiones et Orizonta Describens*. Rome: Typ. Medicea, 1592.

——. *Geographia Nubiensis*. Paris: H. Blageart, 1619.

——. *Géographie d'Edrisi, Traduite de l'arabe en française, d'après deux manuscrits de la bibliothèque du roi et accompagnée de notes par P. Amédée Jaubert*. 2 vols. Paris: Imprimerie Royale, 1836–40.

"Indication de la route de Tuggurt [à] Tombouctou et aux Monts de la Lune: document traduite de l'Arabe par M. [Auguste] Cherbonneau." *Annuaire de la Société archéologique de la Province de Constantine* 1 (1853): 91–101.

Insurrection du sud-oranais en 1881, Bou Amema et le colonel Innocenti. N.p., n.d. [pamphlet housed in the el-Hamma branch of the Bibliothèque nationale d'Algerie]

Jacquot, Félix. *Expédition du Général Cavaignac dans le Sahara algérien en avril et mai 1847: relation du voyage, exploration scientifique, souvenirs, impressions, etc.* Paris: Gide et J. Baudry, 1849.

Joly, Alexandre. *Etude sur le Titteri*. Algiers: Leon, 1906.

——. *Etude sur les Chadouliyas*. Algiers: Jourdan, 1907.

"Joly, Alexandre [obituary]." *Recueil des notices et mémoires de la Société archéologique du Département de Constantine*, 5th ser., vol. 4 (1913): 815–17.

Jomard, François. "Coup d'œil rapide sur le progrès et l'état actuel des découvertes dans l'intérieur de l'Afrique." *Bulletin de la Société de géographie de Paris* 2 (1824): 239–54.

——. "Notice historique sur la vie et les voyages de René Caillié: discours lu à la séance publique de la Société de géographie du 10 décembre 1838." *Bulletin de la Société de géographie de Paris* 10 (December 1838): 330–59.

Jomini, Antoine Henri de. *Précis de l'art de la guerre*. 2 vols. Paris: Anselin, 1838.

Jus, H. "Notes sur le Sahara." *Revue algérienne et coloniale* 1 (October 1859): 49–60.

Ibn Khaldun, 'Abd al-Rahman ibn Muhammad. *Histoire des Berbères*. Translated by William MacGuckin de Slane. 4 vols. Algiers: Imprimerie du Gouvernement, 1852–56.

——. "Prolégomènes d'Ebn-Khaldoun" (in Arabic). Edited by Etienne Quatremère. *Notices et extraits des manuscrits de la bibliothèque du Roi et autres bibliothèques publié par l'Institut Royal de France* 16 (1858): 1–422; 17 (1858): 1–407; 18 (1858): 1–434.

——. "Prolégomènes historiques d'Ibn-Khaldoun." Translated by William MacGuckin de Slane. *Notices et extraits des manuscrits de la bibliothèque du Roi et autres bibliothèques publié par l'Institut Royal de France* 19 (1862): 1–486; 20 (1865): 1–93; 21 (1868): 1–573.

Khodja, Hamdan. *Le Miroir: aperçu historique et statistique sur la régence d'Alger.* [Translated by Hassuna Daghis.] Arles: Actes Sud, 1985.

Labbe, Jules. *Un mois dans le Sahara.* Lille: Jules Petit, 1865.

Lacroix, Napoléon, and Henri Poisson de La Martinière. *Documents pour servir à l'étude du nord-ouest Africain: réunis et rédigés par ordre de Jules Cambon.* 5 vols. Algiers: Gouvernement Général de l'Algérie, service des Affaires indigènes, 1894–96, 1897.

Lagarde, Charles. *Une promenade dans le Sahara.* Paris: E. Plon, 1885.

Laoust, Emile. *Mots et choses Berbères: notes de linguistique et d'ethnographie.* Paris: Challamel, 1920.

Lapasset, Ferdinand-Auguste. *Mémoire sur la colonisation indigène et la colonisation européenne.* Algiers: Bourget, 1848.

——. *Aperçu sur l'organisation des indigènes dans les territoires militaires et dans les territoires civils.* Algiers: Dubos, 1850.

——. *La Guerre en Algérie: instructions sommaires pour la conduite d'une colonne.* Paris: C. Tanera, 1873.

Lapie, Pierre. *Carte comparée des régences d'Alger et de Tunis.* Paris: Picquet, 1828.

——. *Carte topographique et spéciale du royaume d'Alger.* Paris: Houzé, n.d.

Largeau, Victor. *Expédition de Rhadamès: Extraits du journal de route de M. Largeau.* Algiers: Imprimerie de l'Association Ouvrière V. Aillaud et Cie, 1876.

——. *Voyage dans le Sahara et à Rhadamès.* Paris: Imprimerie de E. Martinet, n.d. [1877].

——. *Le Pays de Rirha–Ouargla–Voyage à Rhadamès.* Paris: Hachette, 1879.

——. *Le Sahara algérien: les déserts de l'erg.* 2nd ed. Paris: Hachette, 1881.

——, trans. *La Vengeance d'Ali: poème arabe, traduit par Victor Largeau.* Geneva: Imprimerie de J. G. Fick, 1875.

——. *Flore Saharienne: histoires et légendes.* Geneva: Jules Sandoz, 1879.

Laroche. "Note sur les relations à établir entre l'Algérie et le Sénégal." *Bulletin de la Société de géographie de Paris* 17 (1859): 374–79.

La Sauzaie, Philippe Augier de. *Mémoire au Roi (sur la possibilité de mettre les établissements français de la cote septentrionale de l'Afrique en rapport avec ceux de la côte occidentale, en leur donnant, pour point de raccord, la ville centrale et commerciale de Tumbuctou.* [Paris]: Porthmann, n.d. [1830].

Lasnaveres, Jean-Joseph-Maxmillien. *De l'impossibilité de fonder des colonies européennes en Algérie.* Paris: E. Thunot, 1856.

Layer, Ernest. *Confréries religieuses musulmanes et marabouts.* Rouen: Cagnard, 1916.

Leblanc, Ely. *Choses et gens du Hoggar.* Algiers: Editions P. & G. Soubiron, 1930.

Le Chatelier, Alfred. *Les Médaganat.* Algiers: A. Jourdan, 1888.

Leclercq, Jules Joseph. *De Mogador à Biskra; Maroc et Algérie.* Paris: Challamel Aîné, 1881.

Le Goffic, Charles. *La Rose des sables*. Paris: H. Piazza, 1932.

Lehuraux, Léon. *Nomadisme et colonisation des hauts-plateaux de l'Algérie*. Paris: Editions du Comité de l'Afrique française, 1931.

——. *Le Sahara: ses oasis*. Algiers: Baconnier, 1934.

——. *Les Conquérants des oasis: colonel Théodore Pein*. Paris: Plon, 1935.

——. *Les Français au Sahara*. Algiers: Editions "Les Territoires du Sud," 1935.

——. *Le Sahara algérien*. Algiers: Imprimerie Minerva, 1937.

Lenz, Oskar. *Tombouctou: Voyage au Maroc, au Soudan et au Sahara*. Translated by Pierre Lehautcourt. 2 vols. Paris: Hachette, 1886–87.

Leroux, H. "Notre ennemi le Touareg." *Bulletin du Comité de l'Afrique française* 8 (1898): 272–74.

Leroy Beaulieu, Paul. *Le Sahara, le Soudan et les chemins de fer transsahariens*. Paris: Guillaumin & Cie, 1904.

——. "La Pénétration de la France au Sahara." *L'Economiste français* 8 (December 1906): 828–30.

Liskenne, Louis. *Coup d'œil sur la ville d'Alger*. Paris: Guyonnet, 1830.

Loir-Montgazon (Dr.). "Afrique septentrionale, Was-Reag-Tuggurt." *Revue de l'Orient* 4, nos. 13–16 (1844): 76–82.

Longinus on the Sublime. Translated and edited by William Rhys Roberts. Cambridge: Cambridge University Press, 1899.

de Loverdo, General [Nicholas Michielacato]. "De la régence d'Alger et des avantages que la possession de ce pays peut procurer à la France." *Le Spectateur militaire* 15 (1833): 137–69.

Lucca, Gaudentio di. *Mémoires de Gaudentio di Lucca: où il rend compte aux pères de l'Inquisition de Bologne qui l'ont fait arrêter, de tout ce qui lui est arrivé de plus remarquable dans sa vie et où il les instruit d'un pays inconnu, situé au milieu des vastes déserts de l'Afrique*. 1746. Translated and edited by M. Rhedi. Paris: Hachette, 1972.

Lugan, J.-L. "Relation de l'expédition de l'Atlas." *Revue de Paris* 39 (1832): 5–19, 116–24.

Lyon, George Francis. *Voyage dans l'intérieur de l'Afrique septentrionale en 1818, 1819 et 1820*. Translated by A.-J.-B. Defauconpret. Paris: Gide, 1822.

MacCarthy, Oscar. "Les Touaregs." *Revue de l'Orient* 3 (1856): 135–41.

——. *Géographie physique, économique et politique de l'Algérie*. Algiers: Dubos Frères, 1858.

——. *L'Algérie à l'Exposition universelle de Paris en 1867*. Paris: Bureaux de la Revue de l'Orient et de l'Algérie, 1867.

Mage, Eugène. *Voyage au Soudan occidental, 1863–66*. Edited by J. Belin de Launay. Paris: Karthala, 1980.

Maguelonne, J. "Monographie historique et géographique de la tribu des Ziban." *Recueil des notices et mémoires de la Société archéologique du Département de Constantine* 44 (1910): 213–304.

Maire, René. *Carte phytogéographique de l'Algérie et de la Tunisie*. Algiers: Baconnier, 1926.

Malte-Brun, Conrad. "Coup d'œil sur les découvertes géographiques qu'il reste à faire et sur les meilleurs moyens de les effectuer." *Nouvelles annales des voyages de la géographie et de l'histoire* 1 (1819): 1–104.

——. *Précis de la géographie universelle ou Description de toutes les parties du monde sur un plan nouveau d'après les grandes divisions naturelles du globe.* Vol. 5: *Asie orientale et Afrique.* 5th ed. Edited by M. J.-J.-N. Huot. Paris: Au Bureau des Publications Illustrées, 1845.

Malte-Brune, V. A. "Voyage de M. le commandant Mircher et du capitaine d'état-major de Polignac à Ghadamès." *Bulletin de la Société de géographie de Paris,* 5th ser., vol. 4 (1862): 405.

Mangin, E. *Notes sur l'histoire de Laghouat.* Algiers: Adolphe Jourdan, 1895.

Marcassin, Lucien. *L'Agriculture dans le Sahara de Constantine, 1893–1894.* Nancy: Berger-Levrault, 1895.

Marchand, E. le. *L'Europe et la conquête d'Alger, d'après des documents originaux tirés des archives de l'État.* Paris: Perrin et Cie, 1913.

Marcy, Colonel R. B. *Thirty Years of Army Life on the Border.* New York: Harper and Brothers, 1866.

Marey-Monge, Guillaume-Stanislas. *Expédition de Laghouat, dirigée en mai et juin 1845, par le général Marey.* Algiers: A. Bourget, n.d [1846].

Margueritte, Auguste. *Chasses de l'Algérie et notes sur les Arabes du sud.* 3rd ed. Paris: Jouvet, 1884.

Margueritte, Paul. *Mon père: nouvelle édition, augmentée des lettres du général Margueritte.* Paris: E. Dentu, 1886.

Marin, Chanoine Blaise Eugène. *Algérie—Sahara—Soudan: vie, travaux, voyages de Mgr. Hacquard des Pères Blancs (1860–1901) d'après sa correspondance.* Paris: Berger-Levrault, 1905.

Martin, Alfred-Georges-Paul. *A la frontière du Maroc: les oasis sahariennes.* Paris: Challamel, 1908.

———. *Quatre siècles d'histoire marocaine, au Sahara de 1504 à 1902, au Maroc de 1894 à 1912, d'après archives et documentations indigènes.* Paris: F. Alcan, 1923.

Martins, Charles. "Le Sahara: souvenirs d'un voyage d'hier." *Revue des deux mondes* 34 (5 July 1864): 295–322.

———. *Tableau physique du Sahara oriental de la Province de Constantine: souvenirs d'un voyage exécuté pendant l'hiver de 1863 dans l'Oued-Rir et dans l'Oued-Souf.* Paris: Imprimerie de J. Claye, 1864.

Marty, Paul. *Etudes sur l'islam et les tribus du Soudan.* Vol. 2: *La Région de Tombouctou, Dienne, la Macina et dépendances.* Paris: Ernest Leroux, 1920.

Masqueray, Emile. *Le Sahara occidental.* N.p.: n.p., 1880 [extract from the *Bulletin de la Société de géographie commerciale de Paris*].

———. *Formation des cités chez les populations sédentaires de l'Algérie: Kabyles du Djurdjura, Chaouïa de l'Aourâs, Beni Mezâb.* 1886. Edited by Fanny Colonna. Aix-en-Provence: Edisud, 1983.

———. "Henri Duveyrier." *Bulletin du comité de l'Afrique française* 7 (July 1892): 17–19.

———. "Nécrologie d'Henri Duveyrier." *Journal des débats* (14 May 1892): 3.

———. *Souvenirs et visions d'Afrique.* Paris: Dentu, 1894.

———. *Observations grammaticales sur la grammaire touareg et textes de la Tamahaq des Taïtoq.* Paris: E. Leroux, 1896–97.

Massonié, Gilbert. *Législation algérienne: traité théorique et pratique de la compétence et de la procédure en matière musulmane (Tell, Kabylie, Sahara).* Paris: A. Rousseau, 1909.

Massoutier, C. *Etude sur l'organisation et la conduite des convois des colonnes opérant dans le sud de l'Algérie.* Algiers: Jourdan, 1882.

Maunier, René. "Les Confréries et le pouvoir français en Algérie." *Revue de l'histoire des religions* 113 (1936): 256–74.

Maupassant, Guy de. *Complete Works.* Vol. 12: *Au soleil, or, African Wanderings; La Vie errante, or, In Vagabondia.* Translated by Paul Bourget. Akron, Ohio: St. Dunstan Society, 1903.

———. *Ecrits sur le Maghreb: Au soleil ; La Vie errante.* Edited by Denise Brahimi. Paris: Minerve, 1988.

Maximilien, Jean Joseph. *De l'impossibilité de fonder des colonies européennes en Algérie.* 2 vols. Paris: Librairie Agricole de la Maison Rustique, 1845.

Mayer, Capitaine [E.]. "Quelques notes sur les Touareg du Nord." *Bulletin de la Société de géographie de Toulouse* 7 (1888): 382.

Mazet, Ardouin du. *Etudes algériennes: lettres sur l'insurrection dans le sud-oranais.* Paris: Guillaumin, 1882.

Mehier-de-Mathuisieux, Henri. *A travers la Tripolitaine.* Paris: Hachette, 1903.

Mella, Jean. *Laghouat ou les maisons entourées de jardins.* Paris: Plon Nourrit, 1923.

Mercadier, F. J. G. *L'Esclave de Timimoun.* Paris: France Empire, 1971.

Méry, Gaston. *Une mission chez les Touareg Azdjer.* Paris: Imprimerie réunies, n.d.

———. *Une mission chez les Touareg Azdjer: conférence faite à la Société de géographie de Paris, le 5 mai 1893.* Paris: n.p., 1893. [extract from the *Revue scientifique*].

———. "Renseignements commerciaux sur le mouvement des échanges entre la Tripolitaine et le Soudan central." *Bulletin du Comité de l'Afrique française* 3, no. 9 (3 September 1893): 2–4.

———. "La Météorologie générale et la climatologie algérienne." *Bulletin de la Société de géographie d'Alger* 5 (1900): 410–21.

Milliot, Louis. *Le Gouvernement de l'Algérie.* N.p.: Publications du Comité National Métropolitain du Centenaire de l'Algérie, 1930.

Ministère de la Guerre. *Aperçu historique, statistique et topographique sur l'état d'Alger à l'usage de l'armée expéditionnaire d'Afrique.* Paris: Picquet, 1830.

———. *Tableau de la situation des établissements français dans l'Algérie, 1845–46.* Paris: Imprimerie Royale, 1846.

Moll, L. *Colonisation et agriculture de l'Algérie.* 2 vols. Paris: Librairie Agricole de la Maison Rustique, 1845.

Monod, Théodore. *Méharées: Explorations au vrai Sahara.* 1937. Reprint, N.p.: Actes Sud, 1989.

———. *Le Chercheur d'absolu.* Paris: Gallimard, 1997.

Montagnac, Lucien-François de. *Lettres d'un soldat: neuf années de campagnes en Afrique.* Paris: Plon, 1885.

Montaudon, Jean-Baptiste-Alexandre. *Souvenirs militaires: Afrique, Crimée, Italie.* Paris: Delagrave, 1898.

Montgravier, Azema de. *Lettres à Monsieur le Président de la République.* Paris: n.p., 1849.

Morais, Henry Samuel. *The Daggatouns: A Tribe of Jewish Origin in the Desert of Sahara.* Philadelphia: Edward Stern & Co. 1882 [pamphlet housed at Olin Library, Cornell University].

Morand, Marcel. "Rites relatifs à la chevelure chez les indigènes de l'Algérie." *Revue africaine* 49 (1905): 237–43.

Musil, Alois. *The Northern Hegaz: A Topographical Itinerary.* New York: American Geographical Society, 1926.

Nachtigal, Gustav. *Sahara and Sudan.* Translated and edited by Allan G. B. Fisher and Humphrey J. Fisher with Rex S. O'Fahey. 4 vols. Berkeley: University of California Press, 1971–87.

Naphegyi, Gábor. *Ghardaia; or, Ninety Days among the B'ni Mozab: Adventures in the Oasis of the Desert of Sahara.* New York: G. P. Putnam & Sons, 1871.

Nesbitt, Frances E. *Algeria and Tunis: Painted and Described.* London: Black, 1906.

Nettement, Alfred. *Histoire de la conquête d'Alger, écrite sur des documents inédits et authentiques, suivie du tableau de la conquête de l'Algérie.* Paris: J. Lecoffre, 1856.

Neveu, François-Edouard de. *Les Khouans ordres religieux chez les musulmans de l'Algérie.* 3rd ed. Algiers: A. Jourdan, 1913.

Ney, Napoléon. "Les Relations de la France avec l'extrême sud de l'Algérie et les derniers voyages d'exploration." *Revue des deux mondes* 8, no. 45 (April 1875): 617–32.

"Notes sur le commerce de l'Afrique centrale." *Revue algérienne et coloniale* 2 (1860): 417–20.

Nouveau dictionnaire universel. Edited by Maurice La Châtre. Paris: Docks de la Librairie, 1870.

Palat, Marcel (Marcel Frescaly). *Journal de route et correspondance.* Paris: Charpentier, 1886.

———. *Nouvelles algériennes.* Paris: Charpentier, 1888.

Parisot, Capitaine [A. V.]. "D'Ouargla à el Golea'a: extrait d'une lettre au secrétaire général." *Bulletin de la Société de géographie de Paris* 5 (1873): 322–25.

Park, Mungo. *Voyages dans l'intérieur de l'Afrique, fait en 1795, 1796, et 1797 par M. Mungo Park, avec des éclaircissements sur la géographie de l'intérieur de l'Afrique, par le major Rennel.* Translated by J. Castéra. Paris: Dentu, 1799.

Pein, Capitaine. *Chez les Touareg Azdjer: une reconnaissance à Tarat (juin-juillet 1903).* N.p.: Centre d'Etudes sur l'Histoire du Sahara, 1988.

Pein, Theodore. *Lettres familières sur l'Algérie, un petit royaume arabe.* Algiers: Jourdan, 1893.

Pellissier, Eugène. *Annales algériennes.* Rev. ed. 3 vols. Paris: J. Dumaine; Algiers: Librairie Bastide, 1854.

Perrot, A. M. *Alger: esquisse topographique et historique.* Paris: Ladvocat, 1830.

Petitjean, L. *Le Temps et la prévision du temps en Algérie et au Sahara.* Paris: Masson et Cie, 1930.

Peyré, Joseph. *Proie des ombres.* Geneva: Editions du Milieu du Monde, 1943.

Peyssonnel, Jean-André. *Relation d'un voyage sur les côtes de barbarie fait par ordre du roi en 1724 et 1725.* Paris: Librairie de Gide, 1838.

———. *Voyage dans les régences de Tunis et d'Alger.* Edited by Lucette Valensi. Paris: La Découverte, 1987.

Pharaon, F. *Spahis, turcos et goumiers.* Paris: Challamel, 1864.

Philebert, Charles. *Algérie et Sahara: le général Margueritte.* Paris: Direction du Spectateur Militaire, 1882.

——. *La Conquête pacifique de l'intérieur africain: nègres—musulmans et chrétiens.* Paris: Ernest Leroux, 1889.

Philebert, Charles, and Georges Rolland. *La France en Afrique et le Transsaharien: l'intérieur africain, ce que peut être encore l'Afrique française, pénétration par l'Algérie, question Touareg, chemin de fer transsaharien.* Paris: Challamel, 1890.

Phillipps, Lisle March. *In the Desert, the Hinterland of Algiers.* London: E. Arnold, 1905.

Pichon, Louis-André. *Alger sous la domination française.* Paris: Barrois et Duprat, 1833.

Piesse, Louis. *Itinéraire historique et descriptif de l'Algérie comprenant le Tell et le Sahara.* Paris: L. Hachette, 1862.

Pitois, Christian. *L'Afrique française.* Paris: Barbier, 1846.

Piquet, Victor. *La Colonisation française dans l'Afrique du Nord: Algérie, Tunisie, Maroc.* 2nd ed. Paris: Librairie Armand Colin, 1914.

Poiret, Abbé. *Voyage en barbarie, ou lettres écrites de l'ancienne Numidie pendant les années 1785 et 1786.* Paris: Rochelle, 1789.

Pomel, A. *Des races indigènes de l'Algérie et du rôle que leur réservent leurs aptitudes.* Oran: Imprimerie de Veuve Dagorn, 1871.

——. *Le Sahara: observations de géologie et de géographie physique et biologique, avec des aperçus sur l'Atlas et le Soudan et discussion de l'hypothèse de la mer saharienne à l'époque préhistorique.* Algiers: Association Ouvrière V. Aillaud, 1872.

Pommerol, Jean. *Islam saharien: chez ceux qui guettent (journal d'un témoin).* Paris: Fontemoing, n.d. [ca. 1902].

——. *Une femme chez les sahariennes.* Paris: Flammarion, n.d.

Pottier, René. *Un prince saharien méconnu: Henri Duveyrier.* Paris: Plon, 1938.

——. *La Vocation saharienne du Père de Foucauld.* Paris: Plon, 1939.

——. *Le Transsaharien, liaison d'empire: carnets de l'actualité.* Paris: Sorlot, 1941.

——. *Laperrine, conquérant pacifique du Sahara.* Paris: Editions Latines, 1943.

——. *Charles de Foucauld: le prédestiné.* Paris: Sorlot, 1944.

——. *Au pays du voile bleu.* Paris: F. Sorlot, 1945.

——. *Le Cardinal Lavigerie, apôtre et civilisateur.* Paris: Editions Techniques & Artistiques, 1947.

——. *Histoire du Sahara.* Paris: Nouvelles Editions Latines, 1947.

——. *Flatters.* Paris: Editions de l'Empire Français, 1948.

——. *La Croix sous le burnous.* Paris: La Bonne Presse, 1950.

——. *Le Sahara, les beaux pays.* Paris: B. Arthaud, 1950.

——. *Mission Foureau-Lamy.* Paris: Union Française, 1951.

Pottier, René, and Saad ben Ali. *La Tente noire (roman saharien).* Paris: Les Œuvres Représentatives, 1933.

Poulalion, François. *Mission Alger-Niger (novembre-décembre 1926).* Algiers: Ancienne Maison Bastide-Jourdan, 1927.

——. *Expédition Paul Soleillet.* Algiers: Chambre de commerce d'Alger, 1938.

Powell, E. Alexander. *In Barbary: Tunisia, Algeria, Morocco, and the Sahara.* New York: Century, 1926.

Prax, Jean. "Algérie méridionale ou Sahara algérien." *Revue de l'Orient, de l'Algérie et des colonies* 4 (1848): 129–38, 193–204; 5 (1849): 9–27, 204–25 .

——. *Algérie: commerce de l'Algérie avec la Mecque et le Soudan.* Paris: J. Rouvier, 1849.

Procès du capitaine Doineau et de ses co-accusés devant la cour d'assises d'Oran (août 1857). Paris: Schiller, 1857.

Procès-verbaux et rapports de la commission nommée par le Roi, le 7 juillet 1833, pour aller recueillir en Afrique tous les faits propres à éclairer le gouvernement sur l'état du pays et sur les mesures que réclame son avenir. Paris: Imprimerie Royale, 1834.

Procès-verbaux et rapports de la commission d'Afrique institué par ordonnance du roi du 12 décembre 1833. Paris: Imprimerie Royale, 1834.

[*Supplément aux*] *procès-verbaux de la commission d'Afrique, instituée par ordonnance royale du 12 décembre 1833.* Paris: Imprimerie Royale, 1834.

"Proclamation en arabe adressée par le général de Bourmont aux habitants de la ville d'Alger et des tribus, en juin 1830." Translated by M. Bresnier and edited by A. Berbrugger. "La Première Proclamation adressée par les Français aux Algériens, 1830." *Revue africaine* 6 (1862): 147–56 (Arabic text with French translation made in 1862).

Psichari, Ernest. *Œuvres complètes d'Ernest Psichari.* Paris: L. Conrad, 1948.

"Quelques observations sur les moyens de développer le commerce de l'Algérie avec l'intérieur de l'Afrique, et en particulier sur ceux de se rendre d'Algérie dans le Sénégal en passant par Tombouctou." *Bulletin de la Société de géographie de Paris* 13 (1857): 161–94.

Rabourdin, Lucien. *Algérie et Sahara.* Paris: Challamel Aîné, 1882.

———. *Algérie et Sahara, la question africaine: étude politique et économique, les âges de pierre du Sahara central, préhistoire et ethnographie africaines, carte et itinéraire de la première mission Flatters.* Paris: Challamel Aîné, 1882.

Ragot, W. *Le Sahara de la Province de Constantine: région nord du Sahara.* Constantine: L. Arnolet, 1874.

Randau, Robert. *Le Parfait explorateur colonial.* Paris: Baudinire, 1924.

———. *Isabelle Eberhardt: notes et souvenirs.* Algiers: Charlot, 1945.

Rasch, Gustav. *Nach den Oasen von Siban in der grossen Wüste Sahara: Ein Reisebuch Durch Algerien.* Berlin: A. Vogel, 1866.

Raynal, Guillaume-Thomas. *Histoire philosophique et politique des établissements et du commerce des européens dans les deux Indes.* 10 vols. Amsterdam: n.p., 1770.

Reibell, Emile. *Le Commandant Lamy d'après sa correspondance et ses souvenirs de campagne, 1858–1900.* Paris: Hachette, 1903.

Relation d'un séjour à Alger. Paris: Le Normant, 1820.

Renan, Ernest. "Exploration scientifique de l'Algérie: la société berbère." *Revue des deux mondes* 43 (September 1873): 138–57.

Renou, Emilien Jean. *Description géographique de l'empire du Maroc suivie d'Itinéraires et renseignements sur le pays de Sous et autres parties méridionales du Maroc recueillis par M. Adrien Berbrugger.* Paris: Imprimerie Royale, 1846.

"Réponse aux objections élevées en Angleterre contre l'authenticité de voyage de Caillié à Ten-Boktoue." *Revue des deux mondes* 2 (April 1830): 144–65.

Reveillaud, Eugene. *Une excursion au Sahara algérien et tunisien: angle du nord-est, Djeb-el-Chechar, Khanga-Sidi-Nadgi, Negrine, le Djerid et les Grands Chotts (mer intérieure), la vallée des Beni-Barbar.* Paris: Fischbacher, 1887.

Reybaud, Louis. *La Laine: nouvelle série des études sur le régime des manufactures.* Paris: Michel Lévy Frères, 1867.

Ribourt, F. *Le Gouvernement de l'Algérie de 1852 à 1858.* Paris: E. Panckoucke, 1859.

Richard, Charles. *Etude sur l'insurrection du Dhara* [sic], *1845–46.* Algiers: Besancenez, 1846.

———. *Du gouvernement arabe et de l'institution qui doit l'exercer.* Algiers: Bastide, 1848.

———. *Scènes de mœurs arabes.* 2nd ed. Paris: Challamel Aîné, 1848.

———. *Algérie: de la civilisation du peuple arabe.* Algiers: Dubos, 1850.

———. *Les Mystères du peuple arabe.* Paris: Challamel Aîné, 1860.

Richard, Père Louis. "Journal de route du Père Richard des Pères blancs chez les Touareg Ajjer (1880)." *Travaux de l'institut de recherches sahariennes* 5 (1948): 133–99.

Richardson, James. *Travels in the great desert of Sahara in the years of 1845 and 1846, containing a narrative of personal adventures during a tour of nine months through the desert amongst the Touaricks and other tribes of Saharan people; including a description of the cases and cities of Ghat, Ghadames and Mourzuk.* 1848. Reprint, London: Frank Cass, 1970.

———. *Routes du Sahara: itinéraires dans l'intérieur du grand désert d'Afrique.* Paris: L. Martinet, 1850.

Rinn, Louis-Marie. *Origines berbères: études de linguistique.* Paris: Imprimerie de Chaix, 1882.

———. *Marabouts et khouan: étude sur l'islam en Algérie avec une carte indiquant la marche, la situation et l'importance des ordres religieux musulmans.* Algiers: A. Jourdan, 1884.

———. *Géographie ancienne de l'Algérie: les premiers royaumes berbères et la guerre de Jugurtha.* Algiers: A. Jourdan, 1885.

———. *Régime pénal de l'indigénat en Algérie: les commissions disciplinaires.* Algiers: Jourdan, 1885.

———. *Nos frontières sahariennes.* Algiers: A. Jourdan, 1886.

———. *Les Origines berbères: études linguistiques et ethnologiques.* Algiers: A. Jourdan, 1889.

———. *Régime pénal de l'indigénat en Algérie: le séquestre et la responsabilité collective.* Algiers: A. Jourdan, 1890.

———. *Histoire de l'insurrection de 1871 en Algérie.* Algiers: Librairie A. Jourdan, 1891.

———. *Expédition du Général Salomon dans le Djebel Aourès 539 de J.-C.* Algiers: A. Jourdan, 1894.

———. *Le Royaume d'Alger sous le dernier dey.* Algiers: A. Jourdan, 1900.

Robert, Claude Maurice. *L'Envoûtement du sud: d'el-Kantara à Djanet.* Algiers: Baconnier, 1934.

Robin, Joseph Nil. *L'Insurrection de la grande Kabylie en 1871.* Paris: H. Charles-Lavauzelle, n.d.

———. *Histoire du Chérif Bou Bar'la.* Algiers: A. Jourdan, 1884.

———. *Le Mzab et son annexion à la France.* Algiers: A. Jourdan, 1884.

———. *Soumission des Beni-Yala et opérations du Colonel Canrobert en juillet 1849.* Algiers: A. Jourdan, 1898.

———. *Notes et documents concernant l'insurrection de 1856–1857 de la Grande Kabylie.* Algiers: A. Jourdan, 1902.

———. *La Grande Kabylie sous le régime Turc.* Edited by Alain Mahé. Saint-Denis: Bouchène, 1998. [Originally published as series of article in the *Revue africaine,* 1873–75.]

Rohlfs, Gerhard. *Mein erster Aufenthalt in Marokko und Reise südlich vom Atlas durch die Oasen Draa und Tafilet.* Bremen: J. Kühtmann, 1873.

——. *Adventures in Morocco and Journey through the Oases of Draa and Tafilet.* London: Sampson Low, Marston Low and Searle, 1874.

——. *Voyages et explorations au Sahara.* 1874–75. Translated by Jacques Debetz. 2 vols. Paris: Karthala, 2001.

Rolland, Georges. *L'Oued Rir et la colonisation française au Sahara.* Paris: Challamel Aîné, 1887.

——. *La Conquête du désert: Biskra–Touggourt–l'Oued R'hir.* Paris: Challamel, 1889.

——. *Hydrologie du Sahara algérien: extrait des documents relatifs à la mission de Laghouat, El-Goléa, Ouargla, Biskra, publiés par le ministère des Travaux publics.* Paris: Challamel, 1894.

Roudaire, François Elie. *Rapport à M. le Ministre de l'instruction publique sur la mission des chotts: études relatives au projet de mer intérieure.* Paris: Imprimerie Nationale, 1877.

——. *Travaux de la commission supérieure pour l'examen du projet de mer intérieure dans le sud de l'Algérie et de la Tunisie.* Paris: Imprimerie Nationale, 1882.

——. *La Mer intérieure africaine.* Paris: Imprimerie de la Société Anonyme de Publications Périodiques, 1883.

Rousset, Camille. *Les Commencements d'une conquête: l'Algérie de 1830 à 1840.* 2 vols. Paris: Plon, 1887.

——. *La Conquête de l'Algérie, 1841–1857.* 2 vols. 3rd ed. Paris: Plon, 1901.

Roux-Freissineng, Marcel. *La Liaison Oran-Niger: conférence faite à Oran.* [Oran?]: Heintz, 1926.

Roy, René. *Au pays des mirages.* Paris: Berger-Levrault, 1911.

Royer, Paul. *Les Grands Etablissements de crédit dans l'Algérie et les colonies françaises.* Paris: A. Michalon, 1907.

Rozet, P. [Claude-Antoine]. *Relation de la guerre d'Afrique pendant les années 1830 et 1831.* 2 vols. Paris: Firmin-Didot, 1832.

Rozet, P., and E. Carette. *Algérie.* 1850. 2nd ed. Paris: Bouslama, 1980.

Rozey, Armand-Gabriel. *Cris de conscience de l'Algérie.* Paris: A. Gratiot, 1840.

——. *Esquisse rapide et historique sur l'administration de l'Algérie depuis 1830 et sur la direction qu'y donne le général Bugeaud.* Marseille: M. Olive, 1842.

Sabatier, Camille. *Touat, Sahara et Soudan: étude géographique, politique, économique et militaire.* Paris: Société d'Editions Scientifiques, 1891.

Saint-Arnaud, A. Leroy de. *Lettres du Maréchal de Saint-Arnaud.* 2 vols. Paris: Levy, 1855.

Saint-Arroman, Raoul de. *Les Missions françaises.* Paris: Librairie Illustrée, n.d.

Sainte-Marie, Louis-Marie Rapine-Dumezet de. *Essais historiques sur l'effusion du sang humain par la guerre.* Paris: Buisson, 1807.

al-Selami, al-'Adwani, and Laurent-Charles Féraud. *Kitab el-Adouani: ou le Sahara de Constantine et de Tunis.* Constantine: L. Arnolet, 1868. [Also published anonymously as "Kitab-El-Adouani, ou le Sahara de Constantine et de Tunis." *Recueil des notices et mémoires de la Société archéologique de la Province de Constantine* 12 (1868): 1–208.]

Sand, Georges. *Œuvres complètes de George Sand.* Vol. 5: *Autour de la table.* Paris: Michel Lévy Frères, 1875.

Santini, P. "Contribution d'un médecin à l'étude de *bayoudh* maladie du palmier-dattier." *Archives de l'Institut Pasteur d'Algérie* 15, no. 2 (1937): 51–57.

Sanvitale, Comte H. de. "Tribus du Sahara algérien: les Oueld Nayls de l'Ouest." *Revue de l'Orient et de l'Algérie* 15, no. 1 (1854): 201–9, 274–87.

Savary, Anne-Jean-Marie-René, duc de Rovigo. *Correspondance du duc de Rovigo, 1831–1833.* Edited by Gabriel Esquer. 4 vols. Algiers: Jourdan, 1914.

Savornin, Justin. *Les Territoires du sud de l'Algérie: esquisse géologique et hydrologique.* Algiers: Imprimerie Algérienne, 1930.

Schimper, Wilhelm. *Reise nach Algier in den Jahren 1831 und 1832.* Stuttgart: J. B. Metzler'schen Buchhandlung, 1834.

Schirmer, Henri. "Henri Duveyrier." *Annales de Géographie* 1 (1892): 415–16.

———. *Le Sahara.* Paris: Hachette, 1893.

———. *Pourquoi Flatters et ses compagnons sont morts.* Paris: A. Challamel, 1896.

Scott, Colonel H. L. *Military Dictionary.* New York: D. Van Nostrand, 1861.

Seillière, Ernest. *Introduction à la philosophie de l'impérialisme.* Vol. 3: *L'Impérialisme démocratique.* Paris: Plon-Nourrit, 1907.

———. *Introduction à la philosophie de l'impérialisme: Impérialisme, mysticisme, romantisme, socialisme.* Paris: Félix Alcan, 1911.

Seroka, Joseph-Adrien. "Le Sud Constantinois de 1830–1855." *Revue africaine* 56 (1912): 375–446, 500–565.

Servier, André. *L'Islam et la psychologie du musulman.* Paris: Challamel, 1923.

Shaler, William. "On the Language, Manners, and Customs of the Berbers, or Brebers, of Africa Communicated by William Shaler, Consul of the United States at Algiers, in a Series of Letters to Peter S. Du Ponceau, and by the Latter to the Society." *Transactions of the American Philosophical Society* 2 (1825): 438–65.

———. *Esquisse de l'état d'Alger, considéré sous les rapports politiques, historiques et civils.* Translated by X. Bianchi. Paris: Librairie Ladvocat, 1830.

Shaw, Thomas. *Travels, or Observations Relating to Several Parts of Barbary and the Levant.* Oxford: Printed at the Theatre, 1738.

———. *Voyages de M. Shaw dans plusieurs provinces de la Barbarie et du Levant, Traduit de l'anglais.* The Hague: J. Nmeaume, 1743.

———. *Voyage dans la régence d'Algiers: ou description géographique, physique, philologique, etc. de cet état.* Translated by Jacques MacCarthy. Paris: Marlin, 1830.

Soleillet, Paul. *Voyage de Paul Soleillet d'Alger à l'oasis de 'In-Çalah: rapport présenté à la Chambre de commerce d'Alger.* Algiers: Jourdan, 1874.

———. *Voyage à Ségou, 1878–1890.* Paris: Challamel, 1887.

Soleillet, Paul, and Jules Gros. *Les Voyages et découvertes de Paul Soleillet dans le Sahara et dans le Soudan, en vue d'un projet d'un chemin de fer transsaharien.* Paris: Dreyfous, 1881.

Sommerville, Maxwell. *Sands of Sahara.* Philadelphia: J. B. Lippincott Co., 1901.

Stephan, Raoul. *Isabelle Eberhardt ou la révélation du Sahara.* Paris: Flammarion, 1930.

Stuckle, H. *Le Commerce de la France avec le Soudan.* Paris: Challamel, 1864.

Subtil, Eugène. "Considérations politiques et commerciales sur Ghadamès: suivies d'un itinéraire de Tripoli à Ghadamès." *Revue de l'Orient, Bulletin de la Société oriental* 5, nos. 17–20 (1844): 97–123.

——. "Histoire d'Abd el Gelil, sultan du Fezzan assassiné en 1842." *Revue de l'Orient, Bulletin de la Société oriental* 5, nos. 17–20 (1844): 3–30.

Terrier, A. "Comment on devient explorateur." *Bulletin du Comite de l'Afrique française* 3 (1898): 112–13.

Thoumas, Charles Antoine. *Les Transformations de l'armée française: essais d'histoire et de critique sur l'état militaire de la France*. Paris: Berger-Levrault, 1887.

Tocqueville, Alexis de. *Œuvres complètes*. 2 vols. Edited by André Jardin. Paris: Gallimard, 1991.

——. *Writings on Empire and Slavery*. Edited and translated by Jennifer Pitts. Baltimore: Johns Hopkins University Press, 2001.

Touchard, Joseph Léon. *Travaux et reconnaissances de pénétration saharienne: exécutés dans le sud Constantinois par le cercle de Touggourt, novembre 1904–mars 1905*. Calvisson, France: J. Gandini, 1993.

Trumelet, Corneille. *Histoire de l'insurrection dans le sud de la province d'Alger de 1864 à 1869*. 2 vols. Algiers: A. Jourdan, 1879–84.

——. *Le Corps des interprètes militaires: ce qu'il a été, ce qu'il est, ce qu'il doit être*. Valence, France: Imprimerie de A. Teyssier, 1881.

——. *Les Saints de l'Islam: légendes hagiologiques et croyances algériennes; les saints du Tell*. Paris: Didier et Cie, 1881.

——. *Un drame pour un cheveu: souvenirs intimes de la vie militaire algérienne d'autrefois*. 3 vols. Oran: Imprimerie des Ouvriers Réunis, 1881–84. (Published under the pseudonym C. T. de Fallon.)

——. *Les Français dans le désert: journal historique, militaire et descriptif d'une expédition aux limites du Sahara algérien*. 2nd ed. Paris: Challamel Aîné, 1885.

——. *Blida: Récits selon la légende, la tradition et l'histoire*. 2 vols. Algiers: A. Jourdan, 1887.

——. *Une page de l'histoire de la colonisation algérienne, Bou-Farik*. 2nd ed. Algiers: A. Jourdan, 1887.

——. *Le Général Yusuf*. 2 vols. Paris: Paul Ollendorff, 1890.

——. *L'Algérie légendaire, en pèlerinage ça et là aux tombeaux des principaux thaumaturges de l'Islam, Tell et Sahara*. Algiers: A. Jourdan, 1892.

Urbain, Ismayl. "Le Désert de l'Algérie." *Le Journal des débats*, 27 September 1843.

——. "Le Sahara algérien." *Revue de l'Orient* 2 (1843): 148–53.

——. "Les Zibans, oasis du Sahra algérien." *Revue de l'Orient* 5, nos. 17–20 (1844): 316–19.

——. *L'Algérie pour les Algériens*. 1860. Reprint, Paris: Séguier, 2000.

——. *L'Algérie française, indigènes et immigrants*. 1862. Reprint, Paris: Séguier, 2002.

Vâlet, René-Victor. *L'Afrique du Nord devant le parlement au XIXe siècle (1828–1838; 1880–1881): étude d'histoire parlementaire et de politique coloniale*. Paris: E. Champion, 1924.

——. *Le Saharien algérien: étude de l'organisation administrative, financière et judiciaire des Territoires du sud*. Algiers: Imprimerie "La Typo-litho," 1927.

Vayssettes, E. "Histoire de Constantine, sous la domination turque." *Recueil des notices et mémoires de la Société archéologique de la Province de Constantine* 11 (1867): 241–352; 12 (1868): 255–392; 13 (1869): 453–620.

Vereker, Charles Smyth. *Scenes in the Sunny South: Including the Atlas Mountains and the Oases of the Sahara in Algeria*. London: Longmans, Green, and Co., 1871.

Veuillot, Louis. *Les Français en Algérie: souvenirs d'un voyage fait en 1841.* Tours: A. Mame & Cie, 1857.

Ville, Ludovic Gabriel Alexandre Raymond Joseph. *Voyage d'exploration dans les bassins du Hodna et du Sahara.* Paris: Imprimerie Impériale, 1868.

——. *Exploration géologique du Beni Mzab, du Sahara et de la région des steppes de la province d'Alger.* Paris: Imprimerie Nationale, 1872.

Villot, Etienne-Cécile-Edouard. *Mœurs, coutumes et institutions des indigènes de l'Algérie.* Constantine: Arnolet, 1871.

Vivarez, Mario. *La Zériba du Ben-Oued-Keubbi: projet de fondation d'une factorerie française en Afrique centrale.* Paris: E. Plon, 1878.

——. *Le Soudan algérien: projet de voie ferrée trans-çaharienne* [sic], *Alger–lac Tchad.* Paris: L. Cerf, 1890.

——. *Au sujet du Touât.* Algiers: M. Ruff, 1896.

——. *Pour les venger: un raid sur l'Ahaggar.* Paris, Librairie Africaine et Coloniale, 1897.

——. *La Fécondation du désert: de Biskra au Djebel O'nq à petites journées.* Algiers: J. Bringau, 1925.

Vocabolario degli accademici della Crusca, in questa seconda impressione da' medesimi rineduto, e ampliato, con aggiunta di molte veci autor del buon secolo, e buona quantità di quelle dell'vso. Venezia: Appresso J. Sarzina, 1623.

Voinot, Louis. "La Situation sur la frontière algero-marocaine du Tell lors de l'insurrection des Oulad Sidi Cheikh dans le sud-Oranais (1864–1870)." *Revue africaine* 60 (1919): 399–431.

——. "La Menace des Oulad Sidi Cheikh entre le Tell algérien et les dangers de leurs intrigues au Maroc (1870–1873)." *Revue africaine* 61 (1920): 62–95.

Vuillot, Paul. *Exploration du Sahara: étude historique et géographique.* Paris: A. Challamel, 1895.

Wachi, Paul (Lt.-Col.). "En Algérie: Notes, itinéraires et souvenirs pour servir à l'histoire de la province d'Oran; l'insurrection de Bou Amama (1881–1882)." *Revue tunisien* 8 (1901): 97–104; 9 (1902): 289–317.

Walckenaer, Charles-Athanase. *Recherches géographiques sur l'intérieur de l'Afrique septentrionale.* Paris: F. Didot, 1821.

Walsin-Esterhazy, Louis-Joseph-Ferdinand. *Notice historique sur le maghzen d'Oran.* Oran: Perrier, 1849.

Warnier, Auguste-Hubert. *Des moyens d'assurer la domination française en Algérie: examen par M. le docteur Warnier.* Paris: A. Guyot, 1846.

——. *L'Algérie devant le Sénat.* Paris: Imprimerie de Dubuisson, 1863.

——. *L'Algérie devant l'opinion publique, pour faire suite à l'Algérie devant le Sénat: indigènes et immigrants; examen rétrospectif.* Algiers: Imprimerie de Molot, 1864.

——. *L'Algérie devant l'Empereur.* Paris: Challamel Aîné, 1865.

Warnier, Auguste, and Ernst Carette. *Description et division de l'Algérie.* Paris: Hachette, 1847.

Watbled, Ernest. *Souvenirs de l'armée d'Afrique: Cirta-Constantine; première expédition de Constantine; deuxième expédition et prise de Constantine; épisode de l'insurrection kabyle de 1871; l'armée d'Afrique et les bureaux arabe.* Paris: Challamel Aîné, 1877.

——. *Les Relations de l'Algérie avec l'Afrique centrale.* Paris: Berger-Levrault, 1879.

Wateau, Dr. *Documents pour server à l'histoire des Hamyans et de la région qu'ils occupant actuellement.* Timimoun, 1 June 1914. http://www.mecheria-environnement.org/documents/histoiresdeshmiyanes.pdf (accessed February 2008).

al-Wazzan, al-Hasan ibn Muhammad al-Zayyati al-Fasi (a.k.a. Leo Africanus). *Jean Léon, Africain, historiale description de l'Afrique tierce partie du monde.* Antwerp: Imprimerie de Christophe Planin, 1556.

Westermarck, E. *Ritual and Belief in Morocco.* New Hyde Park, N.Y.: University Books, 1926.

Yusuf, Général [J. V.]. *De la guerre en Afrique.* 2nd ed. Paris: J. Dumaine, 1851.

Yver, Georges. *Documents relatifs au traité de Tafna, 1837.* Algiers: Carbonel, 1924.

SECONDARY SOURCES

Abbas. *Allah O Akbar: A Journey through Militant Islam.* London: Phaidon, 1994.

Abitbol, Michel, ed. "Juifs maghrébins et commerce transsaharien." *Revue française d'histoire d'outre-mer* 66 (1979): 177–93.

——. "Le Maroc et le commerce transsaharien du XVIIe siècle au début du XIXe siècle." *Revue de l'occident musulman et de la Méditerranée* 30 (1980): 5–20.

——. *Communautés juives des marges sahariennes du Maghreb.* Jerusalem: Institut Ben-Zvi, 1982.

Abou-Khamseen, Mansour Ahmed. "The First French-Algerian War (1830–1848)." Ph.D. diss., University of California, Berkeley, 1983.

Abu-Lughod, Lila. *Veiled Sentiments: Honor and Poetry in a Bedouin Society.* Berkeley: University of California Press, 1986.

——. "The Romance of Resistance: Tracing Transformations of Power through Bedouin Women." *American Ethnologist* 17, no. 1 (February 1990): 41–55.

Abun-Nasr, Jamil M. *The Tijaniyya: A Sufi Order in the Modern World.* London: Oxford University Press, 1965.

——. *A History of the Maghrib.* 2nd ed. Cambridge: Cambridge University Press, 1975.

Adas, Michael. *Prophets of Rebellion: Millenarian Protest Movements against the European Colonial Order.* Chapel Hill: University of North Carolina Press, 1979.

Addi, Lahouari. *L'Algérie et la démocratie: pouvoir et crise du politique dans l'Algérie contemporaine.* Paris: Découverte, 1994.

——. "The Failure of Third World Nationalism." *Journal of Democracy* 8, no. 4 (1997): 110–124.

——. *Les Mutations de la société algérienne: famille et lien social dans l'Algérie contemporaine.* Paris: Découverte, 1999.

——. *Sociologie et anthropologie chez Pierre Bourdieu: le paradigme anthropologique kabyle et ses conséquences théoriques.* Paris: Découverte, 2002.

Adeleye, R. A. *Power and Diplomacy in Northern Nigeria, 1804–1906.* New York: Humanities Press, 1971.

el-Adnani, Jillali. *La Tijâniyya, 1781–1881: les origines d'une confrérie religieuse au Maghreb.* Rabat: Editions Marsam, 2007.

Adu-Boahen, A. "The Caravan Trade in the Nineteenth Century." *Journal of African History* 3, no. 2 (1962): 349–59.

――. *Britain, the Sahara, and the Western Sudan, 1788–1861.* Oxford: Clarendon Press, 1964.

Ageron, Charles-Robert. "L'Emigration des Musulmans algériens et l'exode de Tlemcen (1830–1911)." *Annales, économies, sociétés, civilisations* 22, no. 2 (1967): 1047–66.

――. *Les Algériens musulmans et la France, 1871–1919.* 2 vols. Paris: Presses Universitaires de France, 1968.

――. *Politiques coloniales au Maghreb.* Paris: Presses Universitaires de France, 1972.

――. *L'Anticolonialisme en France de 1871 à 1914.* Paris: Presses Universitaires de France, 1973.

――. "Du mythe kabyle aux politiques berbères." In *Le Mal de voir: ethnologie et orientalisme, politique et épistémologie, critique et autocritique,* edited by Henri Moniot, 331–348. Paris: Union Générale de l'Edition, 1976.

――. *France coloniale ou parti colonial?* Paris: Presses Universitaires de France, 1978.

――. *Histoire de l'Algérie contemporaine.* Vol. 2: *De l'insurrection de 1871 au déclenchement de la guerre de libération, 1954.* Paris, Presses Universitaires de France, 1979.

――. *L'Algérie algérienne: De Napoléon III à de Gaulle.* Paris: Sindbad, 1980.

――. *Découvertes européennes et nouvelle vision du monde, 1492–1992.* Paris: Institut d'Histoire des Relations Internationales Contemporaines, [Université] de la Sorbonne, 1994.

――. *Le Gouvernement du général Berthezène à Alger en 1831.* Saint-Denis: Bouchène, 2005.

Ageron, Charles-Robert, and Michael Brett. *Modern Algeria: A History from 1830 to the Present.* London: Hurst & Co., 1991.

Agulhon, Maurice. *The Republican Experiment, 1848–1852.* Translated by Janet Lloyd. New York: Cambridge University Press / Paris: Editions de la Maison des Sciences de l'Homme, 1983.

Ahmed, Saied. "Commerce et commerçants dans le Sahara central: les échanges entre le wilayet de Tripoli et l'Afrique centrale de 1835 à 1911." Ph.D. diss., Université de Provence, 1996.

Ainad-Tabet, Redouane. "Le 8 mai 1945: Jacquerie ou revendication agraire?" *Revue des sciences juridiques, économiques, et politiques* 9, no. 4 (December 1972): 1007–16.

Akinjogbin, Abeagbo, ed. *War and Peace in Yorubaland, 1793–1893.* Ibadan: Heinemann Educational Books, 1998.

Akkache, Ahmed. *La Résistance algérienne de 1845 à 1945.* Algiers: Société Nationale d'Edition et de Diffusion, 1972.

Alatas, Syed Hussein. *The Myth of the Lazy Native: A Study of the Image of the Malays, Filipinos and Javanese from the 16th to the 20th Century and Its Function in the Ideology of Colonial Capitalism.* London: Frank Cass, 1977.

Algergoni, Gianni. "Variations italiennes sur un thème français: la Sanusiya." In *Connaissances du Maghreb,* edited by Jean-Claude Vatin, 111–134. Paris: Editions du Centre National de la Recherche Scientifique, 1984.

L'Algérie dans la violence. Mouans-Sartoux, France: Publications de l'Ecole Moderne Française ados, 1999.

Allan, J. A., ed. *The Sahara: Ecological Change and Early Economic History.* Outwell, G.B.: Middle East and North African Studies Press, 1981.

Alleg, Henri. *The Question*. Translated by John Calder. Lincoln, Neb.: Bison Books, 2006.

Allen, Richard B. "Licentious and Unbridled Proceedings: The Illegal Slave Trade to Mauritius and the Seychelles during the Early Nineteenth Century." *Journal of African History* 42 (2001): 91–126.

Alloula, Malek. *Alger: photographiée au XIXe siècle*. Paris: Marval, 2001.

Alport, E. A. "The Mzab." *Journal of the Royal Anthropological Institute* 84 (January–June 1954): 1–12.

Anderson, Benedict. *Imagined Communities: Reflections on the Origin and Spread of Nationalism*. London: Verso, 1991.

Anderson, Lisa. "Ramadan al-Suwayhli: Hero of the Libyan Resistance." In *Struggle and Survival in the Modern Middle East*, edited by Edmund Burke III, 114–28. Berkeley: University of California Press, 1993.

Anderson, Perry. "Internationalism: A Breviary." *New Left Review* 14 (March–April, 2002): 5–25.

Andezian, Sossie. "Mysticisme extatique dans le champ religieux algérien contemporain." *Annuaire de l'Afrique du nord* 33 (1994): 323–38.

——. *Expériences du divin dans l'Algérie contemporaine: adeptes des saints dans la région de Tlemcen*. Paris: Editions du Centre National de la Recherche Scientifique, 2001.

Aouli, Smaïl, Ramdane Redjala, and Philippe Zoummeroff. *Abd El-Kader*. Paris: Fayard, 1994.

Arkoun, Mohammed. *Essais sur la pensée islamique*. Paris: Maisonneuve et Larose, 1977.

——. *L'Islam: religion et société; interviews dirigées par Mario Arosio*. Paris: Editions du Cerf, 1982.

Arrus, René. *L'Eau en Algérie: de l'impérialisme au développement, 1830–1962*. Grenoble: Presses Universitaires de Grenoble, 1985.

Artaud, Antonin. *The Peyote Dance*. Translated by H. Weaver. New York: Farrar, Straus and Giroux, 1976.

Asch, Ronald B. "Warfare in the Age of the Thirty Years War." In *European Warfare, 1453–1815*, edited by Jeremy Black, 45–68. New York: Palgrave, 1999.

Aumassip, G.. "Autour de la 'mer saharienne.'" *Awal* 8 (1991): 107–17.

Austen, Ralph. *African Economic History*. London: James Currey, 1987.

——. "The 19th Century Islamic Slave Trade from East Africa (Swahili and Red Sea Coasts): A Tentative Census." *Slavery and Abolition* 9, no. 3 (1988): 21–44.

——. "The Mediterranean Islamic Slave Trade Out of Africa: A Tentative Census." *Slavery and Abolition* 13, no. 1 (1992): 214–48.

Austen, Ralph, and Dennis D. Cordell. "Trade, Transportation, and Expanding Economic Networks: Saharan Caravan Commerce in the Era of European Expansion, 1500–1900." In *Black Business and Economic Power*, edited by Alusine Jolloh and Toyin Falola, 80–113. Rochester, N.Y.: University of Rochester Press, 2002.

Auriant. "Notes et documents d'histoire: sur la piste du mystérieux Boutin." *Mercure de France* 177 (1925): 231–42.

Azan, Paul. *Le Duc d'Orléans à Alger et à Oran en 1835: impressions du duc d'Elchingen*. Algiers: Imprimerie de S. Léon, 1906.

——. *Les Grands soldats de l'Algérie*. Paris: Publications du Comité National Métropolitain du Centenaire de l'Algérie, n.d. [1930?].

Ba, Amadou Hampaté, and J. Daget. *L'Empire Peul du Macina*. Paris: Mouton, 1962.

Badawi, Ahmed. *el-Zawiya mukhtariya Awlad Djilal*. N.p.: n.p., n.d. [ca. 2003] (guidebook published by the *zawiyya* of Ouled Djellal).

Bader, Raëd. "L'Esclavage dans l'Algérie coloniale, 1830–1870." *Revue d'histoire maghrébine* 26, nos. 93–94 (May 1999): 57–69.

Baduel, Pierre-Robert. *Société et émigration du Nefzaoua (Sud-Tunisien)*. Paris: Editions du Centre National de la Recherche Scientifique, 1980.

———, et al. *Enjeux sahariens: recherches sur les sociétés méditerranéennes*. Paris: Editions du Centre National de la Recherche Scientifique, 1984.

Baer, Gabriel. "Slavery in Nineteenth Century Egypt." *Journal of African History* 8, no. 3 (1967): 417–41.

Bahous, Malek. *L'Insurrection des Ouled Sidi Cheikh, Si Slimane Ben Hamza, 1864*. Oran: Dar El Gharb, 2001.

Baier, Stephen. "Trans-Saharan Trade and the Sahel Damargu, 1870–1930." *Journal of African History* 18, no. 1 (1977): 37–60.

Baillou, Jean, et al. *Les Affaires étrangères et le corps diplomatique française*. Vol. 1: *De l'ancien régime au second empire*. Paris: Editions du Centre National de la Recherche Scientifique, 1984.

Bairoch, Paul. *Commerce extérieur et développement économique de l'Europe au XIXe siècle*. Paris: Mouton, 1976.

Balandier, Georges. *Political Anthropology*. Translated by A. M. Sheridan Smith. London: Penguin, 1970.

Balibar, Etienne. *Politics and the Other Scene*. Translated by Christine Jones, James Swenson, and Chris Turner. London: Verso, 2002.

Barbier, Maurice, ed. *Voyages et explorations au Sahara occidental au XIXe siècle*. Paris: Harmattan, 1985.

Bardin, Pierre. *Algériens et Tunisiens dans l'empire Ottoman de 1848 à 1914*. Paris: Editions du Centre National de la Recherche Scientifique, 1979.

Baroin, Catherine. "Ecologie et organisation sociale: comparaison de trois sociétés sahariennes (Toubou, Touaregue, Maure)." *Revue de l'occident musulman et de la Méditerranée* 32 (1981): 9–22.

Baroli, Marc. *La Vie quotidienne des français en Algérie, 1830–1914*. [Paris]: Hachette, 1967.

Bataille, Georges. *La Part maudite*. Paris: Editions de Minuit, 1967.

———. *Visions of Excess: Selected Writings, 1927–1939*. Translated and edited by A. Stoekl. Minneapolis: University of Minnesota Press, 1985.

Bataillon, Claude. *Le Souf: étude de géographie humaine*. Algiers: Imbert, 1955.

Baudet, Henri. "Alexis de Tocqueville et la pensée coloniale du XIXe siècle." In *Alexis de Tocqueville: livre du centenaire (1859–1959)*, 121–31. Paris: Editions du Centre National de la Recherche Scientifique, 1960.

Bedjaoui, Youcef, Abbas Aroua, and Méziane Aït-Larbi. eds. *An Inquiry into the Algerian Massacres*. Plan-les-Ouates, Geneva: Hoggar, 1999.

Behnke, Roy. *The Herders of Cyrenaica*. Urbana: University of Illinois Press, 1980.

Bel, Alfred. *La Religion musulmane en Berbérie*. Paris: P. Geuthner, 1938.

Belkaid-Ellyas, Akram, and Jean-Pierre Peyroulou. *L'Algérie en guerre civile*. Paris: Calmann-Lévy, 2002.

Belkhodja, Amar. *Barbarie coloniale en Afrique*. Algiers: Editions ANEP, 2002.

———. *Crimes et famine dans le Sersou*. Algiers: Editions ANEP, 2002.

Bellil, Rachid. *Les Oasis du Gourara (Sahara algérien)*. 3 vols. Paris: Peeters, 1999–2000.

Ben-Ami, Issachar. *Culte des saints et pèlerinages judeéo-musulmans au Maroc*. Paris: Maisonneuve et Larose, 1990.

Benblal, Rachid. *Tlemcen des saints et des savants*. Oran: Editions Dar el Gharb, 2003.

Bénichou, Paul. *Le Sacré de l'écrivain, 1750–1830: essai sur l'avènement d'un pouvoir spirituel laïque dans la France moderne*. 1973. Reprint, Paris: Gallimard, 1996.

———. *Le Temps des prophètes: doctrines de l'âge romantique*. Paris: Gallimard, 1977.

Benjamin, Roger. *Orientalist Aesthetics: Art, Colonialism, and French North Africa, 1880–1930*. Berkeley: University of California Press, 2003.

Benjamin, Walter. "Critique of Violence." *Selected Writings*. Vol. 1: *1913–1926*, edited by Marcus Bullock and Michael W. Jennings, 236–52. Cambridge, Mass.: Harvard University Press, 1996.

Bennassar, Bartolomé, and Lucile Bennassar. *Les Chrétiens d'Allah: l'histoire extraordinaire des renégats des XVIe–XVIIe siècles*. Paris: Perrin, 1989.

Bennoune, Mahfoud. *The Making of Contemporary Algeria, 1830–1987*. Cambridge: Cambridge University Press, 1988.

Bénot, Yves. *Massacres coloniaux, 1944–1950: la IVe république et la mis au pas des colonies françaises*. Paris: Découverte, 1994.

Bercé, Yves-Marie. *History of Peasant Revolts: The Social Origins of Rebellion in Early Modern France*. Translated by Amanda Whitmore. Ithaca, N.Y.: Cornell University Press, 1990.

Berenguer, A. "Documents suédois sur la prise d'Alger (1830)." *Revue d'histoire et de civilisation du Maghreb* 4 (1968): 35–49.

Berger, Anne-Emmanuelle, ed. *Algeria in Others' Languages*. Ithaca, N.Y.: Cornell University Press, 2002.

Bernus, Edmond, et al., eds. *Nomades et commandants: administration et sociétés nomades dans l'ancienne A.O.F.* Paris: Editions Karthala, 1993.

Bernus, Suzanne. *Henri Barth chez les Touaregs de l'Air: extraits du journal de Barth dan l'Air, juillet–décembre 1850*. Niamey, Niger: Centre Nigérien de Recherches en Sciences Humaines, 1972.

———. "Relations entre nomades et sédentaires des confins sahariens méridionaux: essai d'interprétation dynamique." *Revue de l'Occident musulman et de la Méditerranée* 32 (1981): 23–35.

Berque, Augustin. "Esquisse d'une histoire de la seigneurie algérienne." *Revue de la Méditerranée* 7, no. 1 (1949): 18–34; no. 2 (1949): 168–80.

———. *Ecrits sur l'Algérie*. Edited by Jacques Berque. Aix en Provence: Edisud, 1986.

Berque, Jacques. "Qu'est-ce qu'une tribu nord africaine?" In *Eventail de l'histoire vivante: hommage à Lucien Febvre*, edited by Lucien Paul Victor Febvre, 261–71. Paris: A. Colin, 1953.

———. *Structures sociales du Haut-Atlas*. Paris: Presses Universitaires de France, 1955.

———. *French North Africa: The Maghrib between the Two World Wars*. Translated by Jean Stewart. New York: Praeger, 1967.

———. *L'Intérieur du Maghreb*. Paris: Gallimard, 1978.

———. Ulémas, *fondateurs, insurgés du Maghreb: XVIIe siècle*. 2nd ed.. Paris: Sindbad, 1998.

Bessaih, Boualem. *Abdallah Ben Kerriou: poète de Laghouat et du Sahara*. Paris: Publisud, 2003.

Bisson, Jean. *Le Gourara: étude de géographie humaine*. Algiers: Institut de Recherches Sahariennes, Université d'Alger, n.d. [1957].

Blin, Louis. "Les Noirs dans l'Algérie contemporaine." *Politique africaine* 30 (June 1980): 22–31.

———. "L'Algérie et route transsaharienne." *Maghreb Review* 12 (May–August, 1987): 105–13.

———. *L'Algérie du Sahara au Sahel*. Paris: Harmattan, 1991.

Bloch, Marc. *Les Rois thaumaturges: étude sur le caractère surnaturel attribué a la puissance royale, particulièrement en France et en Angleterre*. Paris: A. Colin, 1961.

———. *French Rural History: An Essay on Its Basic Characteristics*. Translated by Janet Sondheimer. Berkeley: University of California Press, 1966.

Boahen, Adu A. "The Caravan Trade in the Nineteenth Century." *Journal of African History* 2 (1962): 349–59.

———. *Britain, the Sahara and the Western Sudan, 1788–1861*. Oxford: Clarendon Press, 1964.

Boetsch G., and J. N. Ferrie. "Du Berbère aux yeux clairs à la race eurafricaine: la Méditerranée des anthropologues physiques." In *Le Maghreb, l'Europe et la France*, edited by K. Basfao and J.-R. Henry, 191–207. Paris: Editions du Centre National de la Recherche Scientifique, 1992.

Bois, Jean-Pierre. *Bugeaud*. Paris: Fayard, 1997.

Bonner, Michael. *Jihad in Islamic History: Doctrines and Practice*. Princeton, N.J.: Princeton University Press, 2006.

Bonté, Pierre. "Segmentarité et pouvoir chez les éleveurs nomades sahariens: éléments d'une problématique." In *Production pastorale et société*, edited by L'Equipe Ecologie et Anthropologie des Sociétés Pastorales, 171–200. Paris: Editions de la Maison des Sciences de l'Homme, 1979.

———, et al. *al-Ansâb: la quête des origines; anthropologie historique de la société tribale arabe*. Paris: Editions de la Maison des Sciences de l'homme, 1991.

———. *Savoirs et pouvoirs au Sahara*. Cologne: Institut für Völkerkunde, Universität zu Köln, 1998.

Bonté, Pierre, Anne-Marie Brisebarre, and Altan Gokalp, eds. *Sacrifices en Islam: espaces et temps d'un rituel*. Paris: Editions du Centre National de la Recherche Scientifique, 1999.

Botte, Roger. "L'Esclavage africain après l'abolition de 1848," *Annales: histoire, sciences sociales* 5 (September–October 2000): 1009–37.

Boualem Bessaih, Abdallah ben. *Kerrion: poète de Laghouat et du Sahara*. Algiers: Editions Zyriab, 2003.

Boubakeur, Si Hamza. "Origines de la guerre du Sud-Oranais contre la France (1864–1900)." *Revue d'histoire maghrébine* 6 (July 1976): 133–49.

———. *Un soufi algérien, Sidi Cheikh: sa vie, son œuvre, son rôle historique, ses descendants*. Paris: Maisonneuve et Larose, 1999.

Bouche, Denise. *Histoire de la colonisation française.* Vol. 2: *Flux et reflux, 1815–1962.* Paris: Fayard, 1991.

Bouderbala, Negib. "Pour un regard froid sur la colonisation: la perception de la colonisation dans le champ de la pensée décolonisée; le cas du Maroc." In *Connaissances du Maghreb,* edited by Jean-Claude Vatin, 423–34. Paris: Editions du Centre National de la Recherche Scientifique, 1984.

Boudjedra, Rachid. *Timimoun: roman.* Algiers: Editions ANEP, 2002.

Boufeldja, Zaïd. *L'Odyssée d'une religieuse au Sahara: scandaleuse mission d'allégresses d'un Dominicain.* Algiers: Société Nationale d'Edition et de Diffusion, 1982.

Boukhobza, M'Hamed. *L'Agropastoralisme traditionnel en Algérie: de l'ordre tribal au désordre colonial.* Algiers: Office des Publications Universitaires, 1982.

———. *Ruptures et transformations sociales en Algérie.* Algiers: Office des Publications Universitaires, 1989.

Bourdieu, Pierre. *The Algerians.* Translated by Alan C. M. Ross. Boston: Beacon Press, 1962.

———. *Les Mozabites.* Paris: Presses Universitaires de France, 1970.

———. *The Logic of Practice.* Translated by Richard Nice. Stanford, Calif.: Stanford University Press, 1990.

———. *Masculine Domination.* Translated by Richard Nice. Stanford, Calif.: Stanford University Press, 2001.

———, et al. *Travail et travailleurs en Algérie.* Paris: Mouton, 1963.

Bourdieu, Pierre, and Abdelmalek Sayad. *Le Déracinement ou la crise de l'agriculture traditionnelle en Algérie.* Paris: Editions de Minuit, 1964.

Bourdieu, Pierre, and Loïc J.D. Wacquant. *An Invitation to Reflexive Sociology.* Chicago: University of Chicago Press, 1992.

Bousquet, Georges-Henri. *Les Grandes pratiques rituelles de l'Islam.* Paris: Presses Universitaires de France, 1979.

Boutaleb, Abdelkader. *L'Emir Abd-el-Kader et la formation de la nation algérienne: de l'émir Abd-el-Kader à la guerre de libération.* Algiers: Editions Dahlab, 1990.

Bovill, Edward William. *The Golden Trade of the Moors.* London: Oxford University Press, 1968.

Böwering, Gerhard. "Règles et rituels soufis." In *Les Voies d'Allah: les ordres mystiques dans l'islam des origines à aujourd'hui,* edited by Alexandre Popovic and Gilles Veinstein, 139–56. Paris: Fayard, 1996.

Bowles, Paul. *The Sheltering Sky.* 1949. Reprint, New York: Vintage Books, 1990.

Boyer, Pierre. *L'Evolution de l'Algérie médiane: ancien département d'Alger de 1830 à 1956.* Paris: Adrien-Maisonneuve, 1960.

Brahimi, Denise. "Voyageurs français du XVIII siècle en Barbarie." Ph.D. diss., Université de Paris III–Lille, 1976.

———. *Requiem pour Isabelle.* Paris: Publisud, 1983.

Brantlinger, Patrick. *Dark Vanishings: Discourse on the Extinction of Primitive Races, 1800–1930.* Ithaca, N.Y.: Cornell University Press, 1993.

Braud, Pierre. *Général Cler: Un oublié de l'histoire.* N.p.: Cercle Généalogique du Haut-Berry, 1995.

Braudel, Fernand. *The Mediterranean and the Mediterranean World in the Age of Philip II.* Translated by Siân Reynolds. 2 vols. Berkeley: University of California Press, 1995.

Brett, Michael. "Mufti, Mrabit, Marabout and Mahdi: Four Types in the Islamic History of North Africa," *Revue de l'occident musulman et de la Méditerranée* 29 (1980): 5–15.

———. "Legislating for Inequality in Algeria: The Senatus-Consulte of 14 July 1865." *Bulletin of the School of Oriental and African Studies* 51, no. 3 (1988): 440–61.

Brett, Michael, and Elizabeth Fentress. *The Berbers.* Oxford: Blackwell, 1996.

Brigol, M. "L'Habitat des nomades sédentarisés à Ouargla." *Travaux de l'Institut de recherches sahariennes* 16, no. 2 (1957): 181–97.

Britsch, Jacques. *La Mission Foureau-Lamy et l'arrivée des Français au Tchad, 1898–1900: carnets de route du lieutenant Gabriel Britsch.* Paris: Harmattan, 1989.

Broc, Numa. "Les Explorateurs français du XIXème réconsidérés." *Revue française d'histoire d'outre-mer* 69 (1982): 237–73, 323–59.

Brower, Benjamin Claude. "A Desert Named Peace: Violence and Empire in the Algerian Sahara, 1844–1902." Ph.D. diss., Cornell University , 2005.

———. "Lutte mystique: un nouveau regard sur les Soufis sahariens dans le XIXème siècle." In *Des voies et des voix.* Edited by Zaïm Khenchelaoui, 59–74. Algiers: Editions du Centre National de Recherches Préhistoriques, Anthropologiques, et Historiques, 2007.

———. "The Servile Populations of the Algerian Sahara Seen through the French Colonial Archives." In *Slavery, Islam, and Diaspora,* edited by Paul Lovejoy, Ismael Montana, and Behnaz Mirzai. Trenton, N.J.: Africa World Press, forthcoming.

Brown, Marshall. *The Shape of German Romanticism.* Ithaca, N.Y.: Cornell University Press, 1979.

Brown, Wendy. *Regulating Aversion: Tolerance in the Age of Identity and Empire.* Princeton, N.J.: Princeton University Press, 2006.

Brunon, Jean, and Raoul Brunon. *Découverte du Hoggar: premier explorateur de l'Atakor n Ahaggar, le lieutenant Cottenest a ouvert le Sahara à la France.* Paris: Compagnie de Recherches et d'Exploitation du Pétrole au Sahara, 1959.

Brunschwig, Henri. *French Colonialism, 1871–1914: Myths and Realities.* Translated by William Glanville Brown. London: Pall Mall Press, 1964.

Bu Aziz, Yahya. *Thawrat 1871: dawr a'ilatay Muqrani wa-al-Haddad.* Algiers: al-Sharikah al-Wataniyah lil-Nashr wa al-Tawzi, 1978.

Bugeja, Manuel. *Au pays des moissons (le Sersou).* Algiers: Fontana, 1948.

Buheiry, Marwan R. "Anti-Colonial Sentiment in France during the July Monarchy: The Algerian Case." Ph.D. diss., Princeton University, 1973.

———. *The Formation and Perception of the Modern Arab World.* Edited by L. I. Conrad. Princeton, N.J.: Darwin Press, 1989.

Bulliet, Richard. *The Camel and the Wheel.* Cambridge Mass.: Harvard University Press, 1975.

Burgat, Marie-Claude, ed. *D'un orient l'autre: les métamorphoses successives des perceptions et connaissances.* 2 vols. Paris: Editions du Centre National de la Recherche Scientifique, 1991.

Burguière, André, and Jacques Revel. *Histoire de la France.* 5 vols. Paris: Editions du Seuil, 2000.

Burke, Edmund, III. *Prelude to Protectorate in Morocco: Precolonial Protest and Resistance, 1860–1912.* Chicago: University of Chicago Press, 1976.

———. "La Mission scientifique au Maroc: science sociale et politique dans l'âge de l'impérialisme." *Bulletin économique et social du Maroc* 138–39 (1979): 37–56.

———. "The First Crisis of Orientalism, 1890–1914." In *Connaissance du Maghreb*, edited by Jean-Claude Vatin, 213–336. Paris: Editions du Centre National de la Recherche Scientifique, 1984.

———. "Islam and Social Movements: Methodological Reflections." In *Islam, Politics, and Social Movements*, edited by Edmund Burke III and Ira M. Lapidus, 17–35. Berkeley: University of California Press, 1988.

———, ed. *Struggle and Survival in the Modern Middle East*. Berkeley: University of California Press, 1993.

Burke Edmund, III, and Walter Goldfrank. "Global Crises and Social Movements: A Comparative Historical Perspective." In *Global Crises and Social Movements: Artisans, Peasants, Populists, and the World Economy*, edited by Edmund Burke III, 1–12. Boulder, Colo.: Westview Press, 1988.

Butler, Judith. "Critique, Coercion, and Sacred Life in Benjamin's 'Critique of Violence.'" In *Political Theologies: Public Religions in a Post-Secular World*, edited by Hent de Vries and Lawrence E. Sullivan, 201–19. New York: Fordham University Press, 2006.

Byrnes, Robert Francis. *Mores, "The First National Socialist."* Notre Dame, Ind.: University of Notre Dame Press, 1950.

Caillois, Roger. *Mythe et l'homme*. Paris: Gallimard, 1938.

———. "Guerre et sacré," *Revue de Paris* 57 (October 1950): 107–16.

———. *Man, Play, and Games*. Translated by M. Barash. New York: Free Press of Glencoe, 1961.

Capot-Rey, Robert. "Le Nomadisme pastoral dans le Sahara français." *Travaux de l'Institut de recherches sahariennes* 1 (1942): 63–86.

———. "Transformations récentes dans une tribu du Sud oranais." *Annales de géographie* 324 (1952): 138–42.

———. *Le Sahara français*. Paris: Presses Universitaires de France, 1953.

———. "Greniers domestiques et greniers fortifiés au Sahara: le cas du Gourara." *Extrait des travaux de l'Institut de recherches sahariennes* 14 (1956): 139–58.

Capot-Rey, Robert, and Philippe Marçais. "La Charrue au Sahara." *Travaux de l'Institut de recherches sahariennes* 10 (1953): 39–69.

Carlier, Omar. "La Guerre d'Algérie et ses prolégomènes: note pour une anthropologie historique de la violence politique." *Naqd: Revue d'études et de critique sociale* 4 (January-March 1993): 32–44.

———, et al. *Lettrés, intellectuels, et militants en Algérie, 1880–1950*. Algiers: Office des Publications Universitaires, 1988.

Caron, François. *Histoire de l'exploitation d'un grand réseau: la compagnie du chemin de fer du nord, 1846–1937*. Paris: Mouton, 1973.

———. *Histoire économique de la France: XIXe–XXe siècles*. Paris: Armand Colin, 1995.

Casajus, Dominique. "La Tente et le campement chez les Touaregs Kel Ferwan." *Revue de l'occident musulman et de la Méditerranée* 32 (1981): 54–70.

———. "Les Amis français de la cause touarègue." *Cahiers d'études africaines* 35, no. 137 (1995): 237–50.

———. "Henri Duveyrier et le désert des Saint-Simoniens." *Ethnologies comparées* 7 (spring 2004). http://alor.univ-moutp3.fr/cercle/r7/d.c.htm (accessed March 2008).

Castoriadis, Cornelius. *The Imaginary Institution of Society*. Translated by Kathleen Blamey. Cambridge Mass.: MIT Press, 1987.

Cauneille, A. *Les Chaanba (leur nomadisme): évolution de la tribu durant l'administration française*. Paris: Editions du Centre National de la Recherche Scientifique, 1968.

Cauvin, Charles, Edouard Cortier, and Henire Laperrine. *La Pénétration saharienne, 1906: le rendez-vous de Taoudeni*. Paris: Harmattan, 1999.

Cazier, Jean-Philippe, ed. *Abécédaire de Pierre Bourdieu*. Mons, Belgium: Sils Maria, 2006.

Chailley, M. "Paul Soleillet." *Encyclopédie mensuelle d'outre-mer* 21 (May 1952): 140–43.

Chaker, Salem. "Langue et écriture berbères au Sahara." *Revue de l'occident musulman et de la Méditerranée* 32 (1981): 71–75.

———, ed. *Etudes Touaregs: bilan des recherches en sciences sociales*. Aix-en-Provence: Edisud, 1988.

Chalmin, Commandant P. *Les Bureaux arabes de leur création à la chute du second empire*. Algiers: Histoire Algérienne, 1954.

Chambert-Loir, Henri, and Claude Guillot, eds. *Le Culte des saints dans le monde musulman*. Paris: Ecole Française d'Extrême-Orient, 1995.

Champault, Francine Dominique. *Une oasis du Sahara nord-occidental: Tabelbala*. Paris: Editions du Centre National de la Recherche Scientifique, 1969.

Charle, Christophe. *A Social History of France in the 19th Century*. Translated by Miriam Kochan. Oxford: Berg, 1994.

———. *La Crise des sociétés impériales: Allemagne, France, Grande-Bretagne, 1900–1940; essai d'histoire sociale comparée*. Paris: Editions du Seuil, 2001.

Charnay, Jean-Paul. *La Vie musulmane en Algérie d'après la jurisprudence de la première moitié du XXe siècle*. Paris: Presses Universitaires de France, 1965.

———. "Action et politique en Islam." In *L'ambivalence dans la culture arabe*, edited by Jean-Paul Charnay, 407–18. Paris: Anthropos, 1967.

Chaulet-Achour, Christiane, and Romuald-Blaise Fonkoua, eds. *Esclavage: libérations, abolitions, commémorations*. Paris: Séguier, 2001.

Chelhod, Joseph. "La *Baraka* chez les Arabes ou l'influence bienfaisante du sacré," *Revue de l'histoire des religions* 148 (1955): 67–88.

———. *Le Sacrifice chez les Arabes*. Paris: Presses Universitaires de France, 1955.

———. *Introduction à la sociologie de l'Islam*. Paris: G.-P. Maisonneuve, 1958.

———. *Les Structures du sacré chez les Arabes*. Paris: Maisonneuve et Larose, 1964.

———. *Le Droit dans la société bédouine*. Paris: Rivière, 1971.

Chemirou, Madjid. "L'Histoire de Bejaia et de sa région de 1833 à 1880." D.E.A. thesis, Université de Paris VII, 2002.

Chenntouf, Tayeb. *L'Algérie politique, 1830–1954*. Algiers: Office des Publications Universitaires, 2003.

———. *Etudes d'histoire de l'Algérie*. Algiers: Office des Publications Universitaires, 2004.

Chenntouf, Tayeb, and Abdelkader Djeghlou, eds. *Eléments de sociologie de l'histoire algérienne, XIXe-XXe*. Oran: Institut des Sciences Sociales, Université d'Oran, 1978–79.

Cherry, Deborah. "Earth into World, Land into Landscape: The 'Worlding' of Algeria in

Nineteenth-Century British Feminism." In *Orientalism's Interlocutors: Painting, Architecture, Photography,* edited by Jill Beaulieu and Mary Roberts, 103–30. Durham, N.C.: Duke University Press, 2002.

Chevaldonné, Hélène. "Le Bureau arabe de Méchéria (Sud-Oranais), 1890–1905." D.E.A. thesis, Université de Provence, Aix Marseille 1, 1988–89.

Chevrillon, André. *Les Puritains du désert (sud-algérien).* Paris: Plon, 1927.

Choutri, Gadhila, ed. *Violence, trauma, et mémoire.* Algiers: Casbah Editions, 2001.

Christelow, Allan. "Saintly Descent and Worldly Affairs in Mid Nineteenth Century Mascara, Algeria." *International Journal of Middle East Studies* 12 (1980): 129–55.

———. "Intellectual History in a Culture under Siege: Algerian Thought in the Last Half of the Nineteenth Century." *Middle Eastern Studies* 18 (1982): 387–99.

———. *Muslim Law Courts and the French Colonial State in Algeria.* Princeton, N.J.: Princeton University Press, 1985.

———. "Slavery in Kano, 1913–1914: Evidence from the Judicial Records." *African Economic History* 14 (1985): 57–74.

Christin, Anne-Marie. *Fromentin conteur d'espace: essai sur l'œuvre algérienne.* Paris: Sycomore, 1982.

Cicerchia, Ricardo. "Journey to the Center of the Earth: Domingo Faustino Sarmiento, a Man of Letters in Algeria." *Journal of Latin American Studies* 36, no. 4 (November 2004): 665–86.

Clancy-Smith, Julia A. "Saints, Mahdis, and Arms: Religion and Resistance in Nineteenth-Century North Africa." In *Islam, Politics, and Social Movements,* edited by Edmund Burke III and Ira M. Lapidus, 60–80. Berkeley: University of California Press, 1988.

———. "In the Eye of the Beholder: Sufi and Saint in North Africa and the Colonial Production of Knowledge, 1830–1900." *Africana Journal* 15 (1990): 220–57.

———. *Rebel and Saint: Muslim Notables, Populist Protest, Colonial Encounters (Algeria and Tunisia, 1800–1904).* Berkeley: University of California Press, 1997.

Clarck-Taoua, Phyllis. "In Search of New Skin: Michel Leiris's *L'Afrique fantôme.*" *Cahiers d'études africaines* 42, no. 167 (2002): 479–98.

Claudot-Hawad, Hélène. "Honneur et politique: les choix stratégiques des touaregs pendant la colonisation française." *Revue de la Méditerranée et du monde musulman* 57 (1991): 11–48.

———. "Ordre sacré et ordre politique chez les touaregs de l'air: l'exemple du pèlerinage aux lieux saints." *Annuaire de l'Afrique du nord* 33 (1994): 223–40.

———. ed. *La Politique dans l'histoire Touarègue* [special issue of *Cahiers de l'Institut de recherches et d'études sur le monde arabe et musulman*]. Aix-en-Provence: Institut de Recherches et d'Etudes sur le Monde Arabe et Musulman, 1993.

Clavel, Marcel. *Fenimore Cooper: sa vie et son œuvre.* Aix-en-Provence: Imprimerie Universitaire de Provence, 1938.

Cleaveland, Timothy. *Becoming Walāta: A History of Saharan Social Formation and Transformation.* Portsmouth, N.H.: Heinemann, 2002.

Cohen, Roger. "News Analysis: Algeria Fails to Curb Killings." *New York Times,* 9 January 1998.

Collinet, Michel. "Le Saint-Simonisme et l'armée." *Revue française de sociologie* 2 (1961): 38–47.

Collingham, H. A. C. *The July Monarchy: A Political History of France, 1830–1848.* London: Longman, 1988.

Collot, Claude. *Les Institutions de l'Algérie durant la période coloniale, 1830–1962.* Paris: Editions du Centre National de la Recherche Scientifique / Algiers: Office des Publications Universitaires, 1987.

Colonna, Fanny. "Cultural Resistance and Religious Legitimacy in Colonial Algeria," *Economy and Society* 3, no. 3 (August 1974): 233–52.

———. *Les Instituteurs algériens, 1883–1939.* Algiers: Office des Publications Universitaires, 1975.

———. *Savants paysans: éléments d'histoire sociale sur l'Algérie rurale.* Algiers: Office des Publications Universitaires, 1987.

———. *Timimoun: une civilisation citadine.* Algiers: Entreprise Nationale de Presse, 1989.

———. *Les Versets de l'invincibilité: permanence et changements religieux dans l'Algérie contemporaine.* Paris: Presses de Science Po, 1995.

Colonna, Fanny, and Claude Ha Brahimi. "Du bon usage de la science coloniale." In *Le Mal de voir: ethnologie et orientalisme, politique et épistémologie, critique et autocritique,* edited by Henri Moniot, 221–41. Paris: Union Générale de l'Edition, 1976.

Colonna, Vincent. *Yamaha d'Alger: roman.* Auch, France: Tristram, 1999.

Conklin, Alice L. *A Mission to Civilize: The Republican Idea of Empire in France and West Africa, 1895–1930.* Stanford, Calif.: Stanford University Press, 1997.

Conte, Edouard. "Alliance et parenté élective en Arabie ancienne: éléments d'un problématique." *L'Homme* 102 (April–June 1987): 119–38.

Cooper, Frederick. "Conflict and Connection: Rethinking Colonial African History." *American Historical Review* 99, no. 5 (December 1994): 1516–45.

———. *Decolonization and African Society: The Labor Question in French and British Africa.* Cambridge: Cambridge University Press, 1996.

Cooper, Frederick, and Ann Laura Stoler, eds. *Tensions of Empire: Colonial Cultures in a Bourgeois World.* Berkeley: University of California Press, 1997.

Copley, Stephen, and Peter Garside, eds.. *The Politics of the Picturesque: Literature, Landscape and Aesthetics Since 1770.* Cambridge: Cambridge University Press, 1994.

Coque, Roger. "Les Vicissitudes d'un mythe: la mer saharienne quaternaire." *Sahara* (Centro studi Luigi Negro) 3 (1990): 7–20.

Coquery-Vidrovitch, Catherine. *La Découverte de l'Afrique: l'Afrique noire atlantique des origines au XVIIIe siècle.* Paris: René Julliard, 1965.

———. *Africa: Endurance and Change South of the Sahara.* Translated by David Maisel. Berkeley: University of California Press, 1988.

———. *L'Afrique et les Africains au XIXe siècle: mutations, révolutions, crises.* Paris: Armand Colin, 1999.

Corbin, Alain. *The Village of Cannibals: Rage and Murder in France, 1870.* Translated by Arthur Goldhammer. Cambridge, Mass.: Harvard University Press, 1992.

———. *The Lure of the Sea: The Discovery of the Seaside in the Western World, 1750–1840.* Translated by Jocelyn Phelps. Berkeley: University of California Press, 1994.

Cordell, Dennis D. "The Awlad Sulayman of Libya and Chad: Power and Adaptation in the Sahara and Sahel," *Canadian Journal of African Studies* 19, no. 2 (1985): 319–43.

———. *Dar Al-Kuti and the Last Years of the Trans-Saharan Slave Trade.* Madison: University of Wisconsin Press, 1985.

——. "The Labor of Violence: Dar al-Kuti in the Nineteenth Century." In *The Workers of African Trade*, edited by Catherine Coquery-Vidrovitch and Paul Lovejoy, 169–92. Beverly Hills, Calif.: Sage Publications, 1985.

——. "No Liberty, Not Much Equality, and Very Little Fraternity: The Mirage of Manumission in the Algerian Sahara in the Second Half of the Nineteenth Century." In *Slavery and Colonial Rule in Africa*, edited by Suzanne Miers and Martin Klein, 38–56. London: Frank Cass, 1999.

Cornell, Vincent J. *Realm of the Saint: Power and Authority in Moroccan Sufism*. Austin: University of Texas Press, 1998.

Côte, Marc. *L'Algérie: espace et société*. Paris: Armand Colin, 1996.

——. *Pays, paysages, paysans d'Algérie*. Paris: Editions du Centre national de la Recherche Scientifique, 1996.

Courtine, Jean-François, et al. *Du sublime*. [Paris]: Belin, 1988.

Crosnier, Elise. *Aurélie Picard, 1849–1933: première française au Sahara*. Algiers: Editions Baconnier, n.d. [1947].

Crummey, Donald, ed. *Banditry, Rebellion, and Social Protest in Africa*. Portsmouth, N.H.: Heinemann, 1986.

Curtin, Philip D. *The Image of Africa. British Ideas and Action, 1780–1850*. Madison: University of Wisconsin Press, 1964.

Curtius, Ernst Robert. *European Literature and the Latin Middle Ages*. Translated by Willard R. Trask. Princeton, N.J.: Princeton University Press, 1967.

Dakhlia, Jocelyne. *L'Oubli de la cité: la mémoire collective à l'épreuve du lignage dans le Jérid tunisien*. Paris: Découverte, 1990.

——. *Le Divan des rois: la politique et le religieux dans l'Islam*. Paris: Aubier, 1998.

Dalton, George. "The Impact of Colonization on Aboriginal Economies in Stateless Societies." *Research in Economic Anthropology* 1 (1978): 131–84.

Danziger, Raphael. *Abd el Qadir and the Algerians: Resistance to the French and Internal Consolidation*. New York: Holmes & Meier, 1977.

Darboise, J.-M., M. Heynard, and J. Martel. *Officiers en Algérie*. Paris: Maspero, 1960.

Dauphin, Cécile, and Arlette Farge, eds. *De la violence et des femmes*. Paris: Albin Michel, 1997.

Daviet, Jean-Pierre. *La Société industrielle en France, 1814–1914*. Paris: Editions du Seuil, 1997.

Davis, Mike. *Late Victorian Holocausts: El Niño Famines and the Making of the Third World*. London: Verso, 2001.

Davis, Natalie Zemon. "The Rites of Violence: Religious Riot in Sixteenth-Century France." *Past and Present* 59 (May 1973): 51–91.

——. *Trickster Travels: A Sixteenth-Century Muslim between Worlds*. New York: Hill and Wang, 2006.

Decraene, Philippe, and Francois Zuccarelli. *Grands sahariens: à la découverte du désert des déserts*. Paris: Denoël, 1994.

Dedieu, Marie France. "Le Bureau arabe de Laghouat, 1859–60." Master's thesis, Université de Toulouse–Le Mirail, 1971.

Dehérain, Henri. *Orientalists et antiquaires: Silvestre de Sacy, ses contemporains et ses disciples*. Paris: P. Geuthner, 1938.

Dejeux, Jean. "Un bandit d'honneur dans l'Aurès de 1917 à 1921: Messaoud ben Zelmad." *Revue de l'occident musulman et de la Méditerranée* 26, no. 2 (1978): 35–54.

Dekker, George, and John P. McWillians, eds. *Fenimore Cooper: The Critical Heritage.* London: Routledge and Kegan Paul, 1973.

Delerive, Roger, and Marc Franconie. *Forts sahariens des Territoires du Sud.* Paris: Geuthner, 1990.

Denis, Pierre. *L'Armée française au Sahara de Bonaparte à 1990.* Paris: Editions L'Harmattan, 1991.

Dermenghem, Emile. *Joseph de Maistre mystique.* Paris: La Connaissance, 1923.

——. *La Vie de Mohomet.* Paris: Plon, 1929.

——. "En marge du culte officiel: les sanctuaires mystérieux d'Alger et de son Sahel." *Sciences et voyages* 51 (March 1950): 97–100.

——. "Le Mzab: un pays, une population, un genre de vies uniques au monde." *Science et voyages* 73 (January 1952): 22–26.

——. "Les Confréries noires en Algérie (Diwans de Sidi Blal)." *Revue africain* 97 (1953): 314–67.

——. *Le Culte des saints dans l'Islam maghrébin.* Paris: Gallimard, 1954.

——. "Entre la 'mer d'alfa' et le désert de sable: le Djebel Amour, un des pays le moins connus de l'Algérie." *Sciences et voyages* 119 (November 1955): 47–50.

——. "Les Filles de la douceur." *Nouvelle revue française* 15 (August 1957): 374–78.

——. "Le Pays de Laghouat et des Larbaa." *Documents algériens* 21 (1957): 161–76.

——. *Le Pays d'Abel: le Sahara des Ouled Nail, des Larbaa et des Amour.* Paris: Gallimard, 1960.

Derrida, Jacques. *Force de loi: le "fondement mystique de l'autorité."* Paris: Galilée, 1994.

Deschamps, Hubert. *Histoire des explorations.* Paris: Presses Universitaires de France, 1969.

Descombes, Vincent. *Modern French Philosophy.* Translated by L. Scott-Fox and J. M. Harding. Cambridge: Cambridge University Press, 1980.

Despois, Jean. "Les Greniers fortifiés de l'Afrique du Nord." *Cahiers de Tunisie* 1 (1953): 38–62.

——. *Le Hodna (Algérie).* Paris: Presses Universitaires de France, 1953.

——. *L'Afrique du Nord.* 3rd ed. Paris: Presses Universitaires de France, 1964.

——. "Les Paysages agraires traditionnels du Maghreb et du Sahara septentrional." *Annales de géographie* 396 (1964): 129–73.

Dessaigne, Francine. *Sonis mystique et soldat.* Paris: Nouvelles Editions Latines, 1988.

Djebar, Assia. *Algerian White: A Narrative.* Translated by David Kelley and Marjolijn de Jager. New York: Seven Stories Press, 2000.

Djebari, Youcef. *La France en Algérie: bilan et controverses.* 3 vols. Algiers: Office des Publications Universitaires, 1995.

Djeghloul, Abdelkader. *Eléments d'histoire culturelle algérienne.* Algiers: Entreprise National du Livre, 1984.

Dondin-Payre, Monique. *La Commission d'exploration scientifique d'Algérie: une héritière méconnue de la Commission d'Egypte.* Abbéville, France: F. Paillart, 1994.

Douki, Caroline, and Philippe Minard. "Histoire globale, histoires connectées: un changement d'échelle historiographique?" *Revue d'histoire moderne et contemporaine* 54, no. 4 bis (January 2008): 7–21.

Dreyfus, Françoise. *L'Invention de la bureaucratie: servir l'Etat en France, en Grande-Bretagne et aux Etats-Unis, XVIIIe–XXe siècle.* Paris: Découverte, 1999.

Drihem, Sakina. "Les Beni Toufout de Collo: une tribu algérienne face à la conquête." Master's thesis, Université de Provence, 1998.

Drinnon, Richard. *Facing West: The Metaphysics of Indian-Hating and Empire-Building.* Minneapolis: University of Minnesota Press, 1980.

Droulers, Charles. *Le Marquis de Morès, 1858–1896.* Paris: Plon, 1932.

Dumont, Louis. *Introduction à deux théories d'anthropologie sociale.* Paris: Mouton, 1971.

Dunn, Ross E. *Resistance in the Desert: Moroccan Responses to French Imperialism, 1881–1912.* Madison: University of Wisconsin Press, 1977.

Dupeux, Georges. *Aspects de l'histoire sociale et politique du Loir-et-Cher, 1848–1914.* Paris: A. Colin, 1962.

Dupuy, Aimé. *L'Algérie dans les lettres d'expression française.* Paris: Editions Universitaires, 1956.

——. "Remarques sur le sens et l'évolution du mot: 'indigène'." *Informations historiques* 3 (1963): 152–57.

Durkheim, Emile. *Socialism and Saint-Simon (Le Socialisme)* Translated by Charlotte Sattler and edited by Alvin W. Gouldner. Yellow Springs, Ohio: Antioch Press, 1958.

——. *The Elementary Forms of Religious Life.* Translated by Karen E. Fields. New York: Free Press, 1995.

Durou, Jean-Marc. *L'Exploration du Sahara.* Arles: Actes du Sud, 1993.

Durou, Jean-Marc, and Marc de Gouvenain. *Le Grand Rêve saharien.* Arles: Actes du Sud, 1997.

Duvollet, P. Roger. *Villages d'Algérie et oasis du Sahara: nouveaux proverbes et dictons arabes.* Vesoul, France: Duvollet, 1987.

d'Eaubonne, Françoise. *La Couronne des sables.* Paris: Flammarion, 1967.

Echallier, J. C. *Villages désertés et structures agraires anciennes du Touat-Gourara (Sahara algérien).* Paris: A.M.G., 1972.

Eickelman, Dale F. *Moroccan Islam: Tradition and Society in a Pilgrimage Center.* Austin: University of Texas Press, 1976.

——. "New Directions in Interpreting North African Society." In *Connaissances du Maghreb,* edited by Jean-Claude Vatin, 279–90. Paris: Editions du Centre National de la Recherche Scientifique, 1984.

——. *Knowledge and Power in Morocco: The Education of a Twentieth-Century Notable.* Princeton, N.J.: Princeton University Press, 1985.

——. *The Middle East: An Anthropological Approach.* Englewood Cliffs, N.J.: Prentice-Hall, 1989.

Eisenbeth, M. "Les Juifs en Algérie et en Tunisie à l'époque turque (1516–1830)," *Revue africaine* 95 (1951): 114–87; 96 (1952): 343–84.

Elkins, Caroline. *Imperial Reckoning: The Untold Story of Britain's Gulag in Kenya.* New York: Henry Holt, 2005.

Emerit, Marcel. *Les Saint-Simoniens en Algérie.* Paris: Belles Lettres, 1941.

——. "Les Explorations Saint-Simoniens en Afrique orientale et sur la route des Indes." *Revue africaine* 87 (1943): 93–116.

——. "La Légende de Léon Roches." *Revue africaine* 92 (1947): 81–105.

——. "L'Abolition de l'esclavage." In *La Révolution de 1848 en Algérie,* ed. Marcel Emerit et al., 29–42. Paris: Larose, 1949.

——. *L'Algérie à l'époque d'Abd-el-Kader*. Paris: Larose, 1951.

——. "Le Problème de la conversion des musulmans d'Algérie sous le Second Empire: le conflit entre MacMahon et Lavigerie." *Revue historique* 84, no. 223 (1960): 63–84.

——. "Les Tribus privilégiées en Algérie dans la première moitie du XIXe siècle." *Annales, économies, sociétés, civilisations* 31 (1966): 44–58.

Ennaji, Mohammed. *Serving the Master: Slavery and Society in Nineteenth-Century Morocco*. Translated by Seth Graebner. New York: St. Martin's Press, 1999.

Epstein, Steven A. *Speaking of Slavery: Color, Ethnicity, and Human Bondage in Italy*. Ithaca, N.Y.: Cornell University Press, 2001.

Ernest-Picard, Paul. *La Monnaie et le crédit en Algérie depuis 1830*. Paris: J. Carbonnel, Librairie Plon, 1930.

Erroux, J. *Les Blés des oasis sahariennes*. Algiers: Institut de Recherches Sahariennes, Université d'Alger, n.d.

Esposito, John. *Islam and Politics*. Syracuse, N.Y.: Syracuse University Press, 1984.

Esquer, Gabriel. *Iconographie historique de l'Algérie depuis le XVIe siècle jusqu'en 1871*. Paris: Plon, 1929.

——. *La prise d'Alger 1830*. Paris: Larose, 1929.

Establet, Colette. *Etre caïd dans l'Algérie coloniale*. Paris: Editions du Centre National de la Recherche Scientifique, 1991.

Etienne, Bruno. *Abdelkader: isthme des isthmes (Barzakh al-barazikh)*. Paris: Hachette, 1994.

Etemad, Bouda. *Possessing the World: Taking the Measurements of Colonisation from the 18th to the 20th Century*. Translated by Andrene Everson. New York: Berghahn, 2007.

Evans-Pritchard, E. E. *Kinship and Marriage among the Nuer*. Oxford: Clarendon Press, 1951.

Eydoux, Henri-Paul. *L'Exploration du Sahara*. Paris: Gallimard, 1938.

——. "Henri Duveyrier." *Hommes et Destins* 7 (1986): 169–73.

Fabre, Jean. *Introduction à la géologie du Sahara algérien et des régions voisines*. Algiers: Société Nationale d'Edition et Diffusion, 1976.

Fanon, Frantz. *The Wretched of the Earth*. Translated by Richard Philcox. New York: Grove Press, 2004.

Farge, Arlette. *Subversive Words: Public Opinion in Eighteenth-Century France*. Translated by Rosemary Morris. University Park: Pennsylvania State University Press, 1995.

Farmer, Paul. *Infections and Inequalities: The Modern Plagues*. Berkeley: University of California Press, 1999.

——. *Pathologies of Power: Health, Human Rights, and the New War on the Poor*. Berkeley: University of California Press, 2003.

——. "An Anthropology of Structural Violence." *Current Anthropology* 45, no. 3 (June 2004): 305–25.

Faroqhi, Suraiya. "Alum Production and Alum Trade in the Ottoman Empire (about 1560–1830)." *Wiener Zeitschrift für der Kunde des Morgenlandes* (Vienna) 71 (1979): 153–75.

——. *The Ottoman Empire and the World Around It*. London: I. B. Tauris, 2004.

——, et al. *An Economic and Social History of the Ottoman Empire*. Vol. 2: *1600–1914*. Cambridge: Cambridge University Press, 1994.

Favrod, Charles-Henri, and Yvan Dalain. *Sahara: à l'heure de la découverte*. Lausanne: Editions Clairefontaine, 1958.

Feraoun, Mouloud. *Journal, 1955–1962: Reflections on the French-Algerian War*. Translated by Mary Ellen Wolf and Claude Fouillade. Edited by James D. Le Sueur. Lincoln: University of Nebraska Press, 2000.

Ferhat, Halima, and Hamid Triki. "Faux prophètes et mahdis dans le Maroc médiéval." *Hespéris Tamuda* 26–27 (1988–89): 5–24.

Fessard, G., and J. Lambert. "Les Problèmes d'adaptions psycho-sociologiques en milieu industriel saharien." *Hygiène mentale* 3 (1960): 191–213.

Fierro, Alfred. *La Société de géographie, 1821–1946.* Geneva: Droz, 1983.

Filali, Kamel. "Le Différend Qadiriyya-Tijaniyya en Algérie." *Revue d'historie maghrébine* 24, nos. 87–88 (1997): 301–14.

———. "Quelques modalités d'opposition entre marabouts: mystiques et élites du pouvoir, en Algérie, à l'époque ottomane." In *Islamic Mysticism Contested: Thirteen Centuries of Controversies and Polemics*, edited by Frederick de Jong and Bernd Radtke, 248–66. Leiden: Brill, 1999.

———. *L'Algérie mystique: des marabouts fondateurs aux khwans insurgés, XVe– XIXe siècles.* Paris: Publisud, 2002.

Finchelstein, Federico. *Transatlantic Fascism: Ideology, Violence and the Sacred in Argentina and Italy, 1919–1945.* Durham, N.C.: Duke University Press, forthcoming.

Fisher, Allen, and Humphrey Fisher. *Slavery and Muslim Society in Africa: The Institution in Saharan and Sudanic Africa and the Trans-Saharan Trade.* Garden City, N.Y.: Doubleday, 1971.

Fisher, Humphrey J. *Slavery in the History of Muslim Black Africa.* New York: New York University Press, 2001.

Foucault, Michel. *History of Sexuality.* Vol. 1: *An Introduction.* Translated by Robert Hurley. New York: Vintage Books, 1990.

Fraguier, Colonel de. "La Crise du nomadisme et de l'élevage sur les hauts plateaux algériens." *Travaux de l'Institut de recherches sahariennes* 9, no. 1 (1953): 71–97.

———. *Les Problèmes humains du Sahara sud-oranais.* Paris: Comité d'Action Scientifique de la Défense Nationale, 1959.

Francis Barker, Peter Hulme, and Margaret Iversen, eds. *Cannibalism and the Colonial World.* Cambridge: Cambridge University Press, 1998.

Frémeaux, Jacques. "Les Bureaux arabes dans la province d'Alger (1844–1856)." Ph.D. diss., Université de Toulouse–Le Mirail, 1976.

———. "Souvenirs de Rome et présence française au Maghreb: essai d'investigation." In *Connaissances du Maghreb*, edited by Jean-Claude Vatin, 29–46. Paris: Editions du Centre National de la Recherche Scientifique, 1984.

———. *L'Afrique à l'ombre des épées.* 2 vols. Paris: Service Historique de l'Armée de Terre, 1993–95.

Frémeaux, Jacques, Daniel Norman, and Guy Pervillé. *Armées, guerre et politique en Afrique du Nord: XIXe–XXe siècles.* Paris: Presses de l'Ecole Normale Supérieure, 1977.

Freud, Sigmund. "Thoughts for the Times on War and Death." In vol. 14 of *The Standard Edition of the Complete Psychological Works of Sigmund Freud.* Translated and edited by James Strachey, 275–300. London: Hogarth Press, 1981.

———. "Why War?" In vol. 22 of *The Standard Edition of the Complete Psychological Works of Sigmund Freud.* Translated and edited by James Strachey, 197–215. London: Hogarth Press, 1981.

Friedlander, Saul. "Themes of Decline and End in Nineteenth-Century Western Imagination." In *Visions of Apocalypse: End or Rebirth?*, edited by Saul Friedlander, 61–83. New York: Holmes & Meier, 1985.

——. ed. *Probing the Limits of Representation: Nazism and the "Final Solution."* Cambridge, Mass.: Harvard University Press, 1992.

——. *History, Memory, and the Extermination of the Jews of Europe.* Bloomington: Indiana University Press, 1993.

Furet, François. *Revolutionary France, 1770–1880.* Translated by Antonia Nevill. Oxford: Blackwell, 1992.

Gaid, Mouloud. *Les Beni Yala et les vérités sur l'insurrection de Mokrani en 1871.* Algiers: Imprimerie Générale, n.d. [1952].

——. *L'Algérie sous les Turcs.* Algiers: Société Nationale d'Edition et de Diffusion, 1974.

Gallissot, René. *L'Economie de l'Afrique du Nord.* Paris: Presses Universitaires de France, 1954.

——. *Maghreb-Algérie: classe et nation.* 2 vols. Paris: Arcantère, 1987.

——. "Minorité ethnique? Les Berbères." *Matériaux pour l'histoire de notre temps* 35 (1994): 21–28.

Gallissot, René, and Lucette Valensi. "Le Maghreb précolonial: mode de production archaïque ou mode de production féodal?" *Pensée* 142 (1968): 57–93.

Garcia-Arenal, Mercedes, ed. *Mahdisme et millénarisme en Islam.* Aix-en-Provence: Edisud, 2000.

Gardel, Gabriel, Bernard Blaudin de Thé, and Jean Dubief. *Les Touareg Ajjer.* [Paris]: Editions Baconnier, 1961.

Gast, Marceau. *Alimentation des populations de l'Ahaggar: étude ethnographique.* Paris: Arts et Métiers Graphiques, 1968.

——. "Modernisation et intégration: les influences arabo-islamiques dans la société des Kel Ahaggar." *Annuaire de l'Afrique du Nord* 14 (1975): 203–19.

——. "Le Désert saharien comme concept dynamique: cadre culturel et politique." *Revue de l'occident musulman et de la Méditerranée* 32 (1981): 78–92.

——. "Un document inédit a propos du massacre de la mission Flatters en 1881." *Cahiers de l'Institut de recherches et d'études sur le monde arabe et musulman* 4 (1993): 49–56.

Gauchet, Marcel. *The Disenchantment of the World: A Political History of Religion.* Translated by Oscar Burge. Princeton, N.J.: Princeton University Press, 1997.

Gaudry, Mathéa. *La Femme Chaouia de l'Aurès: étude de sociologie berbère.* Paris: P. Geuthner, 1929.

Gay, Peter. *The Enlightenment: An Interpretation.* Vol. 2: *The Science of Freedom.* New York: Norton, 1977.

Geertz, Clifford. *Islam Observed; Religious Development in Morocco and Indonesia.* New Haven, Conn.: Yale University Press, 1968.

——. "In Search of North Africa." *New York Review of Books*, 22 April 1971, 10–24.

——. *Local Knowledge: Further Essays in Interpretive Anthropology.* New York: Basic Books, 1983.

Geertz, Clifford, Hildred Geertz, and Lawrence Rosen, eds. *Meaning and Order in Moroccan Society.* Cambridge: Cambridge University Press, 1979.

Gellner, Ernest. *Saints of the Atlas.* Chicago: University of Chicago Press, 1969.

———. "Comment devenir marabout." *Bulletin économique et social du Maroc* 128–29 (1976): 3–43.

———. *Muslim Society*. Cambridge: Cambridge University Press, 1981.

———, ed. *Islam, société et communauté: anthropologies du Maghreb*. Paris: Editions du Centre National de la Recherche Scientifique, 1981.

Gellner, Ernest, and Charles Micaud, eds. *Arabs and Berbers from Tribe to Nation in North Africa*. Lexington Mass.: Lexington Books, 1972.

Gellner, Ernest, and Jean-Claude Vatin, eds. *Islam et politique au Maghreb*. Paris: Editions du Centre National de la Recherche Scientifique, 1981.

Gemery, Henry A., and Jan S. Hogendorn, eds. *The Uncommon Market: Essays in the Economic History of the Atlantic Slave Trade*. New York: Academic Press, 1979.

Genhachenhou, Abdellatif. *Formation du sous-développement en Algérie: essai sur les limites du développement du capitalisme, 1830–1962*. Algiers: Imprimerie Commerciale, 1978.

Genocide in Algeria. Cairo: Front of National Liberation, 1957 [brochure housed at the Bibliotheque nationale d'Algérie, el-Hamma branch].

Germain, Roger. *La Politique indigène de Bugeaud*. Paris: Larose, 1953.

Ghellab, S. "La Tragédie persiste." *El Watan* (Algiers), 6 June 2007.

Ginzburg, Carlo. "Microhistory: Two or Three Things That I Know about It." *Critical Inquiry* 20, no. 1 (autumn 1993): 10–35.

Girard, René. *Violence and the Sacred*. Translated by Patrick Gregory. Baltimore, Md.: Johns Hopkins University Press, 1977.

Girardet, Raoul. *L'Idée coloniale en France de 1871 à 1962*. Paris: La Table Ronde, 1972.

———. *Mythes et mythologies politiques*. Paris: Editions du Seuil, 1986.

———. *La Société militaire de 1815 à nos jours*. Paris: Perrin, 1998.

Gladstone, Penelope. *Travels of Alexine: Alexine Tinne, 1835–1869*. London: John Murray, 1970.

Goldenberg, David M. *The Curse of Ham: Race and Slavery in Early Judaism, Christianity, and Islam*. Princeton, N.J.: Princeton University Press, 2003.

Goldmann, Lucien. *Le Dieu caché: étude sur la vision tragique dans les Pensées de Pascal et dans le théâtre de Racine*. Paris: Gallimard, 1959.

Gordon, Murray. *Slavery in the Arab World*. New York: New Amsterdam Books, 1989.

Goytisolo, Juan. *Landscapes of War: From Sarajevo to Chechnya*. Translated by Peter Bush. San Francisco: City Lights Books, 2000.

Grand'henry, Jacques. *Les Parlers arabes de la région du Mzab, Sahara algérien*. Leiden: E.J. Brill, 1976.

Grant, Kevin. *A Civilised Savagery: Britain and the New Slaveries in Africa, 1884–1926*. New York: Routledge, 2005.

Graffenried, Michael von. *Inside Algeria*. New York: Aperture, 1998.

Gray, J. Glenn. *The Warriors: Reflections on Men in Battle*. Lincoln: University of Nebraska Press, 1970.

Greenfield, Bruce. "The Problem of the Discoverer's Authority in Lewis and Clark's *History*." In *Macropolitics of Nineteenth-Century Literature: Nationalism, Exoticism, Imperialism*, edited by Jonathan Arac and Hariet Ritvo, 12–36. Philadelphia: University of Pennsylvania Press, 1991.

Grévoz, Daniel. *Sahara, 1830–1881: les mirages français et la tragédie Flatters.* Paris: Editions L'Harmattan, 1989.

———. *Les Canonnières de Tombouctou: les français à la conquête de la cité mythique, 1870–1894.* Paris: Editions L'Harmattan, 1992.

———. *Les Méharistes français à la conquête du Sahara, 1900–1930.* Paris: Editions L'Harmattan, 1994.

Gross, David. "Space, Time, and Modern Culture." *Telos* 50 (winter 1981–82): 57–78.

Guerlac, Suzanne. "Longinus and the Subject of the Sublime," *New Literary History* 16, no. 2 (1985): 275–89.

Guilhaume, François. *Les Mythes fondateurs de l'Algérie française.* Paris: Editions L'Harmattan, 1992.

Guiral, Pierre. "Observations et réflexions sur les sévices dans l'armée d'Afrique." *Revue de l'occident musulman et de la Méditerranée* 15–16 (1973): 15–20.

Haarmann, Ulrich. "The Dead Ostrich: Life and Trade in Ghadames (Libya) in the Nineteenth Century." *Die Welt des Islams* 38, no. 1 (March 1998): 9–94.

Hailley, M. "Un grand voyageur nîmois: P. Soleillet." *Acta geographique* (September 1967): 27–33.

El Hamel, Chouki. "'Race,' Slavery and Islam in Maghrebi Mediterranean Thought: The Question of the *Haratin* in Morocco." *Journal of North African Studies* 7, no. 3 (2002): 29–52.

Hamit, Abdoulhadi. *La Piste du commerce transsaharien: étude d'anthropologie économique et historique.* Villeneuve d'Ascq, France: Presses Universitaires du Septentrion, 1998.

Hammoudi, Abdellah. "Segmentarité, stratification sociale, pouvoir politique et sainteté: réflexions sur les thèses de Gellner." *Hespêris Tamuda* 15 (1974): 147–77.

———. "Sainteté, pouvoir et société: Tamgrout aux XVII et XVIII siècles." *Annales, économies, sociétés, civilisations* 35, nos. 3–4 (1980): 615–41.

———. *The Victim and Its Masks: An Essay on Sacrifice and Masquerade in the Maghreb.* Chicago: University of Chicago Press, 1993.

———. "The Path to Sainthood: Structure and Danger." *Princeton Papers in Near Eastern Studies* 3 (1994): 71–88.

Hannache, Ahmed. *La Longue Marche de l'Algérie combattante, 1830–1962.* Algiers: Dahleb, 1990.

Hannoum, Abdelmajid. *Colonial Histories, Post-Colonial Memories: The Legend of the Kahina, a North African Heroine.* Portsmouth, N.H.: Heinemann, 2001.

———. "Translation and the Colonial Imaginary: Ibn Khaldun Orientalist." *History and Theory* 42, no. 1 (2003): 61–82.

Hannoyer, Jean, ed. *Guerres civiles: économies de la violence, dimensions de la civilité.* Paris: Editions Karthala / Beirut: Centre d'Etudes et de Recherches sur le Moyen-Orient Contemporaine, 1999.

Hanson, John H. *Migration, Jihad, and Muslim Authority in West Africa: The Futanke Colonies in Karta.* Bloomington: Indiana University Press, 1996.

Hanson, John H., and David Robinson. *After the Jihad: The Reign of Ahmad al-Kabir in the Western Sudan.* East Lansing: Michigan State University Press, 1991.

Harb, Adib. *Al-Tarikh al-'askari wa-al-idari lil-Amir 'Abd al-Qadir al-Jaza'iri, 1808–1847.* Algiers: al-Sharikah al-Wataniyah lil-Nashr wa al-Tawzi, 1983.

Harbi, Mohammed. "Nationalisme algérien et identité berbère." *Peuples méditerranéens* 11 (April–June 1980): 31–37.

——. *L'Algérie et son destin: croyants ou citoyens*. Paris: Arcantère, 1992.

——. "L'Algérie en perspectives." In *La Guerre de l'Algérie, 1954–2004: la fin de l'amnésie*, edited by Benjamin Stora and Mohammed Harbi, 27–45. Paris: Robert Laffont, 2004.

Hardman, Benjamin C. "Islam and the Métropole: A Case Study of Religion and Rhetoric in Algeria." Ph.D. diss., Temple University, 2005.

Hargreaves, Alec G.. *The Colonial Experience in French Fiction: A Study of Pierre Loti, Ernest Psichari, and Pierre Mille*. London: Macmillan, 1989.

Harrison, Christopher. *France and Islam in West Africa, 1860–1960*. Cambridge: Cambridge University Press, 1988.

Hart, David M. *The Aith Waryaghar of the Moroccan Rif: An Ethnography and History*. Tucson: University of Arizona Press, 1976.

——. *Banditry in Islam: Case Studies from Morocco, Algeria, and the Pakistan North West Frontier*. Wisbech, Cambridgeshire, Engl.: Middle East and North African Studies Press Ltd., 1987.

——. *Tribe and Society in rural Morocco*. Portland, Ore.: Frank Cass, 2000.

——. *Tribalism and Rural Society in the Islamic World*. London: Frank Cass, 2003.

Heers, Jacques. *Les Négriers en terres d'Islam: la première traite des noirs, VIIe–XVIe siècle*. Paris: Perrin, 2003.

Heffernan, Michael. "A French Colonial Controversy: Captain Roudaire and the Saharan Sea (1872–83)." *Maghreb Review* 13, nos. 3–4 (1988): 145–60.

——. "The Limits of Utopia: Henri Duveyrier and the Exploration of the Sahara in the Nineteenth Century." *Geographical Review* 155, no. 3 (November 1989): 342–52.

——. "The Science of Empire: The French Geographical Movement and the Forms of French Imperialism, 1870–1920." In *Geography and Empire*, edited by Anne Godlewska and Neil Smith, 92–114. Oxford: Blackwell, 1994.

——. "The Spoils of War: The *Société de géographie de Paris* and the French Empire, 1914–1919." In *Geography and Imperialism, 1820–1940*, edited by Morag Bell, Robin Butlin, and Michael Heffernan, 221–64. Manchester, Engl.: Manchester University Press, 1995.

Heitmeyer, Wilhelm, and John Hagan, eds. *International Handbook of Violence Research*. 2 vols. Dordrecht: Kluwer Academic Publishers, 2003.

Hell, Bertrand. "L'Esclave et le saint: les Gnawa et la baraka de Moulay Abdallah Ben Hsein (Maroc)." In *Saints, sainteté et martyre: la fabrication de l'exemplarité*, edited by Pierre Centlivres, 149–74. Neuchâtel, Switz.: Editions de l'Institut d'Ethnologie, 2001.

Henni, Ahmed. *Etat surplus et société en Algérie avant 1830*. Algiers: Entreprise Nationale du Livre, 1986.

Henry, Jean-Robert. "Quelques remarques sur le roman colonial en Algérie." *Cahiers de littérature générale et comparée* 5 (1981): 111–21.

——. "Romans sahariens et imaginaire français." *Centre de recherches et d'études sur les sociétés méditerranéennes* (1981): 423–40.

——. "Les Touaregs des Français." *Cahiers de l'Institut de recherches et d'études sur le monde arabe et musulman* 7, no. 8 (1996): 223–38.

——, ed. *Le Maghreb dans l'imaginaire français: la colonie, le désert, l'exil.* [La Calade, Aix-en-Provence]: Edisud, 1985.

Henry, Jean-Robert, and Lucienne Martini, eds. *Littérature et temps colonial: métamorphoses du regard sur la Méditerranée et l'Afrique.* Aix-en-Provence: Edisud, 1999.

Herbillon, Colonel. *Quelques pages d'un vieux cahier: souvenirs du Général Herbillon (1794–1866) publiés par son petit-fils.* Nancy: Imprimerie Berger-Levrault, 1928.

Hertz, Neil. "Lecture de Longin," *Poétique* 15 (1973): 292–306.

Hirtz, Georges. *L'Algérie nomade et ksourienne, 1830–1954.* Marseille: Diffusion P. Tacussel, 1989.

Hogendorn, Jan, and Henry Gemery, eds. *The Uncommon Market: Essays in the Economic History of the Atlantic Slave Trade.* New York: Academic Press, 1979.

Holsinger, Donald. "Migration, Commerce and Community: The Mzabites in Nineteenth-Century Algeria." Ph.D. diss., Northwestern University, 1979.

——. "Trade Routes of the Algerian Sahara in the Nineteenth Century." *Revue de l'occident musulman et de la Méditerranée* 30, no. 2 (1980): 57–70.

Holy, Ladislav, ed. *Segmentary Lineage System Reconsidered.* Belfast: The Queen's University Press, 1979.

Horden, Peregrine, and Nicholas Purcell. *The Corrupting Sea: A Study of Mediterranean History.* Oxford: Blackwell, 2000.

Horkheimer, Max, and Theodor W. Adorno. *Dialectic of Enlightenment.* Translated by John Cumming. New York: Continuum, 1998.

Houdaille, Jacques. "Le Problème des pertes de guerre." *Revue d'histoire moderne et contemporaine* 17 (1970): 411–23.

Hourani, Albert. *Arabic Thought in the Liberal Age, 1798–1939.* Cambridge: Cambridge University Press, 1983.

——. *A History of the Arab Peoples.* New York: Warner Books, 1991.

——. *Islam in European Thought.* Cambridge: Cambridge University Press, 1991.

Hubbell, Andrew. "A View of the Slave Trade from the Margin: Souroudougou in the Late- Nineteenth-Century Slave Trade of the Niger Bend." *Journal of African History* 42 (2001): 25–47.

Hugon, Anne. *L'Afrique des explorateurs.* Vol. 2: *Vers Tombouctou.* Paris: Gallimard, 1994.

Hull, Isabel V. *Absolute Destruction: Military Culture and the Practices of War in Imperial Germany.* Ithaca, N.Y.: Cornell University Press, 2005.

Humbert, Jean-Charles. *Sahara: les traces de l'homme.* Paris: Raymond Chabaud, 1989.

——. *Forts et bordjs de l'extrême sud: Sahara algérien, 1892–1903.* Calvisson, France: Editions J. Gandini, 1993.

——. *La Découverte du Sahara en 1900.* Paris: Editions L'Harmattan, 1996.

Hunwick, John O. "Black Africans in the Islamic World: An Understudied Dimension of the Black Diaspora." *Tarikh* 5, no. 4 (1978): 20–40.

——. *Shari'a in Songhay: The Replies of the Al-Maghili to the Questions of Askia Al-Hajj Muhammad.* Oxford: British Academy and Oxford University Press, 1985.

——. *West Africa and the Arab World.* Accra: Ghana Academy of Arts and Sciences, 1991.

——. *Timbuktu and the Songhay Empire: Al-Sa'di's Ta'rikh al-'Sudan Down to 1613 and Other Contemporary Documents.* Leiden: Brill, 1999.

——. "Aḥmad Bābā on Slavery," *Sudanic Africa* 11 (2000): 131–39.

———. "Islamic Law and Polemics Over Race and Slavery in North and West Africa (16th–19th Century)." *Princeton Papers: Interdisciplinary Journal of Middle East Studies* 7 (2000): 43–68.

Hunwick, John, and Eve Trout Powell. *The African Diaspora in the Mediterranean Lands of Islam.* Princeton, N.J.: Markus Wiener, 2002.

Huyssen, Andreas. "Fortifying the Heart—Totally: Ernst Jünger's Armored Texts." *New German Critique* 59 (spring-summer, 1993): 3–23.

Ichboubene, Larbi. *Alger: histoire et capitale de destin national.* Algiers: Casbah Editions, 1997.

Jamous, Raymond. *Honneur et baraka: les structures sociales traditionnelles dans le Rif.* Paris: Maison des Sciences de l'Homme / Cambridge: Cambridge University Press, 1981.

Jardin, André. "Alexis de Tocqueville, Gustave de Beaumont et le problème de l'égalité des races." In *L'Idée de race dans la pensée politique française contemporaine,* edited by Pierre Guiral and Emile Témime, 200–219. Paris: Editions du Centre National de la Recherche Scientifique, 1977.

Jardin, André, and André Jean Tudesq. *Restoration and Reaction, 1815–1848.* Translated by Elborg Forster. Cambridge: Cambridge University Press / Paris: Editions de la Maison des Sciences de l'Homme, 1983.

Jennings, Lawrence C. *French Anti-Slavery: The Movement for the Abolition of Slavery in France, 1802–1848.* Cambridge: Cambridge University Press, 2000.

Johnson, Douglas. "Algeria: Some Problems of Modern History." *Journal of African History* 5, no. 2 (1964): 221–42.

Johnson, Marion. "Calico Caravans: The Tripoli Kano Trade after 1880." *Journal of African History* 17, no. 1 (1976): 95–117.

Johnston, H.A.S. *The Fulani Empire of Sokoto.* London: Oxford University Press, 1967.

de Jong, Frederick, and Bernd Radtke, eds. *Islamic Mysticism Contested: Thirteen Centuries of Controversies and Polemics.* Leiden: Brill, 1999.

Journet, B. *Nomades de Tombouctou: autopsie d'une colonisation.* Paris: Centre d'Etudes sur l'Histoire du Sahara, 1988.

Joutard, Philippe, ed. *L'Invention du Mont Blanc.* Paris: Gallimard, 1986.

Julien, Charles-André. *Histoire de l'Afrique du Nord: Tunisie–Algérie–Maroc.* Paris: Payot, 1931.

———. *Les Débuts de l'expansion et de la colonisation française (XVe–XVIe siècles).* Paris: Presses Universitaires de France, 1948.

———. *Histoire de l'Afrique du Nord (Tunisie–Algérie–Maroc).* Vol. 1: *Des origines à la conquête arabe (647 ap. J.-C.),* ed. Christian Courtois; Vol. 2: *De la conquête arabe à 1830,* ed. Roger Le Tourneau. 2nd ed. Paris: Payot, 1951–53.

———. *Histoire de l'Algérie contemporaine.* Vol. 1: *La Conquête et les débuts de la colonisation, 1827–1871.* Paris: Presses Universitaires de France, 1979.

Jus, Christelle. *Soudan français-Mauritanie: une géopolitique coloniale, 1880–1963.* Paris: Editions L'Harmattan, 2003.

Kabbali, A., and Y. M. Berger, eds. *L'Elevage du mouton dans un pays à climat méditerranéen.* Rabat: Actes Editions, 1990.

Kaddache, Mahfoud. "L'Utilisation du fait berbère comme facteur politique dans l'Algérie coloniale." In *Proceedings of the First Congress on Mediterranean Studies of Arabo-Berber*

Influence, edited by M. Galled and D.R. Marshall, 276–84. Algiers: Société Nationale d'Edition et de Diffusion, 1973.

——. *Histoire du nationalisme algérien: question nationale et politique algérienne, 1919–1951*. Algiers: Société Nationale d'Edition et de Diffusion, 1980.

——. *L'Algérie pendant la période ottoman*. Algiers: Office des Publications Universitaires, 1992.

——. *L'Algérie des algériens: histoire d'Algérie, 1830–1954*. Algiers: Editions Rocher Noir, 1998.

Kanya-Forstner, A. S. *The Conquest of the Western Sudan: A Study in French Military Imperialism*. Cambridge: Cambridge University Press, 1969.

——. "French African Policy and the Anglo-French Agreement of 5 August 1890." *Historical Journal* 12, no. 4 (December 1969): 628–50.

——. "French Expansion in Africa: The Mythical Theory." In *Studies in the Theory of Imperialism*, edited by Roger Owen and Bob Sutcliffe, 277–94. London: Longman, 1972.

——. "French Missions to the Central Sudan in the 1890s: The Role of Algerian Agents and Interpreters." *Paideuma* 40 (1994): 15–35.

Kanya-Forstner, A.S., and Paul E. Lovejoy, "Editing Nineteenth-Century Intelligence Reports on the Sokoto Caliphate and Borno, or the Delights of a Collaborative Approach." *History in Africa* 24 (1997): 195–204.

——, eds. *Pilgrims, Interpreters and Agents: French Reconnaissance Reports on the Sokoto Caliphate and Borno, 1891–1895*. Madison: African Studies Program, University of Wisconsin–Madison, 1997.

Kaplan, Steven L. *The Famine Plot: Persuasion in Eighteenth-Century France*. Philadelphia, Pa.: American Philosophical Society, 1982.

——. *Provisioning Paris: Merchants and Millers in the Grain and Flour Trade During the Eighteenth Century*. Ithaca, N.Y.: Cornell University Press, 1984.

——. *Farewell, Revolution: Disputed Legacies, France, 1789/1989*. Ithaca, N.Y.: Cornell University Press, 1995.

Kateb, Kamel. *Européens, "indigènes," et juifs en Algérie, 1830–1962*. Paris: Editions de l'Institut National d'Etudes Démographiques, 2001.

Katz, Jonathan G. "Visionary Experience, Autobiography and Sainthood in North African Islam." *Princeton Papers in Near Eastern Studies* 1 (1992): 85–118.

Keenan, Jeremy. *The Tuareg: The People of the Ahaggar*. London: Allen Lane, 1977.

——. *The Lesser Gods of the Sahara: Social Change and Contested Terrain amongst the Tuareg of Algeria*. London: Frank Cass, 2004.

Keller, Richard C. *Colonial Madness: Psychiatry in French North Africa*. Chicago: University of Chicago Press, 2007.

Keyder, Çağlar, and Faruk Tabak, eds. *Landholding and Commercial Agriculture in the Middle East*. Albany: State University of New York Press, 1991.

Khalaf, Samir. *Civil and Uncivil Violence in Lebanon: A History of the Internationalization of Communal Conflict*. New York: Columbia University Press, 2002.

Khenchelaoui, Zaïm, ed., *Des voies et des voix* (Algiers: Editions du CNRPAH, 2007).

Khiati, Mostéfa. *Algérie: l'enfance blessée; les enfants de Bentalha racontent*. Algiers: Editions Barzahk, 2002.

Kilani, M. "La Théorie des 'deux races': quand la science répète le mythe." In *Dire les autres: réflexions et pratiques ethnologiques,* edited by J. Hainard et R. Kaehr, 31–45. Lausanne: Payot, 1997.

Klein, Martin A. *Islam and Imperialism in Senegal: Sine-Saloum, 1847–1914.* Stanford, Calif.: Stanford University Press, 1968.

———. *Slavery and Colonial Rule in French West Africa.* Cambridge: Cambridge University Press, 1998.

———. "Slavery and French Rule in the Sahara." In *Slavery and Colonial Rule in Africa,* edited by Suzanne Miers and Martin Klein, 71–90. London: Frank Cass, 1999.

———. "The Slave Trade and Decentralized Societies." *Journal of African History* 42 (2001): 49–65.

———, ed. *Breaking the Chains: Slavery, Bondage, and Emancipation in Modern Africa and Asia.* Madison: University of Wisconsin Press, 1993.

Klein, Martin, and Claire Robertson, eds. *Women and Slavery in Africa.* Madison: University of Wisconsin Press, 1983.

Komorowski, Zygmunt. "Les Descendants des Soudanais en Algérie et leurs traditions." *Africana Bulletin* (Warsaw) 15 (1971): 43–53.

Labter, Lazhari. *Retour à Laghouat mille ans après Beni Hilel.* Algiers: Editions El Ikhtilef, 2002.

LaCapra, Dominick. *Emile Durkheim: Sociologist and Philosopher.* Ithaca, N.Y.: Cornell University Press, 1972.

———. *History, Politics, and the Novel.* Ithaca, N.Y.: Cornell University Press, 1987.

———. *Representing the Holocaust: History, Theory, Trauma.* Ithaca, N.Y.: Cornell University Press, 1994.

———. *History and Memory after Auschwitz.* Ithaca, N.Y.: Cornell University Press, 1998.

———. *Writing History, Writing Trauma.* Baltimore, Md.: John Hopkins University Press, 2001.

Lacheraf, Mostefa. *L'Algérie: nation et société.* Paris: Maspero, 1965.

———. *Algérie et tiers-monde: agressions, résistances et solidarités intercontinentales.* Algiers: Bouchène, 1989.

Lacheraf, Mostefa, and Abdelkader Djeghloul. *Histoire, culture et société.* Paris: Publication du Centre Culturel Algérien, 1986.

Lacoste, Yves. *Ibn Khaldoun: naissance de l'histoire, passé du tiers monde.* Paris: Maspero, 1966.

———. *La Géographie, ça sert d'abord à faire la guerre.* Paris: Maspero, 1981.

———, et al. *L'Algérie: passé et présent; le cadre et les étapes de la constitution de l'Algérie actuelle.* Paris: Edition Sociales, 1960.

Lacoue-Labarthe, Philippe, and Jean-Luc Nancy. *L'Absolu littéraire: théorie de la littérature du romantisme allemand.* Paris: Editions du Seuil, 1978.

Ladreit de Lacharrière, Jacques. "Un essai de pénétration pacifique en Algérie: les négociations du Général Clauzel avec le bey de Tunis (1830–1831)." *Revue diplomatique* 23 (1909): 240–70, 439–68.

Lafouge, Jean-Pierre. *Etude sur l'orientalisme d'Eugène Fromentin dans ses "Récits algériens."* New York: P. Lang, 1988.

Lagardère, Vincent. *Histoire et société en occident musulman au Moyen Age: analyse du* Mi'yār *d'al-Wansaris*. Madrid: Casa de Velazquez, 1995.

Lahgazi, Abdelaziz Alaoui. "L'Expérience du désert et de l'Islam chez René Caille, Charles de Foucauld, Ernest Psichari et Saint-Exupéry." Ph.D. diss., Université de Provence, 1989.

Larguèche, Abdelhamid. *L'Abolition de l'esclavage en Tunisie à travers les archives, 1841–46*. Tunis: Société Tunisienne d'Etudes du XVIIIe Siècle, 1990.

——. "L'Abolition de l'esclavage en Tunisie: approches pour une histoire de la communauté noir." In *Les Abolitions de l'esclavage de L. F. Sonthonax à V. Schoelcher, 1793–1794–1848*, edited by M. Dorigny, 330–39. Paris: Presses Universitaires de Vincennes, 1995.

Laroui, Abdallah. *The History of the Maghrib: An Interpretive Essay*. Translated by Ralph Manheim. Princeton, N.J.: Princeton University Press, 1977.

Lartéguy, Jean. *Sahara an I*. Paris: Gallimard, 1958.

Lataillade, Louis. *Abd el-Kader: adversaire et ami de la France*. Paris: Pygmalion, 1984.

Laugel, Marcel G.. *Le Roman du Sahara*. Paris: Editions Balland, 1991.

Launay, Michel. *Paysans algériens: la terre, la vigne et les hommes*. Paris: Editions du Seuil, 1963.

Laurens, Henry. *Les Origines intellectuelles de l'expédition de l'Egypte: l'orientalisme islamisant en France, 1698–1798*. Istanbul: Editions Isis, 1987.

——. *L'Expédition d'Egypte*. Paris: Armand Colin, 1989.

——. *Le Royaume impossible, la France et la genèse du monde arabe*. Paris: Armand Colin, 1990.

——. "La Violence dans l'orient arabe." In *L'Histoire inhumaine: massacres et génocides des origines à nos jours*, edited by Guy Richard, 155–71. Paris: Armand Colin, 1992.

——. "L'Islam dans la pensée française, des Lumières à la IIIe République." In *Histoire de l'islam et des musulmans en France, du Moyen Age à nos jours*, edited by Mohammed Arkoun, 483–99. Paris: Albin Michel, 2006.

Lavers, John E. "Trans-Saharan Trade before 1800: Towards Quantification." *Paideuma* 40 (1994): 243–78.

Lawless, Richard I. "L'Evolution du peuplement, de l'habitat et des paysages agraires du Maghreb." *Annales de géographie* 81 (July–September 1972): 451–64.

Lawless, Richard I., and Gerald H. Blake. *Tlemcen: Continuity and Change in an Algerian Islamic Town*. London: Bowker, 1976.

Lazreg, Marnia. *Torture and the Twilight of Empire: From Algiers to Baghdad*. Princeton, N.J.: Princeton University Press, 2008.

Le Cour Grandmaison, Olivier. *Coloniser, exterminer: sur la guerre de l'état colonial*. Paris: Fayard, 2005.

Lefebvre, Georges. *The Great Fear of 1789: Rural Panic in Revolutionary France*. Translated by Joan White. New York, Pantheon Books, 1973.

Lefevre-Witier, Philippe. *Idèles du Hoggar: biologie et écologie d'une communauté saharienne*. Paris: Editions du Centre National de la Recherche Scientifique, 1996.

Le Gall, Michel. "The End of the Trans-Saharan Slave Trade: A View from Tripoli, 1857–1902." *Princeton Papers in Near Eastern Studies* 2 (1993): 25–56.

Leimdorfer, François. *Discours académique et colonisation: thèmes de recherché sur l'Algérie pendant la période coloniale.* Paris: Publisud, 1992.

Leiris, Michel. *L'Afrique fantôme.* Paris: Gallimard, 1988.

Lejeune, Dominique. "La Société de géographie de Paris: un aspect de l'histoire sociale française." *Revue d'histoire moderne et contemporaine* 29 (1982): 141–63.

——. *Les Sociétés de géographie en France et l'expansion coloniale au XIXe siècle.* Paris: Albin Michel, 1993.

Lejeune, Dominique, and Maxine F. Taylor. "Nascent Expansionism in the Geographical Society of Paris, 1821–1848." *Proceedings, Western Society for French History* 7 (1979): 229–38.

Leriche, A. "Les Haratin (Mauritanie)." *Bulletin de liaison saharienne* 6 (October 1951): 24–29.

Lesord, Michel. "Notes sur les pratiques médicales des Harratin d'In Salah." *Archives de l'Institut Pasteur d'Algérie* 15, no. 1 (1937): 51–57.

——. "Le Commerce des plumes d'autruche au Sahara." *Bulletin de liaison saharienne* 45 (March 1962): 33–43.

——. "Evolution des populations sahariennes." *L'Afrique et l'Asie* 57, no. 1 (1962): 11–26.

——. "Les Noirs du Sahara deviendront-ils propriétaires terriens?" *L'Afrique et l'Asie* 60, no. 4 (1962): 36–44.

Lespès, René. *Alger: esquisse de géographie urbaine.* Algiers: Carbonel, 1925.

Lethielleux, Jean. *Ouargla, cité saharienne: des origines au début du XXe siècle.* Paris: Geuthner, 1983.

Létolle, René, and Hocine Bendjoudi. *Histoires d'une mer au Sahara: utopies et politiques.* Paris: Editions L'Harmattan, 1997.

Le Tourneau, Roger. "Occupation de Laghouat par les Français (1844–1852)." In *Etudes maghrébines: mélanges Charles-André Julien,* 111–36. Paris: Presses Universitaires de France, 1964.

Levallois, Michel. *Ismaÿl Urbain: une autre conquête de l'Algérie.* Paris: Maisonneuve et Larose, 2001.

Levi, Giovanni. *Inheriting Power: The Story of an Exorcist.* Translated by Lydia G. Cochrane. Chicago: University of Chicago Press, 1988.

——. "Les Usages de la biographie." *Annales économies, sociétés, civilisations* 44, no. 6 (November–December 1989): 1325–36.

——. "On Microhistory." In *New Perspectives on Historical Writing,* edited by P. Burke, 93–113. Cambridge: Polity Press, 1991.

Lévi-Strauss, Claude. "Guerre et commerce chez les Indiens de l'Amérique du Sud." *Renaissance* (Ecole Libre des Hautes Etudes / New School for Social Research) 1 (1943): 122–39.

Lévy, Bernard-Henri. "*Le Jasmin et le sang.*" *Le Monde,* 8 January 1998.

Lewicki, Tadeusz. *Etudes ibadites nord-africaines.* Warsaw: Panstwowe Wydawnictwo Naukowe, 1955.

——. *Etudes maghrébines et soudanaises.* Warsaw: Etudes Scientifique de Pologne, 1983.

——. "The Role of the Sahara and Saharans in Relationships between North and South." In *General History of Africa,* edited by M. El Fasi, 276–313. Berkeley: University of California Press, 1988.

Lewis, Bernard. *Islam from the Prophet Muhammad to the Capture of Constantinople.* London: Oxford University Press, 1987.

——. *Race and Slavery in the Middle East: An Historical Enquiry.* Oxford: Oxford University Press, 1990.

——. "The Roots of Muslim Rage." *Atlantic Monthly* 266, no. 3 (September 1990): 47–60.

Lhote, Henri. *Les Touaregs du Hoggar (Ahaggar).* Paris: Payot, 1944.

——. *Dans les campements Touaregs.* Paris: Œuvres Françaises, 1947.

——. *La Chasse chez les Touaregs.* Paris: Le Livre Contemporain, 1951.

Liauzu, Claude. *Race et civilisation: l'Autre dans la culture occidentale; anthologie historique.* Paris: Syros-Alternatives, 1992.

——. *Histoire des migrations en Méditerranée occidentale.* Brussels: Editions Complexe, 1996.

——. *Passeurs de rives: changements d'identité dans le Maghreb colonial.* Paris: Editions L'Harmattan, 2000.

——. "Une loi contre l'histoire." *Le Monde diplomatique* 52, no. 613 (April 2005): 28.

——. ed. *Violence et colonisation: pour finir avec les guerres de mémoires.* Paris: Editions Syllepse, 2003.

Liauzu, Claude, and Josette Liauzu. *Quand on chantait les colonies: colonisation et culture populaire de 1830 à nos jours.* Paris: Editions Syllepse, 2002.

Lihoureau, Michel. *Une page de la conquête du Sahara: l'expédition Wimpffen à l'Oued Guir en 1870.* Paris: Editions L'Harmattan, 1996.

Lindqvist, Sven. *Exterminate All the Brutes.* Translated by Joan Tate. New York: New Press, 1996.

Litman, Théodore A. *Le Sublime en France, 1660–1714.* Paris: A. G. Nizet, 1971.

Lorcin, Patricia M. E. *Imperial Identities: Stereotyping, Prejudice, and Race in Colonial Algeria.* London: I. B. Tauris, 1995.

——. "Rome and France in Africa: Recovering Colonial Algeria's Latin Past." *French Historical Studies* 25, no. 2 (spring 2002): 295–329.

——. "Mediating Gender; Mediating Race: Women Writers in Colonial Algeria." *Culture, Theory and Critique* 45, no. 1 (2004): 45–61.

Loutfi, Martine Astier. *Littérature et colonialisme: l'expansion coloniale vue dans la littérature romanesque française, 1871–1914.* Paris: Mouton, 1971.

Lovejoy, Paul E. *Salt of the Desert Sun: A History of Salt Production and Trade in Central Sudan.* Cambridge: Cambridge University Press, 1986.

——. *Transformations in Slavery: A History of Slavery.* 2nd ed. Cambridge: Cambridge University Press, 2000.

——. ed. *The Ideology of Slavery in Africa.* Beverly Hills, Calif.: Sage, 1981.

——. *Slavery and the Muslim Diaspora: African Slaves in Dar Es-Salaam.* Princeton, N.J.: Markus Wiener, 2001.

——. *Slavery on the Frontiers of Islam.* Princeton, N.J.: Markus Wiener, 2004.

Lovejoy, Paul, and Jan S. Hogendorn, *Slow Death for Slavery: The Course of Abolition in Northern Nigeria, 1897–1936.* Cambridge: Cambridge University Press, 1993.

Lovejoy, Paul, Ismael Montana, and Behnaz Mirzai, eds. *Slavery, Islam, and Diaspora.* Trenton, N.J.: Africa World Press, 2009.

Lyndon, Ghislaine. "On Trans-Saharan Trails: Trading Networks and Cross-Cultural Exchange in Western Africa, 1840s–1930s." Ph.D. diss., Michigan State University, 2000.

Lyotard, Jean-François. *The Differend: Phrases in Dispute.* Translated by G. Van Den Abbeele. Minneapolis: University of Minnesota Press, 1988.

Macé, Gérard. *Le Dernier des Egyptiens.* Paris: Gallimard, 1988.

MacKay, D. "Colonialism and the French Geographical Movement." *Geographical Review* 33, no. 2 (1943): 214–32.

Mahadi, Abdullahi. "The Aftermath of the *Jihād* in the Central Sudan as a Major Factor in the Volume of the Trans-Saharan Slave Trade in the Nineteenth Century." *Slavery and Abolition* 13, no. 1 (April 1992): 111–28.

Mahé, Alain. *Histoire de la Grande Kabylie, XIXe–XXe siècles: anthropologie historique du lien social dans les communautés villageoises.* Paris: Bouchène, 2001.

Mahiou, Ahmed, and Jean-Claude Vatin. "En guise d'introduction." *Revue algérienne des sciences juridiques, économiques, et politiques* 9, no. 4 (December 1972): 803–17.

Makdisi, Ussama. *The Culture of Sectarianism: Community, History, and Violence in Nineteenth-Century Ottoman Lebanon.* Berkeley: University of California Press, 2000.

Makdisi, Ussama, and Paul A. Silverstein, eds. *Memory and Violence in the Middle East and North Africa.* Bloomington: Indiana University Press, 2006.

Malek, Redha. *Tradition et révolution: l'enjeu de la modernité en Algérie et dans l'Islam.* Paris: Sindbad, 1993.

Mambre, Emmanuelle. "Henri Duveyrier Explorateur du Sahara (1840–92)." Master's thesis, Université de Provence, 1991–92.

———. "Les Missions d'exploration dans le Sahara algérien entre 1830 et 1902: mise en place d'une stratégie?" D.E.A. thesis, Université de Provence, 1992–93.

———. "Les Touareg du Nord d'Henri Duveyrier: éléments d'une controverse." *Cahiers de l'Institut de recherches et d'études sur le monde arabe et musulman* 4 (1993): 19–23.

Manning, Patrick. *Slavery and African Life.* Cambridge: Cambridge University Press, 1990.

Manuel, Frank E. *The New World of Henri Saint-Simon.* Notre Dame, Ind.: University of Notre Dame Press, 1963.

Marchand, Christel. *Aventurières en crinoline.* Paris: Editions du Seuil, 1987.

Marcos, Fouad. *Fromentin et l'Afrique.* Sherbrooke, Can.: Editions Cosmos, 1973.

Marfaing, Laurence, and Steffen Wippel. *Les Relations transsahariennes à l'époque contemporaine: un espace en constante mutation.* Paris: Editions Karthala, 2004.

Margadant, Ted W. "Tradition and Modernity in Rural France During the Nineteenth Century." *Journal of Modern History* 56 (December 1984): 667–97.

Marmon, Shaun, ed. *Slavery in the Islamic Middle East.* Princeton, N.J.: Marcus Wiener, 1999.

Marouf, Nadir. *Lecture de l'espace oasien.* Paris: Sinbad, 1980.

Marouf, Nadir, and Omar Carlier, eds. *Espaces maghrébins: la force du local? hommage à Jacques Berque.* Paris: Editions L'Harmattan, 1995.

Marrinan, Michael. *Painting and Politics for Louis-Philippe: Art and Ideology in Orleanist France, 1830–1848.* New Haven, Conn.: Yale University Press, 1988.

Marseille, Jacques. *Empire coloniale et capitalisme français: histoire d'un divorce.* Paris: Albin Michel, 1984.

Martel, André. *Les Confines saharo-tripolitains de la Tunisie, 1881–1911.* Paris: Presses Universitaires de France, 1965.

Martin, B. G. *Muslim Brotherhoods in Nineteenth-Century Africa.* Cambridge: Cambridge University Press, 1976.

———. "Ahmad Rasim Pasha and the Suppression of the Fazzan Slave Trade, 1881–1896." *Africa* 38, no. 4 (1983): 545–79.

Martin, C. "L'Affaire Doineau." *Revue africaine* 80 (1937): 171–98.

Martin, Gaston. *Histoire de l'esclavage dans les colonies françaises.* Paris: Presses Universitaires de France, 1948.

Martin, Jean-Clément. *La Vendée et la France.* Paris: Editions du Seuil, 1987.

———. *Violence et révolution: essai sur la naissance d'un mythe national.* Paris: Editions du Seuil, 2006.

Mason, I. L. *A World Dictionary of Livestock Breeds, Types and Varieties.* 4th ed. Wallingford, Oxon, UK: CAB International, 1996.

Maspero, François. *L'Honneur de Saint-Arnaud.* Paris: Plon, 1993.

Massignon, Louis. *Recueil des textes inédits concernant l'histoire de la mystique en pays d'Islam.* Paris: P. Geuthner, 1929.

Mauny, Raymond. *Tableau géographique de l'ouest africain au Moyen Age, d'après les sources écrites, la tradition, et l'archéologie.* Amsterdam: Swets & Zeitlinger N. V., 1967.

Mauss, Marcel. *Sociologie et anthropologie.* Paris: Presses Universitaires de France, 1951.

May, Jacques Meyer. *The Ecology of Malnutrition in Northern Africa: Libya, Tunisia, Algeria, Morocco, Spanish Sahara, and Ifni, Mauritania.* New York: Hafner, 1967.

Mayer, Arno J. *The Persistence of the Old Regime.* New York: Pantheon, 1981.

Mazari, al-Hajd. *al-Hamil: markaz ishʿa thaqafi wa qalaʿa lil-djhad wa al-thawra.* Algiers: Dar al-Hakuma, 1993.

McDougall, E. Ann. "Salt, Saharans, and the Trans-Saharan Slave Trade: Nineteenth-Century Developments." *Slavery and Abolition* 13, no. 1 (April 1992): 61–87.

———. "Discourses and Distortions: Critical Reflections on Studying the Saharan Slave Trade." *Revue française d'histoire d'outre-mer* (December 2002): 55–87.

McDougall, James. *History and the Culture of Nationalism in Algeria.* Cambridge: Cambridge University Press, 2006.

McWilliams, John. *The Last of the Mohicans: Civil Savagery and Savage Civility.* New York: Twayne, 1994.

Meeker, Michael E. *Literature and Violence in North Arabia.* Cambridge: Cambridge University Press, 1979.

Meillassoux, Claude. *L'Esclavage en Afrique précoloniale.* Paris: Maspero, 1975.

———. *Anthropologie de l'esclavage.* Paris: Presses Universitaires de France, 1986.

Melliti, Imed. "La Ruse maraboutique: le statut du hayal et du itlaq dans l'hagiographie des Tijaniyya." *Annuaire de l'Afrique du nord* 33 (1994): 241–52.

Melman, Billie. *Women's Orients: English Women and the Middle East, 1718–1918.* Ann Arbor: University of Michigan Press, 1992.

Merghoub, Baelhadj. *Le Développement politique en Algérie: étude des populations de la région du Mzab.* Paris: Armand Colin, 1972.

Meyer, Jean, et al. *Histoire de la France coloniale.* Vol. 1: *Des origines à 1914.* Paris: Armand Colin, 1990.

Meyers, Allan Richard. "The Abid l-Buhari: Slave Soldiers and Statecraft in Morocco, 1672–1790." Ph.D. diss., Cornell University, 1974.

Meynier, Gilbert. *Histoire intérieure du F.L.N., 1954–1962.* Paris: Fayard, 2002.

Meynier, Gilbert, and Pierre Vidal-Naquet. "*Coloniser, Exterminer:* de vérités bonnes à dire à l'art de la simplification idéologique." *Esprit,* no. 320 (December 2005): 162–77.

Meynier, O. *La Pacification du Sahara et la pénétration saharienne, 1852–1930.* N.p.: Publications du Comité National Métropolitain du Centenaire de l'Algérie, n.d. [1930].

Michalak, Laurence O. "Popular French Perspectives on the Maghreb: Orientalist Painting of the Late 19th and Early 20th Centuries." In *Connaissances du Maghreb,* edited by Jean-Claude Vatin, 47–63. Paris: Editions du Centre National de la Recherche Scientifique, 1984.

Miège, Jean-Louis. *Le Maroc et l'Europe.* 4 vols. Paris: Presses Universitaires de France, 1962.

———. "La Libye et le commerce transsaharien au XIXe siècle." *Revue de l'occident musulman et de la Méditerranée* 19 (1975): 135–68.

———. "Le Commerce transsaharien au XIXe siècle: essai de quantification." *Revue de l'occident musulman et de la Méditerranée* 32 (1981): 93–113.

Miers, Suzanne. *Britain and the Ending of the Slave Trade.* New York: Africana Publishing, 1975.

Miers, Suzanne, and Igor Kopytoff, eds. *Slavery in Africa: Historical and Anthropological Perspectives.* Madison: University of Wisconsin Press, 1977.

Miers, Suzanne, and Richard Roberts, eds. *The End of Slavery in Africa.* Madison: University of Wisconsin Press, 1988.

Miller, Susan Gilson, ed. and trans. *Disorienting Encounters: Travels of a Moroccan Scholar in France in 1845–1846: The Voyage of Muhammad aṣ-Ṣaffār.* Berkeley: University of California Press, 1992.

Minter, David L. *William Faulkner: His Life and Work.* Baltimore, Md.: Johns Hopkins University Press, 1997.

Mitchell, Timothy. *Colonising Egypt.* Berkeley: University of California Press, 1991.

Moniot, Henri, ed. *Le Mal de voir: ethnologie et orientalisme, politique et épistémologie, critique et autocritique.* Paris: Union Générale de l'Edition, 1976.

Monk, Samuel H. *The Sublime: A Study of Critical Theories in XVIII-Century England.* New York: Modern Language Association, 1935.

Monod, Théodore. *Méharées: explorations au vrai Sahara.* N.p.: Actes Sud, 1989.

———. *Le Chercheur d'absolu.* Paris: Gallimard, 1997.

Montagne, Robert. *La Civilisation du désert.* Paris: Hachette, 1947.

Montana, Ismael M. "The Trans-Saharan Slave Trade, Abolition of Slavery and Transformations in the North African Regency of Tunis, 1759–1846." Ph.D. diss., York University, Toronto, 2007.

Monteil, Vincent. "L'Evolution et la sédentarisation des nomades sahariens." *Revue internationale des sciences sociales* 11, no. 4 (1959): 599–612.

———. "Les Bureaux arabes au Maghreb (1830–1961)." *Esprit* 29 (November 1961): 575–606.

Moorhouse, Geoffrey. *The Fearful Void.* Philadelphia, Pa.: Lippincott, 1974.

Morris, David B. *The Religious Sublime: Christian Poetry and Critical Tradition.* Lexington: University Press of Kentucky, 1972.

Mosse, George L. *Towards the Final Solution: A History of European Racism*. Madison: University of Wisconsin Press, 1978.

——. *Fallen Soldiers: Reshaping the Memory of the World Wars*. New York: Oxford University Press, 1990.

Mouffok, Ghania, ed. *Algérie: une saison en enfer*. Paris: Parangon-Aventurine, 2003.

Moussa, S. "Une peur vaincue: l'émergence du mythe bédouin chez les voyageurs français du XVIIIème siècle." In *La Peur au XVIIIème siècle: discours, représentations, pratiques*, edited by J. Berchtold and M. Porret, 193–212. Geneva: Droz, 1994.

Moussaoui, Abderrahmane. *Logiques du sacré et modes d'organisation de l'espace dans le sud-ouest algérien*. Villeneuve d'Ascq, France: Presses Universitaires du Septentrion, 1996.

——. "La Violence en Algérie: des crimes et des châtiments." *Cahiers d'études africaines* 38, nos. 150–52 (1998): 245–69.

Nacib, Youssef. *Cultures oasiennes: essai d'histoire sociale de l'oasis de Bou Saâda*. Algiers: Entreprise National du Livre, 1986.

——. *Une geste en fragments: contribution à l'étude de la légende hilalienne des hautes-plateaux algériens*. Paris: Publisud, 1994.

Nadir, Ahmad. "Les Ordres religieux et la conquête française (1831–1851)." *Revue algérienne des sciences juridiques, économiques et politiques* 9, no. 4 (1972): 819–72.

——. "Le Maraboutisme, une révolution?" In *Méthodes d'approche du monde rural*, edited by Y. Bentabet, 193–207. Algiers: Office des Publications Universitaires, 1984.

Nantet, Bernard. *L'Invention du désert: archéologie au Sahara*. Paris: Payot, 1998.

Nesson, C., Madeleine Rouvillois-Brigol, and Jacques Vallet. *Oasis du Sahara algérien*. Paris: Institut Géographique National, 1973.

Newbury, C. W. "North African and Western Sudan Trade in the Nineteenth Century: A Re-Evaluation." *Journal of African History* 7, no. 2 (1966): 233–46.

Nicolaisen, Johannes. *Ecology and Culture of the Pastoral Tuareg*. Copenhagen: National Museum of Copenhagen, 1963.

Nicolaisen, Johannes, and Ida Nicolaisen. *The Pastoral Tuareg: Ecology, Culture, and Society*. 2 vols. New York: Thames and Hudson, 1997.

Nomades et nomadisme au Sahara: recherches sur la zone aride. Paris: Organisation des Nations Unies pour l'Education, la Science et la Culture, 1963.

Nordman, Daniel. *Profils du Maghreb: essais et études*. Rabat: Université Mohammed V, Faculté des Lettres et des Sciences Humaines, 1996.

——, et al. *Enquêtes en Méditerranée: les expéditions françaises d'Egypte, de Morée et d'Algérie*. Athens: Institut de Recherches Néohelléniques, 1999.

Nordman, Daniel, and Jean Pierre Raison, eds. *Science de l'homme et conquête coloniale: constitution des sciences humaines en Afrique, XIXe–XXe siècles*. Paris: Presses de l'Ecole Normale Supérieure, 1980.

Nouschi, André. *Enquête sur le niveau de vie des populations rurales constantinoises de la conquête jusqu'en 1919*. Paris: Presses Universitaires de France, 1961.

Nussy, Frédéric de. *Caravanes d'Alger au Niger par le Hoggar*. Paris: J. Susse, 1946.

Nye, David E. *American Technological Sublime*. Cambridge, Mass.: MIT Press, 1994.

Oliel, Jacob. *Les Juifs au Sahara: le Touat au Moyen Age*. Paris: Editions du Centre National de la Recherche Scientifique, 1994.

——. *De Jérusalem à Tombouctou: l'odyssée saharienne du rabbin Mardouchée, 1826–1886.* Paris: Olbia, 1998.

Olivier de Sardan, Jean-Pierre. *Les Sociétés Songhay-Zarma (Niger-Mali): chefs, guerriers, esclaves, paysans.* Paris: Editions Karthala, 1984.

Ouatmani, Settar. "La Prise et la destruction de Zaatcha: épisode clé de l'insurrection des Ziban en 1849." *Annuaire de l'Afrique du nord* 36 (1997): 159–65.

Oulebsir, Nabila. *Les Usages du patrimoine: monuments, musées et politique coloniale en Algérie, 1830–1930.* Paris: Maison des Sciences de l'Homme, 2004.

Oussedik, Tahar, *Mouvement insurrectionnel de 1871.* N.p.: n.p., 1984.

——. *Bou-Beghla (l'homme à la mule): le mouvement insurrectionnel de 1850 à 1854.* Algiers: Entreprise Nationale du Livre, 1985.

Owen, Roger, ed. *New Perspectives on Property and Land in the Middle East.* Cambridge, Mass.: Harvard Center for Middle Eastern Studies, 2000.

Ozouf, Mona. *Festivals and the French Revolution.* Translated by Alan Sheridan. Cambridge, Mass.: Harvard University Press, 1988.

Pagniez, Yvonne. *Françaises du désert (oasis sahariennes).* Paris: Plon, 1952.

Pandolfi, Paul. "In Salah 1904, Tamanrasset 1905: les deux soumissions des Touaregs Kel Ahaggar." *Cahiers d'études africaines* 38, no. 149 (1998): 79–83.

——. *Les Touaregs de l'Ahaggar, Sahara algérien: parenté et résidence chez les Dag-Ghâli.* Paris: Editions Karthala, 1998.

——. "La Construction du mythe Touareg: quelques remarques et hypothèses." *Ethnologies comparées* 7 (spring 2004). http://recherche.univ-montp3.fr/mambo/cercle/r7/pl.p.htm (accessed March 2008).

——. "L'Imaginaire coloniale et littérature: Jules Verne chez les Touareg." *Ethnologies comparées* 5 (autumn 2002). http://recherche.univ-montp3.fr/mambo/cercle/r5/p.p.htm (accessed March 2008).

——. "Les Touaregs et nous: une relation triangulaire." *Ethnologies comparées* 2 (spring 2001). http://recherche.univ-montp3.fr/mambo/cerce/r2/p.p.htm (accessed March 2008).

Pankhurst, Richard. "Ethiopian and Other African Slaves in Greece during the Ottoman Occupation." *Slavery and Abolition* 1 (1980): 339–44.

Peabody, Sue. *"There are no slaves in France": The Political Culture of Race and Slavery in the Ancien Régime.* Oxford: Oxford University Press, 1996.

Peirce, Leslie P. *The Imperial Harem: Women and Sovereignty in the Ottoman Empire.* Oxford: Oxford University Press, 1992.

Pelton, Robert Young. *The World's Most Dangerous Places.* 4th ed. New York: Harper Resource, 2000.

Perec, Georges. *L'Infra-ordinaire.* Paris: Editions du Seuil, 1989.

Pérennes, Jean-Jacques. *Structures agraires et décolonisation: les oasis de l'Oued R'hir (Algérie).* Algiers: Office des Publications Universitaires, 1979.

Perinbam, B. M. "Social Relations in the Trans-Saharan and Western Sudanese Trade: An Overview." *Comparative Studies in Society and History* 15, no. 4 (1973): 416–36.

Perkins, Kenneth, and Michel Le Gall, eds. *The Maghrib in Question: Essays in History and Historiography.* Austin: University of Texas Press, 1997.

Person, Jacques de. *Un médecin au Sahara, 1911–1913.* Brinon sur Sauldre, France: Grandvaux, 1992.

Peters, Emrys L. "Some Structural Aspects of the Feud among the Herding Bedouin of Cyrenaica." *Africa* 37 (1967): 261–82.

Peters, Rudolph. *Islam and Colonialism*. The Hague: Mouton, 1980.

Petit, Odette. *Laghouat: essai d'histoire sociale*. Paris: Collège de France, 1976.

Peyerimhoff, H. de. *Enquête sur les résultats de la colonisation officielle de 1871 à 1895*. 2 vols. Algiers: Torrent, 1909.

Peyré, Joseph. *De sable et d'or*. Paris: Flammarion, 1957.

Philips, Miura Toru, and John Edward, eds. *Slave Elites in the Middle East and Africa: A Comparative Study*. London: Kegan Paul International, 2000.

Picon, Antoine. *Les Saint-Simoniens: raison, imaginaire et utopie*. Paris: Belin, 2002.

Pitté, J.-R. "Les Controverses autour de la découverte de Tombouctou au début du XIXe siècle." *Revue historique* 515 (1973): 81–104.

Planche, Jean-Louis. *Sétif 1945: histoire d'un massacre annoncé*. Paris: Perrin / Algiers: Chihab, 2006.

Porch, Douglas. *The Conquest of the Sahara*. New York: Knopf, 1984.

Porterfield, Todd B. *The Allure of Empire: Art in the Service of French Imperialism, 1798–1836*. Princeton, N.J.: Princeton University Press, 1998.

Pouillon, François. "Du savoir malgré tout: connaissance coloniale de l'extrême sud Tunisien." In *Connaissances du Maghreb*, edited by Jean-Claude Vatin, 79–93. Paris: Editions du Centre National de la Recherche Scientifique, 1984.

———. *Les Deux Vies d'Etienne Dinet, peintre en Islam: l'Algérie et l'héritage colonial*. Paris: Balland, 1997.

Powers, David S. *Law, Society, and Culture in the Maghrib, 1300–1500*. Cambridge: Cambridge University Press, 2002.

Pratt, Mary Louise. *Imperial Eyes: Travel Writing and Transculturation*. London: Routledge, 1992.

Praz, Mario. *The Romantic Agony*. Translated by Angus Davidson. Oxford: Oxford University Press, 1970.

Price, Roger. *The Modernization of Rural France: Communications Networks and Agricultural Market Structures in Nineteenth-Century France*. London: Hutchinson, 1983.

Prochaska, David. "Fire on the Mountain: Resisting Colonialism in Algeria." In *Banditry, Rebellion, and Social Protest in Africa*, edited by Donald Crummey, 229–52. Portsmouth, N.H.: Heinemann, 1986.

———. *Making Algeria French: Colonialism in Bône, 1870–1920*. Cambridge: Cambridge University Press, 1990.

Provost, Lucile. *La Seconde Guerre d'Algérie*. Paris: Flammarion, 1996.

Pyenson, Lewis. *Civilizing Mission: Exact Sciences and French Overseas Expansion*. Baltimore, Md.: John Hopkins University Press, 1993.

Ram, Harsha. *The Imperial Sublime: A Russian Poetics of Empire*. Madison: University of Wisconsin Press, 2003.

Randau, Robert. *I. Eberhardt: notes et souvenirs*. Algiers: Charlot, 1945.

Reddy, William. *The Rise of Market Culture: The Textile Trade and French Society, 1750–1900*. Cambridge: Cambridge University Press, 1984.

Redfield, Marc. *The Politics of Aesthetics: Nationalism, Gender, Romanticism*. Stanford, Calif.: Stanford University Press, 2003.

Régnier, Philippe. "Le Mythe oriental des Saint-Simoniens." In *Les Saint-Simoniens et l'Orient: vers la modernité*, edited by Magali Morsy, 29–52. Aix-en-Provence: Edisud, 1989.

——. *Les Saint-Simoniens en Egypte, 1833–1851.* Cairo: Banque de l'Union Européenne, 1989.

Regnier, Y. *Le Petit-Fils de Touameur: les Chaâmba sous le régime français; leur transformation.* Paris: Domat-Montchrestien, 1939.

Rémond, René. *Les Etats-Unis devant l'opinion française, 1815–1852.* 2 vols. Paris: Armand Colin, 1962.

Renault, François. *Lavigerie, l'esclavage africain et l'Europe, 1868–1892.* 2 vols. Paris: Boccard, 1971.

——. *L'Abolition de l'esclavage au Sénégal: l'attitude de l'administration française, 1848–1905.* Paris: Société Française d'Histoire d'Outre-Mer / P. Geuthner, 1972.

——. "La Traite des esclaves noirs en Libye au XVIIIe siècle." *Journal of African History* 23, no. 2 (1982): 163–81.

——. *Le Cardinal Lavigerie.* Paris: Fayard, 1992.

Rey-Goldzeiguer, Annie. *Le Royaume arabe: la politique algérienne de Napoléon III, 1861–1870.* Algiers: Société Nationale d'Edition et de Diffusion, 1977.

——. "Mohammed Ben 'Abdallâh." In *Les Africains*, vol. 12, edited by Charles-André Julien et al., 197–222. Paris: Editions Jeune Afrique, 1978.

Richter, Melvin. "Tocqueville on Algeria." *Review of Politics* 25 (1963): 362–98.

Riesman, Paul. *Freedom in Fulani Social Life.* Translated by Martha Fuller. Chicago: University of Chicago Press, 1977.

Rioux, Jean-Pierre, and Charles-Robert Ageron. *Fins d'empires.* Paris: Plon, 1992.

Rivet, Daniel. "Exotisme et 'pénétration scientifique': l'effort de découverte du Maroc par les français au début du XXe siècle." In *Connaissances du Maghreb*, edited by Jean-Claude Vatin, 95–109. Paris: Editions du Centre National de la Recherche Scientifique, 1984.

——. *Lyautey et l'institution du protectorat français au Maroc, 1912–1925.* Paris: Editions L'Harmattan, 1988.

——. "Conquête et exploration de l'Afrique du Nord." In *Images et colonies: iconographie et propagande coloniale sur l'Afrique française de 1880 à 1962*, edited by Nicolas Bancel, Pascal Blanchard, and Laurent Gervereau, 12–17. Nanterre, France: Bibliothèque de documentation internationale contemporaine, 1993.

——. *Le Maghreb à l'épreuve de la colonisation.* Paris: Editions L'Harmattan, 2002.

Roberts, Richard. *Warriors, Merchants, and Slaves: The State and the Economy in the Middle Niger Valley, 1700–1914.* Stanford, Calif.: Stanford University Press, 1987.

Robinson, David. *The Holy War of Umar Tal: The Western Sudan in the Mid-Nineteenth Century.* Oxford: Clarendon Press, 1985.

——. *Paths of Accommodation: Muslim Societies and French Colonial Authorities in Senegal and Mauritania, 1880–1920.* Athens: Ohio University Press / Oxford: James Currey, 2000.

Roche, Michel Alain. *Hydrogéologie de la haute Saoura, Sahara nord occidental.* Paris: Editions du Centre National de la Recherche Scientifique, 1973.

Rodinson, Maxime. *Les Arabes.* Paris: Presses Universitaires de France, 1979.

———. *Europe and the Mystique of Islam.* Translated by Roger Veinus. London: I. B. Tauris, 1988.

Romano, Ruggiero. *Les Conquistadores: les mécanismes de la conquête coloniale.* Paris: Flammarion, 1972.

Romey, Alain. *Les Sa'id 'Atba de Ngoussa: Histoire et état actuel de leur nomadisme.* Paris: Editions L'Harmattan, 1983.

———. *Histoire, mémoire et sociétés: l'exemple de Ngoussa, oasis berbérophone du Sahara (Ouargla).* Paris: Editions L'Harmattan, 1992.

La Roncière, Charles Germain Marie Bourel de. *La Découverte de l'Afrique au Moyen Age.* 3 vols. Cairo: Société Royale de Géographie d'Egypte, 1924–27.

Rose, Jacqueline. *Why War? Psychoanalysis, Politics, and the Return to Melanie Klein.* Oxford: Blackwell, 1993.

de Rotalier, Bruno. "Les *Yaouleds* (enfants des rues) de Casablanca et leur participation aux émeutes de décembre 1951." *Revue d'histoire de l'enfance irrégulière* 4 (2002). http://rhei.revues.org/document61.html (accessed 12 December 2007).

Rotberg, R. I., ed. *Africa and Its Explorers: Motives, Methods and Impacts.* Cambridge, Mass.: Harvard University Press, 1970.

Rouch, J., et al. *Histoire universelle des explorations.* Vol. 4: *De 1815 à nos jours.* Paris: Nouvelle Librairie de France, 1960.

Roussanne, Albert. *L'Homme suiveur de nuages: Camille Douls.* Rodez, France: Editions du Rouergue, 1991.

Roux, Michel. *Le Désert de sable: le Sahara dans l'imaginaire des Français, 1900–1994.* Paris: Editions L'Harmattan, 1996.

Rowan, David. "Be afraid, be very afraid." *Guardian* (London),2 August 1997.

Roy, Olivier. *Globalized Islam: The Search for a New Ummah.* New York: Columbia University Press, 2004.

Ruedy, John. *Land Policy in Colonial Algeria: The Origins of the Rural Public Domain.* Berkeley: University of California Press, 1967.

———. *Modern Algeria: The Origins and Development of a Nation.* Bloomington: Indiana University Press, 1992.

Ruff, Julius R. *Violence in Early Modern Europe, 1500–1800.* Cambridge: Cambridge University Press, 2001.

Saad, Elias N. *Social History of Timbuktu: The Role of Muslim Scholars and Notables, 1400–1900.* Cambridge: Cambridge University Press, 1983.

Sabry, Mustapha. *L'Empire égyptien sous Mohamed-Ali et la question d'Orient, 1811–1849.* Paris: P. Geuthner, 1930.

Le Sahara: Rapports et contacts humains. Septième colloque d'histoire organisé par la Faculté des Lettres d'Aix-en-Provence. Aix-en-Provence: Publications des Annales de la Faculté des Lettres, 1967.

Sahli, Mohamed Chérif. *L'Emir Abdelkader: mythes français et réalités algériennes.* Algiers: Entreprise Algérienne de Presse, 1988.

Said, Ahmed. "Commerce et commerçants dans le Sahara central: les échanges entre le vilayet de Tripoli et l'Afrique centrale de 1835 à 1911." Ph.D. diss., Université de Provence, 1996.

Said, Edward W. *Orientalism.* 25th Anniversary Edition. New York: Vintage Books, 2003.

———. *Culture and Imperialism*. Rev. ed. New York: Vintage Books, 2007.

Saidouni, Nacereddine. *L'Algérois rural à la fin de l'époque ottomane, 1791–1830*. Beirut: Dar al-Gharb al-Islami, 2001.

Salhi, Mohamed Brahim. "Etude d'une confrérie religieuse algérienne: la Rahmania à la fin du XIXe siècle et dans la première moitié du XXe siècle." Ph.D. diss, Ecole des Hautes Etudes en Sciences Sociales, 1979.

———. "Confrérie religieuse et champ religieux en Grande-Kabylie au milieu du XXe siècle: la Rahmaniyya." *Annuaire de l'Afrique du nord* 33 (1994): 253–70.

Salinas, Michèle. *Voyages et voyageurs en Algérie, 1830–1930*. Toulouse: Privat, 1989.

Salvy, G. *La Crise du nomadisme dans le sud marocain*. Paris: Centre des Hautes Etudes Administratives sur l'Afrique et l'Asie Moderne, n.d.

Sampson, Anthony. "Freud on the State, Violence, and War." *Diacritics* 35, no. 3 (fall 2005): 78–91.

Sanankoua, Bintou. *Un empire peul au XIXe siècle: la Diina du Maasina*. Paris: Editions Karthala, 1990.

Sanders, Edith R. "The Hamitic Hypothesis: Its Origins and Functions in Time Perspective." *Journal of African History* 10, no. 4 (1969): 521–32.

Santner, Eric L. "History Beyond the Pleasure Principle: Some Thoughts on the Representation of Trauma." In *Probing the Limits of Representation: Nazism and the "Final Solution,"* edited by Saul Friedlander, 143–54. Cambridge, Mass.: Harvard University Press, 1992.

Sari, Djillali. *La Dépossession des fellahs, 1830–1962*. Algiers: Société Nationale d'Edition et de Diffusion, 1975.

———. *L'Insurrection de 1881–1882*. Algiers: Société Nationale d'Edition et de Diffusion, 1981.

———. *Dawr al-bi'ah fi al-Jaza'ir*. Algiers: al-Sharikah al-Wataniyah lil-Nashr wa al-Tawzi, 1982.

———. *Le Désastre démographique de 1867–1868 en Algérie*. Algiers: Société Nationale d'Edition et de Diffusion, 1982.

Satia, Priya. "The Defense of Inhumanity: Air Control and the British Idea of Arabia." *American Historical Review* 111, no. 1 (February 2006): 16–51.

Savage, Elizabeth. *A Gateway to Hell, A Gateway to Paradise: The North African Response to the Arab Conquest*. Princeton, N.J.: The Darwin Press, 1997.

Scarry, Elaine. *The Body in Pain: The Making and Unmaking of the World*. New York: Oxford University Press, 1985.

Scelles-Millie, J. *Contes sahariens du Souf*. Paris: Editions G..-P. Maisonneuve et Larose, 1964.

———. *Les Contes arabes du Maghreb*. Paris: Editions G..-P. Maisonneuve et Larose, 1970.

———. *Légende dorée d'Afrique du Nord*. Paris: Editions G..-P. Maisonneuve et Larose, 1973.

Schefer, Christian. "La 'Conquête totale' de l'Algérie (1839–43)." *Revue de l'histoire des colonies françaises* 4 (1916): 22–29.

———. *L'Algérie et l'évolution de la colonisation française*. Paris: Honoré Champion, 1928.

Scheper-Hughes, Nancy, and Philippe Bourgois, eds. *Violence in War and Peace*. Malden, Mass.: Blackwell, 2004.

Schmidt, Nelly. *Victor Schœlcher et l'abolition de l'esclavage*. Paris: Fayard, 1994.

Schwartz, William Leonard. "A Glossary of Franco-Arabic Words." *French Review* 12, no. 2 (December 1938): 138–40.

Schwarzschild, Steven S. "The Marquis de Mores: The Story of Failure, 1859–1896." *Jewish Social Studies* 22 (January 1960): 3–26.

Scott, James C. *The Moral Economy of the Peasant: Rebellion and Subsistence in Southeast Asia*. New Haven, Conn.: Yale University Press, 1976.

——. *Weapons of the Weak: Everyday Forms of Peasant Resistance*. New Haven, Conn.: Yale University Press, 1985.

——. *Domination and the Arts of Resistance: Hidden Transcripts*. New Haven, Conn.: Yale University Press, 1990.

Seddon, David. "Economic Anthropology or Political Economy?: Approaches to the Analysis of Pre-Capitalist Formations in the Maghreb." In *The New Economic Anthropology*, edited by J. Clammer, 61–109. New York: St. Martin's Press, 1978.

Seillan, Jean-Marie. *Aux sources du roman colonial (1863–1914): l'Afrique à la fin du XIX siècle*. Paris: Editions Karthala, 2006.

Sergent, Edmond, and Louis Michel Parrot. *Contribution de l'Institut Pasteur d'Algérie à la connaissance humaine du Sahara, 1900–1960*. Algiers: Institut Pasteur d'Algérie, 1961.

Serman, William. "Denfert-Rochereau et la discipline dans l'armée française entre 1845 et 1874." *Revue d'histoire moderne et contemporaine* 20 (1973): 95–103.

——. *Les Officiers français dans la nation, 1848–1914*. Paris: Aubier, 1982.

Sessions, Jennifer Elson. "Making Colonial France: Culture, National Identity, and the Colonization of Algeria, 1830–1851." Ph.D. diss., University of Pennsylvania, 2005.

Shinar, Pessah. "Note on the Socio-Economic and Cultural Role of Sufi Brotherhoods and Marabutism in the Modern Maghrib." In *Proceedings of the First International Congress of Africanists*, edited by K. Onwuka Dike, Lalage J. Brown, and Michael Crowder, 272–85. London: Longmans, 1964.

Shy, John. "Jomini." In *Makers of Modern Strategy*, edited by P. Paret, 143–85. Princeton, N.J.: Princeton University Press, 1986.

Sigaut, François. *Les Réserves des grains à long terme: techniques de conservation et fonctions sociales dans l'histoire*. Lille: Editions de la Maison des Sciences de l'Homme, 1978.

Silverstein, Paul A. "Regimes of (Un)Truth: Conspiracy Theory and the Transnationalization of the Algerian Civil War." *Middle East Report* 214 (spring 2000): 6–10.

——. "The Kabyle Myth: Colonization and the Production of Ethnicity." In *From the Margins: Historical Anthropology and Its Futures*, edited by Brian Keith Axel, 122–55. Durham, N.C.: Duke University Press, 2002.

Singer, Barnett, and John Langdon. *Cultured Force: Makers and Defenders of the French Colonial Empire*. Madison: University of Wisconsin Press, 2004.

Sivers, Peter von. "The Realm of Justice: Apocalyptic Revolts in Algeria (1849–1879)." *Humaniora Islamica* 1 (1973): 47–60.

——. "Insurrection and Accommodation: Indigenous Leadership in Eastern Algeria, 1840–1900." *International Journal of Middle East Studies* 6 (1975): 259–75.

——. "Rural Uprisings as Political Movements in Colonial Algeria, 1851–1914." In *Islam, Politics, and Social Movements*, edited by Edmund Burke III and Ira M. Lapidus, 39–59. Berkeley: University of California Press, 1988.

Slotkin, Richard. *Regeneration Through Violence: The Mythology of the American Frontier, 1600–1860*. Middletown, Conn.: Wesleyan University Press, 1973.

Smaldone, Joseph P. *Warfare in the Sokoto Caliphate: Historical and Sociological Perspectives*. Cambridge: Cambridge University Press, 1977.

Smati, Mhfoud. *Les Elites algériennes sous la colonisation*. Algiers: Imprimerie d'Ahlab, 1998.

Smith, Tony. "Muslim Impoverishment in Colonial Algeria." *Revue de l'occident musulman et de la Méditerranée* 17 (1974): 139–62.

Sofsky, Wolfgang. *Violence: Terrorism, Genocide, War*. Translated by Anthea Bell. London: Granta Books, 2004.

Souaïdia, Habib. *La Sale Guerre: le témoignage d'un ancien officier des forces de l'armée algérienne*. Paris: Découverte, 2001.

Spaulding, Jay. "Slavery, Land Tenure, and Social Class in Northern Turkish Sudan." *International Journal of African Historical Studies* 15, no. 1 (1982): 1–20.

Stewart, Charles. "Political Authority and Social Stratification in Mauritania." In *Arabs and Berbers: From Tribe to Nation in North Africa*, edited by E. Gellner and Charles Micaud, 376–86. London: D.C. Heath, 1972.

Stoler, Ann Laura. "On Degrees of Imperial Sovereignty." *Public Culture* 18, no. 1 (winter 2006): 125–46.

Stora, Benjamin. *La Gangrène et l'oubli: la mémoire de la guerre d'Algérie*. Paris: Découverte, 1991.

Stora, Benjamin, and Mohammed Harbi, eds. *La Guerre de l'Algérie, 1954–2004: la fin de l'amnésie*. Paris: Robert Laffont, 2004.

Sullivan, Anthony Thrall. *Thomas-Robert Bugeaud: France and Algeria, 1784–1849; Politics, Power, and the Good Society*. Hamden, Conn.: Archon Books, 1983.

Surun, Isabelle. "La Découverte de Tombouctou: déconstruction et reconstruction d'un mythe géographique." *L'Espace géographique* 32, no. 2 (2003): 131–44.

Tambo, D. "The Sokoto Caliphate Slave Trade in the Nineteenth Century." *International Journal of African Historical Studies* 9 (1976): 187–217.

Tangi, Majda. *Contribution à l'étude de l'histoire des "Sudan" au Maroc du début de l'islamisation jusqu'au début du XVIIIème siècle*. Villeneuve d'Ascq, France: Presses Universitaires du Septentrion, 1994.

Temimi, Abdeljeli. "A propos du *Miroir*." In Abdeljeli Temimi, *Recherches et documents d'histoire maghrébine: la Tunisie, l'Algérie et la Tripolitaine de 1816 à 1871*, 109–71. Tunis: Université de Tunis, 1971.

———. *Le Beylik de Constantine et Hadj 'Ahmed Bey, 1830–37*. Tunis: Presses de la Société Tunisienne des Arts Graphiques, 1978.

Terdiman, Richard. *Present Past: Modernity and the Memory Crisis*. Ithaca, N.Y.: Cornell University Press, 1993.

Terray, Emmanuel. *Le Marxisme devant les sociétés "primitives."* Paris: Maspero, 1969.

Thomas, Benjamin Earl. *Trade Routes of Algeria and the Sahara*. New York: Johnson Reprint Corp., 1968.

Thomas, Marc-Robert. *Sahara et communauté*. Paris: Presses Universitaires de France, 1960.

Thompson, E. P. *The Making of the English Working Class*. New York: Vintage Books, 1966.

————. "The Moral Economy of the English Crowd in the Eighteenth Century." *Past and Present* 50 (February 1971): 76–136.

Thomson, Ann. *Barbary and Enlightenment: European Attitudes Towards the Maghreb in the 18th Century*. Leiden: Brill, 1987.

Thornton, John K. *Warfare in Atlantic Africa, 1500–1800*. London: University College London Press, 1999.

Thuillier, Guy. *Bureaucratie et bureaucrates en France au XIXe siècle*. Geneva: Droz, 1980.

————. *Pour une histoire de la bureaucratie en France*. 2 vols. Paris: Comité pour l'Histoire Economique et Financière de la France, 1999–2001.

Thuillier, Guy, and Jean Tulard. *Histoire de l'administration française*. Paris: Presses Universitaires de France, 1984.

Tillion, Germaine. *France and Algeria: Complementary Enemies*. Translated by Richard Howard. New York: Knopf, 1961.

————. *The Republic of Cousins: Women's Oppression in Mediterranean Society*. Translated by Quintin Hoare. London: Al Saqi Books, 1983.

Tilly, Charles, Louise Tilly, and Richard Tilly. *The Rebellious Century, 1830–1930*. Cambridge, Mass.: Harvard University Press, 1975.

Tlemçani, Salima. "Dix ans après le massacre de Bentalha." *El Watan* (Algiers), 24 September 2007.

Todorov, Tzvetan. "Introduction: Tocqueville et la doctrine colonial." In Alexis de Tocqueville, *De la colonie en Algérie*, 9–34. Paris: Complexe, 1988.

————. *On Human Diversity: Nationalism, Racism, and Exoticism in French Thought*. Translated by Catherine Porter. Cambridge, Mass.: Harvard University Press, 1993.

Toledano, Ehud. *The Ottoman Slave Trade and Its Suppression, 1840–1890*. Princeton, N.J.: Princeton University Press, 1983.

————. *Slavery and Abolition in the Ottoman Middle East*. Seattle: University of Washington Press, 1998.

Touati, Houari. *Entre dieu et les hommes: lettrés, saints, et sorciers au Maghreb, 17e siècle*. Paris: Editions de l'Ecole des Hautes Etudes en Sciences Sociales, 1994.

————. "Algerian Historiography in the Nineteenth and Early Twentieth Centuries: From Chronicle to History." In *The Maghrib in Question: Essays in History and Historiography*, edited by Michel Le Gall and Kenneth Perkins, 81–94. Austin: University of Texas Press, 1997.

————. *Islam et voyage au Moyen Age*. Paris: Editions du Seuil, 2000.

Traverso, Enzo. *The Origins of Nazi Violence*. Translated by Janet Lloyd. New York: New Press, 2003.

Triaud, Jean-Louis. *La Légende noire de la Sanûsiyya: une confrérie musulmane saharienne sous le regard français, 1840–1930*. 2 vols. Paris: Editions de la Maison des Sciences de l'Homme, 1995.

Triaud, Jean-Louis, and David Robinson, eds. *Le Temps des marabouts: itinéraires et stratégies islamiques en Afrique occidentale française v. 1880–1960*. Paris: Editions Karthala, 1997.

————. *La Tijaniyya: une confrérie musulmane à la conquête de l'Afrique*. Paris Editions Karthala, 2000.

Tudesq, André-Jean. *Les Grands Notables en France (1840–1849): étude historique d'une psychologie sociale.* Paris: Presses Universitaires de France, 1964.

Turin, Yvonne. *Affrontements culturels dans l'Algérie coloniale.* Paris: Maspero, 1971.

Turner, Bryan S., ed. *Orientalism: Early Sources.* Vol. 1: *Readings in Orientalism.* London: Routledge, 2000.

Tweton, Jerome D. *The Marquis de Morès: Dakota Capitalist, French Nationalist.* Fargo: North Dakota Institute for Regional Studies, 1972.

Valensi, Lucette. "Esclaves chrétiens et esclaves noirs à Tunis au XVIIIe siècle." *Annales, économies, sociétés, civilisations* 22, no. 4 (November–December 1967): 1267–87.

———. "Calamités démographiques en Tunisie et en Méditerranée orientale aux XVIIIe et XIXe siècles." *Annales, économies, sociétés, civilisations* 24, no. 6 (1969): 1540–62.

———. "La Conjoncture agraire en Tunisie aux XVIIIe et XIXe siècles." *Revue historique* 243, no. 2 (1970): 321–36.

———. *On the Eve of Colonialism.* Translated by Kenneth J. Perkins. New York: Africana Publishing, 1977.

———. "Le Maghreb vu du centre: sa place dans l'école sociologique française." In *Connaissances du Maghreb,* edited by Jean-Claude Vatin, 227–44. Paris: Editions du Centre National de la Recherche Scientifique, 1984.

———. *Tunisian Peasants in the Eighteenth and Nineteenth Centuries.* Cambridge: Cambridge University Press / Paris: Editions de la Maison des Sciences de l'Homme, 1985.

———. "La Tour de Babel: groupes et relations ethniques au Moyen Orient et en Afrique du Nord." *Annales, économies, sociétés, civilisations* 41, no. 4 (1986): 817–38.

———. *The Birth of the Despot: Venice and the Sublime Porte.* Translated by Arthur Denner. Ithaca, N.Y.: Cornell University Press, 1993.

Valette, Jacques. "Quelques aspects nouveaux de l'expédition Flatters." *Revue de l'occident musulman et de la Méditerranée* 15–16 (1973): 375–90.

———. "Le Projet de 'mer intérieure' du colonel Roudaire et la politique coloniale de la IIIème République." *Revue d'histoire maghrébine* 7–8 (1977): 251–58.

———. "Pénétration française au Sahara: Exploration: le cas de Paul Soleillet." *Revue française d'histoire d'outre-mer* 67 (1980): 253–67.

Van Der Haven, Elisabeth C. "The Abolition of Slavery in Tunisia (1846)." *Revue d'histoire maghrebine* 27, nos. 99–100 (May 2000): 449–64.

Vatin, Jean-Claude. "A propos de *Le mal de voir.*" *Annuaire de l'Afrique du Nord* 15 (1976): 965–89.

———. *L'Algérie: politique, histoire et société.* Paris: Presses de la Fondation Nationale des Sciences Politiques, 1983.

———. "Exotisme et rationalité: à l'origine de l'enseignement du droit en Algérie (1879–1909)." In *Connaissances du Maghreb,* edited by Jean-Claude Vatin, 161–83. Paris: Editions du Centre National de la Recherche Scientifique, 1984.

———. "Désert construit et inventé, Sahara perdu ou retrouvé: le jeu des imaginaires." In *Le Maghreb dans l'imaginaire français: la colonie, le désert, l'exil,* edited by Jean-Robert Henry, 107–31. Aix-en-Provence: Edisud, 1986.

Verlet, Bruno. *Le Sahara.* Paris: Presses Universitaires de France, 1959.

Vidal-Naquet, Pierre. *Les Crimes de l'armée française: Algérie, 1954–1962.* Paris: Maspero, 1975.

Vigarello, Georges. *A History of Rape: Sexual Violence in France from the 16th to the 20th Centuries*. Translated by Jean Birrell. Cambridge: Polity Press, 2001.

Vikør, Knut S. *Sufi and Scholar on the Desert Edge: Muhammad b. Ali Al-Sanusi and His Brotherhood*. Evanston, Ill.: Northwestern University Press, 1995.

———. *The Oasis of Salt: The History of Kawar, a Saharan Centre of Salt Production*. Bergen, Norway: Centre for Middle Eastern and Islamic Studies, 1999.

Villaret, François de. *Siècles de steppe: jalons pour l'histoire de Djelfa. Deuxième partie: les Oulad Naïl*. Ghardaïa: Centre de Documentation Saharienne, 1995.

Voisin, André. *Contes et légendes du Sahara*. Paris: Editions L'Harmattan, 1995.

Walzer, Michael. *Just and Unjust Wars: A Moral Argument with Historical Illustrations*. 4th ed. New York: Basic Books, 2006.

Watts, Michael. *Silent Violence: Food, Famine and Peasantry in Northern Nigeria*. Berkeley: University of California Press, 1983.

Webb, James L. A. *Desert Frontier: Ecological and Economic Change Along the Western Sahel, 1600–1850*. Madison: University of Wisconsin Press, 1995.

Weil, Patrick. *Qu'est-ce qu'un Français: histoire de la nationalité française depuis la révolution*. Paris: Grasset, 2002.

Weiskel, Thomas. *The Romantic Sublime: Studies in the Structure and Psychology of Transcendence*. Baltimore, Md.: John Hopkins University Press, 1976.

Weiss, John Hubbel. *The Making of Technological Man: The Social Origins of French Engineering Education*. Cambridge, Mass.: MIT Press, 1982.

Westermarck, Edward. *Ritual and Belief in Morocco*. New Hyde Park, N.Y.: University Books, 1926.

Whale, John. "Romantics, Explorers and Picturesque Travelers." In *The Politics of the Picturesque: Literature, Landscape and Aesthetics since 1770*, edited by Stephen Copley and Peter Garside, 175–95. Cambridge: Cambridge University Press, 1994.

Wickins, P. L. *An Economic History of Africa from the Earliest Times to Partition*. Cape Town: Oxford University Press, 1981.

Willis, John-Ralph. *Studies in West African Islamic History*. Vol. 1: *The Cultivators of Islam*. London: Frank Cass, 1979.

———. "Islamic Africa: Reflection and the Servile Estate." *Studia Islamica* 52 (1980): 183–97.

———, ed. *Slaves and Slavery in Muslim Africa*. Vol. 1: *Islam and the Ideology of Enslavement*. Vol. 2: *The Servile Estate*. London: Frank Cass, 1985.

Wolf, Eric. *Europe and the People Without History*. Berkeley: University of California Press, 1982.

Wolff, Mark. "Western Novels as Children's Literature in Nineteenth-Century France." *Mosaic* 34, no. 2 (June 2001): 87–102.

Wright, John. "The Wada–Benghazi Slave Route." *Slavery and Abolition* 13, no. 1 (April 1992): 174–84.

———. *The Trans-Saharan Slave Trade*. New York: Routledge, 2007.

Yacono, Xavier. *Les Bureaux arabes et l'évolution des genres de vie dans l'ouest du Tell algérois (Dahra, Chélif, Ouarsenis, Sersou)*. Paris: Larose, 1953.

———. "Peut-on évaluer la population de l'Algérie en 1830?" *Revue africaine* 95 (1954): 277–307.

———. *La Colonisation des plaines du Chélif.* 2 vols. Algiers: Imprimerie Imbert, 1955–56.

Yook, Youngsoo. "Continuity and Transformation: Emile Barrault and Saint-Simonianism, 1828–1865." Ph.D. diss., University of Washington, 1995.

Zarobell, John J. "Framing French Algeria: Colonialism, Travel and the Representation of Landscape, 1830–1870." Ph.D. diss., University of California, Berkeley, 2000.

Zartman, William. "The Sahara: Bridge or Barrier?" *International Conciliation* 541 (January 1963): 1–62.

Zebadia, Abdelkader. "The Career and Correspondence of Ahmad Al-Bekkay of Timbuctou." Ph.D. diss. University of London, 1974.

Zhiri, Oumelbanine. *L'Afrique au miroir de l'Europe: fortunes de Jean Léon l'Africain à la Renaissance.* Geneva: Droz, 1991.

Zouber, Mahmoud. *Ahmad Baba de Tombouctou (1556–1627): sa vie et son ouvre.* Paris: Maisonneuve et Larose, 1977.

Zouzou, Abdelhamid. *L'Aurès au temps de la France coloniale: évolution politique, économique et sociale, 1837–1939.* 2 vols. Algiers: Editions el Houma, 2002.

Zubaida, Sami. "Is There a Muslim Society? Ernest Gellner's Sociology of Islam," *Economy and Society* 24, no. 2 (May 1995): 151–88.

INDEX

Page numbers in italics refer to illustrations.

Abdelkader, Emir ('Abd al-Qadir ibn Muhyi al-Din al-Jaza'iri), 30, 37, 38, 46, 70, 73, 76, 93, 166, 203, 273n82; Algerian nationalism and, 14–15, 20; allies and followers of, 18, 114; capture and defeat of, 29, 75, 290n27; French vs., 35; at Laghouat, 39; Morocco and, 41; portraits of, 224, 225; as refugee, 36; resistance of, 32–33, 117, 160, 165, 166; Sufism and, 224; western Oran and, 32

abolition, 69, 190; age of, 6, 7–8; in Algeria (1848), 144, 147, 148, 154, 170–72, 175, 177, 186, 195, 301n28, 303n61; ambivalence over, 191; colonial administration and, 171–73, 182, 185–86; Great Britain and, 159; in Mzab, 182–84; reparations and, 171–72; Saharan slave trade and, 159–79; Second Republic and, 143, 170; uneven application of, 175–77. *See also* slaves, slavery; slave trade, slave traders

accommodation, colonialism and, 134, 135, 148, 180–96, 246

African Commission (1833), 20, 21

agriculture, 13, 30, 35; Bugeaud and, 34–35; at Laghouat, 60; native, 112; settled, 32; subsistence, 112; in Tell, 42, 64. *See also* crops; grain; livestock; pastoralism

Aïn-Madi, 39, 44, 60; *zāwiya* at, 203, 264n77, 303n61

Aïn Sefra, 79, 192

Algeria, 55; agriculture in, 13, 30; Arabs in, 62; borders of, 62, 63, 189; civil war in, 5; coastal cities, 31; as destination for former slaves, 167; economy of, 69; exports from, 42; Fanon on, 6; French claims of sovereignty in, 11, 62–63; geography of, 62; independence of, x, 5, 6, 32; interior, 14, 21–22, 31–34; Kabyles in, 62; languages of, 20, 62; Louis-Philippe and, 12–14; as Mediterranean borderland, 6;

CPSIA information can be obtained
at www.ICGtesting.com
Printed in the USA
JSHW020452260620
6360JS00001B/9